More praise for

## DOROTHEA LANGE: A LIFE BEYOND LIMITS

"It takes uncommon insight and self-awareness to write this persuasively about a taciturn woman of labyrinthine complexity. Gordon leaves us to ponder bigger questions about the value and meaning of art over time—and about the exquisite ordinariness that resides deep in the heart of our least ordinary fellow humans."     —Kirk Davis Swinehart, *Chicago Tribune*

"Linda Gordon's biography *Dorothea Lange: A Life Beyond Limits* distinguishes itself by giving us something of a postmodern Lange, one who acknowledges—and even celebrates—the ultimately unknowable inner lives of her subjects."
—Jordan Bear, *Bookforum*

"Gordon's careful and thoughtful biography convinces a reader of Lange's crucial role in the development of documentary photography and at the same time portrays her as a driven and difficult woman trying to balance work, love, and family."     —Barbara Fisher, *Boston Globe*

"Linda Gordon's absorbing biography of photographer Dorothea Lange (1895–1965) should be popping up on lists of 2009's best books. The material is fascinating, and Gordon's presentation sterling. . . . Most impressive is Gordon's ability to explain the visual underpinnings of photography and the reasons why Lange's best work still resonates."
—Deirdre Donahue, *USA Today*

"An absorbing, well-researched and highly political biography of a transformative figure in modern photojournalism."
—*New York Times Book Review*, "100 Notable Books of 2009"

"Gordon's elegant biography is a testament to Lange's gift for challenging her country to open its eyes."     —David Oshinsky, *New York Times Book Review*

"Gordon shows that in Lange's mind her work and her sacrifices were for the American people: 'They were like military service.' "     —*The New Yorker*

"Gordon's moving, intelligent portrait of an artist who set the standard for every socially concerned photographer who followed by depicting the oppressed not as pathetic victims, but as fellow human beings ensnared in circumstances that could and must be changed." —Wendy Smith, *Los Angeles Times*

"[A] riveting portrait of one of America's most renowned photographers. In addition to providing insight into Dorothea Lange's private life (1895–1965) and professional development, Gordon explores the wider context in which she lived and worked. The author's careful scholarship reveals the connection between Lange's work and the sociopolitical environment surrounding her, while still portraying her as a normal, flawed human being. . . . Gordon deftly leads readers through the labyrinth of Lange's life . . . providing a personal, intimate tour of the photographer's life and work. Though largely sympathetic, Gordon doesn't shy away from depicting Lange's sometimes questionable decisions regarding her personal life. A rigorously constructed, entertaining biography." —*Kirkus Reviews*

"Gordon's biography is meticulously researched and pays particular and illuminating attention to her formative years." —Sean O'Hagan, *The Observer*

"Gordon, an accomplished social historian, captures Lange's complexities in context, as few other biographers are likely to do." —Jackson Lears, *American Prospect*

"Gordon's *Dorothea Lange: A Life Beyond Limits* is a masterly biography that illustrates the personal and professional struggles and achievements of a woman who was ahead of her time and who remains overshadowed by her work." —Natasha Clark, *Elle*

"Gordon takes vivid detours through everything from sharecropping to corporate agriculture to New Deal bureaucracies as she follows Lange's trips through the Central Valley and the deep South." —David D'Arcy, *San Francisco Chronicle*

"Lange deserves reconsideration—documentary portraiture is not in vogue these days—and this wide-ranging, richly detailed biography will help." —John McMurtrie, *San Francisco Chronicle,* "100 Best Fiction, Nonfiction Books of 2009"

# DOROTHEA LANGE

## A LIFE BEYOND LIMITS

*Linda Gordon*

W. W. NORTON & COMPANY

LONDON • NEW YORK

Frontispiece caption: Dorothea Lange, probably 1956, by Arthur Dubinsky

For information about permission to reproduce selections from
this book, write to Permissions, W. W. Norton & Company, Inc.,
500 Fifth Avenue, New York, NY 10110

For information about special discounts for bulk purchases,
please contact W. W. Norton Special Sales at specialsales@wwnorton.com or 800-233-4830

Manufacturing by RR Donnelley, Harrisonburg
Book design by Chris Welch
Production manager: Louise Mattarelliano

Library of Congress Cataloging-in-Publication Data

Gordon, Linda.
Dorothea Lange : a life beyond limits / Linda Gordon. — 1st ed.
p. cm.
Includes bibliographical references and index.
ISBN 978-0-393-05730-0 (hardcover)
1. Lange, Dorothea. 2. Photographers—United States—Biography. 3. Documentary photography—United
States—History—20th century. 4. United States—Social life and customs—20th century—Pictorial works.
I. Title.
TR140.L3.G67 2009
770.92—dc22
[B]                                                             2009019639

ISBN 978-0-393-33905-5 pbk.
W. W. Norton & Company, Inc., 500 Fifth Avenue, New York, N.Y. 10110
www.wwnorton.com

W. W. Norton & Company Ltd., Castle House, 75/76 Wells Street, London W1T 3QT

3  4  5  6  7  8  9  0

For Allen

# CONTENTS

## *Part II*

## DEPRESSION AND RENEWAL

## 1932–1935

## *Part III*

## CREATING DOCUMENTARY PHOTOGRAPHY

## 1935–1939

# Part IV

## WARTIME

### 1939–1945

# Part V

## INDEPENDENT PHOTOGRAPHER

### 1945–1965

Nipomo, California, 1936

# "A Camera Is a Tool for Learning How to See . . ."

A camera is a tool for learning how to see without a camera.[1]

The visual life is an enormous undertaking, practically unattainable. . . . I have only touched it with this wonderful democratic instrument, the camera . . . —*Dorothea Lange* [2]

T his photograph, often called *Migrant Mother,* is one of the most recognized pictures in the world. It is not the only one of Dorothea Lange's to win such fame—readers will recognize others in this book. Her photographs often linger in viewers' memories as if their intensity etched itself into the mind. Yet many who are familiar with the photographs do not know the name of the photographer and very few know anything about her. This is partly because most of her photographs were published anonymously, and partly because, when she died in 1965 at age seventy, only a handful of photography connoisseurs grasped her genius and her influence. That has changed: in October 2005 a vintage print of one of her photographs sold at auction for $822,400. (See page 102.) She would have enjoyed the money (she earned little from her photography) and the fame (she savored recognition as much as anyone), but she would have questioned what it meant that a photograph of hungry men at a soup kitchen had become a luxury commodity.

I have come to think of Lange as a photographer of democracy, and for democracy. She was not alone in this commitment, for she had predecessors and colleagues, and today has many photographic descendants. From her family of origin, her two extraordinary husbands, and friends of great talent she absorbed sensitivity, taste, and technique. These people are part of her enabling context, and for that reason this book includes them as major char-

acters. So too the unique cultures of Hoboken, New York, San Francisco, and
Berkeley play major roles in this story.

The greatest influence on Lange's photography, however, was her historical
era, so that also demands attention. Her career developed when the severe economic depression of the 1930s created a political opening for expanding and
deepening American democracy. President Roosevelt's New Deal, responding
to powerful grassroots social movements, made substantial progress in protecting the public health and welfare through regulation in the public interest,
from securities and credit to wages and hours, and through institutionaliz-
ing aid to the needy, such as Social Security. Despite the miseries and fear it
engendered, the Depression created a moment of idealism, imagination, and
unity in Americans' hopes for their country. No photographer of the time,
perhaps no artist of the time, did more than Lange to advance this democratic vision. Her photographs enlarged the popular understanding of who
Americans were, providing a more democratic visual representation of the
nation. Lange's America included Mormons, Jews, and evangelicals; farmers,
sharecroppers, and migrant farmworkers; workers domestic and industrial,
male and female; citizens and immigrants not only black and white but also
Mexican, Filipino, Chinese, and Japanese, notably the 120,000 Japanese
Americans locked in internment camps during World War II. Late in life her
democratic eye reached beyond the United States, as she photographed in
Egypt, Japan, Indonesia, and many other parts of the developing world. There
too her focus was democratic: she photographed primarily working people
through her lens of respect for their labor, skills, and pride.

Most of Lange's photography was optimistic, even utopian, not despite
but precisely through its frequent depictions of sadness and deprivation. By
showing her subjects as worthier than their conditions, she called attention
to the incompleteness of American democracy. And by showing her subjects
as worthier than their conditions, she simultaneously asserted that greater
democracy was possible.

Because her photography was both critical and utopian, its reputation and
popularity have varied with dominant political moods. During the Depression
of the 1930s her photographs became not only symbolic but almost definitive of
a national agenda. The agenda aimed to restore prosperity and prevent further
depressions, to alleviate poverty and reduce inequality. It stood for national
unity and mutual help, and delivered the message that we must indeed be
our brothers' keepers. When a more conservative agenda came to dominate

in the late 1940s and 1950s, Lange's photography became unfashionable, losing currency to more abstract, introspective, and self-referential art. When the
civil rights movement inaugurated several decades of progressive activism,
Lange's photography was again honored and emulated.

As I write at the end of 2008, another major depression makes Lange's
photography as significant as ever, and for the same reasons. We have today
the same need to see—not just look at, but *see*—the struggles of those on the
economic bottom. And we also share some of the 1930s optimism, in our case
built up through widespread, energetic participation in a presidential election, in which the central issue was whether government would shoulder its
responsibility for promoting the health of the society.

It would be a mistake, however, to see Lange's photography as politically
instrumental. Her greatest social purpose was to encourage visual pleasure.
Her message—that beauty, intelligence, and moral strength are found among
people of all circumstances—has profound political implications, of course.
Her greatest commitment, though, was to what she called the "visual life."
This meant discovering and intensifying beauty and our emotional response
to it. Her words about this goal were sometimes corny, but her photographs
were not. Although not a religious woman, she was rather spiritual, even
slightly mystical in sensibility. Yet she never preached and she abhorred the
sentimental.

Because Lange's subjects were often from humble surroundings, some
have assumed that she herself came from among the disadvantaged.[3] To the
contrary, she had educated middle-class parents and operated for sixteen years
a very successful, upscale portrait studio in San Francisco, catering to those of
wealth and high culture. She was married for fifteen years to Maynard Dixon,
a renowned painter. Articles about Lange and Dixon appeared on the society
pages of San Francisco newspapers. Her second husband, Paul Schuster Taylor, was an economics professor at the University of California at Berkeley.

There are other incongruities: This woman born and raised in Hoboken,
New Jersey, and New York City became not only a Californian, not only a lover
of western natural beauty, but an early environmentalist who dared to raise
questions about nature-changing projects such as big dams, which almost no
one challenged at the time. This quintessential city girl became a photographer who specialized in rural America and its farmworkers. She took on an
unusually demanding job for the federal government, on the road for months
at a time, as a disabled woman, lame from an attack of polio when she was

seven years old. Hostile to "feminism," she nevertheless behaved like a feminist throughout her life.

Lange's is also the story of two great love affairs, leading to two unconventional marriages and a houseful of children, and these aspects of her life also carry historical significance. Her first husband, Maynard Dixon, enchanted her with his artistry, prestige, sex appeal, and irreverent personality. Together they were at the center of a bohemian but fashionable community of Bay Area artists and and art patrons. Reversing conventional marital roles, Lange became the breadwinner, while Dixon became increasingly dependent on her, not only financially but emotionally. She was a lone mother during Dixon's many months-long trips, endured his depressions and crude jokes, and lived with the knowledge (and their friends' awareness) of his extramarital affairs. Despite this, they were together for fifteen years, and it was hard for her to make a break. Her second husband, Paul Schuster Taylor, a progressive academic reformer, appears at first to be the anti-Dixon: conventional in appearance, starchy in conversation. Yet he and Lange created an extraordinary romantic, familial, and professional partnership, which lasted until her death thirty years later. In contrast to the archetypical story of a woman's path to liberation, in which she moves from financial dependence on a husband to independence, and in contrast to the story of many other women who sacrifice artistic aspiration to marriage and family, Lange was able to become an artist when she got a husband who could support her. When she was still unknown outside her circle of customers, Taylor thought her photography a work of genius and encouraged her to defy the constraints of wifehood and motherhood. A rare equality shaped their marriage. He taught her about the social problems she was photographing, she taught him to see. Lange's two marriages thus reveal, in their uniqueness, something about how a woman went about transcending the limits that held most women back from this level of achievement.

AS I STUDIED Dorothea Lange, I began to feel an affinity with her work through the concept "documentary," which applies to historical scholarship as well as to photography. There is no standard definition of documentary, but in photography, at least, it connotes both revealing the truth and promoting social justice. These goals fit my historical work. For me as for Lange, however, they need careful qualification. Neither photography nor history simply reports facts. Historians and photographers choose what to include and exclude in the pictures they shape, frame their subjects so as to reveal, emphasize, relate, or separate different elements, and use interpretive techniques to do this. Some will argue, of course, that historians and documentarists have no business promoting their opinions, but that argument rests on the false assumption that it is possible to avoid doing so. History and documentary photography necessarily proceed from a point of view shaped by social position, politics, religious conviction, and the thousands of other factors that mold every human being.

This does not mean that it is appropriate for historians or documentarists to shape their creations as they please, regardless of the evidence. They must try to limit their own biases and must never manipulate evidence or select only the evidence that supports their perspective. When using examples to make a larger point, historians and photographic documentarists must look for the representative, the paradigmatic rather than the exceptional. Yet they must highlight what is most significant and remove detail that impedes the clarity of the main point; if they did not, no one would read a history book and photographs would be incomprehensible. There are disagreements, of course: one person's extraneous detail might be another person's vital evidence. Lange's decisions in framing her photographs are not so different from historians' decisions in writing books or lesson plans.

The camera's capacity to replicate what the eye can see made it appear, originally, to be the ultimate documentary tool. It seemed to be a machine for exact replication, its products machine-made, until the myriad means of constructing photographs were widely understood. Invented just as art steered toward expressing a subjective vision, an individual inner consciousness, the camera seemed limited to representing that which is visible to the naked eye. Honoré Daumier said that "photography described everything and explained nothing." Photographers engaged in some self-delusion along these lines; Walker Evans called documentary "a stark record . . . [of] actuality untouched." Lange did not fuss about exact representation in her photography. Her experience as a portrait photographer left her at ease in retouching an errant hand or shadow, in asking her subjects to move to a different spot or position. Like an historian, she wanted her photographs to emphasize what she saw as the main point and to prevent her viewers from being distracted by details. In her portrait studio she wanted to reveal the inner, not the outer, life and character of her subjects, and she continued the search for hidden truths in her documentary work. She would have agreed with her contemporary, Hungarian modernist photographer László Moholy-Nagy, who said he loved photography because it showed that nothing was as it seemed.[4] This is what she meant by the slogan she so often repeated, "A camera is a tool for learning how to see without a camera." Like many artists, she sought to disrupt conventionalized, clichéd perceptions by revealing less-noticed, often passed-over aspects of the world. Like many historians, I too accept that challenge.

Some artists and critics believed, and many still do, that documentary's instrumental purpose disqualifies it as art. Lange refused this dichotomy. She harbored no doubts about the compatibility of beauty and a concern for justice, or about her ability to fuse them. "I believe that what we call beautiful is generally a by-product. It happens when the thing is done very, very well."[5] Her opinions seem to waver because she often used words loosely, connotatively rather than precisely. She kept on her bulletin board for many years a quotation from seventeenth-century philosopher Francis Bacon: "The contemplation of things as they are, without substitution or imposture, without error or confusion, is in itself a nobler thing than a whole harvest of invention." Yet she insisted that "a documentary photograph is not a factual photograph."[6] She did not see such statements as contradictory because she believed that the truth she sought had an ethical dimension.

One reason the artistic status of photography did not worry her is that for much of her career she did not think of herself as an artist. This humility came from the lingering cultural idea that artistry was an unwomanly aspiration; from her assumption that her first husband, painter Maynard Dixon, was the artist while she was but a craftswoman; from her experience of photography as a business; and, beginning in the 1930s, from her growing sense of social responsibility—she often described her documentary photographs as "evidence."[7] She began as an artisan, continuing a tradition that did not distinguish between art and artisanship. (Her notion that beauty happens when "the thing is done very, very well" could be the artisanal credo.) Her modesty, however, was also sometimes a pose, a coyness, a way of avoiding competition with other photographers who did call their work art. It certainly evidenced no lack of ambition, since the standards she measured herself against were high. But her early disclaimer about artistic ambition, along with her distance from New York, insulated her from the pressures of competing in art as commerce and of seeking the approval of establishment art authorities. It gave her space to develop an autonomous method and style.

In particular, Lange resisted a central motif of photographic modernism, the use of the camera to express her own inner consciousness. To the best of my knowledge, she never made a self-portrait. This indifference to exploring her own inner life through photography appears, at first, surprising, considering that her success as a portrait photographer rested on her ability to express others' inner selves. She was hardly devoid of self-love or pride. I cannot explain this reticence; I can only report that she was driven by interest in the outside world. One of Lange's colleagues, documentary photographer Jack Delano, could have been speaking for her in saying, "I have always been motivated not by something inside me that needed to be expressed but rather by the wonder of something I see that I want to share with the rest of the world. I think of myself as a chronicler of my time and feel impelled to probe and probe into the depths of society in search of the essence of truth."[8]

This inner world/outer world distinction needs to be qualified, however. What Lange saw in her subjects came partly from her own consciousness. Her portraits of sharecroppers and interned Japanese Americans express her emotions as well as theirs. Yet there is a durable distinction between gazes turned inward and those turned outward. Critic Linda Nochlin pointed out that artistic realism arose as a democratic form, originally reserved for representing the common people, deriving from the anti-aristocratic movements of the nineteenth century.[9] Lange's realist approach was itself a democratic form, representing others, no matter how plebeian, as autonomous subjects, most certainly not as emanations of herself. She did this through portraiture. Her documentary photography *was* portrait photography. What made it different was its subjects, and thereby its politics. She looked at the poor as she had looked at the rich, never stereotyping, never pretending "to any easy understanding of her subjects," in the words of Getty museum curator Judith Keller. "Every Lange portrait subject is complex, and to some degree, inscrutable. . . . She never provides any superficial suggestion that we understand that person immediately."[10] That final, impermeable layer of unknowability is the basis of mutual respect and, in turn, the basis of democracy.

FOR ME AS a historian, this book has been a new kind of undertaking. I am neither biographer nor photography expert, and most of my previous writing focused on the history of national policy issues. But once Lange came to my attention, I could not let her go. Lange's life trajectory, though nothing like mine, sounded and resounded themes that resonated with my concerns, forming an obbligato underlining significant episodes and problems in U.S. history.

The book I wrote just prior to this one constituted, perhaps, a step toward biography: By telling a story of events that happened in a small town in just a few days, what historians call a "microhistory," I used a tiny fragment of history to illuminate large themes and problems. Because this book has a larger time frame—two-thirds of the twentieth century—it is both "micro," as it is the story of only one person, and "macro," since it intersects with crucial events and problems of the twentieth-century United States: deadly polio epidemics, the development of bohemian and arts countercultures, the Depression, World War II, the Cold War and McCarthyism, the transformation of agriculture by technology and corporatization, the birth of environmentalism, U.S. foreign assistance, and the civil rights movement.[11] Moreover, her life affords a view of aspects of this history often unnoticed. Her 1920s San Francisco experience suggests that West Coast modernism, even in big cities, was significantly less urban than that in the East—or perhaps that New York's urbanity was only one model of city life. Her 1930s experience showed the centrality of the rural experience to the mid-century United States; by putting farmworkers at the center of Depression history, her photography exposes a major failure of the New Deal. Her experience of the diversity of the West Coast population made her photography particularly insightful about American race and racism. Her own life sensitized her to the inaccuracy of conventional ideals of womanhood. In these and other ways, Dorothea Lange's story forces us to rewrite a bit the history of twentieth-century America.

Lange confronted problems that still hound us today. She faced a conflict common to many women, between personal ambition and public responsibility on the one hand and commitment to children and to family life on the other. She dreamed of a democratic art, accessible to all, and for a brief, intense time, this dream seemed a possibility, because the federal government supported artists as a way of beating back the Depression; that support soon evaporated, however, and art became once again largely a luxury commodity. She endured several timeless personal hardships: disability, a disappearing father, an irresponsible husband, a delinquent son, a criminal brother. She suffered injustices—such as being fired from a beloved photography project although she produced, arguably, its greatest work; and experiencing the suppression of some of her most impassioned photography of protest, unpublished until forty years after her death. She coped with these and other problems in the way that most people do—with impatience, with ambivalence and compromises, with mistakes, with stoicism and irritability, and with resilience.

If Dorothea Lange is a hero, she was, like all real heroes, flawed. She made hard choices, at significant cost to herself and also to others. She behaved at times imperiously. As a mother, she made some dubious decisions. She flirted and maneuvered to promote her work. This is not a biography intended to sanctify her; perfect people belong in fables or hagiography, not in historical biography. My interest is in understanding and explaining, as best I can, the life of a woman embedded in the historical events of her time.[12] This does not mean that I lack interest in Lange as an individual; to the contrary, I find myself often moved by her bravery and capacity for hard work, angry when she hurt others, pained when she was hurt, and awed by her talent, intelligence, and commitment.

The story I tell is limited not only by the areas of my expertise but also by the available source material. Lange did not document her own life. Until she was in her fifties, she did not save letters or keep a diary. Almost nothing that she wrote before 1935 has been preserved, so information about her life before that comes from recorded interviews with her carried out two or three decades later. Once she became a documentary photographer, of course, she created a great deal of evidence, in her field notebooks, correspondence, photographs, and captions. Like any other personal product, the photographs offer information not only about their subjects but also about their maker.

The lack of written evidence about Lange's early life gives her unusual power over its interpretation by a biographer. Forced to rely primarily on her recollections as an older woman, the biographer receives accounts of her youthful experiences only as digested, interpreted, and rearranged by her memory—a notoriously unreliable source—and by her decisions about what to reveal. Like most people, she was an unreliable narrator of her life. I compensate for the fallibility of such recollections with devices well known to historians: noting contradictions in her testimony, comparing her recollections to those of others and to external evidence, reading between the lines, and noticing what she did not talk about. When she did speak, however, Lange's voice, in words as in images, was a strong one. As a result, I may at times accept her account of herself, however unconsciously, when I should not. This fact does not make the biography more celebratory, though, because she is hard on herself in the areas she speaks about most passionately—her photographic achievement. The risk comes from her silences. I try to fill them with what I have learned from those who knew her, but mysteries will remain.

FOR LANGE, AS for most photographers, the most powerful tool was her eye. She learned to use it from her mother and grandmother, her early photographer employers, and from two master artistic observers, her husband, Maynard Dixon, and her close friend, photographer Imogen Cunningham. Cunningham made exquisite close-ups of flowers in which we can see every filament and anther on every stamen. Dixon's prowess as a draftsman was one of the artistic wonders of West Coast art: He could look at a tree briefly and then, from memory, draw not just any tree but *that* tree; he could see the muscular movement on a horse in motion.

All good photography requires visual discipline and imagination, of course. Lange's particular visual intelligence focused on people. In some of her portraits, she seems to have telepathically connected with her subjects' emotions, perhaps because they trusted her enough to reveal something of themselves. That trust was repaid in one valuable currency: Lange's subjects are always good-looking. This was the bread and butter of her studio photography business, of course, but it also became central to her documentary photography. Lange made her documentary subjects handsome not through flattery so much as respect, and when her subjects were farmworkers long deprived of education, health, rest, and nutrition, her respect for them became a political statement. Its effectiveness was doubled because the looks of her subjects drew viewers to her photography, allowed them to take pleasure in it even as it documented misery and injustice. Her photographs delivered both beauty and a call for empathy.

The photographer's eye is a skill, not a physiological organ. Lange loved quotations pointing out that we see with our brains—and have to be taught. She copied out "Seeing is more than a physiological phenomenon. . . . We see not only with our eyes but with all that we are and all that our culture is. The artist is a professional see-er."[13] Her assistants, her family, her friends—all agreed that she taught them, or tried to teach them, how to see. She believed that sight, like most art, consists of 99 percent hard work. The work never ends: The photographer is "continually training his power of vision," she said, "so that he actually knows if the telegraph pole has two cross beams and how many glass cups . . . the things we don't look at anymore."[14]

The worst enemy of seeing is conventionalization, Lange knew, and overcoming it requires vigilance. The more we see the ordinary, the less we notice, because our expectation of what we will see overpowers actual observation, and because we hurry. Skilled seeing requires emptying the mind of false and clichéd responses, responses that the human brain always creates. One neuropsychologist estimates that visual perception is 90 percent memory, less than 10 percent sensory. Perception is thus mostly inference,[15] and a great photographer wants observers not to infer, but to see anew. Lange struggled against conventionalizing in her studio portraiture no less than in her documentary. She criticized one of her own photographs by saying, "That's a passing glance. I know I didn't see it."[16] Lange disdained a photograph that failed to bust through commonsense expectations.

Her commitment to seeing derived not only from artistic openness but also from refusal to pass by uninvolved. The effort of sight fused, for her, with a sense of responsibility to understand and act on the world. Visual imagery can, of course, serve to inflame the worst nationalistic, xenophobic, racist, and misogynist passions. But Lange also believed that pictures can imbue respect and open-mindedness, qualities necessary for democracy. She believed that an imagery of democracy could contribute to building political democracy and that visual education could contribute to an active democratic citizenship.

The responsibility she felt was not to provide solutions to problems, however; she told her students that documentary photographs should ask questions, not provide answers. It is the questioning aspect of Lange's photographs that remains animated today. Many documentary photographs denounce injustice and suffering. The very best are also wondering. They suggest that the photographer does *not* understand everything going on in them. There remains a mystery, and this may be their most respectful and challenging message.

# Part I

---

HOBOKEN AND SAN FRANCISCO

1895–1931

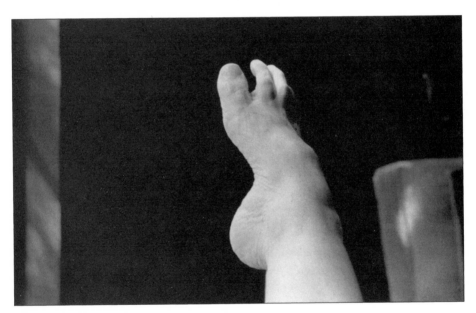

Lange's foot, 1959

# SCENE I

*In 1957, when Dorothea Lange was teaching photography at the California School of Fine Arts in San Francisco, she gave students one of her favorite assignments. Every week, students were to bring in photographs that answered the question "Where do I live?" By this, she did not mean the student's house or apartment, but something deeper. She told them she wanted to see an intimate relation between the photographer and the subject of her or his photography. She pointed out that they could use nonhuman objects to reveal the human, or fragmentary images to refer to wholes. One group of students challenged her to do the assignment herself. What she brought to the class, the only self-portraits she ever made, were several studies of her polio-twisted foot. This is where she lived, she felt— imprisoned in this imperfect body.*

*She explained the assignment this way: ". . . by the time we have looked at them all, we ought to feel that our own homes and hearts, by the view we have been given of the homes and the hearts of others, are not just what they were when we began."[1]*

# I

# Child of Iron, Wounded

Two childhood traumas made Dorothea Lange who she became, or so she believed. The first was polio. She contracted the disease in 1902, when she was seven, before it became epidemic, at a time when physicians had no treatment to offer. She was lucky to escape with her life and her mobility, but she was left with a permanently twisted foot and stiff lower leg. She always limped, and dragged her right foot when she was tired. She applied a powerful will to the project of passing for normal, and succeeded remarkably for many years. The second trauma was her parents' separation five years later. So strong was her anger at her father—a deserting father, as she saw him—that when she moved to San Francisco she took on her mother's maiden name, Lange. So strong even that she never mentioned or saw her father again. These two were the traumas she named. It seems likely that there was a third, so upsetting to her that she never even hinted at it: the suspicion that her father was a crook.

The historian must consider these traumas both as she felt and remembered them and as they "really" happened. But of traumas there is no one reality, no objective way to understand what happened, since what happened takes place partly in the psyche. Parental desertion is one of a child's nightmares, and these anxieties probably never entirely disappear. Any experience is what you make of it, and the adolescent Dorothea felt deserted by her father.

Even as an intensely independent adult, separations or rejections could make her feel orphaned. (It is worth noting that the word *orphan* did not mean in her youth what it means today: in her time, most children labeled orphans still had mothers but lacked fathers.) But it turns out that her father did not "abandon us," as Dorothea repeatedly said. Her parents separated apparently amicably, continued to see each other and share money, and the family never lost its solidly middle-class status.

The polio trauma differs, for it left a visible, debilitating injury. Yet it resembled her parents' separation in creating an invisible emotional wound, one easy to disregard for those of us who have lived in a country now free of polio for fifty years. What's more, it returned to attack her body in middle age.

Dorothea Lange said, "I think it [polio] was the most important thing that happened to me, and formed me, guided me, instructed me, helped me, and humiliated me."[1] No other polio victim of the time would have found this surprising. Polio survivors once had a shorthand that demonstrates this total, permanent impact of the disease: they called themselves "polios." This is not medical shorthand, as when a physician on rounds might say, "Let's look at the broken arm in room three." Polio survivors labeled *themselves*; far from expressing shame, they used the term as a badge of membership in an exclusive club. I have been through the wars, it said. And it indicated a solidarity, one that Dorothea lacked, because polio was still so rare when she was afflicted.

Lange's words about polio's impact on her come from the 1960s, when she was weakened by years of bleeding ulcers and postpolio syndrome and dying of cancer of the esophagus. During her active years, she seemed to have the stamina of a workhorse and at least normal strength, and she hid her disability from others as she tried to deny it to herself. If she was right that polio shaped who she became, it did that jointly with her resilience, her drive, her particular strategies of coping. She saw herself as disabled, by her father's departure as well as by polio, but her response was shaped by a supportive, if sometimes quarrelsome, family and by a character that was anything but disabled. Some children would fade at least a bit under similar stresses. Dorothea became steadily more vivid. She became a charismatic personality, an artistically and intellectually ambitious photographer, a successful businesswoman, a powerful, temperamental, even intimidating presence, and at the same time a human being of unusual sensitivity to others. She developed a keen receptivity to others' emotions, as well as a social conscience and sense of social responsibility. Her gifts, her energy, and her commitments came at a cost. A child thrown into relative independence to an unusual extent and unusually early, she lived with high stress and overwork and she became an adult with a powerful need for control over her environment. To the degree her environment included others, she sometimes needed to control them, too.

DOROTHEA'S LINEAGE WAS homogeneous: all German American. Both her parents were born in New Jersey, of parents who had emigrated from Germany and become middle-class and prosperous.[2] In 1894, her father, Heinrich Nutzhorn,[3] married Johanna Lange, who had Americanized her name to Joan; they probably met at their church, St. Matthew's Lutheran, where she was a soloist in the choir. Their first child, Dorothea, was born at home on May 26, 1895. Heinrich soon became Henry, and, like his father, seemed a go-getter. He spent some time at Northwestern College in Watertown, Wisconsin, formerly a Lutheran seminary, then returned to Hoboken to apprentice in a law firm. In 1891 he passed the New Jersey bar and opened a practice with a partner. Four years later he moved his family from Hoboken to Weehawken, an affluent northern suburb. Weehawken began as a vacation site for New York's rich, a spot where the Palisades above the Hudson River provided cooling breezes and dramatic vistas. (A series of wagon lifts, stairs, and even an elevator designed by Gustave Eiffel, at the time the world's largest, carried residents and visitors from the river to the top of the Palisades.) The Nutzhorns' neighbors were professionals, white-collar workers, the occasional skilled workers (machinists, upholsterers, butchers), and businessmen. As was the norm in their class, Joan Nutzhorn was not employed and housework was done by a maid.

Henry's success rested on Hoboken's prosperity and ethnic makeup.[4] Germans were so dominant there that it is misleading to consider them an ethnic group, which carries the implication of minority status. Teaching German in the public schools was standard and Germans dominated many of the biggest churches, Catholic, Lutheran, and Reformed (Evangelical). The Nutzhorns' church, St. Matthew's, was one of the oldest and most distinguished, with its 150-foot bell tower.

Hoboken's population of 59,000 in 1900 made it a suburb of New York City, whose population was then 3.5 million. But Hoboken was not a bedroom community. Its economy was thriving, a success story based on a greater diversity of enterprises than was typical of growing cities. Its largest manufacturers included Remington Arms, which employed three thousand, a huge dry docks, Cooper Hewitt Electric, and the country's biggest pencil maker. Lipton Tea and Maxwell House Coffee were two of many large importers in Hoboken. Between 1900 and 1905, its factories increased from 194 to 279, and these manufacturing activities gave rise to many mercantile and financial institutions.

In Dorothea's time, Hoboken's soul was its docks. San Francisco's Embarcadero seemed familiar to Dorothea when she first saw it, because Hoboken's riverside had always swarmed with longshoremen and sailors moving from ships to docks to bars and back. Fifty years later, the feel of the Hoboken docks remained vivid enough for Elia Kazan to film *On the Waterfront* there. In Dorothea's youth, Hoboken was the major New York–area steamship terminal, featuring a dozen lines, notably the Hamburg-American Line, which offered express service from Hoboken to Southampton in a record six and a half days. So many immigrants disembarked from these ships that boosters called Hoboken "the city at the nation's front door."

Hoboken also provided for transshipping between sea and rail, and the Lackawanna Railroad provided the fuel—anthracite coal—for this engine of capitalism. In 1907, the massive Erie-Lackawanna train station opened, a Beaux-Arts confection sheathed in lavish ornamental copper, connecting both to the ferry terminal and the new Port Authority Trans-Hudson tunnel train to Manhattan. The wealth of Hoboken and its nearby cities made education and high culture possible, in part because of proximity to New York. It claimed Stephen Crane, Fred Astaire, Jerome Robbins, Alfred Kinsey, and Alfred Stieglitz, the dean of art photography in Dorothea's youth, as native sons.

The Nutzhorns belonged to the elite among Hoboken's middle class. Henry Nutzhorn quickly gained positions of importance: elected Hudson County freeholder, trustee of the most important Lutheran church in Hoboken, officer of the Hoboken Board of Trade, and Republican state representative (at the age of twenty-seven). These offices came to him from family, political, class, and ethnic connections—his father also sat on the church and trade boards. Because of these connections, Dorothea learned early about local politics in all their pettiness and dirtiness. In the state legislature, the two parties made their peace through guaranteeing equality in corruption. Politicians ran gambling, prostitution, racing, and bribery enterprises and sold pardons to criminals, while the state became known as "the Mother of Trusts" for its permissive policy toward holding companies. As New York City had begun to crack down on corruption, some of its greatest barons, such as Jim Fisk and Jay Gould, fled to New Jersey. Nowhere was the graft greater and more brazen than in Democrat-dominated Hudson County. The power behind the county's bosses, magnate Edward F. C. Young, controlled the trolleys, banks, and railroads of the area from the Civil War through the 1890s and doled out lesser properties to his cronies. Becoming careless, legislating too openly in the interests of their criminal and corporate masters, Democratic politicians lost the legislature in 1894 and the governorship in 1896. Within the ascendant Republican party arose a Progressive reform caucus, called the "New Idea" movement, which attacked not only corruption but also subsidies to corporations. The New Idea represented middle-class, professional, and upper-class Protestants, Germans prominent among them, typical of the constituencies of Progressivism throughout the United States. Weehawken, where Henry and Joan and their children now lived, was a center of support for the Progressive reformers, and Henry Nutzhorn counted himself among them. Although they were defeated in 1910, the New Idea movement had increased Nutzhorn's prestige within his community and constituency.

As with many other Progressives, the young Nutzhorn couple was modern and cultured. Their second child, Dorothea's brother, Henry Martin Nutzhorn, Jr., was born when she was six, in 1901, so some kind of birth control was being practiced. The Nutzhorns valued literature and education. The young Dorothea read from the family's volume of Shakespeare's plays. Her father took her once to see *A Midsummer Night's Dream*. When they arrived, there were no more seats, so he stood and she sat on his shoulders through the whole performance. He had a strong back and a strong desire for his daughter to take this in.

Joan, however, was the major communicator of culture. A music lover, broad in her taste, she collected jazz as well as classical recordings; a great reader, she was tuned in to world and local politics, progressive in her opinions and even activist in her orientation. In Weehawken, a uniformed maid relieved her of housework and Joan at times made snobbish remarks about the less cultured. She enjoyed good furniture and a well-decorated home and liked displaying the household's many books. She disliked the way that her sister-in-law Minette, a Ziegfeld dancer, came "shambling up from the train with all her children in tow—it looked too 'Italian,'" and thought that her father had married "beneath" himself in choosing Sophie Votteler. In other ways Joan was liberal, open-minded and restless. She frequently rearranged her house, and once explained that she would move objects and furniture whenever reaching them got to be automatic.[5] This odd and interesting preference was due not just to restlessness or adventurousness but also to an imperative to resist the routine, the taken-for-granted. The same resistance would characterize her daughter, but in Dorothea it would be transmuted into awesome discipline.

The family created art as well as consuming it. Joan was a fine soprano and, when still in her teens, became the paid soloist at St. Matthew's, singing from a classical as well as a religious repertoire. She took Dorothea to hear the renowned Leopold Stokowski conduct an oratorio at New York's elite St. Bartholomew's church. Joan's youngest brother, John George Lange, was a cellist with the Hoboken Quartet, the Haydn Orchestra, and the Dvořák String Quartet. When conducting for Ziegfeld, he met and married Minette, who was then performing in a Victor Herbert musical.[6] A generation back, Joan's great-uncles Otto, William, and Fritz were all lithographers and engravers. They had learned their skills in the old country, and passed them on to two sons, Dorothea's uncles, who also became lithographers. She loved to look at the stones they worked on. They were artisans, yes, but at this time the line between the skilled crafts and the arts was fuzzy, and after a few years they switched their occupational identity in the city business directory to "artist."

Joan's mother, Sophie, was an artisan seamstress, as creative as her brothers. She made all the women in her family a new dress twice a year. She also "turned" the old ones, disassembling the frocks and reassembling them with the inside of the fabric facing out. (This was an indicator of thrift, not poverty.) These were the days when clothing had gussets and plackets, tucks and pleats, even passementerie—elaborate edgings and trimmings of braid, cord, embroidery, and beads. She cut her own patterns, having first marked them out with an old-fashioned pattern wheel on a walnut-topped oval table. The table was covered with little pricks made by the wheel as it marked the paper or fabric, and Dorothea thought it beautiful, like an abstract design. *Grosmama* Sophie was an aesthete; Dorothea remembered that she once said that "of all the things that were beautiful in the world there was nothing finer than an orange. . . ."[7]

Henry and Joan made a fine-looking couple. Henry, handsome and vigorous, was five nine, lean, blond, with gray eyes behind his glasses. As a teenager, Dorothea thought he looked like Woodrow Wilson. Joan was lovely, her features both softer and stronger than his, with a generous nose and mouth, large eyes, an animated face, freckles and a ruddy complexion, a wealth of red-brown hair worn up in a twist. The Nutzhorns were active in their church.

While they were not devout, they practiced and cherished Christian family rituals—singing and playing favorite Christmas music and listening to it on the Victrola, hanging much-used decorations, and cooking and eating elaborate extended-family holiday meals.

DOROTHEA'S CHILDHOOD APPEARS to have been placid for seven years. Nothing threatened to disturb this well-being when the seven-year-old girl came down with a cold in the summer of 1902. But it worsened into what her parents thought was influenza, a potential killer at the time. The young girl was feverish and nauseated, with headache and a stiff neck. But after days of this and then a day or two of feeling better, her legs suddenly buckled while she was walking just a few steps around the house, and soon she could not move her legs at all. Then the paralysis stiffened her whole body. After about a week, the Nutzhorns realized that their daughter had caught infantile paralysis, as poliomyelitis was called in those days. In fact, parents of many children who contracted the disease thought it was a cold or flu, because most polio cases never progressed beyond those symptoms. And since these symptoms came with many other diseases, it is not an anomaly that there is no record of a 1902 outbreak in Hudson County. Entering the body through the digestive system, the virus is often destroyed there by antibodies. Only when it enters the central nervous system does it become destructive, killing motor nerve cells, which cannot regenerate. More confusing yet, sometimes children died before exhibiting clear evidence of paralysis, and at other times the paralysis developed de novo, without any previous warnings of illness. Even the most knowledgeable physicians were confused.

The polio virus is probably ancient, not a new mutation. It had long been endemic—that is, the virus was widespread—but rarely caused much serious disease because children gained a passive immunity through breast-feeding, and later active immunity through exposure. In the crowded slums of London, Paris, and the Lower East Side of New York City, babies and young children were routinely exposed and became immune.

Progress then intercepted this adaptation. When public-health measures improved sanitation, babies were more likely to be spared exposure; then, if exposed at older ages, they lacked immunity. For that reason, polio struck most where standards of hygiene and plumbing were highest, a disease not of the slums but of upscale and rural neighborhoods where water was clean and human wastes either efficiently removed or effectively degraded.[8] In other words, poliomyelitis was an unintended perverse consequence of public health.[9] As living standards rose, exposure to polio was postponed, so that the age of victims climbed. That Franklin Delano Roosevelt came down with polio at age thirty-nine in 1921 was not, by then, completely strange.

But earlier in the century, associations of disease with dirt and poverty clouded the eyes of public-health experts. Despite reports that showed greater polio incidence in better neighborhoods, during the large 1916 New York City epidemic, Commissioner of Health Haven Emerson focused on cleaning up the slums. These assumptions amounted to a moralizing attack on the urban poor, and specifically seemed to blame mothers, since 80 percent of the New York–area cases affected children under five.[10]

The disease soon became known as "the crippler." Although the death rate from polio was much lower than that in epidemics traditionally called "plagues," the crippling and disfigurement made polio differently terrifying. That it almost always attacked children made it the cruelest of diseases. Epidemiologist John R. Paul anthropomorphized the virus as a calculating, strategizing enemy. It "seeks to establish itself in the lymphatic tissue. . . ." It does its best "to get a further foothold in the body of the susceptible child."[11] His semantics eerily match that of the memory of a child polio, the writer Leonard Kriegel:

> I just lay in bed, an eleven-year-old boy who was terrified of the thick somnolent deadness that was creeping up from his ankles. . . . I knew then without even knowing that my life depended upon that thing within me, on whether it had fed enough on my soft, child-muscled body or whether it was simply resting, a quiet pause to cool the ardor of its appetite . . . before it crept on to devour my heart, my neck, my head, even my mind, in its untempered, unrestrained desire.[12]

Neither Dorothea nor anyone close to her left an account of her polio experience, so I have pieced together the typical polio progression from other sources. The onset of paralysis often caused vertigo. One polio remembered crying out, "I can't find my body."[13] The pain was brutal and terrifying. "As the neurons in my body died one by one during those two weeks, I felt relentless pain, like the pain of a tooth being drilled without Novocain, but all over my body."[14] As paralysis ebbed, the pain increased, and there were few painkillers.

Polioed muscles were tender and often in spasm. Every manipulation of the patient—to dress or undress, to wash or massage—produced pain. During the acute phase of the illness, patients were commonly unable to speak, swallow, or control the bowels and bladder.

There was, quite literally, nothing one could do to cure this disease. No reason to be hospitalized. (Middle-class people at the time associated hospitals with the worst of medical care and with death. One physician writing about poliomyelitis referred to the "hospital classes," meaning the poor and disreputable.)[15] If polio attacked the diaphragm, you died, because there were no iron lungs or respirators before 1924. The first reliable U.S. study reported that 17 percent of victims died, but the death rate was higher when polio struck adults or older children. A doctor likely saw Dorothea, for this was standard practice among people of her class and location at the time, but the less he did, the better. Many physicians turned to traditional practices of considerable unpleasantness and no benefit.[16] It is hard to blame them, considering the desperate pleas from parents to do something, try anything.

The eerie paralysis produced a radical separation between consciousness and body, as if the self were imprisoned. Depression often followed. Once active, sociable children were no longer able to play with others. Fear of contagion kept visitors away and led parents to confiscate and even destroy children's most beloved objects—pets, teddy bears, favorite books—in case they were vectors of dirt or germs. Discrete deprivations merged into a pool of loss. Children could even feel guilty: When eleven-year-old Leonard Kriegel could speak again, his first words to his mother were, "Momma, I'm sorry."[17]

When paralysis abated, treatments aimed to prevent deformity through physical manipulation, braces, and painful physical therapy.[18] Dorothea was fitted with a brace for her right leg. It began with a special shoe, a short boot really. Double steel uprights were attached to its shank, running to the upper thigh; the outer upright continued up to a band strapped around the pelvis; it was hinged at ankle and knee, but these hinges could be locked, so as to provide support for maintaining a straight leg and to correct misshapen legs.[19] The steady pressure of the device caused pain, the straps abraded the skin, and the weight of the brace—probably about twenty pounds—fatigued the wearer.

Some paralyzed victims regained full mobility, while others suffered permanently paralyzed legs (this is the single most common polio consequence), arms, stomachs, and, worst of all, diaphragms. In Dorothea's case, the permanent damage—that is, the visible permanent damage—was to her right leg. The muscles shrank, the tendons fixed in tension. Treatment and exercise left her with a right lower leg that was functional but stiffer, weaker, and less well shaped than her left, with a "drop foot" that could not flex into a position perpendicular to the leg. (That foot position was the most common of polio deformities, called *talipes equines* because it appeared hooflike, in extreme cases resembling the bound foot of a woman in old China.) Since the foot was in constant plantar flexion, the posterior muscles and tendons contracted. Dorothea's right foot also took on a bit of *talipes varus*, where the foot turned inward, so that only the outer edge of the sole touched the ground. She would always need to wear two different shoe sizes.

It is difficult to distinguish Dorothea's emotions about her trauma from Joan's, because at the heart of children's polio experience was often a renewed dependence on a caretaker, usually the mother, from whom they had just been developing autonomy. Seven-year-old Dorothea might have been back in diapers, unable to meet any need without her mother, possibly even unable to call her mother, and thus entirely vulnerable. This unnatural and frightening intimacy left a child paralyzed not only in limb, but also inert, without agency. Little knots of misunderstanding might chafe the already-tender child. With the first paralysis, a child was stunned, but the very young might assume it would pass, especially since she experienced her parents as all-protecting. The child might imagine a logical explanation. One child asked, " 'Mama, why does my food all go down into one leg and leave the other one so thin?' "[20] Worse trouble could start here. Knowing that the child needed reassurance, the parents might fib: "You have a cold in your leg." Or misunderstand: One child, experiencing double vision as the polio affected his eyes, told his parents that he was "seeing through" solid objects. They responded that this could not be. So children realized that what their parents said was not necessarily to be believed. In Dorothea, this paralytic dependence strengthened her extraordinary need for independence, a need that came from feeling that dependence was unsafe, unreliable.

With partial recovery came stringent, if not impossible, challenges. Joan emphasized that Dorothea should hide her limp and her distorted leg. Her desire to protect her daughter from stigma communicated her own anxiety at being the mother of a "cripple." The very experience of renewed dependence intensified the child's normal desire to please her mother. This effort was exhausting and often failed. As an adult, Dorothea turned that failure into anger, and condemned her mother for undignified deference to the opinions of others. Yet Joan's shame contributed to Dorothea's lifelong fastidiousness.

She cared little for conventional fashion but much for absolute control over her image.[21]

Returning to school presented new difficulties. There were no programs for "special needs" children. Disability was neither respected nor accepted. Paralysis was often associated with idiocy, and physically and cognitively handicapped children were often placed in the same separate classrooms.[22] Many polios recalled teachers who suspected them of faking or exaggerating paralysis and weakness, and being thus disbelieved worsened the sense of isolation. As other children ran to get outside at recess, the polio child limped slowly down long hallways. Once outside, she would likely stand and watch the games. Some children were instructed not to play with her, and the less well-mannered children stared, whispered, or even taunted the cripple. An older sibling might protect a younger, but Dorothea had only a one-year-old brother. Perhaps there was a loyal, sheltering friend, but friends might also desert.

Could a seven-year-old contemplate life as a "cripple"? Or predict a life with stigma and discrimination? Her parents could certainly contemplate these outcomes. In Dorothea's case, their anxiety ebbed, as she recovered almost complete mobility, but her passage through her parents' panic left a scar, a sensitive area of the psyche then toughened by this resilient child. Decades later, the polio Mia Farrow wrote, "I was nine years old when my childhood ended."[23]

Yet no two polios responded alike. Dorothea's polio experience was shaped by her innate character, and intensified not only her self-discipline and independence but also her determination to transcend the wound.


EXCEPT FOR THE polio ordeal, the Nutzhorns' friends and neighbors might have considered them a model American family. Until it wasn't, and Joan and Henry separated. This event, in 1907, when Dorothea was twelve, became another core part of who she was. She always spoke of her father "abandoning" the family. Mysteriously, she also seemed to regard her father as a criminal, or at least a man of poor character. Some archival research yielded a set of secrets that Dorothea's mother kept from her children in order to protect a faltering man whose success had masked considerable weakness.

In understanding her father as a deserter, Dorothea was fitting her experience into standard early twentieth-century presumptions about marital break-ups. Marriage was understood then, in both law and custom, not as a contract between individuals, but as a contract of spouses with state and church. Marriage was, and still is, a public institution, not a private one—but it was even more so a century ago. The only way out of a marriage contract then was to prove that one party had violated its terms—that is, committed an offense against the law of marriage. Furthermore, divorce required not only that one party to the contract was guilty but also that the other was innocent of wrongdoing. If both were guilty, there was no legal basis for dissolving the contract. As a result, divorce had to be an adversarial proceeding, with one party trying to dissolve the marriage and the other trying to maintain it. Evidence that the wish for divorce was mutual—that is, that there was "collusion" between the parties—would produce automatic denial of the divorce. Evidence of an amicable separation produced the same. One spouse or the other had to sue for divorce.

Divorced mothers faced additional problems: unless they could get support from relatives, they would find it very difficult both to earn a living and care for children. One result was that orphanages at the time were packed with children of living mothers who could not find a way to support them.[24] So mothers were loath to leave marriages, and if husbands left, wives and chil-

1.1. DOROTHEA AND MARTIN NUTZHORN, 1903 OR 1904

dren were often, in fact, deserted, especially since it was difficult to get fathers to pay child support. In this context, all marital separation was commonly named, and perceived, as desertion, even when wives were eager to escape the marriages.

Couples who voluntarily separated, however, might well collude in presenting their story as one of desertion, in the hope of getting financial support from a charity. Desertion, as historian Nancy Cott put it, "was another name for self-divorce."[25] In these early twentieth-century years, numerous husbands dropped in and out of familial households, hiding from public view but surreptitiously visiting and providing financial support. Another common complication of marital separation was ambivalence. Spouses vacillate about separation and divorce today, and they had far more reason to back off from such a precipice then. Today, trial separations and even divorce and remarriage by the same people happen all the time. In 1907, those moves could only be made in secrecy, and children surrounded by secrets often construct stories even worse than the reality.

Henry Nutzhorn did not desert in any of these meanings, however; rather, he fled.[26] Joan might well have been ignorant of his financial finagling until everything collapsed at once. In July 1907, they were evicted from their Weehawken home, their rent three months in arrears. Joan had to sell some jewelry to pay the maid what was owed her. Joan and Henry separated; Joan went with the children to her mother's in Hoboken, and Henry left New Jersey for Flatbush, in Brooklyn. He grew a beard and took an assumed name. A police officer soon arrived at Sophie's home to serve an indictment on Henry, leaving the papers with six-year-old Martin because Henry was not there. The sum of money in question was $4,000 to $5,000, equivalent to $110,000 today. This could not have been only a matter of debt, because criminal indictments for debt, and debtors prison, had long since been abolished in New Jersey.[27] A "special master" appointed by the court in the Nutzhorns' ultimate divorce hearing called him a "gambler" and a "speculator." My best guesses are that Henry gambled with money he had embezzled or with a client's money, or enticed clients into scams, or entered seamy deals that clients offered him.

For the next eleven years Joan Nutzhorn continued to meet him surreptitiously, in rendezvous at restaurants arranged by letter. Joan found employment immediately and she and Henry helped each other financially.[28] In 1914, Henry asked to end their marriage, thus implying that at this point they still had a marriage, but then he reversed his decision. He never came to the house, and for the first seven years of the separation, the children never saw him. Between 1914 and 1918, Joan testified, he saw his children about six times, each visit at a public place, also arranged by letter; he likely felt himself safer after seven years. He brought them gifts. In this period Joan tried to have his criminal indictment nol-prossed, and Henry hinted that perhaps she could pay off the debt. If she considered buying him out of trouble with her own earnings, it would not be the first time a woman sought to rescue a ne'er-do-well man.[29]

The fact that Joan clung to this marriage through eleven years of separation, despite having a decent and stable income of her own, may speak of her continuing affection for Henry, but it was also characteristic of many women's understanding of marriage as necessary to respectability. Finally, in July 1918, she filed for divorce on the grounds of desertion since 1907, which turned out to be an embarrassing mistake. Her deposition not only admitted to their many meetings but also stated that she had lived with Henry "as his wife" in the summer of 1910. She later told Dorothea that she had had an abortion at this time.[30] This could mean that Henry moved back in with his family briefly or that he and Joan had sexual relations once—or anything in between. Whatever the case, she had to amend the divorce petition in March 1919 to date the desertion from September 1914. The divorce became final in December 1919. I could find no trace of Henry Nutzhorn in later years in any location where Joan thought he had been: New York, Delaware, California, Florida, or New Jersey.

Dorothea felt deserted, and the feeling was partly her mother's creation. The intensity of her emotion, however, suggests her own early attachment to her father. This father, who had carried Dorothea on his shoulders throughout a Shakespeare performance, whose success and importance Dorothea was old enough to appreciate, had abandoned his children.

The marital separation changed the children's lives drastically. They moved into grandmother Sophie's house. Controlling, explosive, and a heavy drinker, Sophie would fly into rages, particularly at Dorothea. Her temper grew worse as she aged (and quite possibly as her house became more crowded). She would even hit Dorothea, who, in turn, became furious at her mother, who would not interfere. Dorothea felt herself doubly orphaned, not only by her father but also by her mother. The teenage Dorothea began to build a case against her mother as a weakling, easily intimidated and deferential both to Sophie and to her husband. Fifty years later, she even blamed her mother for overdeference to the doctors when she was ill with polio.[31] Yet Dorothea's cousins Minelda and Joy considered Joan domineering, at least toward her little brother—their father—John.[32] These contrasting appraisals should not be surprising; after all, what daughter can see her own mother objectively? The Nutzhorn/Lange family dynamics led Dorothea to a tangled view of her mother: she loved Joan and sided with her entirely against her father, but she also disdained her passivity. Joan's was not a take-charge personality, and she expressed her fears. Dorothea's own impatience produced an occasional role reversal and she would sometimes reassure her mother. Martin adopted his sister's view, and from the time they were teenagers, Dorothea's and Martin's affectionate name for their mother was "Wuzzy."

Still, the extended family household created when the Nutzhorns moved in with Sophie also bore gifts for Dorothea. Despite her irritability, Sophie encouraged Dorothea and imbued her with cultured tastes. A connoisseur of "fine things," Sophie taught Dorothea to disdain the shoddy, the fake, the cheap; and Dorothea would ever after condemn such objects by saying they were not "fine." Sophie's little sister Caroline, a school teacher, lived there too,

1.2. JOAN NUTZHORN, 1927, *by Dorothea Lange*

and Dorothea called her great-aunt "the only completely reliable person, to me and to the whole family."[33] Joan and Dorothea both relied on Caroline to mediate and to pacify Sophie. Dorothea used Caroline, as she used Sophie, to establish independence from her mother but also to belittle her mother, referring often to Caroline's fine mind and to how her students adored her. When citing Sophie's remark about the beauty of an orange, Dorothea added, "My mother needed an explanation for that. . . . I knew what she meant, perfectly." She blamed her mother for throwing away one of her uncle's lithographic stones, something she believed her grandmother would never have done. "My grandmother knew that I was smarter than my mother . . . more sensitive. . . ."

Joan's work history challenges Dorothea's claims about her passivity. She had been employed in a library before her marriage and she continued to work after marriage, while still cherishing the hope of becoming a professional singer, until she was visibly pregnant—unusual for a woman of her class. Now she got a good job quickly. Between 1902 and 1908, New York City built forty-two public library branches, creating a demand for qualified staff, and Joan was hired at the Chatham Square Branch on the Lower East Side. Her salary (described alternately as twelve dollars a week or fifty-five a month) was twice the typical wage for a working woman (six dollars a week). After working at this job for six years, Joan took a position with the Hudson County juvenile court as an investigator of probation compliance. The court appointment carried significant responsibility and some risk—moving about the city alone, frequently after dark, in the worst neighborhoods. Joan was good at it. Dorothea accompanied her occasionally and saw that Joan "had an uncanny way of knowing if they [the parolees] were in and not answering."[34] So Wuzzy actually provided an example of competence and independence for her daughter.

Adopting the myth of Joan's weakness was functional—it anchored and justified Dorothea's defection from Hoboken and the family. Other Nutzhorns, Vottelers, and Langes stayed there. By leaving permanently when she did, at age twenty-three, and going as far as she went, three thousand miles, Dorothea never quite shed her teenage resentments. She associated the family's Germanness with her mother's alleged obsequiousness: "She had what bothers me in Germans, some kind of a respect for authority that I don't like."[35] But of course this comment about Germans is an ethnic cliché and one more likely to have entered Dorothea's consciousness after leaving Hoboken and living through two world wars.

Joan's employment meant less supervision and greater independence to the adolescent Dorothea. But Dorothea's mythology about her mother as doormat, while inaccurate, also functioned in establishing her own identity as strong. Joan herself contributed to that mythology by assenting to the notion that Dorothea's temperament resembled Sophie's, skipping a generation, as such traits sometimes do. In this family knot, Joan and Dorothea collaborated in building Dorothea's assertiveness. "My mother once said to me," Dorothea recalled, "'You have much more iron in you than I have.' And it's true. I have more iron."[36]

But listen to her very next sentence: "Yet I made a photograph of her, which is through and through my mother, and it reveals that I loved her very much."[37] By speaking of her photographic work as having a mind of its own, as if she were its medium rather than its creator, she was not hedging, but perhaps expressing quite precisely her relation to her mother. As Dorothea's love for her mother welled up and expressed itself despite her best efforts, she was perhaps still struggling to fend off her guilt and shame about ambition, about putting work first, about her iron will.

# 2

# Apprentice to the City

I n the most important ways, Dorothea Lange was an autodidact, self-taught. In this regard, she was in fine company, with Louisa May Alcott, Elizabeth Barrett Browning, Emma Goldman, and Doris Lessing, to name just a few. Dorothea did complete twelve years of public education, as a mediocre student. But from the beginning of her adolescence until she was twenty-three, she was designing and executing, however unconsciously, her own curriculum. Her master teacher was New York City and its lessons shaped her. She might have learned in the same way had she grown up in San Francisco, but the lessons would have been less powerful, for New York was in her time the citiest of American cities. It featured rich and poor, natives and foreigners, whites and people of other colors, bums and aesthetes, slums and mansions, vaudeville and opera, promiscuity and prudery, diverse radicalisms and domineering conservatism.

Dorothea's bridge to that world was her mother. When her husband decamped, Joan Lange Nutzhorn took her twelve-year-old daughter to New York City in 1907—for reasons of practicality but also because Joan herself had no fear of it.

DOROTHEA WAS A pretty child, beautifully dressed and posed in the professional portrait her mother commissioned. She seems thin, intense, and lively, ready to laugh or speak. There is no mark of disability. As an adolescent, she appears a bit more robust, her blond hair long and loosely tied back, her forthright gaze meeting the camera directly, her posture relaxed and self-confident.

That confidence had been put to the test at home. Joan was loving and warm but would not stand up to Sophie, whose temper tantrums grew more frequent. Six-year-old Martin was more often alone with Sophie but he was an easygoing child, and it was the obstinate Dorothea that most provoked her. Joan tried to keep Dorothea away from her grandmother when possible, and this was one of the reasons that, having taken a job in New York City, she decided to send Dorothea to school there. She arranged this by using the address of Dorothea's godmother, Emily Sanderfield, who lived in New York City. So Dorothea and Joan left home together early every weekday morning, riding with the throngs of New Jerseyans commuting to work in the city on the fast ferry to the Christopher Street pier or, after the Hudson tunnel opened in mid-1908, by train. They returned together after the library closed. Dorothea now twelve, was on her own for several hours each day—walking to school after her mother peeled off, later walking from school to the library, where she was supposed to spend her after-school time doing homework in the staff lounge.

Dorothea spent seventh and eighth grades at Intermediate Public School 62 on the Lower East Side of New York City, on Hester Street between Norfolk and Essex.[1] The school was exemplary, owing to both its leadership and its constituency. Lower East Side district school superintendent Julia Richman, a dynamic progressive reformer, had chosen to work with the poor and poorly educated Lower East Side immigrant Jews from Eastern Europe.[2] But the school's effect on Dorothea was not what her mother had hoped. In primary school in Hoboken, Dorothea had felt herself a very good student, quick and bright. Now she "fell from her perch," as she remembered it later, because the students at PS 62 were so smart and diligent. Dorothea later claimed she was the only Gentile among three thousand Jewish children, the only child in school on Rosh Hashanah, and although this was likely an exaggeration, it was the way she felt. But she perceived the Jewish students with more respect than resentment. "They were hungry after knowledge and achievement and making, you know, fighting their way up. . . . They were too smart for me . . . aggressively smart. . . . To an outsider, it was a savage group because of this overwhelming ambition." This understanding had developed over many decades, but the imagery and emotional tone of her memories had been acquired earlier. Bright as Dorothea was, she did not share quite the intense zeal of these newer and poorer Americans for upward mobility and success in America's mainstream institutions. No one was rude to her, she said, but she was always an outsider.[3]

School was only part of her experience of these alien people. Through the windows of "Jewtown," as photographer Jacob Riis had called it, she saw their crowded flats, their multiperson beds, their kitchen sinks doubling as bathtubs and tripling as worktables. "Never a September comes that I don't stop and remember what I used to see in those tenements when they had the Jewish holidays . . . all the women wore *sheitls,* the black wigs, and the men wore beards and little black hats, *yarmulkes.* . . . I just *looked* at everything. I can remember the smell of the cooking too. . . ."[4] She saw the men bent over books, whole families bent over hand sewing. Yet these strange poor people produced the brilliant students at PS 62. She had to reconcile the poverty of the tenements with the abilities of the students who lived in them.

The two years at PS 62 altered Dorothea's self-image. She drew back from school learning; if she had ever imagined herself as a teacher like Aunt Caroline, for example, that goal no longer seemed promising. But later she came to believe that her Jewish classmates and their families had imbued in her their strong ethical standards about what she called the "sacredness of personal relationships" and "greatness in emotions." She took in particularly the Jewish girls' personalities, a new feminine style for Dorothea, for they were often as academically ambitious as the boys.[5]

When she recalled her school days, she never mentioned disability as a factor in her experience. This was always her approach: She experienced her lameness as formative, and reported that it made her feel different from everyone else, but never discussed it—no mention of pain or feeling weak or being stigmatized or taunted.

Increasingly, she dawdled on the way to the library to meet her mother and roamed the streets. In the seventh grade, this precocious child inaugurated her New York persona: walker in the city.[6] She walked long distances, her damaged foot hindering her speed but not her stamina. There was much to see, because in this densely inhabited neighborhood much of life took place on the stoops and the streets—not just buying and selling but also fixing, cleaning, playing, arguing, eating, even sleeping—a way of living outlandish and also exotic to a girl used to middle-class privacy. Her strolls could be grimy, smelly, and occasionally frightening. Returning home alone two nights a week when her mother worked late, she learned to walk carefully around filth, step over drunks, avoid street toughs. Horses and their droppings filled the streets. Thousands died of cholera, typhoid, smallpox, typhus, and diphtheria. Every year, 100,000 were arrested, and 500 children were abandoned. (Her 1950s travels in Asia would remind her of this Lower East Side squalor, and its attractions.)

When she raised her eyes to the buildings, she took in another visual feast. The neighborhood's 170 synagogues were mostly just storefronts, but a few had been built as houses of worship—from Beth Hamedrash Hagadol on Norfolk Street, its architectural simplicity appearing almost modernist, to the ornate Moorish and Romanesque Eldridge Street Synagogue, K'hal Adath Jeshurun. She passed through the remnants of Kleindeutschland, the German district around Tompkins Square Park, the Deutsche Klinik, now Stuyvesant Polyclinic, the Freie Bibliothek, now the Ottendorfer public library branch, and the shooting club, Deutsch-Amerikanische Schützen Gesellschaft, all with elaborately decorative facades in the German Rundbogenstil (round-arched, neo-Romanesque). Turning west to the Hudson, she crossed the "Jewish Rialto," as the strip of Yiddish theaters along Second Avenue was called. Or she might walk up the Bowery, darkened by the overhead tracks of the Third Avenue Elevated, lined with pawnshops, bars, pool halls, and missions. The names of the single-room-occupancy cheap lodging houses and hotels told of their former eminence: the Gotham, the Majestic, the Windsor, and the Whitehouse. Turning west again, she passed the Federal-style town houses of the West Village, originally built for workers and artisans by carpenters using pattern books, now beginning to be reclaimed by bohemians, and she glimpsed some of those unconventional folk on the street.

She would later say that she learned to see on these walks. She exercised the eye that her grandmother had appreciated, the eye that would become her most powerful muscle. The child psychiatrist and documentary-photography critic Robert Coles argued that these experiences both formed and revealed "distinctive elements of her later working style: a willingness to inquire relentlessly, to move with ease from neighborhood to neighborhood; an interest in the ability of extremely hard-pressed families nevertheless to make do; . . . a defiantly rebellious insistence that her own aesthetic and moral interests be affirmed . . . and, particularly, a continual attentiveness. . . ."[7]

Coles is exaggerating slightly, as these abilities took years more to develop. But he is right to see the contribution of the Lower East Side experience to Dorothea's future. It supported her inclination, both innate and family-influenced, toward independence and self-reliance. It confirmed her grand-mother's instruction that looking with concentration could reveal beauty. It taught her that what seemed threatening might prove benign, that a young woman alone in bad neighborhoods might nevertheless be safe. It demon-strated that those who lived in poverty might possess potential equal to that of those who lived in prosperity. And it confirmed a pleasure in being alone. She referred to herself in those days as "a solitary."[8]

Dorothea believed that it was in the Lower East Side that she learned to don her "cloak of invisibility." The cloak enabled her to see without being disrup-tive or unsafe. This metaphor felt quite exact to her, because she repeated it throughout her life. It would become important to her understanding of her photographic method, and it resounds on several frequencies. Imagining herself as invisible calls to mind her mother telling her to work harder at hid-ing her limp and distorted foot. It suggests a child's strategy for staying out of Sophie's way. It expresses her sense that her father could not *see* her, had for-gotten her. The cloak, like that of a flaneur, an observer, claims for herself an active position unusual for a lone young woman. When Baudelaire first used the term, a flaneur was a gentleman and could not be otherwise. No one of the lower classes would have the leisure to stroll and observe, or, allegedly, the detachment required by the Olympian gaze Baudelaire honored. No woman could be safe or respectable trying it. Dorothea Lange was by no means the first to defy that Victorian constraint, but she did so at a remarkably vulnerable age and in an urban tumult.

A lifelong trait becomes clear now: Dorothea loved looking. Her Lower East Side wanderings and her PS 62 failings were introducing her to a new identity as arty. Her grandmother Sophie had said once—in German, but Dorothea had understood—" 'that girl has line in her head,' " which meant that she could see design and composition.[9] Once, looking out at the Hackensack Meadows and seeing wash lines against the sky, she said to her companion, "To me, that's beautiful," and her companion responded, "To you, everything is beautiful." This comment brought her another bit of self-knowledge that she had not previously had.[10] Perhaps she associated it with her pleasure in looking at her uncles' lithography stones.

AFTER GRADUATING FROM PS 62, Dorothea enrolled in Wadleigh High School for Girls. One of only three public high schools in Manhattan and the

Bronx—most were private or parochial schools, and only a small minority of schoolchildren went to high school in those days anyway—Wadleigh was located uptown on 114th and 115th streets at Seventh Avenue, surrounded by the new apartment buildings of the upwardly mobile, including some of the Jewish immigrants who had once lived on the Lower East Side. At Wadleigh, Jews were in the minority, Dorothea a member of the WASP majority. But her heart was not in school and she did not become an ace student here either. She studied Latin, which she barely passed, as well as algebra and geometry, biology, botany, and physics, and English, drawing, and music.[11] Despite some progressive influences—feminist Henrietta Rodman taught there and there was a students' league for woman suffrage—Wadleigh had few of the progressive accoutrements of PS 62. It enforced strict dress and behavior codes, offered little in the arts, and prepared girls for only two wage-earning careers: teaching and clerical work. Dorothea just barely passed her courses. She had the rebellious adolescent's way of considering herself superior even as she earned poor grades. Later, she regretted her educational loss and blamed the pedagogy of the time: ". . . what important years those are and what could have been done for me—because I loved books and I could get things fast—that wasn't done," she mused.[12]

A few teachers captured her attention: one who loved Yeats, a physics teacher with "a good, clean-cut brain," and, above all, Martha Bensley Bruere. Member of a high-society family active in progressive social reform, sister of prominent Progressive Republican Henry Bruere ("his name was in the paper every day," Dorothea recalled), she drew Dorothea to her like a magnet and returned her student's admiration. Dorothea impressed her so much that this straitlaced, serious woman actually cheated for her: "completely undermining her principles . . . she upgraded a paper . . . because I had done so dreadfully . . . which would have meant my failing that course. . . ."[13]

During her four years at Wadleigh, Dorothea became a persistent truant. She spent days on the streets, carrying her books, looking and wandering. Apparently the school never reported her, because her mother never knew, but Dorothea's memory may have exaggerated the extent of her absences. Perhaps she forged excuses.[14] Looking back, she thought that she got away with this because her mother was neglectful, and she thanked God for it. She knew, perhaps subconsciously, that her truancy was not unproductive. She learned the city, and lost her fear of cities. The city she got to know now was far larger than it had been, extending from Harlem to the bottom of Manhattan, and in

1913, the city's subways carried 810 million passengers. Dorothea sometimes walked that whole distance. She saw from the bottom those buildings she had once seen only as part of the skyline as the ferry approached. She saw how differently the rich, the middle class, and the poor lived.

In fact, metropolitan modernity was beginning to blur the cultural lines between classes and ethnicities, by growing a commercial public culture. You could see upscale fashion at Henri Bendel on Fifth Avenue and plebeian styles at Klein's on Fourteenth Street, and an adventuresome teenager could walk through both of them. Electricity was making nighttime itself a spectacle. The Hippodrome, a vaudeville and circus palace built in 1905, sported glittering globes outlined in electric lights, while inside, the dome was circled by bands of light. The new Theater District near Times Square featured more than four hundred entertainment events a year. New York's male "sporting life" continued to expand, featuring gambling, cockfights, saloons, strip clubs, and prostitution. In large areas of the city, women were not safe alone on the streets. But in pockets of this nightlife world, male-accompanied women were as comfortable as men.[15]

Dorothea found a sister in truancy, Fronsie (née Florence) Ahlstrom, also from Hoboken, also using a false address to attend Wadleigh. Dorothea had few friends—in her later musing, she attributed this to a drive that made her different from other girls. She and Fronsie had compatibly rebellious temperaments—and became lifelong friends. Their interests developed jointly as their wanderings became increasingly oriented toward high culture. Between the 1870s and the 1890s, New York had grown from an inelegant, grungy commercial hub to a grand metropolis of culture. As the well-to-do migrated farther north in Manhattan, galleries and museums followed. Central Park, the museums, the public statuary, and the Beaux-Arts architecture could match the attractions of Berlin, if not Paris. The Art Students League enrolled hundreds. The display of nudes was eroding Victorian prudery. Dorothea and Fronsie could visit the Metropolitan Museum, the American Fine Arts Society, the Museum of Natural History, and the many private galleries on Fifty-seventh Street. The Met still clung to a conservative art canon, so the girls would not have encountered Impressionism or Art Nouveau or Edvard Munch there, but they might well have taken in shows of Japanese prints, of Corot and Rousseau, or of the moderns John Singer Sargent and Winslow Homer. The great mansions of the millionaire district—those of the Carnegie, Warburg, Whitney, Harkness, Frick, Pulitzer, Duke, Pinchot, deKoven, Astor, Sloane, and Vanderbilt families—offered pedestrians a catalog of ornate luxury as one walked south on Fifth or Park or Madison avenues. Dorothea had seen first the human hardship created by New York's growth; now she saw the sublime pleasures of upscale New York.

On these walks Dorothea began to see modern art photography. In early twentieth-century New York, the impresario turning photography into an art was her fellow Hoboken native Alfred Stieglitz. Thirty years Lange's senior, Stieglitz came from a different community of Hoboken Germans, the wealthy Jewish Germans, but he shared some of her German culture, albeit of a more elite status. Educated in Germany in the 1880s, he returned to New York in 1890 and worked as a photoengraver, like Lange's uncles. A walker, like Lange, he took his camera outside and photographed lovingly the urban landscape, physical and spiritual. He raised the technical standards of photography, achieving subtleties of texture, tonality, and composition to create stirring images. He expanded the acceptable range of photographic subjects. He developed a style of photography that came to dominate both studio and art photography for several decades. Most importantly, Stieglitz became an impresario who helped get this new style marked as art. Labeled "pictorialism," the technique involved elegantly balanced composition, soft focus, and a small range of tones. The soft focus eliminated unwanted details. It was created with special lenses and, sometimes, by smearing a lens with oil or Vaseline. The low tonality created an aura of mystery or spirituality. After producing negatives, many pictorialists then scratched or painted them to create new effects, disdaining photographs without such handwork as merely a technical product—that is, not art. The style sought to deny the camera, to override its greatest technical capacity—the ability to make sharp images—and instead to make photographs seem painterly. Pictorialism attracted paying clients and audience through picturesque and sentimental themes.

A man of inherited wealth, Stieglitz was also a first-rate entrepreneur. Rejecting the straitjacket of establishment arts preferences, represented at the top by the National Academy of Design, he made three moves that would revolutionize American art—and influence Lange's future development. In 1902 he organized a photographers' group called the Photo-Secession. The name derived from the move by a group of German and Austrian photographers to secede from the academy, a rejection replicated in New York when photographers resigned from the New York Camera Club. Through this group, Stieglitz promoted his pictorialist visual discipline. Members were admitted only by invitation. The privileged included Edward Steichen, then the favorite, Clarence White, and Alvin Langdon Coburn. Two women won this laurel: Gertrude Käsebier and Anne Brigman. Photo-Secession work was to be aesthetically charming, emotionally expressive, and painterly. Next, after editing several older photography magazines, Stieglitz started his own, *Camera Work*, in 1903, the most influential—and beautiful—publication in the field until its demise in 1917.

In 1905 Stieglitz opened a gallery at 291 Fifth Avenue, where he showed modern painting, sculpture, and photography. He brought to New York the work of Rodin, Cézanne, Brancusi, Rousseau, Matisse, and Picasso, as well as African sculpture. He nurtured an important group of American modernist painters who gathered around his gallery. Within a few years, the rebellion begun by Stieglitz generated the Exhibition of Independent Artists, a 1910 show which, for the first time, evaded the National Academy's veto power. It was not a gated community, with judges determining entry, but an open show in which any artist could participate. One hundred and three of them did, making it a major cultural event. Two thousand attended its opening, and a waiting line of over five hundred gathered outside.[16] In 1911 the rebellion grew more overtly oppositional, with a show that required its exhibitors to boycott the Academy's exhibitions. An even greater impact came from the Armory Show of 1913, designed to challenge the Academy openly. It displayed thirteen hundred works by three hundred artists, including all the European modernist greats. The critical attack on this work—that it was formless, immoral, lunatic, anarchic, et cetera—increased the attendance. The show transformed the art world permanently.

Modernism was blooming in all the arts. Dorothea would likely have seen some vaudeville, the dominant entertainment form for at least half a century, possibly at the Union Square Theatre, where one could get a gallery ticket for twenty-five cents. But of much greater interest were the three modernist "little theater" groups that sprouted in New York in 1915: the Washington Square Players, the Provincetown Players, and the Neighborhood Playhouse. Here one could see work by Edna St. Vincent Millay, Floyd Dell, and Djuna Barnes. Lange would have seen modernist art also in new radical publications such as *The Masses*, an arty, socialist monthly. Even if she saw it only on newsstands, she would have noticed its dramatic modernist covers by such painters as John Sloan, Stuart Davis, Maurice Becker, and George Bellows. She might have run into one of the theatrically costumed woman-suffrage parades. Artistic and political modernist streams flowed into the same reservoir of radical ideas.

Dorothea was most stirred, however, not by the art and theater she saw but by Isadora Duncan, who swept into New York like the Greek goddess of her costumes. Duncan's work derived in part from the same source as modernism in the visual arts. Both modern dancers and modern artists were refugees from Victorianism, scholasticism, and Beaux-Arts snobbery, and both experienced the rigid technical standards of their parents' art forms as confining, even suffocating. This is only a partial resemblance, because Armory Show modern art is as appreciated today as ever, while Duncan's dancing is likely to leave today's audiences bored or even annoyed. Dorothea's passion for Duncan makes sense only in its context. And that context includes the fact that Duncan was dancing for women, expressing women's frustrations and aspirations.

Duncan performed in New York in 1908, 1909, and 1911. First a Broadway producer brought her as a novelty, based on her hot European reputation as the "barefoot classic dancer." Her success was such that she then danced, at the invitation of conductor Walter Damrosch, with the New York Symphony Orchestra to Beethoven's Seventh Symphony at the Metropolitan Opera House. This is where Dorothea first saw her; afterward, she tried to see her every performance. "I had never been taken into the upper reaches of human existence before . . . to me it was the greatest thing that ever happened. I still live with that, not as a theatrical performance, but as an extension of human possibility."[17] Duncan literally changed the identity of this teenager still engaged in constructing herself.[18]

It was hard for women to break into many of the arts, but they were leading a revolution in dance. Isadora Duncan, proclaiming that ballet deformed the sacred natural female body, put on a toga, took her shoes off, and became the darling of New York's female arts patrons. It is difficult to appreciate that enthusiasm today. In photographs and drawings, she seems hokey. Dance critic Elizabeth Kendall tactfully calls her dancing "quaint."[19] Today's dancers of every style employ rigorous ballet training, great athleticism, and thin bodies, while Isadora appears in photographs as fleshy, her limbs and torso lax, her movement vague. As Dorothea recollected many years later, "She was rather sloppy-looking, rather fat, with very heavy upper legs, yet with a peculiar grace, not grace as I had preconceived it. . . ."[20] Duncan left audiences awestruck. Although influenced by dancers Ruth St. Denis and Loïe Fuller, she drew most from her extraordinary mother, a San Francisco free spirit, musician, and progressive educator. Mrs. Duncan separated from her husband while Isadora was a baby and supported her four children alone. She taught them romantic poetry, Robert Ingersoll's atheistic romanticism, feminist dress reform, California's pantheistic worship of nature, and a gestural system developed by French acting and singing teacher François Delsarte. Isadora was a product of precisely the San Francisco subculture that Lange, eighteen years younger, would soon enter.

Duncan was very much a partisan and an exemplar of the "new woman" ideology that thrived among modernists and radicals in New York. "Duncan's dances were events through which her viewers recognized themselves as modern," one scholar wrote.[21] Whether the "new women" were feminists or not, all were in high rebellion against Victorian prudery and its double standard. They were assertively feminine even as they dressed in comfortable, bohemian clothing. Duncan affirmed women's sexual desire and sexual rights, even unwed motherhood, and advocated companionate marriage and freedom from household drudgery. She danced in an imagined classical habitat in which women's sexuality was "free."[22] In throwing off Victorian restraints, her sexuality emulated that of the pagan, not the coquette. By wrapping her free spirit in the costume veneer of classicism, she signaled that her performances were high art, avoided the taint of prurience, and maintained the separation of the genteel from the vulgar. Duncan's feminism was the sort that glorified women's difference from men, especially women's alleged instinctiveness, intuitiveness, and "naturally" gentle, earthbound, maternalist nurturing. Duncan signified all these with her physical presence. She bared her body, exalted nature—her California heritage—and celebrated freedom by enacting it in her movements.

DESPITE THEIR HERO WORSHIP, Duncan's young admirers could not glean from her persona any advice on how to proceed, how to become a "new woman." But upon high school graduation in 1912, that was the question Dorothea faced. Her mother expected a plan: a job or more education. Her better-off relatives offered to pay for a teacher-training course. Joan was nothing if not practical at this point, having been a single mother supporting three others now for six years, and she wanted Dorothea to be able to support herself.

To Joan's astonishment, the girl said she wanted to be a photographer. The Nutzhorns did not own a camera and Dorothea had never held one. Amateur photography was booming, especially since Eastman had introduced its light-weight Kodak box camera in 1888; by 1900, you could buy one for five dollars. But Joan could not imagine photography providing economic security—a matter that seemed to her crucial. " 'You have to have something to fall back on,' " Joan said. But Dorothea "knew it was dangerous to have something to fall back on."[23] "A detestable phrase for a young person," she remarked later.[24]

Why such strong words? What dangers was she worried about? One could read a protofeminism in these words, a refusal of the safe path for a middle-class woman, of the job stamped female, and of the straight and predictable road it would put her on. They also might imply defiance of the pressure on young people to choose safety at the expense of growth. One could also read a protoartistic commitment here, a desire not to be tempted into a search for security that would make an artistic vocation impossible.

Despite her lack of enthusiasm, she enrolled, together with Fronsie, in the New York College for the Training of Teachers. Founded in 1887 as a direct response to the influx of immigrants, the school was funded by Grace Dodge and George Vanderbilt. Columbia University president Nicholas Murray Butler brought it into alliance with Columbia in the 1890s and moved it uptown to 119th Street. Its curriculum, like that at PS 62, was influenced by progressive educational ideas, including those of John Dewey, also a professor at Columbia. But the quality of what it offered made no difference to Dorothea. Uninterested, she remained a mediocre student and soon dropped out.

From then on Dorothea Lange designed and executed her own education. Her choice of an employer is one indication of just how ambitious and self-confident Dorothea was. The first photographer she approached for a job was the most prestigious of all, Arnold Genthe. The photographs in his studio window were those of Isadora Duncan, for which he was famous.[25] That he was German helped her find the audacity to ask.

Genthe had been the most famed portrait photographer in the West. He had emigrated to San Francisco in 1895, taught himself photography, and became the "darling of Nob Hill," where the first railroad barons and bonanza kings built their mansions, high above the rowdy, bawdy waterfront. A master pictorialist, he specialized in soft-focus portraits of society women and cultural celebrities. He said of his work: "I believe I was the first professional photographer to give people portraits that were more than mere surface records—pictures that . . . showed something of a real character and personality of the sitter. . . ." Producing what came to be called the Genthe style, he achieved it in part by clicking the shutter when the sitter did not expect it—as Lange would do in her own early studio work.[26] He also made photographs of California's natural beauty, of San Francisco in ruins after the 1906 earthquake, and, most originally, of Chinatown and its residents. Sharing the perspective of so much photography of nonwhites in this era, his take on the Chinese was Orientalist in the extreme—images of dark, sordid, and mysteriously beautiful aspects of pre-earthquake Chinatown, projecting its characteristics as a natural emanation of Chineseness.[27]

He moved to New York in 1911 and quickly developed a similar studio there. Sometime in 1912 or 1913 Dorothea, probably with Fronsie's encouragement, walked in, told him she wanted to learn photography, and offered to do any work at all. The shop was large for a photographer—three women worked there, Dorothea being the youngest. She functioned as general assistant and fill-in person. She answered the phone and received clients, but soon he trained her to change the glass plates quickly, to make proofs, to spot photographs (cover dust flecks or white spots with India ink), to retouch the plates with an etching knife, and to mount pictures. She was also trained to say he wasn't there when he was—that is, to distinguish between those he wanted to see and those he did not. Personal relationships with his clients were central to his success. "Arnold Genthe was an unconscionable old goat," she recalled, "in that he seduced everyone who came in the place. Yes, he was a real *roué*. But . . . very properly a photographer of women because he really loved them. He wasn't at all a vulgar man; he loved women. He understood them. He could make the plainest woman an illuminated woman."[28] (Except for the "*roué*" comment, this, too, described Lange's work fifteen years later.)

Dorothea could not know then that a direct line extended from Genthe to her future husband, Maynard Dixon. Back in San Francisco, Genthe had made a portrait of Dixon: elegantly dressed, his long, delicate fingers holding a cigarette. In return, Dixon had done a cartoon drawing of Genthe photographing a young woman.[29] Just before Genthe left for New York, his friends had given him a farewell party and, as a gift, "amusing caricatures" by Dixon.[30]

From Genthe Dorothea received a view into the world of fineness. "That was a look into a world I hadn't seen . . . a world of privilege . . . command of what seemed to me the most miraculous kind of living . . . everything of the highest expression. A world of Oriental art was in that place"—art Genthe had collected in Chinatown. Once again, Dorothea impressed her teacher, so he began deliberately to educate her. She offered one example: Once "he looked at me and he said, 'I wish you'd take those cheap red beads off. They're not any good.' . . . And I can see them now. They were red cut glass beads. I [had] thought they were nice. I took them off. . . . He was absolutely right. . . ." Lange's interviewer remarked, "Most young girls would weep at that point." To which Dorothea responded, "Not I. Because I knew. Why, my grandmother had taught me better than that. I never [again] wore any costume jewelry. . . ."[31]

The most momentous of Genthe's gifts was a camera—not only the first she had owned but also the first she had held. We can surmise, since Lange did not specify, that it was a used Graflex. First produced in 1907, this was a single-lens reflex camera, in which the photographer, looking down through a black leather hood, is actually seeing through the lens that will expose the film; the image is projected upward by a mirror, which flips out of the way when the shutter is pressed. The shutter speed was adjusted by rotating a ring on the lens, and the aperture was selected by moving a wheel. The Graflex was the camera typically used in portrait studios, and Lange used it throughout her studio career.

After Genthe, Dorothea apprenticed herself, in varying capacities, to seven other photographers. Most lacked his status, and she referred to them in retrospect as "lovable old hacks."[32] But they taught her, or made it possible for her to learn. She worked for six months for Aram Kazanjian's studios, as one of a battery of telephone-solicitation girls repeating " 'Good morning, Mrs. DuPont, this is the Kazanjian Studios calling. Mr. Kazanjian is *so* interested in making a portrait of you and your son together, and we will be in Baltimore on Saturday morning. . . .' " She was able to see the studio process from beginning to end, learning business as well as photography. She learned about people's vanities and how to arrange a bridal veil.[33] Another employer, Madame A. Spencer-Beatty, had lost a photographer right after receiving a well-paid commission, so she sent Dorothea on the assignment "out of sheer desperation." Dorothea's response was characteristic: "I was scared to death . . . certainly not prepared. . . . It was sheer luck and maybe gall. But I had enough insight, you see, by that time to know how professionals behaved on these jobs and what people wanted and didn't want . . . what was the commercial product."[34]

There was a remarkable apprenticeship to an itinerant photographer who actually moved into her Hoboken household. On his door-to-door rounds, he had knocked at the door when Dorothea was home alone, offering a dozen photographs with easel mounts for $2.50 or, for slightly more, photographs hand-colored—distastefully, Dorothea thought. But she found out that he had no darkroom, "and a week later he was ensconced in a little outbuilding that was in back . . . once a chicken coop." From him, she learned how to build a darkroom. He had lived in Italy for three years and introduced her to Italian folding negative-drying racks—he gave her one that she used until glass plates went out. She discovered that "he had been all over Europe, this old fellow, and he had a much better, much richer background that I had expected."[35] The story encapsulates Lange's complex attitudes: snobbish but at the same time open to a down-and-out stranger.

Her last boss, Charles H. Davis, was a celebrity photographer.[36] He did opera singers and fashion, and made a lot of money. After his third or fourth wife sued him for divorce and won everything from him—studio, house, equipment—he had to move downtown to a shabby studio over a saloon, where Lange worked for him, and she could still remember, in the 1960s, "the smell of the beer coming up through the floor." But he draped the room with style and "all his leftover grandeur." He taught her how to pose the model: "the head is placed, and then . . . each finger is positioned. The fingers were very important to him, and he said, 'The knees are the eyes of the body.' . . ." People posed this way, Dorothea saw, "thought they were getting much more for their money than people who nowadays are photographed without knowing it! . . . he would spend two hours and work with every fold. . . ."[37] Another commercial lesson.

In her reminiscence about him, there is a hint of a flirtation. "I became a sort of pet of his; he was very lonely, and he used to take me out to dinner . . . always to the same place, the Lion D'Or, where he would order a very fine dinner and sometimes some of his theater people and his opera people would be there and then I saw how he carried it off." Here was one more way in which she glimpsed the "fine." He did not consider her a talented photographer, and the reason why is telling. "I remember his saying to me, 'You don't know what it is to make a good negative!'" To him, the negative was everything, and making the print was completely mechanical. And already, Dorothea realized "he felt that I didn't like the kind of photography that he did."[38] A remarkable state of affairs—the master aware that the apprentice has her own aesthetic and sense of the craft.

Dorothea also did a stint as a proper photography student, and here too she went to the top: to Clarence H. White, who taught a course under the auspices of Columbia University's Teachers College. She knew his work by then, and "he stood for a certain kind of a photograph that no one else had produced . . . a good deal of poetry and luminosity and a fine sense of the human figure."[39] A contemporary of Stieglitz and a master portrait photographer, he was central to the Photo-Secession group. White was a romantic socialist, of the sensibility of Whitman and the British Edward Carpenter, another poet of democracy. White's studio, decorated with fabric hangings, Japanese prints, Chinese ceramics, and bamboo window screens, was a visual statement of the Arts and Crafts renunciation of the mass-produced. His "first lesson to his students was that art begins with one's everyday surroundings." He rented his Greenwich Village studio from the famous bohemian church, St. Mark's-in-the-Bouwerie, a center for modern dance, of which White was a connoisseur.[40]

White raised pictorialism to high technical standards. He emphasized composition and subjectivity, never representation of the external world, and in this respect his pictorialism, like Stieglitz's, represented a modernist aesthetic. White's influence shows throughout Lange's documentary work, for she made images including large amounts of information legible through easy-to-read composition.

By the mid-1910s, Stieglitz began to reject the pictorialist style and, with his usual controlling temperament, required his colleagues to follow him. White refused and continued to work with soft focus.[41] But he transcended his own style in his teaching. His supreme pedagogical values, like those of John Dewey, insisted that students must explore, finding their own styles and meaning; that a teacher must never impose or assign but should be open to all that is authentic; that there is beauty in the ordinary, in the products of the "folk"; that the artist must honor the natural, the free. Nothing could have suited Dorothea better. "Why he was extraordinary has puzzled me ever since. . . . He was an inarticulate man . . . and he'd hesitate, he'd fumble. He was very gentle and had a very sweet aura. . . . You walked into that dreary room knowing that something was going to happen."[42]

Dorothea did not then recognize how unusual White was in taking women seriously, far more than any male art photographer of his time. His association with Columbia's Teachers College brought him many female students, and his open-minded, nonjudgmental teaching made them comfortable. He taught western landscape photographer Laura Gilpin; the pioneer photographer of African Americans and Appalachians Doris Ulmann; and photojournalist Margaret Bourke-White. In 1924 he wrote an article for *American Photography*—

later reprinted and distributed by the Women's Bureau of Vocational Education —encouraging women to enter photography.[43]

White's assignments focused on observation and composition, rather than on darkroom skills.[44] Abstract still life became the foundation of his classes—like the "five finger exercises and scales of composition," Laura Gilpin recalled.[45] He sent his students to photograph a wrought-iron gate at Columbia, because it was nearby and because they saw it every day but never *saw* it. But he would accept whatever students brought in, which was lucky for Dorothea because she decided "there was no use my photographing that gate, none at all." In fact, she made herself marginal to the class, never bringing in assigned work, refusing to join in the group experience. She later thought she had reacted this way because White was teaching photography as an art, when she thought of it only as an "interesting job, a trade." Perhaps, but she had by now a disinclination to study in a formal setting: She called herself a "self-learner." This puts a positive spin on the trait; the negative version was that her cockiness, her sense of being special, made it hard for her to be just one of a group. That combination of self-esteem and alienation drew from her grandmother's obsession with excellence, and this, too, contained the positive and the negative. Dorothea had high standards and surrounded herself only with well-made, austere, graceful, unpretentious objects—and these adjectives describe her photography as well as any. But the taste for the fine made her a bit of a social snob, as well. In her work as a documentary photographer she could admire the simplicity of peasants, but she could not abide low- and middle-brow commercial culture. "I have a certain snobbishness about things being very first-class, very top-drawer."[46] White influenced Lange significantly, although she recognized it only later. When she herself taught photography, her photograph-the-ordinary assignments, the ones she wouldn't do when she was a student, emulated his.

Dorothea's developing artiness attracted her to artists. Around 1912 she took up with a much older man, a sculptor, "slightly a madman," she recalled, who "fell very much in love with me as a seventeen-year-old girl." He would appear wherever she was, at all hours, "in a state," even at her Hoboken home, where her always-amiable and amenable mother would take care of him and let him stay. "I knew that this was a real artist. And I knew that something was expected of me, but I didn't know what that was." She understood that he loved not her, but what she represented, and also that he was "half a myth" to her. In 1915 she met John Landon, who was about twenty years her senior, active in the famed Pleiades Club. He then became an ardent suitor. "I was the focus of his attention for a couple of years, completely, one hundred percent, three letters a day kind of thing."[47] He sent her poetry. The Hoboken girl with a limp was becoming an enchanter of men. This relationship, too, was mythical, she thought. After Dorothea there was another girl, whom he treated with exactly the same complete devotion.[48]

The Pleiades Club thrilled Dorothea. This Greenwich Village literary society, its members including Stephen Crane, Mark Twain, and Eugene O'Neill, influenced the transformation of the neighborhood from immigrant to bohemian. The club met Sunday nights at the Hotel Brevoort on Fifth Avenue between Eighth and Ninth streets. A favorite inn for visiting Europeans, its café served wine and French food and drew in artists and writers—exactly the kind of hangout Dorothea would rediscover in San Francisco a few years later. Landon took her to high-culture events, such as a farewell dinner for Edward Hugh Sothern and his wife, Julia Marlowe, premier Shakespearean actors of the day. Dorothea remembered Marlowe reading Shakespeare's sonnets. And Dorothea did love words, perhaps as much as images.

It is easy, perhaps facile, to connect Dorothea's attraction to older men with the longing for a father. That she attracted older men, from her employers to John Landon, suggests something else: that her tastes and conversation were becoming sophisticated, and possibly intimidating to men her own age. Bohemian urban subcultures always seemed to open possibilities for women, and they drew Dorothea magnetically. Having found them in New York, she would find them quickly in San Francisco.

DOROTHEA AND FRONSIE loved New York and never imagined living anywhere else. But they were restless, too, and in their day, rich girls took premarriage European cultural tours to complement their formal education. Hard workers, Lange and Ahlstrom saved up money and decided to do the wealthy girls one better: They would travel around the world. The trip was not an escape—Dorothea denied having been unhappy and thought her desire "was a matter of really testing yourself out. Could you or couldn't you."[49] It was to be an adventure, and one not built around photography. Dorothea proposed the plan to Fronsie, who loved it—she was a true sister in adventure to Dorothea.

Both girls' parents opposed the trip at first, but the girls overcame the resistance. If their parents contributed to the costs, it was only a little. Dorothea and Fronsie had very little money, but Dorothea felt confident she could get a job in a photography studio, and Fronsie, then employed by Western Union, thought she could get a job for that company anywhere in the world. Their economic self-confidence, unknown to their mothers' generation, was another sign that they were "new women." Dorothea took the camera that Genthe had given her, thinking to record the sights and, just possibly, earn some money through casual or temporary employment.

They set out early in 1918, while the war still raged. Dorothea had grown up within view of the great steamships docked in Hoboken—her father's office had been quite close to the piers—and to her the ships gave off the smells and sounds of adventure and luxury. So they went by ship to New Orleans. Here they were more thrilled than frightened by the rumors of submarines, a result of the 1917 Zimmermann telegram in which the German foreign minister had proposed an alliance with Mexico against the United States. They had prepared well, getting letters of introduction to friends of friends, who proved most hospitable, putting them up for a time in New Orleans.

From New Orleans, the Southern Pacific Railroad took them to El Paso and Los Angeles, on a route roughly paralleling the old U.S. Route 80, then on to Oakland, where they caught a ferry to San Francisco. The overland part of the trip took six weeks, because they stopped off several times. The travel was mostly comfortable. Train interiors were then embellished with brocade upholstery, beveled-glass doors, inlaid-wood trim, brass fittings, and luxurious cushions. Sleeping cars were the standard on such long trips, and if the two girls had to share quarters with other people, these would certainly have been women. Passengers slept on ironed sheets, even in coach class, and enjoyed individual reading lights, dining cars with real china and silver, and elaborate menus. First-class passengers—which Dorothea and Fronsie were not—were supplied with barbers, showers, valet service, and ticker-tape news. But even coach passengers received service from the famed African American Pullman porters, who made the beds, poured the drinks, and protected women from harassment.

The train ride was a stunning introduction to what the girls hoped would be a round-the-world adventure. Crossing the Rio Grande at El Paso, they soon lost any sight of green, heading into the deserts, dry plains, and barren highlands and mountains of western New Mexico and eastern Arizona. Soon after came their first sight of the giant saguaro cactus forests and the mysterious red mesas, rising so steep and so flat that they seemed man-made. Passing through Tucson, they could see that this was Mexican country. After crossing into California at Yuma, they went to Los Angeles and got their first sight of the Pacific Ocean, then continued up to Oakland.

They crossed to San Francisco by ferry in May 1918. By now, newcomers would have seen no trace of the devastating earthquake of twelve years earlier. Dorothea and Fronsie were used to the steady upward climb of the New York skyline—from the 1890 World Building to the 1913 Woolworth tower. From a Hudson river ferry, there is no point from which one can take in the whole of Manhattan. San Francisco, by contrast, seen from the cross-bay ferry, appears an incomparable natural drama. The forty-seven-square-mile tip of a peninsula, rising anywhere from 150 to 1,000 feet above the surrounding waters, its lower levels often covered by fog, it is utterly photogenic. There were no bridges then, and scores of ferries plying five different routes scooted across the bay, so fast and numerous that thousands of workers were able to commute daily between San Francisco and East Bay cities. Dorothea and Fronsie arrived among these masses at the Beaux-Arts ferry building with its high tower, which had miraculously survived the earthquake of 1906. They marveled at the cable cars, rebuilt after the quake, with eight different lines climbing up and easing themselves down the dizzying steep hills.

Their first adventures, however, were inauspicious. They checked in at a YWCA. The next day, while they were breakfasting at a Compton's Cafeteria, Fronsie's purse was picked of all their money. Undeterred, because there was a friend of Joan's they could look up in Berkeley and because, Lange said, "we knew that we could get money from home if we needed to," they sought advice from the YWCA and were sent to an Episcopal home for working girls, the Mary Elizabeth Inn at 1040 Bush Street, instituted to help and protect working girls. This was a purgatory for these two young "new women." They felt they were "inmates" living in "cubicles," subordinated to rigid rules and Christian sermonizing. One resident got ejected because she missed the 10:00 P.M. curfew and had no choice but to spend the night with her boyfriend—to the horror of the deaconesses who ran the home. With their Greenwich Village disdain for respectability, Dorothea and Fronsie soon got themselves branded as "disruptive elements"; it seemed the table where they ate became the troublemakers' table. Soon they were evicted for unsafe as well as immoral practices—Fronsie left the electric iron on and it burned through the ironing board cover; Dorothea was caught smoking.

The young women made their luck change, however. Once more display-ing their grit, they decided not to call on parental resources but to get jobs and save for the rest of their trip. They managed this quickly. Fronsie did indeed get a Western Union job. Dorothea went to the city directory to find photographic shops and got a job the very next morning at Marsh & Company, a store selling luggage, stationery, cameras, and photographic supplies and providing photo finishing. It was not an easygoing environment. The boss was anxious that his employees be busy every minute. Dorothea took in the orders for developing and printing, but he also expected her to sell enlargements and framing aggressively. She found this obnoxious, but the job was improved by her fascination with the snapshots people brought in for developing. She looked at them as she packed them into envelopes, "and I realized at that time something that's never left me . . . the great visual importance of what's in people's snapshots that they don't know is there. . . . They never see them in any way but personal. One of the things that guided me finally into documen-tary work [was] that over-the-counter experience. . . ."[50] Centrally located at 712 Market, between Geary and O'Farrell, Marsh's turned out to be patronized by many local photographers. One of the first customers she connected with was Roi Partridge, who came in to buy photographic supplies for his wife, the pho-tographer Imogen Cunningham, who soon became a close friend. Dorothea did not know it yet, but her life as a professional photographer had begun just a day after arriving in San Francisco.

# 3

# Becoming a Photographer

When Dorothea Nutzhorn applied for the job at Marsh's, she gave her name as Dorothea Lange. This decision was entirely her own; her mother had not reclaimed the name Lange after her divorce.[1] This renaming was doubly symbolic—of starting a new life, rejecting her father. None of her intimates, including her two husbands and her children, ever heard the name Nutzhorn until after her death. She never communicated with her father again.

The name change did more than clear away the brush in order to build a new life on fresh ground. It was an erasure, a suppression of evidence. There was a practical reason, of course—Lange is simpler, more graceful, and more easily remembered than Nutzhorn. Perhaps Dorothea already envisioned herself as an entrepreneur, a master photographer running her own shop. But these practicalities did not require keeping everyone except Fronsie ignorant of her past. Her merciless fury toward her father came from her sense of abandonment and shame about his misdeeds, whatever they were.

Dorothea loved San Francisco instantly. It was easy to get to know—with its population of about 500,000, it was not a big city to a New Yorker, which is how she now identified herself.[2] Yet it was culturally and politically sophisticated. A business elite was solidly in control of the city, which was no longer the Wild West of the gold rush era. There were five major newspapers, among which the Hearst *Examiner* was the most prestigious. Mike de Young, publisher of the rival *Chronicle*, had already built the first skyscraper. Symbolic of the power structure was Mayor "Sunny Jim" Rolph, who in his nineteen years in office also headed the Ship Owners & Merchants Tugboat Company, the San Francisco Chamber of Commerce, and the Merchants' Exchange. San Francisco's high culture featured an opera, a symphony orchestra, numerous theaters, a fine-arts museum, built by Mike de Young, and an art school, the California School of Fine Arts, built after the 1906 earthquake. The people who created this high culture would become Lange's early photographic subjects.

The gold rush had brought a cosmopolitan mix of people to San Francisco, and in 1918 its diversity—a quarter of its people were foreign-born—remained. These "foreigners," however, were received and categorized quite differently than those in New York. There, for several generations past, immigrants from Ireland, Italy, and Slavic and Mediterranean countries were not considered "white" by the Protestant elites.[3] In California, by contrast, the presence of other subordinated groups—Native Americans, East Asians, Mexicans—meant that all European and Mediterranean immigrants were "white" from the moment they arrived. Italians were especially prominent, bringing good food, good coffee, and wine to the city. Most people "of color," to use a modern term, lived and worked in the countryside, with one big exception: the Chinese, of whom there were some eleven to fourteen thousand in San Francisco. Chinatown was San Francisco's exotic other, and for much of the city's history, residents of Chinese origin were prohibited by law from living outside its five square blocks. Dorothea had seen Genthe's photographs of the district and its people, but the Chinatown Lange saw was entirely new because the earthquake had destroyed the original completely. Afterward, Chinese leaders successfully resisted a campaign to keep them from returning to the city and rebuilt their economy by designing and promoting Chinatown as a tourist attraction. With investments from the Chinese government as well as from Chinese and American commercial interests, developer Look Tin Eli built a new facade for the settlement, a stage-set China with the curved eaves, colorful street lanterns, recessed balconies, and gilded facades that became the prototype for American Chinatowns ever after. Commercial Chinatown seemed much safer to outsiders than the old Chinatown had—few opium dens remained, for example—and it was not long before Dorothea, Fronsie, and their new friends began going there for cheap, delicious food.

IN THIS ECONOMIC and cultural context, Lange would create a portrait studio successful beyond her dreams. She developed a luxury portrait style that suited exactly the intimate taste—even when that taste was not well articulated by customers—of the city's cultural elite. She became the inheritor of Arnold Genthe's clientele as well as of his training and sensibility.

At Marsh's, Dorothea learned about the San Francisco Camera Club and joined it promptly. Between the two locales, she was perfectly situated to meet the right people. But Dorothea's strategic location alone cannot explain how quickly she became *the* portrait photographer for a luxury clientele and a member of a community of artists. Already in 1920 Edward Weston, dean of western photography, made her portrait, a small token of her integration into this community (see figure 4.3). Only her charisma can explain it, or, more precisely, her mixture of charm, ambition, photographic skill, aura of vulnerability, and good looks. By 1920 people who met her knew she was destined for success. As one contemporary remembered her, " 'pretty' is perhaps too strong a word . . . delicacy of features, beautiful eyes and a . . . slim, very attractive build."[4] She compensated so well for her bad leg that it often went unnoticed. "Just a little slide," one friend described it. Roger Sturtevant, who worked as her assistant in the mid-1920s, said it gave a sort of "flow" to her walk.[5]

At the Camera Club, she met a "smart, young, rich" businessman, real estate financier Sidney Franklin, who offered to go into business with her—this after she'd been in San Francisco only a few months. Evidently, he saw commercial potential in her work. She warned him that what she wanted would be expensive, but this did not deter him. Then two other new friends, Joe O'Connor and Jack Boumphrey, who distrusted Sidney Franklin, offered to loan her three thousand dollars, without demanding further involvement in her enterprise. Sidney Franklin released her from her commitment and she opened her own studio.[6]

A Cinderella story like this raises questions unanswerable due to lack of evidence: Were these men her lovers? (Lange never discussed or wrote about such personal matters.) Did the appeal of this young, lone, disabled woman stimulate some male rescue fantasies? What photographs did she make in those first months that stimulated such generosity? How aggressive had she been in looking for such a stake? Evidently, Lange not only attracted men but inspired them with confidence in her photographic and business acumen. Although there was no shortage of portrait studios in San Francisco, photography was still a growing industry and the demand for it could support many more photographers.[7] Furthermore, women did well in this business.[8] The demand favored them, because most purchasers of portraits were women, who often wanted portraits of children and expected women to have a better feel for these intimate images. Supply-side factors also contributed. Portrait studios were marked as a suitable business for women, partly because they allowed women to work from home while continuing to fulfill wifely and motherly responsibilities.[9] (This was one reason that female photojournalists, who could not work at home, were so rare.) Opening a studio did not require licensing, formal training, or large amounts of capital.[10] Photography was a new profession and therefore not defined as a uniquely male skill or tradition. The field's openness was even greater on the West Coast, where no photographic patriarch, not even Genthe in his day, ruled as Stieglitz did in the East, and no western male photographer disdained women's photography as much as Stieglitz did.[11] Although many camera clubs still excluded women, those that accepted them offered substantial resources—darkroom use, classes, libraries, and networking, of particular value to a new photographer eager to make contacts.[12]

With her male friends' money, Lange opened a shop in a handsome old building at 540 Sutter, near Union Square, San Francisco's upscale shopping district. Her studio was in the best possible company: At the front of the building was Hill Tolerton's distinguished art gallery, which sold modern work along with prints by Dürer and Rembrandt. Next door was Elizabeth Arden, a branch of the high-class New York beauty salon (Arden had seized on the term *salon* to replace the less sophisticated "parlor"). These two shops drew in just the kind of people who might be interested in an arty photographer. Lange's savvy, high-rent, high-risk choice announced that she would reach for the top of the market immediately.

Lange made sure to frequent the art gallery, where she charmed wealthy buyers and artists, who then saw and liked her portraits. Before long her clients were, as she put it, the "merchant princes" of San Francisco, the "cream of the trade."[13] No doubt they understood Lange to be Genthe's successor, and Dorothea might well have believed, and fostered the impression, that she was his anointed. This kind of customer was drawn in through word of mouth, not advertising, and although Lange's name was listed in the city business directory starting in 1919, it was missing by 1924, as if she no longer needed to advertise. It helped that her clients connected with one another at society and cultural events. By 1919 Lange's reputation had already spread geographically and customers arrived from Oakland, Napa, Palo Alto, Humboldt County, and San Jose; by 1920 some came from as far away as Salt Lake City, Honolulu, and Seattle.

When translated into today's dollars, her fees seem substantial: Mrs. Wendell Hamon, 1921, sitting and eight prints, $40—worth $411 in 2007; Mrs. Arnstein, 1928, sitting and two prints, $25—equivalent to $296 in 2007.[14] Lange's prestige would likely have allowed her to charge top rates. Her contemporary, photographer Margaret Bourke-White, remarked that "the only way to make 90% of my wealthy clients appreciate the work is to charge simply unheard of prices. . . . It is almost prostituting oneself for money." Lange bought an extremely comfortable armchair for her studio so that " 'my clients will not get up and leave when I name my price.' "[15] Bourke-White was then a leftist, and her class resentment arose not only from her politics but also from her discomfort in an employee position. Lange never expressed resentment of the rich who commissioned her. She did not feel like an employee. On the contrary, she saw herself as an equal and even a teacher to her clients.

Lange plunged into San Francisco's world of professional photographers. Already in 1920, the *San Francisco Chronicle* referred to her as "a photographic artist of great talent, whose work has exceptional quality and feeling, and who has secured a large clientele. . . ."[16] In the same year she became one of the twenty-eight founding members of the Pictorial Photographic Society of San Francisco.[17] She successfully avoided antagonizing the dean of western pictorialist photographers, Sigismund Blumann, soon to become the editor of *Camera Craft*, the West Coast's dominant magazine in the field, and the author of the best-selling *Photographic Workroom Handbook* (first published in 1927, reprinted for many years). He made images of wispy young women gliding through forests, foliage reflected in glimmering lakes, and San Francisco's buildings and shoreline veiled in mist.

Pictorialism can be caricatured—as I have just done—on numerous grounds: for its class and racial elitism, for its sentimentality, for its antiurbanism, not to mention the purist notion that photography should not try to look like a different art form. Some of these complaints involved masculinist sneers at womanly taste. The pictorialist lens not only celebrated the beauty of women and children but also feminized landscapes and urbanscapes, making them nurturant, graceful, and rounded, as opposed to Ansel Adams's later craggy Yosemite, for example. In fact, this gendered opposition is exaggerated.

Most pictorialists were men.[18] Many photographers, like Lange, experimented across the pictorialist/modernist divide. Her style evolved in conversation with her clients, sensitive to what they liked but also introducing them to less conventional approaches to posture, dress, and facial expression.

Lange also wooed her subjects with the elegant ambience of her studio. You entered Lange's studio through the Tolerton gallery, passed to a courtyard with a semicircular pool and a fountain, spitting water out of a lion's mouth, then entered the studio through French doors. The large reception room featured a fireplace, usually lighted, velvet drapes, and a large black velvet couch facing the fireplace. Lange decorated the studio in bohemian style, with exotic Arts and Crafts objects scattered about—a taste she had picked up from Genthe. She turned her studio into a kind of salon. She acquired a Russian samovar, and late every afternoon there was tea and tea cakes from a famous old San Francisco baker, Eppler's, for whoever dropped in. This was served graciously by Lange's receptionist Ah-yee, a beautiful Chinese "mission girl"—that is, she had been educated in a Christian mission school. She had a merry sense of humor and was very popular with Dorothea and her customers. By 5:00 P.M., the "place was full of all kinds of people," taking on the atmosphere of a social event. People made dates to meet "at the couch." They would sometimes roll back the rug, play jazz recordings, and dance.[19] The fact that Dorothea worked very long hours contributed to the social life. She built a darkroom and a retouching workbench in the basement. "I was [there] working most of the time, day and night, Saturdays and Sundays, holidays. . . . That place was my life, and it became the center for many other people who used my studio in the afternoons and the night."[20] She left her door open so that people could enter even if she was in the darkroom, and she would hear their footsteps and come up. Guests got used to her hands, perpetually stained brown by the developer. Fronsie stopped by frequently, and the atmosphere of the studio contributed to her eventual career as a high-design decorator.[21] The arty aura, of course, made the studio more interesting to potential clients. It was the opposite of a sterile cockpit, or the study/studio of a scholar or artist who could not tolerate distraction.

Sometime in the fall of 1919, while working in her basement darkroom, she heard unusually sharp footsteps above her. She soon learned that they were made by the painter Maynard Dixon, who always wore cowboy boots, although she might also have been hearing the taps of the golden-headed cane he carried as a prop. It was not difficult to find out who he was, since he was "easily the most colorful figure" in San Francisco's art world.[22] She then saw him several times in the Tolerton gallery, but she did not approach him, feeling, uncharacteristically, a bit intimidated. The man who introduced them recalled that they immediately radiated mutual attraction. In March 1920, they were married. Impatient readers will have to wait until the next chapter, however, to hear more about their love, marriage, and life together in San Francisco— there is too much to tell to squeeze it in here. And it would be misleading to tell that story first, because it might crowd out the work and world that Lange created for herself.

BY THE TIME she arrived in San Francisco, Dorothea had developed a talent for friendship and projected a warm and dramatic personality. Her manner was subtle—she was not one who held forth or entertained—but she sparkled even as she drew others out. Her charisma derived in part from her originality. The timbre of her voice was high and thin, a little girl's voice at first, its pitch lowering as she warmed to her subject; friends reported that the dash and rhythm of her speech could be mesmerizing, an impression strengthened by her large, expressive eyes. Her conversation combined the arty-intellectual and the ethereal, sometimes even seeming fey. As she aged she grew sharper— "astringent," one friend called her. She dressed eccentrically and dramatically, wearing pants or long skirts and a beret cocked sideways; some said she dressed in costumes.[23]

She was by no means primarily oriented toward men; she developed strong relationships with women and kept them forever. Her charisma drew people to her, but had she not been a sensitive and attentive friend, they would not have stuck. But Dorothea was no feminist. Too young for the first-wave women's movement, she died before the birth of second-wave feminism, so she had little exposure to women's-rights talk. She never complained about sex discrimination, although the fact that she experienced it is undeniable to the historian looking back at her life. Yet after her death, feminists would claim her as a heroine, and they would not be entirely wrong, because her life was in some ways woman-centered: her clients were mainly women; her documentary photography would focus heavily on women and would raise critical questions about gender relations; and she developed close and enduring bonds with women, both photographers and customers.

Many of Lange's female photographer friends became, or already were, illustrious: Anne Brigman, Imogen Cunningham, Consuelo Kanaga, Alma Lavenson, Louise Dahl-Wolfe, Tina Modotti, Margrethe Mather, and, a bit later, Hansel Mieth. But they also faced unique stresses. They shared tips on new developers and groused about difficult clients or ruined negatives, but their talk was not only of photography—in fact they may have wished it were; decades later, Lange would reflect ruefully that she had never had the luxury of a stretch of time in which to concentrate only on photography. The women photographers were preoccupied with how to combine career and artistic development with keeping men happy and taking care of children, or living without husbands and children, which some found equally hard. The solutions they contrived tilted one way and another and rarely lasted; the balances they struck differed, and they no doubt disagreed at times with friends' decisions. How they managed speaks of what was and what was not possible for women at the time.

The "mother" of the San Francisco women photographers was Anne Brigman. Many photographers benefited from her support, including Edward Weston, but particularly women—including Lange. Without Brigman, it would have been harder for the women to win recognition. A generation older than Lange and her other friends, her career was possible because she was divorced and childless. Having gained prestige from her association with Stieglitz— she was one of the two western members of his Photo-Secession group—she ran something of a salon in her Oakland home until she retired to Southern California in 1929. But she also displayed unusual independence. She trekked on her own for weeks at a time through the Sierras, camping out, braving red ants and storms in her search for primeval settings to photograph. Calling herself a "pagan," she photographed nudes—including herself—perched in trees, naked lovers entwined so that they repeated the curves of gnarled trees. The most famous and most suggestive of these photographs, *Cleft in the Rock*, shows a nude woman fitted into the vertical, vaginal crack in a boulder. Then in the darkroom, she would smudge the negatives, scratch out the crotch, scratch in clouds and drapery, morphing her subject into a creature of mythology. She organized a group of women photographers who photographed one another nude, since it was not easy for them to use professional models.[24]

The great photographer Imogen Cunningham became Dorothea's best friend and remained so until Lange's death forty-seven years later. Imogen's husband, etcher Roi Partridge, met Dorothea at Marsh's photo-supply store and invited her home for dinner, saying to Imogen, you really need to meet the young woman I met—"she practically leapt across the counter at me with her eagerness."[25] Imogen and Dorothea made each other and their families into kinfolk, celebrating holidays and outings together. One of Imogen's sons, Rondal Partridge, became Dorothea's apprentice and virtually her adoptive son (as well as a great art photographer himself), and his children became like grandchildren to her. Cunningham influenced Lange's photography (for example, see figures 9.2 and 9.3) and they shared the pleasures and stresses of children, difficult husbands, and, soon, divorces, as well as the need for paying customers.[26]

The adventuresome Dorothea was magnetically drawn by Imogen's unconventionality and rejection of feminine propriety. Nonconformity was Imogen's by inheritance. Her father was a freethinker (that is, an atheist), a vegetarian, a Theosophist, and a believer in spiritualism—communicating with the souls of the dead.[27] She saw her mother as a drudge to husband, children, farmwork and housework, and the lesson she drew was never to repeat that life herself. She became an outspoken feminist. For one portrait, Cunningham made a double exposure, showing her mother's head encircled by an imprisoning crown of kitchen utensils. But she blamed her mother for weakness, rather than her father for his domination. She adored her father, who had home-schooled her and paid for her art lessons. Her photography displayed her father's brand of radicalism. An early self-portrait, made in 1906, shows her lying nude in the grass.[28] In later years, she, like Anne Brigman, called herself a "heathen."[29]

She opened a portrait studio in Seattle in 1910, nine years before Lange did the same thing some eight hundred miles south, and worked with the same sensibility, one Imogen called "expressive portraiture." Cunningham made herself a part of Seattle's art world, as Lange would do in San Francisco. But unlike Lange's, Cunningham's work and ideas grew more daring. She photographed male nudes, including some with their genitals showing. She loved provoking, and continued to love it until she died, at ninety-three, in 1976.

In 1915 Imogen married Roi Partridge, whose work, artistic tastes, and marital expectations were more traditional than Imogen's. He took lengthy sketching trips, not considering Imogen's burden, and seemed resentful of her photography, insisting that photographers had no right to sign their work since it was only an artifact of mechanical reproduction. Their son Rondal calls their marriage an "acid bath."[30] Under pressure from Imogen to earn a living, Roi took jobs first at the advertising agency Foster and Kleiser, where Maynard Dixon also worked, and then at Mills College, but despite his salary, he moved his family to a house in rural Oakland, where water had to be carried up a hill and light was provided by kerosene lamps. Imogen, without a darkroom, did no commercial photography until 1921. She ended the relationship when Roi tried to prohibit her from traveling to New York for a photography commission. We can imagine Imogen's pleasure in her new acquaintance, Dorothea Lange, with whom she shared a drive for independence and photography.

Dorothea was also captivated by photographer Consuelo Kanaga, another free spirit. "She was a person way ahead of her time," Lange recalled, ". . . a terribly attractive, dashing kind of a gal, who worked for the *News* and lived in a Portuguese hotel in North Beach . . . entirely Portuguese workingmen except Consuelo. . . . She had more courage! . . . they could send her to places where an unattached woman shouldn't be seen and Consuelo was never scathed. . . . She had a tripod with a red velvet head cover!" At a mere twenty-one, Kanaga got hired as a newspaper reporter and photojournalist—she may have been the only woman photojournalist in the country then. She gave up this security in 1918 to become an art photographer. Dorothea loved her irreverent spirit: ". . . generally if you use the word unconventional you mean someone who breaks the rules—she had no rules."[31]

Kanaga's and Lange's styles evolved similarly in the 1920s and early 1930s. It may have been in Kanaga's more modernist work that Lange first saw portraits made so close that that the face entirely filled the frame. (See Lange's portrait of a Hopi, figure 5.3.) In the 1920s Kanaga was more tuned in politically than Lange. Working to develop a social-reform photography, she roamed San Francisco streets, photographing street life and poor people. She is best known today as a photographer of American blacks, because these portraits were so unusual at the time. An activist with light, inside and outside the darkroom, she revealed the radiance of dark skin, a quality lost by photographers less skilled with light. Her sensibility toward African Americans, tuned to beauty more than victimization, also influenced Lange.[32] Had Kanaga remained in California, their mutual photographic influence would likely have continued. But they were always in touch, and Dorothea saw her when in New York.

Kanaga's photographic career was truncated by marriages, three of them, and her life journey tells us, by contrast, something about Lange. Her first husband hated city life and insisted that she follow where his job as a mining engineer took him. They soon divorced, and she took off for New York and then Europe. Worried about being single, she soon married an Irish writer, Barry McCarthy. He expected her to remain at home, an entirely irrational expectation since he had no income—his work did not get published. She began an in-home portrait business, but even this threatened him, and once, in anger, he threw out many of her prints. Still she stayed. In 1930 they returned to San Francisco, where he became increasingly alcoholic and abusive. In 1935, finally escaping from McCarthy, she went back to New York, where she married for a third time, to artist Wallace Putnam. Unable to respect her photography as he did his painting, he moved them to an artists' colony in Croton-on-Hudson, where she could not develop a studio business. For the rest of her life she did little photography.

As a photographer, Kanaga was an original. As a woman fenced in, she was not; she could have been Virginia Woolf's fictional Shakespeare's sister, or any woman without a room of one's own. Her need for a husband and her attraction to dominating men interrupted and ultimately shut down her photographic development. Lange, by contrast, managed to combine career, marriage, and motherhood. This was not a matter of political principle. It was just that her passion for photography would not be confined, and neither would her willfulness.

Dorothea was friendly with several other young women photographers in the 1920s, and their stories also highlight the conflicting pressures women faced. The most glamorous was Italian-born Tina Modotti: star of San Francisco's Italian theater, silent-film actress, lover of Edward Weston, activist in the Mexican Communist party, and partner of a Cuban revolutionary in exile in Mexico City. Like any number of other ambitious women of the time, she combined a modernist feminism and revolutionary leftist enthusiasm with pleasure in an identity as companion of charismatic, even heroic men. Her sensibility conceived of male and female as opposite and complementary essences, romanticizing and melodramatizing women's unique receptiveness—a perspective common among bohemian women. Her views about women were like Lange's, reflected in a fun-house mirror, magnified, distorted, and made theatrical. "As far as creation is concerned," Modotti wrote, ". . . women are negative," a comment much like Isadora Duncan's "a woman can [n]ever really be an artist, since Art is a hard taskmaster who demands everything, whereas a woman who loves gives up everything to life."[33]

Taught photography by Weston, Modotti began with close-ups of flowers, bodies, and fruits and vegetables, but by the mid-1920s, she applied the same design principles to photographs of workers and peasants. When she arrived in San Francisco in 1925, she met many of the women photographers, and arranged to use Lange's studio.[34] Returning to Mexico, she threw herself into left-wing activism and into several affairs with important men, including Diego Rivera and Cuban revolutionary Julio Antonio Mella. In 1929 Mella was assassinated in front of her eyes, and she was falsely accused of killing him. Deported from Mexico, she left for Berlin in 1930, then for the Soviet Union, then for Spain; she returned to Mexico under a pseudonym and died there in 1942. Pablo Neruda composed her epitaph. And photography? She produced nothing of any significance after she left Mexico.[35]

Another who opened with fireworks and then faded was Weston's previous model and girlfriend, Margrethe Mather. Lange found her fascinating too. When Weston and Mather met, in 1912, he was a conventional middle-class studio photographer making sentimental portraits of children and landscapes. Mather introduced him to radical ideas—political, sexual, and aesthetic. Her abstracted, close-up details of nude bodies predate and prefigure his, and they made several photographs together, both signing them, something Weston never did again.[36] Mather photographed arts-world celebrities such as Charlie Chaplin, Lillian Gish, Vaclav Nijinsky, and Leon Bakst. In 1930 she became the first photographer to exhibit at the new de Young Museum in San Francisco, an impressive credit for a woman. Yet her photographic career and her stability ended by the mid-1930s, while Weston went on to become one of the great art photographers.[37] Mather's primary sexual and romantic attraction was to women, and she lived with several female lovers during much of her time with Weston. Same-sex love was not at all uncommon among these bohemian artists, and Weston, in turn, had some male lovers. To call this homosexuality would be ahistorical, since this counterculture did not divide people into gay or straight as mutually exclusive identities. Under whatever label, Dorothea was entirely comfortable with same sex–attracted people, and early on hired as an assistant the gay Roger Sturtevant, who went on to become a fine photographer.

Another talented, if less dramatic, photography dropout in Lange's circle was Alma Lavenson. Like her friend Kanaga, she came to photography with economic and educational privilege but despite parental repression. When her wealthy father prohibited her from taking a job after she graduated from Berkeley, she taught herself photography. Her family connections with art dealer and collector Albert Bender got her entrée to the San Francisco photographers' circle; her amazing talent brought her one-person shows at the de Young Museum and at the Brooklyn Museum in 1933—way ahead of Lange in career trajectory. But that year, she married a prosperous attorney, gave birth to two children, and devoted herself exclusively to family, from then on photographing only as a hobby.[38]

Louise Dahl was one of very few women photographers around Lange who made a lasting and prestigious career. She came to documentary photography through friendship with Kanaga. Like Lange, she married an artist and did not consider herself in his league. But by following him to New York, ironically, she became the world-famous fashion photographer for *Harper's Bazaar*, Louise Dahl-Wolfe. Dahl-Wolfe was, besides Lange, the only one of the San Francisco group who worked professionally in photography as a married woman. To do that, one had to have a supportive husband and a strong will.

LANGE'S FRIENDSHIPS WITH clients reveal yet more about who attracted her, about the political influences on her, and about how other married women managed to construct lives outside their families. None of this group of friends was employed, all supported by husbands or family wealth, which gave them leisure—a leisure they spent in political, artistic, charitable, and community endeavors. Their characteristics were not so different from those of the photographers and artists Dorothea knew: love for the arts, cosmopolitan tastes, freedom in moving about the city, liberal sexual standards, appreciation of foreign cultures, and, frequently, leftist politics. They did not garner the renown of Lange, Cunningham, and some of the other photographers, but they were serious and active women. Powerful personality that she was, Dorothea had equally forceful friends.

These friendships grew out of Lange's studio method, its leisurely and conversational pace, and, in turn, these relationships built her business. This is not to say that her friendships were instrumental. She did not need to chase clients—the same ones came back repeatedly, some commissioning family pictures every year, and new clients came when they saw Lange portraits on their friends' grand pianos. It was her friends' culture more than their wealth that attracted Dorothea. Moreover, they chose Dorothea as much as she chose them. What is remarkable here is that this young businesswoman created entirely equal relationships with her elite and culturally sophisticated customers.

Her client friends can be divided into two groups: the urban and the rural. Both groups were high-culture lovers and held liberal attitudes toward everything from elections to child raising. Some of them became, as would Dorothea, advocates of progressive reform under the impact of the Depression. The city women, however, found independence more easily than Lange's photographer friends: Household servants left them free to invest time in "causes" even when their children were young.

Lange's city friends were almost all Jews of German ancestry. Wealthy and powerful, secular and urban, the "Our Crowd" of San Francisco, their ancestors had immigrated in the mid-nineteenth century and built mercantile fortunes.[39] Northern California was open to these immigrants, who counted as white before that status was confirmed for them in New York.[40] They stuck together—they may have been white, but they knew that Christians knew the difference. A widespread "parlor anti-Semitism" excluded them, for example, from the gentlemen's clubs and the high-status women's clubs. Segregation was residential as well. The Gentile aristocracy lived on the three big hills—Nob, Telegraph, and Russian; the richest Jews built mansions in Pacific Heights with spectacular bay views.[41] Their children married one another, producing a complex and encompassing web of family relationships among them. They did not frequent the Jewish neighborhood in the Fillmore District, where Eastern European Jews maintained kosher food stores, bakeries, a Yiddish theater, and political organizations such as the Workmen's Circle.[42]

Consider the interconnected Elkus, Katten, and Kahn families, from which came two of Lange's closest friends, Elizabeth Elkus and Edythe Katten, for their histories are representative of their group. The friends were cousins, because in the 1880s businessmen Albert Elkus and Simon Katten had married two Kahn sisters, daughters of the owner of the leading Oakland department store. All three families parlayed retail stores or garment factories—typical Jewish entrepreneurial beginnings—into prominent businesses and all three produced cultured and politically committed offspring. Albert's father, Louis Elkus, had married Cordelia de Young, sister of the owner of the *San Francisco Chronicle* and founder of San Francisco's de Young Museum, in 1895. Albert, oldest of their eleven children, became a reform mayor of Sacramento in 1921. Another son, Charles de Young Elkus, became an attorney and, with his wife, Ruth, a collector of Native American art. He helped the Pueblo Indians regain control over lands and water that were being usurped by white squatters, and subsidized Indian health care; he became close to John Collier, New Deal head of the Bureau of Indian Affairs, and worked with him to produce the Roosevelt administration's "Indian New Deal" of the 1930s. Through their love for Indians and the West, Ruth and Charles became patrons of Maynard Dixon's art. Albert Elkus, Jr., from the next generation, husband of Dorothea's friend Elizabeth, became a professional musician, composer, professor of music at UCB, and ultimately president of the San Francisco Conservatory of Music.

When Dorothea met Elizabeth and Edythe, both were young, cultured, and well educated, active in charitable and community projects. Although Dorothea never shared their class position, her personality and her artiness made her seem to be one of them. These friendships endured: Decades later, when Edythe was in a hospital having radiation treatment for cancer, Dorothea visited her every night to kiss her good night. When Dorrie, as they called her, was hospitalized, Edythe did the same.[43] When Dorothea was laid up in a New York hospital, she wrote Elizabeth, "I just feel like seeing you and being with you and telling you all my troubles and how disaster overtook me in New York. . . . Get on your slippers."[44] "Slippers" referred to the "slipper club" they formed along with another friend, Minna Blum Neustadt, wife of a prominent New Dealer. The slippers had been gifts from Dorothea. When in town, they met weekly, alternating houses, discussing art, gardening, and politics. Dorothea became so identified with this German Jewish community that several believed she was herself Jewish.

The women's friendships drew in their families. Dorothea's sons Dan and John often played with Ken and Andy Katten and attended the same nursery school. They shared many holiday meals, including Christmas, since these Jews were not at all observant. Edythe's son and daughter-in-law Ken and Jan Katten both sensed the particular intimacy and intensity between Edythe and Dorrie: Jan thinks that there was sexual attraction between them, but no affair, while Ken thinks that his father was jealous of the women's relationship.[45] In Lange's portraits of Edythe, we see a dramatic, austere beauty with large features and a sharp-edged, sculpted hairdo. One set of portraits, made in 1933, shows her bare-shouldered, with a deep décolletage.

The slipper club supported progressive causes. Before her marriage, Edythe Selling had graduated from the University of California at Berkeley with a degree in labor economics. In the 1920s, when Lange's photographer and artist friends were generally apolitical, these women influenced her with their confident, principled commitments. An ardent British Labourite, Elizabeth Elkus taught handicapped children and spoke out on child-welfare issues. Edythe Katten and her husband were active in San Francisco's Socialist party, voting for Norman Thomas rather than FDR in 1932, though they quickly became New Deal supporters.

Dorothea's country friends also came from wealth, and in abjuring city life, they also set an example she admired. Dorothea's young assistant Roger Sturtevant thought of them as back-to-the-earth bohemians who loved the "Isadora Age of sexual freedom. . . ." He exaggerated, but they did go in for skinny-dipping and other "advanced things."[46] The closest to Dorothea, Mary Ann Wilson, was as bohemian as Californians got, and Dorothea and her family visited the Wilsons' Marin County home in Mill Valley so often that a cabin on the property was known as

3.1. EDYTHE KATTEN, 1933

Dorothea's.[47] Mary Ann wore home-sewn, earthy clothing and furnished her rustic house in a spare style—burnished wood tables, oak chairs—that Dorothea emulated. The families shared a love of the natural, which was expressed in allowing the children to swim and play unclothed, their eating and cooking outdoors, and their early-days concern for the environment. Another politically liberal close friend, Gertrude Clausen, migrated through marriage to a ranch in northern California, but her desire for Lange photographs took her to San Francisco at least yearly. She first sat for Dorothea in 1919, when her eldest daughter was born, and whenever a child was born thereafter (there were four more). Gertrude kept the photographs in a brocade album on the piano and told her daughters that in case of fire, that album should be the only thing they tried to save.[48] Gert's daughter Christina became Dorrie's assistant for several years during World War II and her family continued to socialize with Dorothea's children after her death. Dorothea and family also often visited Louise Lovett's parents' farm on Soquel Creek, just east of Santa Cruz. They would camp in a grove of cottonwoods near a stream. Dorothea made beautiful photographs of all the children, especially playing naked in the water, in a fusion of snapshot and pictorialist modes.

CONSCIOUSLY OR NOT, Lange used her studio to strengthen a strategic alliance between the bohemian arts crowd and San Francisco's elite. She sensed that a sector of the wealthy not only respected those who worked to create beauty but also longed to know them, to be accepted by them, to be affected by them. As a class, they were disproportionately responsible for building San Francisco's high-culture institutions: the symphony orchestra, the opera, the ballet, the de Young Legion of Honor.[49] "They gave string quartets in their living rooms or in their drawing rooms, and they educated talent: Yehudi Menuhin . . . Isaac Stern . . ." Dorothea recalled, and she could have added Ernest Bloch, Pierre Monteux, and Joseph Szigeti.[50] Lange made her studio into a site where artists and the liberal rich interacted. The alliance benefited Lange economically and artistically: it built her business and her reputation and allowed her to experiment with a portraiture that was slightly unconventional. Lange's part in building the alliance also helped others, particularly once the Depression deprived so many artists of an income.

Artists have almost always depended on such alliances. Once, artists painted to order, on commission from patrons. In the last few centuries, artists and craftspeople have been able to earn a living at their art only if the wealthy buy their work. Unless they become so famous that their names themselves sell, they have to create what rich people like or can quickly learn to like. This unspoken compact was fundamental to the development of all the arts, not only the visual but also, importantly, music and theater, in San Francisco, as everywhere else.

Lange furthered her connections by agreeing to travel occasionally to photograph people in their homes, a practice not uncommon at the time. Lugging heavy equipment, she went as far as Seattle to photograph the Weyerhaeuser family two or three times. The trips paid off, because she would stay in the homes of her clients, cementing relationships, picking up new clients, receiving the occasional dinner invitation.

Willingness to travel signified Lange's primary orientation: to please her clients. Portrait photography is always client-centered work and success depends on one's ability to sense what the clients will like. "I don't mean pandering to their vanity," she said, but "my personal interpretation was second to the need of the other fellow." Lange's wizardry was that she could often induce them to like what she liked. She stretched their tastes a bit, showed them something unexpected, and she believed that in doing so she was showing them something about themselves that they had not seen before. "I really and seriously tried, with every person I photographed, to reveal them as closely as I could."[51]

Portraits serve both domestic and social aspirations. They signify but also construct family. They provide images that confirm the stability, care, and belonging people desire, and they communicate respectability and dignity to visitors in their homes. They present ideal families and thereby sustain these ideals, often disguising what actual families were like. They give children roots—who does not like to see her own baby pictures? What parent does not wish to be reminded of her children's childhood? In a modern culture with a certain disdain for the old, images of our more beautiful youthful selves shore up the self-esteem of the elderly. At the same time, portraits declare status: military honor, womanly virtue, manly command, and class above all. Thorsten Veblen called the portrait a display of "conspicuous leisure."[52]

Portraits helped people of all social strata demand social respect, but portrait style was often differentiated by class. Photography historian John Tagg has pointed out, for example, that a three-quarter view was typical of portraits made for high-status clients, while straight frontal images characterized those of lower status.[53] Few of Lange's portraits are frontal. Studio photographers in the pictorialist era often used painted backdrops and Beaux-Arts statuary, typically pastoral or garden scenes that betokened access to leisure and beauty, to elevate the status of poorer clients. The nineteenth-century upscale portraitist Nadar began photographing his elite clients, by contrast, against an "unarticulated space" so that they could "disport themselves without script."[54] So did Lange. Her style appeared to her clients as a modern, unconservative kind of elegance. The artistic modernism she had imbibed in New York expressed itself in a taste for simplicity and a rejection of conventional finery. She never draped people and she discouraged formal poses. She did not ask her subjects to smile and she preferred them not to wear suits or gowns, but informal clothes, best of all old clothes, in which they could be more relaxed. She wanted her pictures to be eternal, undated—a desire she would reverse ten years later—so she tried to avoid trendy clothing.[55] She printed her portraits on handmade paper with a deckle edge. And she dated her prints as well as signing them; she wanted this record of her work, even as she discarded her correspondence and any journals she kept.

The finished product was to give sitters the sense that they were representing themselves in an individually chosen manner. Lange offered her elite clientele a portraiture that suggested—or "revealed," she would say—individuality and a deep inner life. She endowed her subject with "interiority," as Allan Sekula wrote.[56] As Alan Trachtenberg put it, she sought the "bodily expression of characteristic inward feeling."[57] No doubt her own not-quite-perfect body had honed her sensitivity to posture and gesture as communicative dimensions. Her slight disability, so slight as to be in no way offensive, may have strengthened her customers' belief in her sensitivity and gentleness. Experiencing her own body as disfigured intensified a soulful quality about her that convinced clients of her power to capture their inner state of grace. They believed that she could make their education, culture, and sensitivity apparent in her images of them. Portraits signaling depth of character were particularly important to the newly rich or middle class and to those who, like Lange's clients, cared more to be identified with high culture than with wealth. Not that they used high culture only for prestige; they were often passionate lovers of music and art. But their cultural commitments were inseparable from the social position they enjoyed.

Culture critic Walter Benjamin argued that photography was a democratic practice because of its reproducibility; and that it abolished the "aura" of prestige surrounding the one-of-a-kind painting. (This judgment was, of course, based on a misunderstanding of how much photographs could be changed in darkrooms.) Thus it is hardly surprising that in the late nineteenth century, portrait photographers began attempting to re-create that aura of self-worth as "character," personality.[58] For the individual, the aura appears to emanate from the subject herself. But the aura also creates social status: the photograph can generate respectability and stand for cultured taste. Framed and set on a piano or a mantel, or collected in a leather or brocade album prominently displayed, it can make an entire home upscale, even prestigious.[59]

The creative force of portraits expresses itself particularly strongly through gendered imagery. Portraits can reassure by marking a woman as appropriately feminine, men as masculine. Portrait photographers develop a sure command of these appearances: how to arrange hair and clothing, how to position their subjects, how to deal with wriggly babies and restless children, how to coax out a desired facial expression. Particularly in Lange's time, women photographers might find these skills easier to acquire because they were consonant with feminine socialization. They decorated their studios invitingly, arranged lighting flatteringly; they seemed to have an intuitive "knack of placement" that revealed inner feelings and family love. They appeared especially gifted at capturing children, landscapes, still lifes, and genre scenes.[60] Lange never defied such expectations of women, but she performed them at what seemed a more sophisticated level. In fact, plenty of male portrait photographers mastered these skills too, but it was easy, given cultural assumptions, to treat them as innate attributes of women. The pictorialist style was particularly evocative of Victorian femininity, and Lange's portraits of women are, on average, mistier than those of men. Her female subjects were more frequently portrayed

3.2. ONE OF LANGE'S PORTRAIT CUSTOMERS, MS. RAENTSCH, 1932

in interior spaces, in part because they were more likely to ask her to come to their homes to photograph. In this regard, the reassuring function may have been particularly desirable, as so many women in this era—particularly those with leisure time to spend—felt anxious about whether their public-sphere activities violated the domesticity that the older culture demanded of women.

So the desired photographic aura required delicate balance and was not easily achieved. To produce a likeness is easy; to "capture" an interior essence requires overcoming the typical human response to the camera, which is to stiffen, to adopt a strained smile, a formal stance, an overdressed demeanor.[61] Lange engaged in a kind of gentle jostling to get subjects to break free of those rigidities. As an assistant in portrait studios in New York, she had been assigned to talk with, pose, and prepare clients. In San Francisco she developed this ability further, unintimidated by artists, intellectuals and big-business and society people, and this confidence and charm, along with her genuine interest in others, improved her product. Through conversation, Lange's liveliness and the substance of what she said induced customers to grow interested in something beyond the camera and their appearance; to loosen up and to engage in an interaction in which, by forgetting themselves, they found themselves.

Lange's interactive method, dependent on the subject to participate in creating the portrait, required patience. She described this often in later interviews. "You have to wait until certain decisions are made by the subject— what he's going to give to the camera . . . and the photographer—what he's going to choose to take. It is a much longer inner process than putting the camera between you and the subject. . . ."[62] She talked a bit of spiritualism, calling herself a "channel," "a cipher, a person that can be used for lots of things. . . ."[63] This kind of talk made her out to be somewhat passive, a trope she would use occasionally throughout her life and one consistent with Victorian conceptions of female nature. She sometimes seemed to understand her work as uniquely, naturally female. To the degree that it suggested passivity or minimized her calculated, disciplined method, the spiritual talk was a performance, even a business strategy. She made many negatives and never hesitated to work them over in the darkroom. Her results came from working long hours, not from her clients' inner lives. She often expected repeated sittings from her clients, an expectation that might have proved annoying but that also flattered them and certified her high standards.

Feminine or not, her portraits could be called intimate. They would not do as publicity photos for movie stars—although glamour photography, using strong lighting, heavy makeup, and elaborate hairdos, got its start in Hollywood just as she opened her studio. She photographed some highbrow celebrities—for example, this photograph of Ernest Bloch— but the images did not sing out *star*. They were designed instead to signal depth of character, uniqueness of personality. Lange could do this even with teenagers, as in her brooding portrait of an adolescent on a horse. (See plate 2.) Displaying yet another feminine skill, Lange grew particularly adept at portraying relationships, most commonly in mother-child or sibling groups, with family members draped over one another informally, but also in other familial couplings, such as this exquisite photograph of a boy and his grandfather.

3.3. Ernest Bloch, 1927

However sophisticated, Lange saw herself as a "tradesman," to use her word. This identity, typical among studio photographers, combined the manual labor and social position of artisan and small entrepreneur.[64] Neither her approach nor her aspiration was that of an artist in the modern sense of that word, although in the past—for example, in the tradition of her lithographer uncles—there was little distinc-

3.4. Katten grandfather
and grandson, 1934

tion between artisan and artist. "It never occurred to me," she said, to do any uncommissioned work—that is, to set her own photographic agenda. That was Imogen's territory.[65] Lange's modest aspirations, exemplified by her choosing not to imagine her work as art, had advantages. It insulated her from the demands and competition of the art market and from the imperatives of establishment art authorities. This insulation was a matter of degree, not an absolute, of course. She studied photography magazines and went to exhibits; she took in what a wide range of other photographers were doing. But for many years she did feel constricted by the obligation to please customers. An art photographer might have rebelled: Walker Evans, for example, thought studio work intolerable because of the "horrors of vanity" of the subjects.[66] By contrast, Lange saw her photography as a service for customers. Although she guided and cajoled, in the end her clients decided what to present of themselves, she believed, and her job was to capture that. They had a right to flattering photographs. What began as a client-centered service, however, would become a powerful documentary technique a decade later.

REMARKABLY, BY 1921 San Francisco's most upscale portrait photographer, most in demand among the rich arty set, was twenty-six-year-old Dorothea Lange. This helps explain how it came about that one of San Francisco's leading artists, and its most dramatic art personality, romanced and married a small young photographic businesswoman, new in the city, who walked with a limp.

# 4

# Maynard Dixon, Bohemian Artist

**M**aynard Dixon, the artist whose sharp steps Dorothea heard above her darkroom, would not only become her lover and husband but would also influence her artistically and culturally. He brought her into the vibrant sociability among San Francisco's bohemian artists and into the natural beauty of California and the southwestern desert. Dixon lived in two clashing worlds—the city and the wilderness. Ultimately, the wilderness won, and he became steadily more bitter as commercialization and suburbanization threatened to devour it; his bitterness would eventually destroy their marriage. But at first, Dorothea's attraction to him vibrated at a pitch she had never before felt. Thus to understand her, we need to understand him.

Dixon came by his cowboy persona legitimately. He was born in frontier-town Fresno in 1875, when it was ranching country.[1] (Later, the town's transformation into the commercial hub of the West's major agricultural district, the San Joaquin Valley, would cause the adult Maynard great distress.) As a boy, he was fascinated by Indians. Fresno was established on Indian land, of course, and Maynard's grandfather had been an Indian fighter. The 1890 Wounded Knee Massacre of the Lakota Sioux mesmerized Maynard, and throughout his life he would study Indian culture, paint Indians, write poetry and stories about Indians, pride himself on friendships with Indians, and venerate the spiritual closeness to nature that he believed abided in Indian blood.[2] He smoked the

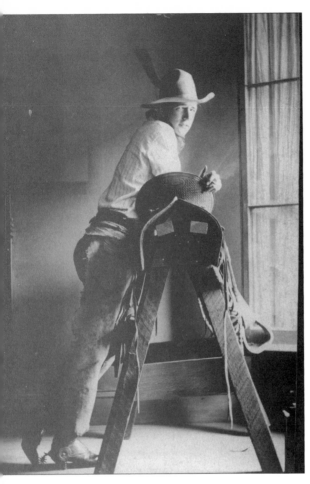

4.1. MAYNARD DIXON, 1895,
*by Isabel Porter Collins*

Indian herb kinnikinnick, in cigarettes that he could roll with one hand.[3] The allure of Indians for Maynard coexisted, as for so many other whites of his time, with racist assumptions about them and other nonwhites.[4] Maynard's Indians were noble savages, their demise part of the inevitable tragedy of advancing civilization. He often painted them among rocks, quite still, as part of nature, reinforcing their stability and distance from the modern. As a grown man, Dixon imagined that he would be more comfortable living with the Indians, because he felt himself unfit for industrial urban capitalism.[5]

Although Maynard grew to love nothing more than camping out alone for weeks, he was by no means a hardy or adventurous child. From his earliest years asthma attacks hounded him, foreshadowing the emphysema that would cripple him at the end of his life. He learned to prefer solitary, sedentary activity, which led to the discovery of his extraordinary talent. Somewhere around the age of five, he began to draw, and his draftsmanship was nothing short of amazing. In 1891 he or his parents sent some of his drawings to Frederic Remington, the premier illustrator of western themes, who responded that Dixon's work was better than his own at that age. Decades later, Maynard would entertain his children by drawing, upon request, and from memory, anything they demanded—horses, Indians, trees, fences, faces, whole rodeos.

Like Dorothea, he was an indifferent student. He dropped out of high school and then out of the California School of Design. But while at that art school he met a group of young artists who introduced him to San Francisco and formed his community for the rest of his life. They included Jimmy Swinnerton, Homer Davenport, Gottardo Piazzoni, and his particular chum, the Mexican Xavier "Marty" Martinez, just returned from studying art in Paris.[6] Dixon benefited from an expanding market for illustrations of the Wild West and became an extremely successful illustrator by age twenty. Before long, he got a job as illustrator for the *San Francisco Morning Call*, and from this base his reputation spread. Soon he was illustrating the work of Jack London and other writers. Gaining in social confidence, he designed a brand for himself—he called it "thunderbird"—with which he marked all his work, and began dressing as a cowboy, replete with boots and a ten-gallon hat.

Dixon's social life in San Francisco's bohemia swirled around wine and cheap food with other artists and writers at working-class dives, a variety of girlfriends, and morning-after hangovers. Marty Martinez took some of the group to Mexico, where Dixon discovered marijuana, to his delight.[7] Compared with what he'd eaten and drunk in Fresno, the fare in San Francisco was a smorgasbord of world food—Chinese, Mexican, Italian. Coppa's restaurant on Montgomery Street, an Italian fishermen's and peddlers' eatery, became this group's hangout, in part because "Papa" Giuseppe Coppa would extend credit to the impecunious artists. They treated their girls with disrespect: when one of them brought along a new woman, the guys would take an under-table vote on her. (Apparently, writer Mary Austin got a negative vote and she wasn't asked again.) A center oval table became reserved for them, and their boisterous presence attracted new customers—well-to-do art lovers, the "slummers," also known as the Nob Hill crowd—who drove out the fishermen. Coppa's bright red walls became literally papered with the overlapping paintings with which the artists paid for their meals. Eventually, in 1905, the artists painted a collective mural on all four walls. The canny Coppa sold as souvenirs the sketches and poems the artists scribbled on the menus and paper tablecloths.[8]

Although most of these young artists made few sales, as the wealthy favored less adventurous work, Dixon's illustration commissions continued and his earnings rose when he was appointed art director of the *San Francisco Examiner Sunday Magazine* in 1899. He was labeled the coming rival of Remington. One of Dixon's early patrons became a father figure: Charles Lummis, editor of *Land of Sunshine*, a California booster publication. He supported Maynard in his break with the family expectation that he would enter ranching and politics. He also helped Maynard to overcome his childhood identity as physically delicate and to construct a manly identity in an occupation—art—with undertones of effeminacy.

In 1900 Dixon, seeking wilderness to paint, found his spiritual home and his trademark subject: the Arizona/New Mexico desert. There, two years later, he would acquire another father figure—the famed John Lorenzo Hubbell, whose trading post at Ganado, Arizona, did so much to make Navajo and Hopi crafts into art commodities. Dixon addressed him as *"Querido patrón."* Hubbell's openness and feeling for art made his home/store a gathering place for artists and intellectuals fascinated with the southwest, and soon he was selling Dixon's paintings, along with blankets and baskets. Before this trip Dixon had associated painting with the Beaux-Arts academic painting that dominated the San Francisco art scene, a style he detested. But he felt increasingly that drawing could not capture the spiritual quality of the desert, so he began to paint. When he returned to San Francisco, he and his friends determined to challenge the conservative artistic canon by establishing a competing organization, the California Society of Artists.[9]

These dissident artists gravitated to a neighborhood—North Beach, and to a particular building—716 Montgomery Street, affectionately known as "the Monkey Block." Dating from 1853, this massive brick and granite four-story building with a central courtyard, originally a lodging house, became an art colony—"a sort of aviary for the strange, nocturnal birds of the city's artistic element"—that marked San Francisco forever. Writers began using it first—Mark Twain in the 1860s, and later Ambrose Bierce, Mary Austin, Ina Coolbrith, and Robert Louis Stevenson. Then painters discovered its spacious second- and third-floor windows.[10] The studios they established became almost collective property, passed on from friend to friend. Dixon became a feature there, almost a totem of the building. A history of the building described him as "a lean, sardonic man with pendulous, thin mustaches, in cowboy boots and flopping hat. He seemed always to have been a child of the Block."[11] The city's many chroniclers delighted in these memories. "You saw them . . . with canvases under their arms, wearing corduroy jackets, paint smeared . . . hurrying along swinging a demijohn of red wine in one hand, a hunk of unwrapped salami or a loaf of French bread in the other."[12]

A Monkey Block residence became, as one observer put it, "the equivalent of a membership card in the poor man's Bohemian Club."[13] Signaling his increasing prominence, Dixon was soon invited to join the rich man's Bohemian Club. The club had been established in 1872 by a group of journalists, artists, and writers who sought company in their irreverent western embrace of modernism. Its early members included Frank Norris, Ambrose Bierce, Jack London, Henry George, and John Muir. By the turn of the century the club increasingly attracted wealthy San Francisco–based businessmen.[14] Taking control of the club, they bought a camp on the Russian River, now called Bohemian Grove, while keeping the "bohemians"—the artists and musicians—to entertain and to add to the cachet of the club. A rowdy western version of an elite men's club, the Bohemians featured camping out, raucous pageantry, cross-dressing burlesque, heavy drinking, and bawdy, often homoerotic escapades. The stunts and elaborate rituals displayed—and still display—college fraternity taste. Nevertheless, the club gave artists direct connections with patrons, and Dixon got his first one-man show there in 1905. Though still relying on illustration for a living, he had begun by 1905 to sell oil paintings to prominent collectors. He was becoming "the darling of the San Francisco cultural circles."[15]

THE EARTHQUAKE OF 1906 destroyed this community—physically, economically, and emotionally. Most artists, museums, and private collectors lost the work of a lifetime. Dixon lost everything except a single armload of drawings. The disaster exiled San Franciscans with centrifugal force. It gave rise to artists' colonies in Carmel, Marin County, Santa Rosa, and Berkeley. And yet, as if delivering a message, the Monkey Block stood. (Only a giant corporation could take it down: It was razed in 1959 and the Transamerica Pyramid, San Francisco's tallest skyscraper, was erected in its place.)

For the next six years, Dixon was part of the diaspora. As Arnold Genthe would do later, he went to New York in 1907, stayed for five years, and quickly duplicated his San Francisco success as an illustrator. His years there were troubled, however, by an unhappy marriage, begun in 1905 in California, to Lillian West Tobey, also a San Francisco painter of significant talent.[16] Lillian designed and sewed costumes for the theater, worked with metal and leather, and dressed beautifully, but her work and reputation have almost disappeared. Soon after marrying, she became depressed and irritable, began drinking too much, and suffered what was then called a nervous breakdown. Thinking to calm her, Maynard moved them to quieter Yonkers—a typical prescription at the time—which was more likely counterproductive than curative. Dixon was not a nurturing partner. He made several long trips back to the desert to paint, leaving Lillian alone, beginning almost immediately after their marriage, and he seems to have done so again in 1910, right after the birth of their daughter, who was named Constance for his mother.

In New York Maynard dived into an intoxicating affair with playwright Sophie Treadwell, eventually the author of nearly forty plays, including the expressionist *Machinal*. Treadwell was also married, and a radical both socially and politically: a women's rights advocate and a journalist who covered the Mexican Revolution. She may well have rejected monogamy ideologically, as Dixon did in practice. Drawn to talented and achieving women, he was besotted with Treadwell and composed poetry to and about her. When she finally ended their relationship in 1917, he wrote in his abbreviated autobiographical notes, "Sophie—real love—desperation . . ."[17]

When he returned to San Francisco and to a Monkey Block studio in 1912, he had developed a new identity as painter and muralist. The great Panama-Pacific International Exposition of 1915, celebrating the Panama Canal and the rebirth of San Francisco, included Dixon's work alongside that of French Impressionists and eastern realists, and he sold several paintings to museums and collectors. With paint and brush, his forms simplified and his work grew more modernist—more abstract, with an economical vocabulary of emotion created by sharper lines and contrasts.[18] Just a few years later, this sensibility would influence Lange's photography.

The return to California did not help his marriage. He continued to cope with Lillian's depression and drinking by absenting himself, and the trips, often now for mural commissions, probably made her more desperate. Meanwhile his asthma worsened and he grew increasingly depressed, as Lillian—now drinking even wood alcohol and Listerine—grew more violent and disruptive. In January 1916 he tried to have her arrested and committed to a hospital—"Attempt to arouse L by arresting her; tragic mistake"—and she responded by trying to shoot him with his own Colt .45. So he left for good, holing up in his studio and at the Bohemian Club, where women were not admitted and Lillian could not get at him.[19] In 1917 he persuaded Lillian to file a divorce suit.[20] She agreed to seek treatment for herself and place seven-year-old Constance in a convent boarding school.

The breakup produced not a release but a collapse for Dixon. "Consie remains with Lillian; conditions very bad—treadmill existence; Sophie returns; the end. Complete misery and despair—verge of insanity." Depression, asthma, and inflammatory rheumatism intensified his despondency over the ruin of the West he loved: "'finished by Henry Ford, the movies, dude ranches, and show business.'"[21] A series of girlfriends tried to nurse him back to health.

He managed to take Consie with him on a trip in the early fall of 1917 to Montana to paint Glacier National Park and Blackfeet Indians, on a commission from the Great Northern Railroad. It was bliss for Consie: "While my father painted, I played with the Indian kids. . . . We children had a play tepee made for us out of Gold Medal flour sacks. . . ." Con-sie was unconsolable when sent back to the convent. "I wanted

4.2. CONSTANCE (CONSIE) DIXON, CIRCA 1920

to stay and become an Indian," she said.[22] Soon Maynard and Lillian agreed to put Consie in the North Berkeley Outdoor School as a boarder, and her parents saw her on alternate weekends. She loved being in his studio, which was filled with Indian blankets, baskets, hatchets, and other artifacts and smelled of paint, turpentine, and the kinnickinnick that he loved to smoke. But on the whole, she recalled, "Daddy-o . . . just tagged me along while he visited his friends."[23] Needing money for the school and for alimony, he took a job with the leading advertising agency of the West, Foster and Kleiser, where Roi Partridge also worked.

SO WHEN DOROTHEA came into his life in 1919, he was just climbing out of a deep hole, operating well beneath his best levels of confidence and energy. Their courtship relieved and reenergized him.[24] Maynard brought Dorothea both urban and rural adventure. They spent many weekends on outings to Marin County and other places accessible by ferry—neither of them had a car or could drive—what he called the "real" California. They hiked, picnicked, and camped out, and Dorothea did these things easily, her energy and stamina unhindered by her bad leg—the only thing she could never do was run. She loved these jaunts, and it is hardly surprising that a person so visual would rapidly learn to love this entirely new landscape. "I did not know the earth," she wrote, "had never known a plant aside from a rubber plant. Now I am me who has explored the country, been involved in deserts, Mtns., plains, prairies, Mtn meadows, granite slopes."[25] (She would become an avid gardener.) If she still harbored plans to continue the round-the-world trip, she easily put them aside.

It is conceivable that this was Dorothea's first fully sexual love affair, that her New York City relationships had been "chaste," although this is not likely. Officially, they lived apart—she with Fronsie in a lodging house on Sutter Street, he in his studio at 728 Montgomery.[26] But they began staying together nights as well, and, of course, socialized in the evenings, after work. She met the approval of the guys at the center table and became a regular part of the group, enjoying the wine and talk and the Tom and Jerry cocktails in wintertime. Dorothea would never be intimidated for long. Furthermore, it was not as if Maynard was introducing a naïve, straitlaced girlfriend to a bohemian life; Dorothea was already part of their countercultural world.

To Dorothea, Maynard was irresistible: a lean cowboy with piercing blue eyes and elegant hands and fingers, graceful and irreverent, surrounded by a group of other dazzling artists. Her photographs of his delicate hands reveal their feminine beauty, too, another side of his allure. He was confident, worldly, somewhat famous—and an older man. Dorothea's close friend Imogen Cunningham, in her typical no-minced-words approach, denounced the relationship because of their twenty-year age difference, but Dorothea, of course, ignored her.

Dorothea had created herself as a stunningly attractive woman. She had big blue-green eyes and a lovely figure. She dressed with care but with eccentricity, her main concern being to stand out. She might wear jeans at work, but never outside. She still covered her leg with pants or a long skirt and had to wear "comfortable" shoes, as the unfashionable ones were called. Yet she was enough in control of her lameness that she asked Imogen and Roi to join her in learning ballroom dancing.[27]

Maynard assimilated Dorothea into his Indian romance. He wrote her poetry, such as this verse:

4.3. DOROTHEA LANGE, 1920, *by Edward Weston*

*And there where they came shyly, brown and barefoot,*
*down the steep trail to the deep-walled spring,*
*dipping up green water with their earthen jars,*
*so do you come now to my waiting heart*
*bringing the sacred vessel of your love*
*to receive the ancient liquid of our life.*[28]

Such a misreading of Dorothea could only mean that Maynard was in love with a fantasy, an Indian maiden—no doubt a recurrent fantasy, now reawakened by Dorothea. She almost certainly did not grasp this, and in any case was absolutely smitten by him. Speaking toward the end of her life, she appreciated him still: "Maynard was restaurant man, a raconteur, a striking personality, graceful, had style, wit, and originality. Much of the wit was defensive. Women loved him. He was no Philanderer, but not monogamous. He was tender to little children. Knew what was true. Loved to tease. . . . never completely at home in the city . . . But coming in from a sketch trip after having worked furiously and walked miles, paint box on back, he was himself. He was a thoughtful husband, loved his little boys."[29] We can see in this recollection how attractive she had found him in 1919, how much she loved him in years after, and how the decades of separation from him had erased or at least subdued her memories of his faults.

They announced their engagement at a tea in her studio in January 1920. Friends were invited, and Maynard was such a prominent figure that newspapers covered it on the arts pages. "Believing that an artist should seek marital happiness with one whose temperament and ideas are the same, Miss Dorothea Lange, 24, portrait photographer and artist, yesterday announced her engagement . . ." Then followed the misinformation that "she graduated from the art school of Columbia University."[30] Dorothea herself might well have been responsible for the claim—she fibbed about her father, naming him on the marriage license as George Warren.[31]

# 5

# Working Mother in Bohemia

The wedding was simple and unconventional. They married on March 21, 1920, in her studio, its French doors open to the lovely little "Spanish court." She decorated with branches from flowering peach and hazel trees and lighted candles. They spoke their vows in front of the large fireplace, with a minister from the People's Liberal Church officiating. No one stood in place of Dorothea's father to give her away. It was a community event, not a family one—only friends attended. Fronsie was her attendant and Roi Partridge was Maynard's. There is no record of whether her mother had been invited, or whether Joan had longed for a proper white wedding in their church in Hoboken, where she might sing. If there was any doubt that Dorothea had become a bohemian, the wedding answered it.

Dorothea and Maynard were a dashing couple, bohemian royalty: he all in black, including a black cape and a black Stetson, and carrying a carved sword-cane (a cane that contained a stiletto); Dorothea in her current favorite color, emerald green, with a beret set asymmetrically on her bobbed hair. Dinner invitations multiplied.[1] An artist friend, Lucien Labaudt, designed some clothing for her, and sometimes she wore a Fortuny gown, an Isadora Duncan–inspired long dress made from one piece of pleated silk (a splurge, but Italian designer Mariano Fortuny was noted for making high fashion affordable).[2]

They took a four-day honeymoon (no record of where) and then moved

5.1. DORRIE ASLEEP, 1920s, *by Maynard Dixon*

into a rented cottage at 1080 Broadway, near Jones Street. These cottages, thrown up after the earthquake, were meant as temporary quarters, but people continued to live in them for decades. They called theirs "The Little House on the Hill."[3] Maynard's brother, Harry St. John Dixon, who became a noted art metalworker, lived in an adjoining cottage with his wife and child. The home would "carry out all the artistic ideals of these two well-known artists," a reporter wrote, Dorothea having explained how she planned to decorate it. A small headline announced BRIDE KEEPS IDENTITY.[4]

There was no question about that: She already had a public identity as a portrait photographer. She loved her work. She was an excellent business-woman. In contrast to her friend Imogen Cunningham, who was so good-hearted that she often allowed customers to pay her with items she had no use for, Dorothea "set her prices, told you in advance what they were, and collected payment systematically," one of her clients recalled.[5] At this time, however, Dorothea and Imogen were not practicing the same vocation: Cunningham was an art photographer, exhibited throughout the country, who did some additional work for customers to earn money. Lange insisted, in interviews of decades later, that she wanted only to fill a need, to please her customers.[6] Yet at the time, in 1920, she had told a reporter that she was "portrait photographer and artist."

There is a contradiction here, but one we need not try to resolve. Identities are frequently contradictory, and that of an ambitious woman in 1920 was particularly inconsistent, even paradoxical. Lange loved photography, relished being a figure of consequence in a community she admired, enjoyed earning her own money. Yet her unacknowledged aspirations leaked out, creating tension between her bohemian free spirits and independent business, and her plan to become a traditional wife and mother. She intended to make their home elegant, orderly, and modern, to cook tasty meals (she got her mother to send her recipes), to raise gifted children. She indulged in a common rescue fantasy: She would be a *good* wife to Maynard, unlike Lillian. She did not expect him to do women's work. They would become a proudly bohemian but nevertheless model family. Maynard wanted this too, but he was also expecting a mother for his unhappy daughter, about whom he felt so much sadness and guilt. This does not mean that his attraction to Dorothea was insincere, but that good-mother was part of his fantasy of what she was like.

Besides, she adored him and knew he was becoming a great painter. The market for both photography and art looked good. So it was no sacrifice at all for her to support Maynard in devoting more time to painting, and he did, first reducing his hours at Foster and Kleiser, then quitting altogether. It eased her mind that in becoming the chief breadwinner, she was, ironically, moving closer to the womanhood and wifehood that she thought appropriate—subordinating herself to his more important career. It was satisfying also because it gave her work a higher purpose—advancing art. He felt wonderful. Dorothea gave him not only more time for painting but also a sturdy reliability and peace, along with her charm and savoir faire. "D's help and confidence. . . . Life in 'Little House'—the garden; breakfast on porch; neighbors," he wrote about his new life.[7]

To get to the "little house" you climbed one of San Francisco's almost-vertical stairways. The couple cut a window into the east wall of the one-room cottage to bring in views of the garden, with its marigolds, geraniums, nasturtiums, and shasta daisies, and they installed a fireplace. They furnished the cottage with cheap old stuff that Dorothea painted—the floor and a chiffonier deep indigo blue; everything else yellow or orange—and she dyed the cheesecloth curtains yellow. Consie Dixon remembered it as "a valiant attempt to fight off S.F.'s dim, gray fogs."[8] The thirty-dollar-per-month rent was all they could afford, because they were paying alimony to Lillian and boarding school costs for Consie, as well as paying off Dorothea's remaining debt to her investors.

The years of their marriage became the time of Maynard's best work and maximum productivity; in their first five years together he painted 140 canvases and sold over 70. He was soon the best-known West Coast muralist. Through murals he moved away from the Impressionism and Postimpressionism of his early painting toward a modernist style. (In this respect he influenced Dorothea and she him: they both developed a fondness for a low horizon line, bold shapes, and simple, stable compositional structures.)[9] His images became less representational and more symbolic—of a West whose loss he mourned. Critics were enthusiastic. In 1924, he won first place in a Los Angeles salon of western art. His buyers included the same cultural elite—the Gerstles, Kahns, Rabinowitzes, Elkuses, Walters—that patronized Lange's studio.[10] Their two careers worked synergistically—Dorothea's studio introduced buyers to his work, and marriage to Maynard increased her prestige.

Dorothea encouraged Maynard to try new ventures. When she learned that he had invented Indian tales for Consie, illustrating them with spontaneous sketches, she suggested turning them into a children's book. This became *Injun Babies,* published by G. P. Putnam's Sons in 1923. A reader seeing the title today might tense up, expecting racist, trivializing, conventionalizing drawings and stories, but that is not what is there. The use of the word *Injun* is obnoxious today, but the protagonists of the seven stories are active, resourceful kids who get in and out of various fixes, often aided by kind animals with magical powers. The children have wonderfully witty, punning names: A-Wáy-She-Go, He-Wánts-Tu-Kwit, No-Páh-No-Mah, O-Só-Sti-Ki.

The fact that Dorothea worked long hours made them more compatible. She did not begrudge him his time in the studio, with friends, or on painting trips. On their joint outings she began photographing outside in natural light. She visited him on some of his solitary trips—"night under stars," he jotted down. In 1921, her mother, with her new husband, George Bowly, came out to meet Maynard, who took the whole extended family, including Consie, on a mule-train painting trip over the High Sierra, through the Owens Valley, and into the Panamint and Inyo mountains. "Glacial meadows and camp fires; C's [Consie's] delight and Wuz's terror [at the steep gorges.]" In a romantic, soft-edged photograph from that trip, Dorothea, seen in profile, is beautiful and happy, seated on the ground and surrounded by high grass. Maynard, standing at her side, is looking determinedly ahead; she is lost in reverie. Of another trip, Maynard wrote, "Great thunderstorm. D's delight."

The Coppa's crowd, now including more photographers, partied a lot. A gag photograph taken by Maynard at a "crazy party" of photographers in Dorothea's studio—a symbolic family portrait—shows Edward Weston standing on one side, Anne Brigman on the other, as the mother and father, holding

Dorothea's camera, which is wrapped in its focusing cloth to represent a baby. The other "kids" are sitting or lying on the floor—Dorothea, Imogen, Roi Partridge, Johan Hagemeyer, Roger Sturtevant (Dorothea's assistant at the time), and Ansel Adams.[11] Prohibition did little to change their recreational habits; in fact, it was so unpopular in San Francisco that the City Board of Supervisors actually ordered the police not to enforce it.

Domestic stability did not, however, erase Maynard's irritability about the crowding and commercialization of the West. The more he painted, the more he mourned the spoiling of natural wilderness. He associated this adulteration of nature with modernism: ". . . art today is full of hokum. . . ." His most common denunciatory term was *hypocrisy*. Modernist " 'self-expression' is just an alibi for idiocy." He felt his own newly simplified style to be integrated, anchored in his personal vision, the "outcome of his inner integrity."[12] By contrast, many other painters appeared to him trendy, painting only for the market. This is, of course, what many artists and intellectuals mean by "selling out," and although the distinction between that and managing to make a living can be fuzzy, nevertheless the distinction is often felt passionately. He saw fashionableness infect collectors and curators as well, a group that included, of course, the portrait customers who supported Dorothea, Consie, Lillian, and himself. Maynard's identity was built around being plainspoken, honest, even vulgar in exposing cant and pretension, and he was quite willing to offend in order to speak the truth. Dorothea had been wowed by his earthy refusal to conform to good manners, and she always respected it, but it would soon become troublesome.

INTO THIS FLUID, easygoing life, an angry intruder arrived. Now ten years old, Consie Dixon had lived the first decade of her life with a mother who loved her but was unable to provide minimally adequate parenting, and Maynard considered it essential to bring her to his new home. We know Consie's experience only from her recollections of fifty years later, but even if only a fragment of the experiences she recounted were true, hers had been a wretched childhood. Her earliest memory was of standing in her crib, rattling the bars and crying, while her parents screamed at each other in the kitchen. Then she would hear her father run down the stairs and slam the door, going off to spend the night at the Bohemian Club. She felt that neither parent wanted her. From as far back as she could remember, Consie knew her mother as frequently hysterical, drunk, and unable to construct a stable life. Maynard and his friends identified the problem exclusively with Lillian's drinking—he called her "his dipsomaniac wife"—while Consie, years later, believed that an underlying mental illness led to Lillian's drinking.

Every so often, Lillian was "sent up to Mendocino or Napa for a 'cure'" and Consie would be sent to friends of the family or boarding school. When she was home, Consie's "each day was about a year long. . . . My mother used to put me out in the backyard and expect me to keep myself amused for hours. I talked to the trees, I talked to the stones, which, in those days, I thought were alive. . . . I used to make little chores for myself, like most kids make mud pies, but that was too quick. . . . I used to grind up old bricks, and then make mud pies. . . . I was in solitary confinement." She recalled despising her mother, finding her "physically repulsive." She clung to her father desperately but he would not intervene. When he couldn't bear being with Lillian any longer, he left Consie there, helpless.[13]

A century later, we wonder why Maynard did not take responsibility for her, but that was not a customary option in 1916, when he left for good. The dominant family ideology did not expect fathers to care for children— although among the poor, many fathers did so—and certainly not an artist. Had he taken her from her mother, he would only have placed her out with another family member, probably his sister Reb. Besides, the ruling standard was that young children needed their mothers, although a child-protection agency would have been alarmed had it seen what went on in Consie's home.

Consie first met Dorothea in 1919, when Maynard took her to one of the tea soirees in the photography studio. Consie recalls being shocked at how young Dorothea looked—her hair in a "Dutch bob," dressed in "worn out riding pants and sneakers." Consie thought she was about sixteen. She did not give Dorothea much thought, since she had "developed a jaundiced view" of the women who wanted to catch her father and "came to the conclusion that he was invulnerable, would not remarry." Like many children of divorce, she expected him to return to Lillian. Besides, she said, "I was madly in love with him myself, and for years my objective had been to get rid of my incompetent mother and move in with Daddy." Lillian first registered Dorothea as a threat and characterized her as a nymphet, a "'little rosebud,'" but Consie knew that description to be "hilarious." She saw Dorothea as "quite aggressive and even somewhat masculine, and a successful career woman . . . no 'rosebud' she."[14]

Still, Dorothea seemed at least marginally tolerable to Consie at first, and she begged to be allowed to live at the "little house." Recently transferred to a day school in San Francisco, she began dropping in uninvited on her way home, staying as long as possible.

Dorothea imagined being a good wife, but not a good mother. She had no inkling of what she was in for with the arrival of an abused ten-year-old who had never had secure parenting and was uncontrollably jealous of this rival for her father. Consie was furious at him for remarrying, but so dependent on his love that she could not express—not even let herself feel— this anger. Her insecurities created no such internal censorship over her feelings about Dorothea, and she treated her stepmother with hostility and sullenness. Dorothea had complementary resentments, unprepared for how a child could come between her parents, let alone how much attention she would demand. As an adult, Consie would realize that Dorothea was only mature enough to be a big sister at best. But the child Consie was afire with jealousy. In this tiny cottage, she could hear all the sexual moans and groans as they "wrastled" with each other, and knew they were doing something unspeakably disgusting.[15]

Dorothea's own childhood led her to expect helpfulness and responsibility from a ten-year-old. Implemented gently, with a reasonably secure child, this expectation might have worked well. Consie enjoyed working in the darkroom, retouching negatives and spotting positives. But Dorothea also asked the girl to do housekeeping chores and responded angrily when she did not oblige. That they lived in such a tiny place did not help.

Maynard, eager to shed the burden of worry about Consie that he had carried, remained an affectionate and playful father but backed out of responsibility for her emotional well-being. He simply handed her over to Dorothea and continued his frequent trips to sketch and paint. He would announce his travel plans, not supposing that Dorothea and Consie should be consulted, let alone exercise veto power, and Dorothea remembered, with considerable resentment, that "he was always going for a month or six weeks but he never came back inside of four months."[16] Even allowing for a bit of exaggeration on Dorothea's part, it is not surprising that Consie felt deserted. Lange felt reluctant to reduce her work hours because they needed the money—and because work made her happy, while Consie did not. So Dorothea coped. She was reliable, always there to provide meals, clothing, homework help, a parental presence, but she sent out a great deal of disapproval toward Consie. Sometimes she exploded, and Consie retaliated. Consie claimed (although some of Dorothea's friends doubted this) that Dorothea lost patience and slapped and hit Consie.[17] Whether she did or not, she was clearly unable to find a way to nurture this unhappy child.

Dorothea made photographs of Consie, as if this were a way to give her love. One shows her on a horse, her hair flying, her body easy, and her legs dangling without stirrups.[18] Several photographs Lange made of Consie in 1923, when she was thirteen, exude complicated emotions. A fine studio portrait of Consie against a wall shows a tall, attractive girl with lustrous hair, looking like a softer, rounder Maynard. She is so pensive, even melancholy, but also so relaxed, that we have to credit the photographer with insight into Consie's pain, even if she could not relieve it.[19] More troubling is a nude torso, with neither head nor legs and thus anonymous: an exquisite fine-textured print of a literally budding adolescent—breasts just beginning to enlarge, the finest sprinkling of pubic hair visible.[20] It seems unlikely that Consie was pleased, and given adolescent girls' typical sensitivity about their bodies, she could well have been seized with embarrassment and fury.

Maynard and Dorothea sent Consie to the Presidio Open Air School, a private progressive school founded by the same wealthy Jewish community

5.2. TORSO OF CONSIE, CIRCA 1923

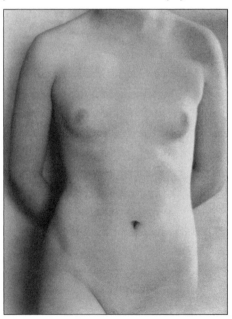

that supported so many cultural institutions.[21] The school director took a John Dewey approach—encouraging children's free expression, teaching through creative activity, and providing individual attention to children. Yet Consie remembered this school too with bitterness: the others were "rich kids," she recalled, who arrived "in limousines with uniformed chauffeurs—and sometimes even footman—and they all had charge accounts at Blums," while she was limited to a one-dollar-a-month allowance. She accused Maynard and Dorothea of sending her to that school so that they could make contacts with potential customers. Consie's anger colors all these memories. There was no action by Dorothea that she would fail to ascribe to a selfish motive. She complained also about her hand-me-down clothes,[22] which one could see, rather, as a comment on their priorities—that they were willing to stretch their budget to send her to a school that they thought would be best for her. Nevertheless, there is an edge of truth to Consie's charge, however distorted, because Maynard and Dorothea did want to feel a part of the cultured community at the school.

The conflicts ebbed when they made weekend outings as a threesome. When they did not head north to Marin, the Dixons often took the train to Carmel, where many artists and writers had settled after the earthquake, and where Maynard visited so often that some thought he was a resident. A village situated in extraordinary natural beauty, its residents in the early 1920s included Robinson and Una Jeffers, Lincoln Steffens and his wife Ella Winter, Jack London, Edward Weston, journalist Ray Stannard Baker, novelists Will and Inez Irwin, author Charles Erskine Scott Wood and his wife, poet and feminist Sara Bard Field, lesbian poet Elsa Gidlow, and George Sterling. Other San Francisco friends often came too, and Maynard like introducing them to campfire-cooked meals.

More often, however, Dorothea was alone with Consie as Maynard continued his trips to the desert to paint. Dorothea could not afford to close down her studio for weeks to accompany him; besides, it was her income that paid for his trips.

Occasionally Dorothea and Maynard escaped together by leaving Consie in the care of others—usually the Wilsons, sometimes Imogen and Roi Partridge—while they trekked on their own. Such farming out of children was not uncommon at the time. In 1922 Consie was "placed out," as the practice was then called, for four months while they stayed on a Navajo reservation at Kayenta, Arizona, where their guides were John and Louisa Wetherill, whites noted as explorers and scholars of the Navajo lands and culture.[23] Dorothea wrote, in what might have been Maynard's voice, "We went into a country which was endless, and timeless, and way out and off from the pressures that I thought were part of life."[24] This memory was with her forever: she bought, probably at the Hubbell trading post, a heavy, wide-ribbed Navajo silver cuff bracelet, dramatic and simple, and wore it every day of her life thereafter.

It was on this trip that Maynard first registered Dorothea's social conscious-ness. At the Tuba City Indian school, the harsh treatment of the children infu-riated her. Further evidence of these emotions appeared throughout the 1920s, notably in her sympathy for Sacco and Vanzetti, Italian immigrant anarchists who were framed and then executed for murder and became the subjects of a large international protest. Their persecution continued a xenophobia and anti-Red hysteria that had begun with World War I and the Bolshevik Revolu-tion. The pro-business conservatism of the decade disgusted San Francisco's bohemians, including Dorothea and Maynard, and had the effect of driving them further away from politics.

Meanwhile, Maynard's very success made him frustrated with the limited western art market. Searching for entrée into the eastern market, they traveled to Chicago and New York in 1923 in search of galleries and museums to show Dixon's work. Trying the Chicago Art Institute, Maynard was shocked to learn that it was booked two years in advance—an indication of the relative parochi-alism of California artists. In New York a gallery put up a Dixon show, but no paintings sold. Dorothea loved being back east and she and her mother got on well, but Maynard responded negatively to the New York art scene: "Hot-house art atmosphere and fake modernisms." They visited the Stieglitz gallery for an O'Keeffe show, and the autocrat of New York art and photography made Dixon even more infuriated: "After listening to exploiter Stieglitz expatiate, and observing so much cleverness and futility, I was glad to quit that stale-air existence and come West."

Maynard's derision did not extend to patrons of his own work, such as Anita Baldwin, despite her ostentatious lifestyle. She had not only bought his paintings but had commissioned him to create murals, including twelve for her Pasadena mansion. This eccentric daughter of Comstock Lode millionaire "Lucky" Baldwin, possibly one of Maynard's ex-lovers, had decided she wanted to write an opera on Indian themes. She invited Maynard and Dorothea to accompany her, later in 1923, on a trip to Indian lands to gather recordings of authentic Indian chants. They agreed and placed out Consie again. Baldwin sent a check for $250 so that Dorothea could buy riding boots and other neces-sities. They traveled in a private railway car with two cooks, two stewards, and Baldwin's bodyguard. Baldwin insisted they travel with all the blinds drawn so no one could see in, and this intensified the heat. Dorothea was frustrated because she could not *look*. Once in Arizona, they camped out in lavish style, having brought tents shaped like Chinese pagodas, colored sands (for the

Hopi to use in sand paintings), peacock feathers (supposedly sacred to the Hopi), caviar, wine, and elaborate food, which Dorothea was expected to cook. Baldwin paid the Hopi to come down to the camp every night to sing so she could find inspiration for her composition.

Dorothea was largely observer and cook, but she also did some of her first noncommissioned photography. As was her practice throughout her life, she destroyed negatives she considered unworthy, and only a few survive. They include a portrait of a Hopi man, cropped and enlarged so that it becomes a high-modernist abstraction; another that could have been a study for one of Maynard's paintings; a meditative shot showing (from the back, prefiguring much of her later work) a line of Hopis in black and white climbing stairs to a mesa, as if proceeding to a religious observance (see plate 3); a Pueblo woman with her chickens; a Navajo mother and child that ranks among her

5.3. HOPI MAN, 1923

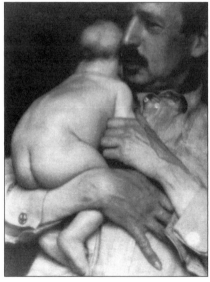

5.4. Dorothea with her sons,
1928–29

5.5. Maynard with his son Daniel,
probably 1925–26

5.6. Daniel Dixon, 1930

most beautiful Madonnas. Other portraits are weaker, owing to her inability to communicate with her subjects. The faces are beautiful and entirely expressionless—the only exception a resentful boy glowering at the camera. Others are modernist abstractions. The best are those taken from enough distance to show what people are doing and how they hold their bodies. Here is a glimpse of what would become a major dimension of her work.

Lange and Baldwin returned to California alone. Dixon, for whom the Indians lived in humility with the natural environment and united individual and community, work and art and play, stayed four more months. His lengthy trips continued throughout their marriage—to New York in 1924, Arizona in 1926, Nevada in 1927, Sacramento in 1928, the Mojave Desert in 1930.

MAYNARD AND DOROTHEA, like her parents, were a modern couple—they used birth control, waiting five years to have their first child. Dorothea never doubted that she would have children of her own, but she was, understandably, cautious: She often worked a twelve-hour day at the studio, then returned to domestic work and a conflicted relationship with Consie. Still, she probably felt she could not wait longer. Twenty-nine, her age when her first child was born, was, in those days, considered extremely late for a first birth.

Daniel Rhodes Dixon was born on May 15, 1925, named for the western writer Eugene Manlove Rhodes, a close friend of Maynard. Maynard and Dorothea's second son, John Goodnews Dixon, arrived on June 12, 1928—his middle name was a whim of Maynard's and was later changed to Eaglefeather. They were beautiful children and, of course, Dorothea made hundreds of photographs of them. Her pleasure seems to make the picture surfaces especially tactile— velvety or glistening, and when she appears in snapshots, she is herself aglow. She loved to photograph them with Maynard, and his gentleness and playfulness shine. One of the most loving shows Maynard holding the baby, his long, fine hands up against the delicious chubbiness of the baby's feet, bottom, and back. Maynard, in turn, made photographs of her with the boys, and through his eye her delight is also unmistakable. As the boys grew older, the family images continued to multiply—typically outdoors shots of swimming, picnicking, and camping—and they vibrate with pleasure. Often the boys are running around naked, and even the adults are skinny-dipping. Throwing off clothes was a symbol of freedom for this generation of bohemians.

As happens to so many women trying to manage work and children, Dorothea underestimated the labor of motherhood. Years later, she recollected "how cocky I was when Dan was born. I well remember the first two weeks at home. After that it was smoother but those two weeks must have been fierce or I would have long since forgotten it, as I have so much else."[25] Her work schedule became staggering. She did housework before heading for the studio—this meant not only cleaning and dressing the boys but arranging their care and schedule, planning meals, and shopping for food. Since the couple had to pay for child care, she needed to earn more, which increased the strain. When she arrived home, of course, there was no time to rest—she turned immediately to cooking, washing the dishes, and spending time with the boys, while Maynard, if he was present, often returned to his work after supper. Maynard was away when John was born; John's original middle name, Goodnews, came from Maynard's words on the phone when he was told of the birth.

Dan and John looked up to their stepsister, who took on some of their care. But their presence did not make things easier for Consie, and one terrible fight with Dorothea sent her away from her home: In 1927, when Maynard was away for four months, one of Consie's jobs was to wash baby Dan's bottle when she got home from school so it would be ready for him. She was late one day, the bottle remained unwashed, and when Dorothea arrived home, she flew into a rage. She and Consie came to blows—Consie bashed her stepmother with a telephone—and both sustained minor injuries. Consie, now seventeen, left to live with Aunt Reb, Maynard's sister. It was not a permanent separation—Consie would live with Maynard and Dorothea again in the future—but for now she was in exile.

Soon the Dixon-Lange household enlarged to take in two teenagers, and this burden, too, fell mainly on Dorothea. The first was John Collier, Jr., later a superb photographer, son of John Collier, Sr., who would be appointed commissioner of Indian Affairs by Franklin Roosevelt. John Senior and Maynard shared a passion for Indians and membership in the American Indian Defense Association—they had collaborated on an article defending the Pueblos—and Maynard and Dorothea visited the Colliers in their homes in Mill Valley and Taos. Hit by a car at age seven, the young John Jr. suffered permanent injury to one arm and his brain, becoming deaf and severely dyslexic and soon dropping out of school. Dorothea found him particularly winning, his disability adding to his appeal for her. Meanwhile, his artistic abilities grew stronger and, as was common practice, his parents sent him to apprentice with Dixon. Off and on between 1924 and 1933, John lived with Maynard and Dorothea and attended the California School of Fine Arts. He adored Maynard, whom he began to address as "Uncle," but spent more time with Dorothea and learned from her to love photography.[26] He bonded especially with Consie, three years his elder, and this friendship fortified her; John often took her side in the conflicts with Dorothea, and internalized some of her animosity toward Dorothea. A decade later, however, Dorothea would get him a photography job at the Farm Security Administration, and for the rest of her life she figured as a mentor not only to John but also to his wife, Mary, a superb photographer as well.[27] In later years, as John aged and his and Dorothea's disabilities

5.7. JOHN COLLIER, JR., SAN FRANCISCO, 1930

worsened, their attachment grew stronger. Their relationship was typical for Lange: not always easy to get along with, she was nevertheless a loyal and generous friend.

Yet another teenager joined the household a few years later, Everett Ruess.[28] To take his measure, consider that this young man, who disappeared at age twenty, was already a noted poet and sketch artist. His mother, Southern California artist Stella Knight Ruess, resembled Dorothea in many ways, including her bohemian values and adoration of Isadora Duncan. Husband and father Christopher Ruess was a Harvard graduate and Unitarian minister. From this background, Everett emerged not only talented but supremely self-confident. Dropping out of UCLA after one semester, he headed for the painter he most admired, arrived at Dixon's studio, introduced himself, and showed Maynard his sketches. Like Maynard, Everett loved the wilderness, romanticized Indians, and enjoyed wandering on his own with watercolors and a writing tablet.

Maynard and Dorothea took him in and he spent about six months with them, intoxicated by the sparkling company of their friends. "The other day I had perhaps the best art lesson I ever had; a lesson in simplicity from Maynard Dixon," he wrote his mother. "The main thing Maynard did was to make me see what is meaningless in a picture and have the strength to eliminate it. . . . This he showed me with little scraps of black and white paper, placed over my drawings. You should try it and follow up the suggestions it gives you."[29] Dorothea mothered and mentored him, taking him along on some of her photographing commissions. We don't know what the boy would have accomplished, however, because of his youthful foolhardiness: In 1934, he set out alone to live off the land in the Utah desert for a year. Last seen at Escalante, he was never heard from again.[30] For a long time, his family and friends assumed he would show up, and only slowly did they slide into grief. Dan and John loved having this big brother, and his disappearance frightened them.

CONSIE DIXON WAS becoming a fine writer, and in 1929, only nineteen years old, she got a job as a reporter for the *San Francisco Examiner*. Her increasing independence and self-esteem lessened friction with Dorothea. As if to fill the emotional space Consie vacated, however, Dorothea and Maynard began to argue more. One of Maynard's biographers writes that "it became common knowledge among their friends that both had started having affairs."[31] Friends interviewed after their deaths were sure that Maynard had had other lovers, but they were less sure about Dorothea; no one, however, had evidence or could name names. In any case, infidelity was only one of the sources of tension. Maynard did not articulate his grievances. He held his emotions close, and never wrote or said anything negative about Dorothea. Everyone who knew her, however, observed how stress had escalated her irritability and controllingness, characteristics that amplified as she grew older. She functioned as what in the late twentieth century was called "superwoman"—trying to do everything, unable to relax.

About Dorothea's grievances we know more: Maynard's absences and remoteness, his scorn for her friends and customers, and his delight in shocking those he considered uptight or pompous. After Daniel was born, they moved from the "Little House" to a bigger place at 1607 Taylor Street, and this allowed Dorothea to invite guests to dinners that became her hallmark—simple food, well cooked, beautifully presented. The guests were often her client friends, valuable professional connections, and she wanted to maintain and develop those. Maynard had no tolerance for these people or for Dorothea's motives. A populist of sorts, he harbored a great deal of resentment for the rich—he liked to announce that their shit smelled the same as anyone else's. He needed the patronage of the wealthy as much as she did, but he could not contain his hostility to the rich and to those who toadied to them. Long a practical joker, he could not resist teasing, baiting, or scandalizing those he found pretentious or pious. Once, he took aside Imogen Cunningham's four-year-old son, Rondal, taught him an obscene verse, and then sent him to recite it to the guests. At other times his jokes seem like fraternity stunts: He found some woman's underpants on the street, "speared them with . . . his swordcane, triumphantly held them aloft, then marched into the dining room, and dropped them into the circle of shocked guests."[32] Another time, he took the society page of the *Chronicle*, which had photos of opening night at the opera, erased the clothes from one prominent woman to make her look naked, then put the paper on her porch.[33] He was famous enough that the guests may have been tolerant. But Dorothea, cringing inside, was left to compensate, uncertain whether to ignore him, to laugh and make light of the situation, or to soothe him.

Dixon's resentments seemed particularly focused on Jews, who formed a disproportionate share of Lange's customers. In unguarded moments he spoke of Jews with pejorative stereotypes. Dorothea must have found this painful—her two best nonphotographer friends, Elizabeth Elkus and Edythe Katten, were Jews. Although Maynard was entirely unchurched—he liked the phrase "cold as Christian charity"—it does not require a religious identity to be anti-Semitic. His own dependence on rich Jews for commissions and sales only made him more resentful.[34]

Some tolerated Maynard's barbs because "temperamental artist" was a recognized category, even titillating. At other times his insults cost him, his hostility to the extraordinary Albert Bender a case in point. The son of a Dublin rabbi, a small, rumpled man with a speech defect, always a "bachelor" (read: gay), Bender had arrived in San Francisco at age sixteen or seventeen and accumulated a fortune in the insurance business. He spent it all on art, uninterested in personal luxuries. He lived in a duplex with his cousin, artist

Anne Bremer, who taught him about art and guided his early purchases. He became *the* insurance person for Chinatown businessmen, a trade he earned by defying the anti-Chinese racism so widespread in California and treating his clients with respect. It paid off: through these contacts he developed an outstanding collection of Asian art. Endearing and generous, he would buy dozens of tickets to a concert and give them away to those he thought couldn't afford them, or discover lovely pieces of Chinese jade and give them spontaneously to friends he encountered. Dorothea liked him very much and learned from him: With Bender as guide, Chinatown became less fearfully exotic, so his company quite possibly contributed to the antiracism she would later display.[35]

Bender patronized many artists, and enjoyed spending time with them, often at Coppa's central table. He provided photographers a service by insuring their cameras. He took chances on the unknown and the unconventional. Never a snob, he endowed a gallery for Roi Partridge at modest Mills College in Oakland, which, as a result, became a leading Bay Area showplace for modern art. Bender was the first of Ansel Adams's several rich patrons, and Adams served for a time as his driver, introducing him into the network of photographers in San Francisco and Carmel, while Bender introduced Adams to the modern art scene.[36]

Bender was the first to purchase Lange's work, thus marking it as art, but remained disinterested in Maynard's work, considering him essentially a poster artist. This reversed the usual perception of Dorothea's and Maynard's work and contributed to Maynard's bitterness, a bitterness that was also estranging him from many of his old friends.[37] Not surprisingly, Maynard detested Bender, considering him one of the "art hypocrites," but also maligning him from his double prejudices against Jews and gays: "effete," "a lisping mincing Jewish homosexual."[38] Some considerable part of their group was gay or bisexual, including Dorothea's assistant and protégé Roger Sturtevant, known as "beautiful boy." Maynard aside, the heterosexual members of the artist crowd regarded homosexuals as just another type of eccentric and threw a protective cloak around them as necessary.[39]

Maynard found his own wealthy benefactor in Beatrice Judd Ryan. An adventurous Australian whose wealthy husband had died young, she could freely follow her attraction to San Francisco's bohemia. She saw herself as a bridge between creative people and the art market, and between traditional and modern art. True to form, Dixon insulted her on their first meeting, suggesting that she was a sycophant, but he warmed to her when he realized that she had the resources and the intention to open a gallery. His talent for charming rich women remained, and theirs became a productive partnership. She sized him up well: "An extremely sensitive man, he camouflaged it with bursts of vulgarity or a sharp tongue—voicing deduction about people that was frequently incorrect." He coached her about how to do a gallery the right way—what artists to invite, who should be on a board of sponsors—and she opened the Galerie Beaux Arts at 116 Maiden Lane. A cooperative venture—patrons who paid seventy-five dollars annually received a painting a year—it became the key location for modern art in San Francisco between 1925 and 1933, a vital alternative to the now-conservative art exhibits at the Bohemian Club, and the source of a good proportion of Dixon's sales.[40]

HAD IT NOT been for the Depression, Dorothea and Maynard's marriage might have stuck, because continued success might have mellowed him and relaxed her. Had it not been for the Depression, however, Americans would never have heard of Dorothea Lange. Because of the Depression and, more important, the social movements it evoked, she reinvented her photography. Her transformation, like the Depression itself, was fitful and gradual. The Depression did not announce itself with the 1929 stock market crash, nor did anyone expect that it would last over a decade, until public spending on a world war brought the economy back to life. It crept into people's lives as an accumulation of bad and then worse news.

Economic depressions produce downward spirals in several ways. They worsen by their own logic: Investment declines produce layoffs, which reduce consumption, which further undercuts investment. Depressions also undercut charity's and government's ability to help. As unemployment grows and businesses shrink, tax revenues and charitable contributions dry up. During the Great Depression, states could not meet their payrolls, and therefore increased the ranks of the unemployed. Construction almost halted, auto sales dropped, public transportation lost customers, and layoffs were imposed; even the docks grew quiet, as there were fewer products to ship. By 1932, unemployment in San Francisco and Los Angeles reached 30 percent and department stores reported nearly a 40 percent decline in sales. By 1934, 20 percent of Californians were living on public relief.

The "economy," long an abstract concept, became a visible human phenomenon. Railroad yards were crowded with hobos. "Bindlestiffs," homeless transients carrying belonging in a blanket roll, trudged along the roads. Men in suits sold apples on the streets. Breadlines grew even longer. In Los Angeles, evangelist Aimee Semple McPherson's church fed forty thousand people a day. Farmworkers' already-scanty wages dropped sharply.

Artists felt the economic crash particularly severely, because they lived on discretionary spending. The art market shrank to almost nothing. Even large museums froze purchasing and cut staffs, and therefore visiting hours. Maynard lowered his price to a fraction of his usual fee in a 1930 bid for a mural in Los Angeles's Southwest Museum, but in the end the museum could not afford it. Disappointed, he sought solace, as usual, on his own in the wilderness, and headed for the Tehachapi Mountains, writing, ". . . growing feeling of oppression,—something ominous and unavoidable impending,—of being caught in slowly closing jaws of a vise, of complete helplessness in face of fate."[41] This left Dorothea alone with work and, of course, with children.

President Hoover tried outdated, inadequate, and even counterproductive measures. He raised tariffs by 52 percent, and tried to balance the budget by raising taxes, despite massive unemployment. To farmers he offered loans and government purchase of surplus, but of such small size that they did not even slow, let alone stop, the agricultural price collapse. He called on private charities to help, just as their donations shrank. At the end of his presidency he provided government financing for banks and insurance companies and some public-works jobs, too late and far too little. Above all, his administration called on the public to tighten their belts and exercise virtue. "People will work harder, live a more moral life," said his treasury secretary, Andrew Mellon. "Enterprising people will pick up the wrecks from less competent people."[42] Those suffering economically found such moralizing insulting and nonsensical, and began to listen to political groups calling for major reform of the economic system.

Those listening included many in the San Francisco arts community. Their interest in socially engaged art grew from Mexican influence. The Mexican Revolution inspired an artistic renaissance, and murals in particular became nearly a social movement; young artists were painting and carving their revolutionary ideals on hundreds of public walls and squares. Diego Rivera had revived the difficult Renaissance technique of fresco and explicitly politicized his art, celebrating Mexico's downtrodden but heroic peasants and workers defending their country's soul against marauding capitalists, generals, and Yankee imperialists. Arts culture in Mexico City was intoxicating, and numerous U.S. artists visited to take it in.[43] The Mexicans' bold and intricately composed integration of folk design and images of working people into their murals fit a budding democratic consciousness among American artists. Even the apolitical Edward Weston was overcome with admiration for "the greatness of Mexican art. Much that I once valued now seems trivial . . . forced, affected, full of effort to be different, smart."[44]

Among many American artists, *los tres grandes*—muralists Rivera, José Clemente Orozco, and David Alfaro Siqueiros—evoked an admiration that bordered on hero worship.[45] Rivera attained celebrity status, a position to which his largeness of personality and body contributed. In California art circles, the Rivera craze included even conservative art patrons.

Dixon was a naysayer. Once the dominant California muralist, Dixon's competitive resentment was fortified by animosity to the organized Left. He also pointed out, quite legitimately, that painters shedding subjugation to European standards were only transferring it to Mexico, instead of developing a style of their own. When artists Ralph Stackpole and Ray Boynton got Albert Bender and shipping magnate William Gerstle to offer Rivera fifteen hundred dollars to paint a mural at the California School of Fine Arts, Dixon gained some support.[46] Rancor at hiring a foreigner during the Depression, when American artists so badly needed work, combined with establishment fury at the Communist content of his work. The San Francisco Labor Council joined the opposition on protectionist grounds. Mainstream art critics condemned Rivera's work as disorganized, lowbrow and showy—one critic called him "the P.T. Barnum of Mexico"—a "mess of odds and ends" that "mean nothing."[47] Dixon, in a sharp break with his friends Stackpole and Boynton, condemned the Rivera "cult" as sycophancy, "Celebrity hounds todying [sic] to him." The Dixon group, which included Frank Van Sloun and Otis Oldfield, also had a legitimate procedural grievance: The funders had conducted a sham competition for the job—Dixon had applied—when they knew it had already been committed to Rivera.[48] But Dixon's denunciation soon became explicitly political: "'He is a professed Communist and has publicly caricatured American financial institutions.'"[49] As Consie later put it, Dixon was a literal reactionary and identified with the old southern aristocracy; while he hated the rich, he "never said a kind word for the laboring classes except out of what he called 'noblesse oblige.'"[50] The opposition forced the withdrawal of the School of Fine Arts commission, but Rivera got the last word: an invitation to paint at the Luncheon Club at the

Pacific Stock Exchange, for which he received four thousand dollars. When the U.S. government refused him a visa because of his communism, his sponsors had the political connections to get the decision reversed.[51]

Despite the opposition, it seemed that all San Francisco feted Rivera when he arrived, along with Frida Kahlo, in November 1930; everyone in the Bay Area art world wanted to meet them.[52] A one-man show of his work opened at the Palace of the Legion of Honor. Rivera and Kahlo stayed in Ralph Stackpole's studio, and Rivera worked there. Maynard and Dorothea socialized with them on several occasions, and Rivera gave Dorothea several drawings.[53] Rivera's style probably influenced Lange's: the monumentalism of the proletarian and peasant figures, the symmetry of composition, the clarity of line and volume. That Rivera combined artistic genius with passion for the oppressed and exploited was not lost on her either.

Frida Kahlo also influenced Dorothea. Today Kahlo appears a fine artist in her own right, her reputation intensified by her beauty, her folk wardrobe, and her tragic health history, and through iconization as a woman of suffering and transcendence of suffering. But in 1930 she was unknown, she was in physical pain, and Rivera promptly began an affair with his San Francisco model, tennis champion Helen Wills Moody.[54] At this painful moment, Dorothea made a quick and intense connection with Frida: here was a disabled woman of great talent, charm, and political commitment, with a philandering artist husband. Like Dorothea, but twelve years younger, Kahlo had contracted polio as a child and emerged with a wizened lower leg, which she hid the same way Lange did—with long skirts. When she was eighteen, much worse befell her: A bus accident left her terribly, irrevocably injured. Dorothea offered Kahlo the use of her photography studio.[55] More important, Dorothea gave her a lifelong gift, one whose value is impossible to overestimate: her doctor, Leo Eloesser.[56] One of the cultural elite of San Francisco and a Lange client, Eloesser was a pioneer thoracic and bone surgeon at the Stanford Medical School, and Lange had consulted him. He was politically left-wing, a physician for Tom Mooney, later a medic for the Republican forces in the Spanish Civil War. It was Eloesser who correctly diagnosed Kahlo's injuries, and in gratitude she painted his portrait at his San Francisco home. He remained her personal physician till her death in 1954.

Even Maynard warmed to Rivera. After completing the Stock Exchange mural, Rivera was reinvited to do the School of Fine Arts mural. In one part of it, he depicted himself and his assistants working on the mural—painting himself from behind, with his extra-large bottom hanging over a scaffold. To Dixon's enjoyment, this gesture demonstrated Rivera's own distaste for sycophants—it was just the type of joke Dixon might have made. In the long run, Rivera's residency helped Maynard. It increased the local demand for murals and thus provided Dixon with more commissions. It brought into greater influence several new collectors and patrons allied with Bender— Gerstle and Pflueger—who were more open to new art than the old guard, such as Fleishhacker, Spreckels, Hearst, and de Young. These new patrons would help rescue several artists as the Depression deepened.[57]

MEANWHILE, THE DEPRESSION hit Dorothea and Maynard hard. Maynard sold no paintings. Dorothea's clientele shrank, and anxiety escalated their irritation and quarreling. Dorothea, aware that their best times occurred in the countryside, suggested a family escape—from the city, from the Depression—to the Southwest. Consie had lost her newspaper job in a Depression staff reduction, so John Collier, Jr., invited her to go along with him to Taos and helped her get work as a waitress and typist for Mabel Dodge Luhan. Consie's upbeat letters induced Maynard and Dorothea to try Taos, where life was less expensive. Mabel Dodge Luhan, a wealthy heiress about Maynard's age, had created a whirlpool of arty people around her, as husbands, lovers both male and female, and hangers-on; she had married Tony Luhan, from the Taos Pueblo, which attracted Maynard. She offered to lend him a studio from among her many properties. "Queen of the Southwest," Dorothea sardonically labeled her.

The Taos plan required investment of money and time. They had to buy a car, their first, and learn to drive it. They had to find a place to live, also accomplished through Mabel Dodge Luhan, who arranged for them to have an adobe house in Ranchos de Taos owned by one of the many who orbited around her, Joe Foster, a writer who had come to New Mexico in search of D. H. Lawrence. Then just as they set out for Taos, novice driver Maynard had a serious accident. In the Santa Cruz Mountains, the car skidded and flipped over. Dorothea and the children were unhurt but he suffered a broken jaw and badly sprained arm. After his brief hospitalization, Dorothea drove the rest of the way. Maynard had to spend his first two months in Taos recuperating, and during that period they spent most of their time as a family. Consie seemed happy in her job, with just the right distance from her family to ease her relations with Dorothea. The boys flourished. They bought six-year-old Dan a pony, but Maynard was frustrated that Dan did not seem to take to riding as naturally as Consie had—it was important to him that his sons become competent outdoorsmen.

After Maynard recovered, socializing began, though it was often only Maynard who indulged. During their earlier trips to the Southwest, Dorothea had made many fine photographs, but now she photographed mainly her family, as she had to stay home with the boys, neither one of whom was in school. Maynard connected with artists who had settled there, many of whom shared Dodge Luhan's and Georgia O'Keeffe's primitivist view of the area as somehow outside modernity. He bonded with Tony Luhan and another Indian from the Taos Pueblo, Antonio Mirabal, whose portrait he had previously painted. Maynard and Dorothea both met the extravagantly costumed Dorothy Brett, an upper-class British artist, friend of the Bloomsbury group and of Frieda and D.H. Lawrence, who had settled in Taos in 1924.[58] Maynard felt artistically stimulated; he marveled at the *penitentes* ("lugubrious walking corpses," he wrote, echoing Daniel's terror at the sight) and watched dances at the nearby pueblos. Predictably, he hated the rush of summer tourists, actually modest by today's standards, and was "not much impressed with Santa Fe—too arty."

Every day, Dorothea drove Maynard to and from the studio Mabel had lent him. Yet even here Maynard felt the need to get farther away from his family. With his old friend Joe Sinel, a San Francisco industrial designer, he took a trip up the Chama River to Abiquiu, Coyote, and "red country"—an extraordinary expedition through a fifteen-hundred-foot-deep multicolored sandstone canyon. Once more, Dorothea and the boys stayed behind. Her housework and child care were arduous: Joe Foster's house had turned out to be an adobe cabin with no running water or toilet; Maynard and the boys loved roughing it, but she did the work.

They stayed in Taos seven or eight months. Maynard was always happier out of the city, and living without modern comforts did not bother him at all. He completed forty paintings, though few sold. But Dorothea did not bond with anyone in the Taos crowd. In San Francisco her life was filled with people day and night, and she had a handful of close friends, while here she was lonely.

AFTERWARD DOROTHEA FREQUENTLY repeated a story about something that did not happen to her in Taos: Only later did she realize that she had come close to meeting the master photographer Paul Strand. She had first encountered his pictorialist work in Stieglitz's gallery, then saw in the 1920s his abstract close-ups and powerful photographs of people on the streets. Strand did the latter surreptitiously, without the consent of his subjects. Attaching a false lens at right angles to his functioning lens, he could face away from his subjects so they did not know they were being photographed. In her own work, Lange would reject such practices as deceptive, but Strand's images expanded for her the possibilities of portraiture, by capturing a broader and less polite range of expression in his subjects. In Taos in 1931, Strand was photographing rocks, plants, and other elements of nature, but he was increasingly attracted by social documentary. A New Yorker, he had joined the Photo League, a left-wing cooperative dedicated to making photography lessons and darkroom access widely available for little cost, and to encouraging socially relevant photography.

As if Strand were a prophet come to reveal the future to someone not yet able to imagine it, Dorothea saw him as a mysterious figure. Someone drove by in a Ford every day at the same time, alone, and returned at the same time, and she assumed he was an artist—by which she meant painter. She did not try to introduce herself. She considered him, she said, "a serious man." This impression reveals her restlessness and self-critical evaluation: she sensed that he was committed to his work, unlike her.[59]

The feeling that she could not be "serious" signaled that she was already imagining a new photography she wanted to do, something more challenging, something transcendent in relation to what she had already done. She blamed herself for not doing it, denying that what held her back was lack of time. Self-censure was a regular Lange refrain, one that became more frequent, ironically, as her achievement grew. In describing her Taos period, this self-blaming reflected her reluctance to challenge being a wife. Thirty years later she understood that wifely condition more fully: ". . . that thing that Paul Strand was able to do, I wasn't able to do. Women rarely can, unless they're not living a woman's life." And she was living a woman's life, of the only sort she knew.

AS WINTER CAME, life in Taos grew harder. Their money was running out.[60] Heavy snow made it hard to drive, so they moved into the hamlet of Taos itself, but they still had no running water, no toilet, no telephone, no heat except for a woodstove. Maynard was wearing three layers of clothes and two pair of gloves in order to paint. Then they were completely snowbound. The boys, now six and a half and three and a half, were restless, and keeping them entertained was a full-time occupation. Dorothea's domestic labor expanded; she was not only cooking and cleaning but keeping the house warm, heating water to wash clothes, keeping the children occupied, shoveling snow, putting on and taking off hats, gloves, galoshes, wet clothes. But she reaffirmed her duty: "I could be of help to Maynard mostly by keeping everything smooth and being happy and making it an enjoyable time and taking care of the children." There was no sign yet of a determination to relinquish that imperative. Her discontent remained an underground stream.

Maynard did not sense her discontent. In his recollection of that 1931 Christmas we feel his pleasure: "Stockings by fireplace; few presents; snug and warm; true Christmas feeling. Hospitality of our neighbors—Miss Kessel invites our boys.—Deer Dance—most ancient ceremony—impressive—sombre. Tony Mirabal in buckskin and buffalo robe. Kiva poles in starlight."

Dorothea began agitating to return to San Francisco. Like most Americans, she had assumed that in a year, or two at most, the economy would improve. Now she recognized that they had not escaped the Depression and would have to reenter it. Maynard resisted until it became too cold for him to paint regardless of how much clothing he wore. They left in January, while the snow was still deep, and trail-blazed the seventy-five-mile downhill road to Santa Fe, driving at the edge of steep canyons, Dorothea terrified but also eager to keep moving. After that, they took their time, driving a southern route through Arizona and Los Angeles. They enjoyed being back in warm country, and Maynard noted the boys "revel[ed] in grass and grapefruit." But soon the sights were ominous: bindlestiffs on the road, in ragged coats, their unshaved faces making them look older than they probably were; many hitchhikers; whole families camped beside their cars, just off the road.[61] As they drove into San Francisco, they saw little boys begging on the streets, some not much older than Dan, a previously unimaginable sight. What they saw, of course, were but the smallest wisps of smoke from the economic disaster, but they were plentiful enough that, as they approached home, their happiness to be there rested on a reservoir of anxiety.

# Part II

## DEPRESSION AND RENEWAL

### 1932–1935

White Angel Breadline, San Francisco, 1932

# SCENE 2

*In the spring of 1932 San Francisco portrait photographer Dorothea Lange looked down from her second-floor studio window and saw the Depression. It's not that she had been oblivious for the previous three years—she could not have been, since her portrait business and her artist husband's sales had suffered mightily. But for such a visual-minded person, the images from her window disturbed her. "The discrepancy between what I was working on . . . and what was going on up the street was more than I could assimilate." Discrepancy was an understatement. Her walls held portraits of the Levi-Straus family, the Freudenthals, the Fleishhackers, the Haases, the de Youngs. The streets below displayed images of unemployed men loitering on corners or standing in breadlines, homeless men huddled around fires or hiding in their bedrolls. They were not only bums in ragged clothes and workingmen's caps but also men in suits and fedoras. She was at the window on this particularly sunny day, making solar proofs of some new portraits. "You know, with those proofs while the image deepens and darkens you have a moment's respite. So I looked out the window. . . ."*[1]

*Luckily, Dorothea's younger brother Martin was in town, himself broke and unemployed. She wanted to take her camera into the streets but she was unaccustomed to wandering the Depression city as a woman alone, "to jostling about in groups of tormented, depressed and angry men . . ."—not to mention bums—and she worried about* damage to her camera.[2] Martin Lange, although rarely purposeful or ambitious, provided just the right company now, being not only a man a but a big and cheerful one, the beloved "Unca' Mucky" to the children. He was willing to walk with her for hours, occasionally carrying "Snappie," her big, heavy Graflex, or her tripod.[3] She worried not only about being hassled in the streets but also about photographing people who had not hired her to do it, who might not even want it. She sensed that these new subjects might be embarrassed or humiliated to be photographed in breadlines, no doubt because she herself saw it as stigmatizing. She could not hide what she was doing, because her camera was large and her setup took some minutes to accomplish. "It makes you very conspicuous," she recalled later.[4] She could not then have imagined spending the rest of her life as a "street photographer."

Accompanied by Martin, she noticed the White Angel soup kitchen. Somehow what she saw made her think, "I'd better make this happen."[5] So she took three shots; "then I got out of there."[6] No one in her immediate community thought much of the photographs. When she put a print on the wall of her studio, her clients either ignored it or said, " 'What are you going to do with this kind of thing?' "[7]

# 6

# Leaving the Children, Leaving the Studio

Dorothea Lange turned onto a new path in 1932, walking in step with her country. Acutely dissatisfied with her marriage and her studio, she sought to expand her photography, but did not dare give up her studio income. Americans were, in general, equally dissatisfied with President Hoover's fundamentalist faith that the market would correct the Depression, but they also saw no way out of it.

Within three years, Lange would close her studio permanently and become a documentary photographer. She would, in fact, re-create what documentary photography meant. She would leave her marriage, having fallen in love with an extraordinary man who was thrilled by the very ambition that caused her guilt and paralysis—a man who, as luck would have it, helped her find a new way to support her children. Her "luck" took place also on a grander scale, created by the whole country's giant forward stride: President Roosevelt's New Deal. It would offer her a wage, a photographic challenge, and a chance to feel part of a movement for social justice. Her new love, Paul Taylor, was a dynamic part of that movement, and their camaraderie ignited and fueled their personal chemistry.

None of this happened easily or smoothly, and in 1932 Lange could not have predicted it; much of that year, she felt that change was impossible. It was as if her shoes had begun to rub and irritate, worsening until she had to take them off. The new shoes were to carry her far, enable her to sprint as never before. But what she gave up for this run was substantial, and painful.


LANGE LATER RECALLED the Taos stay as "a good time for us as people, for the little boys, for me, and for Maynard."[1] This was a false memory, as she had chafed at being housebound and careerless. Neither did the Taos stay solidify her relationship with Maynard. Their return brought the beginning of the end of their marriage—not consciously, and by no means decisively, because Dorothea hung on for three more years.

When they returned to San Francisco, the economic situation was much worse than when they had left. They found their friends "shocked and panicky."[2] The heart of the California economy had almost stopped beating. Agricultural revenue dropped from $750 million in 1929 to $317 million in 1932. Demand for California's oil declined so sharply that the industry was producing 200,000 barrels a day over what it could sell. In the Sacramento area, the payroll of manufacturing industries shrank to one-third of its pre-Depression level. California unemployment surged to 28 percent. Building permits issued in 1933 represented just 11 percent of those issued in 1925. All this despite the fact that California suffered *less* than the rest of the country. Like many others, Lange came to understand that the Depression was unlikely to disappear soon without drastic government action.

The market for art had evaporated. Galleries were closing, including the Galerie de Beaux Arts, Maynard's main outlet. His friend Serge Sherbakov, during his one-man show at the Legion of Honor, was cleaning toilets as a state relief worker.[3] Artists were trying to stay alive by selling directly to the public through outdoor art shows, setting up cooperative galleries, and bartering—one potter traded ceramics for four bushels of apples, an artist gave an oil painting to an obstetrician in return for the doctor's attending his wife.[4] Maynard sold few paintings and had trouble collecting what was owed him from previous sales. Of one hundred easel paintings he had made since the start of the Depression, he had sold twelve.[5] "Work and worry . . . no sales—a dark period," noted Maynard, adding "Kindliness of Jewish friends," referring to purchases of his paintings—a comment suggesting his complicated mixture of need and resentment toward Jews and the rich.[6]

Dorothea's business also declined, despite her wealthy clientele. In 1930 she had earned $1,770; in 1932, she took in only $602. To photograph the

Clausens, for which she charged fifty dollars, she went all the way to Humboldt County, more than two hundred miles to the north, paying her own expenses, something she would have done only for an extremely lucrative job previously. (Imogen's son Rondal remembers Dorothea discussing how long she made that fifty dollars last.)[7] The Clausens noticed her stress. When she arrived at their house, she asked to rest, then lay in bed smoking cigarettes for a long time before beginning work.

Shortly after Dorothea and Maynard returned from Taos, a San Francisco lifestyle journalist produced a puff piece about Dorothea for the *San Francisco News*. It featured a large and attractive photograph of her with her camera, with some of Dixon's drawings of their Taos life collaged around the photo. Dorothea looked "lithe, firm, tanned as a gypsy," dressed in her "blue working jeans and beret," Anna Sommer wrote, fixing Dorothea as a bohemian.[8] At another time such an article—on the front page of the second section—would have produced a flurry of new jobs, a lovely welcome-home gift.

The journalist drew from Dorothea some rather self-righteous—and in hindsight, dubious—pronouncements on wifely duty and successful motherhood. "In local bohemian circles the marriage of Dorothea Lange and Maynard Dixon, noted painter, stands as a shining exception to the proverbial 'tug of war' [that develops when] one artist marries another," Sommer wrote. Since their marriage had lasted, Dorothea became thereby a domestic-relations expert. Asked how it was done, she replied, "Simple . . . an artist's wife accepts the fact that she has to contend with many things that other wives do not. . . . As Maynard's wife, it is my chief job to see that his life does not become too involved—that he has a clear field . . . he needs a certain amount of freedom . . . from the petty, personal things of life." Dorothea was talking about how she thought she ought to behave. In an equally but inversely false claim, she said that she and Maynard lived together "on equal terms." Her ambivalence was making her contradict herself. She knew that providing Maynard with "freedom" burdened her with a double working day, and the journalist knew it, too: "Returning at night to the house on Russian Hill she would shut the door on her work, get dinner and devote the evening to her children. . . . Her distinguished husband, it appeared, divided his evenings with the children and more work."

Anna Sommer labeled both Dixons as artists—yet the article was part of a series called "Their Other Halves." Dorothea tried to finesse the artist identity. She was happy, she said, to describe her work as a "trade": "Too much has been said for and against photography as an art. . . . I don't care whether or not you dignify it with a highbrow name. I think it is more important to find all life interesting than to seek out just the high levels."

Knowing what we know now, it might appear that the lady was a hypocrite. But she was deceiving mainly herself. She had no access to alternative prescriptions for womanhood. Like most women of her time, Lange never imagined that husbands could share child care and domestic work. Her life required trying to do it all, and her peace of mind required convincing herself that it could be done successfully.


DOROTHEA'S SANCTIMONIOUS PAEAN to wifely virtue was a downright sham, because she and Maynard had just decided to live apart—apart not only from each other but from their children. They gave up their Taylor Street home. Maynard moved into his studio and Dorothea into hers. Many artists were doing this at the time because they couldn't manage two rents, but for Lange and Dixon it was a trial separation. They placed out the children, now seven and four, sending them to a school in San Anselmo, in Marin County, that boarded children with private families. For the two adults, both driven to work, giving up the Taylor Street house was only a modest sacrifice. They each had a home, only three doors from each other. But they took the children's only home away.

Had there been no children, Dorothea and Maynard might have developed a de Beauvoir–Sartre kind of arrangement. But there were children. They had previously placed the children with friends when they traveled. Consie had been sent away on several occasions. In 1931, in a first effort to rebond, Dorothea and Maynard had taken a brief holiday from the boys, sending them to stay with friends in Watsonville. But this latest separation was not intended to be brief, and the children were not brought home on weekends, because this would have meant two lengthy round-trips each visit for the parents. (There were no bridges yet and you had to go to Marin County by ferry.) Instead the parents went to the boys. Dan Dixon recalled, "I remember standing outside the place where we lived, waiting and waiting for that black Model A to appear. And when the day was over, I remember watching it go, weeping and weeping as the red taillights receded."[9]

To understand this arrangement, the historian must grapple not only with Dan's and John's pain at the time, their anger as young men, and their recollected sadness as adults, but also with changing standards about mother-child bonding. In the first half of the twentieth century, it was still common for lone mothers, even married employed mothers, to place out their children temporarily, either in private homes or in institutions. Among the poor, this practice (today called foster care) was entirely ordinary. Early in the century, for example, the majority of children in orphanages were not, in fact, orphans, in the meaning of that term today; most had living mothers—single, widowed, or separated—who could not manage to support and care for their children simultaneously. Employed women of all classes often solved child-care problems with temporary placements in institutions, with foster parents, or with relatives. Lange knew of several artists who had done this.[10]

The alternative, organized day care for children, was still rare and still carried the stigma of being a "charity" (today one might translate that as "welfare") intended only for the poor. Such care was characterized by overcrowding, rigid discipline, and poor facilities. Conservative discourse associated day-care centers with Soviet communism.[11] Furthermore, the dominant child-development assumptions of the time held that foster care was the superior choice. In a day-care center, experts reasoned, as in an orphanage, children would be cared for by strangers who were responsible for groups of children; in foster care, by contrast, children would have a mother and a family, possibly even a father. The prevailing child-development wisdom at the time also assumed a somewhat contradictory premise: that separations and shifting caretakers need not be traumatic for children so long as their fundamental physical needs were satisfied. Although most experts today consider children's developmental need for deep bonding with one or two parents to be a timeless and irreducible fact of human nature, that was not the conclusion of childhood experts eighty years ago. Today, foster care is rare among the middle class, although the wealthy send their children to boarding schools and to all-summer camps at very young ages. The practice remains common, however, among immigrants, the poor, and the ill and disabled, and in these cases the state is often an intermediary, licensing and paying the foster parents.

Still, boarding out children was a declining practice in the 1930s, and day nurseries were becoming more common. Previously the Dixon children attended the all-day Golden Gate Nursery School on Pacific Avenue, a modern establishment quite unlike the charity nurseries. Maynard was away from his children as much as he was with them, but his contemporaries did not consider this problematic. A mother, by contrast, was expected never to leave her children for long. But placing out was still common enough that Dorothea felt less external disapproval than private anguish. The very fact that she normally did virtually all the domestic and child-care labor made this decision both more rational and more painful. Later she explained this pithily: it was never "he and I, and the boys [but] myself and the little boys, and he."[12] She agonized, while Maynard did not. "Even now when I speak of it I can feel the pain," she said thirty years later. "It hurts me in the same place as it did then."[13]

There is no doubt about the boys' feelings: pain, fear, anger. Dorothea's were complex. She ached in the same place she hurt when she was twelve and her father left, and yet now it was she doing the abandoning. Despite all her rage at him, was she not repeating his behavior? She recalled her anger at her "wuzzy" mother, who would not defend her against her grandmother, and brooded about how the boarding mother treated Dan and John.[14] Dorothea could not shed her anxiety, and this anxiety led to denial. She spoke of the children's absence in the passive voice, as if she had had no responsibility for making it happen ". . . if the boys hadn't been taken from me by circumstances, I might have said to myself, 'I would do this, but I can't because . . .'"[15] Four years later, she developed the first symptoms of the severe ulcers that would cause so much pain in her later years and would ultimately lead to her death.

Placing the boys, a practice that would be repeated several times over the next seven years, was an only slightly masked indication of Lange's ambition. Her greed was for time and freedom, not money. She could, after all, have kept the boys in her studio. Her drive had previously showed in her willingness to be father as well as mother, to be breadwinner, wife, and child-raiser. This triple labor was a way of supporting Maynard's right to be an artist, but it also reflected her love for her work. It was this ambition, more than sending away the boys, that caused her shame. Ambition was an unacceptable, hidden drive among women, Dorothea being no exception, so she dared not confront it.

The new arrangement also provided her space away from Maynard. She was freeing herself not only of child care but also of care for a husband quite demanding in his own way. Her declarations that his art always came first, she would later admit, were only partly true. After twelve years of marriage, she was fed up with his irresponsibility, his jokes, and his philandering. Maynard was a sexy, romantic mate and friend, but not a good partner. He wounded her repeatedly by his affairs and flirtations. As it became clear that their friends knew about his womanizing, it was harder for her to bear her hurt and humiliation.[16] His frequent long trips not only left Dorothea alone but revealed the limits of their closeness. She was beginning to feel a longing for a missing intimacy. "I knew that this man . . . while he loved me . . . still didn't share the depths of his life with me." And, perhaps, neither did she: "I wasn't really involved in the vitals of the man."[17]

If the separation brought Dorothea more freedom, it gave nothing of the sort to the boys. Dan and John retain, more than seventy-five years later, a deep store of remembered pain. They have never forgiven her. One of Lange's grandchildren called her action "monstrous," having absorbed the anger from her father. John remembers that whenever his mother said, "I met the most interesting people today," he shivered, because it meant that he and his brother were going to be "shipped out" again.[18] The boys missed Maynard, too, but they were not, and are not, angry at him. They counted on their mother, and felt betrayed; they never counted on Maynard, but experienced him as a delightful visitor who arrived bearing gifts. He could *play* with the children as Dorothea, like many busy mothers, could not: with the boys he drew and painted, wrote and told stories, built and manufactured things with his hands, these activities becoming games that ranged from the silly to the mischievous to the ecstatic. The younger Dorothea had loved Maynard's playfulness, and she still did occasionally, but she was increasingly resentful that it was always she who had to be the responsible one. The economic depression made that responsibility, and her aloneness with it, more burdensome.

The most intense reactions I have encountered about placing out the children have come not from Dan and John, but from my own contemporaries, particularly women. When I mention it in conversation or in a lecture, they are shocked. I can tell from their faces and questions that this information changes radically how they think of Lange. As I present these facts, urging listeners to consider them in a historical context, I become worried that I am being perceived as too cool about it, too matter-of-fact. I frequently reshuffle my points, trying to find a perfect balance among my historian's consciousness of the customs of that time, my emotional understanding of the abandoned children's suffering, and my perception of Dorothea's pain and guilt. There is, of course, no perfect balance, only oscillation.

THE RETURN TO San Francisco also confronted Dorothea with another kind of violation and loss. While she was away, her brother Martin, thinking to do her a favor, had rented out her studio for thirty-five dollars a month, expecting that the couple would be happily surprised on their return to get the money. But the renter had trashed the place. He went on a rampage with Prussian blue paint, daubing it all over the walls and furniture; he had smeared it on valuable drawings, including those that Diego Rivera had given her. She had to burn them. Then the tenant had cut his wrists—but survived—and there was blood all over.

She cleaned up, and those few of her clients who still had discretionary income began coming in. Although her "mind was over in San Anselmo most of the time," Dorothea worked as never before.[19]

The family regathered in the summer of 1932. Unlike most others suffering from the economic collapse, they were able to take a blissful vacation. Anita Baldwin loaned them a cottage on her two-thousand-acre, breathtakingly beautiful estate on Fallen Leaf Lake, just south of Lake Tahoe, and they spent the whole summer there, "not a human soul but us"—the four of them, the servants, and Imogen Cunningham and her children, who had become part of the family. Dan and John remember it as paradise. To get there, they went by riverboat to Sacramento, boarding the elegant *Delta King* at dusk, eating in its restaurant amid chandeliers, silver goblets, candlelight, and "stately black stewards in starched white jackets." In the morning they drove the car off the boat and up winding roads into the Sierras. Baldwin owned the whole lakefront on this miniature Tahoe, connected to the big lake by a stream, and she maintained a timbered hunting lodge with a retinue of servants who cleaned and cooked. Maynard built an Indian sweat lodge. The boys ran naked all summer and rarely came indoors. Fallen Leaf was rich in game fish, and they ate what they caught. There were mishaps: John, whom they had begun calling "Chunkin," burned his bare backside in a collision with the potbellied stove on which Dorothea cooked. Maynard caught Dan fooling around with his Colt pistol, and gave him a hiding with a switch. The cabin had no amenities, so Dan got the task of lugging drinking and cooking water up from the lake.[20] Everyone got stronger.

It was in this maximally escapist location, paradoxically, that Dorothea took her first steps toward documentary photography. Wandering through the estate, she tried making Cunningham- or Weston-style pictures of nature: close-ups of young pine trees, stumps, and "skunk cabbage, with big pale leaves and the afternoon sun showing all the veins."[21] This approach was by then a trend: "During the 'twenties and 'thirties," photography historian Naomi Rosenblum wrote tartly, "the sharply detailed close-up of no matter what subject constituted a typical modernist strategy. . . ."[22] Lange had experimented with outdoor photography in Arizona and New Mexico, and now that she had the time to work at it systematically, she expected the pleasure that came with perfecting a new technique. But the pleasure did not come, and she never seemed to like what she produced, although she enjoyed the time alone and the challenge of looking closely at natural beauty.[23] One day, she recalled later, a realization came to her with sudden clarity. She described it as an epiphany, an insight into her own nature. Characteristically, she experienced it in terms of freedom and unfreedom, the great moral and personal theme of her bohemian consciousness at the time. "I was not free when I was trying to photograph those things which were not mine." Freedom required being true to your nature, and this meant feeling photography as a calling, not just a business. "And I then decided that when I went back to the city I would only photograph the people that my life touched."[24]

For a time, however, "the people that my life touched" remained her rich studio clients. She was aware of her dilemma as a craftswoman—that she had to rely on the rich as clients—and wished it could be otherwise. "I enjoyed every portrait that I made in an individual way but . . . photographing only people who paid me for it bothered me." Looking back, she saw her decision clearly: ". . . I was . . . aware that there was a very large world out there that I had entered not too well."[25] But her family depended on her income. Lange announced her new direction with a slight alteration in the business card she made to notify clients that the studio had reopened. Instead of "Portraits in Photography" it read "Pictures of People." This had more meaning to her than to others, since she had always done pictures of people. What had changed was who she identified as subjects. Both literally and figuratively, she looked out her window and the view made her studio seem remote, stifling.

NINETEEN THIRTY-TWO was an election year, but at first the presidential campaign seemed uninteresting. The Democratic platform could almost have been Hoover's, calling as it did for tariffs, sound currency, a balanced budget, and cutbacks in federal expenditure. Many of Lange's friends—both artists and customers—were supporting Socialist presidential candidate Norman Thomas or Communist William Z. Foster, and Lange was sympathetic. As the content of Roosevelt's campaign speeches became more substantive, however, she was attracted to his energy and optimism, as well as to his rhetoric. In April he called for restoring the purchasing power of farmers and finding a way to stop foreclosures when mortgage payments could not be met. In May he suggested that the United States should consider social planning and argued that "we cannot allow our economic life to be controlled by that small group of men whose chief outlook upon the social welfare is . . . that they can make huge profits from the lending of money and the marketing of securities. . . ." July's nomination speech returned to the Party's conservative platform: repeal of Prohibition (supposedly without the return of saloons), cutting government spending, and limiting public works to reforestation projects. After being nominated, however, Roosevelt called for regulation of investment, banking, and utilities, and in September, he defended the right of local governments to own and operate power plants if private utilities were doing a poor job. On September 23 in San Francisco he again denounced the "great industrial and financial combinations" and their "princes of property" who dominated industrial life, although he added that "government should assume the function of economic regulation only as a last resort. . . ." FDR's rhetoric of the "forgotten man at the bottom of the economic pyramid" affirmed what Lange was seeing.[26]

At some point during his campaign, Lange learned that FDR was a polio survivor. She had tamped her polio memories so far down that she rarely spoke of the disease, but now she was undoubtedly riveted, scrutinizing every FDR photograph as if it were one of her own negatives. In a carefully calibrated pre-campaign public-relations move, Roosevelt had arranged an early magazine interview, published July 1931, under the headline IS FRANKLIN D. ROOSEVELT FIT TO BE PRESIDENT?[27] In the usual photographs of FDR, he did his best to hide his infirmity, as did Dorothea. Now one photograph, however, showed his gleaming leg braces, not so different from what hers had looked like, and another revealed his powerful arms and thin legs as he sat in a swimsuit. Roosevelt's way with his disability seemed to Lange of a piece with his activist stance toward the Depression, in contrast to Hoover's calls for patience and faith in market forces.

Lange's own activist inclinations were unleashed by the falloff in her business: Fewer customers released time to think and look. What she saw when she began looking systematically also had consequences: "I knew that if my interests in people were valid I would not only be doing what was in those printing frames."[28] Her idea of the "valid" is packed with implications. Typically, she set herself a challenge. She felt she needed to validate her photography by looking at larger matters. To Dorothea now, the streets were not about San Francisco's charming architecture or dramatic topography, but about the social disruptions palpable everywhere. Memories of the many miles she had walked through New York's Lower East Side, and her increasing comfort there despite its often raucous street life, brought back her confidence as a walker in the city.

Dixon's apprentice and Dorothea's future colleague at FSA, John Collier, Jr., recalled a sudden transformation in Lange: ". . . Dorothea Lange was a highly-paid, rather slick portrait photographer of wealthy women, and she made a good living at it. She was a very good craftsman; she did beautiful work. . . . She was pretty self-centered, and a little bit selfish, and indulgent. About that point she looked down from her window on Sacramento St. and saw a bread-line . . . and something about it triggered some dedication in her. And she walked out of her studio and she figuratively never came back, you know."[29] His understanding of Dorothea was far off the mark, as was his sense of her transition as sudden. But he was right to sense a change in her.

Dorothea's brother Martin had followed his sister to San Francisco in the 1920s. His good looks, easygoing temperament, and mental quickness allowed him to knock about from job to job, and he often camped out in her studio. Seizing him as chaperone, she explored the inner-city streets. They spent hours walking the Mission District, where the city was billeting the homeless. They went to the "slave market," where men gathered, hoping to pick up a few days or a few hours of work. She felt drawn to the breadlines, visually as well as socially, as she would be drawn to the unemployment-compensation and relief lines in the following years. One of her first street photographs, of the White Angel breadline, became one of her most famous.[30] (See page 102.) It changed not only Lange but also documentary photography, as if pulling open a curtain.[31]

Martin reported that she was "awfully hard to get along with"—that is, until she began her street photography.[32] Paradoxically, going into the streets helped her relax. She had been nervous about being in the streets with Depression "bums" but found she felt safe. She had been apprehensive that her method was too slow to capture something important, because she couldn't tell the subjects to hold still—"You know there are moments such as these when . . . you just hope you will have enough time to get it organized in a fraction of a second on that tiny piece of sensitive film"—but she was transfixed by her results. She had been anxious about invading subjects' privacy or evoking

their hostility, but they had not seemed to notice or to object if they did. On such reassurance her whole photographic future rested. "I can only say I knew I was looking at something. . . . Sometimes you have an inner sense that you have encompassed the thing. . . . You know then that you are not taking anything away from anyone, their privacy, their dignity, their wholeness."[33]

Lange's recollection exaggerated the suddenness of this, her first great photograph and her second epiphany, as memory often congeals around particular moments or images.

6.1. HOWARD STREET, SAN FRANCISCO, 1933

A near mishap further emphasizes its accidental quality: she accidentally left the exposed film in the magazine holder of her Graflex, giving it to her assistant Roger Sturtevant to reload. Luckily, he reached inside it while in the darkroom, found the neglected film, and developed it.[34]

This narrative of the accidental White Angel photograph, then picked up by others writing about Lange, implies a sudden leap—or fall—into what became documentary photography. The arresting beauty of that photo did surprise Lange, but it was not an accident. She was consciously exploring a new form of photography. Leaping makes a better story, and Lange herself sometimes employed that metaphor, but it sustains a misleading, romantic view of artists as working from instinct, intuition, as opposed to calculation, deliberation, practice, trials and errors. Moreover, Lange had never confined herself exclusively to studio work and to paying clients. In addition to her southwestern photographs, she had photographed the Chinatown in Carson City, Nevada, where she had gone with Maynard in 1924. At home in San Francisco she produced some striking modernist abstractions, including an image of sheets on a laundry line seen from the back porch of a tenement, a composition and symbolic motif she would use occasionally throughout her life. In 1928 she made a luminous portrait of a San Francisco Mexican-American child, and it came easily. By 1932, she found, "I didn't feel much difference between the portrait sitters and these people" in the streets. Using a painter's metaphor, she said that she saw "out there" as just a "larger canvas."[35] Now she made a Madonna of a young African American mother, much as she had done with the Indian mother in New Mexico.

Also pushing her out of the studio was what she saw in print. Visual images increasingly saturated commercial print culture as new photographic and printing techniques—faster-drying ink and heatset printing, which scorched the ink dry as it was applied—made reproduction of images faster, cheaper, and more legible. Newspapers published regular rotogravure photographic sections, with images ranging from Japanese atrocities to bathing beauties.[36] Glossy magazines, such as *Vogue* or *The Ladies' Home Journal* or *Nash's*, printed page after page of color advertising, some of modernist design (including work by Dorothea's friend Louise Dahl-Wolfe), some of which she would have

6.2. YOUNG BLACK MOTHER HOLDING BABY, EARLY 1930S

disdained as ugly and hokey. She would never try photojournalism or commercial photography, but she was absorbing the new mass distribution of photography and imagining its usefulness for other purposes.

Still, the transition required major readjustments. Studio portraits are made at the request of the subject. Documentary is initiated by the photographer who must surprise, persuade, or manage to be unnoticed by the subject. Many photographers experience their work as requiring a degree of aggressiveness, which in turn requires a degree of confidence, even entitlement. Every street photographer finds her own method of accepting, denying, and performing this aggressiveness. Lange found her method by trial and error.

IN DEVELOPING WHAT came to be called documentary photography, Lange was by no means blazing an entirely new path. She knew the work of Jacob Riis and Lewis Hine. She knew Genthe's photography of San Francisco's Chinatown and Paul Strand's in New York City. In San Francisco, several of her photographer friends had preceded her in taking their cameras onto the streets—Consuelo Kanaga, Alma Lavenson, Louise Dahl, Peter Stackpole, and Willard Van Dyke.

Meanwhile, another network formalized itself as a school of photography, known as f/64, after a small camera aperture that provided sharpness and great depth of field. This group stimulated a West Coast photographic conversation about what was "authentic"—meaning, true to the camera's inherent technology. To the members of f/64, this meant "straight" photography, sharp-edged, as opposed to pictorialism's mistiness, softened forms, classical or historical costuming and poses, and "refined" subjects—the Beaux-Arts style. The "straights" drew a distinction that seems rather arbitrary from today's perspective: Filters, varied lighting, varied chemicals, dodging and burning were acceptable; fuzzy focus, coated lens, scratching the negative, and hand-coloring the print were not. Theirs was an antilowbrow and an anticommercial sensibility.

Initiated in 1932 under Ansel Adams's influence, f/64 took in many of Lange's friends—Imogen Cunningham, John Paul Edwards, Sonya Noskowiak, Henry Swift, Willard Van Dyke, and Edward Weston—and left Lange out. At its first, and only, exhibition, four more were invited in: Preston Holder, Consuelo Kanaga, Alma Lavenson, and Brett Weston (Edward's son)—but not Lange. Her absence offers hints about her identity at the time—still a pictorialist studio photographer.[37] She was not yet widely sharing her street photography.

Like many new ventures, f/64 put out a bombastic manifesto, which overstated not only its significance but also its novelty. What f/64 called "straight" photography, Paul Strand had been practicing for years. Photography scholar Sally Stein called the birth of f/64 and its "straight" idea less a proclamation than a summation.[38]

But f/64 was also a political move, its focus both local and national. Locally, it targeted a particular California photographer, William Mortensen. The "straights" hated his cheesy photographs of models in elaborately staged and costumed classical, Renaissance, and Orientalist tableaux—and also scorned his great popularity.[39]

There was also a national agenda: to bring greater notice to West Coast photography and to disrupt Stieglitz's power to define art photography.[40] The east-west differences in photography reveal something about Lange's uniqueness in the direction she had chosen. Like western painters, most western photographers, both "straight" and pictorialist, focused on the natural rather than urban, manufactured, or industrial landscapes. Western pictorialists placed their human subjects in natural surroundings, rather than in studios.[41] In 1932, Lange's out-of-studio photographic work was urban, and in that dimension her sensibility seemed more eastern. So did her growing concern with social problems. Had she lived in New York, Lange would have joined the radical Photo League when it was established in 1936, an organization that promoted socially engaged photography and provided darkroom use and classes at very low cost to encourage the poor and the working class to try photography. From California, she became one of its official supporters and donated money. Yet less than a decade later, she would become a photographer focused primarily on western rural and farm life—an identity no one, including her, would have predicted in 1932.

But since no one in the West had Stieglitz's drive to control, the western spirit was less coherent, more individualist and democratic, and the organization f/64 soon disappeared. While it existed, however, it helped pull together Bay Area photographers. Their weekends in Carmel were particularly lively—and often raucous. Seema Weatherwax, an amateur photographer and girlfriend of Chan Weston, Edward's eldest son, recalled that "all the boys would get together and we'd have an 'orgy.'" (She was referring more to drinking than sex.)[42] Holder recalled, "We'd go down there on Friday and arrive at night and drink till about 1 o'clock. . . . Saturday was usually spent getting over Friday night." Adams entertained them with pranks: He played the piano once with oranges in his hands, and another time he played the "Blue Danube Waltz" with his rear end.[43]

Dixon and Lange sometimes joined these gatherings, but given this style of recreation, it is hardly surprising that Lange was marginal. She was older than the men, who were mainly in their twenties, and she worked full-time. Moreover, despite her enjoyment of bohemian unconventionality, she liked order, not disorder—Holder called her "very middle class," a pejorative in his vocabulary.[44] And along with the womanizing, the group around Weston operated on a homoerotic frequency that shoved women to the edges of the group.

Although Dorothea claimed to have experienced no resentment about exclusion from f/64, Ansel Adams later recalled that she was very much upset by the slight.[45] Maynard was open about his irritation. By all measure the most explosive of her community, Maynard wanted to send a close-up of his bare ass as a "straight" photography entry to the exhibit, "to say, this is precision for you," but unfortunately the picture didn't turn out well. He did, however, write a scathing letter. He called f/64 slavish, bigoted, contemptible, narrow-minded. He was, and would always be, passionately loyal to Dorothea. He also made a sensible argument: that at this stage in the history of photography, the group should have been exploring all its potentialities rather than clamping down an orthodoxy.[46]

If Maynard was right, Dorothea benefited from not being involved in f/64. The fact that she saw herself as a craftswoman, without pretensions to artistry, protected her from pressure toward an aesthetic orthodoxy. She and Imogen Cunningham were producing both "straight" and pictorialist photography at the same time, and both soft- and sharp-edged photographers were exploring modernist compositions. Insisting that only "straight" photography was legitimate produced wordy, sometimes nasty, and always unproductive debate about authenticity and inauthenticity in photography.

# 7

# A New Deal for Artists

Dorothea, her brother Martin, Maynard, and their friends listened to FDR's inauguration at Ernie's Italian restaurant and bar on Montgomery Street. Martin remembered it as "a big day . . . and [we] had a great laugh over the bartender's comment, 'Best president we ever had.'"[1] Since FDR was a "wet"—that is, an opponent of Prohibition—the artists had supported him and now cheered the prospect of repeal. Except for that, the interregnum between election and taking office—four months at the time—offered nothing hopeful. Roosevelt was silent. Despite the populist rhetoric that would intermittently characterize his appeal—". . . the rulers of the exchange of mankind's goods have failed. . . . They know only the rules of a generation of self-seekers. . . ."—his inaugural speech contained no proposals. His boosterish slogan, "the only thing we have to fear is fear itself," was evidently false to anyone who looked around. Meanwhile, Californians were more aware than easterners of the Japanese invasion of Shanghai and Manchuria, but were not sure yet how the ominous background of Nazi power in Germany and fascist power in Italy would fit into the international picture.

Within days after the inauguration, however, a different Roosevelt appeared. The administration immediately initiated a bank holiday; the Civilian Conservation Corps for unemployed young men; and the Federal Emergency Relief

Administration (FERA) whose head, Harry Hopkins, gave away $5.3 million (equivalent to $84 million in 2007) in his first day on the job.[2] By October 1933, the first large public jobs program, the Civil Works Administration (CWA), announced plans to hire five million unemployed workers. The New Deal was dealing new cards. Even depressed and cynical Maynard noted, "Inauguration of Roosevelt. Hope."[3]

What influenced Lange most in 1933 and 1934 was the combination of government activism and its inadequacy to the need. As is so often the case, it was this juxtaposition of raised hopes and their frustration that stimulated grassroots activism and Lange's own participation in it.

MAYNARD CONTRIBUTED DIRECTLY to lifting San Francisco's spirits. Two heroic bridges were under construction, one stretching over eight miles east to Oakland and Berkeley, the Bay Bridge, and one north to Marin County, the Golden Gate Bridge.[4] When finished, they would transform traffic throughout the Bay Area, until now dependent on ferries. In 1930 Dixon had been commissioned to paint a vision of what the Golden Gate might look like when bridged (a breathtaking aerial view that now hangs in the office of the San Francisco Golden Gate toll plaza), work intended to promote the bond issue. The bridge project's public-relations man, Charles Duncan, was Maynard's brother-in-law, and he asked Maynard to recommend an architect; Maynard's choice, Irving Foster Morrow, got the job and then regularly consulted with Maynard and his artist cohort. The project was controversial. Some thought it disfigured the grand entrance from the Pacific Ocean to San Francisco Bay, while others welcomed it as a monument, a technological tour de force, and a good investment. In an effort to mediate, Maynard organized a "pro and con powwow" for artists in his studio. The chief engineer and Duncan came with maps, drawings, and models. Although many of those present remained opposed, they agreed to make no formal protest, a considerable victory for Maynard and other bridge advocates.[5] Some claim that Maynard and Dorothea ultimately chose the bridge's color: Morrow had had it painted an undercoat of industrial red, and they urged him to keep it that way.[6]

Such projects, systematically pursued, might have helped check unemployment and stimulate consumption in the area. But the state and local governments pursued contradictory economic policies, floating bonds for bridge construction while simultaneously cutting budgets and thereby increasing unemployment. Until federal relief arrived, state and local governments were caught in a vicious circle: unemployment and recession shrank tax revenues and stimulated antitax protests just as the need for relief grew and governments' borrowing capacities declined. San Francisco responded more mercifully than many other cities, but the net effect did nothing to mitigate the underconsumption crisis.[7] Roosevelt made some of the same mistakes. He imposed a 15 percent pay cut on federal employees. His National Recovery Administration was financed by a regressive sales tax, despite the fact that, as the NRA head himself warned, "80 percent of the buying in this country is done by people who earn less than $1800 a year. . . ." Moreover, the NRA failed to control prices, which rose by 10 percent in July 1933 alone.[8]

One program did the right thing politically and morally: relief. Relief was local and personal and created widespread loyalty to Roosevelt. Ignoring accusations of hurried, slapdash decision making, relief boss Harry Hopkins snapped, "People don't eat in the long run, they eat every day." Unlike so many unrealized and underfunded initiatives, the CWA kept its promises and employed 3.5 million by Christmastime, eventually assisting 22 percent of the population. The unemployed cheered the CWA because they almost all preferred jobs to "handouts."[9] In 1935 came the Works Progress Administration, with its $4.8 *billion* budget (the largest peacetime appropriation in U.S. history up until that time), employing 30 percent of the eleven to twelve million unemployed. Because most of its projects involved construction of large public facilities, the WPA became the most visible and popular New Deal program. Its employees put up more than 40,000 new buildings, including courthouses, firehouses, hospitals, schools, and built 350 new airfields, 78,000 new bridges, 800 parks, 1,400 athletic fields, 1,800 public swimming pools, and 40,000 miles of new roads. Equally important, it promoted conservation and public health by reforesting 20,000 acres, planting 20 million trees and bushes, and building 500 water-treatment plants, 1,500 sewage-treatment plants, and 24,000 miles of sewers. In 1938, when disastrous floods hit the Northeast, washing out railroad bridges, highways, and power lines, Hopkins sent fifty thousand WPA employees to work around the clock to evacuate endangered people, build dikes, provide temporary water and power, and then clean the massive expanses of mud that coated the streets and buildings—a federal helping hand never before available.[10] Before long, the WPA would begin reaching artists.

THESE CONSTRUCTIVE STEPS raised hopes but were never large enough to bring the country out of the Depression—only the colossal government spending on World War II did that. The downward economic spiral continued through the decade, with only intermittent upturns, as unemployed, under-employed, and low-wage workers became unable to purchase enough to keep production alive, thereby creating even more unemployed, underemployed, and low-wage workers. Spending even on food fell by almost half. Children roamed San Francisco's streets, visibly hungry. The economic collapse intensi-fied racial and class inequalities. The emergency relief programs—serving 20 percent of Californians—only demonstrated that more government help was necessary.

Adding to the shock was anxiety about fascism. In January 1933, Hitler became chancellor, and in the spring the attacks on Jewish businesses and books escalated. In Italy thousands of Jews were fleeing. The greatest cause for alarm, particularly among Lange's community of friends, many of them Jews, was fascism's growth in the United States. Sinclair Lewis's *It Can't Happen Here*, imagining a fascist coup in the United States, appeared in 1935 to great attention. Many in California thought *fascist* the right label for the alliance of big-business antiunionism with anticommunism, racism, and anti-Semitism. The big growers stirred up a Red-baiting hysteria against union organizers, and hired thugs to threaten or beat up resistant farmworkers. Local authorities frequently supported or, at best, ignored this violent vigilantism. In 1934 a mob six thousand strong, wrought up by claims that Communists were plan-ning to take over, watched as two farmworker organizers were strung up and then released to the ground just before death; vigilantes armed with pickax handles beat many others and kidnapped a dozen. The governor praised the vigilantes, and the *San Jose Evening News*, speaking for the whole Hearst press, editorialized, "The citizens who accomplished that feat were doing their plain duty. . . ."[11] In the Imperial Valley in 1934, an ACLU board member sent to observe enforcement of a federal injunction protecting workers' right of assembly was kidnapped by vigilantes wearing state police uniforms, beaten, and dumped in the middle of the desert. In Santa Rosa in 1935, three hundred night riders tear-gassed the homes of several farmworker organizers, seized them, beat them, forced them to kiss the flag, then tarred and feathered them. In Los Angeles the American Nationalist party and related pro-Nazi groups conducted an anti-Semitic campaign, including sneaking thousands of leaflets into home-delivered copies of the *Los Angeles Times*.[12] There were large Nazi rallies in San Francisco. Several right-leaning Hollywood stars, including Gary Cooper, supported by Hearst money, formed armed and uniformed groups that marched to "protect true Americanism."[13]

Renowned intellectuals began arguing that artists had to lead in the struggle against fascism because it threatened culture itself; that commitment to art necessarily entailed resistance to totalitarianism; and that fascism was anathema to the bohemians' cherished individualism.[14] As artists and intellectuals moved to the Left, photographers had perhaps the most direct route to using their skills in the interest of social justice.

This progressive artistic community developed a "cultural front," in the term used by historian Michael Denning. Disgusted that access to art had become a privilege of the moneyed, while the working and middle classes imbibed primarily commercial kitsch, cultural-front artists sought to create a fine art that was widely accessible. Their mode was uniformly realist, although it included diverse, contradictory, even opposing political and aesthetic streams. Official New Deal art excluded denunciation of inequality and representation of conflict, and instead emphasized national unity and a homogeneity constructed by a narrowed representation of Americanism. But all cultural-front artists made respectful, even honorific images of the "common people." A century earlier, high-art representations of plebeian subjects had expressed the democratic revolutionary spirit of 1848; in the 1930s it often subordinated protest to nationalism. In contrast to the rebellion against America's Protestant provincialism by modernist artists of the early twentieth century, the 1930s style could seem antimodern in its glorification of rural and small-town life. In unison with fascist, Nazi, and Soviet art, many of the cultural front condemned modernism as irresponsible and self-indulgent. Yet cultural-front art incorporated many modernist tastes, notably in its symbolism, simplification and abstraction of form, and repudiation of detailed verisimilitude. Becoming a cultural-front artist did not require recanting high-art sophistication.[15]

That many artists became left-wingers should not be taken for granted as somehow natural, however. True, they respected antiauthoritarian attitudes and practices, defined themselves as outsiders and nonconformists, and claimed to despise mere seeking after wealth. But their "defiant individualism," in the words of historian Jane De Hart Matthews, often kept them at arm's length from politics.[16] Modernism, moreover, influenced them toward the notion that art should express a subjective, individual vision. Maynard Dixon was by no means typical, but he affords an example of the political ambiguity of the 1920s bohemian subculture: Respectful of people who worked with their hands, attracted to Deweyan principles of progressive education, disdainful of Babbittry and prudery, he was at the same time hostile to intellectuals, suspicious of African Americans and Jews, repelled by anything that seemed to him unpatriotic, and unmoved by radical critiques of the United States. Not even his own contempt for commercialism and the power of big money weakened his rejection of organized political action (although if there had been an environmentalist movement, Dixon might have joined it). Furthermore, the economic depression had a literally depressing effect on many, suppressing their energy and engagement; this was Dixon's reaction. Lange's response, by contrast, was a desire to *do* something.

While Lange watched and listened, her client friends, already involved in community service projects and charities, became more political: Edythe Katten was a Socialist party activist, Elizabeth Elkus an ACLU stalwart. Artists and writers of her network, such as Kenneth Rexroth, Bernard Zakheim, Consuelo Kanaga, Willard Van Dyke, Peter Stackpole, and many in Carmel were making and calling others to make socially relevant art. The progressive arts movement was national and the positions being taken by New York artists and writers such as Rockwell Kent, Paul Strand, William Gropper, Stuart Davis, and John Dos Passos were influencing the Bay Area. Zakheim and Rexroth established an Artists' and Writers' Union in San Francisco in 1933, and it was so popular that even Dixon was briefly drawn in. (Ansel Adams was the outlier in his determined opposition to progressive activism and much of the New Deal.)[17]

The Communist party gained widespread respect in this period. Many observers were impressed by glowing reports of the Soviet Union—its industrial growth, the educational and medical institutions it was building, and its resolute antifascist stand—while hearing less about Stalin's crushing of dissent and massacring of peasants. In 1935 the Communist International adopted a strategy of alliance with other progressive forces, which they called a "popular front." In fact, a popular front was already developing spontaneously in the United States, taking the form of alliance between Leftists and New Dealers, and became much larger than the Party sphere. Still, Communists often provided leadership. Although the Party never became large and artists were not numerous among its members, many progressive causes benefited from Communists' energy, discipline, and personal sacrifice.[18]

Lange absorbed this energy directly, as the Monkey Block became a center of Left art activity. She was invited to some Communist party meetings, she recalled. "You wouldn't be told at the first visit that they were party meetings. You would be somewhat flattered and cajoled and it [Party membership] was dangled before you as something that a person like you would be interested in . . . having made photographs . . . I would be valuable." She was being looked over to see if she would make good material. She knew and respected some Communists at this time: "so many people of very good intentions, the best intentions, the best people. . . ." She explained that the reason she "didn't go any further" was that Maynard was so opposed: "He was less socially moved than I."[19]

Dorothea was conflicted. What she felt was not just a stretch, like a rubber cord pulled from each end, but a tug-of-war. She tugged left and tried to haul Maynard with her; he dug in his heels, allowing her to drag him a bit, then yanked her back with his skepticism. Dixon was no fascist sympathizer, but he longed for a return to a preindustrial West, certainly not a growing federal government, and he regarded all organizations as constricting to his freedom. The tugging made Dorothea feel stressed, yet also elated. Despite her words, it is unlikely that she would have deferred to Maynard's objections had she herself been eager to join the Party. Lange would not have been comfortable in a political party demanding doctrinal and strategic obedience, and the CP demanded just that. San Francisco artist Shirley Taschen Triest remarked that "if you didn't do proletarian art, you were just considered beneath contempt."[20] Lange never became active in any organization.

She grew closer to left-wing photographers, though, such as Consuelo Kanaga, who had settled into a studio a few doors down from her. She talked politics with many. A young German photographer couple—Hansel Mieth and Otto Hagel—became lifelong friends. As adventurous teenagers, they had left their homes near Stuttgart (the home of Dorothea's maternal family) to wander Europe; Johanna Mieth took the name Hansel because it was safer for them to pass as two boys. Seeking the land of Jack London, they made their way to California, where they supported themselves as construction workers at Yosemite and as migrant farmworkers throughout the Central Valley. Both began to photograph the conditions and conflicts in the fields; already strongly antifascist in Germany, they soon joined others in the American Left. Moving to San Francisco, Hansel and Otto stayed with Dorothea, she recalled, off and on for six months, and connected to other engaged photography colleagues.

Taking up the new fast-action Leica camera, they gravitated toward photojournalism and moved to New York in 1937 when Mieth got a staff position at *Life,*
joining a small, elite cadre of photographers that included Margaret Bourke-
White, Alfred Eisenstaedt, Peter Stackpole, Carl Mydans, and seven others.
(They married in a double ceremony in 1940 with Robert Capa and his second
wife, Toni Sorel.) The *Life* job did not last long, as Mieth's commitment to
"social" photography did not fit its politics, and she and Hagel returned to
California, bought some property in Santa Rosa, near Jack London's home,
and farmed there for the rest of their lives, committed to a simple, austere life
out of both conviction and poverty. They maintained a close friendship with
Dorothea, who was particularly supportive when they refused to testify before
the House Committee on Un-American Activities.[21]


ARTISTS EAGER TO integrate their political convictions with their work
and to make that work public gravitated to murals. This required government
support. Without it, art remained a luxury article, when it should be a *right*
of the common people, they thought. New Deal relief programs provided an
opportunity to get that support. Although the public works programs hired
primarily construction workers, the white-collar unemployed also got some
jobs: they did cataloging in libraries, inventoried historical records, produced
historical roadside markers, promoted public health, supervised playgrounds,
and helped teachers by working with special-needs children. (Such jobs were
particularly attractive to women, who were otherwise excluded or segregated
into sewing sweatshops.) Soon artists got themselves included, and they began
to create a new political culture that considered art worthy of public support.
The artistic boom of the 1920s meant that even more artists—an estimated
57,000 in the United States—needed help now, and federal programs came
to employ thousands of them—estimates range from ten thousand to thirty
thousand.[22] These included eight Bay Area photographers, not, however,
including Lange.[23]

The very visibility of what visual artists produced added to the political risks
of including them in federal programs, however. To conservatives and others
who did not appreciate the Keynesian argument for government spending,
that artists should be supported by tax money seemed frivolous at the least,
and borderline immoral. So getting the federal work programs to employ artists required agitation and lobbying. In San Francisco, Bernard Zakheim and

Rexroth initiated a campaign to this end. The collapse of sales and commissions and the drying up of commercial-art jobs submerged their internecine feuds, and even Dixon joined. At a meeting in his studio, the group formulated a mural proposal. Ralph Stackpole "knew someone" in Washington and the artists combined their "small change" to send a telegram about their proposal to his contact. They were flabbergasted to receive a positive reply four days later.[24] Stackpole's acquaintance was Edward Bruce, a Treasury Department administrator and painter, who had been agitating for federally funded projects for artists. Gathering support from other New Deal administrators and, crucially, Eleanor Roosevelt and Elinor Morgenthau, wife of Treasury Secretary Henry Morgenthau, who was a close friend of FDR, Bruce became director of the Public Works of Art Project (PWAP) in December 1933.

When the old-guard arts patrons learned of the PWAP money, they moved quickly to seize control. Corporate head and Lange customer Herbert Fleishhacker, member of San Francisco's Board of Supervisors and president of the Board of Park Commissioners, had been stung by criticism of his "last erection," the ugly Coit Tower on Telegraph Hill. He also faced allegations of conflict of interest, since his company had supplied the cement and concrete for the tower construction. So he corralled the PWAP money, originally sought for Golden Gate Park, to put art work in Coit Tower as a means of justifying its existence.[25] Twenty-six artists were commissioned to do Coit murals, including many of Dorothea and Maynard's friends, but Maynard was not among them. Bitter, he called the finished product "a planless mess."[26] (The reason for Dixon's exclusion is unclear, and he might have decided, out of pride and pique, not to apply. Yet he frequently applied to other federal arts projects and was several times rejected. The rejections are hard to understand, since Dixon had developed a strong, simplified style, akin to that used for many murals and posters in the New Deal period.)[27]

The Coit project was a major opportunity—when completed, the Coit paintings would constitute three-quarters of all the murals in California.[28] But within six months, Fleishhacker was ready to destroy them, enraged by the insinuation of left-wing politics into several panels.[29] Zakheim had painted a library where a man pulled *Capital* off the shelf; Victor Arnautoff had painted newspaper kiosks where *The Masses* and *The Daily Worker* appeared; Clifford Wight's painting included the hammer and sickle, among other symbols of political systems.[30] It is striking that the objectionable depictions on the murals involved specific emblems or names. The overall proletarian imagery raised no hackles, or else those hackled were constrained from protesting. Since only the worst offense—the hammer and sickle symbol—was removed, despite other obviously provocative gestures, the result could hardly have functioned better for the politicized muralists had it been calculated: The explicitly leftist signs and symbols took the heat off the core content of the murals, the working class people who had built California.

Maynard did get a WPA commission to paint the construction of Boulder Dam, and spent nine weeks there.[31] Through the eye of a modernist like, say, photojournalist Margaret Bourke-White or filmmaker Sergei Eisenstein, the dam construction would have stimulated a visual exaltation of industrial/monumental design. Not through Dixon's eye: "I decided to make my main theme 'Pigmy man against everlasting rock. . . . Ultimate futility.'" He thought the whole project foolhardy. "The desert will have the last laugh." He also objected, with his usual sympathy for the little guy, to the exploitation and dangerous conditions: "Boulder City like prison camp; armed guards; company houses and concessions; paying with one hand and taking it back with the other. . . . Exhaustion of men. . . . High average of deaths"—aspects of industrial might that other artists often ignored.[32] Dixon's refusal to celebrate these giant icons of industry—in this case, agricultural industry—expressed his antimodernism as well as his instinct to protect nature, an early environmentalism that influenced Lange and that she acted on in her later photography.

Several artists, including the composer Ernest Bloch, a member of San Francisco's artistic elite and one of Dorothea's customers, tried to convince Maynard to take more responsibility for social causes, without success.[33] Dorothea managed to cajole him into painting the urban Depression.[34] As he had led her into the countryside, now she drew him into the cityscape. His paintings *Forgotten Man, No Place to Go, Going Nowhere,* and *Destination Nowhere* show unrelieved gloom: isolated, enervated men, their bodies heavy with fatigue and depression. Their depression, like his, was both external and internal. His asthma was worsening and he was often out of breath when he reached his studio on the top floor of the Monkey Block. He became self-critical: "Like other artists, I had dodged the responsibility of facing social conditions. The depression woke me up. . . ."[35] Connoisseurs differ about the quality of these paintings, but in any case he did not continue in that vein. Concluding that the work was false to him, much as Lange had concluded about her photographs of plants, Dixon returned permanently to painting landscape and Indians.[36]

The federal arts programs exerted a multidirectional force on artists. They allowed many talented people to make art instead of sewing mattresses or building bridges. At the same time, government employment mitigated the disdain with which established artists often regarded the less skilled, the amateurs and beginners. The government also brought art to new populations. Poet and Librarian of Congress Archibald MacLeish said that New Deal arts projects worked "a sort of cultural revolution in America. They brought the American audience and the American artist face to face. . . ."[37] Because the arts projects were often collaborative, they fostered camaraderie, mutual influence, and collective hopes for long-term public support for the arts. In other words, government support for artists was not only a *response* to agitation for relief but also a *cause* of activism, nudging recipients to a more democratic perspective on art. This mood surrounded Lange.

However, with public money came constraints, which Lange would soon experience. The ban on Red propaganda was not the only censorship. In most of the country—New York was occasionally an exception—there was to be no abstract art, no Surrealism, no collage, no Expressionism.[38] These strictures both promoted accessibility and soothed conservative politicians. Ironically, these constraints were identical to those in the fascist countries and the Soviet Union, where the Stalin government tolerated only patriotic, socialist-realist art. Still, along with constraints came freedoms, because government arts projects temporarily reduced the power of the market to force artists to produce only what was immediately salable.

WHILE ARTISTS PAINTED murals, Lange roamed San Francisco's poor and public areas, now as comfortable as she had been on the Lower East Side. If, as she believed, a camera is a tool for learning how to see without a camera, she was teaching herself to see anew. She was learning about society through her camera.

The converse is also true: Her photographic vigor and depth gained from her exploration of the social. *White Angel Breadline* was not a fluke. From 1933 there is a warm close-up of a woman on a food distribution line; from 1934, lyrical, dark images of homeless men sleeping and the unemployed leaning dejectedly against a wall.[39] In 1934, she made one of her most emotional images, a man sitting on a box, head bowed into his hands, next to a perfect symbol of the Depression—an upside-down wheelbarrow. (See plate 4.) She quickly mastered natural light, although she had no light meter (first marketed in 1931; a camera that could synchronize flash and exposure—without which a photographer working alone would be unable to use a flash—was first produced in Germany in 1935). She was finding a new vocabulary of imagery by following her fascination with gesture and body language. Her studio photographs often portrayed temperament and mood through her subjects' bodies, their faces turned aside or in shadow. Now many of her best street photographs showed only bodies. When asked, decades later, to choose the few photographs that best represented her work, she always included one of these early street pictures.

She began to get closer to her new subjects. She made a series of photographs of a homeless man's shaving ritual outside Union Station. He is clean and charming and resourceful in setting up his outdoor toilette. She lugged two cameras, a Rolleiflex using two-and-a-quarter-by-two-and-a-quarter-inch film, and her studio Graflex with glass plates. She hoped to rely on the lighter Rolleiflex in her street photography, but she still found its smaller size frustrating. If she could have managed it, she said, she would have taken an eight-by-ten camera. (Later, when she had a car and an assistant, she preferred to carry three cameras.)

She participated in one fleeting attempt at a collective project. In October 1933 a group of photographers came together to produce activist photography in an organized fashion. Calling themselves the PhotoCommontors (there is no record of what they meant by this term, but I translate it as photographic commentators), they included Lange, Consuelo Kanaga, Willard Van Dyke, Otto Hagel and Hansel Mieth, and Maynard Dixon, who occasionally did some photography. They organized an exhibit of socially relevant photography, but the show closed after just one day, due to American Legion pressure.[40]


AS LANGE WAS tuning in to politics, the intensity of California activism increased exponentially. The turmoil had a spiraling relation to the New Deal: grassroots social movements were responding not only to Depression hardship but also to increased aspirations produced by Roosevelt and his administration, even as these movements sharply challenged the Roosevelt administration. The New Deal benefited California little in comparison to other parts of the country, largely because California remained so agricultural. Through their congressmen and senators, California's big growers, as well as southern plantation owners, got farmworkers excluded from most New Deal legislation, such as the National Labor Relations Act, which protected workers' rights to unionize in industry but not in agriculture. Outside of emergency relief, federal programs in California mainly had the effect of shoring up employers, while doing nothing to get them to share federal aid with workers or the unemployed.

Two statewide political campaigns encouraged political participation. In 1934 Dr. Francis Townsend of Los Angeles led a campaign for federal old-age pensions of two hundred dollars a month for retired people; the plan would benefit everyone, because mandatory retirement would open jobs for younger people, and the requirement that recipients had to spend the entire two hundred dollars each month would stimulate the economy. Townsend's tens of millions of followers constituted a major force in bringing about passage of the Social Security Act. At the same time, the novelist Upton Sinclair inspired the End Poverty in California (EPIC) plan, similar in impetus but more complex and realistic. EPIC would have cut taxes for the poor and middle class and raised them for the rich, acquired unused farms and factories and put the unemployed to work in them, and offered pensions of fifty dollars a month for the elderly, the disabled, and widows with children. Sinclair came close to being elected governor in 1934, supported by most of Dorothea's friends but defeated by a major corporate offensive and one of the most negative, dirtiest campaigns in American history up until that time. Still, Sinclair's near miss added to the sense of possibility that imbued California's atmosphere.

Affected by all this, Lange grew bolder yet, although in these years she still thought that this impulse was something she had to "get out of her system." Instead of wandering she headed for the increasingly frequent and noisy organized protests. Large demonstrations became regular events for her. On May Day 1933, she set herself a specific challenge: ". . . go down there . . . photograph this thing . . . see if I can just grab a hunk of lightning."[41] She set herself a time limit—she would spend no more than twenty-four hours, including time for developing and printing. She had to photograph in a driving rain. The demonstrators demanded freedom for labor leader Tom Mooney, in prison since 1916 for allegedly blowing up a high-voltage tower in support of a streetcar workers' strike. In a campaign reminiscent of that for Sacco and Vanzetti, notables throughout the world—Samuel Gompers, George Bernard Shaw, John Dewey, and Carl Sandburg, to name a very few—called for freeing Mooney. Most left-to-liberal San Franciscans believed he had been framed. (In 1920, a San Francisco police officer had confessed to the mayor that he had helped frame Mooney, but California's Republican governors refused Mooney a pardon.) Lange went to San Quentin to photograph him, portraying him polemically behind the bars of his cell, and one of these photographs appeared on a large poster published by the Tom Mooney Defense Committee.[42]

Did she catch the "hunk of lightning" she was after? Not yet. One photograph has been reproduced often, a police officer in front of demonstrators, his arms across his somewhat thick midriff, looking back disdainfully at the extremely well-dressed crowd carrying signs.[43] She made other pejorative images of policemen, often making fun of their corpulence; this was a left-wing cliché, not particularly thoughtful or illuminating.

Fifty-six of the photographs that Lange took on May Day 1934 have survived. None was of large crowds; she turned back to what she knew, portraits, or tried to make group portraits. But she could not individualize the demonstrators as she did her studio clients. The images at rallies sometimes exhibited striking, modernist composition: a man speaking at microphones, shot from below, almost silhouetted against a light sky; a speaker's head shown next to a star-shaped microphone almost as big as his head; a female speaker whose head is bisected by a mike. When we compare these to her thousands of pictures of the rural poor, they seem both less revealing and less flattering. The faces can appear grimacing, strident. Even when the crowd is cheering, the faces seem histrionic, unattractive. Lange's sympathy for the crowd appears mainly in images of listeners who are quiet and thoughtful, and they include black and Chinese men, children and teenagers. Sometimes she lets us see the signs they carry: DEMAND CASH RELIEF, DOWN WITH SALES TAX, TAX THE RICH FOR UNEMPLOYMENT INSURANCE. These are experimental, uncertain photographs, as she knew.

Soon a mass strike affected Lange deeply, at first by providing a photo opportunity and then by acquainting her with workers' grievances and California's corporate power structure. San Francisco was a port city, dominated by shipping. Even during the Depression, its eighty-two docks handled 250 vessels a day.[44] Beginning in the late 1880s, shipowners' associations had established hiring halls as a device for breaking union power among longshoremen. Every day longshoremen had to show up ("shape up") in the very early morning, in hopes they would be picked for a day's work. The picking was arbitrary and unregulated, so bribery and favoritism ruled. Longshoremen sometimes worked twenty-four to thirty-six hours consecutively, then went days or weeks without work. They had hoped that the New Deal's National Recovery Act, which set minimum standards for various industries, would help them, but it excluded the waterfront as well as agriculture. So the longshoremen struck, asking for nondiscriminatory hiring under union control, safer working conditions, and a raise from seventy-five cents to one dollar an hour, with $1.50 for overtime hours, as a way of spreading the work and checking overlong hours.

The silence of the docks—an eight-mile stretch—seemed to still the whole city. Soon the silence spread several thousand miles, as longshoremen closed down all West Coast ports from Seattle to San Diego from May through July 1934. When the companies hired strikebreakers, truck drivers and warehousemen supported the dockworkers by refusing to move freight to or from the docks. By July, the companies had convinced the mayor to send police to protect strikebreakers. Violence erupted, and on July 5, "Bloody Thursday," two strikers were killed and hundreds injured. The governor then sent the National Guard to occupy the waterfront. The strikers responded by calling a general strike of all San Francisco's workers. For a short time, the strike was so effective that it created a dual-power situation—that is, the unions' strike committee assumed some of the powers of the state, and many citizens recognized it as legitimate authority. The strike committee decided which service and emergency vehicles could move about. Union permits authorized certain businesses and institutions to remain open, in return for honoring union coupons given out to picketers entitling them to food, meals, and other necessities. There was a holiday mood: few streetcars or cars were in the streets, so pedestrians walked and crossed at will; the parks were crowded. The city was on vacation.

Strike opponents built hysteria by charging that Reds were taking over, and leaked the fabricated story that farmworkers were planning to strike in support of the dockers. Although there was no such rural-urban solidarity at the bottom, there was at the top, as growers joined San Francisco capitalists in organizing armed vigilante committees to attack strike supporters and intimidate the public.[45] The general strike petered out, and the dock strike went to arbitration, resulting in substantial union victory. The longshoremen got ninety-five cents an hour and $1.40 for overtime hours, as well as joint union/employer control of the hiring halls, with the union selecting the job dispatcher, who had the final word.

The strike strengthened San Francisco's progressives, and Dorothea's arts community was 100 percent pro-union. Maynard and Dorothea drove and walked around the waterfront, he with sketch pad and she with cameras.[46]

The down-and-out, despondent men in his paintings were replaced now by dogged picketers, sidewalk orators, and strikers whispering plans, beating scabs, and struggling with cops. But Lange's photographs of the strike are inert and marginal to the events. The dockers she photographed could have been anywhere anytime. Much of the action was so fast-moving and so violent that slow-moving Lange could not or would not get close. This was the territory of the new breed of adventurous photojournalists. She would never be able to make photographs of people in action that rivaled her photographs of people in contemplation. By now, her physical limitations were embedded in her photographic style, which was slow, contemplative, conversing rather than shouting, quiet rather than loud. Other limitations may be inherent in still photography. Chanting and yelling often render individual faces as distorted; historian Nicholas Natanson wrote (of another photographer), "an angry camera becomes a demeaning camera."[47]

The relative weakness of these activism photographs may also prefigure a political characteristic of Lange's documentary photography that would become apparent in the next years: sympathetic to progressive causes, Lange was nevertheless uncomfortable with social conflict or organized activism. Drawn to the inner complexity of individuals and the discipline of rendering it visible, she was also politically an individualist. Enraged by social injustice and admiring resistance to it, she conceived of resistance and the heroic primarily in individual terms. Without yet knowing each other, she and Paul Taylor, who would become her second husband and life partner, had a similar reaction to the longshore strike—supportive of the strikers' demands but eager for a settlement negotiated by impartial outsiders.

At the same time, the strike showed Lange something that would be reinforced by Taylor in later years: that prevention of conflict required alleviating the extreme inequality that was increasingly dividing Californians.

THERE WAS SOME family time in the midst of all this, but it was fragmented. Early in the summer of 1933, the Dixons all traveled to Utah. The boys were boarded out on weekdays with a Mormon family in Toquerville—it was as if Maynard and Dorothea were growing accustomed to being together without the kids, even when there was no pressing need to send them away. They told themselves once again that being without them would help to revive their intimacy.

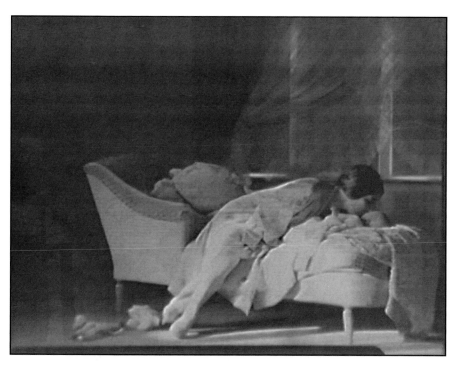

PLATE 1. MOTHER BENDING OVER CHILD, PROBABLY EARLY 1920S

PLATE 2. WICKMAN GIRL, 1932

PLATE 3. HOPIS ON A TRAIL TO PLAZA, 1920S

PLATE 4. SAN FRANCISCO, 1933

PLATE 5. SAN FRANCISCO, 1937

PLATE 6. PINAL COUNTY, ARIZONA, 1940

PLATE 7. EXETER, CALIFORNIA, 1936

PLATE 8. IMPERIAL VALLEY, 1935

PLATE 9. CALIPATRIA, CALIFORNIA, 1939

PLATE 10. NEAR BLYTHEVILLE, ARKANSAS, 1937

PLATE 11. NEAR DOUGLAS, GEORGIA, 1938

Plate 12. Mexican couple, location unknown, 1935

PLATE 13. NEAR WESTLEY, CALIFORNIA, 1939

PLATE 14.
COACHELLA VALLEY,
CALIFORNIA, 1935

PLATE 15.
WAKE COUNTY,
NORTH CAROLINA,
1939

PLATE 16. NEAR WAPATO, YAKIMA VALLEY, WASHINGTON, 1939

PLATE 17. CALIPATRIA, CALIFORNIA, 1939

PLATE 18. IMPERIAL VALLEY, CALIFORNIA, 1937

On weekends, the parents picked up the boys and they camped in a grove of cottonwoods in Zion National Park, a short walk from the river that cut through the canyon. The boys loved every bit of these weekends—hiking, swimming, fetching wood, cooking out, sleeping under the stars, learning bits of campcraft from their dad, watching him paint. (Maynard and the boys would return there in 1939, four years after the divorce—one last trip with dad.) Maynard painted even at night, fascinated by moonlight. Dan recalls being awakened one night by Maynard, who hissed, "Don't move," because a dozen or so rattlesnakes surrounded them, drawn to the campfire by which Maynard was painting. "We lay there, unmoving, heads covered, until the sun came up." (John Dixon suspects that over the years Dan's memory swelled the number of rattlers.)[48] Dorothea and Maynard visited the Boulder Dam construction site, where Dorothea's brother Martin had found construction work.[49] Dorothea made only a few photographs. Natural beauty no longer called out to her to be photographed.

The trip may have served its purpose—because thanks to Maynard's earnings at Boulder Dam, in early 1934 they rented a house again, at 2515 Gough Street at Vallejo, a fine Victorian house in the Cow Hollow district, a few blocks north of Lafayette Park, and brought the boys home. They were overjoyed. John recalled the family gathering in the evenings and listening to music on an old-fashioned Victrola with a crank. To Beethoven's "Turkish March," the boys would "prance and cavort around the room in our pajamas."[50] Now the Dixons economized differently: Dorothea gave up her studio and made the second floor of the house into a work space. She was trying to save her marriage and she thought Maynard couldn't survive without his separate studio, while she could. Later she would be somewhat critical of this and a series of other decisions like it—critical not because she had been suppressing her own work drive but because she thought her sacrifices had not been good for Maynard. "Perhaps the reason that I was never able to give Maynard an uncomfortable time, which he should have had, at some junctures, was that I never felt courageous enough. . . . I wasn't brave enough."[51]

Lack of bravery was not one of Lange's qualities. Her self-criticism indicates, rather, how hard she was on herself, and others, and what marriage meant to a woman at the time. Few women of the time would have felt anything but dread about a marital separation, let alone divorce, particularly when two children were involved. The problem for her was not just the financial and physical burden of single motherhood. It was also the stigma of divorce that prevailed at this time, a stigma that would have extended to the children. It was also guilt, a violation of her sense of virtue and responsibility. Then there was the fear of being an unmarried woman. Being Maynard Dixon's partner was part of the condition of her adulthood and her social standing. As her street photography developed, she became more aware of her ambition, and this made the fear worse, because being ambitious felt unwomanly. Being married confirmed her womanliness—her lovability. Thus, ironically, a professional, economically self-sufficient woman might experience a particularly intense reluctance to become unmarried.

Consciously or not, she feared becoming her mother. Joan's story could have been reassuring: She had found good jobs and had remarried well, to a pleasant man with money. But Dorothea's emotional memory of her parents' separation was that of an adolescent—a memory of desertion.

There was another equally deep set of feelings: love. She loved Maynard and she remained attracted to him. Despite the age difference—he was now fifty-nine and she was thirty-nine—his looks, his spirited unconventionality, his inner directedness, and his extraordinary competence remained *interesting* to her. He was never boring. Aging sapped some of his energy, of course. His lifelong asthma had produced emphysema. He needed oxygen frequently. He was now dependent on her, and that itself was a powerful pull on her loyalty. His diminished vitality, she might have assumed, meant that his days of wandering and womanizing were over.

In late summer 1934, after the marriage-mending trip to Utah and then the strike, Dorothea's mother Joan arrived from Hoboken, this time without her new husband.[52] Her diary recorded a harmonious family. They all met Joan at the station on the morning of Monday, August 6. "Would these fellas [Dan was now nine and John was six] kiss their Grandma? They would not," Joan wrote, "too embarrassed—they wriggled and squirmed until the grandma gave up the effort." Danny was carrying an unfinished gun cut out of a board, and John had a sword. Danny became nervous when they saw a police officer, perhaps influenced by his awareness of the strike violence, and went up to the officer to explain that these were not real weapons. They proudly escorted Joan to their new car. They then embarked on an active schedule: art exhibits, Coppa's for lunch, trips to the shore (probably Marin County) and to Fallen Leaf, again as guests of Anita Baldwin, where Maynard and the boys caught sole, which they roasted in paper. She saw a close family bound by love of art, she wrote.

They returned to San Francisco to await Martin, coming from his construction job at the Boulder Dam site. As always, he introduced a gay mood. Dorothea and the boys adored him. Dan remembers him as "an Apollo," absolutely gorgeous, six-one and slim, engaged in adventurous occupations as a seaman and a high-wire rigger—a man of the same timber as their father. Joan "spent the night talking and laughing and drinking with my two kids. Never knew Dorothy could be so funny." They socialized with Dorothea and Maynard's friends, visited wineries, and shopped at the Emporium and in Chinatown. They took the kids to a Disney movie, and afterward Danny acted out the show, to the great appreciation of his family. As soon as Martin left, the house and even the kids became subdued, Joan thought, which suggests how superficial or wishful was her perception of an untroubled family. She was sad to leave. To have one's children and grandchildren three thousand miles away in 1934 was to see them very rarely.

Soon after Joan left, Maynard became again sullen and withdrawn. He commented that he despised the "postcard scenery" of the "too arty" Lake Tahoe region, and they never returned to Fallen Leaf.[53] Whatever marital glue they had applied during the summer had not stuck. Dorothea was disappointed, though not surprised, that Maynard would not, could not share her desire to be involved in the great events taking place around them. His irritability burdened her, while his dependence made it hard to think of walking away from him. The greatest obstacle to her dream increasingly seemed to be the studio, and her responsibility as a breadwinner. She found herself longing, more every day, to be out in the city with her cameras, but could not do so without an income.

# 8

# Paul Schuster Taylor,
# Maverick Economist

The future second husband of San Francisco's star bohemian portrait photographer could hardly have been more different from her first. From a mischievous western painter dressed like a cowboy and enthralled with the mystique of Indians Lange went to a stiff and slightly ponderous suit-and-tie professor of economics. He was a most unsuitable partner for her, or so one would have predicted. But Taylor was no typical economist. Lange would imbibe his learning and his intellectual approach through an extraordinary partnership that lasted for thirty years, until her death, a partnership sharing qualities with some of the great ones, such as that of Franklin and Eleanor Roosevelt.

Dorothea's two husbands, along with their communities, drew her into new worlds. As Maynard had introduced her to a world of art and nature, so Paul would introduce her to a world of progressive social-justice concerns. In the second marriage, however, the influences were more mutual. Paul taught Dorothea how to think critically and systematically about society, economy, and environment. Dorothea taught Paul to see more acutely the human emotional and aesthetic experience of the political economy he studied. Both already possessed great capacities for patience, discipline, empathy and self-sacrifice, and mutual influence made these capacities grow stronger yet.

ALTHOUGH PAUL FOREVER revered small-farming culture and pioneer roots, he never lived on a farm. His ancestors—English (the Taylors) and German (the Schusters)—were archetypical sodbusters in Wisconsin, but their offspring became educated townsfolk.[1] Paul's mother, Rose Schuster, graduated from the University of Wisconsin in 1885 and became a biology teacher—no small achievement for a woman at that time. His father, Henry James Taylor, earned a law degree, argued before the U.S. Supreme Court, and got himself elected superintendent of schools in Madison's Dane County. When his political career became stymied in Wisconsin, he moved his family to Sioux City, Iowa, in 1887. Paul Schuster Taylor was born there on June 9, 1895, exactly two weeks after Dorothea's birth.

The young Paul grew up in a small city but experienced farm life on his uncle's 120 acres, where he once worked for six months, and through summer farm-labor jobs.[2] He remembered community warmth, egalitarian relations with the help, who ate voluminous meals with the family, and bartering of labor, and from these memories he created a romantic view of family farming that would shape his research and politics.[3] Even Sioux City in his day was a close and closed community of some forty thousand residents. The "diversity" in Sioux City consisted of Scandinavian settlers, white seasonal workers, and Catholics, whom Paul disdained, having been taught that Catholics were "authoritarians," while Congregationalists, like his family, thought for themselves. Paul remembers one "colored" family in town. Paul sang in the church choir, although without any particular religiosity. (As a grown man, he still liked to sing at family gatherings.) His mother home-schooled all four of her children through grade three—not because of any objection to the schools in Sioux City, which were fine, but as a way of continuing her own career.

Like Dorothea, Paul lost his father early, in 1902. His mother, Rose, like Joan Nutzhorn, coped well with widowhood. Unlike Dorothea, Paul was a top student. He was the senior class president in high school, then entered his parents' alma mater, the University of Wisconsin, in 1913, majoring in economics and law. There, too, faculty and fellow students recognized his ability, ambition, and discipline. The caption under his photograph in his junior yearbook was "I can and I will." Influential sociologist E.A. Ross became his hero and mentor. Fired from Stanford for advocating progressive reform, Ross also offended the conservative regents at Wisconsin by encouraging students to listen to Emma Goldman when she came to speak on campus. Paul studied economics under John R. Commons and Richard T. Ely, famous Progressive-era scholars who rejected the ideology that markets are a natural phenomenon and analyzed them instead as arrangements constructed and managed by man-made institutions—notably, governments. This approach, institutional economics, differed from neoclassical economics, which treats the individual, motivated by self-interest, as the unit of economic decision making; it was, instead, an approach that included social and historical analysis, and Paul Taylor never strayed from it.

After graduating in 1917, Taylor enlisted in the Marine Corps as a captain. He commanded a platoon at Bois de Belleau, site of the heaviest American casualties—9,777—in the history of the marines. In the midst of a murderous and futile struggle to take Belleau Wood, on June 13, 1918, the Germans launched a mustard-gas bombardment (all the adversaries were using gas by this time). Mustard was the most lethal of all the gases, and it took twelve hours for the symptoms of the poison to manifest themselves: blistered skin, vomiting, internal bleeding, the stripping of the mucous membrane from the bronchial tubes. Nine hundred men died of this gas in that one battle. Taylor gave his gas mask to a wounded man and was badly injured as a result. He spent three and a half months in a French military hospital recuperating his bronchia and lungs, but his voice and larynx would never completely recover, and he lost the greater part of his sense of smell.[4] Although he was awarded a Purple Heart, his efforts to get his recurrent bronchitis labeled war-related so that he could claim VA medical benefits were in vain.[5] Yet his pride in having been a marine never flagged.[6]

When Taylor returned to the States, he enrolled at Columbia for graduate work. But his injuries still plagued him and a doctor advised him to protect his throat by avoiding cold weather; this sent him from Columbia to the University of California at Berkeley and to his career as a scholar of the West. He completed a Ph.D. in record time and was appointed to the Berkeley economics faculty in 1922. He grew interested in agricultural labor in California and the Southwest and dreamed of complementing Commons's renowned history of industrial labor with a history of agricultural labor.

After four years of teaching, frustrated because he could find no funding for his research, a lucky coincidence launched his career.[7] The great Progressive sociologist Edith Abbott, dean of the most prestigious social-work school in the United States, the University of Chicago's School of Social Service

Administration, happened to stop in Berkeley, accompanied by her sister Grace Abbott, head of the Children's Bureau in the U.S. Department of Labor, and Sophonisba Breckenridge, distinguished senior professor at the Chicago school. The three most distinguished female social scientists in the country, they were veterans of Hull House, the Chicago settlement house opened by Jane Addams, whose residents had developed the social survey method start-ing in the 1890s. They represented the most advanced sector of Progressive social science and reform in the 1920s. It was a coincidence that Paul Taylor met them, but hardly coincidental that this son of a forceful mother and the future husband of two ambitious women was chosen by and attracted to the human dynamo Edith Abbott.

As it happened, Edith Abbott, then directing a Social Science Research Council study of migration, was looking for someone to undertake a study of the rapidly increasing Mexican migration to the United States. Since the Mexicans worked mainly in agriculture, the project was a fit for Taylor. Mexi-can migration was a controversial subject in California at the time, with anti-immigrant nativism confronting the big growers' insistence that they could not produce food without these cheap workers, but Taylor's mentors had taught him that good work might produce opposition. Within weeks after Edith Abbott's visit, at the beginning of the 1927 winter quarter, he was on leave from the university and in the field, his salary paid by the SSRC.

NO ONE IN the United States had studied Mexican immigrants or Mexican Americans at the time, so Taylor's research began with basics. He audited an undergraduate Spanish class, which indicates that from the beginning he planned to conduct interviews as well as collect data. Even more unusual among economists, he decided to make photographs.[8] He bought a new Kodak pocket camera, loaded up his 1924 Dodge, and set out. As would always be his practice, Taylor prepared for field research carefully, collecting available data and gathering letters of introduction from influential people. Nevertheless, his early mistakes show how little was known about Mexican Americans. He did not even know where to find the Mexicans. Someone told him to try Napa, but when he arrived there, he learned that February was too early for farmwork that far north; turning south to Merced and Madera, he learned that he got better interviews with farmworkers in cafés, bars, pool halls, and barbershops than in the fields. He quickly learned that California's

8.1. PAUL TAYLOR INTERVIEWING, PROBABLY 1935, *by Dorothea Lange*

racial segregation could be as extreme as Mississippi's.[9] He collected *corridos*, Mexican storytelling ballads that often contained social commentary. He studied the workings of Texas's white primary.[10]

To consider Taylor's research methods is to begin to understand his compatibility with Dorothea Lange. When he first tried to interview farmworkers, most would not speak with him. He looked and sounded very gringo although his Spanish fluency grew rapidly (in this period, few of these workers knew much English). By trial and error he worked out an unthreatening way to introduce himself, a method that Lange would later emulate. He would approach with a neutral question, such as "How far to the next town?" or "Where can I find gas?" then gradually add questions about what work was available and for how long, working conditions, wages, and housing. The subjects would, of course, want to know why he was asking so many questions. He learned not to say that he was a professor with a research grant, but simply "I'm a teacher," a category that evoked respect without being intimidating. At first his notebook remained in his pocket (for this reason he only used small ones) until the informant gave a concrete answer; then he would say, "Do you mind if I write this down? I have trouble remembering." Unfailingly polite, the Mexicans would say no, and from then on Taylor wrote constantly and speedily, developing a quick shorthand. After leaving the interview, he would sit in his car and write out the interview more fully before his memory of it faded. He became anthropologist, ethnographer, and labor historian as well as economist. Refusing to see these workers as just another production cost, or as members of a homogeneous proletariat, he wanted to understand their aspirations and decisions as individuals with a culture no less honorable than that of their employers.

He also made photographs. "No amount or quality of words could alone convey what the situation was that I was studying. It [photography] was another language, if you will." He would pull down the shades in a room in his Berkeley house and turn it into a darkroom at night. None of his pictures was particularly striking, but each contained a great deal of information. The photographs contained *facts,* Taylor thought. Even more important, they *proved* facts that might otherwise be doubted.

In such unconventional research, Taylor was resisting the impoverishment of economics as it became an abstract, nonempirical, model-building science. He was searching for an economic scholarship that explained human economic lives. This approach reflected his Wisconsin education: a humanistic approach to social science and a fusion of scholarship with commitment to reform. Still, in his use of interviews he went beyond Commons-school economics, toward a distinctive, ethnographic method. Defending that method, he later remarked, "You free yourself from some responsibilities if you can reduce people to numbers."[11]

Like his university mentors, like his sponsor Edith Abbott, and like most social scientists of the Progressive era, Taylor never believed that research integrity required assuming a disinterested perspective. On the contrary, he thought the point of social research was to make things better, and he soon became an advocate for several social-justice campaigns. This sense of responsibility showed itself in an early personal kindness when he met Mercedes Durán, a young Mexican-American woman who impressed him with her potential. Uncharacteristically for a scholar committed to large-scale reform rather than charity, he paid to send her to college. Starting in 1929, she sent him letters from the University of Northern Colorado, written in the beautiful script of someone who had studied penmanship in school; in perfect English, she thanked him profusely and described her ups and downs, and she enclosed her report cards.[12] "One woman told me I could stay with her and when I told her I was Spanish she changed her mind." She experienced conflicts typical of the upwardly mobile: "While I was home the older people weren't very nice to me . . . told grandmother that I was foolish. . . . They all think I'll marry a beet worker. . . . But the young folks were eager to know about college." She was asked to speak at her former high school where, she wrote, "The American [*sic*] people treated me so differently; they acted as if I were a wonderful person they had just discovered. . . . I couldn't realize it was poor Spanish me." The letters form a cameo of the consciousness of a young Mexican American: She called herself "Spanish," as was the custom in the region, to distinguish herself from the migrant Mexican farmworkers, yet referred to them as her own people and called the Anglos "American," a synonym for *white* in the Southwest. Taylor never spoke publicly about this act of charity, nor did either of his wives seem aware of it.

CALIFORNIA AGRICULTURE WAS not farming as Taylor knew it. Frank Norris compared it to mining—extraction, with no concern for long-term consequences: The first yields of wheat were forty to fifty bushels per acre, then dropped to ten or twelve bushels. "When at last, the land . . . would refuse to yield, they would invest their money in something else. . . ."[13] It was also industrial—that is, mass production, with a labor force organized like that in a factory. California agriculture was never dominated by family farms. Most farmworkers roamed the state, harvesting one crop and then another as each ripened. Even stranger to a midwesterner, they were farming a desert. California agriculture required vast amounts of money, construction, and politicking to buy or steal vast quantities of water from elsewhere.

Absentee landlords and giant corporations owned most of California's farmland. The biggest "farmer" in California was the Bank of America.[14] These large growers organized combinations to further their control, winning tax breaks, exemptions from antitrust prosecutions, and tariffs protecting them against foreign agricultural imports. Their biggest problem could not be solved by government alone, however. A fundamental, irreducible difficulty for large agribusinesses was the need for huge inputs of workers for short spells of time, while for most of the year only a tiny fraction of the labor force was needed. For example, in 1935, California growers required 198,000 hands in September, but only 46,000 in January. In fruit, the imbalance was twice as bad: 130,000 needed at peak, 16,000 at trough.[15] Thus temporary labor seemed essential. The growers, as John Steinbeck put it, wanted peons, but wanted to pay them only for the actual days worked. The problem was, to paraphrase Harry Hopkins, that the workers needed to eat all year long.

Growers organized to cope with this problem. They consolidated vertically, combining to own all the processes of growing and distributing agricultural products, from planting through harvesting, processing, packing, and selling.[16] They also organized horizontally, forming in 1926 the Agricultural Labor Bureau, which enabled them to allocate workers according to growers' needs, standardize wage rates, head off strikes, blacklist rebellious workers, and represent growers in dealings with government—to function, in short, as a monopolistic concern.[17] Growers benefited from a system in which California counties provided relief to farmworkers when there was no work for them, thus shifting a burden from employers to taxpayers,[18] but cut them off relief rolls when growers needed labor, so that workers had no bargaining power over wages.[19]

Making this setup still worse for farmworkers and better for owners was the subcontracting system. On most large farms, managers did not hire their own labor, but relied on subcontractors, usually of the same ethnic origin as the workers they recruited. On a large commercial truck farm, for example, a contractor would receive a rate per ton for topping and loading beets, or per acre for harvesting corn. Two layers of management thus extracted profit. Subcontractors might also operate commissaries and saloons where workers received credit, thus keeping them in debt from one payday to the next.[20] Subcontractors also freed growers from policing, hiring, or firing workers themselves.

Growers further held down wages by recruiting—through newspaper ads and leaflets—more labor than needed so as to set up competition for jobs; with jobs scarce, workers could not hold out for higher wages because there would always be others willing to accept the lower wages. Throughout the 1920s, growers typically recruited 40 percent more workers than they needed. A Texas cotton grower told Taylor, "no such thing as too many laborers."[21] Employers also induced workers to arrive *before* the crops were ready for harvest, to provide growers with just in-time labor—but they were not paid until picking began.

By the late 1920s Taylor had become the leading scholarly expert on western agriculture and the only one concerned with the labor force. He traced a seventy-five-year pattern of using foreigners in the fields. Recruiting from around the world was an early form of globalization, in which employers brought cheap labor to the United States instead of exporting jobs as they do today. The Chinese came at first on their own, attracted by discoveries of gold, and turned to farmwork when their prospecting did not pan out. The growers soon became active recruiters, convinced that only the Chinese were reliable: "'. . . nothing [else] can be ordered like a gang of Chinamen and require no further coaching.'"[22] When a wave of racism resulted in the Chinese Exclusion acts of 1882 and 1892, the growers brought in Japanese laborers. They lost their reputation as model workers when they began to save money and buy farmland themselves, often competing with Anglo growers. Another wave of racism stopped Japanese immigration by the 1920s, so Imperial Valley growers then imported Punjabis (called Hindus in California). When immigration quotas limited them, growers turned to Filipinos, who were exempt from a quota, since the Philippines had become a U.S. territory. Southern Europeans were recruited too, and soon there were two dozen nationalities in the California farm-labor force.

In the early twentieth century, growers often insisted that Mexicans were "'chronically indolent'" and would not do the work. Nevertheless, after about 1910, Mexicans became the core of southwestern farmworkers, and employers' appraisals of their qualities changed as a result: "'. . . a fellow easy to handle and very quiet in his living . . . takes his orders and follows them . . .'"; "'. . . the Mexican is not politically conscious, has no political ambitions and does not . . . aspire to dominate the political affairs of the community . . . does not intermarry with Americans. . . .'"[23] Like most immigrants to the United States, Mexicans did not intend to stay, but to earn in order to take money and goods home to their families. More were impelled northward (to Mexico's lost provinces—or México de afuera as they called it) to escape the violence of the Mexican Revolution. Meanwhile, irrigation allowed growers to expand the land under cultivation, thereby creating a seemingly bottomless demand for farm labor in California and Arizona. By 1920 Mexicans made up the majority of California's farmworkers. By the late 1920s there were 368,000 Mexicans, making up 84 percent of the agricultural labor force in Southern California and 56 percent in the San Joaquin Valley.[24]

Figures like these usually came from Taylor's research, as did information about how farmworkers lived. In 1928, a year of excellent harvests, Mexicans earned thirty-five cents an hour on average. Almost every family member was in the fields, old and young, and children very rarely attended school. They lived in shacks, tents, barracks, or *jacales*—huts made of mud, branches, and grasses—without relief from the heat. They drew water from streams, or wells dug by growers, often very close to privies or garbage dumps, so infectious disease was rampant and many children died. They were often paid with scrip, which was accepted only in overpriced company stores, where the quality of food was poor. Recruiters and growers frequently cheated them, promising one wage and then paying a lower one, or promising more days of work than were available, or simply shaving hours from their records. Workers lost wages because they had to carry picked produce to weighing stations and then wait in line to have it weighed. Workers might not know one day whether there would be work the next.

WHITES ONLY signs were common in California, both reflecting and ratcheting up racism. The Depression then produced a nativist hysteria that "aliens" were taking jobs and relief from "whites." The Immigration and Naturalization Service, responding to xenophobic pressure, implemented a "repatriation" program, in which a combination of economic pressure, intimidation, and forcible ejection sent about 300,000 Mexicans (some say 500,000, others 150,000) out of the country between January 1930 and April 1933. Many of those forced out were U.S. citizens.[25] As some Mexicans left, however, others came, because growers continued to employ them. Agribusiness spokesmen complained. One grower insisted, "If I do not get Mexicans to thin these beets and to hoe these beets and to top these beets, I am through with the beet business. The Hindu is worthless, the Filipino is nothing, and the white man will not do the work.' "[26]

Grower confidence in Mexican docility began to erode when, beginning in the 1920s, workers organized strikes. Taylor added strikes to his research topics. Western labor struggles earlier in the twentieth century had taken place primarily in mining and logging camps; during the Depression the battleground shifted to the fields. Nineteen-twenties farmworker unions tended to be local and thus easily crushed by sheriffs' deputies and growers' vigilantes. Then in 1933, some young Communist party organizers threw their energies and talents behind the farmworkers' efforts (which were, at best, disregarded by other unions, most of which supported deportation) and built the Cannery and Agricultural Workers Industrial Union, CAWIU, bringing together workers in lettuce, peas, potatoes, beets, tomatoes, chiles, cherries, strawberries, raspberries, grapes, peaches, pears, and, at the end of the year, citrus fruits—the entire contents of California's cornucopia. During 1933 and 1934, about 130,000 farmworkers participated in 140 strikes across a five-hundred-mile front.[27] The biggest strike erupted in cotton, which by the 1930s was California's most important agricultural product. The cotton region stretched 114 miles long and 30 to 40 miles wide, so it was no small crisis when fifteen thousand workers went on strike in 1933.[28] Growers first tried to prevent work- ers' access to food supplies, but that failed because sympathetic store owners provided credit and donated food; then the growers' men, armed and depu- tized, threatened violence, forced law-enforcement officials to arrest picketers, and ultimately shot at picketers, killing one and wounding others.[29]

The strikes became a war in the fields. The growers fought back with a new organization, Associated Farmers, drawing support from nearly all California's corporate powers—banks, railroads, utilities, and the Industrial Association, California's version of the National Association of Manufacturers. As John Steinbeck wrote sarcastically, "Associated Farmers, which presumes to speak for the farms of California and which is made up of such earth-stained toilers as chain banks, public utilities, railroad companies and those huge corporations called land companies . . ."[30] Associated Farmers wielded often insuperable political power in California. AF blacklisted pro-union workers, and created armed vigilante squads that threatened and beat workers, burned crosses next to workers' camps, evicted them, terrorized their families, and tried to starve them into submission.[31] Farmworkers, in turn, threatened and attacked scabs. In Azteca Hall, strike headquarters in Brawley, police and deputies tear-gassed a meeting, forcing participants out, and then beat them. Vigilantes attacked a mass strike meeting in Pixley, killing Delores Hernández and Delfino Dávila and wounding seven others. The *New York Times* labeled it civil war.[32] The vigilantes were acquitted and sixteen strikers were convicted for rioting. Some charged that the vigilantes and their employers were creating a fascist rural tyranny.[33]

Taylor continued his research on agricultural labor relations—three con- secutive years on leave from the university from 1927 to 1930, then six months in Mexico in 1931—at a cost: although he was tenured, the Berkeley economics department responded to his unconventional work by denying him promo- tions and salary increases. Moreover, his publication rate created resentment among some colleagues.[34] Soon Taylor made more dangerous enemies. The Bank of America had endowed the Giannini Foundation of Agricultural Eco- nomics at the university in 1930 with $1.5 million, an enormous gift for the time. The foundation worked closely with Department of Agriculture agents and the Farm Bureau Federation, the lobbying representative of big growers. The Giannini Foundation's head, the chancellor, and other university leaders met with the growers formally in the Agricultural Legislative Committee and informally in several elite men's clubs.[35] So neither this foundation nor the Agricultural School would support research on agricultural labor. Taylor's stream of publications impugning their exploitive labor policies and, later, the huge water subsidies they got naturally infuriated them. They would later declare him their enemy #1.[36] The growers, well represented among the university's regents, exerted great influence on the whole university system: as John Kenneth Galbraith, a graduate student at Berkeley in the 1930s, described the situation: ". . . the California Farm Bureau Federation and . . . the opulent and perpetually choleric baronage which comprised the Associated Farmers of California . . . told the Dean of the College of Agriculture and the director of Extension what they needed in the way of research and also conclusion. They were heard with attention, even respect. No one was ever told to shape his scholarly work accordingly; men were available who did it as a matter of course."[37] Luckily, Berkeley's provost, Monroe Deutsch, defended Taylor against critics who wanted him muzzled.[38]

Taylor got himself commissioned by the U.S. Senate to investigate the 1933 cotton strike, and produced a report with his graduate student and friend Clark Kerr. Its opening words tell us something of who Taylor had become: a humanist economist. "As the faulting of the earth exposes its strata and reveals its structure, so a social disturbance throws into bold relief the structure of society . . ." Rejecting outside-agitator theory, Taylor and Kerr insisted that the conflict arose from farmworkers' attempts to earn a living. They criticized the Communist party, judging it opportunist and manipulative toward workers, especially those of color, shifting its policy according to orders from above rather than demands from below. They insisted, however, that the Party organizers were not initiating, but responding to, even trying to catch up with, wildcat strikes initiated by the workers themselves.[39]

TAYLOR'S WORK HAD another cost, borne by his family. From this sketch of his life, a reader might not guess that he had a wife and three children. His fatherly absentee record was even worse than Maynard's: From 1927 to 1931 he was on the road most of the time, driving through the San Joaquin and Imperial valleys in California, into Colorado and Texas, to the Calumet region of Illinois and Indiana, and as far east as Bethlehem, Pennsylvania, and into Mexico on a Guggenheim Fellowship, following the migrant workers.

Paul had met his wife, Katharine Whiteside, at the University of Wisconsin. Born in Louisville, Kentucky, she was a pampered child. She later wrote a memoir that began, "No little princess could have had more truly loving and admiring attendants"—her mother and father, many doting relatives, and two black servants. Like Paul's mother, Katharine was a high achiever. At Wisconsin she earned straight A's, swam on a team, performed with a dance group, published poetry in a literary magazine, and rushed one of the "best" sororities. Like Paul she was socially aware and concerned. In 1917, she helped organize a Woman's Peace Committee that gathered two thousand signatures on a petition calling on the president to stay out of the war, and she stood up to being labeled "yellow" by her mother and "pro-German" by her sorority. But she did not get the recognition she wanted; she recalled her hurt when boyfriend Phil La Follette, son of Senator "Fighting Bob" La Follette and future governor of Wisconsin, said she got A's only because "she looks like a million dollars." Unlike Paul Taylor, but like most female students, she had no faculty mentors. Conflicted, she longed to be both an intellectual and a belle.

A cautionary word to readers is now required: almost everything I know about Katharine comes from her unpublished confessional memoir.[40] By the time she wrote it, she was a Jungian analyst with a deeply psychoanalytic view of her life and a national expert in progressive early-childhood and adolescent development. Her expertise may have made her insightful, or she may have reconstructed memories over time, as we all do, and both might be true. She was, without doubt, a self-dramatizing person—so be on guard, reader.

She was both flirtatious and sexually restrained. Paul gave her his fraternity pin before they ever kissed, and she believed firmly "that all caressing must be kept for a very serious declaration of love leading to marriage. . . ." (This was not a wildly unusual standard for a southern college girl at the time, but neither was it typical.) They did not even kiss good-bye when Paul went off to Marine Officers Training School in 1917. She followed Paul to Berkeley in 1921; they married and had what she described as a miserable honeymoon in Carmel: "We had agreed not to have complete intimacy until we were planning to have a baby. . . . The idea of birth control procedures was abhorrent to me." (There are strange contradictions in this prudishness: A few years later, she engaged in several affairs; her mother was a birth-control advocate.) By the end of the two weeks in Carmel, she recalled, referring to Paul's sexual frustration, he was eager to get back to his studies.

Evidently, she and Paul did soon have sexual relations, because she gave birth in 1922 to a daughter, named Katharine, and in 1925 to a son, named Ross, after E. A. Ross.[41] Paul's mother, Rose, and her sister Ethel moved to a Berkeley house nearby and Katharine had to contend with the woman who still commanded Paul's primary allegiance. But Katharine was no doormat. Lovely, chic, a diligent faculty wife with "a country-club style," according to Clark Kerr, she decorated the house well and invited the right people to dinner.[42] Like Dorothea Lange in these years, she was trying to do what a wife should. She also built a life for herself, studying childhood development and helping to start a Berkeley nursery school. She became a bit bohemian: professing free love, reading Bertrand Russell, and attending "natural" dancing classes for mothers and children given by a pupil of Isadora Duncan—a woman who lived with her family in a tent in a eucalyptus grove high in the Berkeley hills and dressed in tunics. Even in the 1920s, Berkeley had its counterculture.

Katharine developed longings for love outside marriage almost immediately upon moving to Berkeley. In her memoir, she confessed to frequent "crushes" on important men.[43] She relished her identity as a free woman and liked telling others about her affairs. In 1926, she had a brief affair with visiting anthropologist Bronislaw Malinowski. In 1927, she began an affair with Herbert Rowell Stolz, her child-development professor and head of a child development institute, and this relationship continued for seven years. Like Malinowski, he was married and had children. Both Katharine and Herbert told their spouses what was going on, attempting to create open marriages. There is no evidence of affairs on Paul's part.

Katharine's third child, Margot, born in 1929, was Herbert's, and it was no secret. Margot learned it herself while still quite young. Quite brutally, Paul's mother, Rose, refused to accept Margot as her grandchild and demanded that Margot be told about her biological father when she was eight—if Katharine or Paul wouldn't tell her, then Mother Rose would.[44] Katharine openly referred to Margot as her "love child," and Margot always knew that her mother "had many men."[45] Yet Paul treated her as his own.

Katharine and Dorothea shared some qualities: willfulness and a capacity for taking risks. Paul Taylor was consistently attracted to vivid and forceful women. But Katharine's aspirations were cramped. She herself and her daughter Margot, as an adult and a psychotherapist, offered the same diagnosis: Katharine Whiteside Taylor was an ambitious woman, thwarted by the gender and family conventions of the time, who sought her "destiny" through attachments to men.[46]

The Berkeley gossip network knew that the Taylors' marriage had to be rocky, and tended to blame Katharine exclusively; but Paul was no less remote, no less irresponsible as a parent, than Maynard. His incessant travel was both a cause and an effect of their friction, signaling both a desire to escape and a denial of his pain and humiliation. This denial, of anger but probably of longings, too, was so effective that falling for Dorothea took him completely by surprise.

# 9

# The Romance of Love,
# The Romance of the Cause

New love is more like a weed than a cultivated flower; it can sprout overnight, even in poor soil. Neither Paul nor Dorothea thought they were open to, let alone looking for, a new relationship when they met, never mind a love that would yield a thirty-year partnership in life and work. But their naturally good chemistry and their much-suppressed emotional longings were fertlized by a feeling for social justice. For Paul this had grown steadily over a decade; for Dorothea it arose from the nation's crisis. By 1935, President Roosevelt was admitting that the Depression was as bad as ever, and calling for permanent economic reform. In doing so, he called into being a sort of government-sponsored social movement.

IN 1934 PAUL TAYLOR learned that Willard Van Dyke exhibited socially engaged art at his 683 Brockhurst gallery in Oakland. Taylor became a frequent visitor there.[1] When he saw some stunning photographs by a woman whose name he didn't know, he got her phone number from Van Dyke and telephoned her to ask if he could use some in his article on the general strike. She asked about the fee. Taylor checked with the editor, who offered fifteen dollars, and Lange accepted. "She was cool. . . . There were no clues that she

9.1. DOROTHEA LANGE, CIRCA 1935,
*photographer unknown*

was suddenly overjoyed at this recognition by a professor whom she had never heard of. . . ."[2]

At her first meeting with Paul there was no spark, unlike her instantaneous attraction to Maynard. Taylor seemed like the professor he was, like a man who would have been uncomfortable with or even repelled by the goings-on at Coppa's. His interest in photography was instrumental: He conceived of it as a forensic technology, a way of documenting wrongdoing.

They fell in love by watching each other work. He was just beginning a new research project on the self-help cooperatives among the unemployed that had sprung up throughout California.[3] These Unemployed Exchange Associations, known as UXAs, were arising across the country and often grew into elaborate organizations. California had some 175 UXAs, with 100,000 members. The largest Bay Area "Hooverville," as shantytowns of the homeless were then called, was "Pipe City," near the railroad tracks by the Oakland waterfront, where hundreds lived in sections of sewer pipe that had never been laid because funding had disappeared. Led by Carl Rhodehamel, an unemployed cellist, composer, and orchestra conductor, Pipe City's down-and-out souls built an impressive UXA, with a labor force of six hundred by early 1933. They operated a foundry, machine shop, woodshop, garage, soap factory, print shop, food cannery, nursery and adult school, and produced goods for sale outside the co-op, with eighteen trucks—rebuilt from scrap parts—making deliveries. All work was credited with one hundred points an hour; there was no distinction between male and female, skilled or unskilled labor; objects were valued by approximating the labor time that went into making, finding, or buying them.[4]

While Taylor was studying the UXAs, Van Dyke approached him, expressing his desire to contribute.[5] So Taylor arranged a documentary photography study. He took five photographers—Van Dyke, his girlfriend Mary Jeanette Edwards, Preston Holder, Imogen Cunningham (all from the f/64 group), and Dorothea Lange—to Oroville, sixty-six miles north of Sacramento, where the Oakland group had established a sawmill.

As Taylor interviewed the workers, his stiffness seemed to disappear, and his interest in his subjects produced exchanges that were more like conversations than interviews. Lange was entranced.[6] The same thing happened to Taylor: he fell for her by watching her work. Her appearance was distinctly unconventional, he recalled—beret cocked sideways, very short hair, dressed in pants. "She just quietly went right to work . . . moved around inconspicuously" with her handheld Rolleiflex.[7] In fact, Lange was so intent on her work that he hardly conversed with her. But as soon as he saw the photographs, he grasped something about Lange's eye. The first photograph she made showed "the back of a man standing, resting on his axe as a man would rest on his cane, facing the forest . . . It is the expression of that man's back that is telling"—resting but feeling good about his labor, breathing in the beauty and smell of the pines.[8] And yet in many of these photographs her approach at this time was still quite like Imogen Cunningham's, moving in close to create modernist compositions. Her documentary style was not born as a sudden revelation.

Lange was not impressed by the UXA; she found it "sad and dreary and doomed." The worst part, she thought, was that the participants had so much hope.[9] She missed the social and political importance of what was going on: people cooperatively deploying their skills and ingenuity to save themselves, and in the process gaining other kinds of skills—organizational, citizenlike.

THESE MISUNDERSTANDINGS WOULD soon be corrected. As they continued to work together, Taylor educated her in the importance of participatory democracy. Under his tutelage, she became the author of the iconic images of the *rural* Depression, a most atypical employee of the Department of Agriculture. "I didn't know a mule from a tractor when I started," she recalled.[10] Maynard had shown her the mountains and desert; Dorothea took him into the slums and working-class neighborhoods; Paul now took Dorothea into the fields.

Taylor was critical of the New Deal's failure to offer anything to agricultural

9.2. DOROTHEA LANGE PHOTOGRAPH,
UNEMPLOYED COOPERATIVE,
OROVILLE, CALIFORNIA, 1935

workers, even though the rural Depression was deeper, more extensive, and more protracted than the urban. One of Roosevelt's campaign promises to the powerful American Farm Bureau Federation, dominated by large-scale growers, was to raise deflated farm prices. Only four days after his inauguration, his bill was introduced; two months later it was law. It paid farm owners to take land out of cultivation so as to allow scarcity to raise prices. As with most legislation, its impact depended on how it was administered, and the old guard dominated local Department of Agriculture representatives. The Agricultural Adjustment Administration's payments for crop reduction were supposed to be shared with tenants, who, in the South and Southwest, constituted 75 percent of all farmers. In practice, most owners not only refused to share payments but reduced production by discharging and evicting tenants, and then often used the AAA money to buy tractors which, in turn, displaced still more tenants. Taylor compared the AAA's impact to the enclosure movement in early-modern rural England, whereby landlords claimed and closed off land once treated as common fields.[11]

Early in 1935, Taylor secured another leave from the university to become field director of California's new Division of Rural Rehabilitation. Working well beyond his instructions, he became a leading advocate for farmworkers. At the same time, Secretary of Agriculture Henry Wallace, pushing a reform agenda in his department, appointed a progressive and controversial undersecretary, Rexford Tugwell, to work on behalf of poor farmers, including tenant farmers. When the department blocked Tugwell's attempts, Wallace gave him a new agency, the Resettlement Administration, later called the Farm Security Administration (FSA).[12] Taylor recognized an opportunity. The Department of Agriculture, fearful of antagonizing its constituency of big growers, had never had a labor division—its critics liked to point out that it knew how many hogs there were in the United States but not how many farmworkers.[13] Moreover, Agriculture Department bureaucrats looked at

9.3. Imogen Cunningham photograph, unemployed cooperative, Oroville, California, 1935

the country through an East Coast frame of reference—for example, Tugwell thought he could help poor farmers by moving them to better land, a nonstarter in California. The fact that California's farmworkers were overwhelmingly people of color, and unable to vote, made them even more invisible to the FSA.

Conditions were desperate, so Taylor moved quickly. He assembled a staff from among those he knew and those with the political influence he needed: Tom Vasey, one of his graduate students; a former University of Wisconsin classmate, Irving Wood; a former banker functioning as an "employer representative"; Edward Rowell, nephew of a university regent and editor of the *San Francisco Chronicle*; a young Mexican American woman to do interviews in Spanish;[14] and Lange.[15] When Taylor asked for a salary for a photographer, the state agency balked. So he hired her as a typist.[16]

They began to drive through California, often in her car, perhaps because Taylor's wife needed theirs. Lange's 1935 mileage-reimbursement requests track her routes: January 1 and 2, Indio, 154 miles; January 3, Indio to San Bernardino, 126 miles; January 4, San Bernardino to Fresno, 347 miles; January 5, Fresno to San Francisco, 183 miles. These trips took longer than they would today because there were no freeways, and by March the heat could stagger even a healthy young man, let alone the children and the elderly who also worked. In the summer, as harvesting peaked, her trips lengthened. She left San Francisco at 5:30 A.M. June 10 and returned on June 28 at 11:00 P.M. She had passed through this landscape before, on route to the desert or the Sierra Nevada, and she disliked it. Vast fields unbroken by trees or houses. Long straight furrows extending to the horizon on flat, dry land, with irrigation ditches and pumps bringing in muddy brown water. Workers moving slowly in groups along the rows, often bent over for thinning or picking, sometimes more upright as they hoed.

Describing her first experience of Taylor's work drive, an energy quite compatible with hers, her complaints thinly disguised her admiration: ". . . we started at six o'clock in the morning and he never thought that anybody should have anything to eat. . . . We discovered that this man didn't know anything about what people require in the way of food and drink and lodging. . . ." Lange's own moralism soon showed: "I also remember all these men ordering dinners that cost $1.75. I thought it was sheer self-indulgence. To work with migratory laborers and then go into a hotel and order a dinner that cost for one person $1.75 was inhuman."[17] Lange's own expense sheets requested, typically, $2.20 for three meals and $2 for a hotel.[18]

Taylor reassured Lange that it might take her awhile to get used to field work, and that she shouldn't worry if she didn't make a single photograph the first day. But she was a natural, Taylor said: ". . . she just quietly walked up to them with her camera. No problems in her relations with the pea-pickers, at all. It went on that way, always." Her comfort as a walker in the city soon made her equally comfortable in the fields and migrant camps. She also began, on her own initiative, to take down pithy quotations from her subjects. "She really had their phraseology, the essence of it," Taylor recalled. She got her subjects to explain "how *they* had been mentally diagnosing" their problems. She learned to carry a small loose-leaf notebook, like Taylor's, in which to take down what became her famous captions.[19] (In the future the notebook would become a symbol of their partnership, because they often shared one, passing it back and forth.) In other words, she immediately grasped the radical democratic edge of Taylor's research method, not just documenting problems from the point of view of an expert but trying, however limited the possibility, to hear the perspective of the farmworkers. She had no idea how unconventional these research methods were.

Lange's own technique evolved. She quickly lost interest in long shots that made the workers appear tiny and peripheral, as if mere accessories to the land,

and wanted to get close, so she had to trek into the fields. She tried a silent approach first. As Taylor described it, she just sauntered up to the people and looked around, then began to fiddle with her camera, and "if she saw that they objected, why she would close it up . . . wait until it appeared that they were used to her, they didn't mind. . . . Then she would take the photograph, sometimes talking with them, sometimes not talking with them. . . . She was naturally very skillful, not playing games, not maneuvering. . . ."[20] It seems odd that Taylor approved of this approach, because it is not transparently respectful. Moving in with a camera without a request that allows the subject to say "Don't take my picture" seems invasive, or, at a minimum, intrusive. Did the farmworkers feel they could say no to Lange? In any case, Lange soon shifted to introducing herself and what she was doing.

Taylor and Lange began to function as a team. Taylor would keep a conversation going while Lange photographed; some of her best photos were of people engaged with him. Taylor also ran interference with employers and overseers who were not happy with researchers interested in their workers. Visualizing, sometimes for the first time, what the scenes of labor and life among these migrants looked like to outsiders, employers realized that photography threatened their interests. Some employers followed them around, with the goal of intimidating workers. Others refused permission for the research group to enter the fields, but with such vast plantations, they could not effectively defend their perimeters.

Learning as fast as possible about farmworkers and about how to make photography under these conditions, Lange's mind, emotions, and body were stretched. She felt a touch of the farmworkers' exhaustion, aches, and distress. Their living conditions sometimes invaded her own body: the heat, the dust, the flies, the fleas, the smell. The solidarity of the team—including Paul—remained in her consciousness when she returned home. So she was tired and sometimes distracted when reunited with Maynard and the children, now ten and seven, who were, again, with foster parents. She was overjoyed to see her boys, but she could not always resist the pull of the darkroom, because without it she could not see what she had done.

TAYLOR DECIDED TO campaign to meet an urgent need: government-built camps to house migratory field laborers. He won over his boss, Harry Drobish, with his idea that decent camps for the migratory workers could pro-

9.4. IMPERIAL VALLEY, CALIFORNIA, 1937

vide the best starting point from which to move toward better hygiene, health care, education, and nutrition. Drobish's superiors turned them down flat, so Taylor asked the FSA for funding for between twenty to thirty camps, later escalating his request to forty-five. The FSA responded that camps would do nothing toward fundamental reform of agricultural labor relations and would amount to government subsidy of the large employers. Both claims were true, and Taylor and Drobish knew it, but to them, on the ground in California, the most immediate priority was alleviating suffering. So they wanted Taylor's survey and report to be maximally persuasive.

Lange had the breath knocked out of her by her first glimpses of farmworkers' living conditions, which were beneath anything she could previously have imagined. They slept in shoddy tents or lean-tos attached to trees or cars. As one farmworker recalled later, "our bedding was always damp, no beds. . . . There was no floor, just the ground. And when it rained, water would just come under and everything was muddy. . . . We had to walk stooped over because if our heads touched the canvas it would spring a leak." Another said, *"No teníamos estufa. No teníamos camas. Dormíamos nomás con cartónes . . .—y a veces en las calles durmiéndonos."* (We had no stove. We had no beds. We would sleep in boxes— and sometimes in the streets.)[21] There was no access to schools, medical care, or legal services. Ironically, fresh fruit and vegetables were beyond farmworkers' budgets and their diet consisted largely of beans and fried dough; there was no milk for the children. Malnutrition, dysentery, and hookworm were epidemic in the camps, and typhoid and scarlet fever were common. In 1936, 80 percent of migrant children had medical problems caused by malnutrition or poor hygiene and the infant mortality rate was high.

9.5. NEAR CALIPATRIA, 1937

Farmworkers often paid growers, typically from four to eight dollars a month, for a place to pitch a tent or park a jalopy. There would be well water from a pump, and, if they were lucky, a toilet and shower for every two to three hundred campers. Owners often hired armed men, frequently deputized by the local sheriff, to patrol the camps, report on suspicious activity (read: union organizing), and forcibly "restrain" resistant workers. At larger camps, they operated company stores, where workers could buy on credit, thus becoming trapped in an endless cycle of debt. For all these reasons many farmworkers preferred just to be near an irrigation ditch or river for water supply. They built shelters of canvas, tin, cardboard, and brush. Toilets were just holes in the ground or spots in the bushes, often dangerously near the water source. Even outside in the open air, the stench could be foul.

Between March and August 1935, working almost nonstop, Lange and Taylor produced five phototextual reports. They knew they had a window of opportunity and were well aware that Roosevelt's relief program could be ended at any time.[22] Lange's increasing responsibilities showed in the fact that the third report was filed as a memo from *her*, not Taylor, a ploy by Taylor to signal her essentialness to the enterprise.

The report did not resemble a government document, for it included not only photographs but also direct quotations from farmworkers. "Somethin' is radical wrong." "My children ain't raised decent like I was raised by my father." "I don't believe the President knows what's happening to us here. Here's all the facts but there's no way we can get it to him." One grower told her, "They want to sleep on the ground—they don't want beds."[23] Since they had to represent the migrant workers as hardworking and capable, Lange began writing some of her own captions: "They have built homes here out of nothing. They have planted trees and flowers. These flimsy shacks represent many a last stand to maintain self-respect." "One-legged man built his house himself."[24]

In making his case, Taylor confronted a policy contradiction that dogged federal relief endeavors everywhere. Relief was for *emergency* conditions only, but migrant farmworkers did not suffer from an emergency. They had lived under these conditions long before the Depression. For a large minority of workers, in fact, relief paid better than any wages they had previously gotten. Relief opponents accused the FERA and the WPA of violating their emergency mission, and, not coincidentally, making it difficult for big growers to get enough low-wage help. They were right. In the San Joaquin Valley, relief "created a de facto minimum wage. . . . Cotton workers making 25 to 30 cents an hour quit their jobs when they could receive 10 cents more per hour on Fresno relief."[25] This was not just a California phenomenon: in the South, relief investigators were "discovering" American poverty as if for the first time; an investigator in Puerto Rico concluded that *no one* there qualified for "emergency relief" because they were no worse off than before the Depression.[26]

TAYLOR SAW THAT relief policy maintained and even exacerbated racial inequalities. Two levels of aid—white and nonwhite—were standard. In San Antonio, for example, whites "needed" thirty-five dollars a month, the authorities figured, while twelve to fifteen dollars represented a fortune for Mexicans because, it was alleged, all they liked to eat anyway was beans, grease, and corn-meal.[27] In Los Angeles County, Anglo families received thirty dollars a month, Mexicans, twenty dollars (although the Mexican families were, on average, larger). When the WPA proposed building houses for Mexican farmworkers, local whites argued that the planned five-hundred-square-foot two-bedroom units with screened windows and doors were too good for the Mexicans.[28]

When Taylor began these investigations, he expected to focus on Mexican and Mexican American farmworkers, and Lange's photographs did this at first. Of the photographs of people in the first report, thirteen featured Mexicans or other people of color, and seven featured people who could possibly be white.[29] Even when her photographs do not indicate ethnicity, her captions did. For example, in Calexico, she copied down what one farmworker told her, "I don' like you make the picture because we have shame thees [sic] house."[30] Lange absorbed Taylor's antiracism but, paradoxically, her urban-ness strengthened it. Familiar with New York's Lower East Side Jews and San Francisco's cosmopolitanism, she neither feared nor disrespected but enjoyed racial diversity.

Only a month later, however, the story changed as Lange and Taylor detected an extraordinary national disaster: the dust bowl migration. No one spoke of a "dust bowl" yet. Taylor knew that "Okies" were entering California as early as 1933, as strikebreakers during the Mexican and Filipino–led cotton strike. In 1935 he realized that it was a mass migration, not a response to a strike-created employment opportunity, a migration that would equal the gold rush.[31] As his team drove eastward to investigate its source, he hired a gas station attendant at the Yuma bridge to provide a daily count of the migrants heading west. This research improvisation initiated what later became more sophisticated data collection: In the five months from June to November, 37,000 migrants entered California on that route; in the next three years, the number rose to 250,000 men (this figure omits women and children and probably Mexicans).[32] Lange, thrilled to be a pioneer investigator, tended in later years to magnify what they had witnessed at the time. "That was the beginning of the first day of the landslide that cut this continent . . . this shaking off of people from their own roots started with those big storms, and it was like a movement of the earth. . . ."[33]

She was right that these people were refugees, uprooted from generations-old farms and dispossessed of all but what they could wear or stuff into jerry-rigged jalopies. Seeking to counter their defamation, Lange and Taylor labeled them "pioneers," producing an article for *Survey Graphic* that they titled "Again the Covered Wagon." (See figure 16.1.) Anticipating Steinbeck's symbolism in *The Grapes of Wrath*, they imagined the flight in biblical terms, as an exodus of the oppressed seeking a promised land. Like runaway slaves, and like those African Americans who were part of the great migration to the North after World War I, the escapees were naïve about the land's promise—about how California would welcome them. (Yet only five years later the despised Okies became the sought-after mainstay of the West Coast defense industry, as Lange would document. The Mexican farmworkers had no such opportunity.)

So in their second report, Taylor delivered a slightly different message, revealing the limits of his antiracism. "Most of the refugees . . . are white Americans." The phrase "white Americans," sometimes "native Americans," appeared frequently in the reports thereafter. It underscored not only whiteness but also the construction of Mexicans as aliens, literally as well as

9.6. On the road between Phoenix and Yuma, Arizona, 1937

9.7. OIL CITY, OKLAHOMA, 1937

symbolically, even those who were citizens. Lange's photographs reflect this changed focus: Of the twenty-three images of people in the second report, only three were of Mexicans. In their desire to awaken the Department of Agriculture to the unprecedented mass migration, they implied that the situation of whites from Oklahoma and Texas was less acceptable than the conditions of Mexican farmworkers; that whites had a right to help that people of Mexican extraction did not. Taylor and Lange did not explicitly call for aid *because* these migrants were white. But the photographs in their context did. Their conscious use of white images to win support for their recommendations reflected an unconscious shock that even whites lived in such terrible conditions. And, of course, the Okies and Arkies sang that tune to Lange and Taylor: "We *did* live like white people." "We ain't no paupers. We hold ourselves to be white folks."[34] White folks dominated the rest of the five reports.

TAYLOR'S UNDERSTANDING OF his responsibility was such that after writing the reports, he campaigned for his recommendations, lobbying journalists, state officials, and university experts. The opposition from big growers and local officials was not only intense but devious, as negotiations with grower DiGiorgio showed. DiGiorgio offered to provide land, water, and electricity for a camp, gratis. In exchange, he wanted his people "to have a voice in deciding who shall be assigned [*sic*] to this camp . . . he does not want reds, Bolsheviks, or a red light district." He wanted, in other words, the feds to build permanent housing that he would inherit when federal camps ended. In that way, he could get at government expense a camp for his workers that he would control. Kern county officials wanted to accept this proposal, but Taylor's allies, familiar with the manipulation of anti-Communist hysteria to prevent farmworkers from organizing, rejected it.[35]

Dorothea eagerly joined Taylor's campaign. She and Maynard knew an editor at the *San Francisco News*, so she invited him and Taylor to dinner, and a week later he published an editorial supporting their recommendations.[36] Taylor was learning about her energy and assertiveness, and the more he learned, the more he grew attracted.

This dinner, and the fact that Maynard went along on several trips as late as June 1935,[37] suggests that nothing overtly romantic was yet happening between Paul and Dorothea—or else that they were not yet ready to own up to a new relationship. On these trips, Maynard was as horrified by what he saw as she was. "Hoovervilles, migrant farm labor, roadside camps; menace of vigilantes in background," he wrote. "Is this my country?"[38] If political differences alienated Maynard and Dorothea, it was because of her growing satisfaction in working for a cause. Maynard's soul was moved when he was alone in the western wilderness. Dorothea's and Paul's souls stirred as they talked to pickers in dusty fields under the baking sun. Sharing that experience generated emotional intimacy. Willard Van Dyke, who saw them together in this period, thought that there was "right away a kind of connection there . . . out of a feeling of, what kind of place is it that lets people be hungry?" Their emotions moved from pity to anger, spurred them, and conquered fatigue, and they recognized these feelings in each other. At the same time, Van Dyke understood, she had been in need of "validation for an approach that she was struggling with as far as this photography was concerned. And Paul gave it."[39]

By the end of the summer of 1935, Dorothea and Paul were making plans to divorce their spouses and marry. However unknown the timing of their relationship, its substance is clear: their attraction merged personal and political excitement. With Paul, Dorothea was entering the adventure of a lifetime. Magnetic attractions like this one are often found in social movements, where the emotions of camaraderie and dedication to a cause can fuse with personal passion. The intimacy developed in these situations— sexual or not—can run very deep. The two were not often alone together, but they were together fourteen to eighteen hours a day. Despite the discomforts of being on the road, and the anguish at witnessing, say, a slight seven-year-old boy dragging a huge cotton sack through the fields, the work was pleasurable, and the pleasure came from hope and from bonding with their *compañeros* of the road. Their sexual attraction soon became obvious. Willard Van Dyke said he had "never seen two people fall for each other the way they did."[40]

Despite their striking dissimilarities, Maynard and Paul both offered Dorothea a fatherlike partner. To the end of her life, she saw herself as a bit of an orphan. Maynard's fatherliness came from his twenty years' seniority and considerable fame. When she met him, she was almost a teenager, out on her first trip away from home, her dreams and aspirations fluid and volatile. He was experienced and self-confident, with multiple skills both masculine and feminine, seemingly fearless, surrounded by fascinating friends, unbound by conventions. Paul proved a different father. Also self-confident and seasoned, also inner-directed and quite willing to defy the standards of his profession, his fatherly reassurance of Dorothea came from solidity and from his absolute certainty in the rightness of what he was doing. Maynard's and Paul's different kinds of masculinity both spoke to that raw spot of anxiety in Dorothea about her ambition. Ambition desexed a woman, as they used to say in the nineteenth century, so an ambitious woman often felt a bigger than life-size need to be reassured that she was feminine and desirable. Both Dorothea's husbands provided this, but Paul celebrated her ambition and found it sexy.

Paul loved her madly. There is more evidence of his feelings than of hers because his letters to her have survived. His passion shows all the more clearly because his words reveal at the same time his formal, somewhat pompous way of speaking, intermittently entering and leaving the realm of the emotional. From a train headed to Washington late that summer of 1935, he wrote:

*Dorothea my dear:*

*If I needed something to make me realize the strength of the ties which draw me to you—this trip seems in a fair way to provide it. Why do I love you? For your complete honesty and integrity. For the clarity with which you see people . . . For the courage with which you face them. For the breadth and depth of your human understanding. For the fineness of your sympathy, which is extended in the same quality to all human beings low & high. (Any exceptions are based upon a sound discrimination).* [Imagine writing this in a love letter!] *For your conception of your own work—your superb achievement, and standards of the excellence and supreme artistry which you can achieve and the relation of your own work to the scientific and social objectives to which it can contribute. For the unalloyed fineness of your personal relations to those with whom you are most intimate. . . . For your gaiety, delicious sense of humor—perspective on one's deepest aspirations and foibles alike. . . .*

He scribbled at the very top, "Not the 'leave-on-the-desk' kind of a letter, is it?"[41] A day later it was, "My heart aches for you, Dorothea." However romantic, his understanding of who she was far surpassed Maynard's at the beginning of his relationship with her.

He signed himself "Pablo," because she had taken to calling him that when they were spending so much time speaking Spanish in the fields. He loved it because it was a lover's nickname. *"Muy buenas noches, mi chaparrito,"* he ended one letter.

Taylor's agenda in Washington had doubled. In addition to lobbying for support for the camps, he began maneuvering to get a photography job for Dorothea that would enable them to continue working in the field together. This put the upright and moralistic Taylor in an embarrassing position, but he was powerless to abandon either his personal or his political passion. He knew that Lange's photography would constitute a powerful tool for progressive reform, *and* he wanted to continue to travel and work in the field with her. He could not bear not to experience that again. He had to leap a high hurdle: married women were being excluded from federal government positions altogether, especially when their husbands were federal employees; and for the two of them to work in the very same program would make it yet more difficult to get that rule ignored or waived.[42] As Taylor was introducing Lange's work around the Department of Agriculture, to universal admiration, he had to confess to his allies in Washington that he was about to marry this photographer.[43]

But persistence was Paul's default approach. He showed her photographs to Roy Stryker, the head of a new rural photography project, who was ecstatic about them.[44] Artist Ben Shahn was present when this occurred and he never forgot the impact of the photographs: ". . . this was a revelation, what this woman was doing. . . . Roy's whole direction changed. . . ."[45] Stryker hired her immediately.[46]

Not even Lange's eloquent photographs persuaded the FSA to build camps for migrant workers, however. Instead, Taylor persuaded Lowry Nelson, San Francisco regional head of FERA, to travel with him to see the farmworkers' conditions for himself. Appalled, Nelson found an unallocated twenty thousand dollars authorized for California relief and got approval to use the money to build two camps.[47] Moving quickly so as to make a start before the growers had time to mount an opposition, Taylor chose sites and appointed Irving Wood to supervise construction and handle community relations—the tough job of pacifying and/or standing up to the growers.

Taylor's hopes for substantial dollar amounts to provide decent housing for all migrant farmworkers never materialized.[48] Tugwell, who had been resistant to the camp idea, went to California in October 1935 and visited the first two camps; commenting, "Well, it works," he allocated ten million dollars for the program, intended to be sufficient to house 150,000 to 200,000 farmworkers.[49] But the new regional FSA boss, Jonathan Garst, was never positive about the camps, the FSA itself was under constant political attack from the Right, and the project was again minimized. By mid-1936, the camp program was reformulated as a set of demonstration projects to serve as a model for some other entity to build. By November 1936, Tugwell was out of office. Ultimately, the FSA in California built only fifteen camps and three mobile camps which traveled by trailer following the harvest.[50]


HAVING DECIDED TO marry, Paul and Dorothea faced difficult tasks: telling their spouses and children, convincing Maynard and Katherine to secure divorces. Paul particularly dreaded telling his mother and aunt, Rose and

Ethel. He wrote to Dorothea with a progress report: "Spoke further to Mother and my sister, doing something along the lines we discussed. . . . I'm sure you will be received in such a way that time can do its work."[51] Paul urged Dorothea to move with him into the house they had rented without waiting for the divorces, pointing out that she could save on rent. "Why not collect the $100 for moving by Nov 1st? . . . Why go to Marge's—do you like her pajamas better?"[52] Dorothea said no. In an odd reversal, Paul was ready to defy the code of propriety, while she clung to the respectable. The divorces were outwardly amicable, but Maynard's journal, terse as always, shows that he was bereft.[53]

The Dixon children had no inkling of the impending separation. In hindsight Dan recalled one signal. "Our backyard had become a kind of playground for the neighborhood kids. We tore it up pretty badly. It was a disaster area—no flowers, no plants, just litter and untended weeds. That wasn't like Maynard and Dorothea. If things had been right for them, our yard would have been cared for." To announce their divorce, they summoned ten-year-old Daniel into their bedroom while they were naked in bed together (the way they always slept).[54] This was supposed to be reassuring. But Willard Van Dyke recalls Dorothea telling a different and more painful version of informing her older son: As she tucked Danny into bed, she explained what she was about to do, and Danny said, "'Well, you got what you wanted again, didn't you?'"[55]

Their friends reacted vehemently. Lange confided the news first to Hansel Mieth and Imogen Cunningham, no doubt expecting support, but both were censorious—a reaction that illustrates the limits of their social liberalism.[56] Just one year before, both Maynard and Dorothea had expressed disapproval when Roi Partridge told them that he planned to divorce Imogen; now divorcée Imogen sent a blistering letter telling Dorothea that she owed it to her children not to leave Maynard.[57] Dorothea and Maynard seemed to their friends an *institution*, a mooring in the insecure Depression world of their crowd. "It was like someone slashing a picture in half," Roger Sturtevant said.[58] Their friends also sensed how Maynard would suffer. They adored his irreverent, dramatic spirit—but they did not have to live with him. Some criticized Dorothea because she was leaving Maynard for a younger man, an interesting twist on the usual older man/younger woman liaisons. Dorothea was hurt by these reactions, but never wavered, any more than she had hesitated to marry Maynard in the face of disapproval. In the end, neither Dorothea nor Maynard lost friends.

The Taylors' breakup was less smooth. Katharine was taken by surprise. Just when she had planned to work on repairing her marriage, she wrote in her memoir, "Paul came home full of joy and explained he had developed a deep love for Dorothea Lange. . . . I really rejoiced and congratulated him." She was trying to honor her free-love ideology, but it collided with her actual emotions, so her account seems inauthentic. Devastated and furious, she claimed that Paul asked her to take Margot and sleep overnight at his "Mother's house for one night so he and Dorothea could have our house to themselves." (This is so out of character that it provokes doubt—though who can know the impera- tives of passion?) Katharine wrote that she complied (she did not mention the whereabouts of her other two children) but afterward became hysterical. In a handwritten insert to her memoir, she added, "Actually became psychotic." Paul called her doctor, she wrote, who sent her to a "sanitarium where I was kept solidly asleep for about 2 weeks." When she left the sanitarium, she appealed to a former lover, William Yandell Eliott, who took her to Inverness, in Marin County, to rest for four days.

When she got home, Paul asked for a divorce. Katharine cried but agreed.[59] She soon learned that her former lover Herbert Rowell Stolz was divorcing his wife and marrying another woman, which only added to her pain. Katharine stored the household goods and went to Carson City, Nevada, for six weeks— with Maynard Dixon. This was his idea, stemming from his "sympathy with his 'Pal o' Misery' "—just the kind of phrase Maynard would use to simultaneously express and hide his grief. In Carson City, Maynard and Katharine became lov- ers, and her memoir noted that his "entertaining stories, often salacious, and interesting incidents about his life in San Francisco's art colony" entertained her and helped her pass the time. She enjoyed watching him paint, and later he gave her a painting of a mountain they had both found beautiful.

Dorothea and Paul married on December 6, 1935, while on the road, a justice of the peace in Albuquerque officiating. They married in the morning and went back to work in the afternoon. As Paul put it, "And our work went on from there, together."[60] There was no honeymoon, but just as political and personal passion joined, so did work and pleasure. Yet the wedding was not really that matter-of-fact or casual. Dorothea spent sixty or seventy dollars (memories may have exaggerated the cost) on a made-to-order beige gabardine suit to get mar- ried in—a big expenditure for Dorothea at this time.[61] She wore, as always, the heavy Indian silver bracelet and her beret.

New lives for Dorothea and Paul required dismantling old ones, of course. There were bruising consequences. Dixon and Taylor children alike were placed out with other families while Paul and Dorothea were on the road and

Katharine was in Nevada with Maynard. Dan and John, at least, were placed together, but the Taylor children were each with a different family.[62] The children's experience could hardly have been more stressful. The "orphan" Dorothea was orphaning the Taylor children, in their view. The Dixon children, already living apart from their parents, felt what seemed to be the permanent dissolution of their home.

# IO

# Blending a Family

For the next thirty years, Dorothea and Paul would do everything possible together, so naturally they influenced each other. They made a marriage of love, commitment, respect, and mutual attraction. There was only one problem: Others were included in this journey. Had they been childless, their relationship might have been as near to ideal as marriages get.

Both Dorothea and Paul treated their ex-spouses with sensitivity and caring, and neither criticized their exes in front of the children. Paul wrote to Dorothea how much he appreciated her "attitude toward K during her last days in California."[1] Maynard and Paul played golf together at least once. Showing me a snapshot of Maynard and Paul sitting on the lawn of the children's school, John Dixon remarked, "This was a very civilized divorce."[2] Dorothea worked at promoting Maynard's work, and got Paul to encourage *Survey Graphic* to use Maynard as an illustrator.[3] Maynard even went on a few photographing and researching trips with Dorothea and Paul after they were a couple, but he admitted that it was not easy for him. On one such trip, Lange recorded, he "threw his hat violently on the ground saying this [amiability] doesn't work. Not when you still love the girl!"[4]

The divorces and remarriage were kept out of the Berkeley courts, but not out of its gossip. Paul particularly feared publicity, worried that the divorce would be used by the growers' organizations to smear him politically. He also found it hard to tell his colleagues. Yet the disapproval mainly smeared Dorothea—the marriage breaker, the husband stealer. Those who knew Paul Taylor could not imagine that he would have been the initiator, although those who knew about Katharine's affairs could sympathize.

Dorothea made a home for the blended family. She found a striking house built just after the 1906 earthquake at 2706 Virginia Street, a two-story redwood, tucked behind and above a larger house, approached by a narrow brick pathway. It contained only three small bedrooms—one for Dorothea and Paul, one for the three boys, one for the two girls—but its large sunken living room focused on a big stone fireplace. Designed by California's most renowned residential architect, Bernard Maybeck, its rustic quality made it cozy.⁵ Rooted in English cottages, the Maybeck style added motifs from California's Japanese and Spanish colonial influences, a sensibility that characterized upscale home building as earthquake refugees moved east across San Francisco Bay. He and his followers, early members of the Sierra Club, designed houses that expressed their conception of harmony with nature—a seemingly unlimited supply of cheap redwood helped—and marked Berkeley's residential landscape permanently. These houses were often dark inside, due to large overhanging soffits, an effect intensified by the natural wood floors, window sashes, and wall paneling, but the views from the windows brought the outside in. From the upper floor of the Virginia Street house you could see a canyon, the campus, and the Bay in the background. That fall of 1935, Dorothea scrubbed and furnished it so that they could move in immediately after their marriage and celebrate Christmas there—a holiday she cherished. She set up a darkroom in the unfinished basement.

She had six children and stepchildren now: Consie Dixon, from Maynard's first marriage, was twenty-five and on her own, but came to the Berkeley home occasionally, especially on holidays. Kathy Taylor was thirteen, Ross Taylor ten, and Margot Taylor just six; Dan Dixon was ten and John Dixon seven. These five children were all placed out with paid foster parents for the winter and spring of 1936. These placements disturb present-day parents even more than the earlier ones. Today's child development wisdom, and most people's common sense, consider the moment of a divorce as the worst possible moment to send children away from their parents. When children fear loss of parents, they need reassurance that their parents won't desert them and that the breakup is not their fault. The four parents involved in this story did not share today's psychological understanding of children's needs, not even Katharine, an expert in childhood development. Rather they assumed, as most early twentieth-century experts did, that children were resilient and adaptable so long as their physical care was good. Progressives in child development at the time were more concerned that children not be deprived of freedom to explore than worried about emotional security.

Today, parents with Dorothea's and Paul's work on the road would be likely to hire a full-time nanny to care for their children at home. Taylor's and Lange's combined salary of $5,800 (worth $87,000 in 2007) was not luxurious for a seven-person household, but they could have afforded a nanny, given the Depression's low wages. They did not choose that option. Live-in servants had been common in the upper-middle class into the very early twentieth century, but by the 1930s only the most elite lived that way. Lange's decision was not conflicted: she simply could not turn down the FSA opportunity. Even had she been able to return home every evening, her child-care options would have been limited. Careers were still uncommon among mothers—poor mothers, by contrast, had jobs, not careers.

So Paul and Dorothea agreed without second thoughts that the children would be placed with others; Maynard took no responsibility and expressed no opinion; Katharine simply announced her intention to head to New York for the year and left the children to Paul and Dorothea.

Where the children would go was a subject of research, discussion, and some vacillation. Dorothea had learned—probably from Katharine—about the Ojai Valley School, a progressive private boarding school located east of Santa Barbara, 350 miles from Berkeley. Paul remained entirely passive about the decision, telling Dorothea repeatedly that he trusted her entirely, was leaving the decision up to her, and had no opinion on the relative merits of boarding school and foster care. Light-headed with love, Paul could not focus on his children, and he had never been accustomed to taking much responsibility for them. He even proposed taking another leave and traveling with Dorothea for a full year.

Dorothea decided against the school in favor of foster care near Berkeley. She made only shorter trips that spring 1936 school semester, so that the children frequently came home to the new blended family on weekends. Ross Taylor and the Dixon boys went to live with a lawyer, Ted Gay, and his wife. The Gays ran a summer camp for kids in the Sierras, and were comfortable as foster parents. The girls were moved several times—none of the three Taylor siblings was placed with either of the other two.

Each of the children's four parents discussed the children's arrangements somewhat differently, but none of them objected. This is how Katharine saw it: "There were of course my children, whom I deeply loved, but whom I would have to leave for a year in order to find myself in a completely new way of life."[6] Like Dorothea, she spoke as if she had no choice. She went to New York to work on a degree in clinical psychology and developed, over the years, a distinguished career in child psychology.[7] She moved from place to place for her studies and her work, with the result that when her children were with her, they, too, were itinerant.[8]

Paul would never speak for the record on this decision. (In his oral history, he barely mentioned Katharine.) This is as personal as an interviewer could get him to be: "After we were married you mean? Well there were family situations to face. There were the children of two families. Yes, it was not altogether easy . . . to pull up stakes of two families and recreate relationships, but on the whole, it was done." He also felt it important that "when he married Dorothea they should be free to work out their relationship without any of the five children involved. . . ." This could be read as not very child-centered, or as an expression of how helplessly in love he was, or, less charitably, as irresponsibility for his children because he assumed that the mothers would make the arrangements. He thought it was *better* for the kids to be away from the new house most of the time because it allowed them to connect gradually.[9]

Dorothea also refused to accept responsibility for her choices, although her guilt leaked out. She reversed the causality, explaining that being separated from the children drove her to work.[10] She suggested to others that the children had gone to a friend's home, never mentioning that she and Paul paid virtual strangers to care for the children.[11] How did this behavior square with her acute sensitivity to the suffering of poor children? Perhaps the comparison made her own children's pain less significant. None of Lange's many interviewers dared press her on the foster-care issue. But her actions spoke loudly. Her drive to take on this adventure, to be free of domestic responsibilities, was as strong as Paul's.

Maynard never commented. He felt neither responsibility nor voice in the matter, and he likely did not even think about what would be good for the children. He never contributed child support—Dorothea and Paul supported all the children.

THE CHILDREN'S EMOTIONAL memories were not unanimous. Since the children were all in Berkeley that first year, they got to know one another on some weekends. None of them had an easy time. Blended families were new and strange. When John Dixon's girlfriend and then wife, Helen, first visited the household, she was amazed and perplexed by the family connections, having never heard of anything so complicated, she told me.

John Dixon's painful memories are vivid. He recalled driving with his mother in their station wagon onto the ferry, then onto the Berkeley pier (the Bay Bridge was not yet open), "crying and shouting, didn't want to go, didn't like this new man who was responsible for her leaving on these trips." Dan, in contrast to his anger about his first placement, in 1932, justified this one to me, remarking that Dorothea and Paul "broke the kids in pretty easy" to their new relationship. Dan and John both remembered friction with Ross, this stranger who had suddenly become a brother; John remembers Ross "jumping up and down on the bed waving a scimitar; a wild man." John has other painful memories: a case of boils, and being terrified when he missed the bus home from school.

The Dixon boys had lost a father. Maynard saw them occasionally, usually along with the Taylor children. In his own way, Maynard tried to minimize the divorce's pain for everyone, and since he had always traveled so much, the boys were not acutely conscious of missing him. Dorothea spoke of him easily and casually, and kept his butcher-block roll of drawing paper in a closet for children and grandchildren to use. Once, the boys had Thanksgiving in Maynard's studio, with their beloved eccentric uncle Harry St. John Dixon, who would sing Scottish songs. Mainly they saw their dad at Dorothea's grand holiday dinners, now crowded with Dixons, Taylors, Partridges, and often academics whom Paul was hosting. The Dixon boys did not always love these Berkeley gatherings. Not only was there tension about executing Dorothea's instructions just so, but Maynard could not be counted on to be polite. "No two women were ever more vulnerable to Maynard's wit," John recalled, than Paul's mother and her older sister, Ethel Rose. Dan described the latter as "still a maiden at fifty or more, and virginal in an upright, corseted way that made her an irresistible target. . . . He twitted them and taunted them and tormented them all the time we were there. . . . If I'd have been Paul, I think I might have punched him in the mouth."[12] Maynard took his sons on one summer camping trip, which they loved. John recounts a vivid memory of Maynard visiting them at the Gays'. As he was helping the boys make some arrows out of wooden shingles, he cut his left hand, the one he drew and painted with. John remembers the blood running down his fingers, and saying worriedly, "Are you okay, Dad, are you okay?" He was anxious about a father wounded by more than a cut to his hand.[13]

Maynard took up with another recently divorced artist, Edith Hamlin, and they soon married. A nurturing woman who subordinated her own painting to care for Maynard as his health declined, Edie became as much of a stepmother to the boys as she could, and they remember her fondly. Dorothea liked Edie, treated her warmly, and felt grateful for her care of Maynard. A few years later, Maynard and Edie moved to Tucson, for the sake of his emphysema, and because he was tired of being a public figure and of playing a theatrical role, Dan explained. They built themselves a log cabin at Mount Carmel, Utah, for the summers. He enjoyed his children but felt no need for regular contact. He wrote them occasional letters, with charming anecdotes and sketches.[14]

Ironically, the Taylor children also felt that they had lost a father. Paul treated the Taylor and Dixon children evenhandedly, but having always considered the children to be Katharine's responsibility, he instantly transferred that responsibility to Dorothea—as Maynard had done with Consie. All five children knew that he would never defend them against her. The result was a whole household of children who sometimes felt unparented. Paul's grandchild Dyanna's conclusion is grim: Paul was simply not focused on his children's well-being. Imogen Cunningham's son Rondal, who remembers the new blended family in their living room, paints a vivid picture of Paul's detachment: Ross playing the French horn, John the clarinet, Dan another instrument, and Paul obliviously writing a report in the midst of it; at other times they might be playing basketball in the living room while Paul napped, then woke and said, "Well, well" or "My, my," always doubling his words, and resumed his work. Dan Dixon characterized Paul's role even more critically: his and Dorothea's partnership was so strong that the children seemed like intruders.

Dorothea, by contrast, could fly into rages, as she had done with Consie. Margot's husband thought she had two personae, Jekyll and Hyde. Kathy, the eldest Taylor child, irritated Dorothea by dressing and behaving in a flirtatious, conventionally feminine way, dreaming of a career as actress or movie star—and also, perhaps, because she resembled Mother Rose in her looks and style. Once when Ross talked back to Dorothea, she slapped his face and said, you won't get insolent with me; yet it was Dorothea who bought him his first instrument, a bugle, and encouraged his formidable musical talent. (He would become the principal French horn player for the San Francisco Symphony Orchestra.) Dorothea worried about her temper and once confessed to her daughter-in-law Onnie that "sometimes I am possessed of the devil." It was not that the Taylor children felt Dorothea favored her own boys; it was just that Paul had ceded all parenting to her, and she could be unpredictably harsh.

Ross's behavior, if Dan's and John's account of it is accurate, signaled his anger. Ross's daughter Dyanna thinks he was his mother's favorite, Katharine's "golden prince"; Margot's husband thought it more accurate to say Ross was his mother's Parsifal, a hero unique and incomparable. He suffered deeply from being farmed out, and from the sense of abandonment by his father. After living with his mother in the second school year after the divorce, Ross asked to be allowed to go live with his father, and his mother allowed it. But he was bitterly disappointed, as once again he could get nothing from Paul, and his only real parent was Dorothea.

Margot became a distinguished psychotherapist, so her recollections were shaped by expertise. The youngest child, she had the fewest emotional resources. She found the "wrath of Dorothea" terrifying, and recalled how she "looked at you with snake eyes." Sixty years later, Margot recounted a bitter memory as if it were yesterday: Once, soon after the new blended family had formed, she was crying—she couldn't remember why—and wanted to be picked up and comforted. Dorothea said no. Margot went crying to Paul, and Dorothea said to her, "No, you won't get anywhere with that." To Paul, Dorothea said, "No, Paul, she has to do this on her own," and Paul complied. (Years later, Margot would come to understand the primal meaning of "on her own" for Dorothea.) Paul would not defy Dorothea, as he never defied his mother, and Margot concluded that if she defied her stepmother, she would be "cut off" from her father; Paul was both father and son to Dorothea, Margot thought, and Dorothea's role in that relationship was to be adored.

It is a sign of this family's complexity that despite these angry and painful memories, Margot felt that she had been Dorothea's favorite, and remembered that Dorothea could be loving, warm, and expressive toward the children. Mary Spivey, a friend of Margot's from junior high, remembered Margot's complaints about how her stepmother intruded, eclipsed whatever the child was interested in, and turned attention back to herself. Mary said that she "met the pain in Margot" before meeting Lange. Yet Mary adored going to Margot's house and experiencing Dorothea's warmth and charisma. "I felt I had come home," she said. Dorothea was always explaining things, something her own children found tedious, but Mary loved it because Dorothea had a way of expressing the feelings "that lay behind things." But those intense feelings for what lay "behind" fed Dorothea's need to control. Once, Mary was helping in the kitchen and picked up a ceramic serving dish to carry it to the dining room; Dorothea took it from her, saying, "Oh no, you must hold it this way to respect its shape."[15]

Paul lost his temper only once: Dan called his mother an old sow and Paul threw him down the stairs—could have killed him, Dan thought. Even if this incident became exaggerated in memory, the message Dan received was clear: Paul would tolerate no serious affront to Dorothea. When Dorothea first joined the Taylor family, she received, as had Paul's first wife, Katharine, a message not to defy Mother Rose. But Dorothea took on the challenge and won. After an initial standoff, according to Margot, it was not long before Dorothea had established her absolute supremacy. Paul visited his mother on his own once a week.

As Dan and John grew up, these tensions gave them a new view of their mother: authoritarian, the "magisterial lawmaker," in Dan's words. "Dictator Dot," they called her; ". . . she governed like a Bismarck,"[16] Dan wrote. There was a great deal of pressure to achieve. Margot told her friend Mary, you don't know what it's like to have both parents in Who's Who; she was fearful of not making Phi Beta Kappa.[17]

The children may have been noticing Dorothea's irascibility more as they got older, but the "devil" Dorothea felt inside her may have been gaining strength. The thrills of that year's developments did not dilute the stresses and pressures of running a house while meeting deadlines.

THE CONTRAST BETWEEN this domestic tyrant and her approach to photographic subjects is so great that at first it was difficult for me to integrate the two. Yet everyone who saw her at home described her as taking control, orchestrating every detail. Her daughter-in-law Helen Dixon described this with maximum charity. Extremely close to Dorothea, Helen loved her, took pride in being her friend, remained living on the Lange/Taylor property even after divorcing John Dixon, and nursed Dorothea as she died. Still, Helen recognized that Dorothea always had a plan and needed to orchestrate others into it.

The least obnoxious venue of this obsessive control was the house: it had to be spotless, and no one was allowed to move anything out of its place or to leave items on surfaces, as she could not bear clutter. Dorothea's intolerance for mess was, however, a modernist design sensibility, not a dirt phobia. She liked simple wooden furniture and not too much of it, preferring bare windows and wooden chairs or canvas director's chairs to upholstered chairs. She placed objects, art, and photographs sparingly and changed them frequently. Her purpose was to encourage looking and noticing, not to allow interiors to become too customary. Her rule was, never have anything in your house that you don't truly like to look at. You only need one set of dishes, she insisted; the best should be used every day.

Her impulse for simplicity was neither spartan nor withholding. She loved to shop, and preferred the interesting to the fashionable. She liked to stand out. Although she frequently rearranged her home, on her body she never strayed from the look she had created for herself in the 1920s, when her San Francisco social circle confirmed her taste for elegance through simplicity. There was one exception: she no longer felt it imperative to cover her lame leg. Moving into a more staid faculty community altered her style not at all. She had bobbed her hair in the twenties, as was fashionable, never grew it out again, but cut it gradually shorter and shorter. She continued wearing a beret, cocked far to one side so as to create an attention-getting asymmetry. She discovered ethnic clothes, mainly Mexican, long before they became fashionable in the 1940s: white embroidered blouses and long, full skirts. On the road, photographing, she wore work clothes: pants and shirts, and often kerchiefs on her head. She liked what she called "fine" things but did not measure their fineness by cost. In 1957 she attended the Academy Awards ceremony with her cousin, film star Hope Lange, who was nominated for Best Supporting Actress for *Peyton Place*; Dorothea crowed about having found a zebra-striped dress at Sears for twelve dollars, only to have people at the event gush, "Who is your designer?"

She was proud of her excellent cooking. She served meals with such spare elegance that Margot recalled them as Japanese tea ceremonies. The price of this fastidiousness was, of course, overworking herself. But she could also improvise. Margot was with her once when she dropped a whole turkey onto the floor. She picked it up, put it back on the platter, and winked at Margot, making it a secret just between them. Margot was delighted.

Dorothea's ritual became particularly elaborate and rigid on holidays; Dan called her "the Bonaparte of the holidays." Hers was a childhood ritual—her mother had also made grand holiday occasions. Christmas gatherings were especially spectacular, choreographed and performed identically each year, but each year adding new layers. Candles in white paper bags bordered the path to the door. Real candles in antique German candleholders burned on the Christmas tree, because this was her *grossmama*'s tradition. (Paul kept a fire extinguisher and buckets of sand at the ready.) She took down the photographs she kept posted on the long white wall of her work space and substituted holiday mementos: family pictures, a child's letter to Santa. Dorothea had a special Christmas outfit—an all white, delicate lace and cotton Mexican dress with very full sleeves, her usual heavy silver Navajo bracelet, and an equally heavy necklace she wore only occasionally. When Paul invited foreigners from the university, she asked them to wear their "traditional native costumes." (I cannot imagine these Korean economists or Egyptian agronomists complying, but perhaps their wives did.)

These were large gatherings, including Maynard and the Partridges, but also guests connected to Paul—sometimes thirty people. The groups grew still larger in the early 1950s, when the children's partners and their children began to arrive. Dorothea did all the cooking—no one else's dishes would do—and decorating, spending so much time that she typically did little photographic work between Thanksgiving and Christmas. There would be two turkeys or one turkey and a roast beef or one turkey and a ham, with many side dishes: creamed onions, yams, mashed potatoes, homemade rolls, vegetables, salad. Simple and earthy cooking, unpretentious but generous, and served with style—an inheritance from Joan. Often there were dueling carvers: Paul, cutting meticulous and thin slices; Martin at the other end of the long table, cutting big chunks—so the boys tried to sit at his end. After the meal came coffee Diablo, served in special cups reserved for this use. As the years went by, the holiday meals grew ever more scripted. "Thanksgiving was warm and wonderful," recalled daughter-in-law Onnie, "but it was Dorothea's show."

The music was also ritualized. Dorothea insisted on playing an old 78 recording of Madame Schumann-Heink singing "Stille Nacht," although family members complained that they could hear nothing but static, with a faint singing voice in the background. The blended family soon added its own songs. From Maynard came "Little Old Man As I Do Tell," the Taylors brought "When Cockle Shells Turn Silver Bells," and Ross liked "Rye Whiskey," also a Maynard favorite.[18] The family lore included codes, secret handshakes, and a nonsense lyric:

*Ve belong to a club vott's fine*
*The president's name is Finkelstein*
*Every night at a quarter to nine*
*Ve get together in a time vott's fine . . .*

It was pronounced with a German or Yiddish accent, and the first line was repeated often in family letters, as an expression of love. If it was anti-Semitic, that was not recognized by the family.

After supper, bells would sound outside and Santa Claus (Paul) would enter through a French door with his bag of presents, including oranges for all the children—oranges he had to fetch from Chinatown in San Francisco because Dorothea insisted that only these would do. He soon added his own rituals: At Thanksgiving he would read aloud Lincoln's original Thanksgiving proclamation, or Daniel Webster's comments on the two hundredth anniversary of the Pilgrims' landing: "The consequence . . . has been a great subdivision of the soil, and a great equality of condition, the true basis, most certainly, of a popular government."[19] (For Paul, there was no distance at all between his personal emotions and his political ones.) He would often add Maynard Dixon's irreverent poem "Death of a Pagan." That Dorothea and Paul had both lost fathers contributed, no doubt, to their mutual pleasure in the bonds of ritual. These occasions provided a structure in which he could express warmth and patriotism and paternalism. They were among the gifts Dorothea brought him.

All this togetherness made life more painful at times for the family member outside the "club vott's fine": Consie. When the blended family formed in 1935, Consie was becoming a political activist. She wrote for a progressive newspaper and supported the longshoremen's union, through which she met Dave Jenkins, a leader in that union. They became a couple and their daughter Rebecca (Becky) was born in 1937. After short stays in Taos, in Woodstock, and in the West Village in New York City, where they lived in a group household with other radicals and artists, she and Dave separated and she returned to San Francisco with Becky.[20] (Dave Jenkins went on to become an important San Francisco labor leader and political activist; had Dorothea's relationship with Consie been better, she would have continued to feel more connected to Bay Area Left politics.)

A loving but unstable mother, Consie was unable to provide emotional security for Becky—she could not keep a job for any length of time, and soon began drinking too much—repeating the pattern of her mother, Lillian Tobey, Maynard Dixon's first wife—and taking up with no-good men, in the opinion of the loyal John Collier, Jr., who rescued her from disasters several times.[21] She made several more short-lived marriages. In the 1940s and 1950s, Consie would have refused the Euclid Street holiday invitations, except for the fact that her daughter Becky loved the ritual, bustle, and warmth. Still, even young Becky felt "the dark cloud" that hung over Consie.[22] It is difficult to reach the core of this family tragedy, but it was probably constructed both by Dorothea and Consie: the stepmother did not extend her usual warmth and hospitality to Consie, and the stepdaughter could not accept what was offered her. But Dorothea held the power, and it is hard to understand her lasting emotional stinginess toward her stepdaughter. It is as if she were stuck in her 1920 jealousy of the girl's hold over her scintillating father.

DOROTHEA'S EMPHASIS ON family togetherness was partly compensatory, as she was on the road so much. It also fit her new location, however. At first Dorothea worried about leaving her beloved San Francisco, the arts community that had stimulated, sustained, and shaped her, and the European-style café life, to become a faculty wife in what must have seemed to her a suburban college town. As a California architect once wrote, "North Berkeley's artistic colony was a health-oriented one and . . . did not associate itself with San Francisco's brawling bohemia at Coppa's den."[23] To her own surprise, however, Dorothea soon learned to love Berkeley's sunnier weather, healthful living, spacious houses, and the benefits bestowed by a great university.

Berkeley was originally part of the approximately 45,000-acre Rancho San Antonio, granted to the Peralta family in 1820 by Spanish governor de Solá. Domingo Peralta built a home on a creek his family named Codornices, meaning "quail"—a creek next to which Lange and Taylor's second home would be located. No Anglos lived there until the gold rush, when the Peraltas sold them some land and then donated more for the first schoolhouse. Anglos started grabbing the land, however, through various deceptive strategems, including a fraudulent survey in the 1850s that stole seven thousand acres and the entire waterfront from Peralta. Ultimately, they bought the rest for $82,000. A small railroad line to the ferry, built at the turn of the twentieth century, made commuting to San Francisco easier, and in 1906 the great San Francisco earthquake sent many survivors across the Bay to settle.

When Lange moved to Berkeley in 1935, it was thriving. The Bay Bridge, completed in 1936, allowed fast travel to San Francisco for a toll of fifty cents. Berkeley spawned a large industrial area near the Bay, and the university enrolled about fifteen thousand students. To Dorothea, a place where you went everywhere in a car, where all the people were white, and where the aromas of Italian and Chinese food were hard to find was not a city. But during the New Deal it picked up other sources of energy. The WPA was stoking the construction industry, building a small amphitheater in Hinkel Park, the Berkeley Rose Garden just across from the Euclid Street house, the Aquatic Park, and the Berkeley Yacht Harbor. Civilian Conservation Corps boys built most of the vast Tilden Park's facilities, bushwhacked fire trails and hiking paths, and planted redwoods and Monterey Pines in the East Bay hills.[24] The university bubbled with activism, most of it left-wing. Historian Henry May recalled, "Campus political argument was carried on between New Dealers on one side and Marxists on the other."[25] The Taylor-Lange home became a site of animated discussions among faculty, visiting scholars, graduate students, California progressives, and agricultural experts. Dorothea listened, learned, and participated when not in the kitchen. Visitors noted that she did no small talk, but plunged into serious conversation. Graduate students in particular loved being there and found the atmosphere lively, relaxed, unsnobbish. Clark Kerr, who visited with Taylor during both his marriages, described Dorothea as informal, unconcerned with people's status, oblivious to fashion, the complete opposite of Katharine.[26] Walter Goldschmidt, who became a distinguished anthropologist, and his wife Gayl felt comfortable dropping in of an evening and inviting Paul and Dorothea to grad-student parties. Walter Goldschmidt lived with them when he taught for a term at Berkeley, and he saw their differences and the complexities of their connection. While Paul was "angry" at injustice, Dorothea had a spiritual approach, he said. "She was no radical, but a sentimental liberal, a flower child a generation before flower children were born. . . . She had a tough streak. . . . I admired it but I didn't like it." They arrived at the same opinions from different points of view, Goldschmidt noted, "two very genuine people . . . who really cared about the world . . . on the same wavelength."[27]

It is noticeable, however, that none of these guests mentioned the children.

# Part III

CREATING

DOCUMENTARY PHOTOGRAPHY

1935–1939

LANGE AT WORK, CIRCA 1935, *by Rondal Partridge*

# SCENE 3

"*I found a little office, tucked away, in a hot, muggy early summer, where nobody especially knew exactly what he was going to do. And this is no criticism because you walked into an atmosphere of a very special kind of freedom. That's the thing that is almost impossible to duplicate or find. Roy Stryker was a man with a hospitable mind. You know there is a word élan. There was something that I would understand better myself if it applied to one of us only. But it didn't. It caught. And it caught like it was contagious. What you were doing was important. You were important. Not in the way in an organizational chart, not that way at all. You had a responsibility. Not to those people in the office, but in general. As a person expands when he has an important thing to do. When you were out in the field you found your way, but never like a big-shot photographer, not as the big magazine boys do it now. We found our way in, slid in on the edges. The people who are garrulous and tell you everything, that's one kind of person, but the fellow who's hiding behind a tree, is the fellow that you'd better find out why. So often it's just sticking around, not swooping in and swooping out in a cloud of dust; sitting down on the ground with people, letting the children look at your camera with their dirty, grimy little hands, and putting their fingers on the lens, and you let them, because you know that if you will behave in a generous manner, you're very apt to receive it. I don't mean to say that I did that all the time, but I have done it, and I have asked for a drink of water and taken a long time to drink it, and I have told everything about myself long before I asked any question. 'What are you doing here?' they'd say. 'What do you want to take pictures of us for?' I've taken a long time to explain, and as truthfully as I could. They knew that you are telling the truth. Not that you could ever promise them anything, but it meant a lot that the government in Washington was aware enough even to send you out."*[1]

—*Dorothea Lange*

# 11

# Father Stryker and
# the Beloved Community

Between 1935 and 1939, Lange spent most of her working time—a time broken by several layoffs—making documentary photography for the Farm Security Administration. Their work represented at once the most advanced, farsighted dream of the New Deal and its most ahistorically nostalgic, with the result that it created a paean to the New Deal's most ineffective program. But this is not how it felt at the time. The FSA photography team was a "beloved community," to use a phrase from the southern civil rights movement of the early 1960s. Like family members, the photographers subordinated their individual careers for a time to a collective social-justice project at once patriotic and intimate. Also like families, there were disagreements and inequities. Yet everyone on the staff knew that they would seize an opportunity to do it again.

ROY STRYKER, HEAD of the FSA photography project, was another of Lange's "fathers." His own father, a radical Populist in Great Bend, Kansas, once interrupted the family prayers, shouting, "'Damn Wall Street, damn the railroads and goddamn Standard Oil.'"[1] After serving in World War I, he enrolled in Columbia University—as Taylor had—where he studied economics under Rexford Tugwell, who "set his mind afire." Like Lange, Stryker walked in the city. He saw poverty and discrimination, and he wanted to do something about it. As an adjunct instructor at Columbia, he took his students on "revolutionary field trips" into the city—to union meetings, printing plants, slaughterhouses, and slums. And he began collecting pictures that would allow his city students to learn about agriculture and rural life. Then Tugwell hired him to assemble a "Pictorial Sourcebook of American Agricultural History." Stryker became obsessive about collecting old pictures, his pockets always bulging with notes and references on three-by-five-inch slips of paper. The book never appeared, but the project grew into something much more important.

The FSA arose out of conflict within the Department of Agriculture.[2] Progressives in the Department were enraged that the Agricultural Adjustment Act of 1933 (discussed in chapter 9) ended up victimizing hundreds of thousands of farmworkers. The guru of these progressives was Rexford Tugwell, Stryker's former professor, a prolific author, and the charismatic undersecretary of Agriculture. He threatened to resign unless the department enforced sharing AAA benefits with tenants and sharecroppers.[3] At the same time, a storm of militant social protest movements, on both the Left and Right, made it harder for Roosevelt to stick to his conservative alliances. Tugwell did not get the progressive enforcement he wanted—on the contrary, liberals were purged from the Department of Agriculture—but he did get, on May 1, 1935, a new agency, the Resettlement Administration (RA), which was independent of the Department of Agriculture, established by presidential order. It was a "poor man's Department of Agriculture," and it could never have been inaugurated within the antidemocratic Department of Agriculture.[4] To head it, Tugwell chose a complete outsider: Will Alexander, a minister, president of Dillard University in New Orleans, and the leader of what there was of a white southern antiracist movement. There could hardly have been a more provocative appointment. As assistant administrator Tugwell appointed another progressive, C.B. Baldwin, a Henry Wallace loyalist. So from the moment of its birth, the RA was the target of anti-Roosevelt opposition.

The RA had at first no independent appropriation and had to hustle for funds from emergency relief programs, although the RA's whole premise was that rural poverty was not an emergency because it was chronic.[5] The progressive Agriculture Department network, Paul Taylor included, saw its task not as emergency relief but as a permanent democratization of land ownership and use, a policy that would be called "land reform" elsewhere.[6] Tugwell built his agency rapidly, enlarging it from twelve employees in April 1935 to sixteen thousand by the end of the year. Its main program, however—resettlement of the poorest farmers on better land and in suburban garden towns—required suitable land to move farmers onto, which could only have been obtained through buying or taking land from large plantations and ranches, and the RA had no authority to do this. Due to political attacks on "collectivist" alternatives, the FSA clung mainly to archaic family-farm and small-town projects. The RA also provided loans for modernization, grants in cases of natural disasters, and loans to producer and consumer cooperatives. But these programs developed only on a small scale, and any slight improvement in agricultural conditions was produced mainly by emergency relief.

Despite its weakness, the RA immediately evoked political attack from the Right, squeezing it in a political pincers: strong opposition yet little accomplishment. Tugwell resigned in November 1936 in order to free the agency from his taint as a leftist. The program was moved into the Department of Agriculture and renamed the Farm Security Administration the following year—a title whose vagueness was precisely the point. This move made the FSA literally surrounded by its enemies, protected only by the man at the top—Secretary of Agriculture Henry Wallace.

Despite opposition, the FSA managed some impressive initiatives. Its "home supervisors," for example, were supposed to advise farm women on nutrition, clothing, and hygiene. The supervision could be patronizing, but through the supervisors' reports back to the FSA, farm women tried to educate Washington about their problems—notably poor health, ranging from abscessed teeth to corneal ulcers to venereal disease to infant diarrhea, pellagra, and malaria.[7] The FSA then embarked on substantial medical-aid programs. It introduced group medical-care programs in some drought states, setting up nonprofit HMO-type corporations that hired physicians, dentists, and nurses. The FSA justified this program with the finding that poor health was a widespread cause of improverishment and, thus, of defaults on loans.[8] The field workers also recognized the inverse: that poverty caused ill health. In twenty-nine states, the FSA contracted with state medical associations to provide care to the rural poor.[9] Even more controversially, the FSA cooperated covertly with the Birth Control Federation of America—Margaret Sanger's organization—to provide contraceptive advice to its clients and to residents in migrant labor camps. "One FSA official put it this way: 'We are doing this service as emissaries of the Lord, if you please, and never as emissaries of Uncle

Sam, who does not officially know we are doing it.'" Migrant farmworkers were among the eager beneficiaries of this service.[10]

The most intense opposition targeted the FSA's very modest attempts to provide services to black as well as white farmers.[11] Growers complained that loans to blacks were "killing what little thrift and initiative our negroes had to start with," that even agreeing to meet with negroes "tended to grant them certain privileges which . . . make the [racial] situation more serious. . . ."[12] Powerful Senator Harry Byrd of Virginia was irate when he learned that the FSA was paying poll taxes for its southern clients. FSA administrator Baldwin responded that he was proud to do this: ". . . we took the position that a person couldn't be a good citizen without being a voter."[13]

On the whole, though, the FSA was forced to defer to the department's racism. Even racial liberal Will Alexander, head of the FSA, approved segregating not only FSA projects but even information about them—for example, issuing press releases about aid to black farmers only to the black press. The same principles guided the FSA's distribution of photographs. The first FSA traveling exhibit omitted all images of blacks except for one Lange portrait sanitized of its context and caption, and even this was objectionable to the Texas staff. A Grand Central Station mural composed of twenty FSA photographs by Ed Rosskam showed not one black face, although it was mounted by a black assistant.[14] Even when Florence Loeb Kellogg of the magazine *Survey Graphic* specifically asked the FSA for photographs showing racial diversity, she did not get them.[15] Such racism saturated New Deal agencies. Almost no government photography showed whites and blacks together.[16] Throughout the public arts projects, administrators told artists to observe southern racial codes.[17]

The photography project, intended as a minor appendage of the FSA's public-relations section, became, unexpectedly, its most influential activity. Tugwell established the project in 1935 to help neutralize or counteract the inevitable conservative attacks, and he hired his former student, Roy Stryker, to head it, encouraging him to "turn to new devices, the movie and the still picture and other things. . . ."[18] Many federal agencies were using photography to promote their work to the public. At first, Stryker ordered up images of land, machinery, crops, and especially land misuse and mismanagement, as well as pictures that promoted FSA programs.[19] It was only when he saw Lange's pictures, he said, that he realized that agriculture was more than "machines, homemade harrows and so on." He then began talking to his photographers about the "sociological implications" of what they saw.[20] However great Lange's influence, it would not have been absorbed had Stryker not been the creative, open-minded man he was. Lange thought he had a "hospitable mind."[21] His leadership created an extraordinary, eccentric, and capacious project: a public photographic record of America's rural life. It was extraordinary because of the quantity and quality of the photographs; eccentric because of its administrative location; capacious because Stryker included social and even political aspects of life as well as agriculture.

STRYKER'S PROJECT ALWAYS functioned on a shoestring. At peak in 1939, Stryker's staff totaled twenty-one. There were three female typist/stenographers; three male laboratory technicians; Ed Rosskam, hired to design publications and exhibits; five or more photographers; and six assorted employees with titles like draftsman and assistant photographer, all male. Stryker was a political appointee, but all the others had civil service ranks—CAF-9 for Rosskam, CAF-6 for the photographers, CAF-4 for the lab guys, down to CAF-1 for the most junior.[22] The annual budget at its simplest was:

| | |
|---|---|
| salaries | $ 38,460. |
| travel | 11,000. |
| procurements | 13,525. |
| salary increases due to reclassification | 3,540. |
| Total | $66,350.[23] |

Stryker knew that newspapers and magazines were publishing pictures as never before, and he set out to supply them, further kindling the print media's interest in photography. Journalists and photojournalists came to depend on FSA material; they would telephone to request specific images or drop by just to browse.[24]

Stryker spoke of his role with a modesty partly real and partly a pose: "I'm the guy who sat in the middle. I kept the store." In fact, his flexibility, seat-of-the-pants procedures, and lack of sophistication in photography were assets, because they left him open to new insights and initiatives and saved him from the arty and the elegant: ". . . it was so fortunate," he wrote, "that . . . we were some distance from the 'salons' of New York. . . ."[25]

Stryker did not look for extensive photographic skill when hiring. Asked how he picked photographers, Stryker responded that he looked for curiosity, a desire to know.[26] His first hire was a former student at Columbia, Arthur Rothstein, who became a fine technician and set up a decent darkroom—at his arrival, the Department of Agriculture's darkroom was so antiquated that it could not even handle film, only glass-plate negatives.[27] A New York Jew, the son of immigrants, Rothstein was some twenty years younger than Stryker. A product of New York's meritocratic high school system and a quintessential first-generation Jewish American, Rothstein was a "type" that Stryker had come to know and respect at Columbia. (He took an FSA job because he was discouraged by anti-Semitic rejections at medical schools.)[28] Stryker then took in journalist Carl Mydans, also Jewish, but he stayed at the FSA only a year, recruited away by *Life* magazine.

Then came two young artists, Walker Evans and Ben Shahn. Both were bestowed upon Stryker by an extraordinary woman whose influence on the photography project is little known. Ernestine Evans (not related to Walker) had been a writer and children's book editor, one of the first Americans to publish on Diego Rivera. Then she moved into a position at the FSA for which she was overqualified, not an atypical experience for women at the time. Well connected in international art circles, especially with documentary photographers and filmmakers, she gained a reputation as someone "always pioneering new ideas in the new agencies" of the New Deal. She got Walker Evans a significant photography assignment—taking the photographs for Carleton Beal's book on Cuba.[29] Evans came from a wealthy family, grew up with servants, attended boarding schools and Williams College, and then spent time in Paris. His elegance of style and manners won him influential friends, notably the arts philanthropist Lincoln Kirstein, and enabled him to move "with ease up and down the social ladder in New York."[30]

Evans shared a studio with his good friend Ben Shahn in a relationship that must have involved the attraction of opposites.[31] In their photography, Evans savored the stillness and formal beauty of vernacular architecture and lined faces, Shahn the fleeting, the marginal, taking a narrative approach, a possibility created by his fast Leica camera. An immigrant from Jewish Lithuania and a Leftist, Shahn was already a serious painter in the 1920s, having worked as an assistant to Diego Rivera on the Rockefeller Center murals (destroyed at Rockefeller's insistence because of their Red content). He, too, came to Stryker at Ernestine Evans's recommendation. When Shahn saw Lange's photographs for the first time, he was shaken by their power, thinking, this is fantastic and I want to do something like this.[32] So Stryker just put a camera in his hands and said, "Go." His technique was terrible, most of his early work was out of focus, or underexposed, or overexposed, but Stryker learned to love his eye and figured, absolutely correctly, that he would learn to use the camera wisely.[33]

Later more photographers joined the project, notably the multitalented Jack Delano, born Jacob Ovcharov in Kiev, a composer and artist as well as photographer; Russell Lee, who wanted to be a painter until he picked up a camera for the first time in 1935; Ed Rosskam, also a painter before becoming a photographer. Gordon Parks, the only nonwhite photographer on the team, arrived at the bitter end of the project. Parks was not actually hired by the agency: a Rosenwald Fund Fellowship supported him as an intern. (No other photographers, not even neophytes, had served as interns without salary.) Even then, Stryker was reluctant and had to be persuaded to take him in; the FSA darkroom workers didn't want to process film for him. Two other women were hired by Stryker: Marion Post Wolcott in 1938, Esther Bubley in 1942. So this was a white men's space that Lange entered, although she did not meet the others for a year and never met some of them, including Jack Delano.

Making the group even odder was the fact that most of them hailed from urban or immigrant backgrounds, and five of the eleven major photographers were Jews. Had it not been for the FSA project, some of them would have grav-itated toward the left-wing New York Photo League. Instead these urbanites featured rural folk as symbols of America. Moreover, because of their focus, the images and concept of the Depression in American minds were more rural than they would have been otherwise. This aberration contributed to the particular form of democratic populism that characterized New Deal political culture: imagining the nation and its citizens as rooted in farms and small towns. Thus even as FSA photography expanded the nation's sympathy for the needy and support for New Deal programs, it may also have hampered an understanding of the roots of the crisis. Because structural reform of Ameri-can agriculture failed, the Department of Agriculture's net impact on rural society was to drive several million more off the land and into urban poverty.

Lange began doing FSA work well before her appointment was official.[34] California state and California federal rural aid officials were so interlinked that Stryker, the local FSA representatives, the state relief people, and, for a time, Taylor pooled funds from several agencies to pay her. The arrangement made sense because several agencies were using her work, and Stryker was using Taylor's work.[35] In the spring and summer of 1935, Taylor and Lange were working on the reports for the California SERA. In September they went to see the first FSA camp at Marysville, north of Sacramento, which was being built in response to their reports. Sometimes she filed for reimbursement of expenses, sometimes he did.

She earned $2,300 yearly, more than twice the Depression's average full-time salary, which was then $1,137 a year; 77 percent of American workers earned less than she did, and the average female white professional at the time earned about $676 a year. Yet her salary was discriminatory. She earned what photographers Arthur Rothstein, Paul Carter, and Theodor Jung got. Yet Rothstein, just graduated from college, was twenty years younger than Lange, and his only photography experience was the Columbia University Camera Club; Carter, the son of the head of the FSA's Information Division, and Jung were both very young and Stryker fired them after less than a year because they did not show any aptitude. Mydans, twelve years younger than Lange, a journalist who had just discovered photography, earned $2,600; Walker Evans, eight years younger than Lange, was already in the public eye as a photographer, and he earned $3,000. Although Stryker had been bowled over by her photographs, he set wages in line with the ideology then justifying why women were paid less: that she was not responsible for a family and had a husband to support her. Her relation to Taylor further relieved Stryker of any responsibility to pay her equally. (That she had had no male breadwinner for the past fifteen years did not distinguish her from millions of other working women who had families to support.) Moreover, when the FSA budget tightened, Stryker viewed Lange as the employee who could most easily make do with less income.[36]

On the other hand, Lange's location in California brought her a few perks that the others did not have. Having closed her San Francisco studio, she had no darkroom. While she worked with Taylor for the state of California, he arranged for her to have access to a UC/Berkeley darkroom. Then she built a darkroom in the Virginia Street basement, and the FSA agreed to give her twenty-five dollars a month to cover water and electricity, insurance on her cameras, a small fraction of the rent, and a bit of depreciation compensation.

THESE PHOTOGRAPHERS MADE by one estimate 272,000 photographs, by another 100,000, and no one has been able to look at them all.[37] So much film, so many negatives and prints piled up around the office that no one could keep track. Like the best parts of the New Deal, the work was hectic, fluid, volatile—in a nice slip of the tongue, Lange called it "a state of foment."[38] But in retrospect, everyone in the shop considered the disorganization a necessary condition of their creativity.[39] Given the sense of urgency the Depression and New Deal engendered, it is not surprising that Stryker limited the proportion of his budget spent on archiving and record keeping.

Stryker was above all an educator, and through his respect for education and his insistence that it become an essential part of the FSA documentary project, he raised the level of what the photography revealed. He read widely and assigned readings to his staff, including the antiracist 1936 *Preface to Peasantry*, a study of the sharecropping system by southern white sociologist Arthur Raper, a professional friend of Paul Taylor who also spoke out against lynching.[40] Everyone in the Washington shop, including the clerical workers, was included in Stryker's educational requirements. "He used to give us homework," secretary Helen Wool recalled. "He told me to read Beard's *History of the United States* and if I didn't understand it then I wasn't ready for pictures. . . ."[41]

The educational process flowed through discussions and critiques of particular photographs, meetings with scholars and with those writing the WPA guides to individual states,[42] and Stryker's lectures. Carl Mydans remembered being assigned to go south and "'do cotton.' . . . I put my camera together and drew my film and got an itinerary and I came in to say to Roy that I was on my way. He greeted me goodbye, wished me luck, and then . . . said, 'By the way, what do you know about cotton?' . . . I said 'Not very much.'" Stryker told his secretary to cancel Mydans's travel reservations and talked to him about cotton through both lunch and dinner and well into the night—". . . about cotton as an agricultural product, cotton as a commercial product, the history of cotton in the South, what cotton did to the politics and the history of the United States, and how it affected areas outside the U.S.A."[43] City-bred Arthur Rothstein was assigned to do ranching country, but not before "he had lived cattle with me, because it was in my blood," Stryker said.[44] Only Walker Evans insisted that Stryker never influenced his work in any way. Located in California, Lange received less of Stryker's tutelage, but she had Taylor's.

Stryker gave his photographers "shooting scripts"—"My God, I used to drive you mad with those outlines," he recalled—and they were at first strictly agricultural. For example,

I. Production of foods . . .
   a. Packaging and processing of above
   b. Picking, hauling, sorting, preparing, drying, canning, packag-
      ing, loading for shipping
   c. Field operations—planting; cultivation; spraying
   d. Dramatic pictures of fields, show "pattern" of the country; get
      feeling of the productive earth, boundless acres.
   e. Warehouses filled with food, raw and processed, cans, boxes,
      bags, etc. . . .[45]

This changed after a meeting with sociologist Robert Lynd in 1936, who urged
them to investigate sociological questions. The meeting produced a research
protocol, such as might be prepared for a dissertation proposal. Lynd suggested they ask, "Where can people meet? . . . Well-to-do . . .? Poor . . .?" He
advised them to look at garages, filling stations, stores, lodges, cafés, country
clubs, railroad and bus stations, and the streets. "Do women have as many
meeting places as men?" What is the "relationship between time and the job?"
and "How many people do you know?"[46]

Stryker's scripts were not commands, however. His grace and genius lay
in educating but then trusting his photographers. They soon learned not
to fill specific orders if good pictures would not result. Whatever Stryker's
directions, John Collier recalled, they all photographed 90 percent "between
the lines."[47] They wrote Stryker long letters, and occasionally telephoned, to
explain new tacks they were taking. As Stryker explained, the photographer
is "the man on the ground in the end, and we used his judgment because all
those photographers I got to know I could trust their judgment."[48] As Lange
put it, they used the camera in exploratory way and did not function as illustra-
tors of something they already knew.[49]

Despite the academic-style homework, FSA taste in photography was deliberately vernacular and anti-elitist. Stryker called himself "an illiterate humanist."[50]
This might have created problems for a portrait photographer to the arty elite
like Lange, but she adapted quickly, having already learned to photograph outdoors without access to controlled lighting and neutral backgrounds. Besides,
Stryker's condemnation of arty photographs was mainly a political tactic. He
banned the word *composition* from the shop, and he called photographs he liked
"swell," but this folksiness was aimed at heading off right-wing charges of elitism. At the same time, he sought art-establishment support against conserva-

tives who labeled his project an FDR propaganda agency. He tried and failed to get a Museum of Modern Art exhibit for FSA photography. (Walker Evans did get a one-man exhibit there, through his friend and promoter Lincoln Kirstein, but this event brought little benefit to the Stryker family, because Evans would not credit the FSA, even on the photographs he made on its nickel.)[51]

Gradually, FSA photography began to attract critical notice. In 1936, *U.S. Camera*, an influential photography magazine, published two FSA pictures, by Lange and Rothstein, as well as exhibiting them in its annual salon in Rockefeller Center.[52] Several dozen exhibits, including those at the prestigious College Art Association convention and several big-city art museums, featured FSA photographs.[53]

Individual FSA photographers were not usually identified in publications or exhibits. In this respect, the FSA photography threw its weight against modernism, against the historical trajectory of art toward focus on an individual artist. This attempt to make individual *auteurs* disappear also arose from the anti-elitist orientation of the project and its participation, despite its odd location in the Department of Agriculture, in the widespread public democratic arts activity of the New Deal. Collective attribution of authorship seemed appropriate in photography because of its association with mechanical reproduction—although the similarity among FSA photographs by different people is not always greater than the similarity in New Deal painted images. Despite the camaraderie of the photographers, however, they chafed at being deprived of individual recognition, and every one of them who continued to work in photography moved toward building individual bodies of work. It was as if photography with a collective *auteur* could not be art.

There also remained the debate about whether documentary photography could be art. There had been numerous historical challenges to the museums and galleries that decided what was art, and in the 1930s documentary photography was forcing its way in. Rarified definitions of art, and the distinctions between art and persuasion, were losing traction. The "straight" photography of Paul Strand, Edward Weston, and Ansel Adams was being acclaimed—and if a photograph of mountains could be art, why not a photograph of agricultural fields or Hopi Indians? Even Stieglitz had photographed some plebeian subjects. Inversely, Romana Javitz, curator of photography for the New York Public Library, was arguing that every work of art is a document, an idea commonplace today among cultural-studies critics but one that was strange at the time to all but historians and archivists.[54]

The ambiguous position of documentary photography, however, created political problems for Stryker. He could not justify his budget if the funds went to creating art, and he could not justify the documentary function if the pictures were not factually correct. The expectation that a camera, and its operator, were reproducing objective reality led to recurrent heckling of photographers who arranged their subjects, as a painter would arrange a still life, chose unexpected angles and foci, cropped photographs, or corrected mistakes. Tugwell dismissed the issue, saying that whether the photographs were art is "incidental to our purpose,"[55] but Stryker knew the matter was not so simple. To repel political attacks, he had to ban "artifice" in the making of photographs, although artifice is central to art, both as a word and as a cultural phenomenon. And he had to make the images free to popular publications, a practice that detracted from their art status in an economy that already featured a luxury art market. He had to require his photographers to produce many overtly propagandistic and evidentiary images—of FSA houses, cabins, settlements, and fields, of the pressure cookers FSA gave out and their grateful recipients. And he ultimately fired Walker Evans because he would not make these. Much as he appreciated fine photography, and was often awed by what his photographers could produce at their best, Stryker was quite prepared to serve his employers at the expense of photographic integrity or artistic sensibility.

STRYKER'S TEACHERLY IMPULSES and fatherly style helped the staff to bond—not as a democratic unit but as a family, with Stryker as father. He was a good father, praising and admonishing his children, protecting them from outside attack, fighting for their wages and the ever-newer equipment they demanded, protecting their freedom of artistic and political expression when he could, reining them in when necessary to keep the FSA afloat. When the budget shrank, Stryker tried to find work for his kids, not only within the government but in the new photography magazines.[56]

Stryker was a quick study in the bureaucratic fight for survival. He insisted that users of his photographs credit the FSA, standing up to a major news and photo agency and to other government agencies to establish this principle—a policy that also built the esprit and solidarity of his photographers.[57] He repeatedly fended off budget cuts and other threats to his operation. He described one in his usual comic but completely serious fashion: "Had a bad attack of budgetitis a couple of days ago. Fischer [his immediate boss] had a terrible fever, short breath. Hope to hell it doesn't become chronic next year."[58] As his project gained recognition, he would threaten to move it to another part of the administration when his superiors tried to cut his budget.[59] "I have never had to back down on a fight"—an extraordinary record for a federal employee, which he explained by adding that he also knew when to keep his mouth shut. He survived losing his protector, Rexford Tugwell, who had "held an umbrella over him."[60] His staff thought he loved to have the phone ring with a "fight on the other end of the line." He denied this but took pride in his street-fighting skills. "I have been cornered a couple of times and . . . I showed my fangs."[61] But he added, proudly, "I never kicked the guy below me, never!"[62]

The bonds among the staff were those of a social movement. Interviewed in the 1960s, the photographers all remembered the FSA as the best period of their lives.[63] As John Collier, Jr., put it, "It was not a job. It was a devotion. . . ."[64] When Lange said the group was held together by loyalty, John Vachon responded, "Loyalty! It was practically a cult. . . ."[65] Dorothea said it was like joining an order.[66] But it was not a hermitic order—they floated in a bigger sea. "All Washington was in a state of wonderful excitement," Lange recalled on one of her visits there.[67] Ben Shahn described it as feeling "completely in harmony with the times . . . a total commitment. . . . It was pure."[68]

The photographers also loved the FSA work because it developed their photographic proficiency. As Lange put it, ". . . you had people who expected something of you behind you, and you had to develop. . . . You have to produce, not that anyone was going to be rough on you if you didn't, but it was a real obligation." It helped that Stryker praised them. Even his criticism was charitable: "He would say, so and so is tired, I can see it in the pictures . . . staying out too long, working too hard."[69]

These comments came decades later, when nostalgia had shaped memory. They never again had such fun with their work, so naturally they remembered it as more perfect than it was. You can hear them in their interviews, minimizing and explaining away grievances and conflict. It is allegedly a healthy practice to remember positive more vividly than negative experience, but not permissible for the historian.

Several photographers, notably Shahn and Evans, experienced Stryker's fathering as dictatorial and authoritarian. Stryker had a gruff style, bawling out his photographers in an avuncular voice disguised as humorous. When

Delano wired Stryker asking for a day off to get married, Stryker replied, "No." This was a joke.[70] He was often sarcastic. He wrote to Rothstein, "Why not cut this out of the letter and paste it on your hat so that I won't have to write it in every letter?"[71] To Lee, he wrote, "If TX is no better than you make it out, I don't know why the hell you want to stay down there. Will you please get the hell into the next state."[72] Stryker was not afraid to make "hard" decisions, as in firing Carter and Jung.

More disturbingly coldhearted was Stryker's refusal to hire Lewis Hine, who was, more than any other individual, the father of American photography of the poor. His extraordinary contribution to early twentieth-century progressive reform would be hard to overestimate, yet by 1938, at age sixty-four, he was broke, unemployed, and on relief. His son was hospitalized after an accident and his wife's untreatable asthma was getting worse. Hine wrote Stryker repeatedly asking for work at the FSA, a logical place to turn since the whole project rested on Hine's legacy, but Stryker always refused.[73]

Photographers were angriest about how Stryker killed photographs— sometimes because they had objectionable subject matter, as when Rothstein photographed in a whorehouse or Shahn captured police brutality on film, but mostly because Stryker considered them of poor quality. At first he would clip the corners of negatives he judged weak or flawed, then later punched holes in them; some have estimated—wildly, I think—that he killed as many as 100,000.[74] Stryker defended this triage as essential because making prints was the lab's most time-consuming work, but the photographers failed to understand why he could not put the inferior negatives aside without ruining them. Gordon Parks considered Stryker's hole punching "barbaric," "because there is no way of telling, no way, what photograph would come alive when."[75] It took years of pressure from the photographers to get him to quit this practice,[76] and the fact that Parks, who didn't arrive until 1942, complained suggests that Stryker may never have quit entirely (although it is possible that Parks knew about the practice from seeing old negatives).

In these gripes we can hear artists' desire for control over their work. Despite their social-movement consciousness, they also wanted to control their photography. Most of them would have preferred to do their own developing and printing, and Lange in particular tried to wangle a way to do this. She complained bitterly about not being able to see prints soon after they were made, so that she lost the opportunity to appraise what she had done and to make improvements immediately. She hated the decontextualization of her work, notably the fact that her captions were never published or exhibited. It galled them all to have their work purged; Stryker's censorship alienated their labor, they felt, and stole from them some of the satisfaction of working for social justice.

The very nature of the photography project discriminated against women. Many kinds of obligations made it difficult for women to be on the road for months at a time. Men could have wives taking care of homes and children. Men could also have wives, or their functional equivalent, as assistants on the road. It was such standard procedure for wives and girlfriends to travel as assistants to the male photographers that Mrs. Vachon once said in surprise to Lange, "You mean you didn't have a writer with you?"[77] Jack Delano's wife Irene, Edwin Rosskam's wife Louise, and Russell Lee's wife Jean, traveled with and assisted their husbands; Grace Falke Tugwell worked in the FSA as an assistant to her husband. The female partners helped with captioning, while Lange was always both photographer and caption writer; Louise Rosskam, for example, would stand next to Ed, taking notes as he photographed.[78] All the wives interviewed said "we" when referring to the photography project.[79] Lange took along an assistant when her husband was not with her on the road, but this was a photographic helper, not an assistant who would wash clothes, write captions, send letters to relatives, shop for food, and make sandwiches. Of the photographers, only Lange had children, only Lange was disabled; yet when Paul could not accompany her, she paid for her help from her own wages.

Only four female photographers ever worked for the FSA, most in later years, and most for very short times: in addition to Lange, there was Marion Post Wolcott, hired in 1938; Marjory Collins, hired in 1942; and Esther Bubley, hired in 1942. Louise Rosskam, a first-class photographer, was never on the payroll, although Stryker "gathered in" and distributed many of her photographs. Most of Bubley's work in the FSA file was done on her own as she tried to convince Stryker to take her on as a photographer.[80] In other words, the FSA got good photography from several women without having to pay them wages. Marion Post Wolcott, a rich and beautiful young woman of twenty-eight, was treated in a teasing and protective manner. She traveled alone and, as a result, encountered overt discrimination: local officials and regional FSA staff, especially in the South, would refuse to do the advance work she needed, such as helping her figure out where to go.[81] Stryker and the other photographers joked about these problems. She "suffered from being a very attractive girl," Stryker said, and Rosskam commented that he could recognize Marion's pictures "because the men are always leering at the camera."[82] Stryker called Lange, by contrast, a "matriarch," showing his lack of nonclichéd categories by which to understand and describe an assertive woman. (He also called other women around the office matriarchs, such as secretary Helen Wool.)[83] Despite her skill, despite her geographical distance from Washington, Lange could not shed the burden of womanness that structured both work and home relationships, as would become clear over the next years. Yet despite the considerable burdens, Lange was embarking on the great adventure of her life.

# 12

# On the Road: California

From 1935 to 1941, Lange was almost constantly on the road, photographing agricultural labor. These were the years when she established without ambiguity that documentary photography could be art and that she was an artist.

She did this by fusing documentary photography with rural sociology, becoming a visual sociologist. She had a private tutor—Paul Taylor, a master teacher who trained a large handful of rigorous and empathic social scientists.[1] He also made her an historian of rural labor and inspired her to another achievement—creating visual narrative. She began in California, where farming was heavily industrialized, then traveled to the southern plains, where remaining smallholders and tenant farmers were facing ruin, and from there into the southeastern states, where agriculture remained most primitive.[2]

She also invented a way to put words and images together by quoting her photographic subjects. When she copied their words, she often arranged them on the pages of her notebook like free verse.[3]

*Seems funny to me we got*
*so much of everything,*
*including good men with*

*good bodies, and we can't*
*make a living. Its an*
*unfair deal. I can't figger what*
*its all about*

She was writing found poetry.

DURING THE SCHOOL years, she and Paul tried to return home daily, or after a few days away, whenever possible, so as to see their children frequently. Even so, Lange was responsible for all of California, an immense state, 770 miles long. For every hour of photographing, she spent several hours in a car—cars being the only way to get to small towns and rural areas while carrying heavy equipment. The freeways had not yet been built, so the roads were often slow and narrow; the cars were not air-conditioned and the scorching dust flew in through the open windows.

The heat usually structured her daily schedule. She had to get out in the fields very early, because it was cooler then, because that's when farmworkers started, and because of the light. "The hours to knock off are 10:30 to 3:30," Lange said. But she wanted to show wilted plants, and if she waited until late afternoon, they would have perked up again.[4] So she also tried to photograph the heat: "This here is a blast of light . . . This is a town and nobody is out, it's too hot but this one little figure, and it shows the way he walks with his head and his hat down . . . touching that heat."

The photographers stayed in cheap auto courts where the windows usually had no screens to keep out mosquitoes, chiggers, and flies. They often did not sleep well. They used the telephone to stay in touch with home infrequently, because long-distance calls were expensive and they had to account for every call on their expense sheets. (The mail service was faster than it is today, however.) Russell Lee believed that being on the road cost him his first marriage.[5] They sought motels that advertised " 'ice-cold running water' " and looked for bathrooms that could be transformed into darkrooms.[6] Irene Delano said that being on the road was not so hard because they were young,[7] but Dorothea wasn't. She was forty when she set out, the oldest of the FSA group.

She was chronically tired. She made mistakes because she was so tired at night: "I load up the films and transfer the exposed ones to the boxes at night. Last night made a slip and got the holders mixed." There "weren't any

Saturdays and Sundays . . . nobody thought anything of working all day and traveling most of the night and working the next day. . . . You had to write up your notes at night . . . pack up your film . . . write letters to Roy . . . be at the next town to get a wire from him."[8] You had to keep track of which caption matched which exposure, but sometimes your days were so busy that you wrote the captions only weeks or months later, after the proof prints arrived back from Washington.[9]

She had to develop new skills for work on the road. Some were physical and relational—carrying heavy equipment, working faster, communicating with potential subjects. Some were intellectual and artistic—finding means to represent both individuals and their social/economic/environmental situation in the same photographs.

She got some respite at the ranch of a new friend. Taylor had connected with Sam Hamburg, an unusual Left-leaning grower who supported farmworkers, allowing them to camp on his land during strikes and providing food and water. After the federal camp project fizzled, he built his own decent housing for his workers. Even his children were not sure how he got away with what he did, particularly because he was a noncitizen immigrant Jew. The Hamburg place in Los Baños, northwest of Fresno, was the only place in the whole valley where Lange and Taylor could stay, welcomed and safe. A man with an outgoing, warm personality, Sam gave his friends nicknames: Paul was "doc," Dorothea was "queenie."[10] The deepest bond became that between Dorothea and Sam, who made an instant affective connection. Within minutes of their introduction, "they were talking like soulmates," his daughters recollected. The two shared an ability "to see the whole arc of things . . . talking in a language of visionaries." (He dreamed of founding a cooperative cotton farm in Israel.)[11] Dorothea made several portraits of him, and this is a connection that, I sense, could have become a romantic one under the right circumstances, though there is no evidence that it did. Sam's radical thinking intensified her sympathy for farmworkers.

She carried three different cameras: a Graflex that used film packs that could be exposed in rapid succession by pulling paper tabs, a Zeiss Juwell fitted to take twelve sheets of film at a time, and a Rolleiflex that used roll film with twelve exposures. The Juwell and Graflex produced negatives of 3.25 by 4.25 and 4 by 5, respectively, two to three times the size of the Rolleiflex negatives of 2.25 inches square. (She occasionally worked with a 35-mm camera later, for the sake of speed and because she was weaker and could not carry the heavy ones, but she often considered it a nuisance because you had to hold it up to your eye, making it hard to talk to people.) She wanted all three cameras loaded with film, ready to grab a fleeting shot. So she learned to take along an assistant when possible.

Paul served as assistant when he could, but soon she recruited a paid one, Rondal Partridge, the teenage son of her best friend, Imogen Cunningham. She had known him since he was a year old. When Imogen and Roi divorced in 1934, the families became even closer. They celebrated every Thanksgiving, Christmas, and Easter jointly. Rondal, his twin, Padraic, and their older brother, Gryffyd, were like cousins to the Dixon and Taylor children, and Rondal was another son to Dorothea; she loved him, and he loved her, to the end of her life.[12]

Rondal was already interested in photography, had already worked as Ansel Adams's assistant, and went on to become a master photographer. She paid him one dollar a day, plus all expenses, which she took out of her allowance of four dollars; she was abstemious and he liked the romance of life on the road.[13] They bought groceries instead of eating in cafés. At the auto courts where they spent nights, he frequently slept outside in his sleeping bag, preferring the cool to a mattress. He remembers being lulled to sleep by the roar and bang of the Southern Pacific. When they registered, the managers sometimes looked skeptically at this couple, the forty-year-old woman and twenty-year-old guy, and she once registered as "Dorothea Lange and fancy man."[14]

Rondal describes his job as "mainly driving, being enthusiastic, and accepting anything."[15] Driving was a constant, because she wanted to be free to look out the windows. She would nag him to slow down, which he hated, and ask for sudden stops when she saw something interesting. They would get out of the car, approach slowly, set up her tripod—although she also carried her Rolleiflex around her neck—and this activity often attracted children. They would beg to have their pictures taken, then run to tell their parents, and she would follow and "palaver," as Rondal put it, with the adults.

Like everyone who worked with her, he was awed by an interviewing technique that combined her natural charm with what she learned from Paul. She did not begin with "union" questions about the provision of water and toilets, or wages; these would alarm workers fearful of retaliation. She would inquire instead about the routes they traveled, how their cars held up, children's ages. She might complain of the heat, ask for a drink of water, and then take a long time to drink it. She might be seized upon by the talkative ones, but she reminded herself to focus equally on those who withdrew, because, she said,

"Sometimes in a hostile situation you stick around, because hostility itself is important." In fact, Rondal recalled, she would not stop to photograph if she hadn't the time for interviewing, often passing up promising sites if she knew she could not proceed at a leisurely pace.

Then she would ask if she could "take their pictures" and they almost never refused. She would explain that she worked for President Roosevelt and that the photographs aimed to increase support for public aid and jobs. Most subjects understood perfectly, and many specifically asked her to send the photographs to the president. At first they would pose, but she would take so long—deliberately, I feel sure—walking around to calculate the right angle and distance, that they would go back to what they had been doing. She would move her setup several times, often ending up as close as three or four feet from her subjects. As Ron came to understand, "her presence was the most important thing" about her work. He considered her a magician with people.

Every so often, she would return to the car and hurriedly write down what people had said. "She just locked it into her head and got it down in the right order," always matching the quotation to the right subject, Ron recalled.

*A human being has a right to stand*
*like a tree has a right to stand.*

ALWAYS A PORTRAIT PHOTOGRAPHER, Lange turned toward the poor the same eye, the same flattering angles and easy-to-read composition she had previously directed toward the rich. Her most famous pictures—a tiny proportion of her photography—were composed by massing simple forms—triangles, ovals—and fell comfortably inside conventional, vernacular, Christian visual culture. Many of her photographs, by contrast, display considerably more complexity of composition.[16] But not even the simpler photographs reduce tensions or smooth contradictions. (See plates 6–11.) Her attraction to human personality and complexity did not subside when her subjects were poor. Where she once catered to the rich by traveling to their homes to photograph, now she went to lean-tos and shacks.

The point of this photography, however, was to show people in their contexts, unlike the void backgrounds of her studio portraiture. She produced, of course, the establishing shots, showing the scale of the agriculture. She used the rhythm of the plowed ruts and ridges and the rows of plants to increase

12.1. Meloland, Imperial Valley, 1939

12.2. Filipinos cutting lettuce, Salinas, California, 1935

visually the size of the fields. She included tiny farmworkers, mules, and tractors in these field shots not only as a gauge by which to measure size but also
to show the impersonality of these enterprises where workers never met the
boss and did not know many of their coworkers. Her disapproval of this agricultural system is unmistakable when you hold these photographs next to the
romantic, even saccharine images she occasionally made of family farmers.

The farmworkers' context had two sites, fields and camps, corresponding
to labor and living conditions. She photographed systematically from one
crop to another: 177 photographs of cotton, 171 of peas, 54 of carrots, 32 of
potatoes, 41 of lettuce—and these are underestimates.[17] Much of the work
she illustrated was stoop labor. People are bent over picking cotton, pulling
carrots, digging potatoes, thinning lettuce, cutting cabbage and cauliflower.
Their bodies are part of the earth, their faces hidden from view by their
focus on the ground and the hats they wear to ward off some of the sun and
heat. She had become an ethnographer: ". . . the hat is more than a covering
against sun and wind. It is a badge of service . . . linking past and present."[18]
In many of these photographs, the composition represents, symbolically as
well as empirically, the relation of the worker to the earth—for example, in
the upside-down U's of the pickers in the endless rows of plants silhouetted
against the immense sky. In images of carrying, workers drag cotton sacks, or
lug bushel baskets, wooden crates, armloads of tied carrots; their bodies lean
off center to manage the weight.

Then the visual narrative she constructed takes us to the moment at which
the class conflict becomes most visible: weighing the produce. The workers
want the highest possible weight for what they've picked, the managers the
lowest. All parties are watching each other and the scale intensely. Sometimes
the workers as well as the weigh masters are writing—the former on much-
used scraps of paper, the latter in account books.

Other photographs call into question *who* is working. Lange documented
children and old people doing heavy work. Her captions label some subjects
as grandmothers, lest there be any ambiguity about their ages. (See plate 20.)
These pictures produced furious letters of denial, as when one county probation officer claimed that Lange's photograph—of a child with a cotton sack
waiting to go to work at 7:00 A.M.—could not have been made during the
school term.[19]

The farmworkers' biggest problem was not overwork but underwork, lack
of waged hours. Growers preferred four hundred pickers working for five days

12.3. COACHELLA VALLEY, CALIFORNIA, 1937

12.4. SOUTH TEXAS, 1936

to one hundred working for twenty days. So Lange documented people waiting hours and days for work to begin. She photographed mechanization and other forms of rationalization, seeking visual metaphors for the economic integration big growers were introducing—for example, packing vegetables and fruits in the fields rather than carting them to packing houses or sheds. Her attitude toward these changes was critical. In the Soviet Union at this time, photographers and artists were making glorified images of heroic peasants, female as well as male, driving tractors and combines. In Lange's pictures, the machines that dwarf the drivers—tractors—are part of the problem, not the solution. This dismal orientation clashed with the more positive approach the FSA wanted, since, after all, the machines had been paid for by the Department of Agriculture.[20]

Many California photographs focused on farmworkers' appalling living conditions. Lange squeezed in as much detail as possible, considering her images to be political ammunition: "This camp site belongs to one of the large growers of Kern Co. who is strongly opposed to the Camp program. For this reason these negatives will be valuable here," she wrote Stryker.[21] Frequently, one needs a magnifying glass to extract fully the information out of her photographs, and it would require pages to write down everything that Lange made visible. (See figures 9.4 and 9.6.) The photographs show the garbage next to the lean-tos where people sleep, the cast-off materials of which the thin and fragile shelters were constructed, the metal tubs used for bathing and cooking, the dangerous methods of providing heat, the families in the open, with no shelter at all. The best grower-owned camps featured one-room wooden cabins, which never included plumbing or electricity, typically had no windows, and often contained a woodstove. When it rained, the ground was puddled and muddy, and sometimes the entire camp would be flooded. She photographed privies—typically crooked wooden shacks with doors that didn't close—often very near the water supply. One ironic photograph shows a privy on the outskirts of Bakersfield, constructed of gas station signs, one of which reads, OF ITS KIND . . . UNSURPASSED ALWAYS.

Lange showed with particular detail the migrant women's endless struggle to create cleanliness and order: wash hanging on a line, a washtub leaning against the outside of the hut, bedding draped on the roof to air out, a garbage dump neatly dug at a fifty-yard distance. They were defending not just civility but civilization itself. (See plates 12 and 13.) They did this work not only as individuals and families but as a larger community of travelers. Mutual aid spread not only within encampments but also among groups traveling in tandem. They shared tools, utensils, water, food, sociability. In the Imperial Valley in June 1935, Lange copied this down:

*Hooverville 2 yrs, wintered here,*
*If they's ever been a cross word*

*I haven't heard it. When one has*
*they all has. I can't explain—*
*Each and every one has sympathy*
*for the other cause they've all been*
*the same.*

The children worried her particularly, and put her anxiety and guilt about her own children in a new perspective. Most of the migrant children were not in school: some were rejected because their health was too poor; Mexican children were discouraged from attending or even formally excluded. Those who were in school frequently arrived hungry and sometimes seriously malnourished. "Children dressed in rags, their hands incrusted [*sic*] with dirt, complexions pasty white, their teeth quite rotted. . . ." Lange recorded in her field notes. Polluted water, taken from irrigation ditches and wells next to privies, sickened children especially, and there was typhoid and meningitis.[22] Pellagra was not uncommon, nor was it due to ignorance: One mother in Kern County told Lange, "'I'm not on the diet agin it, cause I have to eat what I can get.'" Field-working children were lucky to have an eight-hour workday—in beets, the hours were frequently ten to fifteen hours a day.

Lange's photographs began to lure reporters into the great agricultural valleys, and their words echoed her pictures: "loathsome," "unimaginable filth," "festering sores."[23] But images of squalor alone are too wretched and too inanimate—or the people in them too distant—to create the outrage and the "do something" response she and Taylor wanted. Lange learned that images of individuals did that more effectively, and that the individuals could not be too beaten down. For example, many viewers react with particular distress to her image of a toddler covered with flies. It is as if the visual desecration of a child's satiny skin, shot close up, works as a symbol more forcefully than group misery. Lange returned to her portrait specialty because it was what she loved most and did best, but also because she sensed its persuasive power. Her portraits performed political work that the more impersonal shots of terrible living conditions could not. Her portraits showed people who were somehow better than their conditions. They were accustomed to better: "'I never lived this way before . . . But I do now and I can't help it.'" And they deserved better. As one farmworker told her, "'Average man wants to live a little bit decent.'" And sometimes they were angry. "'We are not here because we <u>like</u> it. This place is the result of <u>conditions</u>.'"

12.5. IMPERIAL VALLEY, CALIFORNIA. 1935

LANGE'S APPROACH WAS not only a method but also a democratic way of seeing. Like all documentary photographers of her time, she shared the popular-front aesthetic known as social realism. Celebrating the "common man," she represented the people who worked the land as model citizens. The most wretched sharecroppers and homeless migrants were salt-of-the-earth citizens. They worked hard, deserved respect, and merited the rights and power of a citizen in a democracy. Moreover, these common folk had complexity and gravitas equal to that of the rich and the educated. In Arthur Miller's words of this era, "the common man is as apt a subject for tragedy in its highest sense as kings were."[24]

Nineteen-thirties social realism and its respect for working people were simultaneously an international and a nationalist phenomena. In the United States, influenced by both Mexican murals and regionalist Americana, this aesthetic featured bulky-muscled, sweaty workingmen and their earthy female helpmates. In this highly urbanized country, paradoxically, the wide distribution of FSA photographs popularized rural images, and that ruralist version of America then intensified a populist nationalism that, in turn, popularized the style. FSA photography sometimes resembled Soviet socialist realism, with its sturdy peasant women wearing head scarves and Stakhanovite men pouring steel.[25] Spinning socialism in a racist direction, the Nazis—who, after all, called themselves "National Socialists"—shared this aesthetic: their art and photography also featured muscular workers and sturdy women, in a confounding convergence of political cultures that seemed antithetical. In other words, the social-realist style arose from both Left and Right, its nationalist and populist content allowing it to cross ideological boundaries.

American social realism came in several versions. The upbeat, mainstream style, found in post office murals, most resembled the Soviet, signaling confidence that hardworking Americans would overcome all obstacles to restore prosperity and a healthy future for their children. Its emphasis on national unity across class lines paralleled Soviet hammer and sickle ideology, emphasizing the unity of workers and peasants. A more highbrow style, modernist photographic abstractions of large industrial forms, as in the work of Margaret Bourke-White, owed much to the avant-garde art and design of 1920s Soviet Union and Weimar Germany. The American Left version of social realism was, in keeping with Marxist theory, more industrial than rural, and stressed exploitation and suffering, behind which lay the promise of a workers' uprising. Its images of oppression often appeared in prints, especially woodcuts, reproduced and circulated in magazines, pamphlets, and posters. The FSA version served the agency's agenda of agrarian reform.

Lange's version of social realism stands out, first, in its racial politics. Despite her and Taylor's decision to feature Okies in the 1935 California reports, her FSA photography featured people of color prominently. Historian Nicholas Natanson calculated that approximately one-third of her photographs showed people of color, a proportion greater than that of any other FSA photographer until Gordon Parks joined the crew.[26] The qualities of those images, treating subjects as attractive, intelligent, hardworking, and trustworthy, were as important as their quantity: white people rarely saw respectful images of black or brown people in the mid-twentieth century.

In the main, all social realists honored workingmen and their families. Lange's work, however, and that of later FSA photographer Esther Bubley stand out for their gender politics, a refusal to accept the myth that the nuclear family was the only "normal" family form and the muscular man the quintessential worker. Among the migrant farmworkers, communities of interdependence often constituted fractured or extended families and unrelated groups of fellow travelers. Lange photographed so many lone parents with children that we might consider her particularly drawn to such families. Her captions sometimes called attention to nonstandard family forms, such as "Age 70, she came from near Greeley, Nebraska, with sister age 65, nephew age 30, and brother age 68." Where she did show intact nuclear families among migrant farmworkers, husbands and fathers often appeared weakened, reduced from head-of-family confidence, more fragile than the mothers and wives. This was by no means a "feminist" reading of family scenes, but, rather, an insight into the impact of traumatic insecurity on men; these images contrast with those she made in the Southeast, which feature more stable—though equally poor—sharecropper families. (See chapter 15.) Nor was it an expression of animosity toward men. Lange's male subjects often ooze sex appeal. None of her photographs is more tender than her many—strikingly many—images of fathers with children.[27] (See plate 19.) Her attraction to paternal love may have derived from her own identity as fatherless, but it must be seen also as an openness to the more egalitarian, less conventionally gendered family forms that became more common and more honored later in the century. This this was one of several indications that Lange's visual sensibility picked up new democratic possibilities that many did not yet sense.

Her photographs of the handsome homeless could be said to argue a New Deal analysis of the Depression. Refusing to search for the causes of poverty in individual character, the dominant approach several decades previously, New Deal relief rested on the premise that the economic crisis was structural. The economy, not the people, needed moral reform. Because the Depression crisis had thrown so many respectable working- and middle-class people into poverty, it became clear that those who appeared disheveled might well be entirely upright, their economic wretchedness no longer a sign of weak character. To the victims, then, New Deal relief provided no moralizing, only money and jobs.[28] To support this policy visually, to subvert centuries of blaming poor people, required showing that they worked hard, maintained good morals, and behaved with restraint. One of Lange's visual metaphors for this discipline was order, a composition both aesthetically and morally reassuring, achieved through careful, often centered framing of subjects, and the use of landscape or tidy agricultural fields to provide restful background. To counteract the chaos of the migrant camp, she emphasized stable elements,

12.6. PORTERVILLE, CALIFORNIA, 1936

and these were often female-centered: mothers with children (perhaps the most universal symbol of the human order), the repetition of homely tasks—washing, cooking, grooming—despite obstacles.

Like other 1930s social realists, Lange ennobled, monumentalized, even exalted working people. Her poor people are virtuous and resilient, rarely resentful, never lazy or violent. They evoke respect, as did her 1920s portraits of the rich. Perhaps more important, her images of farmworkers, as those of her studio customers, show individuality and complexity, and this usually saves the photographs from rank sentimentality. The standard adjective applied to her subjects is *dignified*, but at least equally compelling is the fact that they are *interesting*. Lange's desperate farmworkers are simultaneously victimized and vibrant; often sexy—both women and men—vigorous, animated, or contemplative. They may be depressed, but not only depressed. Her subjects sing, play banjos and guitars, dance. The children are excited and curious; the grown-ups laugh. She copied out a song she heard:

*Oh I wisht I was a handsome bitch*
*I'd never be pore, and I'd allus be rich*
*I'd sleep all day and I'd work all night*
*and I'd live in a house with a big red light*
*Oh onct a month I'd take a rest*
*and drive my customers wild!*

The most destitute women walking the highway could be well dressed, the migrant workers often well groomed even as they slept and ate on the ground. Her subjects are thoughtful and intelligent; they are using intellectual as well as emotional and physical faculties to figure out how to survive.

Lange sought out mixed emotions, mixed character. Photography "ought to be contradictory," she maintained.[29] Her portraits grip the viewer through their internal tensions, between the disordered lives of their subjects and the integrity and stability of their composition; between their subjects' deprivation and their richness of personality. However broke and broken, her subjects remain captivating, and capable.[30]

In yet another dimension, Lange's work resembles Soviet socialist realism: its concentration on active labor. Of course many of her finest and most well-known images are portraits of people conversing, resting, thinking, or watching her warily. But others show her attraction to how people work. She saw skill, ingenuity, even creativity in the labor despised by so many: people making a kitchen from a campfire and a bucket; pulling boll weevils off cotton blossoms; picking strawberries with a soft touch so they do not bruise; leaning far off a ladder high in fruit trees while moving heavy citrus fruit into a shoulder bag. Influenced by Maynard Dixon's attraction to skilled physical labor and disdain for paper pushers, by the time she entered the FSA that orientation had become for her habitual.

There remained a tension between the portraits she could do best and the social context required for the agency's political agenda: portraiture required close-ups, which often eliminated context. She became adept at portraiture in context, but also at building up the context with captions, which she developed far beyond Stryker's original instructions. She became the model captioner for other FSA photographers. Explicitly rejecting the notion that "a picture is worth a thousand words," she was frustrated that exhibits and publications almost never used her captions. She did *not* want her photographs to be time-less insights into human universals, the icons so many of them have become. ". . . Every photograph . . . belongs in some place, has a place in history—can be fortified by words," she argued.[31] "I'm just trying to find as many ways as I can think of to enrich visible images so they mean more. . . . A purist would just put not a line. . . .[32] (*Purist* was for her a word of opprobrium.) Her captions were substantive, not literary, and they did not repeat information contained in the photograph.[33]

Unsurprisingly, her captions owed a lot to Taylor. For example:

> Salinas Valley, California. Feb. 1939. Large-scale commercial agriculture. This single California County (Monterey) shipped 20,096 carlots of lettuce in 1934, or 45% of all US carlot shipments. . . . Production of lettuce is largely in the hands of a comparatively small number of grower-shippers. . . . Labor is principally Mexican and Filipino in the fields, and white American in the packing sheds.[34]

Or:

> Kern County, November 1938. Night street meeting of cotton strikers near end of defeated strike. Strikers receive 75 cents per 100 lbs.; demanded $1. In 1910 cotton growers in Imperial County advertised for pickers in the Southwest to come to Imperial Valley to pick for $1 per 100 lbs.[35]

AS LANGE BEGAN her FSA work in 1935, the California agricultural labor market was being reconstructed by the "dust bowl" immigration of "Okies" and the deportation of Mexicans. Actually, the drought refugees were not mostly from Oklahoma, but from a number of plains states. What made them "Okies" was their whiteness, as distinct from the customary farmworkers. Their mass migration westward agitated California's politics in contradictory ways. Their whiteness made their sufferings more shocking to the elite. Both political sides—conservative growers and liberal reformers—virtually erased from public discussion the equally suffering Mexican, Filipino, Japanese, Chinese, and Indian agricultural laborers. At the same time, the "Okie" label became so pejorative that it threatened their whiteness. They were so "low-grade" that in the estimation of many white Californians, they seemed a different race. The farmworkers' roadside camps were often called "jungles," a word later applied pejoratively to black urban neighborhoods.

Before the "Okie" migration, growers had argued that white people simply would not do the backbreaking labor that Mexicans and other nonwhite people would. The Depression then showed the growers that white people *would* do that work.[36]

Having learned that lesson, the growers hoped that the so-called Okies would provide a less volatile labor force, in contrast to the strike-prone Mexican and Filipino farmworkers.[37] But the Okies presented another problem—they were not planning to return to the plains states. Many Mexicans did their employers the favor of "disappearing" to Mexico when there was no work. Many lived fully binational lives, trying to earn money in the United States that could create economic betterment for their families in Mexico. As Taylor and Lange were among the first to discover, the Okies, by contrast, were refugees who could not return to their homeland, convinced that the land they had fled could not be recovered for farming by small farmers with no resources. They had no choice:

*Makin a livin*
*even this kind of a livin*
*beats starvin to death.*
*Back there we like to starve to death.*

They aimed to resettle permanently and to own land. "They would squat . . . and sift the dirt in their hands and say, 'All we want is a little bit . . . of this good dirt.' They'd never seen such soil . . . such fruit . . . such magnificent abundance *pouring* out of the land. . . ."

Okies were privileged workers in California agribusiness, receiving higher wages and better jobs. Filipinos could get jobs in asparagus and lettuce, but not peas, for example, and the crops you picked made a considerable difference in earnings.[38] Okies frequently asserted their white supremacy to Lange: "You turn over everything to the sheenies—" But their race talk, like all race talk, expressed a complex variety of relationships. Sometimes they were expressing class anger in racialized terms: "A white man that will work for the wages a farmer can pay is worse than a nigger." Most often it was a complaint about the erosion of their status: "We *did* live like white people." "We ain't no paupers. We hold ourselves to be white folks." They were asserting self-respect and demanding respect from others, albeit through invidious comparison to people of color. They had few other ways to argue for respect. Their understanding of "white," in a vocabulary recognized throughout the United States, was not merely colloquial but functional. It set up whiteness as an ideology, a fantasy that mythologized poor whites' commonality with men of power, an identity that worked to assuage the insults of poverty, illiteracy, and political weakness. Their words rang of injured pride and rage at the undeserved misery in which they were living.

New Deal progressives like Lange and Taylor believed they could not afford *not* to exploit racialized sympathy for the Okies as a means of mobilizing support for better treatment of farmworkers in general. Taylor wrote, "It should be understood that with this new race, the old methods of repression, starvation wages, of jailing and intimidation are not going to work. These are Americans."[39] Such talk confirmed the idea that Mexican Californians were aliens. One white migrant told Lange:

> *Tain't hardly fair.*
> *They holler that we ain't citizens*
> *but their fruit would rot*
> *if we didn't come.*

He was right that they were being effectively deprived of citizenship. Okies were rarely treated as badly as people of color, but their rights were routinely violated. NO MEXICANS OR OKIES signs appeared on many establishments. Not only the private sector but even government denied them the entitlements of citizenship. All were discouraged from sending their children to schools, using local hospitals, or exercising rights to old-age assistance or general relief. Children's protective service agencies ignored them. They were disfranchised and unprotected by protective labor legislation. They were denied many federal citizenship rights as well: no workman's compensation, no Social Security old-age pensions. Just about the only New Deal program to treat farmworkers as citizens was emergency relief, and despite federal policy, local relief administration often rejected farmworker applicants. As one migrant said to Lange:

> Now I want to ask you a question
> Can you tell me whose entitled
> to this relief and why —
> It's broke me up — I used to have
>     furniture

The FSA's attempts to bring farmworkers into citizenship enraged the growers. As a local FSA staff member recalled, the FSA "was probably the most unpopular organization that Washington could have possibly sent out here."[40] Growers charged that "California would have no migrant problem if it were not for the activities of the Farm Security Administration."[41] Growers' economic power and control over state and local officials enabled them to resist or scuttle FSA initiatives. Watching the growers block the camp program was a political education for Lange. If she had not previously understood their power, she did now. She wrote to Stryker, ". . . what goes on in the Imperial Valley is beyond belief . . . [the area] has a social structure all its own. . . . Down there if they don't like you they shoot you . . . beat you up and throw you in a ditch. . . ." She informed Stryker that she would not travel alone there.[42]

You might think that the growers would have welcomed the FSA camp program. It subsidized them by assuming some of the costs of maintaining their labor force. But their fears of farmworker unionization dominated. Since they saw any refusal to work for any wage offered as evidence of Red influence, they argued that the camps would serve as breeding grounds for communism, by allowing organizers to hold meetings, recruit the allegedly simple migrants, and create conspiracies. In general, the improved standards of the federal camps would make workers too demanding.[43]

The growers were right that better facilities elevated farmworkers' sense of what they deserved, for the FSA camps seemed to them like paradise. The typical camp provided metal shelters or tent platforms arranged around utility buildings. Clean water came out of numerous outdoor faucets; the central buildings featured flush toilets, hot and cold running water, showers, and laundry and ironing rooms. There were garbage cans. The facilities that created the greatest delight were the baths and showers. When someone noted that one new arrival took three baths in one day, the farmworker replied, "If you had had to go without a bath as long as I have . . ." A local FSA employee reported that a woman who had just arrived in a camp "stood under the shower all afternoon, crying, drying herself, and going back into the shower. . . ."[44] The camps operated day-care centers, infirmaries, and first-aid centers, garages and workshops with tools and, often, skilled mechanics. Families typically paid ten cents a day and were required to contribute two hours work a week.[45] The camps were far from luxurious and sometimes ill-conceived, as in Arizona, where the FSA built prefabricated houses of metal that become hot as ovens.[46] They offered little privacy and supplied no food, but compared to the grower camps or the roadside, they were high civilization.[47]

The growers were also right that the camps made it easier for farmworkers to act collectively. Campers elected governing committees that established and enforced rules. They planted cooperative gardens, held classes, published newsletters.[48] Above all, they traded information, grievances, and gossip. The camps functioned in some ways as citizenship schools, analogous to those created by the civil rights movement twenty-five years later.[49] Had there been many more FSA camps, they could conceivably have changed California's politics and power structure. Arvin camp manager Tom Collins believed that the camps led many residents to register and vote in state and national elections. He called his job the "'repatriation of American exiles,'" meaning exiles from the nation, from citizenship.[50]

The word *citizenship* does not appear in Lange's captions, but the concept directed her images and captions nevertheless. Her respectful portraits of farmworkers showed them to be thoughtful, hardworking, responsible—visually demonstrating their citizenly capacity. When she could, she used words to this end as well, captioning one portrait of father and baby "Future voter & his Mexican father." She copied the words of a female farmworker: "I want to go back to Mexico but my children say, No we all born here we belong in this country. We don't go."[51] Had the photographs been available to their subjects—lacking any control over her work, Lange had no way of sharing the pictures with her subjects—they might have helped construct as well as represent citizenship. Lange's was not just a legal but a stronger, more demanding meaning of citizenship: active participation in self-government. So she was particularly interested in the governance of the FSA camps. Her pictures

12.7. SOUTHERN SAN JOAQUIN VALLEY, CALIFORNIA, 1936

focused not only on camp facilities but also on bulletin boards, sewing clubs, and camp council meetings, representing them as exercises of citizenship. She made extensive notes on the proceedings of such a meeting and captioned the matching pictures, "the beginnings of democracy."[52]

The growers' charge that the camps offered a "harbor for agitators" was also true to an extent.[53] Communists did indeed try to recruit among farmworkers, although not all the Communists were outsiders and not all the agitators were Communists. The Communist-led union UCAPAWA (United Cannery, Agricultural, Packing, and Allied Workers of America) established regional headquarters in at least one FSA camp. Carey McWilliams even saw the camps as an "initial step toward a collective agricultural economy." [54] But the majority of camp residents were more depressed than furious, suspicious of collective action and uncomfortable with the rhetoric of class conflict. Besides, their patriotism tended toward racism. Okie political culture differed in these respects from that of Mexicans, and the union organizers had overestimated Okie potential for collective protest.[55]

Meanwhile, the FSA Left had the opposite fears—that the camps not only subsidized employers but could serve to police workers. Fred Soule of the California FSA complained about "thoroughly-policed, thoroughly-regimented camps . . . and the death of the democratic, cooperative, morale-lifting and self-guiding spirit. . . ." Lange also perceived dangers, as in her take on Tom Collins: "a slim, dark, wiry, nervous fellow . . . intensely close to the people, and it got so when he hoisted the American flag over that camp every morning it was his camp and he protected it from the outside world and he was just master of it, although he was dedicated to the benefit of the people. It was one of the most curious combinations. . . ." Paul Taylor feared that the camps would "freeze" the migrants as an "army of cheap and plentiful labor. . . ."[56] The farmworkers understood this:

> *I'm not a kickin'.*
> *I'm being tuk care of*
> *but if I should live to be a hundred, this way,*
> *I'm not getting ahead noways.*

But Taylor would not ignore immediate sufferings for the sake of a long-term, and radical, agenda. Besides, the Left critics had no alternative to offer.

Taylor found intolerable, however, the camps' racial discrimination: almost all took in only whites. His protests failed. Even the mythologized Tom Collins, role model for the camp director in Steinbeck's *The Grapes of Wrath*, turned away blacks. The segregation was illegal, but tolerating it was Department of Agriculture policy. People of color knew it and did not try to get in to the camps. Threat of deportation made Mexicans fearful of encountering authorities of any kind. The whites-only policy was enforced not only from the top but also from the bottom—by residents. The all-white Arvin camp council voted that "Negroes, Mexicans, and Filipinos be placed in a separate unit"—which did not exist.[57] There is bitter irony here, because the impetus for the camps came from Mexican and Filipino strikes, but the program they won by their activism was closed to them.

Always hoping for incremental improvement, Taylor would not criticize the FSA camps publicly, not even their inadequate numbers. Even *Survey Graphic*, for which Taylor was a regular writer, found his article on the camps "superficial and too rosy—a look at a few small spots where a little something has been done; but it disregards the big problem . . . at no points takes up the criticisms of the RA. . . ."[58] Taylor revised his piece and the magazine published it, but it still dodged the large questions.

Lange's photographs similarly flattered the camps. This perspective was an occupational hazard among government insiders trying to create reforms against powerful interests: They had to work so hard to put small programs in place that they became proud of limited, even drop-in-the-bucket achievements, and pushed the overall failure out of mind.[59] On the other hand, the pride and optimism that led to the fantasy that he was making a dent was also what kept Taylor going, and he supported farmworkers until the day he died. Of course he was frustrated, writing in an emotional tone unusual for him, "At times one is fairly heartsick."[60] But had he continually reminded himself how slim were his chances of success, he might well have quit.

Lange was less patient. Always "emotional," as critics have called her, she was also more introspective and self-critical than Taylor. She rarely dodged big questions or settled for fractional gains. Blaming herself for imperfect photography expanded to blaming herself for photography not strong enough to change a policy. Her appraisal of what determined the quality of her photography changed as her photographic wisdom grew. In 1936, she felt emotionality as a negative: "I make the most mistakes on subject matter that I get excited about and enthusiastic. In other words, the worse the work, the richer the material was."[61] In later years, she came to think the opposite: that her best work arose from her deepest feelings.

But Paul's concrete policy goals never displaced her own photographic ones. As she moved irrevocably into documentary, her primary commitment to photography grew. What drove her and made her most excited was the challenge to make photography maximally revealing—to show truths not evident to the superficial eye, ear, or mind.

To her, the camps not only provided shelter but prefigured the freedom that was her artistic as well as social ideal. While her 1920s bohemian sensibility imagined freedom as absence of restriction, now she understood that government might have to act to nurture freedom. To her, the FSA camp project had a utopian dimension. As scholar Carol Shloss put it, ". . . in a world where the state has become a private police state, the only freedom is to be found in enclosure, in space that protects people from the vigilance of those who want to frighten them into quietness and submission."[62] There could be no freedom without a home, Lange perceived, without a place of mutual respect, of stability, even a step toward rootedness, for people shattered by insecurity. The experience of the homelessness of migrant workers gave deeper emotional resonance to an assignment she used later as a teacher, to photograph "where you live." Even a temporary moorage could reduce anxiety and raise the quality of living above mere survival.

Women's mental health in particular required a minimum of domestic order. That the camps provided a bit of decency—showers, toilets, laundry rooms—reverberated with Lange's visceral love of homemaking. Her own itinerancy, however privileged her conditions in comparison with those of her subjects, intensified her commitment to the FSA camps. Never a feminist in the sense of challenging gender, she believed that women were meant to mother and to make homes. "I hope through these pictures to express or to delineate or to reveal my love for women and their function," she said. "Not only my love for women but my respect for their function. . . ."[63]

An aroma of rescue mission in Lange's and Taylor's visions of the camps evokes the question, did they see themselves as saviors of the farmworkers. Probably, but not in a simple way, because they understood that the camps functioned in part as a pacification program, responding to farmworkers' strikes by providing temporary aid, as opposed to higher wages and union bargaining power. As a middle-class urbanite photographing the uneducated, often darker-skinned rural poor, often in the company of an academic who wrote about the poor, was Lange like an anthropologist studying natives in their "primitive" society? Her "invisibility" trick, her skilled "palaver," may well have increased the inequality of the transaction. Did some viewers find her images titillating? These problems are not easily avoided. Lange knew that good documentary requires both intrusiveness and emotional distance. She also knew that her photographs often elicited outpourings of charity. To condemn documentary photography on account of its inequality is to say that no privileged person can ever help others less fortunate through creative work. And that is patently untrue.

Lange's and Taylor's work contributed to at least one major political development. Lange's sympathetic photographs of farmworkers, along with the growers' arrogance, built public condemnation of big-grower rule in California. This public opinion contributed to the election of progressive Democrat Culbert Olson as governor in 1939 (over notoriously antilabor incumbent Frank Merriam), which delighted Taylor and Lange.

OVERT CLASS CONFLICT in California's vast plantations, however, threatened to rip apart Lange's stitching together of objective reporting and propagandistic advocacy. After a relatively peaceful 1935, Lange began to experience agricultural strikes firsthand and up close. She was not assigned to cover them, but she wanted to, felt she needed to.

In June 1936, 2,500 Mexican citrus workers in the Imperial Valley walked out when they heard that the growers had just received a two-million-dollar cut in freight rates. Strikers beat up strikebreakers and growers responded with armed warfare. Orange County was in a "state of siege," with four hundred armed guards, commanded by former "football heroes" from USC, ordered by the sheriff to shoot to kill. Two hundred workers were arrested and locked into a stockade built by the growers; food trucks sent by strike sympathizers in Los Angeles were hijacked and dumped.[64]

Afraid to venture into the Imperial Valley, Lange thought she could photograph a strike in Salinas, "salad bowl of the world," which supplied 90 percent of the nation's lettuce. The sheriff and police chief there literally abdicated to Associated Farmers, which established a general staff to run the battle, swearing in 2,500 of their supporters as deputies. This army of "clerks, service station operators, shopkeepers," in John Steinbeck's words, "dopes and suckers" of the big growers, arrested hundreds of farmworkers, forcibly stopped picketing, and brought in strikebreakers.[65] In Salinas, too, the growers built a stockade in advance of the strike. Carey McWilliams wrote, "I came across a strange sight . . . a concentration camp protected by barbed wire fencing, strong gates, and sentry posts or towers. . . . One might say the camp symbolizes the prevailing model of labor relations in shipper-grower circles. . . ."[66] When local officials raised questions, the growers reassured them: "but of course we won't put white men in it, just Filipinos."[67] The growers' strategy of segregating workers by race was effective, and the resultant disunity made strikers unable to resist the violence directed against them. Once again, Lange drew back from this violence.

Two years later, in 1938, she did try to cover a conflict in cotton, by now California's leading crop.[68] Associated Farmers threatened retaliation against any grower who offered wage concessions, and refused to accept Department of Labor mediation. There were too many hungry migrants to prevent strikebreaking, and the strike collapsed.[69] In a letter to Stryker explaining why she could not photograph what was happening, Lange wrote in a distraught tone,

"The tail-end of a long heart-breaking strike, unsuccessful . . ."; since there was no one in the fields except "strike breakers . . . it was too dangerous to go. . . ."[70]

As in San Francisco in 1934, Lange's attempts to document social conflict consistently failed.[71] Her few photographs of strikes lacked intensity and provided little information. Her problem was partly inherent in war photography, summarized by Robert Capa as, "if your pictures aren't good enough, you're not close enough." Lange could not get close enough—it was dangerous to do so, neither side trusted her, and she did not move quickly. For strikers, the very existence of photographs was dangerous and could lead, at the least, to being blacklisted out of work. Strike photographs by her more adventurous young friend Otto Hagel were not much better. Lange's photographic temperament, however, suggests that she had no affinity for overt conflict, let alone violence. She raged at the growers, of course: The inequalities were so great, the methods used against the workers so violent and unfair, the power concentrated in the hands of the growers so overwhelming. Her photographs, however, wept more than they raged.

# 13

# *Migrant Mother*

It is fitting that Lange's most famous photograph, one of America's most famous photographs, showed a drawn, hungry farmworker mother of extraordinary beauty. (See page xii.) This was Lange's signature: beauty in expected places. Yet this specific picture, like *White Angel Breadline* (see chapter 6), was almost accidental, its creation an exception to everything we know about Lange's usual practice.

Florence Thompson, the subject of *Migrant Mother*, as the photograph has become known, was an Okie, but she was a Native American Okie, born in 1903 in a Cherokee reservation in Oklahoma—in a tepee, she reported.[1] Both her biological parents were Cherokee, but her father, Jackson Christie, abandoned her mother before Florence was born. Her mother then married Charles Akman, a Choctaw, whom Florence came to regard as her real father, and they settled on a farm near Tahlequah, Oklahoma. At age seventeen, Florence married Cleo Owens, and a few years later the young family moved to California, where her husband worked in sawmills and fields in Porterville, Oroville, and Merced Falls. He died in 1931, leaving her with five children, and pregnant with her sixth. She worked in the fields by day and as a waitress by night, and in 1933, she became pregnant again, this time by a prosperous Oroville businessman. Fearful of having this illegitimate child taken from her by welfare authorities, she returned to her parents in Oklahoma to give birth, but in 1934, the whole extended family moved to Shafter, in California's Central Valley. Florence worked in the fields, from Redding in the north to the Imperial Valley in the south. There she entered a relationship with James Hill, with whom she had four more children as they followed the crops. When Lange saw her, Hill and the boys were off trying to get the family car fixed.

Lange usually had an assistant with her and worked on a schedule; she made this photograph alone and she almost passed up the opportunity.[2] She was driving north on U.S. 101 on a cold and miserable rainy day in February 1936, returning from a month of working on the road alone. She was exhausted, "worked out," and eager to get home to her family, figuring on seven more hours of driving. About two hours beyond Santa Barbara, near the small town of Nipomo, she saw a small hand-lettered sign, PEA-PICKERS CAMP. (Nipomo is in the coastal foothills, an area less hot and more rainy than the Central Valley, so cool-weather crops could be grown there.) She ignored the sign and kept on driving for twenty miles, almost to San Luis Obispo, but something kept pulling her back. She conducted, she recalled, an argument with herself:

> Dorothea, how about that camp back there?
> What is the situation back there?
> Nobody could ask this of you, now could they? . . .
> Haven't you plenty of negatives already on this subject? *Isn't this just one more of the same?*
> Besides, if you take a camera out in this rain, you're just asking for trouble.

The chance nature of this photograph, however, resulted from the kind of luck that comes only with years of practice. The atypical was conditioned by the habitual. Lange's fleeting glance caught something important because her eye was so trained. Then a second part of her photographic discipline took over: a sense of responsibility—to document conditions and seize visual opportunity. She turned around and drove back—like a "homing pigeon," she recalled.[3]

Arriving back at the camp, she learned that a freak cold snap had killed the peas, so there was no work. As Thompson's grandson recounted later, retelling the story he had heard so often from his grandmother, "The look of hunger was already in the camp; within a week death would be there too. First, the very young, and the very old. Soon the locals would descend on the camp, arresting some, beating others, but scattering all to the four winds." Lange saw a lean-to of torn canvas stretched from two short stakes in back to two higher stakes in front, the stakes held by ropes pegged into the ground. The only furniture visible in it was a suitcase with an empty pie plate resting on it and a small open trunk. Inside was a family group: a mother with a baby at her breast, two very young children, and a sullen teenage girl. Something about them attracted Lange. Very tired, she abbreviated her usual conversation with subjects. She learned that the mother was thirty-two, that the family had been living on frozen vegetables stolen from the surrounding fields and on birds that the children killed—and that 2,500 people in this camp were in similar desperate circumstances.

Lange typically made two kinds of portraits—those that captured the subject in direct engagement with the photographer and those made as the subject had become enough accustomed to the camera that she began to ignore it. *Migrant Mother* was of the latter. It was one of a series of six or seven photographs, and from their variety, it is clear that Lange asked the mother and children to move into several different positions. She began with a mid-distance shot. Then she backed up for one shot, then came closer for the others.[4] She moved aside a pile of dirty clothes. (She would never embarrass her subjects.) She then moved closer yet, focusing on three younger children and sidelining the teenage daughter out of the later pictures altogether.[5] Then this master photographer of children made the unusual decision to ask the two youngsters leaning on their mother to turn their faces away from the camera. She was building the drama and impact of the photograph by forcing the viewer to focus entirely on Florence Thompson's beauty and anxiety, and by letting the children's bodies, rather than their faces, express their dependence on their mother. It was the same compositional strategy that made *White Angel Breadline* so powerful.

Feeling that she had captured what she could of this moment, Lange then returned to Highway 101 and drove home to Berkeley. When she developed the negatives, she knew she had something strong, and she offered the photographs to the press. The *San Francisco News* published two of them on March 10, 1936. In response, contributions of $200,000 poured in for the destitute farmworkers stuck in Nipomo.

*MIGRANT MOTHER* HAS been so often reproduced that critics call it an icon. It was used for a thirty-two-cent postage stamp, in political campaign literature, in advertisements for all sorts of commodities, for charity fund-raising, and for magazine covers. The Black Panthers put an Afro on the mother. A right-wing Web site compares it to Josef Goebbels's creation of the storm trooper icon Horst Wessel.[6] When I asked my university students if they knew who Dorothea Lange was, almost all said no. But when I asked them to tell me their visual images of the Depression, many described this photograph. Within that association, its meaning varies: it can connote victimization, the irrepressible resilience of Americans, or the selflessness of mothers. The picture could be said even to stand for the nation, much as Marianne stands for France—*Migrant Mother* is the enduring, ultimately invincible nation enduring a terrible collective tragedy. It functions as an *"aide-memoire* for activating a 'structure of feeling.' "[7]

The image evokes several powerful historical ideas and clichés about motherhood, all of them highly ideological. Her children lean on her because she is a pillar of strength. Not only do they lean on her but there is no space separating the four members of this family; they have become, as they began, one flesh. The mother's worry expresses her need to nurture and protect them at any cost. Nothing will induce her to walk away from her motherly responsibility. Like so many other mothers, she has worked hard but reaped no reward or security. She is overpowered by circumstances she cannot control. She is absolutely innocent of any blame. We somehow know that she has already done her utmost and is in danger of running out of survival strategies. She may even strengthen associations of women with weakness, as she is paralyzed with anxiety rather than active. Other iconic meanings call uniquely on the Christian tradition: *Migrant Mother* is a Madonna, of course, a mother holy because she is pure and asexual. More, she is at the center of a holy family.[8]

Photography scholar Sally Stein, however, suggests that if the photograph were only a Madonna, it would have less power. She argues that the photograph also contains a tension that has added to its force, however unconsciously. Stein points out that the mother is so merged with her children as to be in bondage, locked in through this visual compression. Mothers are workers, and Lange, as the quintessential photographer of working people and one who found motherhood hard work, was exquisitely aware of that. But motherhood is indentured labor, not free. It is love itself that imprisons. Moreover, as Stein points out, her arm and face push forward of her children. She is alone in a crowd, looking away from the others, like the man in *White Angel Breadline*. Her children use their hands to touch her, but she does not return the gesture.

Moreover, Madonnas usually look at their child; *Migrant Mother* does not. The "picture lacked most of the sentimental cues that make the mother and child formula work, or work easily, as secular variant of sacred conviction," Stein concludes.

Lange herself sometimes wondered why this photo in particular became so much used; she knew it to be a fine photograph, but she had made many others of equal strength. Why a specific image is unusually gripping remains mysterious, but, as Stein argues, *Migrant Mother*'s inner tension, precisely its lack of resolution, contributes to its power. Lange made flattering photographs, but her tastes did not run to conventional prettiness. She was exquisitely sensitive to embodied emotion, but she also probably felt the complexity of Thompson's anxiety because it was hers, as well. Nothing in Lange's personal life was as fraught as her own motherhood and she lived with contradictory impulses every day.

ANTI—NEW DEAL Republicans frequently charged that FSA photographs were slanted. Roy Stryker defended them by insisting on their truth, but not all his staff shared his literal-minded definition of truth. So he had been burned when the anti-Roosevelt press discovered that FSA photographer Arthur Rothstein had moved a steer skull a few yards to make a more powerful image of the drought.[9] In response to another conservative attack, Stryker denied, mistakenly, that Lange had posed the family members in *Migrant Mother,* his denial implying that to have done so would be cheating. He complained when Lange retouched the photograph, removing a fragment of Florence Thompson's thumb that intruded into the composition. Forty years later, a scholar accused Lange of staging a June 1938 photograph of another family by having thrown something on the ground that would cause a toddler to turn around and look at it.[10] Yet at times, Stryker instructed his photographers to stage photographs. "If possible," he wrote Rothstein, "get . . . Debt Adjustment Committees at work (even if staged). . . ."[11]

Why was retouching or staging a suspect technique? Why did these issues matter? They arose because the common understanding of photography as mechanical reproduction collided with the political weight of documentary photography in the Depression. This concern for authenticity, as critic William Stott discerned, pervaded 1930s political culture, including both visual and textual arts.[12] The documentary mode matched the federal government's increasing reliance on empirical data in promoting its policies. The very effectiveness of politically engaged photography stimulated opponents to challenge its authenticity. From a different political perspective, Stryker shared their assumptions, and used a courtroom analogy: that his photographs functioned as evidence, building a case for federal policy. He aimed at "annexing the emergent prestige and authority of professional photojournalism to the already established 'scientific' reliability of experts in social science. . . ."[13] (Stryker knew that he could never justify funding his photography project if its products were considered art.) Forensic or news photographers might have agreed that they should not retouch or rearrange their subjects, but they could not avoid framing each photograph so as to include or exclude; the viewer can never know what is just outside the frame.

Seventy years later, this concept of authenticity seems not only vague and superficial but ideological. Prohibiting rearranging a group so as to make a more compelling portrait rests on a concept of truth as immediately evident to the senses, never requiring analysis and understanding. This concept would make truth captive to common-sense, conventional appearances, while Lange was determined to disrupt the constant temptation to see conventionally, in order to provoke deeper questions. Lange's FSA colleague Jack Delano argued, "It isn't something you happen to see, a documentary photograph is an expression of the essence of what you are seeing."[14] Lange managed photographic scenes so as to expose truths not readily accessible. She loved a Chinese proverb: The eyes are blind to what the mind does not see.[15]

This approach derived, of course, from portraiture and the idea that individuals had inner natures, sometimes hidden but capable of exposure under the right conditions. What she was now documenting was not, of course, individuals alone, but individuals in social conditions and relationships: "the full meaning and significance of the episode or the circumstance or the situation. . . ."[16] By using people as her subjects, she believed, she could better communicate those conditions and relations, and by moving them into the kind of classic composition and revealing postures that she liked, she made them more expressive.

SEVERAL DECADES AFTER the photograph was made, a journalist searched out Florence Thompson and discovered that she was a "full-blooded" Cherokee. This fact adds to the ironies of the photograph's trajectory. Its reputation grew because it symbolized white motherhood and white dust bowl refugees. If Lange had interviewed Mrs. Thompson at greater length, would she have learned her history and origins? It is not clear whether Thompson was claiming an Indian identity at the time. Would the photograph have had such popularity if viewers had known that its subject was a "woman of color"? Lange would have welcomed this knowledge. But would Stryker have distributed it?[17] Probably not.

Within a decade, certainly by 1955, when it was published in the Museum of Modern Art's *Family of Man,* the photograph of Florence Thompson had traveled the world. As public property, it was available for any person or corporation to use for any purpose whatever without fee. In 1958 Thompson and her family saw it in *U.S. Camera* and wrote to the magazine to complain, and their letter is in itself a fascinating document, suggesting how even those of limited education might use the language of rights to assert themselves:

> *This photo since has been displayed In the Palace of Fine Arts San Francisco, also Two Years ago it was called to My attention that it appeared in Look Magazine . . . [and] in U.S. Camera. . . . Since I have not been consulted . . . I request you Recall all the un-Sold Magazines. . . . You would do Dorothea Lange a great Favor by Sending me her address That I may Inform her that should the picture appear in Any magazine again I and my Three Daughters shall be Forced to Protect our rights. Trusting that it will not be necessary to use Drastic Means to force you to Remove the magazine from Circulation Without Due Permission to Use my Picture in your Publication I remain*
>
> > *Respectfully*
> > *Florence Thompson*[18]

Lange was shaken—frightened and miserable that her photograph had caused grief.[19] Of course she had earned no money from the image and could not control its use, so Florence Thompson had no grounds for a suit. But Thompson's anger is understandable: She felt that she had been stereotyped as a *Grapes of Wrath* character, an Okie, and that she gained nothing from the photograph, and she assumed that Lange had profited handsomely. Thompson also charged that Lange had promised and failed to send her a copy, and had guaranteed that the photograph would not be published. These claims are dubious, because Lange knew well that all FSA pictures could be published, because Lange never promised to send copies, and because FSA photographers never took names, in keeping with project guidelines. Once Lange's relationship to the photograph was clarified, Thompson and her family withdrew their complaint, and today Thompson's daughter speaks positively about the making of the photograph: "She asked my mother if she could take her picture—that . . . her name would never be published, but it was to help the people in the plight that we were all in, the hard times," Peggy McIntosh says. "So mother let her take the picture, because she thought it would help."[20]

Nevertheless, Thompson's feelings deserve respect. Her description of the encounter helps explain how she understood it: "a shiny new car" approached; "A well-dressed woman got out with a large camera."[21] Lange's car was not likely to have been shiny after many days on the alternately muddy and dusty roads around California fields, and she was equally unlikely to have looked well dressed. Thompson's memory, like all memory, had no doubt modulated over the years. But her emotional memory was true, because Lange clearly came from another world. She was a woman driving alone, her big camera a mark of authority. And what this woman took—photographs—belies Lange's view that she was not taking anything from her subject. In capturing Thompson and her children, ragged and worn, Lange may have taken a bit of their pride. As one Okie told Lange, "I never have wrote back home and told my folks that we live in a tent. I've wrote that we're well and such as that but I never have wrote that we live in a tent."[22] These feelings raise questions of social ethics. Is it best to capture a farmworker in her ragged dress so that she will evoke pity and, possibly, help? Or to allow her the opportunity to present herself as she wishes? Does the former make the subject doubly victimized, first by the society and economy, then again by the documentarian? Thompson may have felt like the Mexican farmworker in Calexico who did not want to be photographed because "we have shame thees house." (See chapter 9.) As a black minister told Robert Coles in 1963, "I wonder about who's doing the 'documenting,' and what a person has in mind to see . . . will they document our tears but not our smiles? . . . I know we need outsiders to lend us a hand. . . . But . . . we'll end up appearing the way the Klan people want us to appear—as bad off as animals, and all the time whining, like a cat or dog."[23] Florence Thompson felt that she had been portrayed that way, and had been humiliated.[24]

Lange did not share any of these ethical doubts. Like her mother and her husband, she felt a responsibility to help. True, her approach to Thompson had deviated from her typical use of conversation, even "seductiveness," as one critic put it,[25] to mitigate a subject's stiffness or shame. Approaching Thompson that day in February, she was too tired to seduce and probably became pushy. But although often introspective about photography, Lange never worried about potential harm to subjects. She was so sure that she was doing good that there was no room for such doubts.

Florence Thompson did not have an easy life after the photograph. As she charged, she got no benefit from the picture; more broadly, her life points to the failure of Lange's and Taylor's hopes for economic democracy. Thompson remained for some time a farmworker, struggling to support her ten children. In 1978, a reporter for the *Modesto Bee* discovered her living in a mobile home and interviewed her; she again complained that she should have received some money and threatened a lawsuit. She was then living on $331.60 a month from Social Security, with an extra $44.40 for medical expenses. In 1979, another journalist, Bill Ganzel, included her in a larger project of tracking down Depression photographic subjects. She was in the news again in August 1983, when she was terminally ill with cancer, heart disease, and the effects of a stroke, and one of her sons informed a reporter that the family couldn't handle the $1,400 weekly medical expenses. In the end, Lange was able to help Thompson's family in a small way: The publicity surrounding this article stimulated contributions amounting to more than thirty thousand dollars. Thompson died in September 1983.[26]

# 14

# On the Road:
# The Dust Bowl

The dust bowl is a defining national legend, of mythic status in American history, and Dorothea Lange helped construct that myth. It was the dust bowl that made Lange an environmentalist; Taylor would expound during their long hours on the road, but it was what she saw that crystallized his teachings into emotional understanding. Dorothea understood all things best by seeing.

The visual metaphors in Lange's dust bowl photographs tell an environmental story. At the core of Lange's developing environmentalism was a narrative—of relations between people and nature, each altering the other. The earth itself comes first. She tried to photograph a few dust storms but rarely captured the swirling dust, which made her images seem merely fuzzy.[1] She got better effect from the dunes of dust, the drifts that covered fences, farm equipment, storage cellars, even the first-floor windows of houses. More importantly, she showed causes: the vast plowed fields where once prairie grass grew, now defenseless against the wind; the men on tractors, ripping up the soil yet again despite the years of failure.

A second theme, desertion, begins with the parched fields, naked and exposed, deserted by all vegetation. Then the pictures move on to human desertion: abandoned farmhouses, forgotten plows, relics of human society. There are the vacant central squares of towns, the wide main streets nearly

14.1. NEW MEXICO, SPRING 1935

empty of vehicles, the stores boarded up, their signs peeling. Several FSA photographers worked in the drought-stricken plains, but no one matched Lange's images of the human costs of the disaster.[2]

*That year the spring come and found us blank.*

A third theme repeats Lange's Depression specialty: dejected men. In the dust bowl area, these are typically groups of men in conversation—the drought area consisted of small towns where people knew one another. (By contrast, the images of dejected unemployed in her San Francisco photographs express not only their hopelessness but also their isolation, signaling Lange's growing anxiety about cities.) The men appear by the sides of the empty, silent main streets. They are all gaunt. Some stand, some squat, some lean on cars. Some are in overalls, but many wear better trousers, clothes for going to town, because there is no farmwork for them to do. They all wear hats, some of straw,

14.2. CALIPATRIA, IMPERIAL VALLEY, 1937

some fedoras, some cowboy hats. Many attend morning movies for a few cents because there is nothing else to do. In these towns, there are no women, an absence that tells an important story: When there was no farmwork for men to do, they idled with one another, while the women were working harder than ever, trying to keep homes, bodies, clothing, food and water clean; trying to put together meals with little food in the larder or money in the coffee can; trying to keep animals alive and human spirits a margin away from crippling depression.

On the farms and on the road, however, women are plentiful, and they reveal another Lange theme: the female heroic. They work in the fields along-side men, then feed and clean their families. They exemplify Lange's and the popular front's gender sensibility: They are the stronger sex but never seek to lead, to displace men, or to ask men to share their female chores. They are often without men, but not by choice. When women and men appear together, the men often seem more depressed. Of these two photographs, Lange, with her customary drive to simplification, preferred to cut the husband out, focusing on the woman's steely gaze. The result is an image less of pity than of determination.

Next in the story came the farmers' decision to leave, a decision she could not photograph but recorded in her field notebook, for example, "That drought put the fixins to us." To represent their migration experience, Lange used distance shots of auto caravans, usually stopped, because Lange's relatively slow camera could not catch them in motion. The passengers in their ragged

14.3. Blythe, California, 1936

14.4. BLYTHE, CALIFORNIA, 1936

clothes stand or sit outside the hot cars as they wait—for the car radiator to cool off, for water, for a repair, for a used auto part. Close-ups reveal how the jalopies are packed—household belongings tied to or hanging from every surface of the car. (See figure 9.6.) Sometimes the vehicles are small pickups with homemade canvas roofs sheltering the people in the back. Other images focus not on the vehicles but on the families themselves—the new pioneers, Lange and Taylor wanted to tell us. Their trips may not have been quite so dangerous as those of the previous century, but they remained arduous. The men are haggard, not only worried but sometimes a bit glassy-eyed, possibly on the edge of cracking; they may well be dehydrated or suffering from heatstroke. The men are always driving. Women, children, and elderly folk crowd in elsewhere, the women often holding and feeding babies by bottle or breast. The children have dirty faces, legs, feet, and clothing.

The families camp, often right on the side of the road. We see their ingenious makeshift constructions: a sheltering canvas strung to trees, open fires or small stoves, improvised cooking systems, and multitasking vessels used for cooking, washing dishes, washing clothes, bathing. Once camped, the women are at the family center, working and directing the work of others. The men and older boys might have been absent on errands or looking for work. Occasionally, only children are in the camp, because adults and youth are in the fields. The children mix play with looking after younger children and fetching water. In reference to several such scenes, Lange noted in her captions that drought refugees were "mingling" with Mexican farmworkers, and she photographed groups of Mexican and Okie children playing together—obviously an event rare enough to elicit notice.

Families and groups often drove in tandem, because their cars broke down so often. At other times, groups formed in roadside encampments, where they could share resources and exchange information. Their culture required mutual help and generosity, no matter how severe their deprivation. Inversely, theirs was also a culture of resignation. "It is not for us to understand/Just leave it all in jesus hand." "Don't be what you ain't/Jes' be what you is . . ./If you're just a little tadpole/Don't try to be a frog."[3] Yet Lange also encountered critical awareness of that resignation: "'Fellers like myself haven't got brains enough to be as sore as they ought to.'"

PAUL TAYLOR KNEW as much about the disaster as any other agricultural economist, perhaps as much as those farmers who lived through it. He became the leading New Deal expert on the Okie migration, "a churning documentary engine producing facts and statistics regarding the catastrophe," as historian Kevin Starr put it.[4] Part of Taylor's skill and insight was understanding the environment as a story, in which nature and humans changed each other. To Taylor, "environmentalism" required sensitivity to that human-nature interaction so as to find a way not merely to preservation but to sustainability.

The area hardest hit by dust was not, in fact, Oklahoma; the core of the dust bowl included only the tip of the Oklahoma panhandle and took in more of Texas, Kansas, and New Mexico. The whole dust bowl—comprising one hundred million acres—reached as far north as North Dakota and Montana and as far east as western Louisiana. Nevertheless, the name "Okies," originally used by journalist Ben Riddick of the very conservative *Los Angeles Times,* stuck to all these refugees as they made their way west in search of work.[5] Among them were an unknown but large number of those who, like Florence Thompson, were American Indians; and there were also several thousand African Americans, although these people were always called just "colored" or "Negro," never Okies.

*We've been "tractored out."*

Taylor traced the dust bowl to the 1870s, when white settlers began to erode the "bison ecology" in which the Plains Indians lived. Ignoring the typically dry conditions of this semiarid region, which received between half and one-third the rain of typical American farmland, settlers homesteaded and plowed the earth. They uprooted the prairie grasses that held down the dry soil, some of them, like mesquite, sending roots down 150 feet. With that kind of sod, the winds would stir up dust but never rip off the soil altogether. Heavy rains in the 1880s fostered the delusion that plowing the land would actually increase the rainfall—the slogan "Rain follows the plow" even gained support among scientists. Realty and railroad companies promoted settlement by whites by promising an inexhaustible shallow underground water belt that could be tapped. The Department of Agriculture recruited homesteaders, but under the Homestead Act of 1862, each family was allowed only 160 acres, later increased to 640, but even this proved not enough in this arid region.[6] The Department of Agriculture provided instruction in dry farming, explaining that proper plowing would prevent evaporation. "The soil is the one indestructible, immutable asset that the nation possesses. It is the one resource that cannot be exhausted. . . ."[7]

Crop failure, along with a predatory, speculative market in land, ruined many homesteaders, and family farming soon gave way to absentee ownership, large-scale commercial agriculture, and tenant farmers.[8] By 1910, 53 percent of the farmers in Texas were tenants, 62 percent in Oklahoma. Cotton was the major culprit.[9] As cotton production moved west, those with capital accumulated larger tracts of land and more settlers were forced into tenancy.

14.5. CHILDRESS COUNTY, TEXAS, 1938

As the size of farms grew, and as the Depression lowered farm prices, it became cost-effective to mechanize and displace these tenants. "The west is being re-fenced," Lange wrote in her field notes, referring to the enclosures that had displaced European peasants. Those tenants who hung on were being deprived even of small plots for vegetable farming and small stock raising when owners insisted that every square foot of earth be devoted to the commercial crop. In the five years preceding the drought, between 1925 and 1930, a million acres of grasses were being destroyed every year.[10]

Consolidation of land ownership also changed farm technology. Earlier farmers had used the lister plow, which cut a furrow down its center so that the loosened earth fell symmetrically to both sides, and left untilled ridges as barriers to wind. When farmers sought greater productivity, they switched to faster one-way disk plows, a set of parallel sharp disks that reduced clumps more and turned all the soil to one side. These one-way plows could handle heavy stubble and hard sunbaked soil, and as mechanization advanced, they could be fitted with attachments for seeding. But they left a more finely pulverized surface layer, more vulnerable to the wind.

Mechanization was not just the cause but the cause and effect of the ecological destruction. Faced with overcapitalization, excessive expansion of acreage, and periodic droughts, landowners saw mechanization as their only hope, oblivious that it was also their undoing—"destroying the Garden in the search for the Garden."[11] Many tenants reversed the analysis, in the Luddite tradition, treating mechanization itself as the problem. "Tractors should be in the bottom of the river. They ain't nothing but starvation for the people." Some were more practical: "Tractor farming IS the cheapest way of farming but I'll say this about it—it ought to be adjusted so one man can't farm so much land."[12]

Then the Agricultural Adjustment Act made matters worse: growers, paid not to plant, evicted their tenants, and used the AAA money to buy tractors. As one former tenant explained, "My landlord said he could make more renting [his land] to the government, and so he couldn't let me have the place."[13] A migrant told Lange, "I reckon the AAA gypped me out of my share and put me on the road."[14] Then growers adopted the California model, hiring wage labor instead of tenants. The employers owed nothing to the wage workers, not even regular work. One tenant's meditation on being "let go" resembled Marx's punning snarls at "free" labor:

> They're fixin to free all us fellow.
> Free us for what. Free us like they
> freed the mules. . . .

After transcribing this, Lange wrote, "He speaks for his class."[15]

So the 1930s droughts, the worst in U.S. history, found the earth of the southern plains naked. Unrelenting heat—the summer of 1934 saw thirty-six days straight with a temperature over one hundred degrees in the Great Plains—further dried the soil. There were fourteen major dust storms in 1932, thirty-eight in 1933, and seventy-two in 1937. It was often dark at midday. Paul Taylor, speaking in his unique humanist/economist voice, wrote, "Like fresh sores which open by over-irritation of the skin and close under the growth of protective cover, dust bowls form and heal. Dust is not new on the Great Plains, but never . . . has it been so pervasive and so destructive. Dried by years of drought and pulverized by machine-drawn gang disk plows, the soil was literally thrown to the winds which whipped it in clouds across the country. . . . They loosened the hold of settlers on the land, and like particles of dust drove them rolling down ribbons of highway."[16]

The black blizzards and drifts of fine soil not only made farming impossible but poisoned entire communities: the dust made everyone itch, made housework a Sisyphean task, destroyed machinery, caused illness and sometimes death. Oklahoma lost one-quarter of its soil; thirty-five million acres of formerly cultivated land were made unarable by the end of 1934. Half of Oklahomans were on relief, and in some counties, 90 percent were.[17]

Taylor and Lange liked the metaphors *social erosion* and *human erosion* to describe the correlate and consequence of soil erosion. Lange photographed the multiple erosions . . . and then the departures. These were not people on a trip. They were leaving forever and often had to discard what they could not stuff into a vehicle.

SO THEY BECAME "Okies." Many started their journeys with hope. They traveled in every direction, including north and east, seeking urban as well as rural work. But most went west because they had heard of farmwork available there, from reports of earlier migrants or from California growers' widely distributed recruiting fliers. "I heered tell of this here irrigation, plenty of water and plenty to eat." Most of them traveled on Route 66, the iconic Will Rogers Highway, which took them across the Texas Panhandle, through the middle of New Mexico and Arizona, and to the California border at Needles.

Highways carry immense symbolism in the United States, and Dorothea Lange used and changed that symbolism. Like the railroad, the highway means motion, mobility, and escape. As railroads are the great theme of the blues, brought north by African Americans, so highways go with bluegrass and country-western music. Railroads are public; you ride with strangers and you're just a passenger. In the car, the head of the family becomes also the driver, and the experience is overlaid with several layers of masculinity: The machine itself, the control of the powerful machine, and the long highway stretching before one's eyes all imply freedom and adventure. In Lange's vision, the highway changes character. The machine carrying people along it is not powerful; it is an overloaded, aged jalopy, running anything but smoothly, not fast, and frequently breaking down on the road. Her many images of used-car and salvage lots, of men under raised hoods, confirm the feebleness of the jalopies and symbolize the human disrepair and wreckage. These vehicles also expose the domestic, the private female space, to the public: buckets and washtubs and lanterns hanging from ropes, high chair and table strapped onto the hood, bed linen and pillows rolled and bound on top, children leaning out the windows, grandparents cradling babies. The view of the highway ahead is ambiguous: It still leads to the future and the unknown, but it is lonely, barren, surrounded by sage, tumbleweed, nettles, barbed-wire fences. The highway and its vehicles now speak of failure, loss, and masculinity reduced.

Lange also photographed those fallen to the nadir of masculinity, forced to walk or hitchhike. Nothing is as lonely, even pathetic, as the men and even families moving down the barren highways without a car.

*Can't make it*
*ate up the car, ate up the tent,*
*living like hogs*

Itinerant life was harder on the women. If the family was working, the women worked double—in the fields and in the camp; if there was no work, their burden was differently heavy as they tried to feed men and children—they were not so much cooks as magicians, conjuring meals out of the poorest and fewest of ingredients. They worried about the children's diet and health. As one migrant explained to an interviewer, "Where the men say, 'To hell with the clean clothes, I'm too damn tired,' the women will insist on trying to keep clean, and so may work from three to five hours longer than the man."[18]

When they had to move on, they had an established, efficient routine. The men would get rid of the bedsprings and other articles too bulky or heavy to take. Benches were knocked apart into their separate boards so they could be loaded and reassembled at the next stop. Everyone carried something to the car, and they all knew exactly where each piece went. The bedding was placed on top, some articles were tied on the side, and the tents were packed on the trailer. Their ingenuity was impressive. One photograph shows luggage carriers attached to the running boards and loaded with boxes, clothing stuffed in bags

14.6. U.S. 80 near Lordsburg, New Mexico, 1938

attached to the front fenders, boxes with cooking equipment on the floor of the
backseat, and bedding on top of the backseat, with children on top of that.

CALIFORNIA'S UNION ORGANIZERS sometimes claimed that the Okies
were hopelessly individualistic and incapable of solidarity, in contrast to
Mexican farmworkers. It was true that Mexicans were more experienced with
unions and grassroots activism. But Lange saw and showed collective spirit
among the Okies, too: their generosity and mutual help, their love of singing,
and, above all, their shared religiosity.

Still, they were refugees, their communities shattered. Citizenship, in
Lange's and Taylor's understanding, involved relationships not just between
individuals and government but also between individuals and their community. Life on the road made community fleeting at best. One of Lange's cap-

tions, written in a dry, social science tone, read, "Constant movement does not favor the development of normal relationships between citizens and community, and between employer and employee nor the proper functioning of democracy."[19] In so many ways, citizenship rests on having a home, a "settlement," as it was called in early America. What historian Kevin Starr calls the "Tobacco Road canard," the insinuation that Okies were incestuous, degenerate, sexually immoral, stupid "white trash" who would cause the hereditary decline of the California population,[20] derived, if it had any truth at all, from the erosion of community standards.

With this image to combat, Lange thought "a photograph should be above all a promoter of consequences."[21] Her captions became argumentative, though maintaining a documentary voice. About a group of men in Hardeman County, Texas, she wrote a fifteen-paragraph caption, which included a number of direct quotations from them. All seven were on relief and told the usual story of eviction, but Lange elicited more information from them: "None of us vote. It costs us $3.50 poll tax for a married man and wife to vote in Texas." "We used to go to church when we had better clothes." "The big landowners are on the WPA Committee, and they want us cut off so we can work for them for a few days at $1.50 a day harvesting their wheat. But if a man gets a job, he'll lose his WPA card; it'll take him a month to get back on WPA after the work is over, and another 20 days until he gets his first check."[22] Just as she selected her strongest photograph from among many of the same subjects, she framed her questions and then selected quotations to make points, as writers and scholars do. There is no doubt as to her purpose: to show how citizenlike were these farmers deprived of citizenship.

Soon the Okies' citizenship was directly challenged by the Los Angeles police. The number of migrants, as always, exceeded the work available, and the desperate people had no choice but to head for towns and cities and apply for relief. To discourage the migration, the state legislature authorized excluding those "likely to become public charges." In December 1935, the Los Angeles Chamber of Commerce proposed that transients be convicted of vagrancy and put to hard labor.[23] The legislature then toughened its antivagrancy statutes to provide that vagrants could be arrested and "lent" to growers to work off their fines.[24] Antimigrant rhetoric escalated toward hysteria. A Los Angeles columnist thought the state should quit building and repairing roads as a way of keeping them out, and claimed that Rome fell because of migrant paupers.[25] When none of these methods proved effective, Los Ange-

les chief of police James E. Davis, already notorious for his tolerance of brutality and intolerance of "Reds," met in January 1936 with representatives of
the city prosecutor and the chamber of commerce and decided to fingerprint
all adult vagrants and residents of "jungles." He asked housewives to report
any beggars they saw. But nothing drove them back. "They won't go," Lange
wrote in one of her captions, quoting a caseworker for transients in Imperial
County, "until they get so hungry that there's nothing else for them to do . . .
not twenty-five percent will go."[26]

Failing to stem the flow, Chief Davis took direct action. On February 3,
1936, he deployed policemen to sixteen entry points into California from Arizona, Oregon, and Nevada to stop all cars and determine if the passengers had
"definite purpose" and "visible means of support." He asked county sheriffs
to deputize men to staff this "bum blockade." Migrants were to be given the
choice to turn back or serve thirty to eighty days at hard labor. This extraordinary and entirely unconstitutional move repeated an established Anglo
strategy of trying to exclude "aliens." Used against the Chinese, Japanese,
Mexicans and Filipinos, the strategy was repeated throughout the Depression
in several attempts to lengthen the residency requirement for relief.[27]

Not all sheriffs were willing to enforce the blockade, and naturally the governors and attorneys general of the states that the migrants would be returned
to—most frequently Arizona—were not pleased. But the blockade functioned.
The Los Angeles mayor and the governor ruled that the blockade was legal.
Representatives of the chamber of commerce spoke to the press as if they
were elected authorities. Davis claimed that the state would save three million
dollars in relief money and one and a half million that the vagrants would have
stolen.[28]

Stryker asked Lange to hunt down some photographs of the blockade, but
she did not succeed, explaining that the migrants were terrified of being photographed, for fearing they would be identified as "aliens" and arrested or
deported.[29]

The ACLU brought suit, and after two months Davis withdrew his "foreign
legion," as opponents called his border patrol. (The blockade was ultimately
ruled unconstitutional by the U.S. Supreme Court in *Edwards v California*.) But
other unconstitutional practices continued. Paul Taylor kept in his files a State
Board of Public Welfare directive of December 1936, urging county boards
to seize migrants' cars—"A part of the plan for the stabilizing of migrants
is that we take from them the easiest mode of transportation, which is the

automobile"—sell them, and use the money to send the people back to where they came from.[30]

Meanwhile, the chambers of commerce and the California Citizens Association continued to ratchet up the anti-Okie fury. In today's understanding, of course, Okies are simply "white." But in 1930s California, they were another race, of "degenerate" and "degraded stock." A California health official announced in a 1938 speech that Okies were "incapable of being absorbed into our civilization. . . ."[31] Many Anglo Californians grouped Okies with Mexicans, Filipinos, Japanese, Chinese, and "Hindus" as illegal aliens. The denunciation of the Okies anticipated another Lange subject, the anti-Japanese fury of five years later, and raised her consciousness still further about race hatred and how quickly it could be incited.

# 15

# On the Road: The South

L ange made her most sensuous FSA photographs in the South. The southern pictures seem to contain not only sights but also the smells, the humidity, the green, and the heat. When you compare them to those of the drought and dust area and the California agricultural valleys, you can feel the different natural environments with all the senses, as well as the environment's links to human relations.

The southern photographs were also her most beautiful. This may be because of the heat, which forces bodies to relax and move slowly. It may also be because her subjects were more rooted. Their rootedness made them comfortable in their skins, which made them good photographic subjects. But their rootedness resulted from lack of freedom, not from beloved tradition or contentment. Lange's son Daniel summarized how she saw it: "Up until then, most of her work had been done in areas where Depression had shaken apart any form of social order. But in the South, a social order remained, and it held so tenaciously to those who lived under it that to photograph the people she discovered that she had to photograph the order as well." Lange responded, "I couldn't pry the two apart. . . . Earlier, I'd gotten at people through the ways they'd been torn loose, but now I had to get at them through the ways they were bound up."[1]

The FSA photographs represent the South as more fixed and unchanging

15.1. MEMPHIS, TENNESSEE, 1938

than other regions. Photographs of the dust bowl and West Coast regions could not avoid showing the transformation of land and the wandering of people. These were less visible in the South. Walker Evans's photographs are at one extreme in this respect: motionless. His portrait subjects, lined up in front of the walls they had built, tell us that they live just like their grandparents and great-grandparents and will never live otherwise. His love affair with folk architecture recapitulated the stillness. Every FSA photographer, including Lange, made a few of these "Evans shots." Lange's portraits, however, typically avoided Evans's frontality and made everyone handsome. She chose attractive subjects, but she also found the attractiveness in everyone. An approach born of insight, it had become habit from years of portrait work, and was reinforced by her democratic politics.

The photographs also reflect the beauty of the southern countryside. All the FSA photographers responded to this, and with some surprise. None of them were previously familiar with the South. The southern images they imagined from the reading Stryker assigned consisted of backwardness, ignorance, poverty, and racism. Compared to the orderliness and flatness of the California plantations and the bleakness of the parched prairies, the southern landscape was a feast of natural and human-made vistas. The rough plank or log houses and barns seemed to have grown out of the earth like the trees, the stone chimneys clung to the sides of their houses like off-center spines, and the porches rested on stems of stacked rock. Dirt roads curved up and down the

15.2. PERSON COUNTY, NORTH CAROLINA, 1939

hills as if they had emerged gradually over decades from the trampling down of weeds by those taking their daily work routes. Adding to the absence of a boundary between people and nature was the fact that so much of life's work took place outside, not only the farming but also cooking, washing, mending, braiding hair, building, conversing, resting. Even environmental damage could be beautiful, as in a shot of a badly eroded Negro cemetery.[2]

But these impressions also created a trap for the unwary documentary photographer. More then other American regions, the South could seduce a photographer into the picturesque. Because of its economic and social "backwardness," romanticism crept in not only to FSA landscapes but also to photo-

15.3. CHATHAM COUNTY, NORTH CAROLINA, 1939

graphs of people. Urban photographers could not always resist seeing "simple" lives rich in community and tradition, happily absent the commercialism and tension of modernity. Their romance featured the very "backwardness" that the FSA hoped to remedy. Even Lange, a photographer of people, was moved to record the delicate patterns in the log or board houses, the tobacco barns, the fences, the laundry on the line, the wildflowers. At the same time, a bucolic photograph could disrupt clichés, as with a sharecropper, of a class often assumed to be illiterate, sitting under a tree on his home-built chair reading a newspaper.

The FSA respect for southern popular culture was at once a democratic political stance and a sentimentalizing of a "simpler" folk. It had a tinge of colonial Orientalism, the images sometimes reminiscent of *National Geographic*'s photo spreads on premodern societies. Evans's pitiless, spare gaze saved him from sentimentality. Lange's gaze, even in her rare frontal compositions, showed more mercy but avoided sentimentality by its emphasis on individual personality and complexity. The sharecroppers of her photographs are typically contemplative or conversational, and, because they are so often black, convey an antiracist message. Photographing African Americans in the South could endanger them, and this increased the occurrence of suspicion, even hostility toward the photographer. Far from avoiding those glances or suppressing those images, Lange saw in them evidence of pride and autonomy. (See plate 10, for example.)

It was more difficult to show the violence that held southern society in place. Looking at Lange's mellifluous southern landscapes and lyrical portraits, one could forget that this was the land of lynching and the "legal lynching," of the Scottsboro "boys." Racism was not a holdover from slavery, but a thriving activity, continually reproduced but also adapted to new conditions, just as racism was reproduced and adapted by the industrial agricultural economy of the West.

Directives from Department of Agriculture superiors, and the southern Democratic politicians whose political support Roosevelt needed, prohibited open critique of racism in the photographs. No blacks and whites in social contact, no references to racial oppression, no images of racial inequality or abuse of blacks were to be shown.[3] The photographers themselves killed photographs that could provoke racist reprisal and disguised the identities of interviewees.[4] Still, the photographers were shocked by what they saw—Jack Delano sent Stryker "two disgusting postcards bought in a drug store" and told him to put them in a "shame of America" file—and broke the rules when they could. They photographed WHITES ONLY signs and African Americans giving way to whites on the sidewalk. This transgressive photography met resistance and even physical threats. Arthur Rothstein reported to Stryker that when he asked to get "pictures of miners and steel workers in the Birmingham area . . . it was as though I had asked them to raise their employees' wages." When he drove to a mine to photograph without permission, "a foreman . . . took Tom and me into custody . . . shotguns surrounded us . . . someone would have thought we had tried to blow up the place."[5]

In one extraordinary image of a plantation owner and his croppers at a country store, Lange succeeded in replicating the power structure visually, both on the picture plane and in the three dimensions it represents. (See plate 25.) A plantation owner stands next to the porch of a Mississippi general store, dominating the image from just right of center, with one leg set aggressively on the bumper of his car, looking off to his right.[6] Behind him are five black men, probably his share croppers, sitting and standing on the porch, in postures almost exaggeratedly unassuming, withdrawing, small, even frail by contrast with the white man. As the white man makes himself, and is made by Lange, as large as possible, so the black men are shrinking themselves. The photograph lets us *see* the relations of power and deference on a southern plantation. Some viewers had no trouble understanding this image as subversive. One letter to a newspaper complained that ". . . indicative of the agency's [FSA's] vivid pink trend . . . is Miss Lange's cunningly posed portrait of 'The Plantation Owner. . . .' "[7]

In response to such attacks, Stryker's staff sometimes exercised verbal as well as visual censorship. Once someone excised a phrase from a Lange caption: "Old Negro—the kind the planters like. He hoes, picks cotton, and is full of good humor."[8] On the other hand, the office staff did not interfere with a Lange caption that included a direct quotation: "A tractor pioneer of the Mississippi Delta. In 1927 he had 160 colored tenant families working his land, in 1936 he won thirty Farmall tractors and employs thirty families on day labor basis. He says, 'Now I can make money. Hours are nothing to us. You can't industrialize farming. We in Mississippi know how to treat our niggers.' "[9]

To get around the stricture on challenging racism, FSA photographers emphasized cross-race similarity. This was not only a tactic; it was also the dominant analysis of the South among progressive New Dealers, including Paul Taylor. To the FSA progressives, the South's main feature was the tenant

PLATE 19. AMERICAN RIVER CAMP, SACRAMENTO, CALIFORNIA, 1936
(HAPPY FAMILY)

PLATE 22.
SOUTHERN
SAN JOAQUIN
VALLEY, 1936

PLATE 23.
SOUTHERN SAN JOAQUIN
VALLEY, 1936

PLATE 24. SHOOFLY, NORTH CAROLINA, 1939

PLATE 25. MISSISSIPPI DELTA, NEAR CLARKSDALE, MISSISSIPPI, 1936

PLATE 26. STRIKE MEETING, YUBA COUNTY, CALIFORNIA, 1938

PLATE 27. MARYSVILLE, CALIFORNIA, MIGRANT CAMP, 1935

Plate 28. Near El Paso, Texas, 1938

and sharecropping system, which imprisoned whites and blacks alike. This analysis, accurate but incomplete, was convenient to the Roosevelt administration's policy not to confront racism, though it still evoked fury among southern planters and their political representatives. Although Lange and Taylor also stressed parallels between white and black farmworkers, and tenancy as the root problem, they were more conscious of the salience of race than others in and around the Department of Agriculture.

Lange's images of southern labor are mainly of blacks. Moreover, discontent as usual with simple condemnation, she showed the racial intimacy that constituted the reverse face of the southern racial system. She showed whites and blacks, even tenants and owners, working together in the fields. She photographed children playing and bonding across racial lines, white and black farmworkers relaxing at stores, and, above all, the extraordinary similarities between poor blacks and whites. Her captions told what she could not show, underlining complexities: "The three year old white girl at intervals slapped and switched the little Negro girl about her age and once called her a damn fool; but between these outbursts the children played together peaceably . . ." One black tenant "goes to the white folks church and sits in the front row. She wouldn't go if she had to sit in the balcony."[10]

*When you work a sharecrop*
*you supposed to do all the work*
*he supposed to supply all the 'terials*
*They don't do what they supposed to do*


IF THE MAJOR MASCULINITY THEME of the drought area was dejection, in the South it was the sweat-drenched labor of tenant farmers and sharecroppers—except here it was women's theme, as well. *Tenancy* was a generic term that could include all farmers who worked someone else's land, excluding wage laborers, and in this sense sharecroppers are a kind of tenant. More commonly, *tenant* referred to someone who paid cash rent, supplied his own tools, animals, feed, and seed, and kept all his produce for sale or consumption; a sharecropper was supplied by the landlord and turned the crop over to him, receiving, in turn, a share of it. Sharecropping dominated east of the Mississippi.[11] In theory, croppers received a "furnish" of seed, food, animal feed, et cetera, from the owner each year and used the owner's tools and plows. They repaid this debt after their crop sold, theoretically at an average 10 percent interest, but since the advance had been theirs only part of a year, they were effectively paying much higher interest, often up to 44 percent.[12] In return for use of the land, they also gave the owner a proportion of the crop— sometimes half, sometimes a third.

A crucial aspect of the system, at the core of the South's "backward" character, was that there was no free market in labor. Farmworkers often moved from one landowner to another in search of better terms, but in practice sharecroppers were often indebted to their owner and not free to leave until they had paid off their debt.[13] Plantation owners typically ran their own commissaries, or company stores, so sharecroppers had to buy at inflated prices. Forced to put up a future crop as collateral for an advance of supplies, an arrangement known as the crop lien system, a sharecropper could owe even his own part of the crop to the landlord or store owner. Sharecroppers lived on land belonging to their landlord and could be evicted for any or no reason. Their livelihood often depended on fishing, hunting, and gardening on the owner's land, a "privilege" they would lose if evicted. As if all that were not binding enough, owners were able to dictate changes in tenancy contracts year by year according to what benefited them.[14] Landlords further cheated tenants by making only verbal contracts, keeping false commissary accounts, and fixing the scales they used to weigh the crop.

The system could not have survived democracy, but there was none. In the "solid South" less than half, and often less than a quarter, of *white* tenants could vote, because of poll taxes, literacy tests, and other devices designed to disenfranchise; almost no blacks could vote. Large landowners dominated all aspects of local government, including tax collection, criminal justice, education, and transportation.

Because labor was so cheap, few planters mechanized. In 1930, there were approximately one thousand tractors on all southern plantations, as opposed to eleven thousand in California.[15] The productive power of an Iowa farmer was seven to eight times that of a southern farmer.[16] "The field tools used by the typical tenant farmer would not seem strange to Moses and Hammurabi," Taylor's friend Arthur Raper wrote.[17] Lange showed the reliance on animal power—oxen, mules, and the occasional horse pulling wagons containing logs, people, and every conceivable kind of load.[18] Neither government nor planters bothered to provide education or medical care to the poor because they did not need an educated or healthy workforce. Southern farms were becoming "westernized" as sharecroppers were forced to become hourly wage laborers, usually migratory. In 1939, planters hired airplanes to drop recruiting flyers in Florida. Growers recruited workers just as they did in the West, gathering more than they needed or would pay. One operator used the same words as a California grower: "You can't have too much labor. You just can't have too much."[19] These workers followed the crops just as those in California did.[20] In June 1937, Taylor estimated that between one thousand and fifteen hundred workers, most of them former croppers, were being taken from Memphis down to the Mississippi Delta to chop cotton.[21] Lange photographed truckloads of farmworkers ferried to hours or days of work in distant locations, noting that they were not paid for travel time. One of Lange's subjects explained it, and she transcribed his words as a found poem:

> Soil Consoleration would
> pay you for your corn . . .
> Then they knocked out the corn.
> Rather than go into the Soil
> Consoleration they won't let
> you plant no corn.
> We needs bread thru the winter
> We want to raise hawgs.
>    They want all theyselves.
> They aint begun to fill those houses
> They want day labor, haul em
> from town.
> He's got some on the place
> but the biggest
> he gets em out of town.

The FSA considered soil erosion one of the causes of southern poverty and backwardness, and Lange obediently made dozens of photographs of erosion.[22] The timber industry in the South was particularly destructive, and she photographed barren, cut-over land. In such photographs she added human consequences in her captions. About the cut-over land, for example, she noted, "The tract extends for thirty-seven miles. A lumber industry owner did no replanting and cut out in 1931 after eighteen years of operations. They employed approximately 3000 men."[23]

This backwardness once led experts to conclude that southern agriculture operated not only in a preindustrial but also a precapitalist system. This was not the case. These plantations had been tied in to the world economy since their establishment in the seventeenth century and continued those ties in the twentieth, as suppliers of international trade and borrowers from global lending institutions. In 1934, a third of southern cotton plantations were owned by banks and insurance companies; in the cotton belt, absentee ownership was at 60 to 70 percent.[24] Southern "backwardness" was created by modern capitalism.

Lange became aware of this contradiction—that the rural South could be part of a global economy even as its workers knew only their local community—through her conversations with subjects. She was shocked to find that a Gordonton, North Carolina, woman had never heard of California[25] and that a "colored plowboy" on a Texas cotton plantation had never heard of Joe Louis.[26] This was changing, Lange observed as she listened to the aspirations of her interviewees. The woman who did not know about California had heard of Amelia Earhart and wished she could travel. "I've never been nowhere except to Durham and Danville. All I've seen is corn and tobacco— and a houseful of children." An old black sharecropper thought her sixty-nine-year-old husband deserved a pension and would have liked to let their land "rest" every other year.[27] A black father working in the sweet potato fields with his thirteen-year-old daughter wanted to send her to high school.[28] A mother, proud that her children were doing well in school, wanted to send them to college.[29]

The FSA did help some sharecroppers, predominantly white ones. Arthur Raper found that an FSA program in Greene County, North Carolina, produced much-improved nutrition, increased home production of canned fruits and vegetables, eggs, milk, bread, and meat; it built twenty-six new school buildings (segregated) and organized several 4H-type clubs (segregated), a county library system, a bookmobile, a motion-picture projector, and a hot-lunch program—even a small cooperative, HMO-like medical-care program.[30] Results like these made Dorothea and Paul comfortable creating propaganda for the FSA when asked.

But at the same time, they documented FSA corruption, which was particularly widespread in the South. One group of displaced sharecroppers were, to Lange's and Taylor's disgust, *refugees* from a nearby FSA resettlement community, Dixie Plantation, where local Department of Agriculture official Yates was cheating them. "Never had a settlement for last year's crop—no statement—no receipt, no gin tickets," a sharecropper told Lange; living on credit at the store, they could not even find out what they were being charged for their purchases. About Yates, they reported, "Bad as on a plantation." "He owns a store in Shelby, Bolivar Grocery and Supply. He's a planter hisself." He told them the federal government required them to turn in all their animals to him. Another Agriculture agent, Stirewalt, had forged their names on government checks and kept the money.[31]

LANGE DISPLAYED A more ambivalent attitude toward another part of the South's "backwardness," its local general stores/gas stations, usually conjoined in the same structure. She photographed them nearly everywhere she went because they were natural social centers, and the images are picturesque: dilapidated board structures with porches, on which men—rarely women, who, as usual, were busier—sit on boxes to relax, smoke, and visit. On the facades are metal commercial signs advertising Coca-Cola, Pop Kola, Orange Crush, Armour Fertilizer, Texaco, Chesterfield, Old Gold, Raleigh, and Camel cigarettes, and snuff; there are also hand-lettered signs, such as these:

LIBITY.

CASH GROC.

M. POPE.

Crates of empty green glass Coca-Cola bottles are stacked outside.[32]

She very rarely shot inside homes, not only because of her dislike for flashbulbs but also because she did not want to embarrass or endanger her subjects by asking to come in. Once, she listened to an entire sermon from outside the window of a black church, reluctant to intrude.[33] Besides, her subjects usually spent their days outside, even if they were not in the fields. So her photographs could show men sawing, hammering, and stretching gunnysacks to make the bins for transporting tobacco. The women and children are seen churning, sewing, hairdressing, pumping water, cooking, feeding and watering animals, gathering eggs, killing chickens, and nursing babies. Kids are playing in the dirt. The photographs are full of dense activity.

Hesitant as always to make anyone look bad, Lange photographed some rundown homes, but most appear neat. One historian claimed that her photographs show that blacks are neater than poor whites, and Lange thought the black women did more decorating and flower gardening, but in general the sharecroppers' tiny houses all look tidy.[34] Clean laundry hangs on the line. Nearby wild-flowers and tubs of flowers on the porches bloom profusely. Very occasionally, there is a vegetable garden. Household vessels and tools rest in precise patterns on outside shelves or hang from nails. Describing one of her photographs years later, she pointed out "the dignified, almost queenly gesture of a cotton tenant farmer's wife. . . . It's the quality of the gesture."[35] Did she avoid the wretched? She could not or did not show what they ate: corn, sweet potatoes, fatback; nor could her photographs show pellagra, hookworms, or anemia.

She used housing to depict both inequality and beauty. The croppers usually lived in dogtrot houses, with an open passage from front to back through the center of the house, one room on either side, although many had only one-room cabins. Lange's lens lingered over the grain on the unpainted boards, the bits of bark clinging to the rough-hewn four-by-fours, the carved joints, the flow between indoors and outdoors, as well as the impromptu construction, the houses resting precariously on rocks to provide airspace under the floor. A painted house, a two-story house, or one with sanded boards marked a rich person.[36] Some planters still lived in the old mansions, and Lange recorded the pretentiousness of their columns, grand entryways, and second-floor verandas. Most old plantation houses were decrepit and unoccupied, or occupied by tenants. Houses, like highways, are dense with symbolism in Lange's photographs: a white woman tenant sitting on the collapsing front steps of a former "big house" surrounded by eroding fields;[37] a black teenage woman sitting on her porch, staring disconsolately out at the photographer through the bars made by beautifully trained butter-bean vines secured to the porch roof. (See figure 15.1.)

The most visible sign of economic transformation in her photographs is the automobile.[38] Unlike their significance in the plains and California, however, where they were a means of travel to find work, for southern sharecroppers cars meant escape, literally. The deference black pedestrians had to offer whites on the sidewalk did not extend to the road, a further attraction of cars for African Americans. But many cars went unused, for lack of money to buy gas or license tags. One black woman sharecropper, clearly the household's financial manager, told Lange, "I always say rations and clothes come before riding. . . ."[39]

ON HER FOUR southern trips, during the summers of 1936 to 1939, Lange focused on three major agricultural products—cotton, tobacco, and turpen-

15.4. PERSON COUNTY, NORTH CAROLINA, 1939

tine. She documented the cycle of production for each crop as best she could, given her schedule.[40] On her last trip, she executed an unusually fruitful commission, working in collaboration with social scientists at the University of North Carolina, which yielded a photo-textual study of tobacco production. An extraordinary group of social researchers had gravitated to the University of North Carolina, drawn together by distinguished sociologist Howard Odum and his Institute for Research in Social Science. Established in 1924 with Rockefeller Foundation money, it was dedicated to studying southern society, with a particular, though quiet, emphasis on race. The energetic Odum started the *Journal of Social Forces*, which was to become influential in the field, and made the UNC sociology department and the UNC Press nationally eminent, particularly as a hub of interracial and antiracist scholarship.[41] Editor Wil-

15.5. LANGE INTERVIEWING, GREENE COUNTY, GEORGIA, 1939

liam Couch began including FSA photographs in the press's books. Odum's colleague Arthur Raper knew Taylor's work and showed Paul and Dorothea around Greene County in 1937.[42]

The Odum group included Margaret Jarman Hagood, a woman of considerable achievement, who became a nationally known statistician and birth-control advocate.[43] When Lange showed up, Hagood was just finishing a study of white sharecropper mothers, *Mothers of the South,* which produced some surprising findings. Eighty-eight percent of the women, for example, preferred field work to housework—so much for "protecting" women by trying to keep them in their homes. Yet even when they worked in the fields alongside men, as at harvest time, it never occurred to them to ask that men share in the housework. They had little or no expectation of being able to "improve themselves," but they agonized when their poverty deprived their children. Like Lange's, Hagood's portraits defied the stereotypes of "tobacco road" degenerates. But Hagood interviewed only white women. Surrounded as she was by the Odum network's racial liberals, she may have had charitable feelings toward blacks, but she was unwilling to include them as "mothers of the South."

Hagood requested some FSA photographs for her book, and Stryker sent her both Lange and Marion Post Wolcott. Hagood was a strong partner for Lange, not only because she offered better access to subjects but also because her methodology resembled Taylor's, but with a feminist slant, even offering birth-control information.[44]

Tobacco was the main crop in the region. Because of the nature of the plant, and because of North Carolina's history and geography, there were more small farms and fewer large plantations here than in the deep South, or the cotton South. Lange was photographing and interviewing workers who knew and controlled every aspect of tobacco production. Her respect for their labor shows in the detailed "general captions" she wrote. Lange was not there for the planting, so we first see the tobacco in June, when it was about two feet high. Lange shot close-ups of tobacco plants to contrast healthy plants to those with wilt, for which there was no remedy at this time. The worms were particularly bad this year. Photographs show the croppers picking them off, pointing out that they sometimes lie on the underside of top leaves, or hide deep in the center of the plant. A father and his toddler daughter move through the rows together, he topping and suckering and she worming; she appears proud when she finds two worms. Children partici-pate in all the farmwork—in the fields, barns, house, and yard, tending chickens and gathering eggs, cul-tivating vegetables, and working in every aspect of the tobacco culture. The boys particularly took pride in their skills, and sometimes bragged about how good they were.[45]

Meanwhile, farmwork-ers were also building and repairing tobacco barns, which required frequent upkeep. The average life of

15.6. PICKING OFF WORMS, PERSON COUNTY, NORTH CAROLINA, 1939

a barn was fifteen to twenty years, because the fires burned out the bricks in
the flues. Most were built of logs, but an especially prosperous grower might
have had one built of planks. Workers also built and repaired tobacco slides
or sleds. These containers, about five feet by two feet, were made of burlap
hung from a wooden frame. Their bottoms are like sleds, with planks placed
on end beneath each container to skid along the muddy paths from fields
to barns. Occasionally the sharecroppers built a giant wooden dolly to move
several sleds at once. Lange saw them topping tobacco—breaking off the tops
of plants before they blossom except for a few that are saved for seed. One
elderly man bragged that he could do two rows, swinging from right to left, as
fast as he could walk, even as he accurately topped the plants to ten, twelve,
or fourteen leaves—whichever he chose.[46] At first ripeness, priming started.
Because the bottom leaves ripened first, this was stoop labor and exhausting
as well as skilled. The leaves were loaded into the sleds, which were pulled
and pushed by men or by mules, or both. Women and children took over next,
carefully bunching the leaves, tying their stems together, then stringing them
upside down on sticks to be hung in the barns for curing.

Firing and curing of the tobacco came next, a delicate process. Because
the wrong temperatures or timing could spoil a crop, this operation had to be
monitored twenty-four hours a day, and there was often a "bed shed" for the
use of the man who tended the fires at night.

There is a special feeling of care and attentiveness in these photographs, as
if Lange were trying to reproduce the care with which farmworkers handled
the crop on which their living depended. The barns are treated particularly
lovingly, as if, having now understood the logic of their construction and their
function as a part of the production process, she cared for them more than
for less productive buildings. The materialism of her photographs and captions speaks of her respect for sharecroppers' expertise and experience and
her refusal to treat manual labor as unskilled.


OUT OF TENANTS' and sharecroppers' frustration grew an important labor
and civil rights movement, a movement that, despite its ultimate failure, left
a vital legacy. Arkansas sharecroppers, aided by a few outside organizers,
including a few Communists and, unofficially, some FSA people, organized
the Southern Tenant Farmers' Union.[47] Eighteen sharecropper organizers
first met in July 1934 and planned a secret association, a vigilante group of

sharecroppers "punishing dishonest landlords and oppressive managers and riding bosses" with nighttime attacks.[48] Accustomed to violent reprisals, their subsequent decision to go public required extraordinary courage. Supported by two local small businessmen, trusted white socialists, they formed a union, aiming to better their conditions through collective bargaining with planters. Their meetings often included prayer, hymns, and oaths of loyalty. They took place outside or in friendly homes, not only to avoid violence but also because planters padlocked the doors of churches and schools to keep them out, and the locations were revealed only to trusted members. As in much of the civil rights movement two decades later, members were required to leave their shotguns at home despite the likelihood of armed attacks.

Risking an integrated union so as to head off the inevitable divide and conquer strategy of the local power structure, they asked that tenants share in AAA payment and that evictions be prohibited; the Department of Agriculture retaliated in support of the planters, on the grounds that the union was a Communist conspiracy duping ignorant sharecroppers. (Roosevelt's legislative clout depended particularly on Senator Joseph Robinson of Arkansas, Democratic majority leader.) Despite violence and eviction threats from landlords, sheriffs and local racists, the STFU grew. After a few months, it claimed 1,400 members, and by early 1935, 4,500 to 5,000. Locals arose in Missouri, Oklahoma, Texas, and Mississippi, the membership totaling 20,000 to 25,000 at peak.

Lange was one of several FSA people who got access to the STFU. She was escorted to meetings by a trusted member after giving assurances that she would photograph no individuals without their permission. So she photographed only sparingly, and rarely showed interracial groups. Only white leaders allowed her to make their portraits—president J.R. Butler and secretary H. L. Mitchell—although she photographed several unnamed black activists. STFU's nighttime meetings once led her to try to use a flashbulb, which she immediately regretted. Trying to follow directions on a very dark night, she got lost and asked for help from a man who "started to talk," she recalled, "and tell us his life story and I got out a camera with a flash gun. . . . I don't think he'd ever seen a camera, let alone this thing that goes off in his face . . . he was so frightened that he just didn't move, I fired off . . . five negatives, one after another, he was just paralyzed. [Voice drops] I've often thought afterward, how really, what a terrible thing I did. . . . Do look at that picture . . . etched out of the black, what an awful thing it was to do that. . . ."[49]

One unanticipated result of the violent repression of the STFU was a cooperative farm, which particularly attracted Taylor, an ardent supporter of farm co-ops. A grower evicted twenty-one families without notice and left them camped on the roadside. Local officials refused them relief. To help, the STFU decided to build a cooperative farm, calling in aid from Memphis white allies who led them to Sherwood Eddy, an upper-class New England missionary and religious writer. When Eddy arrived in Arkansas to investigate, he was arrested by local deputy sheriffs and held without charge, warned not to help "these damn niggers who won't work."[50] But he had powerful friends: the U.S. attorney general, Homer Cummings, got him released, and then Reinhold Niebuhr helped him raise the money to buy two thousand acres at Hillhouse in Bolivar County, Mississippi, just across the river—the croppers considered Arkansas just too dangerous.[51] Here, the STFU established the Delta Cooperative Farm in March 1936, with twenty-four families, of which thirteen were black.

When Lange and Taylor first drove up to the co-op in their dusty Ford station wagon in early July 1936, they were a sight. Even here in deep Mississippi, Dorothea dressed eccentrically, and some other visitors to the cooperative worried about how she would be received. They needn't have: Her usual technique, moving about unobtrusively, absorbed in her camera preparations, made her subjects comfortable with her presence. Paul's back was hurting (hardly surprising after so many weeks on the road), and Dorothea wanted him to rest it; she asked for help from members of the co-op, who laid boards across sawhorses, on which he stretched out—a perfect icebreaker.[52]

Her photographs and Taylor's notes document an extraordinary social experiment, one so inspiring that they returned in 1937 and 1938. The cooperators were particularly proud of their houses, and Lange photographed them dutifully. Built of weatherproof boards instead of logs, they featured screened windows and porches, curtains in the windows, and a water pump by each. The cooperators also built a store and a community center that housed a library, a clinic, and school and meeting rooms. They recruited a nurse and a doctor to provide medical care to people who had never had any. They developed adult-education programs and enlisted American Friends Service Committee volunteers to work at construction, child care, and chopping cotton, prefiguring the thousands of northerners who came to help in the civil rights movement two decades later. To head off violent attacks, the members defied southern white racial etiquette only gingerly: black and white members lived on opposite sides of a road, and children attended segregated schools. Since the white children got eight months of schooling in classes half the size of those the black children attended for only four months, the group set up a supplementary education program for the black children. Co-op meetings and community facilities—the store, clinic, church, and credit union—were integrated. Visitors were housed in the same place whatever their race, as when researchers Arthur Raper, white, and Charles S. Johnson, black, appeared together. The members got around the ban on calling African Americans Mr. or Mrs. by addressing everyone by his or her first name. At the end of the first year, each family had earned $328, plus $122 in deferred credits for their labor in preparing the land and constructing houses—more than they had ever earned before and more than twice the current average tenant income.[53]

Lange's unabashedly enthusiastic photographs emphasized racial integration—at work, in meetings, at leisure. She showed white and black men working together, but, strangely, made no photographs of women. Perhaps they were doing less field work here than in the past—it was the nearly universal aspiration of sharecroppers that wives devote full time to housewifery and motherhood—and Lange continued uncomfortable shooting indoors. But the absence of women in the STFU pictures may also reflect the fact that because Lange was so positive about the project, she accepted photographing what she was shown on an official tour, rather than exploring on her own. Her California-bred respect for the bravery of union people was confirmed here, but typically her view was sentimental rather than strategic. "Union organizer means somebody of importance. These are the beginning seeds, the martyrs of the union movement, martyrs, that's the word I'm looking for. . . ."[54]

She was disappointed. Delta lasted only seven years. Its land was poor, the co-op was never able to become independent of philanthropic gifts, and in 1942 it folded into a larger co-op in Holmes County, Mississippi. The STFU was broken by planters' and sheriffs' violence and threats of retaliation that croppers could not survive. Its FSA supporters could not prevent STFU members from being defeated through terror—threats, arrests, floggings, and lynchings. Nevertheless, Taylor contributed financially to the STFU for decades, even when it was only a shadow of its former substance.

Neither the STFU nor the Delta Cooperative evoked Lange's best work. Most of the co-op pictures are posed—a black child and a white one jointly holding a large melon, black men and white men gathered around a tractor.[55] The rest are unpeopled images of progress—better houses, a co-op store, neatly plowed fields, a sign announcing an educational program. There are a few STFU portraits, but I suspect Lange destroyed negatives that were unsuccessful or dangerous to their subjects. The best, again, are portraits of leaders already publicly known and thus unafraid to be photographed.[56] Celebratory photography was never Lange's forte.

Lange had seen racism, but nowhere was it as terroristic as here in the Deep South. Seeing southern white brutality up close deepened her respect for those who stood up to it, but also increased her understanding of why so many did not.

> . . . when I look at the Farm Security [photographs] in the south . . .
> I thought, these are the people who are stirring themselves 20 years later.
> —*Dorothea Lange, 1965*

Her transcontinental experience—observing race relations in western, central, and eastern farmlands—provided an unparalleled understanding of how racism and labor exploitation strengthened each other. This was, of course, a partial understanding, one that missed many of the cultural, sexual, and psychological impulses that animate racism. In the late 1930s, however, the Lange-Taylor analysis was far ahead of the understanding of most other progressive white Americans.

Lange's ability to communicate that visually was imperfect, she knew—and the more masterful a photographer she became, the more self-critical she grew. Convinced that words needed pictures and that pictures needed words, Lange and Taylor decided to produce a photo-textual book that would summarize in vivid and simple terms their holistic view of American agriculture and the radical historical crisis facing it. It would be a visual history of landowners, field workers, and the earth itself.

# 16

# *An American Exodus*

Sometime in the late 1930s, Lange and Taylor decided to sum up their work together. They envisioned a collaboration as personal as it was public, as historical as it was a call for reform. Taylor wanted to develop his vernacular, nonacademic voice, his ability to persuade. Lange wanted to move documentary photography toward what she considered its culmination, a narrative that completely integrated images and text. The result was *An American Exodus*, published in 1939, a high point in photo-textual storytelling, the fullest synthesis of images and words yet achieved, according to some critics.[1] The project was also a celebration of their partnership and a chance to produce something tangible that was theirs, jointly and equally.

Luckily, they enjoyed the process, because the book never got the attention it deserves. Appearing a few months after World War II began in September 1939, the book got lost in the dire headlines. Moreover, it lacked commercial appeal. It told several centuries of history; it was not billed as an exposé; its goal was agrarian reform, not a cause likely to grip the interests of those who bought photographic books. By contrast, John Steinbeck's *The Grapes of Wrath*, strongly influenced by Lange's images, appeared shortly before *American Exodus* and became a sensation. Twentieth Century–Fox immediately bought the rights and rushed a film, with a major star and director, into production. It would receive seven Oscar nominations and win two.

*An American Exodus* deserves a fresh look, not only because it is a very good book but also because it marks Lange's new photographic ambition, the creation of visual narrative. She had long focused on how grouping and arranging photographs could expand their meaning. Biographer Henry Mayer wrote, "Lange had come to realize that the language of photography might employ a sophisticated grammar of sentences and paragraphs, but the FSA spoke only one word at a time."[2]

Photo-textual books had recently become a new genre. Illustrated books and photography books had long existed, of course; the novelty was in making text and images equal and so meshed that their impact transcended either medium alone.[3] The first to attract significant public notice was the product of another photographer-writer couple, Margaret Bourke-White's and Erskine Caldwell's 1937 *You Have Seen Their Faces*, a sensationalist take on southern sharecroppers. The authors were well known—the world's first famous female photojournalist, whose modernist photograph of a dam on *Life* magazine's first cover promised that industrial power could conquer the Depression, working with the author of many novels, notably *Tobacco Road*. But it was the book's lurid words and images that created a stir. Lange detested the book. Its subjects are abject, wretched, and degenerate; the South appears a human swamp, its victims " 'numbed like their own dumb animals.' "[4] Bourke-White seemed unable to pass a disfigured person or a sick child without photographing her. Few in the book do any work. Blacks appear only as imprisoned, lazing about, or stupid. In one of the "quotations," a black woman says, "I got more children now than I know what to do with, but they keep coming along like watermelons in the summertime."

To Lange's and Taylor's fury, these quotations were fabricated; as Bourke-White and Caldwell forthrightly admitted, the words expressed "the authors' own conceptions of the sentiments of the individuals portrayed...."[5] Although Lange and other photographers edited images and quotations, there was a qualitative difference between them and Bourke-White and Caldwell. Jacob Riis often arranged his dark scenes and sometimes paid his subjects.[6] Walker Evans simplified his subjects' kitchens by removing objects. Jack Delano of the FSA explained to Stryker that he killed photographs of Negroes that could "be interpreted unfairly."[7] Lange and Taylor edited quotes: "If you die, you're dead, that's all" was extracted from a much longer caption and the original context gave it different meaning, complaining that the county would not help pay for decent burials for the poor.[8] For all these documentary photographers, the editing aimed to produce more beautiful and more respectful images, never to fabricate or sensationalize. Lange and Taylor would make their indignation at the Bourke-White/Caldwell method explicit in their own book: "Quotations which accompany photographs report what the persons photographed said, not what we think might be their unspoken thoughts."

After *You Have Seen Their Faces,* the next photo-textual book to appear was by the patrician Archibald MacLeish, poet, ardent New Dealer, and future Librarian of Congress. His *Land of the Free* published 62 FSA photographs, 33 of them Lange's, to critical approval. This book, more than any other single factor, established the FSA as a producer of art, but it rested on a contentless and sentimental patriotism that Lange disliked.[9] Its text bore little relation to the photographs;[10] MacLeish merely juxtaposed photographs on right-hand pages with some banal free verse on facing left-hand pages. He (or someone at the FSA) committed an atrocity on one Lange photograph. MacLeish took her image of a plantation owner and his sharecroppers (see plate 25), shamelessly cropped out almost everything except the white man, and turned him into a salt-of-the-earth American farmer, an icon of grassroots Americanism.[11] The transformation of that photograph exemplifies the futility of seeking authenticity or veracity in photographs, and provides evidence for Lange's conviction that photographs do not "speak for themselves."[12]

The most enduring of these photo-textual books was journalist James Agee and photographer Walker Evans's *Let Us Now Praise Famous Men.* Following Lange and Taylor's volume by two years, it ultimately became acclaimed by a highbrow as well as a middlebrow audience, a rare occurrence. At first, however, it also met a cold reception, appearing at a time as inauspicious as Lange and Taylor's, September 1941, after the fall of Europe to the Nazis. Agee's overlong, confessional, self-centered text—in which he agonized over his role as "spy," thereby foreshadowing postmodernist scholarship—outraged critics. Profiling three white tenant families, it separated photographs and essay entirely. Evans's photographs of individuals, families, barren kitchens, and wooden shacks are hushed, contained, and simplified, revealing the similar beauty of weathered boards and faces—both appear timeless, unchanging. *Let Us Now Praise Famous Men* is ahistorical, asocial, and apolitical. It ennobles the poor but offers no help in explaining why they are so poor or in changing their destiny. Lange and Taylor sought, in contrast and perhaps in naïveté, to end poverty. While Agee and Evans's book presented only whites, the first two chapters of *An American Exodus* focused on African Americans and included

Mexicans and Filipinos.[13] The book might have won greater popularity had it featured only "Okies."

AN AMERICAN EXODUS rested on "a tripod of photographs, captions, and text," as Lange put it. The book's design is on the whole conservative, making its substantive innovations more easily legible. A classic font was used for the text, not one of the sporty scripts fashionable in the 1930s and 1940s. The photographs are presented uniformly: bled to the edges, occupying usually the top three-quarters of the page, captions beneath. The paper is thick, semiglossy, and cream-colored. But one innovative aspect of its design signals its democratic politics: Inside the front and back covers quotations from farmworkers are presented in a collage, end to end, like wallpaper, producing an effect like that of a Greek chorus.

One critic called Lange's layout a "Cubist approach."[14] This is a stretch, but a fruitful one. Lange's photography is representational, a classic example of American social realism; nothing could contrast more with the Constructivism, Surrealism, and montage being explored by European photographers of her time.[15] *An American Exodus* is resolutely antiart, expressing both Lange's self-conception at the time—documentarist, not artist—and its communicative, political purpose.[16] Yet by juxtaposing images, quotations, hand-lettered signs, newspaper ads, data, and brief excerpts from authorities, Lange was doing something akin to what Cubists did: breaking up objects, analyzing them, and reassembling them in a form that calls attention to their construction by denaturalizing the whole; presenting objects not from one viewpoint, but from a multitude of viewpoints, so as to say more about the object than you can see at a glance. She used layout to produce a new syntax. After finishing the manuscript, she insisted on overseeing every detail of production.[17]

The book did not find a publisher easily. Dorothea asked John Steinbeck to contribute an introduction or preface, but he refused—a rather stingy response, given his indebtedness to her photographs.[18] Unstoppable, Dorothea may well have promised publishers a Steinbeck introduction anyway.[19] Even so, the book was rejected by Random House and Viking, among other publishers, until Reynal & Hitchcock, a distinguished New York publishing house, took it.

The story line of *An American Exodus* reversed Lange's learning process: as she had traveled west to east, the book travels east to west, from the older to the

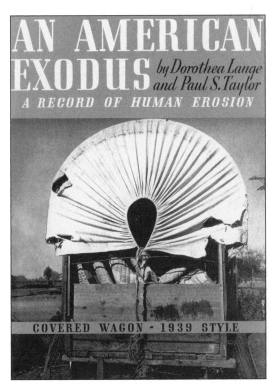

16.1. *AN AMERICAN EXODUS* COVER, 1939

newer parts of the nation. Images of highways show how "on the road" bears a variety of meanings in American history, implying the expansion of the United States, the movement and mobility so central to American culture, the automobile as a symbol of freedom and as transportation to a better life. The movement at the climax of the narrative is the mass migration of displaced tenant farmers from the drought-ridden southern plains to California—hence the title.[20]

A story in six chapters, the book's mainspring is cotton. Its subtitle, *A Record of Human Erosion,* with its metaphoric use of an environmental term, signaled that the book was not about crops or conservation, but people. The cover photo was a rear view of a wooden auto trailer, with a top made of circularly stretched canvas—what we see is a covered wagon, one of the most sacred images of Americana. The message is that the exodus consists of pioneers, not bums.[21]

In all six chapters, photographs, accompanied by captions, precede the text.[22] Each chapter begins with an iconic picture of a region: For the Old South, piles of baled cotton; for the "last west," the endless highway, of course. Some of these introductory pictures aim to undermine clichés—the dust bowl chapter begins not with an image of a dust storm, but with a grain elevator, directing attention to what had created the dust bowl. In a typical Lange democratic gesture, captions mix the authority of experts with that of farmers: "The collapse of the plantation system, rendered inevitable by its exploitation of land and labor, leaves in its wake depleted soil, shoddy livestock, inadequate farm equipment, crude agricultural practices, crippled institutions, a

16.2. *An American Exodus, 1939*

defeated and impoverished people." "A piece of meat in the house would like to scare these children of mine to death." "There's lots of ways to break a man down." Some captions make theoretical points: "Old forms remain, but they are changed at the core."

In content as well as design, Lange's photographs are restrained. There are sad children, dejected men, and long-suffering mothers, but there are more hardworking, attractive, thoughtful, animated people. The message was, in Taylor's words, "These people are worth helping."[23] Lange selected the photographs with great discipline, to advance the story rather than promote her artistic reputation. *Migrant Mother* is not included.[24]

The narrative explains that rural poverty was a product of history, not nature. Although agricultural prosperity in the Old South came from mechanization—the cotton gin—there was no incentive to mechanize farming, due to the cheap labor provided by slavery and then by sharecropping. Neither was there incentive to preserve the environment, so the soil became exhausted and the monoculture gave birth to invulnerable pests like boll weevils. The reign of cotton produced the worst damage—85 percent of cotton was produced on plantations, including the largest in the world in Mississippi's Bolivar County. As the dry prairie was plowed up, the tenant system took over there too, but without even minimal paternalist obligations to dependents. As a result, many tenants survived by traveling in search of seasonal work. As cotton prices collapsed in the 1930s, growers began to buy row-crop tractors, evict sharecroppers, and rely on casual wage laborers. Lange treated a grain silo as if it were a church, suggesting that large-scale farming, devouring ever more land and people, had become an object of worship. The plowed prairie was defenseless against dust storms that stripped away the soil. So farmworkers had to leave their homes for good, heading to Arizona and California, where there had never been an economy of family farms, to join the migrants in the fields of the vast agribusinesses, typically owned by absentee capitalists.

Lange and Taylor were proud of the book and worked to promote it. They celebrated its appearance at dinner with progressive Wisconsin senator Bob La Follette, Jr., Paul's college friend. Through historian Mary Beard, Dorothea tried to enlist Eleanor Roosevelt's support, but she only managed to get a one-sentence mention in the First Lady's weekly column, "My Day."[25] Photographers, however, recognized its importance. Ansel Adams wrote Dorothea with his usual warmth and charm and unusual high praise: "Your book has been looked at, read, studied, observed, pulled apart and put together again, and glanced through, raced through, micromatically poured [*sic*] over and macroscopically examined . . . it is the most successful of all the documentary projects produced to date . . . its soundness, its fairness, and its integrity. . . . A supurb [*sic*] job throughout."[26] Edward Weston wrote, ". . . the most important book of its kind that I have seen. In truth it is in a class apart. . . . This sounds like a patent medicine testimonial but it is nonetheless sincere."[27] Unexpectedly, the left-wing Paul Strand was critical. He found the text weighted more heavily than the images, which he thought merely illustrated the text, and he criticized some less than excellent photographs.[28] The latter criticism was quite right, for Lange chose photographs because of what they showed. Adams and Weston did not mind, because they did not see the book as art at all, while Strand, committed to the possibility of socially critical fine art, objected. New Dealers and left-wing magazines loved it, but it got few reviews overall. The book sank quickly into oblivion.

The muted reception of *An American Exodus* proved harder for Paul than for Dorothea. As is often the case for artists, the process provided enough pleasure for her. Dorothea knew that she had advanced a new genre. Her characterization of what they had done—"on the way to true documentary technique," she wrote to Stryker—is all about development.[29] Taylor, his eye on policy, saw the book's lack of notice as one more failure—along with his attempts to get decent housing for migrant farmworkers, Social Security benefits for farmworkers, or agricultural cooperatives; in the future, he would fail to stop the theft of water by the big growers. A few years later, they both understood that the book's rapid disappearance was a sign not only of the New Deal's decline but, more specifically, of the defeat of the FSA's goal—a democratic agricultural policy.

# 17

# Dorothea and Roy

From 1935 through 1941, Lange's relationship with Roy Stryker was as intense as any excepting those with her family. Two strong personalities, they loved and respected each other but frequently clashed. Historians of the project, along with its staff and intimates, apportion the blame differently.

To Roy Stryker and his supporters, Lange was a superb photographer, but came with a high maintenance cost. She often demanded special treatment. She tried several times to go over Stryker's head when she couldn't get her way with him. She treated the office staff so peremptorily that some of them dreaded her appearance in Washington. Her technical skills were by no means the equal of her mesmerizing vision; her negatives were often defective and, worse, she denied the problems and resisted questions intended to help her solve them. She promoted herself, egged on by an interfering husband who believed she could do no wrong.

To Lange's defenders, Stryker's insistence on centralized control over all photographic activity and distribution made no sense given the politics and problems of the West. Lange worked harder than any other FSA photographer. Her photography contributed disproportionately to the influence of the project, but she did not get the deserved recognition, remaining a virtual unknown (outside of the photographic community) up until her death. Stryker resisted and may have even resented her ideas for deepening the photographic critique of injustice.

To this author, the charges leveled against her seem accurate, but her assertiveness was misunderstood, often due to sex discrimination, and not only regarding her salary. In a double bind, she was stereotyped as a sentimental woman but also blamed for not behaving like a woman should. Much of the relationship would have been better had she been around the FSA office more. Yet she herself expressed no bitterness, not at the time, not even later. She knew that what she gained from this job far outweighed her aggravation.

Still, her four off-and-on years working for Stryker displayed the ups and downs of a clumsy love affair. Filled with arguments about schedule, reimbursement, assignments, and proposals, their letters ripple with hurts, frustrations, and affection, thinly disguised on both sides—by Stryker's banter and Lange's flirtation. Their relationship was neither sexual nor romantic, but its intensity was nevertheless palpable. Both were passionate in their commitments and their mutual admiration. Besides, Stryker was her entrance ticket to the most exciting gig imaginable for a documentary photographer.

CONFLICTS THAT HAD nothing to do with Lange surrounded the FSA photography project. Stryker fought life-or-death struggles to defend the project, against both anti–New Deal congressmen and his Department of Agriculture superiors. Then there was the normal office stress: layoffs, hirings, supply shortages, urgent requests, high-pressure darkroom work, and the herculean task, which grew ever larger, of filing photographs with a system that allowed them to be found again. Only the office staff could grasp the whole array of problems, because all the photographers were on the road most of the time. No one, however, was as removed as Lange, who visited the Washington office only five brief times while on the payroll.[1] She asked to be brought to Washington more, but Stryker did not accommodate her.

Had Dorothea not been connected to Taylor, whose expertise created his own agendas, had she not been so accustomed to being her own boss, and had she been socialized into the culture of the Washington FSA office, she would no doubt have dealt with Stryker differently—as an employee. Instead, their fervent mutual commitment to the work created clashes. These skirmishes never eroded their mutual appreciation. Their many long letters make it clear how much they esteemed each other. They also communicated through photographs. Stryker remembered his elation whenever a box of film came in from one of his field photographers, particularly Lange.

Conflicts caused by distance began almost immediately. In her first letter to Stryker, she asked for money for a darkroom and tried to set her own schedule and itinerary for travel. Stryker responded negatively to both.[2] He experienced her requests as presumptuous from the beginning, and these requests never let up. But she had good reasons for many of them, and another professional in her position might have been equally demanding, if perhaps more tactful.

Consider her grievances about control of photographs: It was difficult, if not impossible, to see what she produced, to learn from her mistakes, if she could not see prints promptly, and so she repeatedly asked to develop her own film and make one set of prints before sending the negatives on. Ansel Adams, not directly involved but speaking for several of the FSA photographers, pleaded with Stryker to change his policy, but Stryker continued to insist that all prints be made and all negatives stored in Washington.[3] So Lange had to wait weeks, sometimes months, to see prints, delays caused by bottlenecks in the office. She sent negative numbers to Stryker to request copies, but she could not be sure the numbers were right, so she either had to rely on his judgement— "choose the best of these," she instructed—or try to describe what she thought the image corresponding with a negative number should be.[4]

Sometimes Lange's mail to Washington got lost, usually in the office. Once Stryker sent her a batch of prints to be captioned, but she had already done that work, hours and hours of it, and sent the captions with the negatives. Occasionally a negative precious to Lange could never be found in Washington.[5] Publishers asked her for photographs, but she had to tell them to wait for prints from Washington. She sometimes proposed using the same negatives for multiple purposes—a magazine, an exhibit, a government report—but Stryker vetoed that because each party usually insisted on a unique photograph.[6] When the editor of an important academic press asked to use some of her photographs, she dutifully told him to contact Stryker; when he did that, Stryker sent mostly photographs by others.[7] Lacking ownership of her own work was personally frustrating. "I have nothing at all to show for my 3 years of government work in the way of prints," she complained, exaggeratedly, to Roy.[8] She knew her mastery was growing but couldn't document it.

She was often squeezed between the San Francisco and Washington FSA offices, for those in San Francisco were no happier than she was with Washington's control over pictures made in the western region. When Frederick

Soule, head of information for the FSA's California region, arranged to go with Dorothea to cover a cotton strike, she felt it necessary to reassure Stryker that she would "go through all the necessary motions of working with him. . . . But I won't let it get to the place where he writes my program."[9] To Stryker's consternation, the regional office requested at one point to hire its own photographer; and his resistance only intensified when he discovered that the photographer in question was Mary Jeanette Edwards, Willard Van Dyke's girlfriend and Lange's former assistant.[10]

Lange missed out on much headquarters camaraderie. As she missed Stryker's briefings, so she missed debriefing and critique sessions.[11] As the staff expanded and contracted because of budgetary changes, she was not there to welcome newcomers and say good-bye to those leaving. Despite the flux, the photographers bonded tightly when they intersected. They sometimes paired up and traveled together—Evans and Shahn, Rothstein and Lee, Rosskam and Delano, for example—an opportunity Lange did not have, although she extended hospitality and the use of her darkroom to any photographer who came to California.

The Lange-Stryker relationship was constructed primarily through correspondence, and her peremptory and superefficient style, a voice common to overstressed women trying to be all things, evoked resentment. She wrote to one of the secretaries, "Enclosed a list of things I need. Please push it through with no delay, all you can, Yours, Lange." Multiply that by the many things she requested—a developing tank, developing chemicals, lenses, flashgun, paper, an assistant, contribution to home darkroom expenses, reimbursement for local purchases, permission to keep negatives, getting proof prints quicker, paying Ansel Adams to print for her, a raise to $2,600—and irritation grew. They perceived her as a diva.[12] In face-to-face discussions, she would have been able to make her requests more softly, to listen to and sympathize with budget problems, to charm her coworkers, and Stryker might have been better able to explain his constraints. Her efforts at a light tone could not disguise her intensity: "Miss Slackman said in her letter that you were making the prints for me. Please mister that idea is no good. This show is the most important photographic show we have. . . . I couldn't afford to show prints, unsigned, which I have not even seen." Enthusiastic and hard-driving, she proposed photographic subjects more often than any other photographer, and began to do so almost immediately after being hired. "We have a chance to score and I'm anxious to make use of it," she wrote Stryker.[13]

She did not accept defeat easily, so she found it hard to respect bureaucratic hierarchy. She sent pictures out occasionally without authorization. When she was laid off in October 1936, she went over Stryker's head to write the FSA's director of information, M. E. Gilfond, "There is a job . . . which should be done right away. I need the time and the authorization from you to do it . . . a democratic experience of unusual social interest and national significance." (Gilfond, of course, sent this letter over to Stryker.) She sent another suggestion to Walter Packard (who sent the letter to Grace Falke Tugwell, who sent it to Gilfond, who sent it to Stryker).[14] These were not only the aggressive and ill-considered moves of someone unaccustomed to bureaucratic channels, but the impatience of someone accustomed to being an entrepreneur, without a boss. Lange apologized and promised not to do this again. But she could not stop making suggestions, even though aware of her possible insubordination: "Is this all out of my province? Excuse," she scribbled on the margin of a letter to Stryker packed with ideas for projects. Yet she executed boring assignments without a murmur of complaint because, as she put it, it was the American public that set her these chores—in her mind, they were like military service.[15] "Have a date with a farmer late this afternoon . . . to photograph spreading of grasshopper bait"—and this was by no means unusual.[16] She put up with being graded on report cards (on which her ratings were by no means stellar)[17] and holdups in getting her wages and travel expenses.

She was self-promoting, but not inordinately so. She sent Stryker a copy of a request from Edward Filene, the Boston department store owner, philanthropist, and New Deal supporter, who wanted a Lange photograph for his desk. (Who wouldn't show her boss something like that?) She nagged Stryker repeatedly about a raise and once again went over his head, arguing for the raise by telling Gilfond she had an outside job offer.[18] She was galled that less skilled male photographers made more money than she did. She let Stryker know about the many direct requests she received for pictures. But she made no demands to be recognized by name in the many publications that printed her work. And she was by no means as self-promoting as Walker Evans, who refused to do assignments that did not advance his art and reputation.

A double standard appears in Stryker's dealings with Walker Evans and Lange. Stryker cherished talking with Evans, admired his personal elegance, and thought his photography extraordinary beautiful. But Evans could not work in a bureaucracy. As one historian put it, "Evans' way was to disappear for months at a time, keep no clear records of where he had been or was going, and finally to reappear with a small number of the finest photographs ever taken."[19] In a passive-aggressive manner, he would not argue with Stryker; he simply did not do his assignments, refusing altogether to write captions. Stryker nagged him constantly about his low productivity.[20] Other FSA photographers resented Evans's bigger paycheck despite this lower productivity and refusal of assignments that they executed obediently. Ultimately, Stryker found Evans's arrogance insupportable. "I had grown up considerably," Stryker said, implying that his infatuation with Evans had been immature; "He treated Arthur [Rothstein] very snottily, very nasty to him, and Arthur . . . you see, he wasn't his kind"—a reference to Evans's anti-Semitism.[21] Even Ben Shahn, Evans's close friend, recognized his snobbery: When Evans was broke, he went to his sister to borrow money; when Shahn was broke, he got a job drawing pots and pans and bicycles for department store ads, and when Evans heard about this, he "looked upon me disdainfully," Shahn recalled.[22]

Lange's interactive mode, by contrast, was direct. She argued and pestered, while Evans just ignored his boss. But she never refused an assignment.

Grievances about equipment also rankled. At headquarters, numerous cameras, lenses, even the newly invented light meters were shared by the photographers. Excluded from this pool of equipment, Lange sometimes made specific requests—for a Goerz Dagor III short-focal-length lens, a Schneider wide-angle lens, and other devices—which she either did not get or did not get quickly. She was resentful when she learned that Walker Evans got an expensive new lens for his camera.[23] Lange could not buy her own supplies of paper, chemicals, et cetera, but had to ask Washington to buy and send them to her, which created delays that other photographers did not experience. And she sometimes complained about the quality of what she got: the paper had defective emulsion; the developer was inferior. If she ran out of something while traveling, her only alternative was to buy materials at her own expense— she could not be reimbursed. She had difficulties getting her payroll status straight, problems that would have been more easily solved had she been in Washington.[24]

Stryker recognized that some of Lange's requests were legitimate and tried to accommodate her. After first assuming that Taylor could get her continuing access to a university darkroom, he then agreed to budget twenty-five dollars a month for the expenses of a darkroom in her house, to cover water and electricity, insurance on her cameras, a small fraction of the rent, and a bit for depreciation. Once he sent her a personal check for some extra-large paper for which she could not be reimbursed.[25] He put up with her reluctance to shift technology: In late 1938, she was still using large-plate film, resisting his requests to get her camera refitted for three-and-a-quarter- by four-and-a-quarter-inch film, making it hard to get supplies for her. He bit his tongue in letters to Lange even more than he did with his male photographers, whom he sometimes bawled out roundly, albeit usually with a bit of humor.

Complaints from Washington about the clarity of her film are more difficult to evaluate. The Washington staff charged that her negatives sometimes arrived streaked, muddy, gray, stained, grainy, or any combination of these. Lange believed that they were damaged by the heat and humidity. Stryker responded that other photographers working under similar conditions did not have that problem.[26] Ansel Adams, who did some developing for Lange when she was on the road, supported her explanation. He said he could smell the marshes and the mildew when he opened the film, "all fogged up with humidity and mold. . . . Films will take heat but they won't take humidity." A master of photographic technology, Adams called Lange "an excellent craftsman . . . a profound respect for her work."[27] The tension worsened when lab workers complained that Lange blamed them for her poor negatives. (Yet when Adams's assistant Seema Weatherwax ruined some of Lange's negatives, she reported that Dorothea was understanding and reassuring.)[28] No one can adjudicate this dispute now. Lange may well have been erratic, turning out both excellent and flawed work. In her studio photography, she could filter out whatever was less than excellent. In many ways, she was a perfectionist. Her tremendous volume of photographs resulted from long hours of work, not quickness. Stryker criticized her for making too many exposures of the same image and instructed her at least to weed them out before sending them in (something she could have done more easily if she had been allowed to make her own prints).[29] "One thing is certain," Stryker wrote Russell Lee in 1939 about an impending Lange visit, "she cannot work in the laboratory. If she does, I shall have to hire a whole new laboratory force."[30]

TO SOME OF the FSA staff, Lange seemed larger than life; she took up a great deal of the air and space when she was around, and seemed to command that people defer to her. But some of this reaction would have been different had she been male. Jonathan Garst wrote Stryker about her, ". . . . dealing with fighting cocks, race horses, and lady artists, you will have to make arrangements that they win once in a while."[31] The shift in the gender of the metaphors, from cocks through racehorses to ladies, speaks eloquently of their mixed feelings about Lange: egotistic, powerful, high-strung. Even her virtue intimidated the men. Rosskam remarked that she was a "saint . . . [who] over-awed me a little bit," because of her passion for helping the needy.[32]

The conflicts take on new perspective in comparison to the experience of Marion Post Wolcott. She was raised by a wealthy feminist mother who volunteered in Margaret Sanger's campaign for birth control and, after a divorce, moved to Greenwich Village—had she been in San Francisco, she would have been one of Lange's customers. The young Marion was a serious modern dancer and socialized with members of New York's experimental Group Theatre. While at the University of Vienna in 1933, she met photographer Trude Fleischmann, who loaned her a good camera. Her friends in Vienna were left-wing artists horrified by Nazism. She returned to New York, where she joined the League Against War and Fascism, helping Jews, including Fleischmann, to escape Europe. In 1937, after having done a few assignments for the Associated Press, she got hired as a staff photographer for the *Philadelphia Evening Bulletin,* and her male colleagues threw spitballs at her and put cigarette butts in her developer. Her assignments, not surprisingly, confined her to covering fashion and special features.[33] (This brief experience as a photojournalist must have made the FSA seem a feminist paradise.) In 1940, Margaret Bourke-White and Mary Morris, who worked for the New York progressive newspaper *PM,* were still the only female photojournalists in the United States.[34]

At the FSA, Marion Post was not only female and pretty but also a "girl" and decidedly upper-class. The men were kind, admiring, and protective. Since she traveled alone, Rothstein persuaded her to get an ax for protection. Both protective and censorious, Stryker lectured her on how to dress and behave—and sometimes he was right. She began traveling in South Carolina in a convertible with the top down, tanned from the sun, with "a very bright-colored . . . head scarf [and] jangly earrings. . . ." Her subjects, she recalled, "began dragging their kids away and thought . . . that I was . . . a modern gypsy in an automobile [who] would come in and kidnap their children. . . ." (Lange also wore head scarves, but on her the look was eccentric or practical, not exotic.) Stryker had to warn Post how dangerous it was for a southern black man to be seen with an unaccompanied white woman. The darkroom men in the office disrespected and patronized her, but they also gave her more help than they did the male photographers.[35]

Post's and Lange's strengths differed considerably. Post was more adventurous, more outspoken about female freedom, and more willing to be intrusive—qualities that reflected her class background. She could be impetuous, while Lange made deliberated decisions.[36] Post photographed a strip club and a miner taking a bath.[37] Her biting photographs of the very rich at leisure are among the most challenging images in the FSA file.

When you examine the two women's experiences closely, a paradox emerges: Post was more articulate about sex discrimination, and seemed to harbor more unconventional aspirations for a woman, but she overcame discrimination less well and displayed a softening flirtatiousness that Lange did not have. Post sent a photograph to Stryker to prove she was tough: it shows her lying on her side on a muddy and rocky road along the Kentucky River, changing a tire by using a fence post propped on rocks to jack the car up. The photograph makes her resourcefulness cute, like the word *feisty*, which treats bravery and assertiveness in women as fetching. Post's letters were witty and coquettish: "What really ruins my disposition [in New England in winter] are the icy cold toilet seats. . . . I practically took to sleeping in my clothes. . . . And no miss fancy pants underwear either. Long, wool and ugly."[38] But then Post entered a marriage that seemed almost patriarchal by comparison to Lange's: Lee Wolcott not only insisted that Marion quit her job but also required Stryker's shop to go back and relabel every photograph she had made with her new, married name. She never photographed professionally again. The similarities between her story and those of Consuelo Kanaga and Alma Lavenson suggest that Lange was the more independent, even transgressive woman, despite her seemingly conventional views about women's nature.

Although respected more than Post Wolcott, Lange nonetheless faced discrimination at the FSA. When she and Taylor married, the personnel office redid all her paperwork to change her name to Taylor—she ignored this and never used that name, just as she had never used the name Dixon (although others applied it to her at times). Hers was not just a "professional name" but her only name, exceptional in the 1930s and 1940s. Yet with Stryker, she did a strange thing: for the first year and a half, she signed her letters to him just "Lange." She had never done this before; she had always used her full name— Dorothea Lange—in her portrait business. Clearly, she wanted to signal her professionalism and independence from Taylor, and to be treated like one of the guys. Starting in February 1937, by which time she had met Stryker twice in person, she signed "Dorothea," and addressed him as "Roy." But she never wrote him about her children, buying a new house, her friends, or not feeling well, as his male photographers did. When she had an appendectomy, he found out well after the fact.

Yet the emotionality of Lange's relationship with Stryker is obvious from their correspondence. She was especially hurt that Stryker never visited her on the road or in California. Stryker dictated long letters to his photographers, providing feedback on photographs and further instructions and advice. He complained to them about Washington bureaucracy in general and his specific enemies in particular. At one point, he instructed Lange to destroy a particularly frank letter about the Department of Agriculture and told her to write him at his home address because he did not want their correspondence to fall into the wrong hands.[39] This trust established an intimacy that intensified her longing for him to see her at work, to meet the regional office staff, to allow her to host him. But he never came. He often felt he could not leave Washington, complaining to her "how they move in on you the minute you get across the District Line. . . ." But Lange knew that he traveled to see other photographers, some as far west as Arizona. The rejection wounded this woman who felt deserted by her father. Once, Stryker promised to meet her in the Southwest and spend a week traveling with her, but it never happened. In April 1937, he said he would join her in Albuquerque in May. In May, he promised to find a way to meet her in the South.[40] In June, she was pleading, "You went with Rothstein, you went with Lee, you went with Mydans. And how about me?" Perhaps conscious of sounding like a child, she then lightened the emotional tone by commiserating with Stryker about "the tyranny of little men" who were threatening the project's budget and who forced him to stay as "watchdog" in the office. But her complaints about his neglect sounded an orphan theme. "How about a letter to your little stepchild?" she wrote.[41] In her flirtatiousness, she was an orphan, not a seductress.

Why wouldn't Stryker, usually a nurturing mentor, go to her? Perhaps he was resentful, jealous, or ill at ease when it came to Taylor. But without a doubt he misunderstood Dorothea: He confused her assertiveness with manipulative behavior, when, in fact, it arose from neediness and passion for the work.

The photography project was white as well as male. Gordon Parks was the only person of color ever to photograph for Stryker, and he did not even draw a salary. Born in Fort Scott, Kansas, in 1912, he was just fifteen when his mother died and he became a wanderer, working as a waiter, bartender, and semi-professional basketball and football player before deciding to try fashion photography. Jack Delano noticed his work at an exhibit on Chicago's South Side and helped him get a grant from the Rosenwald Fund. One of the few liberal foundations to fund African American educational work at this time, it gave Parks a stipend to intern at the FSA photography project. Stryker explained his reluctance to accept Parks, even at no cost, in terms of the District of Columbia's segregation.[42] (Stryker often adopted this passive, buck-passing stance about racism; he claimed to be interested in the "Negro problem" but distributed photographs of whites because "we know that these will receive much wider use.")[43] The effect on Parks, however, was mobilizing: As he put it, "I came back roaring mad and I wanted my camera and he [Stryker] said, 'For what?' And I said I wanted to expose . . . this discrimination."[44]

LANGE'S POSITION IN the FSA was further complicated because she was half of a powerful couple. Taylor's authority was imbedded in Stryker's first letter to Lange: he would be happy, he assured her, to work with Taylor in deciding what she should photograph. It was an indication of a taken-for-granted sexism, an extraordinary relinquishing of control, and an acknowledgment of Taylor's prestige. Taylor participated in all the early negotiations about her work, a role he yielded in later years—except when Lange was directly thwarted. It was Taylor who first suggested that the FSA pay Ansel Adams to make prints from her negatives. It was Taylor who first proposed that she head to Southern California to photograph the camps for migratory workers.[45] Taylor accompanied her on many trips and all of her visits to Washington.[46] Stryker expected to be head of a family, but Lange had another powerful protector. She did not always handle this ménage-à-trois with delicacy.

Taylor's influence meant that he could find his own money and authorization for trips on which he could accompany Lange or she him.[47] From the summer of 1936 to 1941, he worked as a consultant economist for the Social Security Board, with the agenda of getting farmworkers covered by the Social Security Act. His efforts were in vain, because Democratic politicians had already promised large growers in the South and West that farmworkers—who included the majority of the country's people of color—would continue to be excluded. But the job allowed him to shape his itinerary to match his wife's assignments, and he was completely honest about this: "It also happens," he wrote his boss in the spring of 1937, "that . . . Mr. Stryker has just ordered my wife to take the field through the South this summer in her car. I believe that the results of our work . . . together in the past have amply justified this [joint] method of work . . . as efficient, and economical to the government. . . ."[48]

Lange frequently passed on to Stryker information and interpretations she got from Taylor. Feeding the boss intelligence that he would not otherwise receive had underscored her reputation as privileged and self-important. She once informed Stryker that Secretary of Agriculture Henry Wallace was preparing a tenancy bill.[49] She had the audacity to lecture Stryker: ". . . the significance and use of the negatives which I have made on this theme [displacement by mechanization, which Wallace was emphasizing] might escape you."[50] Taylor sometimes received requests for photographs for congressional reports and hearings, and Lange would therefore ask Stryker's permission to work on them. Paul wanted to give one of her prints as a gift to a Social Security official, and Lange asked permission for that, too.[51]

Yet Taylor's influence could not save her job in the end. Stryker let her go and rehired her several times when under budget pressure. Dorothea appears saintly in her patience with repeated layoffs, canceling of trips at short notice, travel authorizations delayed and withdrawn. As she prepared for a trip to start in February 1936, Stryker suddenly wired that she had to be on the road by January 27. So she hurried and then, on January 23, he wired that the trip was canceled. Two weeks later, it was on again. In October 1936, she was laid off, but in January 1937, she was urgently summoned back to work, although she had not been put back on the payroll. In early March, Stryker told her to prepare for a trip to the Pacific Northwest. She planned routes and made arrangements with regional FSA people, only to have Stryker cancel this trip and instead send her to the South. In September, Stryker laid her off again, this time with a month's notice so that she could finish captioning her summer photographs. In June 1938, Stryker told her that if Ben Shahn quit, as anticipated, he would rehire Lange, but instead he hired Marion Post.

Finally, in October 1939, he telephoned Lange while she was on the road in Oregon to notify her that she was being "terminated" as of January 1, 1940. A four-page letter written the next day detailed his budget problems but offered no explanation of why she was the photographer to be cut. Lange left no written account of her feelings, but we know how hurt she was from an extraordinary personal letter from Jonathan Garst, western regional FSA director, speaking also for Walter Packard, former FSA chief, an emotional plea to Stryker to rehire Lange. Garst discussed all that she had given, her "whole-souled" commitment; reminded Stryker that Taylor was "the father of our migratory camp program"; pointed out Taylor's personal sacrifices for the cause, including the low university salary that resulted from his defiance of the state's agricultural powers; and characterized Taylor and Lange as "hard up" because they supported a large family. In a remarkably emotional tone for such a letter, he referred to the deep hurt caused to both Dorothea and Paul: "Paul Taylor is apparently still violently in love with Dorothea . . . anything that would hurt her feelings would have very much more effect on Paul's feelings than anything that was done to him directly." He admitted that "Dorothea with her pell-mell enthusiasm may be at times difficult to work with" and suggested offering her part-time, seasonal work (as a way of saving face for Stryker).[52] Stryker would not budge: "I selected for termination the person who would give me least cooperation in the job that is laid before me." Then, defending himself not against Garst, who had said nothing about Lange's artistry, but against his own barely suppressed consciousness of the foolishness of his decision, he added that "judgments of art are highly subjective."[53]

Lange's assertive, interfering temperament cannot justify, or even explain, Stryker's decision. No amount of Lange's interference—especially since it arrived from three thousand miles' distance—could have outweighed the value of her work. Her photographs contributed most to the cause they shared; her captions set the standard for the other photographers. Stryker should have put up with her.[54] Stryker's decision can be explained only by his greater comfort with his male protégés and less assertive female ones. Firing Lange seems of a piece with his rejection of Lewis Hine. Having made the decision, he went on to impute corrupt motives to her: He withheld her final check until all her equipment had been returned. She asked to get her cameras cleaned at FSA expense and he said no.[55]

Controlling her feelings, she responded graciously, as she had to every previous layoff.[56] Perhaps because she had been laid off so often, she hoped that this one, too, might be reversed. It never was.

The FSA photography project was disbanded finally in 1943, the victim of conservative attacks and a wartime budget. The achievement of its last two years never equaled that of 1936—1939. Roy Stryker and many of his staff went on to magazine, corporate, or fashion photography. Lange postponed those options as long as she could and continued to find small pieces of government work for the next five years. This is not because she was a paragon of selflessness, but because the FSA experience represented exactly what she wanted to do. Whatever their grievances, every FSA photographer, including

Lange, spoke of it as life's high point. Lange, in fact, never ceased trying to create a similar project—a team of photographers working collectively at the highest technical and aesthetic level to change the world. The loss of her FSA job would have been infinitely more painful had she known that such a project would never again emerge.

# Part IV

---

WARTIME

1939–1945

San Francisco, 1942

# SCENE 4

*In 1942, the U.S. Army hired Dorothea Lange to photograph the pro-
cess of incarcerating 120,000 Japanese Americans on the grounds that
they might be disloyal. Throughout her work on this project, Lange was
harassed by the same army that had hired her, but she developed a
particularly adversarial relation with a Major Beasley (referred to by
some as "Bozo Beasley"). Observing the critical quality of her photographs, he tried to find cause to fire her. He was particularly infuriated
by her photographs of hothouse sheds in a camp where the sun shining
through the glass panes cast prison bar–like shadows on the garden-
ers working there.[1] Once, Beasley thought he had caught her out in
taking a negative—this was forbidden; all negatives were to be held by
the army—because he found an empty negative sleeve. She had indeed
taken some of her negatives for her own use, but, through sheer luck, not
this one; he called her in and confronted her with the empty envelope,
but she shook it and the negative fell out.[2]*

*Another time, Beasley almost did catch her in a serious infraction.
She gave photographs to Caleb Foote, a leader in the Fellowship of Reconciliation, an interdenominational Christian pacifist organization,
one of the tiny number of groups to oppose the internment. Paul Taylor
was already an active member of a local effort to resist the internment,
the Committee on American Principles and Fair Play, and met Foote
through that connection. Foote used the Lange photographs—one of a*

*young Japanese American girl and another of the stables being used to*
*house the internees—in a pamphlet denouncing the internment. Beasley*
*saw the pamphlet and called her in. Once more, she was unexpectedly*
*lucky. It seems that the prints she gave Foote had already appeared in a*
*U.S. House of Representatives committee report (the Tolan Committee*
*on Defense Migration), thus putting the images into the public domain.*[3]
*She could claim that the committee report was Foote's source.*

# 18

# Family Stress

Being fired brought hurt but also relief to Lange, and she looked forward to a slower tempo. The expected relief did not materialize. There were new on-the-road photography commissions and serious family crises, and it cannot be coincidental that she suffered her first serious health problems since childhood at this time.

Late in 1939, Lange took another rural photography job documenting labor migration for the Bureau of Agricultural Economics, which requested two months' work on a "w.a.e." (when actually employed) basis.[1] The BAE's leash was shorter than Stryker's, and as a result her photography did not match the FSA achievement. There are fewer portraits, fewer pictures of field labor, and more of the terrible living conditions of migrant farmworkers, children in particular. As required, she also documented the better conditions in the FSA camps. But these photographs also reflect Lange's own feelings—burned out, less optimistic, even despairing. There are some beautiful portraits. (See plate 6.) But many of the best BAE photographs are so sad, they are nearly pathetic, and when Lange's photos are sad, the emotion seems to overflow the picture plane. They also seem angrier. This was the only time she photographed people as wretchedly unattractive as those in Bourke-White's *You Have Seen Their Faces*. Bitterly, she captioned the batch from which the next two images come, "Children in a Democracy."[2] Despite her abiding loyalty to the camp

18.1. SOUTH OF ELOY, PINAL COUNTY, ARIZONA, 1940

project, her photographs raise doubts about whether most farmworkers' lives had improved at all during the New Deal.

Lange once again seemed finely tuned to her country's mood, for her 1939–1940 photography expressed the contraction of New Deal hopes and the growing fears of war. Like most liberals, she was horrified by the Nazis and fascism but not eager for war. In June 1939, on a trip to New York, she was shocked to hear "an American 'storm trooper'" haranguing a crowd from a soapbox at Columbus Circle.[3] Ominous international events intruded into her field notes, as, for example, in a caption reading "Close-up of door of Prophecy Tabernacle. Photograph made on the day Holland, Belgium, Luxembourg were invaded by the German armies."[4]

In some ways the FSA spirit continued. By now an agriculture expert, Lange made long essays out of some of her "general captions," on topics such as alkaline or hardpan soil, cultural traditions of the migrants, housing options, and family budgets. One was a twenty-six-page paper with data from BAE research. She also introduced issues the BAE did not ask for, such as prejudice toward migrant farmworkers and race segregation in the camps.[5]

As war buildup brought new jobs and the Depression receded, and it became evident that government work was petering out, Lange applied for a Guggenheim Fellowship. Edward Weston had held one in 1937 and 1938, Walker Evans in 1940 (and Paul Taylor in 1930). Henry Allen Moe, president of the Guggenheim Foundation, who would go on to chair the Museum of Modern Art trustees' photography committee, had previously connected with Taylor.[6] What influence Paul exerted for Dorothea is unknown, but her appli-

18.2. SOUTH OF CHANDLER, MARICOPA COUNTY, ARIZONA, 1940

cation, written October 1940, evolved from their joint thinking. "The theme of the project is the relation of man to the earth and man to man, and the forces of stability and change in communities of contrasting types."[7] She would study three communities: a Mormon village in Utah, Amana cooperatives in Iowa, and Hutterites in South Dakota.[8] She got the fellowship. Thrilled to have financial support for a project of her own for the first time, she plunged into the work, usually with Paul's company, during the summer of 1941.

Working now without government supervision, she promised to send photographs to her subjects.[9] Otherwise, her methods remained the same. Her field notes contain data (South Dakota, "a state in which one third of the population has been on relief, in which 75% of the banks have failed, and in which taxes have become delinquent on approx 1/3 of the taxable land"), self-criticism ("very bum careless snapshots in the old town"), and verbatim quotations from her subjects ("We've seen the rough"). By September, back in Berkeley developing and printing, she wrote Moe, ". . . feel that I am on my way, ideas fortified."[10]

BUT VERY SOON she had to write Moe to ask for a postponement. Family troubles overwhelmed her, not because she collapsed from worry but because she didn't. Instead, she became again the fixer, the superwoman on whom the family depended.

One trouble was already several years old. Just as the boys grew old enough that she no longer needed round-the-clock child care when she was gone, Daniel became, in his own words to me, a "desperate and delinquent" adolescent.[11] Starting in 1938, when he was thirteen, he began skipping school and became insolent and defiant. Dorothea was worried enough to consult Maynard, who recommended placing him out again, away from the city, imagining that frontier life and hard work would straighten Daniel out. A sheep rancher and his physician wife in Smith Valley, Nevada, took him, but sent him back after a few months. Paul and Dorothea then tried Black Mountain College, hoping to harness Dan's interest in poetry and the unconventional, but he only lasted eight months there. In the fall of 1940 Dorothea wrote that "the progress of my work has been completely blocked. I find my own home a slum. . . ."[12] This choice of word speaks volumes about her need for domestic order; it likened her family chaos to the deprivation and squalor she had so often photographed, and expressed her sense that Daniel was disordered. He was indeed uncontrollable. He frequently did not come home at night, and he spent several teenage years as an off-and-on street person, keeping warm in libraries, eating out of dumpsters, occasionally dropping by home for food. He was never violent, but he was arrested several times for stealing. Once he stole and hocked his mother's typewriter, and another time her Rolleiflex.[13] There is not much mystery about the target of his rage. He felt that all his parents had deserted: his father to the desert, his stepfather to the university, his mother to her field work or to the darkroom—Dan remembered her disappearing to the studio for twelve-hour stretches, probably an exaggeration but emotionally accurate.

The whole family saw a psychiatrist who worked for the Oakland Public School District. Paul and Dorothea had great faith in him, but Daniel calls him "a villain." He pronounced Daniel psychotic and recommended institutionalization, a suggestion Dorothea vetoed. Ultimately Dorothea and Paul applied "tough love" and locked him out of the house. When he appeared, Dorothea would feed him but not allow him to stay. Dan felt close to Rondal Partridge, who was only eight years older, and Rondal offered to take him in, but Dorothea and Paul vetoed this. Then came a preposterous marriage: He met a girl in a dime-a-dance place, was immediately infatuated, and proposed to her on the spot. While his parents slept, he "borrowed" the car and drove to Reno, where they married. Returning, she asked him to let her stop at her "home," which turned out to be a seedy hotel, and told him to wait in the car. She never came back.

Dorothea was in agony. Then Paul offered a solution: the army. Dan had been rejected by the draft because of bad eyesight. Paul "pulled strings" with the Berkeley draft board and got him drafted anyway. But this didn't work either: by the end of the war, Dan was in the stockade at Fort Knox, having been repeatedly AWOL.

Dan worked his way back to a close relationship with his mother and became a successful writer who collaborated with her on several projects, but he did not get there easily. He carried a great deal of guilt; as late as 1954 he referred to the "whole, ugly truth" about himself, and called himself "in some degree a cripple."[14]

John, three years younger, was relatively composed, enjoying basketball in the park and biking around Berkeley, but he naturally resented the attention his brother's bad behavior got. He still felt keenly the loss of a father. John described Paul as "distant—no this is too strong, because he was not unapproachable," but he never felt emotionally involved with his stepfather.[15] Dorothea worried that he had little ambition or passion for what he would like to "become," so she nagged him.


BEFORE DAN CAME to his senses, another of Dorothea's dependents fell into delinquency. Her brother Martin was caught embezzling from the California state unemployment compensation agency.

Baby brother Martin, six years Dorothea's junior, had often trailed his dynamic big sister and she had often looked after him.[16] He followed her to San Francisco just a year after she arrived; he changed his name to Lange soon after she did; he absorbed her politics; he bought her and Paul's first Berkeley house when they moved to a bigger one. In the 1920s, Dorothea and Maynard provided his home base between jobs and apartments. He had high energy of a sort so different from Dorothea as to make the two of them a stereotypical older/younger sibling dyad: as she was ambitious and disciplined, he was fun-loving and seemingly free of ambition; as she was independent, he was dependent.

Martin worked first for Pacific Gas and Electric, then as a seaman, then at odd jobs in Yosemite National Park—he was talented and absorbed skills quickly. In 1934 he got a job as a high-line rigger with the Boulder Dam construction project. He developed a romantic and adventurist version of "Wobbly" attraction to masculine, risky jobs and the brave men who did them.[17] The teenage Rondal Partridge was infatuated with Martin, and remembers that he could build a boat from scratch. To Dan and John, he was playful "Unca' Mucky" and his arrival was always cause for celebration. He was a loving uncle, and occasionally visited the boys when they were with foster parents. Dan remembers him as "an Apollo," absolutely gorgeous, about six one and slim, and John, even as a man of eighty, resembles him. Once he built a miniature zip line across Dorothea and Paul's living room with a basket in which the kids could travel back and forth across the room. A "good-time guy," he drank a lot, threw money around unwisely, attracted many friends and "lots of ladies."

In 1941 Martin, then an office manager for the California Division of Unemployment Compensation, was caught in a four-person ring that was arranging unemployment-compensation payments to sixty-nine fictitious employees of dummy corporations.[18] His three partners in crime were hardly riffraff: Leonard Sledge was dean of Placer County Junior College; Raymond F. Killian was the principal of Templeton Union High School in San Luis Obispo; Albert Jilk was Killian's cousin. The police considered Killian the "brains"; he pulled in Martin, whom he had met at Boulder Dam.

The news of the crime broke on the front pages on September 12, 1941, although Dorothea knew it earlier when Martin telephoned from jail. She was shaken. Her brother was repeating their father's disgrace, some thirty years later. She knew Martin was weak, yes, but she also knew him as a warm and loving man. At this moment he became another of her children. That night, she recalled, she got drunk and ruined a negative by leaving it with water running all night—the only time she had ever been so careless.

But the humiliation and anger made her active, not paralyzed, and she devoted herself 100 percent to the case. Someone else might have refused responsibility for an irresponsible brother. Instead, Dorothea became even more invested in controlling and supporting him, and he cooperated—no matter how much she nagged him, he came to her and her alone when he was in need. As late as the 1960s, ill with cancer, she told an interviewer, "Even now I'm not absolutely sure that I'm not going to have to take care of him."[19] She and Paul found the money to pay for his bail and a top lawyer, and he got off easy. While Killian was sentenced to one to five years in San Quentin, Martin Lange got six months at a county road camp and ten years' probation.[20] Dorothea told no one outside her family of Martin's crime, while Martin spoke of it easily. Within the family, she argued that Martin would never have stolen from the needy, that because he stole only from a state agency he was a criminal but not a bad person. "He's done some pretty terrible things *against himself* [emphasis added]," she told an interviewer.[21] They were both repeating childhood roles.

She did not pick up a camera or enter her darkroom for three months.

FOR THESE FAMILY troubles and the years of punishing work, she paid with her body. Already in 1936, when she was on the road for most of the year, she had reported ulcer symptoms—severe, burning abdominal pain. How long the symptoms had been building, how long she kept them to herself, can no longer be determined. In 1938 she had an emergency appendectomy, but it did nothing to relieve her more chronic symptoms. She had severe and protracted bouts of pain in 1940. Soon after her brother's arrest, she developed the first symptoms of an esophageal constriction that would hound her for the rest of her life. She did not consult a doctor about these symptoms until 1943, when X rays found no cause for the pain. (She did not get an accurate diagnosis until 1945.) From now on, her work would be continually interrupted by painful illness—until the balance shifted and her ailing would be occasionally interrupted by feeling well.

In the early 1940s she also experienced the first symptoms of post-polio syndrome, and once again physicians did not understand what was happening to her. The syndrome was unknown then, not recognized as part of a post-polio pattern until the 1970s.[22] This second coming of polio produces muscular weakening, fatigue, muscle atrophy, and pain from joint degeneration, but individual experiences vary.[23] For Dorothea, fatigue was the most pronounced symptom,[24] although she would yet prove herself capable of some marathons of traveling photography.

Despite illness and crises, in 1940 Dorothea made a new home for the blended family—one she would have for the rest of her life. She had never had a long-term nest. Even in Hoboken she had lived in three different locations. Then marriage to a man with wanderlust, followed by her own itinerant work, left her longing for stability and order. Virginia Street was too small. So they bought a new house, bigger and with extraordinary grounds.[25] Decorating it cost much of her energy but gave pleasure in return. As her son-in-law Donald Fanger put it, one of Paul's gifts to her was this chance to be architect of family and home.[26] The house at 1163 Euclid Avenue in Berkeley is an eccentric redwood occupying an unusual lot on a steep hill, the backyard flowing into semiwooded Codornices Creek. As if in personal thanks to Lange, the WPA had built a rose garden with a terraced amphitheater and 220-foot-long redwood pergola directly across Euclid Avenue.

The house was designed in 1910 in the Maybeck style.[27] The floor plan was rambling and asymmetrical. Dorothea removed carved moldings from the fireplace to simplify the lines of the main room. She displayed only a few of her growing collection of Arts and Crafts objects at a time, so as not to violate her simplicity principle, but she frequently rearranged furniture and objects, so the house continually revealed new articulations of its spaces. Most of what she collected was *used* for cooking and eating, and if they were not regularly used, she would give them away. For every meal the dining table held a centerpiece of candles or pottery or flowers—sometimes a blossoming branch or wild grass that Rondal brought. As her assistant Christina Page Gardner recalled, "The house always had cleanliness and Shaker-like orderliness . . . the furniture moved from room to room. . . . It had the same mysterious quality of the wall sconces which puffed into flame spontaneously and magically in 'Beauty and the Beast.' Dorothea had the same qualities. Magical is the only word."[28] Her son-in-law Donald Fanger found the house filled with tranquillity.

For Dorothea, the setting was as beloved as the house itself. From the kitchen, where Dorothea spent many hours, a winding path took you down past a picnic table and benches to the creek.[29] She created a thick but informal garden, and over the years the spaces, shapes, and colors created by plants were elaborated by beautifully placed driftwood and rocks (Paul was frequently hefting her finds into and out of the car). She had a deck built off their bedroom, overlooking the back garden, and from this vantage point, she developed an intense emotional relationship with a live oak—she photographed it repeatedly over the next decades. In the right light, the tree could seem to enter the bedroom, which contained only a bed and a single chest of drawers. From John's bedroom at the top of the house, he could see the Golden Gate Bridge.[30]

When they moved in, she created a small workroom for herself with a table along one side and the flat drawers she needed built in. Above it a long corkboard held the photographs, newspaper clippings, and other images she wanted to take in at the moment. When Ross Taylor left home, his bedroom became her darkroom. Five years later, in 1945, Paul surprised her with a precious gift—an adjoining lot. This purchase not only guaranteed that their backyard would flow unobstructed into the park but also allowed her to have the "room of one's own" she had so longed for, her first and only adequate work space. She designed a studio of about fourteen by twenty-two feet, featuring a wall of sloping frosted glass over the worktable and a wall of standard windows along the opposite side, with a darkroom at the end. She added a slender couch and some canvas director's chairs. She could now put two doors and twenty-five yards between herself and the demands of house, Paul, and children.

# 19

# Defiant War Photography: The Japanese Internment

After the verdict in Martin Lange's trial, Dorothea asked to get her Guggenheim reinstated. But the world did not permit. Just as her thoughts were returning to rural cooperative colonies, the Japanese bombed Pearl Harbor, the United States was at war, and the government commissioned her photography once again.

On the West Coast, a racial hysteria against Japanese Americans was building rapidly. The first calls for massive internment came from long-standing anti-Japanese groups, big growers, and California politicians.[1] The mass media, building on a century of racism against East Asians, raised the fever by alleging that a Japanese American fifth column was signaling Japanese ships from the mainland, a charge that the secretary of war considered without merit.[2] Lange and Taylor suspected something that has since been confirmed: that Associated Farmers, the organization of big commercial farmowners in California, supported the internment in order to gain cheap purchase of Japanese-owned land.[3] Politicians joined the fear mongering, and on February 19, 1942, President Roosevelt issued Executive Order 9066, resulting in the incarceration of 120,000 Japanese Americans.

To Lange's surprise and confusion, the U.S. Army's Western Defense Command offered her the job of documenting this internment photographically. She and Taylor never thought an internment necessary or justified. Taylor was

already a prominent member of one of the few local groups to resist the internment, the Committee on American Principles and Fair Play, originating at the
University of California at Berkeley.[4] Lange felt that a photographic record
could be valuable, might possibly even make the process more humane. So
she asked for a second postponement of her Guggenheim Fellowship—not
knowing that she would be unable to take it up again for ten years—and took
the job. The more than eight hundred photographs she produced were so
unmistakably critical that the army impounded them for the duration of the
war and quietly placed them in the National Archives thereafter. "Impounded"
was written on some of the prints in the archives, but luckily not on the negatives. Few of them were known to the public until 2006.[5]

So why did they hire her if they were so nervous about a photographic
record? I have never been able to find any documentation explaining this decision, but my guess is that they thought a photographic record could protect
against false allegations of mistreatment and violations of international law.
They did not, apparently, register that such a record carried the risk of con-
firming allegations that were true. A measure of how important it seemed to
prevent such an exposure was that the internees in many camps were forbidden to have cameras. One distinguished Japanese American photographer,
Toyo Miyatake, smuggled a lens and a ground glass into Manzanar, built a
camera box from scrap wood, disguised it as a lunch box, and photographed
clandestinely.[6] An unknown number of internees did likewise. We owe some
of our information about camp life to their initiative and courage.

Lange's photographs, had they been shown, would have been one of a very
few critical voices among the almost unanimous acceptance of the internment
by non–Japanese Americans. Writer and editor Carey McWilliams remarked
that you could count on your fingers the number of "whites" who spoke publicly against sending Japanese Americans to concentration camps.[7] Even the
liberal children's writer Dr. Seuss contributed a racist anti–Japanese American cartoon.[8] The Communist newspaper *People's World,* representing a group
hardly strangers to government repression, called the internment a " 'job well-
done . . . was dictated by military necessary,' " and the Party suspended its Japanese American members for the duration of the war.[9] Many of Lange's friends
and colleagues supported internment, and it is a measure of her principles
that despite her admiration for the president, despite her antifascism, she did
not fall for the government's assurance that the internment was necessary to
achieve victory. A few ministers and rabbis, pacifist groups like the Fellowship

of Reconciliation and the American Friends Service Committee, parts of the
ACLU, Socialist party leader Norman Thomas, and African American leaders
such as C. L. Dellums and Bayard Rustin expressed opposition. The NAACP
newspaper *Crisis* called the internment racist.[10] But fear mongering and hyper-
patriotic rhetoric intimidated potential protesters.

Lange's opposition grew, of course, from her FSA experience, but, then, so
did the army's decision to hire her. Whoever made the decision probably knew
nothing about the content of her work, only that an excellent government photographer lived in California and was available.[11]

The internment photographs need to be seen not only as a passionate protest against racism but also as the first of Lange's several exercises in war photography. War photography is usually defined as that focused on the battlefield
or its immediate consequences, and as a form of photojournalism. In this
sense, it was an almost exclusively male activity at this time, requiring speed,
physical bravery, physical strength, competitiveness, a taste for hard living,
until Margaret Bourke-White, as adventurous a woman as they come, broke
the barrier. Documentary photography, by contrast, had a feminine aroma, the
scent of empathy, bruised idealism, even sentimentality. Lange's coverage of
the Japanese American internment was both.

The greatest of recent war photographers have been liberals or leftists,
motivated by opposition to war. They were often constrained by military as
well as civilian censors, aware that images can be vital weapons. Embedded
photographers—this is a new word but not a new position—understood
also that the "wrong" photographs could undermine the nation's security. In
the embedded situation, censorship is so ordinary that it can become taken
for granted, even unnoticeable. Much heroic war imagery results not from
intrepid photographers daring the line of fire but from photo ops set up by the
military establishment. Lange was embedded in much the same way in the
FSA. She accepted the censorship that came with that job because she identified with her employers' constraints. Her history as an official government
photographer makes all the more impressive her resistance when working for
the U.S. Army.

IMPERIAL JAPAN'S BOMBING of Pearl Harbor provoked understandable anger, but the internment arose not out of war strategy but out of racial
thinking. General DeWitt, head of the Western Defense Command, wrote,

"The Japanese race is an enemy race and while many second and third generation Japanese born on American soil, possessed of American citizenship,
have become 'Americanized,' the racial strains are undiluted. . . ."[12] In other
words, what made Japanese Americans untrustworthy was in their genes. The
contrasting treatment of German Americans was evident even in photography: The Office of War Information hired an FSA photographer to produce
positive images of a largely German American town to head off outbreaks of
anti-German sentiment.[13]

The Western Defense Command was at first reluctant to undertake this
massive roundup and imprisonment because of doubts that the army had the
human and financial resources to do it. Once evacuation was ordered, that
problem of state capacity was solved by delegating the work of organizing
and staffing the assembly centers to the Works Progress Administration, the
major New Deal relief agency.[14] Even more disgusting to Lange must have
been the fact that the West Coast FSA office was assigned to organize evacuation.[15] Had this remained the plan, Lange's position would have been even
more difficult, given her loyalty to the FSA, but a few weeks later the army
created the War Relocation Authority (WRA) to conduct evacuation and run
the camps.[16] It is a sign of the widespread approval of the internment that
programs once at the progressive edge of the New Deal were expected to help
run this morally rotten enterprise.

Lange did the job with her usual unmatched intensity, hurrying out of fear
that she might be fired at any time. She started to photograph the moment
the roundups began on March 22, although she was not on the payroll until
April 2. She worked sixteen-hour days, often seven days a week, for four and
a half months, all the while living with fears about Dan, her abdominal pain,
her muscle aches and fatigue, and the need to maintain a facade of neutrality
in her dealings with army brass.

But she needed help now more than ever. She could not drive for hours
without rest, as she had frequently done in the 1930s. To work quickly, she
sometimes kept four cameras in the car and counted on an assistant to see
that each was always loaded with film. Whenever possible she still used
a tripod, which had to be unfolded, set up, folded again, and carried. She
needed a boost to get on top of her car. On return drives she often slept from
exhaustion.[17] Rondal Partridge was now in the navy, so Dorothea asked Christina Clausen Page to help her.[18] The twenty-two-year-old daughter of one of
Lange's oldest studio-client friends, just graduated from UCB, Christina had

recently married aspiring photographer Homer Page. With photography thus surrounding her, Christina jumped at the chance to "apprentice" with Lange, as Partridge had.[19]

Lange's job was more stressful yet because of censorship, aimed not at national security, as claimed, but to preclude unflattering images. Concerned to orchestrate news and photographs concerning the internment, the army hired a PR firm[20] to manage news releases and appointed loyal journalists as PR officers for the assembly centers. A colonel set out rules: "One thing that is absolutely taboo, pictures of machine guns in the towers. . . . Pictures of forts that bring out our military police in a favorable light, show them to be strong, healthful men, but not Gestapo and that sort of thing. . . . It is a matter of holding down publicity and letting out only that which would be in aid to inform the public of what is happening to bring us the favorable light. . . ." He warned particularly about news that might reach "the Japs" and South America. "As to news going across the water to the enemy . . . that might bring reprisals if it's not right." As to South America, "Fact is, we've always told them we live by the democratic way that's the way you should live so don't play along with the other boys. Now, the thing is about our situation here they will probably wonder."[21]

Not only watchtowers but also barbed wire, armed guards, and anything suggesting resistance within the camps were forbidden subjects. Despite credentials from the WRA, Lange was frequently refused access to what she was supposed to photograph. Guards would demand to see her credentials repeatedly, making her lose precious time waiting. Tellingly, none of her assistants were ever asked for credentials, putting the lie to any claim that security was the concern. Evidently not everyone in authority wanted photographs to be made at all. The guards threw at her any regulation or security claim they could invent or adapt to stop, slow down, or censor her work, and arbitrarily declared certain spaces off-limits.[22] MPs followed her, harassed her, and tried to keep her from talking with internees, roughly enough to frighten her at times.[23] Christina suspected that witnessing this made the internees more willing to cooperate with Lange. Army bureaucrats challenged her mileage records, meal and gas receipts, and telephone calls. She was required to turn over all negatives, prints, and undeveloped film from this work and to sign a notarized agreement that she would have no further access to them.[24]

The internment offered Lange a second opportunity—after *An American Exodus*—to create a photographic narrative. That narrative never appeared because she lost control of the images, but her photographic strategy can be pieced together. (In the book of these photographs we edited, *Impounded,* Gary Okihiro and I organized the photographs as we think she intended, telling the story from the point of view of its victims, from life before Pearl Harbor to Manzanar, and in that book I provide a fuller account of her work than is possible here.) She began with a strategy that the WRA never intended, photographing Japanese American life in the context of California's society and economy before evacuation—that is, establishing their Americanness.[25] (In film, these would be called establishing shots.) She was able thereby to demonstrate the respectability, Americanism, work ethic, good citizenship, and achievements of these people now being treated as criminals. She showed children reading American comic books, saluting the flag, playing baseball;

19.1. RAPHAEL WEILL SCHOOL, SAN FRANCISCO, 1942

housewives who could have been Betty Crocker; teenage boys dressed in the coolest fashion; young men in U.S. army uniforms; beautifully gardened homes both upscale and modest. This was a standard antiracist approach of the time—invoking the melting-pot ideal in which immigrants become identical with all other Americans (and in this denial of difference, it clashes with more recent diversity and multicultural ideals). To demonstrate "Americanness," she produced several visual vignettes of families, such as the Shibuyas of Mountain View, a town at the southern end of San Francisco Bay. We see them relaxing with a pet dog in front of their white Colonial-style house and working in their fields, which were as meticulously tended and as clear of weeds as their lawn. Captions to portraits detail the achievements of the family: one son attended Stanford Medical School, another graduated from the UC College of Agriculture with a degree in plant pathology; their father "arrived in this country in 1904, with $60 and a basket of clothes," and now grew prize chrysanthemums for select markets. She ended this caption and many others with the words, "Horticulturists and other evacuees of Japanese ancestry will be given opportunities to follow their callings at War Relocation Authority centers where they will spend the duration."[26] Did she believe this? Did she feel obligated to include it? Or by including it was she trying to hold the government to its promises? One extrapolation seems justified: that the censors might look as much to the words as to the pictures and that she could appease them through captions. It is also possible that she was trying, perhaps not entirely consciously, to influence the army authorities themselves.

Next she photographed the roundup: registration orders posted on walls and telephone poles, people tagged and issued instructions: bring linen, dishes and utensils, clothing, only what you can carry, but no pets, no camera, no cars. She documented a hurried last harvesting, a last load of laundry, the garage sales, a last-minute wedding to keep sweethearts from being separated.[27] Then they waited in lines with their suitcases for buses or trains to take them to temporary assembly camps. In this, her "chapter two," she wanted the viewer to see the "process of processing."[28] Once the people were lined up for registration, inspection, and evacuation, their previous lives seemed to disappear. A population stratified by class and many other identities, like all populations, was now homogenized. Lange made fewer individual portraits of these people once they had boarded buses and trains, because the MPs would not let her get that close.

Here we meet a motif, both visual and emotional, that runs throughout the internment photographs: waiting in line. It is Lange at her best, creating a visual metaphor for the deindividualization of the prisoners. The Japanese Americans line up for their preliminary registration; they wait in chairs or stand waiting before tables at which officials ask questions, fill out forms, give out instructions. Sometimes soldiers guard them. Then they are tagged: the head of each family receives a number with a tag for each member of the family. Father is 107351A, mother 107351B, children C through F, from oldest to youngest, grandmother 107351G, and so on. (See page 303.) Then they wait for buses or trains to carry them away. Their belongings also form queues on sidewalks and dirt roads. Lange is taking us into a brave new world of rationalization and control, featuring the industrial and technological forms of domination later described most influentially by Foucault. We see now that what is being stolen is not only farms and education and businesses and jobs but also personal identity. Individuals are registered, numbered, inoculated, tagged, categorized, and assigned. They are divided up, segregated, exiled, inspected, billeted, surveilled. They are herded. A curfew is imposed and roll call is held every day at 6:45 A.M. and 6:45 P.M.[29] A high barbed-wire fence surrounds them; in every direction they see armed guards and watchtowers; searchlights trace huge illuminated circles all night; camp police patrol night and day.

Even in this condemnation of dehumanization, however, her photographs refuse simple generalizations. "These people came . . . dressed as though they were going to an important event," she recalled, "but always off in a little group by themselves were the teenage boys. They were the ones that really hurt me the most, the teenage boys who didn't know what they were. The older people have more of a way of being very dignified in such a situation and not asking questions. But these Americanized boys, they were loud and they were rowdy and they were frightened"—many were just Daniel's age, dressing like him, covering their anxiety with cockiness as he did.[30]

Despite being infuriated, she retained her typical restraint, as did her subjects. There are very few tearjerkers, like this girl weeping at the train station (figure 19.2). It is precisely this commitment to the discipline of her craft, not permitting emotion to drown the evidence, that makes the photographs so compelling as a collection. Instead of uniquely painful moments, the photographs document queue after queue, barrack after barrack, interspersed with symbols of internee creativity and resourcefulness. So the impact is from the whole, not from the individual photographs; the repetition proves the point.

"Chapter three" takes place in the temporary assembly centers. The first

19.2. Oakland, California, 1942

one she saw—the Tanforan Racetrack in San Bruno—left her staggered. She needed to make her own home beautiful, even artful, and she was aware of the same impulse in Japanese Americans. (Fifteen years later, visiting Japan and appreciating its characteristic design elegance, she saw the origin of this sensibility.) Arriving inmates passed through two lines of troops with rifles and fixed bayonets pointed at them as their belongings were searched for contraband. Each family received a broom, a mop, and a bucket to clear away the omnipresent dust, but it returned within hours of being swept away. Thousands suffered irritated eyes from the dust. Each individual received a mattress tick bag, which they filled from a huge straw pile near the grandstand.[31] Tanforan resident Jean Kariya's family of five occupied the stable of one racehorse, she recalled. (Occasionally, very large families got two rooms.) "The place still smelled of hay and horse manure. The stable had been hurriedly swept and spray painted over cobwebs and dust."[32] Parents had no privacy from their children and not much from neighbors, since the thin walls did not extend to the ceiling. Stables were supplemented by barracks, averaging from ten to fourteen rooms each, with fourteen or so barracks to a block. Lack of insulation and ventilation made the cubbyholes in which they lived freezing in winter and sweltering in summer. Dust, mud, ugliness surrounded them. Nothing to do. Lines for breakfast, lines for lunch, lines for supper, lines for mail, lines for the canteen, lines for laundry tubs, lines for toilets. The most common activity was waiting.

The camps disrupted families. There were no family meals: each block had a mess hall, typically serving meals in two shifts to eight hundred people at a time. The hurried meals eroded good manners and replaced the ritual of Japanese cooking and serving with mere feeding of the body. Strange food— definitely not Japanese—was doled out, sometimes from large garbage cans, onto plates the internees held out as they moved along the line. One month, Jean Kariya remembers, they were served tripe twenty times. The communal laundries (there were no washing machines, only tubs and washboards, and frequently no hot water) and showers were chronically short of soap and hot water, and there was no decent provision for washing diapers. The showers and latrines were communal, a condition that inmates, especially women, found very difficult. The toilets consisted of a bench with several holes, with no partitions between seats; at one camp, the long trough always flushed all at once, so if you were sitting at the low end of the bench, you got splashed; hardly surprisingly, there was widespread constipation.[33] Without family privacy, the chief influence on children became peer culture; parental authority diminished, offending many parents. Children lost some of their dependence on parents, who neither fed them nor set the rules. Teenagers ran in packs through the camp.

Lange's sensitivity to dejected men reemerged. Her pictures testify to the idleness, humiliation, and domination that corroded masculine self-esteem. Almost every aspect of the experience undercut customary manly identity: Men were no longer breadwinners; they could no longer be strivers to better their families. Men lost authority; the whole interned population, men, women, and children, were leveled in their subordination to the army. Everyone had to ask permission to do almost anything; no one had to ask a father's or husband's permission anymore. Men were as domestic as their wives and mothers; there was no way to go into the outside world. Although many of the men sought energetically to reproduce their work lives in the camps, in agriculture, art, carpentry, or medicine, they could extract only limited benefits from their labor. Other men, whether as a result of temperament or of their skill set, responded with idleness, low energy, and depression.

To some extent the camps created a zero-sum enterprise—while men lost power, women and children gained in autonomy. Women slid into organized camp activities as much, if not more than, men. Living in barracks, they saw as much of neighbors as of their husbands, and spent more time with other women. In their degree of autonomy, they often experienced a leveling upward, in that the most independent women set the norm for womanly behavior. This was by no means an entirely happy or appreciated development, however. As in the Depression, when men's unemployment was so severe, women were by no means always pleased to gain in autonomy and power at the expense of husbands. Meanwhile, the camps deprived women of sources of identity and pride. They no longer cooked, as there were no family meals. They could not easily individuate their living spaces or make them into places of peace, quiet, and beauty. And above all, their authority as mothers diminished.

Manzanar, the last "chapter," was the only long-term internment camp Lange was able to visit, because others were not yet open.[34] Located just west of Death Valley and just east of the Sierra Nevada, the place suffered extremes of weather: The snow-covered mountains looking down from the west did nothing to cool the one-hundred-plus-degree summer heat, and there were neither trees nor hills to break the fierce winds, whether icy or hot. These barracks could not keep out the weather, either, constructed as they were of quarter-inch boards covered with tar paper.

In this desert, Lange showed, internees worked to create civilization, their ingenuity recalling that of migrant farmworkers. They decorated their "apartments" with curtains, rugs, pictures, and flowers. They built room dividers, shelves, closets, chairs, benches, and tables out of scrap lumber. They cleared the brush, then planted and irrigated both vegetables and flowers. They built libraries (although nothing written in Japanese was permitted), produced camp newspapers (whose contents were censored by the army), and put on talent shows. They created rock gardens and set up art classes in both Western and Japanese styles. They organized sports and folk dancing.

The project was not entirely thankless, for Lange received gratitude of a personal nature. A number of Japanese Americans grasped what she was doing and thanked her after their release. Dorothea and Paul went to visit one family in Utah, and Paul said it "was like old home week. . . . When I went [there] with her, they received us like—well, like guests." Every Christmas, they received cards from former internees. After Dorothea's death, the Japanese American Citizens League gave Paul Taylor a honorary plaque, but he thought, "That was for Dorothea, probably more than for me. . . ."[35]

IMPOUNDING THESE PHOTOGRAPHS deprived Americans of a more accurate and complex view of World War II and of our national strengths and weaknesses. Visual images always help construct political attitudes. World War II became a proving ground for photojournalists, and their heroic and celebratory photographs shaped the national memory of this "good war." Movies in the heroic mode sometimes shifted this memory toward the sentimental. Whether raising the U.S. flag at Iwo Jima, holding a wounded GI buddy, or flying bombing runs from England, Americans were standing up against tyranny, saving the rest of the world from it.

Defining Japanese Americans as an enemy was itself partly a visual process. The Japanese face was imprinted on the public through posters, grafitti, atrocity films, cartoons, and caricatures. The epicanthic eye fold and prominent teeth in particular became visual tropes for a despised, allegedly untrustworthy, and now enemy "race." The racist images then circulating were particularly authoritative to a public only just beginning to be saturated with photographic images. Entering a stream of anti-Japanese racism on the West Coast, photography both intensified and reshaped racial categories, molding "Japanese" as a "visual field" signifying disloyalty and treachery.[36]

Of course it is a myth that race is readily visible. Store owners put up signs identifying themselves as Chinese or Filipino because they understood the uncertainty of physiological categories, especially to outsiders' eyes. *Life* published two marked-up head shots to teach "Americans" how to tell the Japanese from the Chinese. Rounding up the Japanese Americans depended on the cooperation of the census bureau in providing the army with supposedly confidential population numbers and the outlines of Japanese neighborhoods.[37] Still, getting Japanese Americans to report and register without the army having to apprehend them in their homes relied in part on their understanding that they could not hide, that they could be identified visually and turned in by the "American citizens"—that is, the "white" citizens. Thus the internment strengthened the racial content of American nationalism. Lange was the first of several major photographers who tried to challenge this with countervailing images, but no other photographer so explicitly damned the internment policy. Her photographs rank with the best war photography.

LANGE DID NOT see these photographs for over twenty years. In 1964, just one year before she died, already very ill, she went to the National Archives to look at them. She had braced herself with low expectations because she had compromised her photographic standards in order to record everything she could. For once, she relaxed some of her tendency to self-criticism regarding the photographs: "I had never had a comfortable feeling about that war relocation job . . . the difficulties of doing it were immense . . . but really it's surprising what I did. . . . Gosh I'd worked . . . and some of them are beautiful, some of them are really compelling pictures, not a very great many, but the factual ones are also there. . . . In 1967 it will be 25 years since that thing happened, and I think it would be time to make a television documentary to say, *this is what we did* [emphasizing each word] how did it happen, how could we?"[38]

# 20

# Unruly War Photography:
# The Office of War Information
# and Defense Workers

Apparently, news of the War Department's displeasure with Lange's work on the internment did not reach other agencies, because the Office of War Information hired her for six projects between 1942 and 1945.[1] Despite the bitterness left by her War Relocation Authority experience, the state of the war made it impossible for her to refuse: The Nazis were on their way to Stalingrad, Rommel had captured the strategic port of Tobruk in Libya, Italian torpedoes were destroying British submarines in the Mediterranean, the Japanese had captured Burma and were headed for India, and, unknown to the Western press, the Nazis had begun extermination of the Jews at Auschwitz.

In this period of wartime propaganda, movies were of highest priority, now that eighty million Americans a week saw films, but OWI also required still photographs for its glossy magazine, *Victory*, published in six languages for distribution abroad.[2] Lange and Ansel Adams supplied many of its pictures. Both supported the war effort fervently, but once again Lange clashed with her government employer. Although the OWI swallowed up the FSA photography project, the work did not feel like a continuation to Lange. Her convictions aligned her with a progressive faction in OWI that wanted to promote a democratic ideology, seeking to continue and even advance the New Deal. The dominant OWI group, however, would countenance nothing that suggested social division in the United States and sought to limit OWI messages to those of national unity and determination. FDR himself announced that Dr. New Deal was dead and Dr. Win the War had taken over. When OWI progressives published the small photo-textual pamphlet *Negroes and the War,* at a time when the armed forces were still segregated, it came under heavy assault, despite offering mainly handsome images of African American successes and counseling patience.[3] At the same time, congressional Republicans charged that the OWI was just another Roosevelt self-promotion vehicle.[4]

Lange found OWI products offensively simplistic. Many American allies, even those entirely dependent on U.S. aid, agreed. A photographic exhibit sent to England, with text by Carl Sandburg as captions, was roundly panned by British critics: ". . . the rather grandiose Americanese of Sandburg's text met with considerable criticism . . . the nativist streak, amounting almost to jingoism, when seen by overseas eyes, would not have promoted better transatlantic understanding. . . ." The OWI's glamorous shots of women war workers with perfectly coifed hair and makeup, intended to assuage fears that they were losing their femininity, did not go over well where women were sleeping in bomb shelters.[5] The OWI's propaganda operation even used and defanged Lange's FSA work. In one case, a 1939 photograph of a typical run-down North Carolina country store/filling station with a group of young men goofing off on the porch was transformed into a World War II poster by cropping and superimposing a message: "*This is America . . .* Where a fellow can start on the home team and wind up in the big league. Where there is always room at the top for the fellow who has it on the ball ★ This is *your* America! . . . *Keep it Free!*"

Lange had made five photographs of the scene, showing about a dozen figures, several in baseball uniforms, preparing to play with a local league; mugging for the camera, they began picking up and swinging one guy by his arms and legs. In the original context, these images signaled the economic backwardness, inactivity, and racism of the rural South. At the far end of the porch, distinctly removed from the others, was a black man who did not participate in the roughhousing, but sat tight with a tense smile. In the poster, both sides of the image and were cropped and it showed only young white men standing in manly, confident but relaxed postures, ready to play the quintessentially American game.[6]

The OWI built a campaign around unity in diversity—"Americans All, Immigrants All" was the slogan—aimed at countering Axis propaganda that the U.S. treated minority groups no better than its opponents. With her usual enthusiasm and assertiveness, Lange sent suggestions to her supervisor, Jess Gorkin. Trying to compromise, she would not deny American inequalities or exclude people of color, but proposed a story about Negroes who had escaped or surmounted some of the cruder forms of discrimination. Other suggestions included the Chinese working in the shipyards, and the crops being grown for lend-lease—with "Mexicans, Filipinos, Indians, Negroes, boys and girls . . . war prisoners and Jamaicans . . . participating in the harvest to feed the world."[7] None of these requests was approved. The only diversity Lange was allowed to show was white ethnics.[8] This concept of diversity fit an expansion of the category "American" developing at this time, seen in many World War II

20.1. BRACEROS, 1942

movies, to include Jews, various categories of Slavs, even Greeks, as American and white. Their inclusion only confirmed the exclusion of nonwhites. She did manage some photography of the Mexicans on the OWI tab. The federal Bracero program recruited 125,000 Mexican workers into the United States every year to work for the war effort, placing them in jobs in agriculture and on the railroads. We see these young men arriving, hopeful at their first glimpse of the USA. But to the best of my knowledge, the OWI never used these.[9]

Lange fumed at restrictions and hassles resembling those of the internment job. She had to get separate credentials from the Western Defense Command, the U.S. Navy, the San Francisco Police Department, and the Port of Embarkation Authority.[10] When she wanted to photograph North Beach from the top of Telegraph Hill, she was told there should be no photographing at all from hills, roofs, or windows. And how could she photograph fishermen when no photography was allowed at any time on the waterfront? Before she could send her photographs to Washington, they had to be reviewed and censored by army, navy, Coast Guard, and Port authorities. Her complaints reflect also the chronically subversive potential of photography, and the resultant anxiety that it produces in authorities.

Overall Lange did six OWI assignments: photographing Italian, Spanish, and Yugoslav Americans, UCB student life, the Volunteer Land Army's vegetable seed production, and, finally, the opening of the United Nations in San Francisco. The photos reflect her persistent attempts to go beyond her orders. Regarding Spanish Americans, captions explain that they traced their settlement back to a Mexican land grant to Juan Manuel Vaca in 1843 and that Spanish farmworkers, recruited by Hawaiian sugar companies, supported the Spanish Republic against the fascist coup; they "call themselves 'Fighters for Democracy, not only for Spanish democracy but for democracy anywhere.'" But they were also pleased to take over the leaseholds of interned Japanese Americans, she dryly pointed out.[11] This, of course, is not what was shown in *Victory*. There one sees a mother from a family that operated five ranches; the restored seventeenth-century mission church of San Juan Bautista; a pastoral vision of a Basque sheepherder with his herd under snowcapped mountains; and a generic shot of shipyard workers—the last two photographs probably by Ansel Adams.

The Italian and Yugoslav American work was similarly bland, a tone that may have resulted not only from OWI strictures but also from Lange's own idealization of family farms and small-town life. The relative weakness of the

OWI photographs also raises the question of whether the strength of her FSA pictures derived in any part from the helplessness of the subjects. Poor farm-workers were, to a degree, captive subjects, living exposed lives with little privacy, often deferential toward elites. And some of the revelatory punch of the FSA photographs derived from the tension between the subjects' economic dishonor and their honorable appearance as captured by Lange's camera. The OWI subjects suffered no such deprivation. In general, Lange's best mode in these years was the tragic, not the contented. Yet her photographs of prosperous and optimistic defense workers, made without government supervision, would be stunning.

Lange's assignment to photograph the University of California and the student body presented no problems. Her feeling for the Berkeley campus shows in loving photographs of the beautiful bark texture and branch shapes of a eucalyptus tree (brought to California from Australia), of the Italianate campanile nestled against the East Bay hills, and of students making architectural drawings, experimenting in a petroleum lab, playing woodwinds in the band, and relaxing on the union terrace.[12] But even here she could not resist going beyond her instructions, adding in a smaller feature on foreign-born students.[13]

LANGE'S BEST WAR photography emerged when she was freed from the government payroll. In 1944 she worked with Ansel Adams on a commission from *Fortune* to cover defense shipbuilding in Richmond, California, and then on her own made a series on the war's impact on Oakland. By then it looked to be only a matter of time before the Axis was defeated, so her anxiety on that front was diminished. Always seeking complexity, she focused on radical changes the war brought to the California home front, the making of a "new California."

Defense workers were arriving by the tens of thousands. In Richmond, a shipbuilding harbor just north of Berkeley, a single Kaiser plant—the biggest shipbuilding facility in the country—built more Victory and Liberty ships than any other U.S. location, and once built a ship in five days. Richmond's population was 23,000 in 1940; then 90,000 defense workers arrived. Oakland absorbed 82,000 new residents. Military bases proliferated. Twenty-three million tons of war materiel and 1.6 million military personnel shipped out through the Golden Gate.[14]

Many farmworkers seized the defense-work opportunities, so Lange was often photographing the same social groups she had portrayed in the 1930s. As she wrote, the migratory workers now slept under a roof while the Negroes came by the truckload from the cotton fields. The majority of these were "Okies," but many African Americans and some Mexican, Chinese, and Filipino Americans managed to get hired, and the racial complexion of the Bay Area changed radically. Oakland had previously included 8,000 African Americans, but by 1950 it held 42,000. Richmond, an almost exclusively white town in 1940, had 6,000 at the end of the war.[15]

This "second gold rush" gave money to the masses, not just lucky prospectors and merchants. Billions in defense contracts lifted consumer spending, finally ending the Depression's deflation and unemployment. The boom also created hardships that good wages could not quickly solve. The many women employed—about 25 percent of shipyard workers—were often harassed, rather than supported, by their male coworkers. Housing could not keep up with demand and even well-paid workers lived in overcrowded apartments, garages, cars, or tent encampments that reminded Dorothea of migratory farmworkers' camps. Workers often took turns in the same beds. Black workers in particular encountered discrimination, especially in finding housing. In schools, sixty children were frequently assigned to one teacher. Lack of child-care provision and the fact that schools operated with shorter hours in three or even four shifts left children often unsupervised. In fact, the whole of Richmond lived on shifts: Three times a day, somewhere between twenty and forty thousand workers crossed one another, some leaving, some coming to work.[16]

With all this happening just outside her door, Lange felt her OWI work to be trivial. "I was working on the wrong thing. . . . In this war booming world . . . the vast upheavals of peoples, and the radical and profound changes . . . I had to go in the country and do apricot and prunes and do simple living under the grape arbors for the Spanish."[17]

She wanted to be at the heart of world events. In another life, would she have been attracted by photojournalism, even battle photography? Probably not, because that would have required giving up some of her core technique and turning to faster cameras, faster film, and fleeting glimpses. For *Fortune*, Adams and Lange proposed to document twenty-four hours in the life of shipyard workers (although their photography was actually a composite of many days' work), and she soon realized that this *was* at the heart of world events.

20.2. OAKLAND, CALIFORNIA, 1942

These workers were servicemen and women just like those at Anzio or Guam.

The shipyard workers Lange photographed are positively heroic. She saw their pride in the work. She made some classic "Rosie the Riveter" photographs; now the culture shared her taste for powerful, even tough female figures, as the defense industries' need for labor stimulated propaganda lauding women's strength, stamina, and patriotism. *Fortune* published her pithy captions, unlike the FSA or OWI, and she could comment on the diversity and strange juxtapositions created by the war: "Son of an Oklahoma Indian chief, now a Kaiser machinist." A Chinese woman "hasn't missed a day's work in two years." An elderly Okie woman "has a son in France, works as a common laborer."[18]

Never one to avoid contradictions, however, Lange complicated the story of the "good war."[19] For the new workers, prosperity and difficulty coexisted. Workers now had money to spend. Local merchants prospered, especially bar owners and landlords. Despite discrimination, blacks found Richmond and Oakland far better than Texas or Arkansas, and none wanted to leave afterward. As to women defense workers, "Hitler got us out of the kitchen," said one of them.[20] Benefit-

20.3. RICHMOND, CALIFORNIA, 1942

20.4. OAKLAND, CALIFORNIA, 1942

ing from male-level wages and working conditions, working-class women had more spending power, and this, along with the experience of living without husbands, made women less deferential and tractable. Class markers faded as working-class women bought stylish clothes.

But these hardworking patriots lived in barracks on the mud flats next to the Bay. Families reeled, pushed off balance by missing men, round-the-clock shift work, lack of privacy, lack of housekeeping resources, and women doing the "double day"—paid work for one shift, unpaid housework for another shift. All this made children anxious and, with schools operating on shifts, disruptive. Overloaded sewers backed up and paved streets cracked under heavy traffic. A small polio epidemic broke out in 1943.[21]

The photographs signal her mixed feelings. She worried about leisure time spent shopping rather than conversing, singing, or building things. "Can life be 'abundant' without being 'good'?" she asked. She captured with exquisite sensitivity the personal tensions arising from the radical disruption of family life and family balance of power. (See plate 36.) Couples argue and friends bicker.[22] Like her photograph of the plantation owner and his croppers, this "argument in a trailer court" photograph made visual composition represent social relations. She fretted about anomie among the tens of thousands of workers pulled abruptly out of their communities. "The New Californians, they have no roots, but they take over," she wrote.[23] "Oakland. It was a HOME TOWN, once." "NO ROOTS NO ROOTS . . . the new and raw frontier—its barrenness its meanness its homelessness its blight." Lange was a worrier. Just as her need for control arose from personal anxiety, so this anxious vision derived as much

20.5. RICHMOND, CALIFORNIA, 1942

from her and Paul's romance with small-town community as from the defense
workers' own concerns. She captioned several pictures of workers leaving a
plant, "Notice how these people are entirely unrelated to each other. This is
the story of these times and the shipyard."[24] But this is an overreaction. To me,
the people in this famous photograph look tired and eager to get home but not
particularly alienated from one another. As in the 1920s she had absorbed Maynard's mourning for the loss of wilderness, as in the 1930s she had absorbed
Paul's mourning for lost family farming, now in the 1940s she mourned the
loss of the more intimate, homogeneous Bay Area she loved so much. She may
have projected these concerns onto the defense workers.

Returning to the city streets, a subject she had not touched for almost a
decade, Lange developed a new photographic exercise, a method that practically invited projecting her feelings onto subjects: She stood on the street
*without* a camera, watched passersby, and speculated about their relationships
and feelings. "A young couple having a quarrel, a grudge kind of a quarrel.
He's ready to talk it over but she won't." "I think her hands are in fists in
those pockets." "Hostile reaction to hatred. The good thing about it is that she
stands up to it, which I like about it." These projections could be far-fetched,
and faintly similar to Bourke-White's captions, in which she expressed what
she thought her subjects meant. But Lange never published her projections;
for her they were rehearsals for deepening the photographs themselves.

Moreover, she intended her photographs to raise questions, not provide
answers. Drawn to images that transgressed gender and race codes, she sometimes made slyly humorous photographs. A blonde with a stylish pageboy is
a mail carrier—with a flower tucked into her post-office cap. A well-dressed
young white woman with perfectly coifed hair and a black man in work clothes
and a railroad cap emerge from the same market, carrying loaded grocery
bags.[25] Shopping is no longer exclusively women's work. A woman, a black
man, a white man, all in hard hats, window-shop at a Richmond department
store. At an Oakland newsstand, men in business suits browse next to men
in overalls with lunch pails.[26] Several dozen men sleep in an all-night movie
house.[27] One photograph conveys the absolute absurdity of a Kaiser auto dealer
who elevated automobiles on his roof, as icons for worship.

TWO PHOTOGRAPHERS COULD hardly be more different than Lange and
Ansel Adams.[28] They would drive to Richmond in Ansel's car, and Christina

Page, who was again assisting, recalled that Dorothea kept saying, "Don't drive so fast." Dorothea liked to go ten miles an hour so she wouldn't miss a photo op, while Adams was interested in distance views. Dorothea kept pushing in his car lighter to light her cigarette and it refused to heat up. He pushed it gently once and it popped out red-hot. Chris and Dorothea made eye contact, recognizing this as Ansel's rapport with the inanimate: all machines worked perfectly for him, while Dorothea never felt the master of her equipment. His station wagon was loaded with equipment and it took him quite some time to unload and set it up; he was accustomed to photographing things that did not move. Dorothea carried only a Rolleiflex, an extra film bag, and a notebook, and began shooting the minute she was out of the car, losing herself in the crowd immediately. "She had a peculiar facility," Chris remembered, "for just melting away and for not seeming to be photographing at the same time that she was sticking a camera in somebody's face." As Dorothea put it, "I have this gray coat that I put on and I just disappear. . . ."[29] Ansel waited for the right light before photographing, for light was in some ways the subject as well as the means of his pictures; Dorothea would photograph anytime there was enough light to make an exposure. While Adams captured "the grandiose aspects of a great shipyard," she got "the intricate aspects of workers' lives."[30] Dismayed at how she continually ventured beyond *Fortune*'s assignment, he nevertheless appreciated her ability to cut through red tape and "was glad to go along on her coattails."[31] They had one thing in common: every day, as soon as they returned, both went straight down to their darkrooms to see what they had got, a freedom Lange had had to do without for years.

Adams and Lange quarreled all their lives. Rondal Partridge thought they were like feuding stand-up comics or the bickering partners on cop shows. Both were a bit intolerant of others' approaches to photography.[32] On matters of politics, the disagreements were fundamental. Lange could be very judgmental and Ansel provoked her, sometimes mischievously, by asserting his imperviousness to matters of social justice. She once responded, "Are you still worshipping the same Gods of Beauty and Truth?"[33] His devotion to the Sierras communicated an outdoorsy quality, which led to his friends' surprise when they became aware of his high standard of living and social connections. He had a knack for creating alliances with the very rich, such as Albert Bender and arts patron David McAlpin, a banker member of the Rockefeller family and the Museum of Modern Art board. In a moment of Imogen-like sharpness, Dorothea asked him, when she first saw the spectacular lot he bought in Carmel, "Do you feel you deserve it?"[34] Her competitiveness often showed particularly vividly in her relationship with Ansel. After Ansel described a plush party he'd attended in New York, she said to him, "You really *like* rich people, don't you?'" Adams understood perfectly: "What she meant was that I gravitated towards luxury. There was something to that. . . ." By contrast, he found her taste unnecessarily austere.[35]

Adams entirely misunderstood Lange's politics and background. He once described her as coming from a ghetto or near-ghetto background. It was her social commitments that most alienated him. He told an interviewer that ". . . all the people she knew were . . . very party line. . . ." He was unsure whether she "leaned to Leninism or Trotskyism . . ." but knew that she had "a very strong dedication to the party ideal . . . like an orthodox priest, you know, orthodoxy." Backing down a bit, he acknowledged that she was not "an actual *member* of the Commie Party," but her sympathies were socialistic, always favoring the "underdog. The underprivileged. The breadline people, which is no personal criticism of the people. . . . But also there are a lot of people getting welfare for the privilege of loafing, and that just drives me nuts."[36] Adams experienced the Left as unpatriotic: "I am so *goddam* mad over what people from the left tier think America is. Stinks, social and otherwise, are a poor excuse and imitation of the real beauty and power of the land and the real people inhabiting it."[37] Adams liked his emotions and his photographs unmixed, critic Sally Stein points out; he did not like irony or conflicting desires.[38] When Rondal Partridge made a series of photographs of Yosemite in the 1960s, contrasting the park's grandeur to the automobile and commercial inroads that threatened it, Adams disapproved. Lange, like Partridge, found rich material precisely in such contradictory stories.

Given these differences, it is striking that Adams's slurs against Lange coexisted—or alternated—with appreciation and respect. Adams deeply respected, championed, and promoted her photography.[39] He was one of the first to publish her work—as an example in one of his textbooks. He defended her against FSA accusations of shoddy technique. He tried to persuade Stryker to let her make and keep prints in California. He promoted her: His biographer Mary Street Alinder found that he mentioned "her name at every opportunity in print as well as in person." He brought her work to the attention of Beaumont Newhall, a scholar and patron of photography also in the Rockefeller and Museum of Modern Art sphere. He and his assistants did darkroom work for her. Despite railing against social-justice advocacy, he registered Lange's total commitment to exploring the possibilities of visual communication.

A SIGN THAT the New Deal was dead, its beloved community scattered, was that Paul could no longer regularly travel with Dorothea. With gas and tires rationed, neither of them traveled as much, but he took occasional trips to Washington, and while gone he still wrote love letters. His memories put her by his side, he wrote from the train, "but I would prefer it if the upper berth were more crowded." He sent droll greetings to the children—"Tell Dan to bathe Blazes [their dog], and John to read Stuhldreyer's letter after the Wis-Yale game"—and he reported on family work that Dorothea had assigned him. On a trip to New York, he saw a lot of her mother, whose second husband had recently died. One day, Joan and her sister Minette met him in Princeton "and had a big day of it." He reported having worked out a financial plan with his daughter Kathy, mediating between her desires and Dorothea's controlling directives. He would give Kathy seven hundred dollars for her last year at Swarthmore ("I added $100 'because it was the last year.' Is that OK?"), plus something unspecified when school ended, while she tried to get a "theatre job," plus half the cost of her trip west and a twenty-dollar gift.[40]

The letters also testify to what Lange had taught him. In Washington, friends took him to breakfast in Rock Creek Park—"open fireplace and leaves on the ground, and floating from the trees like snow in the wind, and drifting downstream, thick on the surface of Rock Creek." Another time, he wrote, "The sunlight has that rich golden tinge, and you are perhaps hoeing in the garden, and sprinkling the lawn."[41]

# Part V

---

INDEPENDENT PHOTOGRAPHER

1945–1965

LANGE-TAYLOR FAMILY PHOTOGRAPH

# SCENE 5

*In 1957, the Lange-Taylor extended family began to rent a cabin on the coast of Marin County. Located one mile south of Stinson Beach on a rocky point protruding into the Pacific, the area was called Steep Ravine by locals. On the point were ten rustic cabins, built in the 1930s as a getaway for the family of local congressman and landowner William Kent.[1] Dan and his wife, Mia, had visited one and described it enthusiastically. Dorothea fell in love with it on her first visit. It was rough: only cold water, a woodstove, no radio, a single room with a small sleeping loft.*

*She and Paul drove up on many weekends, accompanied by various combinations of children, grandchildren, in-laws, and close friends like Imogen Cunningham, Rondal Partridge, and their families. She always took a camera, of course, and when not around her neck, it hung from a nail just by the door. She photographed the rocks and the ocean but mainly the people in their relation to the rocks and the ocean. She thought of these photographs as snapshots and private at first, but by 1964, the Steep Ravine cabin had become the site for an ambitious new photo essay. It was published only posthumously, so we have only a partial understanding of how Lange would have shaped it. She spoke about it in 1964 and 1965 to an interviewer.*

INTERVIEWER: *Let's talk about families and the untellable. I read a sentence of yours that people don't photograph families.*

DOROTHEA: *Yes. That's a kind of sore place, a hurt place because I, who realize the great potential that there is in photographing your family, I haven't done it either. I have had a lot of photographs of family groups on Christmas cards, an emptier form of telling you about the family I don't know. Communication, zero. The things that are very near to you are very difficult. To photograph your family is a very unfamiliar road, there is no road.*

But she insisted that the project "didn't have the subject 'the family.'" Her family would stand in for a universal. She read aloud a quotation that she had copied out, without identifying its author. "'We cannot all love our fellow men except in the most abstract way, but we can . . . always try to connect. . . . The sense of connection is like a muscle. Unused it withers, exercised it grows.'"[2]

The subject of this photography project was "freedom, the circumstances under which people, children and their parents and their friends feel unlocked and free. What brings that about. It wouldn't necessarily have to be just my family, it was planned to be kept to my family because it's simpler to make a small book revolving around a few people. I tried to show something of the growth process . . . I'm not making it so that anyone who looks at this show will be acquainted with Helen or John or say how cute is Lisa . . . it's the growth process, in this light, in this air, under these trees, which is the main thing, and life is the obligato that flows, comes in and out."[3]

# 21

# Surviving in the Cold

As the hopefulness of the New Deal and the massive war effort dissolved into McCarthyist repression, Lange seemed to embody—literally, take into her body—the country's political decline. Severe and occasionally bleeding ulcers and esophageal constriction kept her in great physical pain for long stretches of time and made it so hard to eat that she several times lost a dangerous amount of weight.[1] Pain and fatigue produced a depression she had not experienced before. In July 1954, she wrote to Edward Steichen in a despairing, self-pitying vein:

> The time has come when I must face the sickening fact that I have not made the photographs in all my long years of struggle to do it that claim place in the Family of Man. . . .
>
> I always operated on the basis that my good working years were always ahead of me. Everything I ever did was always (in my mind) just preliminary. A bad mistake. . . .
>
> So I write you confessing that I am a bum, unreliable and inconstant.[2]

Of course she was wrong about what she had already accomplished, and she was wrong about the standards of the "Family of Man," but she was not exaggerating her physical weakness. She would never again be an entirely well woman.

Lange's documentary photography had both expressed and shaped 1930s political culture, in which working for social justice was not only urgent but a thrilling adventure as well. Only a decade later, she was out of harmony with the rising political trends and her photography was less circulated and less appreciated. Like Franklin and Eleanor Roosevelt, she assumed that the New Deal agenda would resume after the war, that the country would move toward racial equality, fair treatment of farmworkers, health insurance, even a guaranteed standard of living for all. Instead, the postwar decade brought a backlash against progressive policies. The Cold War and a hurricane-force resurgence of anticommunism brought with it a culture of fearful conformism. An intolerant patriotism defined all dissent as disloyal. This repression seized hold of the national body and squeezed the life out of a few and the courage out of many. Organized opposition became mainly local and tentative, because those who resisted publicly were often punished severely. The political chill seemed to drain Lange of bodily force.

The repressive mood affected all Americans, but the narrowing of cultural possibility squeezed artists and intellectuals particularly viscerally. Few members of Lange's community—artists and scholars—shared the values that came to be called McCarthyist, but many were silent. Those who did not go along leaned into ironic and alienated identities—Beat writers, Abstract Expressionist painters, cool jazz musicians, noir filmmakers. Lange's visual earnestness and faith in "the common man" seemed ever more naïve to both high- and lowbrow taste.

THE SPRING OF 1945 brought Lange a last celebratory OWI job, to cover the founding UN conference in San Francisco in May and June 1945. This first act of an internationalist dream was also a last act of New Dealist vision; it inspired her but went sour immediately. Before it began, on April 12, Roosevelt died. Despite his visible weakening during the war, many Americans felt him to be immortal, as the generic good-father president. Millions wept privately and often publicly. It seemed fitting to Dorothea that the president died at Warm Springs, Georgia, where he had established a polio-treatment facility and often visited with other "polios." And it fit the increased saturation of the culture with visual imagery that a widespread icon of this national grief was a photograph, published in *Life*, of CPO Graham Jackson playing the accordion, tears running down his face, as the president's body was carried away.[3] Dorothea's grief came with a particularly painful ulcer attack. Both she and her physician suspected she should not take on the UN job.

But Lange was incapable of turning down an interesting photography project, especially one honoring an historic occasion and the culmination of hopes for peace. Once again, however, she was prevented from doing a proper job by the people who hired her to do it. In an odd similarity to the internment photography, security men confined her to a gallery and refused to allow her to get close to the delegates. She tried to catch delegates on the street as they entered and exited, which made the job more strenuous. She carried on for the full two months. Her ulcer symptoms escalated to the point that she needed morphine for the pain. By late August she was hospitalized with life-threatening internal bleeding.

One further blow completed the uncanny convergence of Lange's personal, political, and photographic experience: these UN photographs, along with her other OWI work, were lost forever. After the New York office of OWI closed, victim of conservative attacks, no one could ever again find her photographs. The only remnants of her OWI work are the images that appeared in *Victory* and a few negatives she held back, which remain with her estate at the Oakland Museum.[4]

Lange's physical collapse in 1945 was only the first of a two-decade-long series of health crises, to which she responded with great physical resilience, until she could not.[5] In 1945 a physician diagnosed a gallbladder disorder; surgery in August revealed that her pancreas was inflamed, and it was "drained." But her pain, nausea, and vomiting continued until she began hemorrhaging and returned to the hospital, her family and friends collecting blood donations in a panic—she required twenty-three transfusions. At one point, her fever was so high, she was irrational. A more thorough gastrointestinal exam turned up a duodenal ulcer, and an antacid diet was prescribed.[6] She slowly healed and returned home on November 11, just in time to welcome Dan home from the army. She was rehospitalized in January, in late February, and in mid-March 1946, each time pronounced cured, until the problems recurred. Even when relatively stable, she could not talk or eat much without terrible nausea, and she vomited frequently. A hospital physician suggested that she had anorexia, and she consulted a psychiatrist. Finally, having confirmed the ulcer diagnosis, surgeons performed a gastric resection, removing much of the acid-bearing part of the stomach, and it seemed to work: Dorothea healed rapidly and came home after two weeks.[7] Again, the good result was temporary. Without today's strong acid suppressants, her ulcers periodically reappeared, and continued acid reflux produced esophagitis, constriction of the esophagus, which made it difficult for her to swallow food. This would continue on and off for the rest of her life. Physicians would repeatedly dilate her esophagus with a rubber tube called a bougie, in the hopes of producing a lasting reopening of the gullet. In 1950 and again in 1951, she received cobalt radiation treatment to destroy the ulcer and reduce acid production. These treatments produced a year of relief, sometimes two, but the symptoms always returned.

Not surprisingly, Dorothea entered a protracted period of depression in the mid-1940s. All her government work had been directed toward change, from Paul's specific causes to their larger ideals, but very little had been achieved, and now the government was disavowing those ideals. As a photographer, she was caught in a downward spiral: unable to photograph now, she feared that she would never be able to photograph again and this made her more depressed and less able to photograph. She felt that her illness was punishment for having been a bad mother. She sought consolation in domesticity, gardening, buying a sewing machine and making curtains, as if to reassure herself of her motherly capacity. Her stepdaughter Margot remembered her making a voluminous skirt with many pleats, spending hours and hours sewing red trim onto it, as a way of tolerating the pain. She cooked, although she could eat only tiny amounts at a time. She continued the antiacid diet. She gave up smoking with little apparent difficulty. Never much of a drinker, she would sip a bit of scotch and soda through a straw. She read eclectically— Dickens, Lewis Mumford, André Malraux, William Saroyan, Carl Sandburg, photography journals. "A total loss," she said about these five years. A colleague of Paul's referred to her in 1949 as a "semi-invalid."[8] But her family and friends recall very little complaining. It was as if she had compacted to a more minimal self, her desires shrinking along with her body. The physical changes were extraordinary. By age fifty, photographs show, she looked like an old woman—a result of years of work in the hot sun, combined with pain, poor nutrition, and weight loss.

Lange was at one of her lowest moments when Maynard died in 1946. He had settled in Tucson with Edith Hamlin, his third wife, who soon became also nurse, chauffeur, and breadwinner. Dorothea felt grateful that Edith was there. As he grew weaker, Edith contacted friends, and a small stream of them came to visit, including Ansel Adams and even Sophie Treadwell, whom Maynard had not seen for twenty-eight years. When Dorothea got the news of his death, she was in the hospital, being prepared for surgery on her esophagus. An emotional Dan telephoned, said "Dad's dead," and hung up. Dorothea literally got up from her hospital bed and went home. She was not surprised at the news—he was seventy-one and his emphysema had been worsening for years. He had long had to use oxygen, and toward the end he needed it twenty-four hours a day. Although she had not seen him for several years, her pain was still sharp. She had always loved him.

WITH ONLY A bit of exaggeration, Dorothea claimed that she did not pick up a camera for five years. This is partly because she continued to do all the cooking, cleaning, and gardening—like so many women in the period, she never seemed to think that a husband should do domestic work. She turned down most photographic invitations and commissions. She cropped her hair short, and kept it that way for the rest of her life, as if eliminating any drag on her energies. She worked in her studio, as absorbed with photography as ever. She pulled prints and contact sheets out of drawers, putting them on walls and in piles all over the floor, reorganizing them. Concentrating on how photographs speak to each other—". . . pairs amplify and extend the meanings . . . like a sentence of 2 words"—she was reclassifying them thematically. Her unpretentious and mainly upbeat themes included "Killing Time," or relaxation; "Pleasantries," photographic jokes; "Indescribables," motifs that could not be expressed in words; "Home is Where . . ."; and, she later added, "Death and Disaster."[9]

Reorganizing her files constituted a review of her oeuvre and it produced, oddly, a rebirth of ambition despite her invalidism. A desire that she had been suppressing for many years began to break through an internal prohibition— to recognize herself as an artist. It was a dream she had repeatedly expelled from consciousness but never squelched. It heightened her anxiety, of course, but it probably also contributed to her return to active photography at the end of the decade.

Surprising everyone close to her, Lange rebounded in the 1950s. She emerged, paradoxically, as a much-esteemed photography doyenne even as her photographs were no longer fashionable. Limited in her ability to photograph intensively, Lange became a key participant in the national community of top art photographers—something the government work had never left her time to do.

She was sought out by Magnum, the world's most prestigious photographers' agency. Founded in 1947 by Robert Capa, Henri Cartier-Bresson, David "Chim" Seymour, and George Rodger, all foreign-born, all leftists, Magnum brought together photographers through a labor-union consciousness, aiming to bargain collectively for fees and win photographers' control of their work. As a group, these photographers represented a new generation, influenced particularly by the possibility of action photography with fast cameras such as the Leica. Attracted to speed, both in their war photography and in Cartier-Bresson's desire to "trap" moments of action, they also shared a masculinist romance of photography as adventure. Nevertheless, they revered Lange's work; the aesthetic valorization of working people in her photography resonated for them with the socialist and antifascist experience of Europe, from which they had all emerged. They invited her to become a contributing member, and she agreed. Magnum was never able to get assignments for her— her work no longer had a commercial market. But several Magnum people remember her as the only outsider who put energy into the project, stopping by the Magnum office whenever she was in New York. In her no-small-talk way, Lange always managed to initiate conversations they enjoyed, conversations that were "philosophic," not technical, "about how societies work, how cultures change."[10]

She was a central figure in the founding of *Aperture* magazine and in an historic photographic conference. Ever since f/64, Ansel Adams had wanted to develop a high-end photography magazine. He pulled together private and corporate underwriting for a 1951 conference of photographers to discuss the state of their art and to create a magazine. Never before or since has such a group been assembled. One hundred and fifty photographers came together at the Aspen Institute for Humanistic Studies for presentations and panel discussions, but no "technical shop-talk" was allowed. "Every meal . . . was a symposium. No table was large enough to accommodate all who wanted to sit together. . . . " One of the conferees said, "I had to expand or explode."[11] The conference contributed to Lange's recuperation through the respect she engendered and the attention she commanded from the nation's finest photographers. It also yielded a lasting product: the magazine *Aperture*. A committee including Lange, Adams, Nancy Newhall, and Minor White committed themselves to get it off the ground.[12] On the first issue's cover was Lange's photograph of the conference itself.

At the conference, some of the intense debates involved Lange centrally, and they afford a glimpse into her developing photographic thinking. Lange and New York photographer Berenice Abbott were identified as advocates of "realism," but their differences at the conference indicated Lange's temperamental antipathy to ideology. They were of the same generation, and both had absorbed bohemianism in Greenwich Village, but Abbott went to Paris when Lange went to San Francisco. Abbott's arts scene there was more avant-garde than that of San Francisco. Like Lange, she photographed artistic and cultural figures, such as Jean Cocteau and James Joyce, but she also worked for photographer Man Ray and became a promoter of the photography of Eugène Atget. Returning to New York, she, too, became a supporter of the left-wing Photo League; she, too, did some New Deal government work; and she, too, considered documenting the changing world her fundamental calling. Also like Lange, she found a supportive partner, Elizabeth McCausland, a leftist art critic, who did much to promote her photography. But because of her location, Abbott remained a photographer of New York City, and her work did not resonate with Depression-era nostalgia for a rural and small-town world.

At Aspen, Abbott hotly condemned abstract photography, a judgment Lange never shared, despite her own realist bent. Lange was open to a capacious range of styles. Nevertheless, she emphasized photography as communication. As part of that goal, she advocated narrative, an aim usually, although not necessarily, requiring realism. She argued for contextualized and historical photographic series, which could tell stories of change, as she had tried to do with *An American Exodus* and her World War II work. To illustrate, she sketched an imaginary "shooting script," telling the story of the conference itself.[13] The listeners, intrigued, asked her to give them a complete script, but she responded that it would have to emerge from a photographer's engagement with the subject, or it would hold back "the possibility—and the necessity—of growth."[14] Each photograph might expose new insights and lead, therefore, to further photographs, unpredictable in advance. Emphasizing that the photographer must follow her subject material to new discoveries, Lange hardly sounded like someone who for four years had executed shooting scripts written by a nonphotographer who almost never saw what the photographers saw. (Fortunately, Stryker had sensed that he got the best work by respecting photographers' autonomy.) Lange's practice—an amalgam of her portrait method, involving interaction with her subjects, and her documentary method, in which she tried to use visual imagery to communicate social reality—had not changed so much as her articulation of it. What was important, however, was her insistence on openness to new information and ideas coming from engagement with the world outside herself. This is a photographer who, for all her fascination with personal relationships and inner character, never made a self-portrait.

This complexity appeared also in her teaching, another new departure. At least twice, she taught a Saturday-morning photography class for fourteen weeks at the California School of Fine Arts.[15] Although the course was open to all, most of her students appear to have been experienced photographers, such as Allen Willis, later called "dean of African American filmmakers"; George Ballis, who would produce a large body of photographs and films about California activism; Carolyn Mason Jones, an accomplished photographer of the performing arts; and Michael Bry, a much-published photographer of San Francisco's beauty. Beginners may have been too intimidated to sign up.

Her teaching method seems indebted both to Clarence White and to Roy Stryker. At some point during the course, she distributed the poem "Theory," by the poet Wallace Stevens,[16] and "Person-to-Person," by Tennessee Williams, a 1955 statement of his artistic credo. Although unlike Williams in her interests and themes, Lange identified with his imperative to connect with audiences. He denounced subjective, narcissistic writing that "has not yet mastered its necessary trick of rising above the singular to the plural concern, from personal to general import."[17] This is the core of Lange's refusal of *only* subjectivity. She asked of photography that it set up communion or at least conversation, not only between photographer and viewer but also between viewer and photographic subject. Photography thereby becomes a medium in which the viewer is an active participant.

And yet what she wanted her students to do was by no means impersonal. She began the course by interviewing each of the students—twenty in one class—individually. She titled the course, "Where Do I Live?" She then organized it around that question, requiring students to bring in photographs that answered it.[18] She assigned the observational exercise she had developed for herself, which she called " 'finger-exercises' in seeing." They were to take notes on the street, guessing at the stories of passersby. Another assignment required using nonhuman objects to reveal the human, a form of Lange's much-used visual synecdoche. "We ought to know beyond a doubt that to some people . . . this desk or this garden, this bottle of pills, this racing form or this box of candy is home. . . ." In finding "the location of the heart," she pointed out, searching the face alone can be misleading.

As she had done at Aspen, she was asking students to find a way to express their own vision and the reality of the outside world simultaneously. The challenge was sterner yet because of her insistence that they "not make the kind of picture that bulwarks a popular conception. . . . True exploration into the possibilities of the photographic medium raises questions that are not answered."[19]

The challenge represented Lange's own photographic development and the theoretical discussions about photography that she had participated in, from f/64's emphasis on the "straight," to the FSA project's fusion of authenticity and propaganda, to her wartime efforts to represent and promote national unity against fascism without sacrificing her dissenting eye and visual questioning. She was trying to impart to her students a way of doing photography that could be simultaneously subjective and objective. It was in one of these classes that students challenged her to reveal where *she* lived, and she produced the portrait of her twisted foot—an act of self-revelation unique for Lange and one that must have affected the students deeply.

Did this challenge come across? It would take a study of her students' photography to know whether they were able to act on the complexity she asked for. Their letters were grateful. Several spoke of Lange's extraordinary visual memory. They got better at making photographs, one student wrote, "because of your remarkable ability to keep track of what each one of the huge tablefull was doing and remembering all he had done before." Another student praised "the unusually responsible consideration you gave to the problems of each individual . . . refusing to let me substitute verbal communication for photographic communication."[20] Altogether, her teaching file suggests that she was a gifted teacher for advanced photographers, and this is consistent with what her many assistants thought. As to how she would have worked with beginners, there is room for doubt, given her remarkable lack of interest in the mechanics of cameras.

PAUL TAYLOR ALSO suffered from the convergence of Dorothea's life-threatening illness and the burial of the New Deal. At times he thought he might lose her, an unbearable idea, which only reinforced his drive to work as a way of managing the worry. He also had superb powers of concentration and a prodigious sense of social responsibility. He would continue to support farmworker causes with words and cash for forty more years, until his death in 1984. In the 1940s, however, as war jobs and the Bracero program suppressed farmworkers' activism and pushed them off the public agenda, Taylor became a leader on California's most critical social-environmental issue: water. The 1902 Reclamation Act had authorized the federal government to construct dams, reservoirs, and canals to make arid western lands arable, financed through interest-free loans and other subsidies. The law provided that an individual owner could receive only the water needed to irrigate 160 acres. That proviso had rarely, probably never, been enforced, and its disregard constituted a subsidy of enormous value to California's big growers. Without federal water projects, there would have been no San Joaquin Valley or Imperial Valley agriculture.

Taylor, ever on the side of the little guy, thought it a gross injustice that taxpayer-subsidized water furthered corporate agriculture's dominance. Also concerned with resource conservation, he formed an alliance with Interior Department attorney Arthur "Tex" Goldschmidt, brother of Taylor's graduate student Walter Goldschmidt. The tenacious Taylor agitated for enforcement of the 160-acre rule for the next forty years. Although right in law, he tended to sidestep the facts that California had never been primarily a family-farming state and that much of the state was too dry to make small farms viable. Yet his die-hard agitation on this issue had the benefit of exposing the power of the big growers.[21] His water campaign further antagonized those who already considered him an enemy—agribusiness and their conservative political and academic representatives.

He annoyed them even more through his activism in reform Democratic politics. After supporting FDR's son James Roosevelt's unsuccessful 1950 campaign for governor against Earl Warren, his most intense involvement was with the campaign of a forceful woman, Helen Gahagan Douglas. Glamorous Broadway and Hollywood actress, wife of film star Melvyn Douglas, she had been active in New Deal causes. In 1938 she had visited migrant camps with Lange and Taylor, hosted fund-raisers for farmworkers, and organized a Christmas party for five thousand farmworkers' children.[22] Dorothea photographed her when she was an alternate delegate to the opening UN conference, and the two dynamic women made a quick and enduring connection.[23] Paul actively supported her first political venture, a campaign for Congress from California's

Fourteenth Congressional District in 1944; she won and served three terms. In 1950, enraged by what she saw on a tour of water projects with Taylor and Lange, she ran for the Senate, with the 160-acre limit as a major plank in her platform. Taylor functioned as an adviser to that campaign.[24] Dorothea and Paul were disgusted by Nixon's 1950 victorious campaign against her, which relied on the most odious and dishonest McCarthyist smears: Nixon called her a Communist in every way conceivable and at every moment possible (and said very little else), while at the same time smearing her with Hollywood's licentious reputation—she was, he said, "pink right down to her underwear." Nixon's support came particularly from California agribusiness, and Gahagan Douglas's forthright pro-labor and pro-environmental positions—in other words, her alignment with Paul Taylor's causes—intensified Associated Farmers' determination to defeat her at any cost.

Taylor's western enemies were among the founders of what we now call McCarthyism. It originated not from the Cold War, but in prewar conservative congressional opposition to the New Deal. It became an institution of state in 1938 when Congressman Martin Dies, Jr., of Texas transformed a House Committee established to investigate the KKK and pro-Nazi activity into a witch-hunt against alleged Communist influence in the New Deal.[25] By repeating this claim over and over, the Dies Committee and the FBI helped create a new consensus that socialist and communist ideas were un-American. Their targets took in all of Lange's employers and government allies—the FSA and other progressive endeavors in the Department of Agriculture; California's programs of relief, public housing, and minority rights; and the OWI.

The twirling noose of the anti-Communist frenzy swung closer and closer to Taylor and Lange. In 1943, parrying criticism of his own Nazi sympathies, Dies named thirty-nine federal officials as disloyal and sought to get Congress to stop their paychecks, including Taylor's close ally Arthur "Tex" Goldschmidt.[26] The FBI sought to discredit Taylor himself through invasive investigation and surveillance, interviewing several dozen people, including every employer but also every California enemy of Taylor's, mainly the big growers.[27] The Bureau checked to see that his divorce and remarriage were properly legal and obtained his credit rating—they not only got one from California but went back to Madison, Wisconsin, for a credit report on Taylor as a college student. Searching for a criminal record, an investigator was reduced to reporting a parking violation "in front of home in no parking zone," Berkeley, 1937, "dismissed without prejudice."

The FBI alleged that he was a member of several "un-American" organizations, including the Communist party, the Joint Anti-Fascist Refugee
Committee, and several groups that probably did not exist, listed because of
investigators' mishearing or their informants' misunderstanding.[28] The charge
that Taylor was a Communist is patently absurd, as anyone who worked with
him knew, since he was explicitly anti-Communist and argued for socioeco-
nomic reform as a means of preventing or challenging Communists' appeal.
Taylor's FBI file shows that Associated Farmers and its allies were the source
of these allegations.[29] Once, Taylor walked into the university on a Saturday
and found an FBI man inside his office. Taylor's cool "Can I help you?" produced no answer—"he wriggles and wriggles and wriggles . . . makes all sorts
of crazy apologies." Anxious to get out, the intruder said that he could see
Taylor was busy, to which Taylor wickedly replied that, on the contrary, he had
plenty of time.[30]

The FBI dossier on Lange, much thinner, consists mainly of copies from
Taylor's and others' dossiers. She is referred to variously as Doretha, Dorthea,
Dot, and Mrs. Taylor. In a guilt-by-association memo that would be comical if
it had come from a less powerful source, the FBI implied that the Guggenheim
Foundation was disloyal because it had had granted fellowships to Broadway
composer Marc Blitzstein, song composer Earl Robinson, and Carey McWilliams, as well as to Lange and Taylor.[31] One of the Associated Farmers sources
charged that "by adroit use of lighting, composition and subject matter, Mrs.
Taylor had conveyed a very dismal and depressing view of exploitation of migratory laborers by large and wealthy agricultural interests."

McCarthyism invaded Paul and Dorothea's lives directly in its campaign
to drive New Dealers and leftists out of the universities, an effort particularly
strong against the University of California. Associated Farmers helped produce this campaign, too.[32] When the state legislature set up a "little Dies committee," known as the Tenney Committee after its chair, university president
Robert Sproul, fearing an attack on his faculty, calculated that a loyalty oath
could ward it off.[33] In late June 1949, all university employees were ordered
to sign an oath that they were not Communists, or face dismissal. (Universities usually impose unpopular decisions during summers, when faculty and
students are dispersed and cannot easily organize opposition.) Sproul had
miscalculated. A strong network of faculty from all eight campuses refused
to sign, protesting this attempt to limit academic freedom and pointing out
that they had already all signed oaths of allegiance to state and federal con-

stitutions. Taylor was among them, and his daughter Margot was a member of the student movement supporting them. After a protracted and complex struggle that sapped the energies of hundreds of scholars, a compromise was accepted by almost all, including Taylor; several dozen resisters were fired but ultimately won reinstatement and back pay.

Thirty years later, Paul Taylor still felt guilt about having joined the signers. "Dorothea was going through some of her very difficult months and years in and out of the hospital . . . I would have been out on the street, looking for a job somewhere else . . . Whether I am just hiding behind a woman's skirts—well, you can put it anyway you like, but that was a factor . . ."[34] His metaphor, "hiding behind a woman's skirts," suggests not only his need to support Dorothea but also his sense of having been unmanly. His problem, of course, was that either option—giving in or being fired—would have made him unmanly in that cultural moment. Yet in the same interview, he explained his decision in terms of his own political priorities: ". . . it was just not my battle. I choose my battles. I never . . . 'scattered' my efforts . . . for all the causes that I believed in. . . . The easiest way for your opponent to undercut you . . . is on *his* ground rather than on *your* ground." This was a lesson he learned in the marines, he said. "I have been unwilling to offer them any openings. . . ."[35]

McCarthyist poison soon reached Lange's photographic community directly. It scored a direct hit on the extraordinary Photo League of New York, which she supported financially and, when in New York, with her time. A proudly left-wing program, inspired by the 1920s German worker photography movement, the League was a grassroots cooperative providing access to photography for the poor and an atelier for already-practicing photographers.[36] It operated a photographic school and workshop with great success for fifteen years, training as many as fifteen hundred photographers.[37] It bought chemicals in bulk and passed the savings on to individual members, provided darkroom access, loaned and rented out cameras, offered classes for low fees, sponsored lectures and exhibits, and produced a newsletter, *Photo Notes*, with high-quality articles.[38] Paul Strand—Lange's favorite photographer—exerted the greatest artistic influence on the League, but its prestige was such that virtually every important name in photography was listed as a sponsor, not only those on the Left but also Lange's friends Ansel Adams and Edward Weston.[39] Fund-raising parties featured performances by Zero Mostel, Woody Guthrie, Pete Seeger, Carl Reiner, and the Katherine Dunham Dance Company.

Lange gave a talk at the League in 1939, offering advice on getting work published and critiquing members' photographs. She endowed a scholarship for a photography student—its first recipient was Lou Stoumen who went on to an Academy Award–winning career. The League mounted a Lange exhibit. She got Aaron Siskind's "Harlem Document," a group project documenting black life in Harlem, included in the exhibit curated by Ansel Adams at San Francisco's World's Fair.

Dedicated to democratizing photography and encouraging documentary, and including many Communists, the League was unsurprisingly vulnerable to McCarthyism. At first, when Attorney General Tom Clark listed it as a subversive organization in 1947, artists and photographers rushed to defend it and membership doubled. But in 1949, Angela Calomiris, an FBI informant who had briefly appeared at the League—to get help from Sid Grossman in salvaging poor negatives in order to complete a commercial job she had undertaken—denounced it as a Communist front. She charged that Sid Grossman had tried to recruit her into the Communist party, a dubious allegation, since he barely knew her. Nevertheless, her claim worked not only to smear the Photo League but also to delegitimatize the Left, by implying that the very act of asking someone to join the CP, a legal organization at the time, was treasonous. Conservative journalists such as Westbook Pegler, Walter Winchell, and Fulton Lewis, Jr., repeated denunciations at high volume. Frightened, members resigned, including Ansel Adams, Barbara Morgan, and Beaumont and Nancy Newhall.[40] Paul Strand, Dorothea Lange, and Edward Weston remained steadfast, but fear of persecution intimidated too many members, and as the McCarthyist repression continued, the League formally folded in 1951—a relic of a bygone, more hopeful age, like Lange herself.

EDWARD STEICHEN INTENDED his 1955 blockbuster "Family of Man" exhibition at the Museum of Modern Art as resistance to McCarthyism, the Cold War, and the nuclear-arms race. In the massive job of collecting photographs, Lange functioned at first as an associate curator, in substance though not in name.[41] The failure of Lange's influence contributed to a paradox: the exhibit delivered an ambiguous message—preaching international brotherhood but also celebrating the superiority of the American way of life.

Edward Steichen was in some ways the heir to Stieglitz. Born in Luxembourg, but only eighteen months old when he came with his parents to Michigan, he was both American and cosmopolitan. Mentored by Stieglitz, he became a renaissance photographer, expert in military, advertising, fashion, and glamour as well as art photography. (Some of the best-known photographs of Greta Garbo, Marlene Dietrich, Loretta Young, Joan Crawford, and Gary Cooper are Steichen's.) A man of progressive convictions, he curated a thirty-two-page section of FSA photographs for the *U.S. Camera Annual* of 1939, admiring Lange's photography in particular. During both world wars, he worked for the military developing aerial photography.

In 1947, Steichen got the job heading MoMA's photography department, a contested hiring decision. Many photographers and critics had expected the position to return to Beaumont Newhall, who, like Steichen, had spent the war doing military aerial photography. The museum, opened in 1929, was funded largely by Rockefeller money, and the Newhalls were part of the Rockefeller/MoMA network, close friends of Ansel Adams and his Rockefeller-scion patron, David McAlpin. The Newhalls had become a power in the photography world.[42] Their supporters, including Lincoln Kirstein, considered Steichen a sellout to lowbrow and commercial culture.

During Steichen's early years at MoMA, the Cold War drew the United States into a real war. The United States intervened in Korea in 1950, ending up facing Chinese troops and suffering severe losses. Nuclear war with the Soviet Union threatened. The McCarthyist hysteria limited antiwar sentiment to a tiny minority, but a somewhat larger public came to support nuclear disarmament. Hoping to build that support and convinced that photography could prove persuasive, Steichen hatched an idea for a photographic exhibition that could simultaneously encourage global peace and bring more people and income to the museum.[43] (Ironically, MoMA was at this time accepting covert funding from the CIA to mount exhibitions calculated to make positive propaganda for the U.S. side in the war against communism.)[44] Lange shared Steichen's belief in photography's progressive persuasive potential, although watching California's anti-Japanese hysteria had made her understand it as a difficult task. However naïve Steichen's thought that his exhibit could actually change the world, his hopes were at the heart of what documentary photography has been about. Lange would argue, in fact, that strengthening the public's visual critical skills was an essential precondition for democracy.[45]

Steichen got the title "The Family of Man" from his brother-in-law, poet Carl Sandburg, who had quoted Lincoln's words in his biography, and Lange loved it. As soon as she heard of the plan, she volunteered to help and began showering Steichen with ideas. He was quick to accept her assistance: ". . . you have been appointed, and have accepted, the western section of the United States . . . jubilantly recorded. . . ."[46] In their bantering but serious correspondence, she assumed the same voice she had used with Stryker—flirtatious, devoted, insecure but assertive. Steichen became another father figure. "Ask me to do anything, including the improbable and the impossible, also the unreasonable. . . . Scold, and be in bad temper, if you feel that way." Later, it was "I am needing to hear from you. . . . Perhaps you are not enthusiastic. Perhaps you are even not approving. I need to know or I am . . . not certain of my ground."[47] She sent photographs, suggestions for finding photographs, and drafts of letters for Steichen to send. She reminded him of what was missing—fear, love, belonging.[48] She influenced him to hire the young California photographer Wayne Miller as an assistant; then, concerned about photographers who could not afford materials, she got Miller to obtain a small fund from MoMA to help impoverished photographers submit prints.[49]

By now we recognize her familiar pattern: enthusiasm, more suggestions and more ambitious suggestions than her boss wanted. Miller cautioned Steichen, "I don't know if you fully realize how completely she has thrown herself into this show. She is not one to be able to do something with ease or moderation. . . . If you don't utilize her . . . fully . . . you will be having an unhappy Dorothea on your hands."[50] She organized three West Coast meetings to solicit photographs,[51] but little that she gathered ended up in the exhibition. Many of the photographers at the meetings resented being asked to relinquish control over photographs to Steichen and having their photographs chosen for "content" rather than sheer artistic quality.[52] (Lange, by contrast, was accustomed to such capitulations.) Wayne Miller got most of what was used by leafing through millions of photographs from the files of *Life,* Magnum, and other large photographic archives, including even Sovfoto. Yet Miller believed that Lange's concern with the overall "message" brought coherence to the exhibition.[53] John Szarkowski, who succeeded Steichen at MoMA, thought the strength of the exhibition resulted from her "insisting that [Steichen] settle for nothing less than a work of vaulting ambition."[54]

"The Family of Man" exhibit opened in 1955 to a slightly improved political atmosphere: McCarthy had overstepped by Red-baiting the U.S. Army, undermining some of his ability to intimidate, while nuclear buildups were raising anxieties about war. The exhibit broke all previous attendance records for art shows. More than 250,000 people saw it in New York, and six editions of the show then circulated to other U.S. cities and thirty-seven countries. The book version, a best-seller, is still in print. But it was panned by many reviewers, and their criticisms reveal how much the popular-front style had lost prestige. Conservative critics such as Hilton Kramer condemned its sentimentality, middlebrow taste and "message" orientation—this was the moment when Abstract Expressionism reigned supreme among the New York literati.[55] But Leftist Roland Barthes agreed with Kramer that its "pieties" about the unity of mankind served as "a self-congratulatory means for obscuring the urgency of real problems under a blanket of ideology. . . ."[56] Decades later, New Left critics Allan Sekula, Eric Sandeen, and Abigail Solomon-Godeau argued that it presented the liberal face of the Cold War, implicitly endorsing an evolutionary, even teleological story of humanity progressing to its current pinnacle—the American family.[57] The overall impact of the exhibit was saccharine, and reactionary in its literal sense of trying to go back into a nostalgic harmonious age that had never existed.

The message that all people are alike "under the skin," an extension of the "Americans All" OWI theme, and that peace could prevail if people learned to avoid prejudice, ignored the more significant obstacles to peace—economic and social inequality. If you understood America only from this exhibit, you would be bewildered to learn that in that very year the Montgomery bus boycott launched the civil rights movement. No images of political conflict, social movements, or strikes were included. Solomon-Godeau points out that the only images from the realm of "politics" show people putting ballots in boxes, a narrow and quintessentially American definition of politics.[58]

The exhibit presented universals at the expense of history. No photographs were dated. No captions identified place; locations were specified only by nation—an ideological statement about the superiority of nation-states to colonies, empires, tribes, and a further deindividualization of subjects. Displaying repeatedly the beautiful photograph of a young Peruvian flute player created a leitmotif that further emphasized the upbeat, universalist message. Just as the pictures were decontextualized, so were the quotations that replaced Lange's typically informative captions. Compiled by Dorothy Norman, photographer and protegée of both Steichen and Stieglitz, the biblical, literary, and folkloric captions functioned as pop spirituality. The approach disguised international inequalities. In this context, the family of man becomes a biological given, not a product of human-created culture; even such matters as courtship, marriage, play, house building, and suffering are determined by our biology.

The show was actually more nationalist than internationalist, despite its claims. The vast majority of the 503 photographs were American. Its human-ism was strikingly religious in tone, reflecting the unique religiosity of the United States.[59] It placed a white American family at the center of the exhibit, not just a family but a farm family of four generations—with photographs of ancestors on the walls—positing thus a false ideology about family life in the United States in 1955. In the book, this idealized American family sits directly opposite a largely unclothed Bechuanaland family. (Africans and other non-white peoples were mainly represented as primitive.) Could there be a more explicit visual statement about the direction of civilization?

Its gender politics were particularly conservative, consistent with the cul-ture of the times: Cold War political culture pressured women to devote them-selves exclusively to husbands, children, and homemaking. In the exhibit, images of young love were followed by marriage, pregnancy, childbirth, breast-feeding, and other mother-child bonding in an inevitable sequence. Near the close of the exhibit, viewed after the audience had been shocked by the huge six-by-eight-foot color photograph of a nuclear explosion, seven elderly couples looked out at viewers (Dutch, Chinese, Canadian, German, Sicilian, American Indian—and another American couple, white, identified simply as from the "U.S.," for they were the prototypical Americans), each one atop a caption reading "We two form a multitude." Marriage thus not only propagates humanity but might, somehow, save us from destruction. Images of labor feature big male biceps, daring high-rise construction work-ers, men wielding heavy tools, building railroads, smelting metal, dragging in fishnets. Mother-and-child, pietà images suggest universalism among Eskimos, Native Americans, American blacks, and a *Vogue* model (or is she a lady millionaire?). These messages about what was supposedly universal did not accurately describe what was happening in the developed world—such as the increasing numbers of women in the wage labor force and in higher education and the widespread use of birth control as large families became economically impossible.

The exhibition, like many since then, was designed to control the flow of spectators, to prohibit them from wandering among the photographs and thereby creating their own juxtapositions. The enforced path was circular, rep-licating the cyclical organization of the photographs—birth, childhood, mar-riage, reproduction, family, old age, death, birth—an ahistorical, eternal order. This order was, moreover, visually teleological: when looking at young lovers, one saw the large families ahead, for example. One decision brought together the insistence on crowd control and upbeat tone: a photograph of a lynching was removed after two weeks because, Wayne Miller thought, it caused the flow of spectators to stop and created a bottleneck.[60] Yet it was in August of that year that fourteen-year-old Emmett Till was lynched.

Much of this conservatism, however, was not a new Cold War product but a continuation of New Deal and World War II political culture. Depression family-values talk emphasized men's natural role as family heads and women's as domesticity. The stresses of war, paradoxically, produced similar responses: Although women's employment and men's absence eroded women's reliance on male heads of household, government and media always represented that state of affairs as an emergency and continually referred to women's dependence on men when soldiers returned. As the melting pot of Depression and war assimilated people of European-immigrant backgrounds to Americanism, non-Europeans continued to be treated as non-American. War nationalism invoked a rhetorical universality, as did "The Family of Man," by ignoring the barriers to equality that rendered universalist rhetoric hollow.

Lange had argued to make "The Family of Man" more complex, even a bit subversive. Some of her influence shows—for example, the nine father-child photographs (including her *First Born*). Her own *Migrant Mother* and *White Angel Breadline* were encapsulated within a series on calamities. But Lange ideas that did not make it into the exhibit might have shifted its meanings considerably. She argued that evil lived in the family of man and that the show should include more conflict, war, and other violence.[61] She wanted the exhibition's textual material to quote from President Eisenhower's 1953 inaugural address: "The men who mine coal and fire furnaces and balance ledgers and turn lathes and pick cotton and heal the sick and plant corn—all serve as proudly and as profitably for America as the statesmen who draft treaties or the legislators who enact laws. This faith rules our whole way of life."[62] A hackneyed and masculinist piece of rhetoric, it nevertheless sounded the New Deal voice and resisted the McCarthyist voice. Steichen originally asked Lange "and your good husband" to draft a call to photographers that laid out the "over-all plan," and the version he sent out incorporated most of Lange's text. She wanted to begin the exhibition with six larger-than-life-size naked figures, one of each sex of three "races." (Experts at that time taught that humanity consisted of Caucasians, Negroes, and Asians.) She wanted "working people's bodies," not models—that is, naked, not nude.[63] But nakedness was not acceptable in the 1950s; Harry Callahan's nude of his pregnant wife was weeded out,[64] and the only flesh shown was the breasts of African women—signifiers of primitivism.

Nevertheless, Lange's enthusiasm about "The Family of Man" was unqualified. That enthusiasm reflected in part her never-quite-realized longing to belong to the art establishment. She had received some of that acceptance when Steichen included her work in a Museum of Modern Art show of six women photographers in 1949. But her California location, her long-term government employment, her continued commitment to advocacy, and her realist photography kept her, she felt, marginal rather than central in art photography. MoMA was its center.

Yet her enthusiasm also arose from her astute appraisal of the exhibit's impact, something the critics failed to grasp. Those who saw and loved the exhibit or book felt it, however unconsciously, as an affirmation of possibilities for peace and interracial respect, and as an endorsement of the United Nations—of New Deal international policy. It asserted the beauty of people of color. It undermined xenophobia, making foreigners appealing in their strangeness. It even showed a bit of racial diversity in the United States.

Ultimately, Lange supported "The Family of Man" because she believed it was the best that could be done. She was not a purist. Temperamentally, and in accord with Paul, she believed that you offered what you could and celebrated the bits of progress that could be achieved. Besides, the Lange of 1955 was not the same person as that of 1935, nor was the world she lived in the same. The decade from 1945 to 1955 had frightened her at every level—physical, emotional, political. She knew that her photographic style was no longer trendy and, worse, her photographic ideas no longer on the national agenda. She understood her body's fragility and fatigue; she could no longer breathe fire.

DURING ONE NEW YORK trip for "Family of Man" work, Dorothea collapsed in her hotel room due to internal bleeding from her ulcers. She had been scheduled to speak to the American Society of Magazine Photographers, and when she failed to appear, Steichen phoned her hotel room. He and Wayne Miller rushed to her. Carrying her out, they took her by cab to Lenox Hill Hospital, where she once again received emergency blood transfusions. Steichen held Dorothea in the cab, and she recalled gratefully, "'Steichen has the most marvelous protective hands.' "[65] Being comforted in this moment of terror reaffirmed her experience of him as a father.

She was stuck in New York at Lenox Hill Hospital for some time. Paul came, but she could not get to Dan's wedding to Mia. Dorothea minded this loss greatly, as she loved ceremony, thought Mia delightful, and savored Dan's transformation out of his very difficult years. She wrote what Mia recalled as a wonderful "welcome-to-the-family letter."[66]

Another trauma on another trip to New York was to the good: Dorothea was there when her mother died at age seventy-nine, when she who so often felt herself an orphan actually became one. It was a gift that mother and daughter, long separated by a continent, were now together through some of the dying. Dorothea left no record of her emotions at the time and she rarely spoke about her mother at all.[67] Silence was her response to most of the greatest emotional events of her life. As mother-daughter bonds go, theirs was neither the closest nor the most distant, but their love and appreciation was mutual. Dorothea always kept a photograph of Joan on her dresser. Joan's instinct was to soothe, and she played the same role with her daughter that she had with her mother: Perhaps unbeknownst to Dorothea, Joan sometimes soothed the victims of Dorothea's sting, telling Margot, for example, to forgive her stepmother because "she can't help it."[68] Dorothea did know that Joan had given her considerable gifts: generosity and competence and discipline, love of music and ritual, a taste for stylish hospitality and home decor, an open mind, a capacity for empathy, an appreciation for different cultures, and, not least, the confidence not to overvalue respectability. Characteristically, in their first decades apart, it was her own photographs of Joan that "revealed," Dorothea said, her love for her mother.[69] Once she had a large family and created grand holiday meals, Dorothea would send a daily card to her mother from mid-December through Christmas so that Joan would feel "with us and by us."[70]

Yet as Dorothea suffered the loss of a mother, pain and frightening collapses, family brought new pleasure into her life. John married Helen, who became extremely close to Dorothea; Ross, Katharine, and then Margot married; and they all had children. Dorothea became the grandmother of twelve.[71] Three of these young families and seven of the children lived nearby. Dorothea's greatest pleasure in her later years came from these grandchildren. She could spend hours with them in the garden or at the ocean, looking at weeds and sticks and shells, teaching them to see.

# 22

# Working for *Life*

In 1952, Lange tiptoed back into photography, and by the late 1950s she was working intensively again, her schedule now eased by the fact that all the children had left home. Her physical condition after 1945, always more a remission than a cure, leaves one awed by her continuing accomplishments. "I've always had immense physical reserves, for a person who has such a bad body, very strong."[1] This is an understatement.

Now free of regular employment, she designed topics and approaches ambitiously and produced work of great beauty and significance. Professionally, the new ventures proved disappointing, because she was trying to sell her photo-essays to *Life,* entering a world of corporate mass journalism. In other words, she could not in fact be an independent photographer as long as she wanted paid work; Paul was happy to support her, but traveling for photography, now her habit, was expensive, and, besides, she needed paying work for her identity as a professional. With the end of government work, Henry Luce's *Time/Life/Fortune* conglomerate represented a key outlet for photography, and many FSAers had worked there. Individual photographers were supporting their calling by acceding to a corporate sensibility, and often, as in the case of Luce's empire, a conservative political one.

In theory, *Life* published just what Lange wanted: photo-essays rather than individual photographs. But the working arrangements turned out to constrain her artistic integrity even more than the government had. Editors wanted photographers to dump thousands of pictures in their laps, then leave on the next assignment, not even consulting, let alone casting a vote, on the selection of photographs, layout, text, or overall message in the published piece.[2] While Stryker had admonished Lange not to send him too many pictures, *Life* editors saw about seven thousand a week, from which they would select two hundred for publication. Moreover, months of photography could be bumped at the last minute by breaking news. In Lange's work for *Life,* two of her four commissions got published in a form that she disliked, two were rejected altogether after she sent in photographs, and at least two proposals were turned down before any photography was done. Luckily, since Lange never did exactly what she was commissioned to do anyway, many of the photographs live on in spite of *Life.*

This photography was shaped not only by *Life* but also by Lange's own stage of life—older and fragile—and by history. Far removed from the New Deal's orientation toward building a better future, the dominant strands of American political culture were now defensive, seeking safety in the status quo and protection against threats to it. Nostalgia pervaded all four of Lange's projects, and that spirit made her think she could produce material *Life* would want. It was nostalgia for an imaginary past, of course. It was a nostalgia that had already underlain the last years of FSA work, when Stryker was calling for cheerful photographs, and now Taylor's family-farm romance and Lange's unease with the anomie of cities strengthened it.

Her first project profiled three Mormon towns in Utah, and she envisaged a local exhibit as well as a *Life* feature. She had been in Utah often: with Maynard, for the FSA, and with Paul, and now she planned to realize her Guggenheim project. Although she knew just what she wanted to do for *Life,* her new sense of herself as feeble led her to gather three coworkers.[3] She wanted Paul with her in case of health disasters. She wanted her son Dan because he was beginning to work seriously on becoming a writer and she could help him.[4] She wanted Ansel Adams because of the subject matter. She felt that the inhospitable natural surroundings, mountains and desert, were fundamental to the culture of these villages—and no one could capture that except Ansel.[5] This turned out to be a mistake. Not only did she and Adams quarrel, as usual, but Paul and Dan's presence exacerbated the disagreements.

Starting in 1952, Lange and Taylor studied the area and chose three towns with different economies: Toquerville, a bit of a ghost town, populated primarily by old people; Gunlock, remaining a subsistence-farming community; and St.

George, transformed by a new highway into a tourist stop.[6] Lange envisioned
a coherent, orchestrated photo-essay, in four "movements," each with different tempo, which would allow her to bring out the distinct character of each
town. Toquerville, which means black in the local Indian language, would be
introduced at night, an adagio in a minor key. "Concentrate on old people and
houses. Photograph in a subdued and fading light." The second movement,
to be photographed in "high summer light," was Gunlock; its themes were
"everybody knows everybody," "satisfied with what we have," "the simple both
in the light and in the material." Quoting one of her Gunlock subjects, she
wrote, "'... knew you was as safe as if you was in God's pocket.'" The third
movement would sound the interactions of past and present—the desert, an
old road or trail, the graveyard, but also a neon sign. The fourth movement
would be St. George, its light "hard and brilliant." "A few decades ago money
was practically unknown," she wrote, but now there were twenty-three motels
and the numbers who slept in them equaled one-quarter of the town's population. It had become "a place to sleep, a place to eat, a place to service the car, a
place between two other places—Los Angeles 832 miles, Salt Lake 237 miles."
Importantly, she did not condemn St. George's residents, but praised them
as brave in adapting to the commercial economy, pioneers venturing into
the unknown. She planned meticulously, outlining photographs in "progres-
sions," like a film storyboard. She relied on her trademark synecdoche—that
is, using pieces to reveal wholes: "the hymn book ... the window ... the white
pierced ear ... bread ... the neon sign ... the cornice ..." Ever the bossy one,
she made lists for Adams, too.[7]

When they began photographing in 1953, Adams was "tremendously
pleased with the way the Mormon project is shaping up. In spite of the
difficulties of working with Dorothea in the field—due to her extreme
intensity . . . she has a great and important concept, and I am very glad
to be a part of it." But he disliked her "sociological cerebration," while she
found his "idealistic individualism" irresponsible.[8] Then a gaffe by Taylor and
Lange made Ansel furious. Taylor had sought permission to photograph from
a Mormon bishop and thought he had received it; but the elders' approval
had not reached the potential subjects and, worse, Taylor had said the photographs were for an exhibition and had not mentioned publication in *Life*.[9]
Without doubt, he misled their subjects. He and Lange were accustomed to
government field work, in which they never got formal permissions for photographs or quotations, never discussed publication plans, and never expe-

rienced resentment. Tension arose again because Adams wanted his close friend Nancy Newhall to write the *Life* piece. Lange vetoed this. She was not fond of Nancy, intimidated by her upper-class, girls-school confidence and competitive with the Newhalls' acclaim by elite patrons.[10] More important, Lange strongly wanted—in fact, *needed*—the job for Dan because she hoped it would boost him into the writing career he sought.

Acceding but annoyed, Adams withdrew entirely after the photographs were printed, leaving everything else to Lange. Out of a staggering 1,100 images they made, she delivered 135 to *Life*. When the feature appeared in December 1954, only a quarter of those were included, of which more than three-quarters were hers,[11] adding to his irritation. *Life* staffers wrote mawkish captions that, along with the photos used, stereotyped the villages. For Toquerville, there was an empty house, a sagging fence, and an explanation that "the Mormons kept themselves apart from the changing world, believing that they are God's Chosen People." In Gunlock, children played and danced, women bore canned goods and flowers, the whole town gathered at the church.[12] The headline ST. GEORGE HAS TAKEN UP WORLDLY WAYS hardly pleased the Mormons.[13] (The headline turned out, ironically, quite fitting, for St. George was the closest town to a thirty-two-kiloton bomb tested at Yucca Flats, Nevada, later in 1953, the fallout resulting in marked increases in cancer and other radiation-caused diseases.)

*Life* voided Lange's vision of the complexity of social change. Sympathetic to the Mormons, she saw them not, as many do today, as a conservative, autocratic society, but as a minority church rejecting corporate commercialism and dedicated to simpler living and strong community, "an enduring embodiment of the frontier spirit."[14] The best of the Utah photographs document in pairs Lange's unease about commercialism and a consumerist reconstruction of women's domesticity. A gaggle of girls riding a horse contrasts with the containment of a mother and daughter in their kitchen. A compact real cowboy squats, tired but graceful, while a huge neon cowboy advertises a truck stop.

Dorothea had antagonized Ansel about Nancy Newhall for naught, because only a bit of Dan's language was included in the captions, and he got no credit. Still, the Utah project marked the beginning of a turnaround for Dan. *Modern Photography* soon paid him five hundred dollars for an article including some of his mother's photographs and he became his mother's collaborator on several further projects. He felt that from this point on "she partnered him to climbing out of the mess."[15]

The quarrel with Ansel was painful for Dorothea, who loved him despite her inability to refrain from needling him. They never worked together again. Yet despite their impatience with each other's politics, technique, and method, they remained good friends to the end. Adams, always genial and generous, continued to praise Lange and her work. They were always in touch and he was attentive during her health crises. When he was hospitalized in 1962, she wrote, "'It is my turn to tell you that I wish for you the very best under all circumstances and also that I have loved you right or wrong.'"[16] He felt the same.

LIFE TOOK UP another Lange proposal, a profile of Ireland's County Clare.[17] Feeling stronger, she went there with Dan only—Paul came for a short visit toward the end of their stay—arriving at the beginning of September 1954 and staying six weeks, mainly in Ennis, population seven thousand.[18] She made 2,400 photographs, seeming not to need to rest. Dorothea took a malfunctioning camera for repair and thereby met a young photographer, Dennis Wylde, who drove for her when Dan was not available. He said that he learned more about photography from her than from any other source. He was particularly impressed by how tenaciously she would pursue a shot she wanted, climbing on her car or any available elevation and returning repeatedly to a spot day after day. (He even said she had climbed a tree, hard for me to imagine.)[19] Dan's lack of discipline appeared again; he "gathered impressions," without formal interviews or taking notes. Dorothea was not pleased that much of his gathering of information was done through "roistering" with the locals in the pubs (there were sixty-five of them in tiny Ennis).[20]

Lange sought in Ireland what she had sought among the Mormons: the community created by village life and family farming. As in Utah, she read, then studied the area first without a camera and listed images symbolic, descriptive, and analytic: "the milk cow is the center around which this economy thrives/ the bicycle and the raincoat/ the farmer and the milk can/ the farmer and his tools, spade, flail and scythe/ the fire and the pot/." She made categories: "emigration; congregations; the temperament and the weather . . ." and categories within the categories: "congregations: the church, the creamers, the fair." And she established perspectives: "what one sees from the door; the four walls of a room; what one sees as work goes on; work in the hayyard."[21] The photographs celebrate labor—a man pulls a hay cart, women cook on hearth fires of

22.1. COUNTY CLARE, IRELAND, 1954

dried turf, buskers sing at the country market, farmers fight the foxes that eat the lambs, a shoemaker and a priest serve people's needs—everyone works, young and old. Lange was implicitly comparing the rooted poverty of Irish peasants with the uprooted poverty of migrant farmworkers: She saw Irish peasants as stable and happy, even as their children went barefoot to school and women carried water in pails. Her captions become more lyrical. Less rushed, she developed more personal relationships with subjects, as she had done in her San Francisco studio. She was enjoying herself.

Nothing roughed up her misty, romanticized take, not the arduous labor, the poverty, or the emigration of so many of County Clare's young to the

22.2. COUNTY CLARE, IRELAND, 1954

22.3. COUNTY CLARE, IRELAND, 1954

United States. There is no hint of inequality among social classes.[22] Lange's decision to focus on an area relatively isolated from economic development left the Ireland photo-essay without the sense of historical change that provided the narrative tension of the Mormon story. Yet no place in Europe had been immune from global economic change, and a skilled sociological interviewer would have seen its impact, however subtle or unapparent. Lange had those skills but did not use them. She settled for a pastoral romance: ". . . no hurry . . . no sense of want, or wanting, or urge to buy more and more, [or] bombardment of new goods and advertising. . . ."[23] In fact, the sparkling consumer goods of modern metropolises came in regularly, by mail or as gifts from the millions in the Irish diaspora.

However romantic and unrealistic, Lange's Irish peasants would never be confused with Russian or Italian peasants—or Mormons. They belonged specifically to Ireland.[24] John Szarkowski told her that he felt the damp wind blowing out of one photograph. Back home, Lange hung a photograph of a Irish girl in the rain on her front door, intending that Irish rain and gloom and mud would make Berkeley sunshine more treasured. Ireland's beauty induced her to make landscapes, but she thought only one of them good: ". . . pure Ireland . . . it's a poor landscape but it's the only one that I made there that gave the feeling . . . once in a while the whole earth smiles for a minute. . . ."[25] The best Irish photographs were, of course, portraits. (See plate 37.)

*Life*'s headings expressed Lange's romance: SERENELY THEY LIVE IN AGE-OLD PATTERNS; A WILD AND RUGGED COUNTRY TESTS A MAN'S BEST; THE QUIET LIFE RICH IN FAITH AND A BIT OF FUN. Many of the impoverished Irish would call this blarney. Then a last-minute news story reduced the Ireland spread by about 50 percent. Once again, Dan's text was not used and he got no credit line. Dorothea was furious.[26]

LANGE AND TAYLOR'S nostalgia for a less corporate society may have been backward-looking in one respect, but in another it produced a vital forward-looking concern—for environmental protection. Lange was an early environmentalist, well before the movement gathered political power. She had absorbed Maynard's love of the desert and his hatred for the soulless greed of developers, Ansel Adams's love of the Rocky Mountains and the Sierra Nevada, Paul's and the FSA's concern for a democratic rural economy and sustainable agriculture, Paul's expertise about water politics; and to these, she added her own alarm at the costs of rapid, unregulated urbanization. Expressing a point of view extremely off center in the 1950s, when dams seemed the essence of progress, she sent *Life* a photo-essay on the social cost of a dam. Today, this *Death of a Valley* photography would command widespread interest and agreement. In 1957, *Life* would have none of it.

In Solano County, northeast of San Francisco, the Bureau of Reclamation acceded to demands for more water and power by proposing a dam project near the town of Monticello, thirty-some miles west of Sacramento. The commercial center of the fertile Berryessa Valley, an oasis alongside Putah Creek in an otherwise-dry area, Monticello had one store, two filling stations, a small motel, and one roadside café. Its farmlands produced pears, grapes, walnuts, alfalfa and other grains, and herds of cattle and horses. In springtime, wildflowers carpeted the valley floor and hillsides, and California poppies spilled into the town cemetery. Dam construction began in 1953, and ten years later the large valley was covered by 1.6 million acre-feet of water, creating the second-largest man-made lake in California (after Shasta Lake). The reservoir provides recreation, aqueducts send water to agribusiness in the Central Valley, and the dam generates electricity for Pacific Gas and Electric Company's power grid.

The dam project came to Lange's attention not only through Paul, ever alert to what he saw as water theft, but also through her son John and brother, Martin, both of whom worked on the dam. She proposed a photo-essay on "before and after" the dam to *Life* and got a commission for one thousand dollars. She recruited Pirkle Jones, who had processed the Mormon film for Ansel and Dorothea, as an assistant.[27] They started immediately, in order to capture the village before flooding, so she was working under pressure, against fatigue. A local photographer described her: ". . . she was tired . . . her face and her eyes were alive. She was a tiny, little thing. . . . She had a crippled leg. If you didn't know it, you wouldn't notice it, hardly, except when she was tired, when she sort of pulled that leg along."[28]

In 1957, Lange sent *Life* 175 photographs, including 13 five-by-seven color transparencies—one of the few times she ever worked with color film. The "before" images are even sweeter than the Irish photographs, her feeling for the valley mixed with personal longings. ". . . the valley held generations in its palm," she wrote. The photographs—I speak of hers and Jones's jointly—make the viewer want to walk in this valley and smell the alfalfa and the orchards and the manure. The contrasts between "before" and "after" are almost too simple: an old cemetery thick in wildflowers, for example, and the cemetery

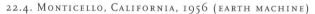

22.4. MONTICELLO, CALIFORNIA, 1956 (EARTH MACHINE)

22.5. DOROTHEA LANGE AT MONTICELLO, 1956 OR 1957, *by Pirkle Jones*

after it had been bulldozed and the bodies exhumed. The disruption of a culture is encapsulated in Lange's only portrait of an animal—a terrified horse caught in a field being bulldozed. (See plate 40.) As with her greatest images of humans, she made the beautiful animal's body the bearer of the anxieties of the whole community. *Life* declined to publish any of this material.[29]

BETWEEN TRIPS TO the valley, Lange worked on an intensely urban photo-essay, and once more produced something that *Life* would not touch.[30] But this venture projected the mirror image of her Utah/Ireland/"Death of a Valley" sensibility. She had been ambivalent about the "new California" even at the height of its World War II prosperity, and this anxiety had fed her idealization of traditional small communities. This very urban woman had become anxious about the callousness of the big-city environment, an anxiety escalated by her increased sensitivity to racism. Often in Oakland, she saw how the roaring defense-dollar economy had brought in tens of thousands of workers who

were then spit out by the unemployment that followed from the demobiliza-
tion at war's end and the steady deindustrialization afterward. Lange saw also
that the racial tolerance that war production had encouraged was too thin to
support policies that could combat the racialized urban poverty resulting from
so much unemployment.

To tell this story she developed a visual profile of the work of an Oakland public defender.[31] She had been musing about the legal system since
Martin Lange's arrest, and about how defendants who lacked money and
know-how could get legal representation. The accused, often African Americans, contrasted sharply with the sharecroppers she had photographed in the
South. Both groups were abused, she thought, but the new Oaklanders lacked
supportive and disciplining family and community as they faced unfamiliar forms of race prejudice.[32] The northern, urban structures of racism were
also less visual, so she wanted to embody it through human interaction. The
public defender series carries the anxiety and critique through its narrative
dynamic, as her own worries about the social transformation of the Bay Area
mixed with the high tension of courthouse events.

She found a public defender with eight years' experience, Martin Pulich,
whose charisma, dedication, and intensity attracted her, and she followed
him from morning to close of day for months.[33] His motive in agreeing to
become her subject was to create public understanding of the necessity for
what he did, and she expected to be taught, so it was a good fit. She honored
his commitment to the presumption of innocence, but she also registered the
difficulty in maintaining that presumption.

These photographs rely heavily on fragments to stand for a whole experience. Among the most well known are a nighttime close-up of the back of a
Black Maria, gleaming ominously despite its dented doors; a jail guard's waist,
keys hanging from it, in front of the locked grilled door of a cell; the feet of
an acquitted man, walking lively down the courthouse steps. Remarkably, she
charmed a judge into letting her photograph in the courtroom. She said that
after several weeks, she "set up a view camera in front of my seat with a long
bulb so that I was separate from the camera, and the bulb would open and
close without a sound, so it looked like someone had left the camera there."[34]
In these photographs, women sit in courtrooms, holding infants, waiting for
hours; a defendant glares suspiciously at Lange; others slump in holding cells.
Pulich's intensity made him a good subject for Lange, the master of posture
and gesture: seen over a client's shoulder, intent on his interrogation, as they

22.6. OAKLAND, 1957

confer in a closed room; lightly touching the back of a convicted client as he is
led away; head bent over law books; intervening sharply in mid-trial. Perhaps
some unconscious doubts about the legal system surfaced in her image of
the judge's face, a huge American flag behind him, representing justice but
also intimidation. (See plate 38.) But this skepticism did not extend far. The
photographs display a grand sympathy for the defendants, even as Pulich
tells her how many lie and deceive and "thwart the believer." But she neither
interviewed nor gathered information about them. She learned, for example,
that 85 percent of Pulich's cases were settled by plea bargain. She did not ask
under what pressure these defendants were induced to accept a deal in lieu
of a trial and a chance to plead not guilty. Perhaps she so admired Pulich that
her focus shifted to him and away from his clients; perhaps reaching out to
the defendants seemed beyond her physical capability now. Whatever the reason, the message of the public defender series is more ambiguous, its critical
edge duller than that of her FSA work.[35]

AIMING AT PHOTOGRAPHS lighter and publishable, Lange tried her eye on something charming: San Francisco's cable cars. Here, her nostalgia was mainstream: Everyone wanted to preserve this feature of San Francisco. Sold to *Pageant* for a tourist audience, the photos were also an homage to the city she loved. The cable cars encapsulated the city's drama: hills so steep that newcomers feared to drive on them, shining views of the Bay and two awe-inspiring bridges, the precipitous descent to the Embarcadero. Yet the very smallness of the cable cars, their human scale, suggested the city's intimacy. "The cable car," Lange wrote, "is almost like an animal. . . . They hop on and off as [if it were] a little pony saddled and ready to go."

*Pageant* published thirteen photos in March 1957, with text by San Francisco columnist Herb Caen. The 946 negatives Lange made, however, were, as a whole, disappointing. "I thought this was going to be a cinch, just a lark, but it wasn't a bit, it was hard to do." She prepared carefully, as always: "The hills exaggerated, vertical—by Hasselblad—Graflex, try at noon." Her list included

22.7. OAKLAND, 1957

22.8. BERKELEY, 1957

the Bay, various nationality groups, the fog, the gloves of the gripman, bread and sausages, Sun Yat Sen, and Bop City, a landmark jazz club. She captured well the riders alighting and stepping off the moving cars, hanging on to poles from the running boards, but not the steepness or the sensation of being pulled up and down.[36] A photographer like Margaret Bourke-White might have made close-ups of the cable-car machinery or figured angles that would show the awesome slopes of the streets. Lange gravitated, as always, to the people, making portraits of riders and workers, but she had little to say about them, aside from their seeming obliviousness to one another, signaling the anomie that characterized Lange's worry about city life.

She could not get back to the San Francisco she had loved thirty years previously. She had changed, and was no longer a carefree bohemian, no longer connected to the city's counterculture. So had the city changed, its population having grown by 50 percent, tourists forming a higher proportion of its occupants on any given day, its flavor increasingly corporate. Lange was no longer a San Franciscan, but her friends who remained San Franciscans did not live in the city she remembered, either.

22.9. WINTERS, CALIFORNIA, 1952

IN 1957, DOROTHEA gained a restorative site of delight and contentment—a cabin on the ocean in Marin County. For Lange, it became more than a retreat; it was a veritable idyll. She liked to watch and listen to the water, to study the life in the tide pools, and to photograph there. She and Paul went there many weekends, often with a few grandchildren—it was too small for the whole extended family to sleep there—sometimes with friends. The cabin, called Steep Ravine for its location, came to stand for freedom.

Throughout the 1950s, both at the cabin and in the Euclid Street backyard, Lange made photographs of her domestic surroundings and of her extended family, which had now multiplied. She made numerous still lifes. That of her kitchen recapitulates the migrant farmworker's kitchen (see plate 13), a testimonial to women's work and pleasures and reassertion of sisterhood among women. Many photographs of her garden speak of another source of work and pleasure. She made loving fun of Paul and expressed equally loving sympathy for Helen Dixon, John's wife, during her second pregnancy.

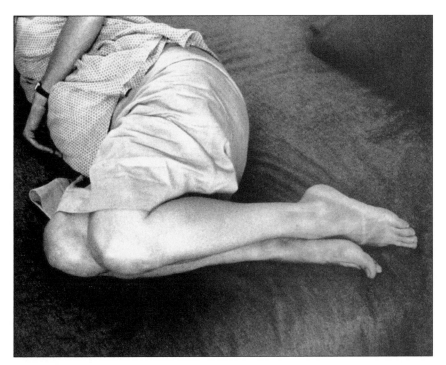

22.10. WINTERS, CALIFORNIA, 1955

This new photography was simultaneously an appreciation of family, a withdrawal from travel, and an artistic challenge—to turn family snapshots into photography that could communicate far beyond family. It would become her final project, but another adventure would intervene first. She would finally make the trip around the world that she and Fronsie had dreamed up in 1918.

22.11. PAUL TAYLOR, BERKELEY, 1957

# 23

# Diplomat's Wife

For several decades Paul Taylor had configured his work whenever possible to join Lange in her projects. That pattern reversed starting in 1958. Taylor worked as a consultant on agrarian reform in the underdeveloped world from 1952 through 1967 and she accompanied him on three of these jobs, spending many months abroad.[1] On these trips she was no longer a coworker, but a wife. Taylor was greeted and escorted by government officials, translators always at his side. He took her along to official dinners and tours when he could. Lange worked at photography on her own, walking the streets when that was possible and otherwise riding in a taxi or with a chauffeur, but she could not speak the languages, could not understand the cultures, and did not know the rules of safety or courtesy. Had Lange taken these trips at a younger age, or had she been a healthy sixty-year-old, she might have made these travels more productive despite the obstacles. Her photography was enriched and diversified by new visual influences. The exquisite design sensibility of some Asian cultures, the communal quality of village life, the beauty of the farms and farm homes, the arduous labor of peasants, the frequent subordination or even invisibility of women, the luxury of the ruling elites—having seen these, she saw America anew. As it was, however, although she produced some stunning photography, her body of work from these trips was not comparable to her U.S. photography; and the travels probably worsened her health.

To family and closest friends, Dorothea's assertiveness and Paul's devotion suggested that he was the one who loved more, who shaped his life to fit hers. No one reading her travel journal could be so sure of that. Weak, in chronic pain and enduring frequent major health crises, she would, on balance, have preferred to stay home. She had many reasons: She wondered if she could photograph in strange, underdeveloped places. Her garden had never been lovelier, a quiet life never more desirable. Her darkroom work went slowly and she had backed-up demand for exhibition prints. Above all, she had five grand-children nearby. "Gregor will be 6 years old on Monday! No teeth in front. Dee in the 1st grade. Leslie can tell wonderful fairy stories, with all shades of expression . . . Andrew can *sing* and Paulie just smiles and smiles."[2] Aside from photography, the grandchildren were her greatest source of pleasure, especially because with them she felt she could repair her maternal history. (She would miss major family events while she was gone: Two more grand-children, Lisa and Seth, were born. John and Helen decided to move back to Berkeley and live temporarily in her studio until they found something better, a move that brought three of the grandchildren right next door.)

Lange consulted her doctor, quite possibly hoping he would prohibit the trip, but instead he said, "What's the difference whether you die here or there? Let's go."[3] And there was an attraction: she had been outside the United States only once, to Ireland and England, and her youthful dream of going around the world had been halted by a San Francisco pickpocket.

Paul pitched the 1958 trip as a grand adventure—eight months, twelve countries. He "eased" her into these trips, she recalled; disavowing any desire to pressure her, he would let her know how sad and lonely he would be with-out her, then add that he had "just left some [travel] material on your desk for you . . . to look at when you have time."[4] Once she seemed to agree, he would leave all the trip preparations to her because, as she put it, "my liege is entirely absorbed in water and power."[5]

Her travel journal shows a side of Paul Taylor that was previously only visible to the immediate family. He would not be distracted from his work. Yes, he adored Dorothea; no one revered her genius more. But he could put her needs out of his mind when immersed in the issues he cared about. Like all love, Taylor's was partly selfish: he wanted her with him. She knew this: ". . . in some peculiar fashion [he] is ruthless and non-comprehending. Part of me he banishes. . . . I plead, but he cannot and will not change. I must give, and do."[6] She was repeating what she criticized herself for doing to and for Maynard: "I should have been a more critical and less agreeable wife."[7] These trips expose Dorothea's controllingness to a different light, showing it to be entirely compatible with willingness to defer, even sacrifice, on matters important to her husband.

So she spent many months between 1958 and 1963 on long and exhausting trips, despite weakness and pain, because he wanted her company. She packed and repacked dozens of times; spent days alone in hotel rooms, writing hundreds of postcards and letters; sat through official dinners that she could not eat; and engaged enthusiastically in tourism and shopping with Paul. By contrast, the foreign work represented a new career for Paul Taylor and it energized him. As Dorothea weakened, he got a second wind. Yet this second career, ultimately, smashed his aspirations once again. Having lived through the defeat of an agricultural New Deal in the States, he then relived that defeat abroad. Lange, no longer invested in government work, but also emotionally braver, recognized this first and more unsparingly.

FOR TAYLOR, THESE foreign consultantships continued his New Deal work. He was among a number of Department of Agriculture people who began to work abroad as New Deal programs shut down, and some of them, progressives like Taylor, wanted to foster rural democracy abroad. They perceived that the huge inequalities in landowning in countries like the Philippines, Indonesia, Vietnam, and Pakistan stood in the way of political democracy and freedom. In the end, their advocacy of land reform stalled as badly in the Third World as it had in the United States, stymied by the Cold War and the American government's determination to protect its anti-Communist allies no matter how corrupt, brutal, and antidemocratic. Paul Taylor's appraisal was less blunt, in part because he enjoyed the work. But there is plenty of evidence of his frustration, and his denial of the overall futility of what he did was like that of a soldier unable to acknowledge that he had sacrificed for a futile and unjust war. Besides, Taylor was a never-say-die activist, who campaigned for agricultural democratization to the end of his life, in 1984, and never quit believing that the United States could help poor countries if its foreign policy were only a bit smarter.

That Taylor was working for the State Department even as the FBI was investigating him for disloyalty was not an unusual contradiction in American Cold War politics. Many in Washington knew him to be staunchly anti-

Communist, arguing for land reform and democratic participation as the only way to stop Communism. In this perspective, he was a Cold War liberal, never questioning the need to check Soviet influence. But liberal opposition to Communist authoritarianism varied, and Taylor, unregenerate New Dealer, valued economic and social democracy as much as political freedom. In fact, he believed that without that democracy, political freedom was uncertain, if not impossible. He had seen that unrestrained corporate power threatened democracy and civil liberties. When critics of the big growers in California compared their rule to that of fascism, he listened, even if he did not use that word himself.

What Taylor wanted for the United States came to be called land reform (or, more broadly, agrarian reform) when it was prescribed for the Third World. It included not just redistribution of land but also credit for small farmers, rent controls for tenant farmers, higher wages for landless farmworkers. His international agenda flowed from his commitment to small farms as part of the ground of American democracy. By the early 1950s, the success of Japan's land reform, designed in part by Taylor's Ph.D. student William Gilmartin and imposed by the United States after its victory in World War II, made it seem a promising strategy for other countries where the United States had economic or strategic interests.[8] His foreign consultantships connected him to old allies, including Wolf Ladejinsky, a former McCarthy victim now working for U.S. AID in Vietnam.[9]

Agrarian reform was to be accompanied by "community development." For Taylor, this meant popular participation in decision making, a radical democratic idea pioneered by the settlement-house movement and continued later by the civil rights and farmworker movements. Taylor believed that agrarian reform could be accomplished only as a grassroots movement.[10]

This vision did not resemble what the United States actually did. The State Department leadership, concerned to stimulate economic growth so as to lessen the attraction of Communist-promoted radical redistribution, cared little about democratization. It feared not only the Soviet challenge but also liberation movements in the former European colonies, which it believed to be supported by Soviet rubles and Chinese yuan. U.S. foreign aid and technical advice had counterinsurgency as its purpose: lessening the appeal of nationalist and leftist movements. In one country after another, rulers were too dependent on landowners to cross them, even after accepting multiple millions of U.S. dollars supposedly contingent on reforms. The traditional elites of these small countries were more successful in using the United States for maintaining their power and wealth than the United States was in using reform to resist the popular appeal of Communism.

Taylor wrote report after report on the need for democratic agrarian reform, but his recommendations were never implemented. He tried without success to get aid funds cut when rulers blocked reform.[11] The State Department refused to publish the 1967 report it had hired him to prepare, on "Communist Strategy and Tactics Employing Peasant Dissatisfaction. . . ."[12] Soon Taylor and the other New Dealers working abroad gave way to a younger generation formed by Cold War thinking, with no experience of the New Deal era.

In the years since the disastrous U.S. intervention into Vietnam, critical scholars have shown that American expertise functioned more to suppress than to advance democracy. Most blame the State Department, the Defense Department, the CIA and, sometimes, the big foundations. Taylor, his thinking formed prior to the Vietnam debacle, would, in retrospect, blame the Department of Agriculture, with which he was, of course, intimately familiar.[13] If he was wrong to let the others off the hook, he was calling attention to a neglected dimension of the problem. The Department of Agriculture men were accustomed to representing large farmers for whom mechanization and heavy use of chemicals were cost-effective. They tended to write off peasants who were not immediately convinced to try new methods, and failed, Taylor saw, to understand peasants' rational reluctance to experiment.[14] Agriculture's Foreign Advisory Service sought to increase productivity as an alternative, rather than a complement, to land reform. It also disdained cooperatives, which could have brought poor farmers economies of scale—though Taylor was skeptical of the department's view that bigger was always more productive, and instead he favored cooperatives.[15] The "green revolution" thus exacerbated inequalities and increased land monopolization, sending hundreds of thousands of ruined peasants to swell the urban shantytowns. Worse than diplomats and soldiers in their disregard for social structure and environmental sustainability, the Department of Agriculture was interested only in modeling short-term costs and yields.[16]

Yet Taylor aided these antidemocratic projects. He knew his recommendations to be futile, he knew how corrupt and tyrannical were many of the rulers he encountered, and he knew the power of large plantation owners in agrarian societies. Despite disappointment and frustration, he never refused these consultancies. In the United States, he combined research with advocacy, campaigning even for causes his employers called "lost," such as better wages and living conditions for farmworkers and the 160-acre water limit.[17] He did not attempt this regarding foreign policy, and would have lost his consultant jobs if he had. To do the foreign consulting, he had to resign himself to functioning as a government agent, his usually strong ethical passions muted.

LANGE, WITH HIGH hopes, packed a great deal of film for the trip. And at their first stop, Tokyo, she was upbeat. She bought a 35-mm camera and experimented with it. She was impressed by Japanese design consciousness, produced and displayed even in manufactured goods: "These department stores [she had just been to Takashimaya] are like museums of contemporary life." In the Japanese countryside, she saw "the Art of farming . . . the curves and shapes of the fields . . . where the fruit is tied in little bags, on orchard islands" and, of course, the grace of the workers.

But the second stop, Korea, shook her confidence. She had seen far more poverty than most Americans, but she was not prepared for "Third World" wretchedness. The war that divided the country had ended, but the suffering had not. An orphanage "wrung my heart, turned my stomach, and rocked my complacency. . . . Infants, lying in their dirty boxes, with running sores. . . . Tiny gray-white bundles of sick flesh that I could not bring myself to touch. . . ." She also noticed Korean hostility to mixed-blood, notably Negro-Korean, children. In Vietnam she photographed an American GI with his mixed-race baby, whose future she thought in doubt.[18] Yet racist clichés that she would have rejected in her own country appeared in her early observations: "Human life is cheap in Korea. . . ." Speaking of Manila, she wrote, "People look like jungle creatures."

However painful the poverty, she wanted to see it, but her handlers struggled to keep her isolated. In Korea "they took us by the back of the neck like puppies and put us out there on the government thing which was like living in the suburbs." When she walked about on her own, she attracted crowds who, at a minimum, blocked her line of sight and sometimes made her frightened: "a pushing mob of children, and curious adults . . . I am surrounded, my clothes examined, my hair stroked." She had lost her cloak of invisibility.[19] In Asia she could not be the walker in the city she had been in New York and San Francisco.

As a result, the Asian photographs do not offer the critique found in her travel diary. But her own reluctance also played a part. She had never liked making images of wretchedness or filth, and she did so in the 1930s only because it was her assignment and because she believed it might help her subjects, while here in Asia nothing constructive would have flowed from such images. One has a sense that she was making photographs as a diplomat's wife, discreet, tactful, deferential.

She often saw pictures she could not photograph because she was in a moving train or car. "Twice yesterday I saw what could have been a recording," she wrote, and her aural rather than visual metaphor conveys her sense that she was blindly reflecting, rather than interpreting, what she saw. She would ask drivers to stop, but they would refuse or pretend not to understand. "I sit in that car, cameras on my lap, and seethe."

Repelled by the arrogance and privileges of the Americans and their disrespect for Asians, she picked up visual signs of inequality, such as the bench in front of a PX on which Korean soldiers were not allowed to sit.[20] She was disgusted by the behavior of American soldiers with their Korean girlfriends, their radios drowning out even the street hubbub.[21] Her greatest discomfort was in Vietnam. Visiting there in the midst of Diem's repression campaign—a

23.1. KOREA, 1958                    23.2. EGYPT, 1963

23.3, PALESTINE, 1958

reign of terror in the countryside, where prizes were offered for turning in the names of neighbors and relatives, and where jailing or simply shooting suspected Vietminh sympathizers was commonplace—she called it a police state. She found her handler there obnoxious: "We are in the hands of . . . Sergeant Droopy-drawers, old Redneck, Sergeant Jug-ears, an imperious, egotistical, conceited old Big Game Hunter with a twisted outlook." Even the circumspect Taylor registered an official complaint about this man, and hoped that their "Vietnamese interpreter could not understand the stream of English talk that this fellow would let loose . . . disparaging the Vietnamese. . . ."[22]

From her peripheral perspective on these U.S. aid programs, Dorothea was less likely than Paul to blame only individuals. "There is something here that is at the core, rotten," she wrote. In Vietnam, she wondered, ". . . if American aid moved out of Asia . . . If they had the courage to stand up to us and deny us our intentions would, in the long run, these countries be in a better position to take their place among nations? Are we weakening them at the source? Are we interrupting the course of their development? . . . We are like a conqueror nation."

But these negative comments appear only in the travel journals and in letters to family, not in her photography—on these trips, she only photographed beautiful things. Awestruck by Asian aesthetics, she made thousands of fine pictures and wrote hundreds of pages about her observations. "The landscape teems with brown people, in Korean white, sharp, distinct, slow-moving, solitaries and in groups, squatting, studded with frames loaded, the bearer buried, peering from under his load . . . the little brown boys with dragonfly nets, bright-colored nets . . . the loads the women carry on their smooth black heads . . . the conformation and ploughing design of the rice patties [sic]." She was also analyzing what she saw, ecologically: ". . . all these ways in which men move in their environment, and use it, and how it supports their life. . . ."

As always, her photographs recognized farm labor. One of its motifs was carrying—done occasionally by pack animals but more frequently by people's backs or heads. Grace, in movement or at rest, was an equally powerful motif, continuous in Lange's photography since her studio days. The most published of Lange's Asian photographs are supremely elegant—the hand of a Javanese dancer, the perfect symmetry and smoothness of a Korean child's face. Always haunted by feet, in Asia as in the United States, she used them as metaphors for labor, endurance, and grace in Asia. (When she returned home she organized a sequence she called "conversations with feet.") (See plates 45–48 for my attempt to replicate this.) She similarly used bodies, in Asia as in the United States, as metaphors for relationships and tenderness. Her portraits often featured children, because they were more approachable than adults. She managed to catch them in noncute moments—of reverie, anxiety, suspicion, or silliness. Both the children and the women she sought to photograph were often hiding, and she photographed that hiding, making it a central theme and part of the identity of her subjects, to the degree that hiding became a metaphor for the photographer's position as outsider. (See plate 42.)

When I studied the Asian photographs, I was on guard against intimations of an Orientalist take on an exotic and "backward" people, because there

is so much of that in other observations by First World visitors. I did not
see much of this. Lange made, of course, many photographs of unfamiliar
practices—veiled women, turbaned men, women carrying heavy loads on their
heads, women with nose rings, naked toddlers (she had always loved naked
children), Javanese dance. Yet the images do not titillate or mystify. Lange
was interested less in the exotic than in the mundane. Her camera was more
often pointed at farmworkers working in fields, women chatting in groups,
and the omnipresent traffic of people carrying their loads. She photographed
temples and minarets but more often the homes of poor people, paying close
attention to how they were constructed. She registered the many domestic
tasks performed outdoors, such as cooking, car and bicycle repair, washing
clothes, and marketing. Her attitude toward Asian women is similar to her
take on American women: they are represented as mothers, workers, farmers,
craftswomen—but their labor is heavier than that of Westerners.

As if in compensation for the photographic limitation, Lange looked exten-
sively at folk art. "We purchased and purchased. Paul and I certainly love to do
this. . . ." Shopping also provided escape from officials, who would tell them
nothing of use anyway, Paul thought. Paul was even more eager to acquire
artifacts than Dorothea,[23] but she was a connoisseur. In Vietnam, she got silk
dresses made for all the daughters, daughters-in-law, and granddaughters (but

23.4. VIETNAM, 1958

not Consie or Becky); from Indonesia, she wrote Helen, "You will be wearing sarongs for the rest of your life."[24] For themselves they bought useful items, which Dorothea then used regularly. This flowed from principles both ethical and aesthetic. The objects she (or they) cherished were the actual furniture of people's lives, part of their everyday culture. They were objects displaying the union of form and function, of use and art, the essence of Dorothea's elegant simplicity of taste.

She sometimes enjoyed the luxury extended to an American diplomat, but at other times she tolerated miserable conditions because of Paul's determination to see the real countryside. In the big cities, they stayed in luxury hotels. In Chiang Mai, Thailand, the State Department set them up in the elegantly furnished palace of the former prince. But after staying in a rural inn in Korea, she was picking fleas off of her body. In a "Rest House" in Siwa, Egypt—a wealthy oasis and home of an honored oracle in ancient Egypt, but a deserted archaeological site in 1958—they slept on dirty sheets covered with flea powder and went entirely without food on one day.[25] The soft food she could eat was often hard to get. Toilet facilities were a severe trial, especially with her recurrent intestinal problems. They took long bumpy rides in open jeeps (350 miles to Siwa from Cairo), becoming coated with dust. Dorothea endured terror as they rode with maniac taxi drivers and flew in dicey airplanes. This was far harder than the San Joaquin Valley or the dust bowl.

Paul thrived on the work, never tired, never homesick, always eager to reach the next place. He met important men, who treated him with respect and occasionally with honorifics, and on the small planes he delighted in riding in the cockpit with the pilot. "Paul enjoys officialdom"; "he loves this life," Dorothea wrote. On the whole, she responded with her usual resilience and criticized herself when she was irritable: "I always find something these days to complain about and use as a weapon against his devotion to work. I find it limiting and monotonous, and I'm rebelling after 23 years." If there was rebellion, it never lasted. She wished she could skip some of the formal dinners and griped that he was so involved with his work that he wasn't hearing what she was saying, but she never minded being alone. When included, she loved seeing him at work; recalling her first introduction to him as he interviewed research subjects, she appreciated his skill at what he did. About a lecture at the Seoul Chamber of Commerce, she wrote, "He was just as fine as could be. . . . His dignity and simplicity were moving. . . . My love for him sometimes overwhelms me."

Plate 29. Alabama, circa 1938

PLATE 30. DURHAM COUNTY, NORTH CAROLINA, 1939

PLATE 31. NEAR EXETER, CALIFORNIA, 1936

PLATE 32. DOS PALOS, CALIFORNIA, 1938

Plate 33. Centerville, California, 1942

Plate 34. Manzanar Internment Camp, 1942

PLATE 35. OAKLAND, CALIFORNIA

PLATE 36. TRAILER CAMP, RICHMOND, CALIFORNIA, 1942

PLATE 37. COUNTY CLARE, IRELAND, 1954

Plate 38. Oakland, California, 1957

PLATE 39. CONTRA COSTA COUNTY, CALIFORNIA, 1956

PLATE 40. MONTICELLO, CALIFORNIA, 1953

Plate 41. Philippines, 1958

PLATE 42. PAKISTAN, 1958

PLATE 43. KOREA, 1958

Plate 44. Egypt, 1963

PLATE 45. NEAR EUTAW, ALABAMA, 1936

PLATE 46. SOMEWHERE IN ASIA, 1958

PLATE 47. WINTERS, CALIFORNIA, 1954

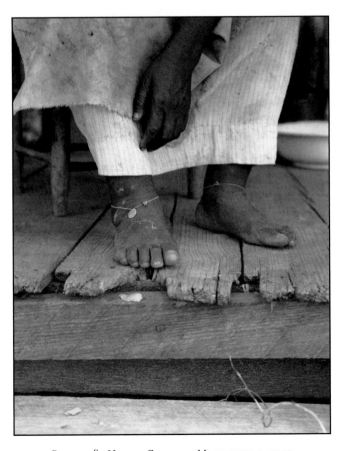

PLATE 48. HINDS COUNTY, MISSISSIPPI, 1937

BUT ILLNESS LAUNCHED surprise attacks; and increasingly, feeling good was the surprise and discomfort the norm. At the very beginning of this 1958 trip, on the flight from Honolulu to Wake Island, the burning pain from her ulcers was so great, she feared she would have to turn back. Pain never let her alone long. "My whole insides really hurt. . . . I wonder whether I will break down completely and if I can see this trip through." "I endure pain a part of every day. This leaves exhaustion. It hurts me, it hurts me. Sometimes, if I am alone, I cry out." Once, alone in Pakistan, she had an attack of dysentery in the night that "left me fragmentated. . . ." She was not often well nourished.

These complaints were articulated only to her journal, not to her husband. Right next to her on that first flight, he did not know she was in pain. He should have known, because he knew that she protected him. "For one who had such physical distresses, prolonged over so many years, she never laid it on anybody else," he commented.[26] She was well aware of the expenditure of energy that this stoicism required. She wrote to Margaret Bourke-White, who suffered from Parkinson's disease, "We are inclined . . . to crawl into our dark holes, and if we do not inflict our suffering upon others we regard our responsibilities as performed."[27] Reading her journal next to his recollections suggests Paul's self-absorption. Nothing dampened her spirits, he recalled, their "interests dovetailed so beautifully . . . there was never any, 'Oh, I wish that we could do something else.'" She thought he wasn't hearing her.

Despite her physical condition, she obliged Paul by agreeing to visit five more countries as tourists when he finished his work. First, they went to Moscow, where they were greeted as honored diplomatic guests and confronted with obstructionist bureacracy, the two sides of official Soviet culture. Tickets for the Bolshoi Ballet and other performances appeared daily, but Paul was not allowed to meet with other economists and economic-development experts. They then went to Germany, passing through East and West Berlin and visiting both her and his ancestral locations—Stuttgart and Kaiserslautern. In Germany, a thicket of mixed feelings sprouted. Hearing the language evoked irascible Uncle Fritz, magnificent *Grosmama* and the sound of her sewing machine, Nettie's "big, open plain face, the big nose, and how they clucked together when she came of an afternoon to visit *Grosmama*." She found ten Vottelers, her mother's family name, in the Stuttgart phone book, but she did not try to meet them. "Let sleeping dogs lie," she wrote enigmatically, perhaps wanting to avoid the risk of finding Nazi sympathizers

among her forebears—it was only thirteen years since the fall of the Third
Reich. Nazism and the Holocaust were much on her mind. Even after hearing a concert of Bach cantatas, she wrote, "Was it 6,000,000 Jews they
exterminated?"

They bought a VW in Stuttgart and drove west through Switzerland, and
had a serious argument on the way: Dorothea wanted to go to Paris, but Paul
insisted on traveling instead to the location where he had been gassed in
World War I, Belleau Wood. (Apparently there wasn't time for both.) Dorothea
had underestimated Paul's desire to return there—his battle service, injury,
self-sacrifice and patriotism wrapped into one very large emotion.[28] He found
the battle site just as he remembered it, even a wine cellar that had served his
unit as a first-aid station. This threw Dorothea into a self-pitying irritability—
for which she promptly criticized herself: "You imagine yourself persecuted,
you attack in a rain of petty criticism, spoken and unspoken. . . . You set
yourself up as a Paris-sort-of-a-person. This is not true, but it is *revenge*." She
never got to Paris, never saw its treasure of photography and modern art.

Finally, they stopped in London to see Margot and her husband, Don
Fanger, and then again in Chicago to see Paul's daughter Kathy. When they
arrived in San Francisco, Dorothea's exhaustion almost dissipated at the sight
of John and Helen Dixon and Ross and Onnie Taylor, with five grandchildren,
who met them at the airport.

TAYLOR DID SOME consulting trips alone but managed to get Dorothea to
accompany him on two more, to Ecuador and Venezuela in the summer of
1960. Despite the evidence, Paul continued to hope that he could convince the
State Department to do its foreign aid right, to make use of indigenous social
strengths and support genuine democracy. Venezuela under the former leftist Betancourt encouraged peasant unions that impressed Taylor. In Ecuador,
by contrast, Taylor and Lange were both extremely critical of U.S. policy.[29]
Guayaquil was a "city of the deprived," Lange wrote, ". . . as ugly and terrible a
city as one can experience. . . ." U.S. foreign aid to South America was a "crude
deal of which we are ashamed as we walk the streets," and the hostile stares
confirmed their unease. She saw a bit of salvation when they reached peasant
villages because, despite terrible poverty and filth, she saw there "a relationship of man to environment that felt good, and deep." The peasants were so
"earnest, so serious, so poor and sweated, so willing to raise their work-worn

23.5. ECUADOR, 1960

hands and arms for the *communidad*." However romantic, her longing led
to a most material wish: "Couldn't there be a place in the world where [the
pressure of] making money would be lifted?"[30] She was growing even more
skeptical that Paul's ideals could prevail.

Physical misery accompanied her again: riding hours through the Andes
in an open jeep, dust in her eyes and mouth, and a nose itching from scabies.
She was relieved to sit out one of these side trips and stay in the hotel: ". . . my
drive, my spirit, have deserted me," she wrote. "Paul is . . . relentless. There is
no give."

In 1961 Dorothea successfully resisted a trip. "My Liege expects me to join
him. . . . I want to work quietly in the darkroom with no one here to disturb
(no 160 acres). . . ."[31] There was a last trip, however, in 1963, and it was the
hardest. It was supposed to be easier because they would stay mostly in one
place—Paul had just retired from UCB and went to teach for a semester at the
University of Alexandria, at a Ford Foundation–funded Institute on Land Settlement. Egypt in 1963 had been a republic for a decade, and President Gamal
Abd el-Nasser, a nationalist of worldwide influence, was committed to land
reform. Moreover, the vehemently anti-Communist Nasser had brought Egypt
into the nonaligned movement in 1955, an effort by Third World countries to

escape the Cold War between the great powers and to take an independent course. This, too, attracted Taylor.

Having endured another spate of pain and hospitalization in 1962, Dorothea didn't want to go, and Paul knew it. But he was committed to the trip and she could not desert him. Was he reckless and selfish? He could not turn down these invitations. She had been so vigorous in their life together, so resilient after numerous health crises, and so uncomplaining, that he did not understand her ailments as life-threatening.

In Alexandria the university provided an apartment and a house servant, Hussein, as well a car and a driver, Aly Agua. Dorothea cooked, and shopped at the markets, a time-consuming undertaking but one she welcomed as a source of photographic opportunities. But the street crowds here were overtly hostile, a sign of developing anti-Americanism. (After Nasser nationalized the Suez Canal in 1956, the United States and Israel had committed themselves to his overthrow.) Children threw pebbles at her. One bystander demanded that she photograph something beautiful, as opposed to poor people on the street. Aly told her what she must have known about poor and ragged people everywhere: " 'When the people see the cloth-es is all broke [translation: When the photographs show people in ragged clothes]—the blood goes upside-down.' "[32]

With more opportunity to observe ordinary people than on the previous trips, Lange grew increasingly conscious of the status of women. "The little girls take the babies on their backs very early and from then on all their lives." When she learned of events where women were not allowed, she took critical note but nevertheless described this lightly in a postcard sent home: "I shall not come home wearing a face-veil, but considerably chastened."[33] Lange's ideas were challenged here: her rosy view of "traditional," less individualistic societies collided with disturbing evidence of women's subordination. Like many Western travelers, of course, she oversimplified the meaning and function of women's veiling and seclusion, unable to see the rewarding women's communities that sometimes resulted or the ways in which women, although subordinated, were not entirely powerless. Taylor's less romantic, less ideological understanding of gender produced more accurate insights. For example, having noticed rural women's lack of enthusiasm for mechanization of the home, such as washing machines and gas ranges, he asked questions and thereby came to understand it. What happened in homes was dependent on the mechanization of field labor, because women "found little reason to save time and labor in the home so long as the saving was to be spent in labor in the field."[34]

On this supposedly easier trip, Dorothea faced a truly terrifying health crisis. She began suffering not just painful ulcer attacks but a kind of wasting: with chronic diarrhea and the repeated closing of her esophagus, she could not nourish herself and began again to lose weight drastically. She wrote Margot that she was holding up her clothes with safety pins. In March 1963 a new symptom appeared: intermittent high fevers, which abated after a few days on antibiotics. In July, visiting Iran on their way home, Paul awoke one morning in Tabriz and found her babbling and delirious; she had to be hospitalized for five days. A week later in Teheran, another hospitalization occurred. None of these fine, often American-trained physicians could find a source of infection. The worst crisis hit August 2, while they were in Switzerland, driving west. As her fever climbed, Paul drove frantically late into the night to get her to a hospital in Interlaken.

Here the physicians began intravenous feedings and blood transfusions, but they refused to administer antibiotics, reasoning that previous diagnoses had failed to determine the source of infection because antibiotics so quickly reduced the microorganism that was torturing her. The gamble paid off. She had malaria.[35] The standard treatment began to work, but slowly, because the disease had been so long neglected and she had become so sick and depleted. On the eighth day she was still receiving IV feedings and transfusions.

She remained in the Interlaken hospital for three weeks. Paul would stay in her room all day, then move to a nearby hotel to sleep.[36] Paul felt it was paradise. This sentiment expressed his relief that there was, finally, a strategy to make her well and doctors he trusted. He loved the crisp, sun-filled air and the view from Dorothea's window. Equally likely, being forced to sit still, to stop activity, to find the patience that her severe illness and debilitation now demanded, had a tonic effect on him. As she gained strength, her mood got better and better.

When she was preparing to leave, she recalled, the doctor "said to me, 'What would you like?' And I said 'doctor, I would like ten years,' and he said 'I believe you can do it. I believe you'll have your ten years.' . . . They had gone over me and had discovered that of all that had been done to me . . . it was working and it was functioning, and there was no reason that, with care, it wouldn't hold up for ten years."[37] She held on to this as if it were a promise. Now sixty-eight years old, she desperately wanted to stay alive. Feeling well for the first time in many months, she was once again imagining new photographic projects and the pleasures of home.

Yet on her release, they still did not go straight home. Paul wanted always to see more and do more, and her elation at feeling better and at the physician's promise made her acquiesce. Five days after leaving Interlaken, her fever spiked again, and she had to begin taking quinine once more. Even then they did not stop. In early September in the Netherlands, still on quinine, she was walking around and visiting museums. Once back in the United States, they made three stops before returning to Berkeley. Paul took off almost immediately to Chile and Iran, leaving Dorothea to enjoy her grandchildren and her darkroom.

TOWARD THE END of the first Asian trip, Dorothea reviewed what she had accomplished, commenting, ". . . that very excellent photographer was not present. . . . There was a half-sick, cold and world-weary old woman, with eyes not so dull as most. . . . She could have met the possibilities she carries within her. But she did not make that movement." In Asia, Lange had often felt visually empty. "The 'secret treasury of my heart' is dried up," she wrote. One morning back in Berkeley, she destroyed ten days' worth of her Asia photography.[38]

Typically, she thought she should be able to suppress pain and fatigue with willpower and condemned herself for weakness of character. "What I shall do here," she had written at the outset of the first trip, after her bouts of pain on the first flight, "depends upon what is in me and how courageous I am." But that was not true—lack of courage was not the problem. Lange's demands on herself were so unreasonable as to be warped, for in truth she had attempted the impossible.[39] Even had she not been so physically drained, she was working blind in unfamiliar societies, when her skill rested on being able to understand the culture and context of her subjects. (In Ireland, at least she had been able to talk to people.) Photography curator Therese Heyman thought the foreign trips were a waste of Dorothea's time. Dropped into a culture she did not understand, Dorothea could not know if what she was seeing was typical or unusual, so she had no choice but "to rip it off," by which Heyman meant not literal theft but the figurative theft through representing a culture superficially.[40] Looking back a few years later, Lange acknowledged the problem: "I didn't know what I was looking at." "Japan

23.6. VIETNAM, 1958

went over my head."[41] This understanding lay behind her warning to "look out for the picturesque. . . ."[42] The cultural barriers may have been more unexpected because of her commitment to family of man–style universalism. She wanted to reach a core of human oneness beneath a surface of cultural diversity. But such common humanity—women's care for children, children's playfulness, family unity—is often banal. Indeed, the commonality could be superficial and the differences more profound.

Her work abroad was further limited by the auspices under which she traveled. Had she been escorted by indigenous documentary photographers or democracy advocates instead of State Department and military men, the photography might have been different.

There are dissenting opinions. The photography establishment, including Grace Mayer and Ansel Adams, praised the Asia photographs.[43] Many of them exquisitely beautiful, their appropriation of Asian art styles addressed connoisseurs. They were immediately understandable as art, in contrast to how her photographs of American poor people appeared in the 1930s. The Third World pictures conveyed no burdensome sense of responsibility or political purpose; they did not appear documentary. But Lange stuck to her overall negative judgment. Her young assistant, Richard Conrat, told her that he thought the Asia work honest but on the whole unsuccessful, and she agreed.[44]

Her judgment was far too harsh. True, her achievement might have been no less great had she never left the United States, and the trips increased her suffering and may have shortened her life. But if the Asian and Latin American photography were all she had ever done, it would be a major achievement. As it is, we inevitably compare it to her American work. And in an historical vein, the relative weakness of the Asian photographs was fitting: Lange was quintessentially American, so it should be no surprise that her greatest work was conditioned by a heroic, democratic moment in American life, her lesser work by a period more self-interested and frightened than generous.

## 24

# To a Cabin

The historian sees Dorothea Lange in 1955 as a woman entering her last decade, but she, of course, did not. She began to think of herself as a dying woman, I suspect, only after her diagnosis with inoperable cancer of the esophagus in August 1964. Her medical crises and hospitalizations had begun in 1945, twenty years before she died, but she always rebounded. Her physical and emotional resilience, her capacity to put up with pain, and her Swiss doctor's 1963 promise of ten more years made her expect more time than she had. By the end, however, she saw what the historian sees: that hers was a life with an extraordinary concentration of great work into a single decade, 1935–1945. You could view this as a loss—a life with its creativity cut cruelly short. Or you could view the years of ill health as a price paid for the all-out effort of that decade, a Faustian bargain. Or you could view it as, I believe, she herself did at the end, as the life trajectory of a woman who seized an extraordinary opportunity and wasted none of it.

The historian must not, however, let the heroic achievements of Lange's most productive period, or the bouts of ill health that began in 1945, obscure the more human-scale achievements of her later years. Her greatest intensity went into designing her one-woman show at MoMA. She made sure to stay alive until it was completed, but never saw it—it opened a few months after her death. After decades of relatively little acclaim, she understood it as a belated invitation into the exclusive club of photographers recognized by the art establishment as artists.

Even bracketing that exhibit, her productivity in her last decade outstripped what her health would have suggested. San Francisco TV station KQED made two films about her for National Educational Television; this required submitting to many days of taping and filming in her home, sacrificing privacy and rest. She created several photo-essays from her Asian trips and started two photographic books, which were published posthumously: *Dorothea Lange Looks at the American Country Woman* and *To a Cabin*.[1] Equal respect is due to efforts that did not succeed, such as her continuing campaign for an urban photography project—a gift she wanted to give to America and to younger photographers. And indeed, a group of young photographers photographing the civil rights movement reached out to her for advice and help, recognizing her photography as their inspiration, connecting her New Deal liberalism directly to a New Left just being born. The cutting short of that connection reveals what was lost with her illness and death, what might have been gained had she lived or kept her energy only a few years longer.

Driving herself as hard as she did may have shortened her life, but she chose the path and did not regret it. This meant that in some ways she also chose how to die. One of the last things she said to Paul was, "It's a miracle, that this comes at the right time."[2] There is an unexpected meaning to her "right time" here, because it preceded the actual MoMA exhibit. She needed to create it, but apparently did not need to see it. She was

24.1. BERKELEY, 1959

willing to die without knowing the judgment of the art-photography world. Two readings of this statement are possible: it suggests her recurring lack of confidence, now an anxiety about the critical reception of her show, her fear that she never became a great photographer; or, more likely, in my view, that she knew the value of her work and needed no ultimate sanction from an establishment.

IN THE EARLY 1960s McCarthyism was palpably weakening. Charges of communism were losing their power to repress dissent. Several dynamics came together to advance this opening up of political possibilities, of which the most important was the civil rights movement (which then gave birth to antiwar, women's rights and gay rights movements). From the legal battle against school segregation and the Montgomery bus boycott of 1956, it expanded to sit-ins at lunch counters in 1960, the Freedom Rides of 1961, and the voter registration drives of 1963 and 1964. Awed by the activists' commitment to nonviolence, even in the face of violence toward them, Lange was particularly moved by her understanding that this heroic struggle came from among the very people she had interviewed and photographed, who had seemed so beaten down.[3]

A Supreme Court headed by Earl Warren overturned not only segregated schools but also prayer in schools, HUAC witch-hunts, literacy tests for voting, laws prohibiting mixed marriage and contraception; it guaranteed lawyers for poor defendants and required police Miranda warnings. The Twenty-fourth Amendment, banning the poll tax, which Lange had so often denounced, was making its way through Congress and then the states. The movement begun by the children of the communities she had photographed in North Carolina, Mississippi, and Arkansas was changing America.

Kennedy's election in 1960 let more light into dark places, as much because of his rhetorical and personal charisma as because of his policies. The Kennedys brought in a new cultural style—chamber music and French food in the White House, among other signs of elite taste—which captivated Lange. Lyndon Johnson's creation of a National Endowment for the Arts to provide some federal support for artists was cause for elation in someone who had experienced New Deal arts funding. So was his War on Poverty. Ironically, the new policies that appealed most to Taylor—the Peace Corps, the expansive foreign economic assistance programs, and the Nuclear Test Ban Treaty—resulted from Cold War competition with the Soviet Union, which was actively supporting independence movements in Africa and denouncing the treatment of African Americans.

(The policy record was of course not homogeneous, and Taylor was critical of cutting taxes for the wealthy and surreptitiously entering a disastrous hot war in Vietnam.)

The great expansion of public universities after the war intersected with all these changes, stimulating an upswing in student activism. Berkeley students, frustrated by giant lecture courses and what felt like assembly-line education, were picking up some of the courage of their African American peers. In 1960, a small group picketed Huac hearings in San Francisco, but when police attacked the peaceful demonstrators with clubs and high-pressure water hoses— suggesting that California was not entirely different from Alabama—a much larger demonstration formed the next day. This gratified people like Taylor and Lange, who had felt the hot breath of the witch-hunting monster.

24.2. BERKELEY, 1964

Lange wished she could roam the UCB campus to photograph the student radicals,[4] but she hadn't the strength. Her ulcers and esophagus condition flared up repeatedly, until by 1964 she was quite weak. By now, she had been in poor health for almost twenty years, during which time she had also suffered from misdiagnoses (gallbladder, pancreas, anorexia). Time after time, she had rebounded. In the spring of 1964, she undertook a demanding trip to New York and Washington, came home weak and in pain, and did not rebound. By July, her esophagus had closed so much she could not swallow. This time, the attempts to dilate it led to the discovery, in August, of a malignant and inoperable tumor.[5] She hoped for a last stint of photographing and ordered a new camera, a Leica, two lenses, and other items she had longed for. She never used them.[6] She continued to photograph sporadically, but this was not a time for her to try new equipment. Paul, in shock, continued to hope that she could regain some strength if only she would rest, so for a time during that fall of 1964, he discouraged visitors. He wanted to nurse her himself. She, however, wanted to work and soon broke through Paul's protective cordon, returning to her studio for a few hours at a time.

She now depended on a new assistant, Richard Conrat, a twenty-three-

24.3. BERKELEY, 1964

year-old photography student who stayed with her to the end. He looked back on his two years with her as an extraordinary opportunity.[7] Conrat proved an excellent partner in preparing the MoMA exhibition, because of his politics as well as his skills. Drawn to Lange because of her photography of social commitment, he came into her life as she was moving away from that, both in her Asian work and her family photography, so he became a voice of conscience to her. He was willing to challenge her, and she responded openly and thoughtfully, not defensively. The MoMA show may well have been better because of Conrat's presence in her life.

Meanwhile, a producer who had just finished films on Ansel Adams began filming Lange. Her state of health required a labor-intensive method: filming her in her own work space as she carried out whatever was on her agenda. Each day, the film crew would telephone to see if she felt well enough to let them come. The intersection of the exhibit preparation and the film project produced a treasure for the historian and for photography lovers, because the tapes capture Lange's intermittent, months-long running commentary on her photographic thinking. Although she could hardly have been oblivious to a film crew in her living room, and she was to some degree performing, the

KQED recordings are the more valuable because she was at times explicating her thinking to nonphotographers. At other times she was addressing future generations of photographers. She had a historical sense of herself, as a figure within a coherent and continuing process of photographic development. Her words and her method of preparing the show combined to create a unique summation of her visual thinking.

She began by selecting groups of images: ". . . a single photograph, it's provocative, it's an idea, but if you can do two or three maybe you make of that a phrase and if you can do it in ten maybe it's a sentence. It's a hard obscure language, but it's worth studying." Relations among photographs constituted a visual grammar or a musical piece. An image might be dominant or only contributory, or several might be perfectly balanced; one might amplify the other, or they might sound in unison; photographs might proceed logically or historically one from the other. The goal was not photojournalism, she insisted, but "closer to the literary form of essay." Grouping was not the same as "cataloguing, not putting them into pigeon holes of organization." For example, she rejected a distinction between images of people and of nature, in a shift from her three-decades-earlier self-description as "Photographer of People." Now she insisted that the human and inhuman are part of a single repertoire of expression. "You can photograph a tree, certainly it isn't human, but you who are doing it are human, and your understanding and the reason for doing that tree are strictly human motives." Thus her photographic categories were becoming more symbolic than representational. She also enunciated what some might call a postmodernist approach to her work, acknowledging that photographic meanings change over time. She rejected images that had become hackneyed from overuse, losing their power to break through conventionalized seeing, and she actually tore up numerous photographs.[8]

Lange knew that her photography had been labeled "sentimental." Conrat asked her about this boldly: "Some people seem to think that poverty is inherently sentimental, that there is a kind of pathos in the filming of people in disadvantaged conditions. How can this ever be avoided?" Sentimentality is shallow emotionalism, she replied; images deepen when they force a recognition of something new. When photographs made her think "oh god, how many times have you seen this. . . . He's doing a rehash of a rehash of a rehash of something that wasn't very deeply grounded at the beginning," then, she said, "that's sentimental: a superficial thing, a too readily recognizable thing, an over-familiar thing."[9] Lange wanted to seduce viewers into seeing something for the first time.

Lange did not connect allegations of sentimentality to conventional notions of female sensibility. She may not have registered that these accusations have been particularly directed at women, and at explorations of the domestic, the intimate, the emotional. Walker Evans, for example, used the phrase "photographing babies" as a synonym for selling out artistic integrity.[10] The sentimentality charge also targeted Lange because her subjects worked and lived off the earth rather than in factories or offices. To the degree that FSA photography was sentimental, that quality derived from its ennobling the poor and the downtrodden and romanticizing rural life, and it appeared in male as well as in female photography.

Several critics have read off the strong emotional content of Lange's work as naturally, femininely instinctive and intuitive. George Elliott wrote in the catalog for her MoMA show, "For an artist like Dorothea Lange the making of a great, perfect, anonymous image is a trick of grace, about which she can do little beyond making herself available for that gift of grace."[11] Another described her as a piece of white photosensitive paper, or "an unexposed film," onto which light and shadow marked impressions.[12] Lange contributed to her reputation as instinctive through her own passive metaphors for her work, describing herself as a channel. Creative workers of all kinds and both sexes use such metaphors. Lange saw herself as both passive and active, aware that she worked, as most artists do, with both spontaneity and calculation, and that spontaneity comes from skill acquired from practice, much as dancers develop muscle memory.

Recognizing the tension between specificity and universalism, Lange sought to resolve it through balance: "The better the work, the more ways there are of interpreting it . . ." but "If it is too particular and too personal, then your observer, you give him nothing." She disliked her photographs becoming icons and for that reason wanted to leave the *Migrant Mother* photograph out of the MoMA show. "Some things you do get a life of their own. . . . They cut loose from the person who made them, marched off so you don't have any relationship anymore." Moreover, for Lange, the universality of an icon dishonored the subject by erasing the person's own particular story.[13]

She thought she could unite her universalist, family-of-man theme with the diversity of actual people. She constructed a wall for the MoMA show that she called "the human face": ". . . the idea of that wall is that we have only one universal language that we all understand and that is in the reading of the human face." The tension remains, however, unresolvable. Without uniqueness, human subjects lose dignity. As critic Clive Scott put it, "the photograph . . . refuses to lie down, to be an illustration . . . to depict the purely social. . . ."[14] Yet documentary gains much of its power through viewers' recognition of kinship with the subjects. Moreover, the more contextualized, the more dated the images. While rejecting the overused, Lange yearned nevertheless for eternal life for her images.

Yet photographic icons deserve a defense. They function to create what Raymond Williams called an *"aide-memoire* for activating a 'structure of feeling.' "[15] However often *Migrant Mother* appears, she connotes a worried mother, poor and under stress. The image of raising the American flag at Iwo Jima invokes a generic wartime heroism as well as that of a particular war, and the naked Vietnamese girl burning from napalm invokes the excruciating pain of all wars as well as that of the Vietnam War. Iconization makes its subjects into "types"—that is, individuals come to stand for certain categories, but this is an inevitable response to contextualized portraiture.[16] It is harder to make them "types" but not stereotypes—something Lange often achieved.

Despite her commitment to social context, Lange resisted being defined as a reformer photographer, sometimes rejecting even the term *documentary*. At other times, she accepted the term but argued about its definition: "Documentary photographers are not social workers. Social reform . . . may be a consequence, because it can reveal situations and can be concerned with *change*." The photographer "is a witness . . . not a propagandist or an advertiser."[17] This view was unnecessarily defensive; what makes propaganda is in part its context—even one of Ansel Adams's sublime photographs of the Sierras function sometimes as propaganda for wilderness preservation. Besides, at other times Lange defended propaganda—it was not unusual for her to contradict herself. The defensiveness reveals that even now, as she prepared for an exhibit that would label her definitively as an artist, she could not free herself of a lingering concern that documentary photography was second-class. The photography labeled "art" in her formative years—that of Pictorialism, f/64, Strand and Weston and Adams—excluded what she did. She knew that her best work was done as a government employee—a status oxymoronic with that of artist.

That Lange did not make self-portraits was fundamental to her personality, her values, and the culture of her times. She was impatient with a photography that was about its maker: ". . . many artist photographers' alliance with the world is very slight. Their alliance is to themselves and their effort is to translate the outside world in terms of their needs."[18] Lange did not lack vanity and ambition, but the mysteries that drew her were outside herself.

AS PHOTOGRAPHERS KNOW but the public rarely appreciates, curating an exhibition requires extensive work. Lange's labor was greater because this show would take place at the summit of art, and because she knew she was shaping her reputation. Nevertheless, she was not merely selecting the best of a lifetime of photographs. Tired as she was, she intended to advance her photography by presenting visual stories and conversations. It meant excavating tens of thousands of contact sheets, negatives, and prints and choosing a tiny fraction to show, then deciding how to group them and in what order. She had to consider the printing specifications for each one, their size, whether and how they should be matted and framed, how hung and on what kind of walls. She had to go to the Library of Congress and the National Archives to see the bulk of her work, which she did not own or possess.

John Szarkowski made two trips to Berkeley to work with her on the forthcoming show, in December 1964 and August 1965. Knowing her diagnosis, he was at first worried about how to negotiate with a dying woman. On arriv-

24.4. LANGE WITH SZARKOWSKI, BERKELEY, 1964 OR 1965

ing, he was alarmed to find that she had already planned the show in her mind. Once they began working, however, he found it easy and natural; she was comfortable with disagreement and argued strongly herself. After the first visit his letters became looser, teasing, even flirtatious: "Go ahead, get mad. I warned you . . . However I cannot really bully you . . . because . . . I am in love with you, which puts me at a great disadvantage."[19] He felt her charm and also knew how to handle her.

MoMA had mounted five one-person photography shows previously, featuring Walker Evans, Paul Strand, Edward Weston, Henri Cartier-Bresson, and Edward Steichen. Lange was not at all sure she matched up to this company, in good part because she knew that many high-art curators and critics did not think she did. Szarkowski's visits were themselves a recognition, although not so great as it would have been a few decades later, since he was still a junior figure in the photography world. The gossip from MoMA, however, was that Szarkowski had not wanted to do this show.[20] With pain and weakness adding to her stress, it is not surprising that she was anxious about the exhibition. "I was scared, really scared." "It gives me the cold chills." But not so scared that she held back.[21]

At first, Szarkowski recalled, Lange wanted an Asia wall, an Ireland wall, and an Egypt wall.[22] She thought photographic groupings should be historical and narrative, as in *An American Exodus*, while Szarkowski envisaged groupings based on visual themes. She argued fiercely: "Listen to me young man, you were in knee pants and I was there the day that men first lined up to get their first social security payments." "You're getting my back up just a little by pronouncements. . . ." She would not allow her photographs to "lose the argument" to universalistic images of human nature. "What's the background of the white owner sitting on the porch. Who's doing his work for him?"[23]

Yet Lange also balked at an instrumental, reform-minded vision of the show. Her former protégé, photographer Homer Page, suggested that her MoMA show serve as a model for the urban photography project she was pursuing. Lange refused. She did not wish her show made into an appendage to a social-justice movement, and she wanted the artistic acclaim she was due. She would not let Szarkowski strip her work of its political content, but she would not let it be reduced to visual sloganeering, either. She did, however, write a statement to be mounted at the end of the show: "I would like to add a line to encourage persons interested in using a camera to concern themselves with making photographs of the life which surrounds them, to raise his sights to include what's going on about us, to use the cameras to show this awareness."[24]

The better she got to know Szarkowski, the more she respected his opinions. Compromises became easier. He convinced her, for example, to include *Migrant Mother.* "This exhibit is not being done for these 50 people in the photographic community who could fill out a pretty good sketch of Migrant Mother." Her response then illustrated the fruits of their collaboration: "Yeah, okay, that one picture belongs to the public but let's put her in some unexpected place, in some relationship, give her a new both interpretation and understanding."[25]

Unable to make many of the final exhibition prints, she turned over most of the negatives to the man who had done the printing for "The Family of Man" exhibition, Irwin Welcher.[26] He worked fast because he knew how important it was to her to be able to see the prints before sending them to MoMA. She wanted them on a polycontrast paper to avoid high-gloss, stark blacks and whites; he resisted this decision at first but then acceded and even found a spray coating that would enhance the detail; she was happy with the result. To her last days, she argued for her choices to Szarkowski, especially about the juxtapositions of the photographs, because she knew that mounting an exhibit always led to further changes. Then she sent him a gift: a cake of soap, two Idaho potatoes, and a gong from a Korean Buddhist temple for his new daughter, thanking him for "an immense partnership."[27]

LANGE HELD BACK just enough energy from the MoMA show to pursue the dream she had nurtured since the FSA closed down, a collective several-year photography project about urban life. Her work in Richmond and Oakland showed the need, and her model was, of course, the FSA photographers' beloved community. Now the civil rights movement and the Kennedy presidency made the dream, called Project One, seem possible again.

She had broached the idea publicly in 1952 in an interview with Jacob Deschin of the *New York Times,* in 1955 in a *U.S. Camera* interview, and in 1958 to Magnum. In December 1962, on her way to Egypt, she stopped in New York to talk to Henry Allen Moe of the Guggenheim Foundation about it, to no avail. She wrote a new proposal and took it when she traveled to New York City in May 1964 for the MoMA photography center opening, at which two of her photographs appeared.[28] She sought support from the Ford Foundation and Steichen. Convincing Ben Shahn in New Jersey and Szarkowski in New York to bring together groups of photographers, she found support for her idea but would not compromise her vision. The assembled photographers envisioned a focus exclusively on the poor, a focus she considered simplistic and shallow. She thought, rather, that ". . . our decade of unprecedented 'prosperity' has many faces, there are many forms of privation within prosperity. . . ."[29] The time had come, she said, to photograph "affluence—whose other face is poverty." From Taylor, from her FSA work, and from Asia, she had learned that poverty is a relational phenomenon, a product of inequality rather than an absolute or a marker of underdevelopment that modernization would correct. Still, alongside this Marxist-inflected analysis remained her more spiritual allegiance. "There is poverty within us, poverty of spirit that allows the other poverty," and both poverties needed documentation.[30]

Meanwhile, even as she was getting nowhere with Project One, Lange began campaigning for Project Two, a permanent national photography center where photographers working collectively could expand the powers of the medium. She looked for university as well as foundation sponsorship but insisted on autonomy within a university; she believed that if fine-art photography became lodged only in university art departments, it would be cramped, possibly even stifled. Her animosity to photography's becoming captive to art reveals another aspect of her mixed feelings toward high art—yearning to belong but unwilling to surrender her vision of photography as communication. Floating the idea that the new Kennedy Library incorporate a photographic center, she was trying to arrange a meeting to this end with Beaumont Newhall, Ansel Adams, and Szarkowski just two months before her death.[31] Taylor continued to work for such a project after her death. He lobbied administrators and faculty at UCB to create such a photography center; he started a commission of notables in the photography world, and it further developed and circulated Lange's proposal, with a budget of $400,000 per year for five years.[32] The project was never realized. What Lange had feared came to pass: Photography came to be taught mostly in art departments devoted to training photographers or other academics.[33] Lange was after a humanistic visual education for everyone, as much for those who would look at pictures as for those who would make them.

In 1964, Lange seemed likely to join forces with some young photographers awakened by the civil rights movement and hoping to form an "FSA-type" cooperative group like her Project One. They saw her as their model, while she, thrilled by the movement, was of course ready to jump in as adviser and sponsor.[34] Matt Herron and others involved organized a meeting, but she had to cancel because of a hospitalization. Their correspondence continued, and they sent her drafts of proposals for comment. Facing the same difficulty that Lange had in obtaining funding, they rewrote their proposal to focus entirely on the Student Nonviolent Coordinating Committee's voter registration and citizenship schools; Herron moved his family to Jackson, Mississippi, to work on it full-time. The civil rights organizations understood the power of photography, both to document the violence used against them and to communicate their spirit to potential supporters. One photography curator likened the power of these images to that of the freedom songs.[35] Lange was never able to meet with them. Her illness cost all of us something that would have been extraordinary: Lange photographs of the southern civil rights movement.

For her own photography in the last year of her life, Lange was overwhelmed with offers of help. In response to news of her scheduled MoMA show, those who knew how ill she was—and word traveled fast—responded with a generosity that signaled the affection and respect she engendered.[36] Dorothea was taken aback. "I was scared, really scared [of being able to prepare the exhibit], but my God the people who are ready to come help me, you'd be amazed, and such magnificent offers."[37] Her race—between cancer and the exhibit—became a collective project.[38] Letters poured in and friends and admirers "lined up" to help, she said with a kind of awe, offered to print for her, to help her sort and file photographs, even Nancy Newhall, with whom she had always had a tense and competitive relationship.[39] These were gestures of gratitude and respect, of course, but also desire for intimacy; previously Dorothea's need to control had not always left space for such overtures from others. In her weakness, others could take initiatives. Above all, many saw her photography as a national resource and felt that all America had an investment in this show coming off well.

EVEN NOW, DOROTHEA was not left free to concentrate entirely on her own work, or even her dying, because of worry about the mental health of her stepson Ross Taylor. The most conspicuously talented, and quite possibly the favored child of the blended family, he had become an internationally known musician, ending his career as the principal French horn player of the San Francisco Symphony Orchestra.[40] When Dorothea came into his life, he was ten, and his mixed experience with her was typical among her stepchildren: She blew up over small infractions, but she was the one who noticed and encouraged his musical talent. At fifteen, he played Mozart's Third Concerto for Horn with the UCB Symphony Orchestra, conducted by Albert Elkus. Just as Paul had "pulled strings" to get Dan into the army, he arranged to get Ross into the army band so he would not be in combat.[41] After the war, he studied at Juilliard, and in his second year there played with the New York Philharmonic. He married Anne Wegman, affectionately known as "Onnie," a concert singer and the daughter of San Francisco Symphony Orchestra's second violinist. In 1950, he joined the Cleveland Symphony Orchestra and in 1955 the San Francisco. Extremely productive, he became a highly regarded teacher and made over 150 transcriptions and arrangements for different instrumentations.

Paul and Dorothea were, of course, delighted when he returned to the area with Onnie and their three children. But Ross had hesitated to make the move because of friction with his stepmother, and the fact that Dorothea did not take an instant liking to Onnie. Onnie's feelings were divided: She found Dorothea generous but also intimidating. The Ross Taylors tried to limit their Berkeley visits to the big holiday occasions.

A tense and brittle personality, Ross never had an easy time with his conductors. He considered Cleveland's George Szell dictatorial, San Francisco's Enrique Jordá an inferior musician, and Jordá's replacement, Jozef Krips, also inadequate. Ross dealt with stress by drinking, and in San Francisco he began an extramarital affair. He showed symptoms of what his sister, psychotherapist Margot Fanger, considered adult-onset manic depression. Medication brought some relief inconsistently. In the early 1960s, his depression intensified and his manic periods became more frequent and more extreme. He could not stop talking and inhabited "another world," imagining himself "with the greats of all time," an alarmed Dorothea wrote to Margot.[42]

Despite the family's alarm and vigilance, Ross was found dead at age forty-one in September 1964, a death attributed to mixing liquor and psychoactive drugs. Many considered it a suicide, although some family members insist it was an accident, but in any case the combination of mental illness, drugs, and drinking was toxic. His death devastated many: his mother, Katharine; his father and stepmother; his wife; his two sisters, especially Margot, who felt very close to him; his children, aged twelve, ten, and six; his friend Rondal Partridge, who had tried to save him; and his musician colleagues.[43] Coming shortly after Dorothea's cancer diagnosis, the loss devastated Paul and Dorothea.[44]

THE LAST YEAR of Dorothea's life and the progress of her disease were documented, inadvertently and impressionistically, by the KQED taping. Twice weekly the miserable dilations of her esophagus in an effort to make eating possible.[45] Cobalt radiation therapy at Merritt Hospital five days a week for six to eight weeks. She was emaciated, and for pain she took Librium—a tranquilizer, not a potent painkiller. (She clipped a newspaper article about Cicely Saunders, a founder of the hospice movement, who advocated using heroin for pain in the terminally ill.) She located herself for a caller as "sitting on my couch of pain."[46] For the first time, she and Paul had Thanksgiving dinner alone. Yet once again, the cobalt therapy seemed to help and she returned to work on the exhibit.

In the fall of 1964, she could work steadily on some days, taking little breaks, eating snacks. "I think I've gotta stop a few minutes, because I am beginning to get little knots again." She would eat cheese cut into little pieces and some buttered bread and even gained some weight. She joked. Family members sang to her, "Golden Vanity" and "Lowland, Lowland," and she complained, "Nobody asks *me* to sing I notice."[47] She laughed about the fact that Imogen Cunningham still didn't drive, "still going around on buses. With cameras. But she's very smart about hitching rides . . . it's something like a monkey going from tree to tree. She'll call you up and say I'm coming to see you. Someone is dropping me at your gate. I'll only be there twenty-five minutes because someone is picking me up."[48] With the filmmakers, she discussed factional fights at KQED and with Conrat discussed what public radio could be. She was still cooking, though mainly for others, and giving away her treasures to her children. Margot admired some blue bowls from Egypt, and Dorothea insisted that she take them all: "Giving one is no good."[49]

She became increasingly dependent on Helen Dixon for help—cleaning, shopping, cooking, providing gossip, and bringing the grandchildren over. Many friends and neighbors also pitched in. By the winter of 1964, she could eat only ice cream and liquids, especially Helen's chicken soup. Being denied food was what she found hardest.[50] She had shifted from Librium to Percodan, but she continued to do some gardening. On some days, her energy level made some expect her to beat the cancer.[51]

And she continued to be gripped by the civil rights movement, which went a good distance to overcome her anxiety about sharp conflict. These good feelings—feelings that boosted her will to live—were temporarily crushed by a repression very close to home. The dean of students at Berkeley banned from campus the information tables at which students recruited for political causes, notably the civil rights movement, which was now appealing for volunteers to go to the South and participate in nonviolent resistance. The dean's move, foolish as well as unjustified, created the Free Speech Movement, which gained overwhelming student support from the Right as well as the Left. The chancellor, Paul's former student and collaborator, Clark Kerr, defended the dean's thoughtless order. In early December 1964, with students conducting a sit-in, he panicked. Instead of listening and negotiating, he ordered police to remove the students, a task accomplished with dogs and considerable brutality. Dorothea and Paul were horrified. Just a few years before, they had been thrilled when he became chancellor.[52] Now Lange predicted, correctly, that the violence would never be forgotten, "Clark Kerr will never get out from under that image," she said.[53]

The downward slope of her energy was erratic rather than steady, and the Berkeley fiasco probably contributed to a low point in early December. She had Paul write a letter to the children, explaining that Christmas would be minimal and that she had to overlook some birthdays—things that might be normal behavior from others were for Dorothea a signal of defeat.[54] But she sprang back again, and Christmas turned out festive after all. "We said it would be quiet, but it made itself, and came out pretty much as always, as the family made it for us. You would have had a wrench," she wrote Margot, "to see Wim [Onnie's father] and Paulie [Ross's son] play duets. . . . Ross . . . was here with the music. . . ."[55]

In February 1965 came another family blow: Dan and Mia were divorcing. They knew how badly Dorothea would take it and had kept the news from her for several months. Dorothea loved Mia and thought the divorce another of Dan's failures. She never knew that John and Helen also divorced—they told no one until after Dorothea's death. By March, she was "losing ground everyday a little. . . . I've always had immense physical reserves, for a person who has such a bad body but it won't last too long. . . . Sometimes it comes over me in a wave but generally it's all right. I've accepted it, I have to find the right way through it, you know, so it isn't horrible, and I have help."[56] But some of this was wishful thinking. She became more irritable and once actually hit out at Paul. "I watch my temper every second . . . I am not ready. The other day, I turned around, I punched on Paul. And I saw myself do it, real Jekyll and Hyde . . . it's that opium that I take."

Yet she prepared for death as carefully as for a photo shoot. She dictated to Paul a list of those to whom she wanted to bequeath photographs and art objects. One list contains seventy-one names, from family and closest friends to Rexford Tugwell, Arthur Raper, and Romana Javitz, and other scraps of paper hold more names. She usually specified a particular photograph for each individual. To the Clausens went a photograph of her beloved live oak. Phil Green of KQED was to get a photograph of an endless highway. To cousin Minelda she bequeathed an Egyptian woman. Some, like John Szarkowski, were invited to choose the print they wanted. As people visited, she gave them items on the spot: pottery, baskets, wall hangings. Two years after her death, Paul was still distributing these gifts.

Another list surfaced in her papers, made before the cancer diagnosis, yet part of a summing up before death. Titled "People who loved me," it could have seemed egotistical to those who did not know her well. Those who did, however, knew that Dorothea was driven by ambition but also by self-doubt and the early lesson that only self-reliance is reliable; she was never entirely able to trust that others could be counted on. As the list grew, it became a larger statement of gratitude, the acknowledgments for a life. It started in Hoboken, listing "mother, uncle John, Sophie," "little brother for goodness," Caroline "for reliance," and Fronsie " for companionship . . . her vision, my trust." She listed her godmother, Emily Sanderfield, "for patience and quietude," photographer-employer Spencer-Beatty "for grit," and "Genthe for?" She remembered two New York boyfriends—"Landon for devotion, sculptor for love." (Had she forgotten the sculptor's name?) The list told me some things I already knew, such as her continuing sense of Martin as "little brother," and some things that were surprising, such as the question mark after Genthe's name, and the distinction between love and devotion on the part of boyfriends. Her adult family members had no reasons after their names, a strong statement in itself, and, surprisingly, she placed Steichen between Maynard and Paul. There was no mention of Stryker; perhaps she had not completely forgiven him after all. Last on the list were "the power of prayer" and "Isadora Duncan for a lift unto the heavens clear of the known earth." She was acknowledging gifts, remembering whom she loved as much as those who loved her. Perhaps her closeness to death also accounts for her reference to prayer, the first since she was a child.[57]

LANGE'S LAST PROJECT was a photo-essay about freedom. Its material subject was her extended family—in two locations: the garden at Euclid Street and the Steep Ravine cabin. But she insisted that the project was not about family, or love, or togetherness, or natural beauty, but about freedom and growth: "The circumstances under which people, children and their parents and their friends, feel unlocked and free. What brings it about?"[58] Attempting to visualize a utopian moment, she drew on the bohemian values of her youth and her abiding anxiety about urban life. At the same time, the project came from her grandmotherhood; young children were central to it because their capacity for freedom is so close to the surface and their growth so visible. Over the years, she had many times photographed a favorite tree in back of the house, a live oak, and its growth fused in her visual consciousness with that of her grandchildren. Her photographic plan incorporated that tree, her garden, the cabin, and the rocky Marin coast as symbolic elements. But now she understood these environments through a Spinoza-like, pantheistic sensibility, seeing the sacred in all living things.

24.5. GRANDDAUGHTER LISA, BETWEEN 1957 AND 1964

You approach the Steep Ravine cabins from a high cliff, looking down at a spectacular piece of rocky shoreline. Their cabin was the closest to the ocean and "the spray sometimes comes right to the door," Dorothea wrote delightedly.[59] Considering the dramatic setting, the place was quite accessible— only one hundred yards from where you left the car. Dorothea had no trouble with the walk until very late in her life, when general weakness, not her bad

24.6. STEEP RAVINE, BETWEEN 1957 AND 1964

leg, made her need help. Once during a big storm, she and Paul drove up to the cabin to see "the ocean in full action . . . the seas . . . came over the dunes and into the village of Stinson itself." Paul loved to sit with his back against a warm rock to do "his solitary thinking," Dorothea reported.[60]

Dorothea believed that people changed when they came to the cabin. They moved and stood differently—sliding into what she had called in her studio period their "natural body language." The children became more independent, less restless, and did not fight. They explored and invented games. The water was too cold for most adults, but Paul sometimes waded in with the grandchildren. Dorothea made hundreds of photographs of children there— her grandchildren, Partridge grandchildren, visiting children. Sleeping space was limited, so she and Paul formed the habit of taking several grandchildren at a time to the cabin for a weekend; sometimes their parents drove out for the day on Sunday. These times figure vibrantly in the grandchildren's memories. They *occupied* the site, made it theirs. In Dorothea's photographs, they are collecting rocks and shells, climbing, throwing rocks into the water, splashing, digging, watching tide-pool animals, reading in the sun, reading in a sleeping bag, collecting driftwood, balancing on a floating log, eating, napping. This is where Dorothea taught her grandchildren to see, they all remember. They picture her hunched over pebbles, seaweed, or small plants that usually went unnoticed. Here they could misbehave, refuse to fall asleep, with only mild reproof from Dorothea and Paul. These interactions were not necessarily ecstatic or intense, but they were by no means casual; in such exchanges, she was adding another dimension to freedom and growth: intimacy. Besides, the interactions were material for photography, and that was never casual for her.

Cabin life brought memories of trips with Maynard—swimming naked, camping, setting up a tepee. Now the children wore bathing suits, but the meaning was the same. Children entered a space where restrictions were relaxed. Leslie Dixon thought, in retrospect, that Dorothea and Paul were not cautious enough about watching the children as they played by the ocean.[61] If this is true, it speaks of Dorothea's strong impulse to let the children be unrestrained.

24.7. LANGE WITH GRANDDAUGHTER LISA, BETWEEN 1957 AND 1964

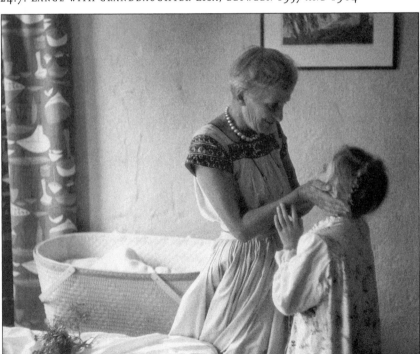

She used trips to the cabin to redo her flawed mothering. Her single-mindedness about this was so clear that everyone around her understood the behavior as compensating the grandchildren for what her children did not get. Some considered it expiation of guilt, but that is not quite right. Her retrospection was leading not to guilt, I think, because she knew she could not have made different decisions, but to sadness, about what she had lost as well as what she had denied her children.

She also understood that her family had invented "the cabin." "Listen," she wrote in one of her meditative notes to herself, "we build up the cabin in our minds, we <u>create</u> the myth of THE cabin in order to fill our <u>human needs</u>. Way deep back we <u>know</u> that these are a sad and sorry string of poor little shacks, with dirty windows, leaky roofs, staring blankly down over the rocks at the cold and restless sea. But our spirits thrive because here we have room to expand and generate and create our world."[62]

Dorothea's second-favorite place was her garden. She wished KQED could film there, but the background noise was too high. She conducted personal relationships not only with the live oak but with many of the garden's inhabitants. She was attached to a chopping block from an old Berryesa ranch that ended up in her garden. She gave some of her flowers names, reporting that "Miss Nettie O'Melvany" (daffodil) was "being sulky" this year and that "Miss Milly von Hoboken" (phlox) was in good health. She cherished a stump: "That's a very old friend of mine. When I pass that, I pat it . . . you know, like a friend." It was a gift in repayment of some photographic equipment she gave to a young photographer. "It was so heavy, and now through erosion, wind, rain, it's become much lighter. Isn't that funny what time does?"[63]


DOROTHEA SPOKE FREELY of dying, often in metaphorical language but without self-dramatization or apparent despair. She remarked that the silver Navajo bracelet she had worn every day for over forty years had worn away and now weighed much less, like the tree stump.[64]

After Szarkowski's last visit, she began losing the battle against dehydration and required intravenous liquids. The dehydration damaged her body systems. She tried to make plans for Paul—her love and her need to take charge mixed as she wrote one of his Asian contacts, requesting that Paul be invited on a big trip soon after her death, perhaps to Yemen.[65] Characteristically, she tried to control her dying as long as she could. She hated hospitals, having spent at least a year of her life in them, and insisted on staying home when her doctor wanted her hospitalized. She managed that until October 8, 1965, when she said to Paul, "We're licked," and accepted hospitalization. On the afternoon of the tenth, her physician said, "She has finished her work," but she remained energetic enough to spend an hour with her two sons and their wives in both serious and joking conversation, Dorothea saying, "I may be here three weeks yet." But she soon began hemorrhaging, then stopped breathing at 4:37 A.M., October 11. Her last words were, "It's in scale."[66]

# 25

# Photographer of Democracy

The moral function of art itself is to remove prejudice, do away with the scales that keep the eye from seeing, tear away the veils due to wont and custom, perfect the power to perceive. —*John Dewey* [1]

A portrait is a lesson on how one human being should approach another.—*Dorothea Lange, 1965* [2]

D
orothea Lange was America's preeminent photographer of democracy. She was also a woman of great passion. Passion is often associated with intimate relationships, particularly romantic, sexual love, and Lange's two marriages were both love affairs of intensity. Managing those relationships as well as two children and four stepchildren, a small business of her own, then one of the most demanding jobs imaginable, not to mention disability, gave rise to conflict, pain, and lasting hurt to others. Lange was no perfect woman. Her children bore some of the costs of her prodigious photographic contribution. Always insecure in some emotional dimensions, she could be manipulative, controlling, bossy, and explosive as well as generous, loyal, perceptive, and kind. She was sometimes at her worst with those closest to her. Some may judge her choices harshly, but no one can dispute that they were hard choices. Such a life could be a bit easier today, when there is less sex discrimination and more support for working mothers, but it would still, and perhaps always, be stressful. The responsibility I take is not to judge Lange or excuse her, but to present her in the round, so to speak. She constructed her life, as we all do, through choices and constraints. What was exceptional was her talent and her willingness to reach beyond limits.

Lange was equally passionate about democracy. Her greatest contribution was in seeing it not only as an American achievement but as an ideal not yet

reached, one that she had a responsibility to promote. She came to understand this responsibility as requiring her to act—against racism, against the
particularly intense exploitation of farmworkers, against the environmental
destruction of not just nature but also of community and beauty.

Her deepest passion, however, was for photography. In 1954 she responded
to an appeal by *U.S. Camera* to name the twenty-five greatest photographs of
all time. Her list included two that were indictments of injustice—a lynching
and police attacking strikes at Republic Steel in 1937. But mostly she listed
images of great beauty—a Stieglitz of popular trees, a Cartier-Bresson of
children playing, an Ansel Adams of Alaskan mountains, a Max Yavno of a
crowded beach, a Eugene Smith of Spanish women in mourning. Her tastes
were always eclectic, capacious. She loved to look—at everything.

Yet she was not tempted by the avant-garde. Unlike her close friend Imogen
Cunningham, unlike her European contemporaries Man Ray and Moholy-
Nagy, unlike Diane Arbus, she was not a photographer trying to startle. She
did not try collage, Surrealism, multiple exposure, or dizzying angles; her
ironies were soft and even her images of suffering were somehow hopeful.[3]
She rarely deserted classical compositional structures and elegant portraiture
as she made images of poverty full of information so as to provide evidence of
injustice.

Lange's most consistent aim was communication, but not by any means
exclusively in efforts to persuade. This goal prevailed as well in portraits of
studio clients and of Asian peasants. She disliked narcissism: ". . . you're not
talking to yourself, you're talking to others. And that's the difference between
being a professional and being an amateur."[4] Conceiving of herself partly as
an educator, she taught visual as much as social acuity. "If you can come close
to the truth there are consequences from the photographs. I'm not talking
about social work. It can be in the area of something that is extraordinarily
beautiful for its own sake . . . the consequence of its beauty is in the transmis-
sion of it."[5] In pursuit of communication, Lange recognized the limits of what
photography could do. She wanted her pictures "fortified" by words, and she
regretted that viewers rarely took in her words.

She rarely separated her artistic from her social commitment. Her vision of
democracy included democratizing art, making it possible for art to become
a public resource, part of the national heritage, as well as a luxury commodity. Having experienced the New Deal's expanded program of public arts, she
never stopped trying to find support for public photography. For her, there

was no "pure" art, as for Paul Taylor there was no "pure" scholarship, if purity meant avoiding citizenly responsibility. I am inclined to think that "pure" art is a myth, arising from a conception of the artist as floating unmoored to her society. Lange, by contrast, made no attempt to camouflage her moorings. Independent and original, she was nevertheless shaped by experience both individual and historical, from polio to the Cold War.

The democracy Lange honored was a particular, historical kind, not a timeless one. She was a member of a 1930s and 1940s popular front that joined liberals, leftists, industrial unionists, and some populists at a moment of unique political opportunity. These groups created the grassroots political pressure that pushed the United States some distance toward economic as well as political democracy.

But Lange's work transcended the popular-front vision. Influenced by the cosmopolitanism of her San Francisco artists' community, by multiracial California, and by Paul Taylor, Lange developed a commitment to antiracism that was extremely unusual among whites at the time. The California context also taught her that "race" in the United States was a matter not only of white and black but of many other groups as well, with unique histories. She made portraits of people of color that were rare at the time, portraying them as individuals, thoughtful, complex, and dignified (the hackneyed term cannot be avoided). They neither defer nor posture, at a time when mainstream white images of people of color were undignified in the extreme. They are hardworking and rational actors. They often display uncommon grace and elegance of movement; she could make bodies as expressive as faces. Lange and Taylor ceded some ground to political opportunism by featuring white "Okies" in their appeals for better treatment of farmworkers, but they did not surrender their commitment to advocating for "nonwhite" populations. They both challenged—Lange with particular bravery—the internment of 120,000 Japanese Americans, an extreme violation of both citizens' and human rights. They intended their work in Asia to continue this antiracism on an international scale.

Lange's respect for the farmworkers she was hired to photograph was part of a more general respect for labor. She refused to measure skill hierarchically. Where she could converse with her subjects, as in North Carolina, she took the trouble to learn what they did and to expose the expertise, planning, and problem solving involved.

Her assignment to document farm labor provided her the opportunity to bring women's work into visibility. Her moorings did not include a women's rights movement; the last one had peaked and then dwindled not long after she left her childhood home, and second-wave feminism arose after her death. So it is hardly surprising that she retained some Victorian notions of women as naturally nurturant, instinctive, self-sacrificing, and all-around softer than men—despite the fact that she herself was not like this. Her photography, however, subverted those beliefs. Her female subjects bear little resemblance to the stereotypical feminine; instead they are judicious, competent, and often powerful, like her male subjects. Few of her female subjects tip their heads in flirtatious, little-girl appeal. Their "domestic" labor is clearly arduous and skilled.

Despite her many images of suffering and sacrificing mothers, a modern and open attitude toward family structure shows in Lange's photographs. Just as she thought that her photography "revealed" her unrecognized love for her mother, so the photography "revealed" unconventional forms of family. Late in her life, Lange recognized that the gender ideology of her youth no longer fit. Speaking of a photograph of a shipyard worker made in 1944, Lange remarked, "She represents the emergence of another era, of a change in the way women live . . . the growth in political development."[6]

Lange was also more farsighted than most New Dealers in her environmental sensibility. At a time when the man-against-nature ethos still dominated, she saw and tried to show the cost of environmental destruction—the cost not only to "nature" but to human community and quality of life.

Lange's remarkable ability to see incited her to dream of more than she could accomplish. To the end of her life, she longed for more time to work—not just more years to live but also time without interruptions. Always self-critical, she felt she was just beginning to explore the potential of still photography. And yet she enjoyed this restlessness. Admitting that she was "constantly restless and probing and frantic," she nevertheless affirmed her choices: "that way of life and working keeps you alive, no boredom descends on you. You're right out on the thin edge, all the time, where you're unprotected, defenseless, where it's going to hurt you, but you're there by choice."[7]

LANGE LEFT MANY descendants, and I had the good fortune to interview some of them. I was impressed not only by their generosity and openness toward me but also by their scrupulous and balanced perspective on her. No one would suggest that she was easygoing, yet her children, stepchildren, and grandchildren spoke of her warmth, her encouragement, and what they had learned from her, as well as of her infuriating need to control. All found their sense of her changed a bit when her biographer Milton Meltzer discovered the truth about her father, finding in it a clue to her insecurities. Paul Taylor in particular was deeply hurt that she had not trusted him with that truth. He continued to live with Dorrie, in a sense, for years after her death, as he parceled out her gifts, disposed of her photography and papers, and promoted her ideas. But he never ceased his activist intellectual work, and he continued advocating for land reform and supporting American farmworkers as they finally built a union—the United Farm Workers.

The most alienated family member was the one who agonized most over Dorothea's death: her stepdaughter Consie. She decided that it would be hypocritical to attend the memorial service, but remained tortured, never fully at rest with that decision.[8] Paul, always judgmental, responded angrily to Consie's refusal, and as a result of his response, Consie would not attend his memorial, either. For her, the family only brought pain.

AT LANGE'S DEATH, a stream of obituaries and other tributes began to appear in newspapers, magazines, and letters to Paul. The *San Francisco Chronicle* and the Japanese American *Nichi Bei Times* put her death on the front page.[9] A memorial service held a few weeks after she died drew hundreds. Dan Dixon spoke eloquently for the family. Critic Allan Temko spoke, repeating the widespread belief that she was responsible for the color of the Golden Gate Bridge and praising her eye for beauty, even in "humble cooking utensils assembled nobly at a primitive family hearth." The California Wind Quintet played a Mozart quintet arranged by Ross Taylor. Christina Page Gardner memorialized her by mentioning three news items: Sonoma County, where she lived, was to get $200,000 in federal aid to build portable dwelling units for farmworkers; the last claims for damages to Japanese Americans from the internship were paid; and "Two Ku Klux Klansmen, who were acquitted in the nightrider killing of a Negro educator last year, attacked a Negro photographer yesterday and were promptly jailed. The photographer was also arrested." Most telling, perhaps, is that Christina did not need to say more—everyone knew these events' relevance to Lange.

Yet outside the Bay Area, she was well known only in the world of photography at the time of her death. The *New York Times* obituary repeated a common mistake about her work: DOROTHEA LANGE IS DEAD AT 70; CHRONICLED DUST BOWL WOES. Tributes by people who knew her well were, of course, more accurate: For Magnum, Wayne Miller wrote, "Although physically small and at times fragile, she was a giant made of spring steel."[10]

Her recognition has grown steeply since her death, and in the first years, Paul was partly responsible. Promoting her became a job almost as important as his advocacy of the 160-acre limit. He tried several strategies for getting an urban photography project started. He systematically gathered information from Dorothea's photography friends to create an exact chronology of her life. Whenever journalists, scholars, or curators wanted information, he wrote them at length.

It does not diminish his work to recognize that Lange's fame would have developed even without him. She was "discovered" by the progressive activists of the civil rights, the anti–Vietnam War, and the women's movements during the 1960s and 1970s. Today, her work is part of the classic canon of American art and international photography. Her name is frequently invoked to refer to a classic, realist feel in documentary, as in "There's a Dorothea Lange feel to his pictures."[11] The National Endowment for the Humanities includes Lange photographs in its mass distribution of American art to schools.[12] The famed German art publisher Taschen includes a chapter on Lange in its collection on twenty-five *Photographic Icons*. Her photographs are staples in textbooks, articles, and on Web sites about the Depression in particular and American history more generally. *Migrant Mother* is often included as the only nonjournalistic iconic photograph in a group including images of raising the flag at Iwo Jima, the spaceship *Challenger* explosion, JFK's son saluting his father's coffin, and the Kent State shooting.[13] It is an icon in many countries besides the United States. The high-gloss art market has now taken in her vintage photographs and they regularly sell for six-figure sums.

Since so much of her work is in the public domain, it is repeatedly used for purposes alien to hers. Consider just the single photograph, *Migrant Mother*.[14] Both profit and nonprofit businesses raise funds by selling prints of it, at prices from $9.98 to $755. At least one enterprise offers a "colorized" print of *Migrant Mother*.[15] Others sell postcards and notecards featuring it. The photograph has been used to promote the Socialist party, the Black Panther party, the ACLU, myriad NGOs, academic conferences, and women's movement and charity appeals and events. It appears on the Web sites of several countries and as the cover of an issue of the *Archives of Pediatric Adolescent Medicine*.[16] It advertises Samsonite luggage, antiwrinkle cosmetics, the Jehovah's Witnesses, the Salvation Army, the Gap, and hundreds of commodities. It is featured on GodWeb. Lange was right that it was no longer her photograph.

Much of her photography was originally published as authorless, so many fewer people know her name than know her photographs. But that, too, is changing. She figures repeatedly in halls of fame and on lists of great women, schoolchildren's heroes, and photographs that changed the world; Governor Schwarzenegger announced her induction into California's Hall of Fame in 2008.[17] She is the subject of dozens of dissertations and theses, thousands of college papers and school reports. There are plays about her, both amateur and professional, and several films. A public elementary school has been named for her in Nipomo, California. Her name is used as a comparison or metaphor, almost always complimentarily, to invoke a certain style and substance: realist photographs of the poor, photos where composition and bodies indicate anxiety or hard work or both, with restrained beauty.

What Lange would have considered her biggest failure was not personal but collective: that an urban photography project never materialized. More than seventy years since the New Deal, the United States has not generated large-scale public support for photography or the arts in general. Documentary photography thrives nevertheless, though very few practitioners can earn a living by doing it. Photographs and critics frequently mention Lange as source and inspiration. The next-best thing to Project One was the 1990 initiation of the twenty-thousand-dollar Lange-Taylor Prize for documentary collaboration between a photographer and a writer, supported by the Center for Documentary Studies at Duke University.[18] Winners have documented daily life in the Mississippi Delta, the struggle to survive in Cuba since the fall of the Soviet Union, Mayan survival in Guatemala City, Salvadoran street gangs, and living with mental illness.

DOROTHEA LANGE'S PHOTOGRAPHS have never been more immediately relevant. I never anticipated finishing this book under economic conditions resembling those she felt and illustrated. As I write, many are calling for "another Dorothea Lange" to document and communicate the impoverishment and fear that so many are experiencing. Yet her photographs have had an extraordinary impact even in the most prosperous of times; they may well live forever. There will always be a need to be reminded that beauty can be found in unlikely places, that we must learn to see beyond the limits of the conventional and the expected. Such indelible images mean more, not less, if we understand how they came to exist. They were produced not by a faultless genius who could remain above the wounds, failings, and sins that afflict the rest of us, but by a fallible and hardworking woman. They were produced also by the historical times she lived in, times optimistic and pessimistic, times that honored generous, compassionate, and respectful impulses of Americans and times that encouraged the closed, fearful, and intolerant. Lange's photographs will always evoke the best of American democracy.

# LANGE'S PHOTOGRAPH
## CAPTIONS

page xii. Destitute pea pickers in California. Mother of seven children. Age thirty-two.

9.4 Ditch bank housing for Mexican field workers. Imperial Valley, California.

9.5 Water supply: an open settling basin from the irrigation ditch in a California squatter camp near Calipatria.

9.7 Family of nine from Fort Smith, Arkansas, trying to repair their car on road between Phoenix and Yuma, Arizona. On their way to try to find work in the California harvests.

12.1 Near Meloland, Imperial Valley. Large scale agriculture. Gang labor, Mexican and white, from the Southwest. Pull, clean, tie and crate carrots for the eastern market for eleven cents per crate of forty-eight bunches. Many can make barely one dollar a day. Heavy oversupply of labor and competition for jobs is keen.

12.2 Filipinos cutting lettuce.

12.3 Filipino crew of fifty-five boys cutting and loading lettuce.

12.4 Cotton weighing. South Texas.

12.5 "Cleanliness." Southern California. Oklahoma refugees camping in Imperial Valley, California.

12.6 1936 drought refugee from Polk, Missouri. Awaiting the opening of orange picking season at Porterville, California.

12.7 Cotton picker. Southern San Joaquin Valley, California.

14.2 *Waiting for the semi-monthly relief checks at Calipatria. Typical story: 15 years ago they owned farms in Oklahoma. Lost them through foreclosure when cotton prices fell after the

*These captions are taken from Lange's "general captions" that apply to more than one photograph.

war. Became tenants and sharecroppers. With drought and dust they came West—1934–1937. Never before left the county where they were born; now, although in California over a year, they haven't been continuously resident in any single county long enough to become legal resident. Reason: migratory agricultural laborers.

14.3 Drought refugees from Oklahoma camping by the roadside. They hope to work in the cotton fields. There are seven in family. Blythe, California

14.4 Drought refugees from Oklahoma camping by the roadside. They hope to work in the cotton fields. The official at the border (California-Arizona) inspection service said that on this day, August 17, 1936, twenty-three car loads and truck loads of migrant families out of the drought counties of Oklahoma and Arkansas had passed through that station entering California up to 3 o'clock in the afternoon

14.5 Power farming displaces tenants from the land in dry cotton area. Childress County, Texas Panhandle.

14.6 The highway going West. US 80 near Lordsburg, New Mexico.

15.1 Butter bean vines across the porch. Negro quarter in Memphis, Tennessee.

15.2 Young sharecropper and his first child. Hillside Farm. Person County, North Carolina.

15.3 Tenant farmer. Chatham County, North Carolina.

15.4 Construction detail of double log cabin of Negro share tenants. The cowhide was hung there after being dried on a barn to be used as floor covering. Shelf shows churn, also bucket of water in which baby's bottle is kept cool. Person County, North Carolina.

15.6 *Mr. Whitfield is topping, and at the same time worming. The children are looking for worms. The 3-1/2 year old girl found two. Her father says she is learning, but she is a little too rough with the tobacco leaves and bruises them. The children like to go to the field with their father. When the mother goes, the oldest girl has to stay at home with the baby. The mother has helped a "right smart" this year because Mr. Whitfield has been "falling off." She thinks it is because he is so worried over paying the doctor and the hospital bills.

18.1 South of Eloy, Pinal County, Arizona. Ten-year-old migratory Mexican cotton picker. He was born in Tucson. He is fixing the family car. He does not go to school now, but when he did go was in grade 1-A. Says (in Spanish) "I do not go to school because my father wishes my aid in picking cotton." On preceding day he picked 25 pounds of Pima cotton.

18.2 On Arizona Highway 87, south of Chandler. Maricopa County, Arizona. Children in a democracy. A migratory family living in a trailer in an open field. No sanitation, no water. They came from Amarillo, Texas. Pulled bolls near Amarillo, picked cotton near Roswell, New Mexico, and in Arizona. Plan to return to Amarillo at close of cotton picking season for work on WPA.

24.1 Home.


### Inserts

Plate 5. "Skid Row." Howard Street, San Francisco, California.

Plate 6. Cortaro Farms, Pinal County, Arizona. Migratory cotton picker on Cortaro Farms.

Plate 7. Migratory woman, Greek, living in a cotton camp near Exeter, California.

Plate 9. A grandmother from Oklahoma. She works in the California pea fields. Calipatria, California.

Plate 10. Cotton worker in Sunday clothes. Near Blytheville, Arkansas.

Plate 11. Near Douglas, Georgia. "You don't have to worriate so much and you've got time to raise somp'n to eat." The program to eliminate the risk and uncertainty of a one-crop system meets the approval of this sharecropper. She sits on the porch and sorts tobacco.

Plate 13. Tent interior in a labor contractor's camp, showing household equipment. Near Westley, California.

Plate 15. Zollie Lyon, Negro sharecropper, home from the field for dinner at noontime, with his wife and part of his family. Note dog run. 1939, Wake County, North Carolina.

Plate 16. *One of Chris Adolph's younger children. Farm Security Administration Rehabilitation clients. Came to the Yakima Valley in 1937 from Bethune, Kit Carson County, Colorado. He owned his own farm there and he had lived there all his life. Drought forced him out with his wife and 8 children. His wife had been a school teacher. . . . "I've broke thousands of acres of sod. The dust got so bad that we had to sleep with wet cloths over our faces."

Plate 17. Calipatria, Imperial Valley, in Farm Security Administration (FSA) emergency migratory labor camp. Daughter of ex-tenant farmers on thirds and fourths in cotton. Had fifty dollars when set out. Went to Phoenix, picked cotton, pulled bolls made eighty cents a day with two people pulling bolls. Stayed until school closed. Went to Idaho, picked peas until August. Left McCall with forty dollars "in hand." Went to Cedar City and Parowan, Utah, a distance of 700 miles. Picked peas through September. Went to Hollister, California. Picked peas through October. Left Hollister for Calipatria for early peas which froze. Now receiving Farm Security Administration food grant and waiting for work to begin. "Back in Oklahoma, we are sinking. You work your head off for a crop and then see it burn up. You live in debts that you can never get out of. This isn't a good life, but I say that it's a better life than it was."

Plate 18. Migratory Mexican field worker's home on the edge of a frozen pea field.

Plate 19. Destitute family. Five children, aged two to seventeen years.

Plate 20. A grandmother washing clothes in a migrant camp. Stanislaus County, California.

Plate 21. Daughter of Negro tenant churning butter.

Plate 22. Loading cotton.

Plate 23. Loading cotton.

Plate 24. *Beginning at the bottom of the [tobacco] plant, the leaves are stripped; usually 2 or 3 bottom leaves are removed at one priming. Only the rip[e] leaves are primed, and ripeness is determined by the color of the leaf. When ripe, the leaves are pale yellow in color, although they are often difficult to distinguish from the green leaves. Hence the job of priming is something of an art, which is left to the men of the family, or to those "women folks" who are skilled at it. In the field picture, the men are priming for the second time, the "first primings," or sand leaves, having been removed.

Plate 25. Plantation owner.

Plate 27. Migrant agricultural worker in Marysville migrant camp (trying to figure out his year's earnings). California.

Plate 30. Roadside meeting with Durham County farmer. North Carolina. He gives road directions by drawing in dirt with stick.

Plate 31. Drought refugees from Texas encamped in California near Exeter. Seven in family.

Plate 32. "Victory through Christ" Society holding its Sunday Morning Revival in a garage. Dos Palos, California. Testimony: "He's such a wonderful savior, Glory to God. I'm so glad I came to home. Praise God. His love is so wonderful. He's coming soon. I want to praise the Lord for what he is to me. He saved me one time and filled me with the Holy Ghost. Hallalulah! He will fill your heart today with overflowing. Bless His Holy name."

Plate 45. *Negro tenant family who barely lives on the earnings of fifty dollars a year. They pay a standing rent. There are five children working; ages from seven to fourteen. The older children cultivating, the younger children hoeing and chopping.

# ACKNOWLEDGMENTS

This book, more than any other I've done, rests on the generosity and knowledge of others, some old friends and some new acquaintances. In fact, my first thanks go to someone I never met, Henry Mayer. A superb biographer, he had embarked on a study of the life of Dorothea Lange when he met premature death from a heart attack. Some of his many friends sought a writer who could make use of the materials he had collected, their path led to me, and I rather hesitatingly agreed to consider the project. In doing that I met his wife, Betsy Anderson Mayer, a woman of uncommon generosity who gave me not only his papers but also his splendid collection of books of Lange's photography. Betsy also became a friend and I am pleased finally to be able to thank her with this book.

I could not have written this book without the help of Dorothea Lange's descendants. I want to thank them not only for their time but also for their thoughtful answers to my many questions, some of them intrusive. Many of them impressed me with their nuanced, judicious, and balanced appraisals and memories. I want to thank the late Daniel Dixon, and to express my regret that he did not live to see this book and tell me what he thought of it; Helen and John Dixon; Donald and Kate Fanger; Becky Jenkins; Katharine Taylor Loesch; Betsy, Meg, and Rondal Partridge; Dyanna, Onnie, and Paul Wegman Taylor. Others who were part of an extended Lange/Taylor family offered help, too, and I want to thank Mary and Malcolm Collier, Nora Elliott, Christina Gardner, Walter Goldschmidt, Pirkle Jones, Jennifer McFarland, Ray Marshall, Edee and Jack Mezirow, Helen Nestor, and the late Alan Temko. Lange's previous biographer, Milton Meltzer, was kind enough to talk with me when I was in an early stage of research.

Scholars of Lange and in related fields also provided a great deal of help. I am especially grateful to Sally Stein, not only because her work on Lange is brilliant but also for providing me with an empty apartment for several weeks of work at the Getty Research Institute. Others read sections of the book for me and saved me from errors and/or gave me tips and materials; my thanks to Tom Bender, Arthur Bleich, Gray Brechin, Nick Cullather, Pete Daniel, Ellen Eisenberg, Donald Fanger, Jess Gilbert, Rosie Hunter, Hadassa Kosak, Judith Walzer Leavitt, Lewis Leavitt, David Ludden, Eric Meeks, Melissa Milewski, Greg Robinson, Anne Firor Scott, and Mike Wallace. In working with me on Lange's photographs of the Japanese American internment for *Impounded*, Gary Okihiro was able to improve slightly my photographic sophistication and understanding of the Japanese American internment. I thank him also for his willingness to undertake a project with someone who was at first a stranger.

Allen Hunter, Elinor Langer, Bob Weil, and Laura Wexler read the whole damn thing, and their comments were invaluable. Barbara Forrest, Judy Leavitt, and Allen looked at photographs with me and reduced somewhat my tendency to agonize over choices. Helen Dixon, Becky Jenkins, Betsy, Meg and Rondal Partridge, and Dyanna Taylor helped me over and over again. Joyce Seltzer has my continuing gratitude for helping me become a better writer. A million thanks.

I want to thank also the archivists and graduate students who helped me with the research: Robin Doolin, Drew Johnson, Alice Hudson, Andrew Lee, Bill McMorris, Marcela Echeverri, Jack von Euw, Ivy Klenetsky, Melissa Milewski, Ana-maria Quezada and Micaela Sullivan-Fowler. Michelle Chase did some painstaking scans for me. Archivists Beverly Brannan and Nicholas Natanson not only helped me find materials but as scholars, educated me as well.

The collective thanks I owe are no less fervent. First and foremost to my treasured colleagues in the history department and to colleagues from other departments from whom I have learned. Thanks to the NYU graduate school for providing me with some time to write this book. Thanks to the Cullman Center at the New York Public Library for a year's fellowship and nurturing conditions for work. Thanks to the staff of W. W. Norton, especially Lucas Wittmann for his care and thoughtfulness with incessant details and Tom Mayer (in a lovely coincidence, the son of Henry Mayer, whose project I am in some sense completing). To Judy Dater, Gail Saliterman, Barrie Thorne, and the late Peter Lyman, thanks for putting me up. And my gratitude also to those who have heard me talk about Lange, displayed interest, and offered comments or asked difficult questions. These include many who just listened to lectures but especially friends whose intellectual rigor, aesthetic sensibility, and sense of justice have shaped my writing. Thank you to Allen Hunter above all, and to Ros Baxandall, Dick Cluster, Suzanne Desan, Sara Evans, Nancy Falk, Barbara Forrest, Susan Friedman, Ed Friedman, Linda Kerber, Alice Kessler-Harris, Elinor Langer, Judy Leavitt, Lewis Leavitt, Gerda Lerner, Elaine Tyler May, Molly Nolan, Elizabeth Schneider, Joyce Seltzer, Shifra Sharlin, Charlotte Sheedy, Erik and Marcia Wright.

Finally, I have been blessed with an agent from heaven, Charlotte Sheedy. My editor, Bob Weil, is a rare jewel today, an editor who edited every page of my third-from-last draft, and the book is much better because of his superb skill and sensibility. Thank you, thank you, Bob and Charlotte.

# NOTE ON PHOTOGRAPHS AND QUOTATIONS

Choosing which of Lange's tens of thousands of photographs to include in this book was not an easy undertaking. I accomplished the task only by concluding that it was impossible to illustrate the full range of her subject matter and technique. I used several intersecting criteria for the selection: I wanted a balance of well-known, slightly known, and unknown photographs. I wanted to represent her range of subjects along several lines: in sociological terms—e.g., women and men, young and old people; in aspects of life—e.g., labor and living conditions; in geographical terms—e.g., East and West, U.S. and foreign; in genre—e.g., portraits, still lifes; in themes—e.g., relationships with others and with the photographer; in political and ethical concerns—e.g., social injustice, environmental destruction. My choices were further limited by a need to keep the cost of the book and my own expenditure under control. My apologies to those who find their favorite Lange photographs or themes not included.

The photographs are not presented strictly chronologically. Because some photographs must do double duty—for example, illustrate both genre and subject matter—I deliberately placed some where they fit my discussion of an issue rather than where they fit chronologically.

Sources for the photographs are identified separately after the notes.

In much of this book, I relied on taped interviews, sometimes transcribed, with Lange, her colleagues, and her family members. In quoting from interviews, I have corrected spelling and punctuation and have eliminated ellipses, "uh," and pauses so as to make the statements easier to understand. Quotations from written sources are given exactly as they appear in the original.

# NOTES

LoC             Library of Congress, Prints and Photographs Division. All Lange images have the prefix LC-USF34-, followed by the photograph number cited.

MD              Maynard Dixon

MD Diary        Chronological notes by Maynard Dixon in box 2, Dixon Papers, mss. 73/8, Bancroft

MM              Milton Meltzer

NARA            National Archives, College Park, Maryland

OM              Oakland Museum Dorothea Lange Archive

OWI             Office of War Information

PST             Paul Schuster Taylor

PST Bancroft    Paul Schuster Taylor Papers, mss. 84/38, Bancroft Library, University of California/Berkeley

Riess           Suzanne Riess, ed., "Dorothea Lange: The Making of a Documentary Photographer," interview transcript, Berkeley, 1968, for the University of California/Berkeley Regional Oral History Office, Earl Warren Oral History Project

Riess/PST       Suzanne Riess, ed., "Paul Schuster Taylor: California Social Scientist," interview transcript, 3 vols., Berkeley 1973, for the University of California/Berkeley Regional Oral History Office, Earl Warren Oral History Project

RP              Rondal Partridge

RS              Roy Stryker

RS mss.         Roy Stryker papers, University of Louisville, also on microfilm at LoC

TH              Therese Heyman. All her interview transcripts are at OM

UCB             University of California/Berkeley

UNC             University of North Carolina, Southern History Collection photographs

### Introduction: "A Camera Is a Tool for Learning How to See . . ."

1. Lange believed that Max Ernst was the author of this phrase but she was not sure and I was unable to track it down.

2. KQED 6.

3. Many of those familiar with the *Migrant Mother* picture took from it, unconsciously, the impression that it is a photograph of Lange herself, and they imagine her as a poor, Mother Earth sort of woman.

4. Evans quoted in Naomi Rosenblum, "Documentary Photography: A Historical Survey," in *Changing Chicago: A Photodocumentary* (Urbana: University of Illinois Press, 1989), 8; Daumier and Moholy-Nagy quoted in John Szarkowski, ed., *Looking at Photographs* (New York: Museum of Modern Art, 1973), 72, 88.

5. KQED 16.

6. Riess. All further quotations from Lange in this book come from this oral history unless otherwise noted.

7. Nat Herz, "Dorothea Lange in Perspective: A Reappraisal of the FSA and an Interview," *Infinity* 12, no. 4 (1963): 10.

8. *Jack Delano, Photographic Memories* (Washington, D.C.: Smithsonian Institution Press, 1997), 215.

9. Linda Nochlin, "The Realist Criminal," *Art in America*, September/October and November/December 1973, 58.

10. Judith Keller, ed., *Dorothea Lange: Photographs from the J. Paul Getty Museum* (Los Angeles: J. Paul Getty Museum, 2002), 100.

11. Linda Gordon, "Biography as Microhistory, Photography as Microhistory: Documentary Photographer Dorothea Lange as Subject and Agent of Microhistory," in *Small Worlds: Method, Meaning, and Narrative in Microhistory*, ed. James E. Brooks, Christopher R. DeCorse, and John Walton (Santa Fe: School for Advanced Research Press, 2007).

12. This is neither a psychological nor an art-historical analysis, for which I am not trained. Luckily I have been able to rely on some superb scholarship about Lange's photography: Robert Coles, untitled essay, in *Dorothea Lange, Photographs of a Lifetime* (Millerton, New York: Aperture, 1982); James C. Curtis, "Dorothea Lange, Migrant Mother, and the Culture of the Great Depression," *Winterthur Portfolio* (1986): 1–20; James Curtis, *Mind's Eye, Mind's Truth: FSA Photography Reconsidered* (Philadelphia: Temple University Press, 1989); Jacqueline Ellis, *Silent Witnesses: Representations of Working-Class Women in the United States* (Bowling Green, Ohio: Bowling Green University Popular Press, 1998); Therese Thau Heyman, ed., *Celebrating a Collection: The Work of Dorothea Lange* (Oakland, California: Oakland Museum, 1978); Therese Thau Heyman, Sandra S. Phillips, and John Szarkowski, eds., *Dorothea Lange: American Photographs* (San Francisco: San Francisco Museum of Modern Art and Chronicle Books, 1994); Karin Becker Ohrn, *Dorothea Lange and the Documentary Tradition* (Baton Rouge: Louisiana State University Press, 1980); Elizabeth Partridge, ed., *Dorothea Lange: A Visual Life* (Washington, D.C.: Smithsonian Institution Press, 1994); Naomi Rosenblum, "Modernist Eye, Responsive Heart: The Work of Dorothea Lange," in *Dorothea Lange: The Human Face* (Paris: NBC Editions, 1998); Carol Shloss, *In Visible Light: Photography and the American Writer, 1840–1940* (New York: Oxford University Press, 1987); Sally Stein, "On Location: The Placement (and Replacement) of California in 1930s Photography," in *Reading California: Art, Image, and Identity, 1900–2000*, ed. Stephanie Barron et al. (Los Angeles: University of California Press, 2000); Sally Stein, "Passing Likeness: Dorothea Lange's 'Migrant Mother' and the Paradox of Iconicity," in *Only Skin Deep: Changing Visions of the American Self*, ed. Coco Fusco and Brian Wallis (New York: Harry N. Abrams, 2003); Sally Stein, "Peculiar Grace: Dorothea Lange and the Testimony of the Body," in *Dorothea Lange: A Visual Life*, ed. Partridge; Sally Stein, "Portraiture's Veil," in *Dorothea Lange: The Human Face* (Paris: NBC Editions, 1998); William Stott, "Introduction to a Never-Published Book of Dorothea Lange's Best Photographs of Depression America," *Exposure* 22 no. 3 (1984): 22–30; Karen Tsujimoto, *Dorothea Lange: Archive of an Artist* (Oakland, California: Oakland Museum, 1995); Charles Wollenberg, *Photographing the Second Gold Rush: Dorothea Lange and the Bay Area at War, 1941–1945* (Berkeley: Heyday Books, 1995).

13. KQED 24.

14. She went on to say, "He also trains his vision not to interpret in terms of what he *guesses* is the situation. . . ." KQED 14.

15. Richard Gregory, quoted in Atul Gawande, "The Itch," *The New Yorker,* June 30, 2008, 63.

16. KQED 17.


## Scene 1

1. Letters from students in OM and in JDC.


## 1. Child of Iron, Wounded

1. Riess, 17. This interview is my source for all of Lange's childhood memories, unless otherwise cited, but only direct quotes are attributed in the notes.

2. Bernard Friedrich Nutzhorn, Dorothea's paternal grandfather, came from Württemberg in 1859, calling himself a carpenter, but by 1864, when he became a U.S. citizen, he was operating a grocery store in the New York neighborhood now called SoHo. He married Dorothea Margaretta Fischer, born in Hannover, Lower Saxony, and brought to the United States by her parents. He soon bought property, moved to Hoboken, and opened a liquor warehouse as well as a grocery store. When he died in 1900, he left $15,000 in real estate and $500 in personal property—these amount to more than $332,000 and $11,000, respectively, today (not bad for an immigrant). They had three sons, and the second, Heinrich Martin Nutzhorn, born in 1868, became Dorothea's father. At about the same time, Friedrich Lange, Dorothea's maternal grandfather, emigrated from Oldenburg, also in Lower Saxony, and his future wife, Sophie Votteler, from Stuttgart. When they met, Sophie was a widow with a child—her first husband, Stefan Woll, had died young of consumption. She married Friedrich in 1866 and gave birth to five more children with him. He, too, was in business, a tea merchant in partnership with his brother Carl in Manhattan. Their first daughter, Johanna, born in 1873, became Dorothea's mother.

3. Dorothea's father had been married previously, but his wife died in childbirth, along with the infant, a year after they married.

4. Hoboken information was taken from the following sources: *History of the Municipalities of Hudson County, New Jersey, 1630–1923,* vol. 1 (New York: Lewis Historical Publishing Co., 1924); Patricia Florio Colrick, *Hoboken* (Charleston, South Carolina: Arcadia Publishing, 1999); Andrew L. Yarrow, "Hoboken," *New York Times,* November 15, 1985; and census publications.

5. HM interview with Joy Lange Boardman, October 14, 1999.

6. John was the father of the film actress Hope Lange (1931–2003), Dorothea's first cousin. Therese Heyman interview with David Lange, February 15, 1978, transcribed by Zoe Brown, in Dorothea Lange Archive, OM (cited).

7. Riess, 1.

8. The polio virus is excreted in human stools; the virus could enter the digestive tract through

contact with infected water or sewage or dirty diapers. John Rodman Paul, *A History of Poliomyelitis* (New Haven: Yale University Press, 1971), 1–2. This understanding of the transition from endemic to epidemic polio has now been challenged, however, by the finding of high polio rates in Uganda and India; see Anne Finger, *Elegy for a Disease: A Personal and Cultural History of Polio* (New York: St. Martin's Press, 2006), 46. In the first large American outbreak, 71 percent of the cases occurred in well-to-do or moderate-income families; see Vermont State Board of Health, *Infantile Paralysis in Vermont* (Burlington, Vermont, 1924), 23.

9. In New York City, for example, the incidence of polio was highest in bucolic Queens and Staten Island, lower in Manhattan.

10. Tony Gould, *A Summer Plague: Polio and Its Survivors* (New Haven: Yale University Press, 1995), 5; Paul, *Poliomyelitis*, 13; Fred Davis, *Passage Through Crisis: Polio Victims and Their Families* (Indianapolis: Bobbs-Merrill, 1963), 36–38; Marc Shell, *Polio and Its Aftermath: The Paralysis of Culture* (Cambridge: Harvard University Press, 2005), 67.

11. Paul, *Poliomyelitis*, 2–3.

12. Leonard Kriegel, *The Long Walk Home* (New York: Appleton-Century, 1964), 8. My description of a child's polio experience is also taken from Raymond Leslie Goldman, *Even the Night* (New York: Macmillan, 1947)—the polio memoir of a writer born in the same year as Lange, 1895, who developed the illness in 1899. Other useful polio memoirs include Alan Marshall, *I Can Jump Puddles* (Cleveland: World Publishing, 1956); Turnley Walker, *Rise Up and Walk* (New York: E. P. Dutton, 1950). Several studies synthesize many interviews and memoirs: Shell, *Polio and Its Aftermath;* Edmund J. Sass, *Polio's Legacy: An Oral History* (Lanham, Maryland: University Press of America, 1996; Finger, *Elegy for a Disease;* Davis, *Passage through Crisis;* Vermont State Board of Health, *Infantile Paralysis in Vermont;* Jill Lewis, unpublished memoir, and interviews with Jill Lewis, March and April 2007.

13. Quoted in Finger, *Elegy for a Disease*, 56–57.

14. Ibid.

15. Muirhead Little, "An Analysis of a Series of Cases of Infantile Paralysis, with some Notes on Treatment," *British Medical Journal* 2(1900); 581.

16. The mildest included applying "counter-irritants," such as mustard plasters or cupping, aimed at reducing the "congestion" of the spinal cord by bringing the blood to the surface, but physicians also tried bloodletting, withdrawing spinal fluid, purgatives, and enemas. Some of the more up-to-date experimented with using disinfectants inside the body; one tried a nasal spray of hydrogen peroxide, another ammonium salicylate. Others injected urotropin or Adrenalin into the spinal column. Still others used electric current. Naomi Rogers, *Dirt and Disease: Polio Before FDR* (New Brunswick, New Jersey: Rutgers University Press, 1992), 87 ff.; G. M. Hammond, "The Restoration of Vitality to Muscles Which Have Been Completely Paralyzed from Poliomyelitis," *Transactions of the American Electrotherapy Association* (New York, 1892), 161–67.

17. Kriegel, *The Long Walk Home*, 14.

18. One man recalled in his memoir how his left leg, having become two inches shorter than his right, was stretched. His mother and a nurse stood by his head, holding down his arms

and shoulders, while the doctor pulled down on his leg. Fifty years later, this polio recalled it as "an Inquisitional rack." Goldman, *Even the Night,* 9; further examples in Gould, *A Summer Plague,* Part II.

19. HM interview with Joy Lange Boardman; Robert W. Lovett, M.D., *The Treatment of Infantile Paralysis* (Philadelphia: P. Blakiston's Son & Co., 1917), 46 ff.; John Ruhräh, M.D., and Erwin E. Mayer, M.D., *Poliomyelitis in All Its Aspects* (Philadelphia: Lea & Febiger, 1917), chapter XII; F.P. Millard, D.O., ed., *Poliomyelitis* (Kirksville, Missouri: Journal Printing Co., 1918), chapter V and p. 116.

20. Shell, *Polio and Its Aftermath,* 41.

21. KQED 10 and 12.

22. Marshall, *I Can Jump Puddles,* 12.

23. Quoted in Shell, *Polio and Its Aftermath,* 30.

24. Linda Gordon, *Heroes of Their Own Lives: The Politics and History of Family Violence* (New York: Viking, 1988), chapter 4.

25. Nancy F. Cott, *Public Vows: A History of Marriage and the Nation* (Cambridge: Harvard University Press, 2000), 38.

26. All of the information regarding the divorce comes from papers pursuant to the divorce proceedings, copied by Eileen Thompson for HM. The interpretation of what transpired, however, is entirely my own.

27. To the best of my knowledge, Hudson County criminal records and local newspapers contain no account of the charge against Henry.

28. In December 1907, Joan passed on money from her librarian's wages to him. Two years later, Henry gave her money and a commitment to supply eighteen dollars a week, telling her that he was now earning "a little money in real estate." Still, he and Joan sold the property at 62 Hudson Street, his father's grocery store. In 1914, he was sending seven dollars a week from "the west," where he was working, still under a different name.

29. In 1916, Henry Nutzhorn was in Wilmington, Delaware, a salesman for the Pennsylvania and Delaware Development Corporation (probably a real estate venture). There, in 1918, apparently by coincidence, John Lange, Joan's younger brother, ran into Henry; Henry announced that he had given up any plans for a family life with Joan; John angrily responded, don't you realize that you've been keeping my sister "in a hole"—that is, keeping her from meeting someone. Yet Henry met with her several more times.

30. CD to MM, September 9, 1976. Photocopies of these letters were given to me by Consie's daughter Becky Jenkins.

31. "Although I was a little child, I hated it," she recalled; Riess, 5. But it is unlikely that a very ill seven-year-old would have thought this; it was probably an impression formed later in her life.

32. Milton Meltzer, *Dorothea Lange: A Photographer's Life* (New York: Farrar, Straus and Giroux, 1978), 21–22.

33. Riess, 1–4.

34. Ibid., 7, 60.

35. Ibid., 5.

36. Ibid., 6.

37. Ibid.

## 2. Apprentice to the City

1. Today, Seward Park High School occupies the site.

2. Richman created playgrounds, lunch programs, health and eye examinations, and special programs for foreign-language-speaking and gifted students. She converted her own house into a social center for teachers.

3. Riess, 13.

4. Ibid., 82.

5. Lange quotes as recounted to author by CG and in her interview with TH, August 26, 1975; Susan Glenn, *Daughters of the Shtetl: Life and Labor in the Immigrant Generation* (Ithaca, New York: Cornell University Press, 1990), 208–9, 220–21.

6. I refer, of course, to Alfred Kazin's *A Walker in the City*.

7. Robert Coles, untitled essay, in Dorothea Lange, *Photographs of a Lifetime* (Millerton, New York: Aperture, 1982), 10.

8. Riess, 23.

9. Ibid., 2.

10. Ibid., 19.

11. Her highest grades were 80s but many were in the 60s. Milton Meltzer, *Dorothea Lange: A Photographer's Life* (New York: Farrar, Straus and Giroux, 1978), 15; Meltzer's information was taken from her school record, now at Louis D. Brandeis High School Annex, 165 West 65th St., New York, N.Y.

12. Riess, 24.

13. Ibid.

14. Meltzer, *Dorothea Lange*, 17.

15. Kenneth I. Jackson, ed., *The Encyclopedia of New York* (New Haven: Yale University Press, 1995), 1137.

16. Arthur Frank Wertheim, *The New York Little Renaissance: Iconoclasm, Modernism, and Nationalism in American Culture, 1908–1917* (New York: New York University Press, 1976), 135.

17. Riess, 60.

18. I wonder if Lange ever knew that she and Duncan were born on the same day, May 26.

19. Elizabeth Kendall, *Where She Danced* (New York: Alfred A. Knopf, 1979), xiii.

20. Riess, 61.

21. Elizabeth Francis, "From Event to Monument: Modernism, Feminism and Isadora Duncan," *American Studies* 35, no. 1 (1994): 25: see also Ann Daly, "Isadora Duncan and the Distinction of Dance," *American Studies* 35, no. 1 (1994), 5–23.

22. In fact, Duncan's choreography, her look, and the relation of her choreography to her music were carefully composed.

23. Riess, 27.

24. Doud, DL, May 22, 1964.

25. Nat Herz, "Dorothea Lange in Perspective: A Reappraisal of the FSA and an Interview," *Infinity* 12, no. 4 (1963): 10.

26. Genthe, quoted in L. Victoria de L'Arbre, "Photography in California: 1900–1910," in *Images of El Dorado: A History of California Photography, 1850–1975*, ed. Joseph A. Baird (Davis: University of California, 1975); Oscar Lewis, *Bay Window Bohemia* (Garden City, New York: Doubleday, 1956), 180–83.

27. Anthony W. Lee, "Picturing San Francisco's Chinatown: The Photo Albums of Arnold Genthe," *Visual Resources* [Amsterdam] 12: 107–14; John Kuo Wei Tchen, *Genthe's Photographs of San Francisco's Old Chinatown* (New York: Dover, 1994).

28. Riess, 28–29. At least one person close to the adult Dorothea believes she had an affair with Genthe.

29. Portrait is LoC negative LC-G399-0004; drawing is LC-G405-T01-0138.

30. Arnold Genthe, *As I Remember* (New York: Reynal & Hitchcock, 1936), 119.

31. Riess, 28, 30–31.

32. Ibid., 45.

33. Doud, DL.

34. Riess, 32–34.

35. Ibid., 45–46. Lange did not mention the name of this photographer.

36. Davis was an upstart competitor of the well-known Napoleon Sarony. As was common in the late nineteenth century, he began as a lithographer and switched to photography in the mid-1860s. He photographed Oscar Wilde and reputedly paid Sarah Bernhardt fifteen hundred dollars to pose for him.

37. Riess, 48–49, 51.

38. Ibid., 50.

39. Ibid., 37.

40. Bonnie Yochelson, "Clarence H. White, Peaceful Warrior," in *Pictorialism into Modernism: The Clarence H. White School of Photography*, ed. Marianne Fulton (New York: Rizzoli, 1996), 18, 26, 54.

41. White sought to redefine pictorialism more inclusively: " 'Pictorial photography is simply a name applied to photography that really has . . . construction and expression' "; Christian A. Peterson, *After the Photo-Secession: American Pictorial Photography, 1910–1955* (New York: W. W. Norton, 1997), 86.

42. Riess, 38.

43. New York City had opened a path for women photographers earlier, with the 1859 establishment of Cooper Union, a *free*, privately endowed college of architecture, art, and engineering that accepted women students from the beginning. Many of White's female students became professional photographers. Naomi Rosenblum, *A History of Women Photographers* (New York: Abbeville Press, 1994); Peterson, *After the Photo-Secession*, 104.

44. "I don't think he mentioned technique once, how it's done, or shortcuts, or photographic manipulations," Lange stated. Riess, 39.

45. Gilpin, quoted in Yochelson, "Clarence H. White, Peaceful Warrior," 66.

46. Riess, 75, 76, 86.

47. Ibid., 64–69. Lange called Landon president of the club, but its records show a Landon as first vice president in 1917–1918. Pleiades Club Collection, box 2, folders 6–9, Fales Special Collections, Bobst Library, New York University. Thanks to Melissa Milewski for research on the Pleiades Club.

48. "I think we conjure up and invent people, and then whoever happens to be there is the recipient of our imagination. . . . It wasn't really me. I must have been aware of that, too, because I always pitied him just a little," Lange said. Riess, 68.

49. Ibid., 80.

50. Doud, DL.

## 3. Becoming a Photographer

1. Martin, Dorothea's younger brother, also took the name Lange after joining his sister in San Francisco.

2. Information on San Francisco from the following sources: U.S. census; T. H. Watkins and R. R. Olmsted, *Mirror of the Dream: An Illustrated History of San Francisco* (San Francisco: Scrimshaw Press, 1976); Jerry Flamm, *Good Life in Hard Times: San Francisco in the '20s & '30s* (San Francisco: Chronicle Books, 1978); Judd Kahn, *Imperial San Francisco: Politics and Planning in an American City, 1897–1906* (Lincoln: University of Nebraska Press, 1979); Charles Wollenberg, *Golden Gate Metropolis: Perspectives on Bay Area History* (Berkeley: Institute of Governmental Studies, 1985); William Issel and Robert Cherny, *San Francisco, 1865–1932: Politics, Power and Urban Development* (Berkeley: University of California Press, 1986); Robert O'Brien, *This is San Francisco: A Classic Portrait of the City* (San Francisco: Chronicle Books, 1994), a reprint of his columns from 1939 ff.; Gray Brechin, *Imperial San Francisco: Urban Power, Earthly Ruin* (Berkeley: University of California Press, 1999).

3. For a discussion of regional variations in the meaning of "white" in the United States, see Linda Gordon, *The Great Arizona Orphan Abduction* (Cambridge: Harvard University Press, 1999), chapter 3.

4. TH interview with Willard Van Dyke (1977), OM.

5. TH interview with Roger Sturtevant, n.d., OM.

6. Doud, DL; CD to MM, September 4, 1976.

7. Twenty-six photographers were listed in the 1919 city business directory, not counting the commercial and view photographers, flashlight photographers, photographic colorists, or suppliers of photographic equipment.

8. By the year 1900, there were already 3,500 women listed as photographers in the U.S. census.

9. Laura Wexler, *Tender Violence: Domestic Visions in an Age of U.S. Imperialism* (Chapel Hill: University of North Carolina Press, 2000), 210.

10. Colleen McDannell, *Picturing Faith: Photography and the Great Depression* (New Haven: Yale University Press, 2004), 46–47; Melissa A. McEuen, *Seeing America: Women Photographers Between the Wars* (Lexington: University Press of Kentucky, 2000), 2–3.

11. Sally Stein, "Starting from Pictorialism: Notable Continuities in the Modernization of California Photography," in *Capturing Light: Masterpieces of California Photography, 1850 to the Present*, ed. Drew Heath Johnson (New York: W. W. Norton, 2001).

12. Naomi Rosenblum, *A History of Women Photographers* (New York: Abbeville Press, 1994), 150, 156; Rosenblum, speech at the Amon Carter Museum, Fort Worth, Texas, 1990. In the decade between 1910 and 1920, the California Camera Club organized yearly trips to Yosemite and mounted exhibits.

13. Riess, 18.

14. Lange's records make it impossible to calculate her fees, but before the Depression she had no economic problems, even when she was supporting two children and a husband.

15. Quoted in Vicki Goldberg, *Margaret Bourke-White: A Biography* (New York: Harper & Row, 1987), 71–72, 87.

16. *San Francisco Chronicle*, January 22, 1920.

17. *Camera Craft* 27 (1920): 378.

18. Rosenblum, *A History of Women Photographers*, 155.

19. Christina Page Gardner, "The Contemplation of Dorothea," unpublished manuscript, author's possession; CD to MM October 25, 1976.

20. Riess, 92, 89.

21. TH, Roger Sturtevant. Dorothea's own reputation as an interior decorator was such that in 1926, when artist Otis Oldfield got married, he asked her to create the decorations. Doud, interview with Ruth Oldfield, AAA; Beatrice Judd Ryan, "The Bridge Between Then and Now," typescript of memoir, unpublished manuscript, University of California/Berkeley Library, 24.

22. Ryan, "The Bridge Between Then and Now," 13.

23. HM interview with Greta Mitchell, July 24, 1998; Doud, TH; HM interview with Joy Lange Boardman, October 14, 1999.

24. This kind of sexual daring was more common among female photographers than one might suppose. Rosenblum says that Lange was one of this group, but I have never seen a nude photograph of Lange; Rosenblum, *A History of Women Photographers*, 164.

25. Imogen's son Rondal Partridge and his daughter Betsy Partridge described this incident to me, Rondal quoting what his father had said.

26. They developed a pattern of not talking about work, in a mutual but unarticulated strategy to defend their friendship against the tensions that could have arisen from Dorothea's drive and occasional bossiness and from Imogen's occasional resentments and caustic tongue. In one of her less straightforward comments, Cunningham remarked, "Dorothea and I have always been such friends that we are more liable to talk about our offspring than about our work." KQED 2; IC to Minor White, May 20, 1964, Imogen Cunningham Papers, AAA.

27. When Imogen was four, her father moved the family to the Puget Sound Co-operative Colony at Port Angeles, Washington, on the Strait of Juan de Fuca. This was the first of several utopian communities established in Washington that derived their social philosophy from pre-Marxist socialist thinkers like Charles Fourier, Robert Owen, and Edward

Bellamy. The Cunninghams could not make a living there and moved to Seattle a few years later, where Isaac began a wood and coal business.

28. Richard Lorenz, *Imogen Cunningham: Ideas Without End* (San Francisco: Chronicle Books, 1993), plate 1.

29. Like Dorothea, Imogen knew very early on that she wanted to be a photographer, and bought herself a mail-order camera while a college student. From 1907 to 1909 she worked for the studio of Edward Curtis, famed early photographer of western landscape and American Indians. Upon her graduation, her college sorority gave her a fellowship of five hundred dollars (sisterhood indeed!) and she went to Dresden in 1909 to study photographic chemistry at the Technische Hochschule. Here and in Paris, she saw the best of European modernist photography and realized that composition interested her more than chemistry. Stephanie Bart, "Imogen Cunningham: Fame, Personality, Work" (B.A. thesis, Ohio State University, 1976), 64.

30. HM interview with RP, July 7, 1999. As if in confirmation, he appears handsome and slightly sneering in a Lange portrait.

31. Riess, 88. Unless otherwise cited, the information on Kanaga is taken from Barbara Head Millstein and Sarah M. Lowe, *Consuelo Kanaga: American Photographer* (Seattle: University of Washington Press, 1992).

32. Kanaga's reputation was such that Langston Hughes, on a visit to Carmel, came up to San Francisco so Kanaga could photograph him. Millstein and Lowe, *Consuelo Kanaga*, 33–35. She traveled to the South in 1948 and 1950, where she made some documentary photographs of black workers, but was not able to work there long enough to perfect a way of using her portrait style in the fields.

33. Both quotations from Amy Stark, ed., *The Letters of Tina Modotti to Edward Weston* (Tucson: Center for Creative Photography, 1986), 30.

34. She had hoped to have the place to herself, but "the photographer was there—*all day long*—developing, printing, spotting—you know how nervous I get working with people around." (Not a particularly appropriate response to the woman who had generously offered to share her space.) "Tomorrow night we gather at Consuelo's," she wrote in one letter. Ibid., 40, 42.

35. It is ironic, as historian Naomi Rosenblum points out, that she declined to try photojournalism during the Spanish Civil War because she considered it men's work. Rosenblum, *A History of Women Photographers*, 170.

36. Imogen Cunningham, years later, called Mather the "first and best influence" on Weston, saying she educated him to photography's possibilities when he was only a "slick commercial photographer and an expert retoucher." IC to Phyllis Masser of the Metropolitan Museum of Art, November 12, 1970, quoted in Lawrence Jasud, "Margrethe Mather: Questions of Influence," *Archive* [Center for Creative Photography] 11 (1979): 55.

37. Hard living and lack of economic security gave Mather chronic health problems, and she began to use opium and alcohol heavily. In the 1940s she developed multiple sclerosis; she died in 1952. Beth Gates Warren, *Margrethe Mather & Edward Weston: A Passionate Collaboration* (New York: W. W. Norton, 2001); Van Deren Coke, "The New Vision in Europe and

America: 1920–1950," in James Enyeart, ed., *Decade by Decade: Twentieth-Century American Photographs from the Collection of the Center for Creative Photography* (Boston: Little, Brown, 1989), 19–34.

38. Susan Ehrens, ed., *Alma Lavenson: Photographs* (Berkeley, California: Wildwood Arts, 1990); review by Susan J. Cooke, *Woman's Art Journal* 16, no. 2: 40–41.

39. Often refugees from the defeated 1848 German revolutions, many joined the gold rush, found little gold, but soon discovered that they could make more reliable fortunes by supplying the miners. In the nineteenth century virtually all goods had to enter through the port of San Francisco. This was the origin of the Levi Strauss fortune as well as those of the Gerstle, Salz, Sloss, Freudenthal, Kahn, and Elkus families, among others.

40. One historian thought that "the Jews in the American West in the second half of the nineteenth century were the freest anywhere in the world." Fred Rosenbaum, *Visions of Reform: Congregation Emanu-El and the Jews of San Francisco, 1849–1999* (Berkeley, California: Judah L. Magnes Museum, 2000), 41.

41. One such, the Haas-Lilienthal house, is now a museum, one of the attractions recommended to San Francisco tourists.

42. Jerry Flamm, *Good Life in Hard Times: San Francisco in the '20s & '30s* (San Francisco: Chronicle Books, 1978), chapter 5.

43. Edythe Katten loathed her parents' spelling of her name and much preferred "Edith." For help in untangling these family connections I am indebted to Jonathan Katten, Anne Katten, and Jonathan Elkus.

44. Lange postcard (of a Dürer) to Elizabeth Elkus, from Lenox Hill Hospital in New York City, dated April 23, 1954, box 2, folder 43, Albert Israel Elkus Papers, Bancroft. Elizabeth Elkus was described by another friend thus: "If you know her even a little bit, if you're in trouble, she's just the person who comes to help you out in the most unofficious way, so that you wouldn't even know you were being helped. She's that kind of a person." Suzanne Riess, ed., "Sketches of an Improbable Ninety Years," interview with Helen A. Salz, University of California/Berkeley Regional Oral History Office.

45. HM interviews with Jan Katten, February 16, 2000, and Ken Katten, March 4, 2000.

46. JM interview with Roger Sturtevant, February 1977, OM, 31, 36. I have never been able to identify JM. Unfortunately what Sturtevant went on to say tends to undermine his credibility: "The women at that time who were sexually free went around figuratively [*sic*] raping males and doing Greek dances and being, what do I want to say, being spiritually superior."

47. *Mill Valley Herald* clipping, n.d., from JDC. An amateur painter, Wilson hosted lavish roast beef dinners for her artist friends every weekend; CD to MM June 21, 1976. It was from Mary Ann Wilson that Dorothea adopted the beret that she wore for the rest of her life.

48. Gardner, "The Contemplation of Dorothea."

49. Maynard's daughter Consie remarked, "Everything that was culture in S.F. in those days was supported by the old Jewish families. The Walters, the Haases, the Raases, the Arnsteins, the Kattens, the Salzes, the Zellerbachs, the Strausses." CD to MM, June 23, 1976. Referring to the analogous crowd in New York, Benita Eisler calls it "upper bohemia": Benita Eisler, *O'Keeffe and Stieglitz: An American Romance* (New York: Doubleday, 1991), 342.

50. Riess, 118–119.

51. Ibid., 90–92.

52. Quoted in Allan Sekula, "Photography Between Labour and Capital," in Leslie Shedden, *Mining Photographs and Other Pictures. A Selection from the Negative Archives of Shedden Studio, Glace Bay, Cape Breton* (Cape Breton: Press of the Nova Scotia College of Art and Design, n.d.), 23.

53. John Tagg, *The Burden of Representation: Essays on Photographies and Histories* (Amherst: University of Massachusetts, 1988), 35–36.

54. Max Kozloff, "Nadar and the Republic of Mind," quoted in Vicki Goldberg, ed., *Photography in Print: Writings from 1816 to the Present* (New York: Simon and Schuster, 1981), 132–35.

55. She gave Gertrude Clausen a kimono to throw over her suit to relax the lines of the composition. Yet she also posed her once looking away from the camera so that the then-fashionable Psyche knot of her hair would show. Gardner, "The Contemplation of Dorothea."

56. Allan Sekula, "The Body and the Archive," *October* 39 (w1986), 3–64.

57. Alan Trachtenberg, "Likeness as Identity: Reflections on the Daguerrean Mystique," in *The Portrait in Photography*, ed. Graham Clarke (London: Reaktion, 1992), 173–92, 189–90.

58. One scholar calls this the "auratic sign of middle class rights." Shawn Michelle Smith, *American Archives: Gender, Race and Class in Visual Culture* (Princeton: Princeton University Press, 1999), 54.

59. Max Kozloff argued that because of these mixed functions, photographers are often caught between "the memorial aims of the image . . . and its type-casting function," the former realist, the latter symbolic. Kozloff, "Nadar," 130. Lange integrated those two aspects of portrait function well.

60. Rosenblum, speech at the Amon Carter Museum.

61. Smith, *American Archives*, 55.

62. Riess, 54.

63. Doud, DL.

64. Sekula, "Photography Between Labour and Capital," 194.

65. Riess, 92. In what might have been a veiled dig at Lange, Cunningham said, "Most of the people that I photograph are people whose image both psychically and physically mean[s] something to me and that is the reason that I am an un-money making photographer." IC to James McLeod, box 4, July 11, 1970, IC Papers, AAA.

66. Quoted in Max Kozloff, *New York: Capital of Photography* (New Haven: Yale University Press, 2002), 39.

## 4. Maynard Dixon, Bohemian Artist

1. Biographical information on Maynard Dixon was taken from: *Anatomy of a Frontier Town: Maynard Dixon's Fresno* (Madera, California: Madera Method Foundation Press, 1995), a collection of primary sources based on the journal of Maynard Dixon's mother, Constance Maynard Dixon; Wesley Burnside, *Maynard Dixon: Artist of the West* (Provo, Utah: Brigham Young University Press, 1974), Linda Jones Gibbs, with Deborah Brown Rasiel, *Escape*

*to Reality: The Western World of Maynard Dixon* (Provo, Utah: Brigham Young University Museum of Art, 2000); Donald J. Hagerty, *Desert Dreams: The Art and Life of Maynard Dixon* (Salt Lake City: Gibbs Smith, 1998); Grant Wallace, "Maynard Dixon: Biography and Works," California Art Research, WPA Monograph, WPA Project 2874, vol. 8, 1937; Jayne McKay, *Maynard Dixon: Art and Spirit* (2007 DVD, available from www.maynarddixondoc .com).

2. HM interview with Edith Arnstein Jenkins, September 4, 1998.

3. Winona Tomanoczy, "Remembrances of a Friend," in Maynard Dixon, *Images of the Native American* (San Francisco: California Academy of Sciences, 1981), 80.

4. Maynard's father Harry, a Confederate officer, moved to California with a group of other Confederate loyalists fleeing Reconstruction and established an "Alabama colony" near the San Joaquin River. Harry St. John Dixon Papers, Southern Historical Collection, University of North Carolina at Chapel Hill. Bringing his old party loyalty into a new context, he became active in California's Democratic party. Harry Dixon had sufficient prestige and power that he could get away with refusing to fly the U.S. flag; he compromised by not showing the Confederate flag, either—instead, his wife, Constance, sewed a medieval banner as a means of flying something unobjectionable. He named his second child Rebecca so they could call her "Reb," thus offering him an intimate means of expressing his political attachments.

5. "I have friends among them I would prefer to many a white man." Zeb Stewart, "Do You Know Maynard Dixon?" from the audiovisual program at the California Academy of Science Exhibition 1981; Dixon papers, mss. 73/81c, box 2, Bancroft.

6. Oscar Lewis, *Bay Window Bohemia* (Garden City, New York: Doubleday, 1956), 195.

7. TH interview with RP and CG, August 26, 1975, OM.

8. By the 1870s, San Franciscans patronized hotels and restaurants in unusually high numbers. Barbara Berglund, *Making San Francisco American: Cultural Frontiers in the Urban West, 1846–1906* (Lawrence: University Press of Kansas, 2007), 31–33; Warren Unna, *The Coppa Murals: A Pageant of Bohemian Life in San Francisco at the Turn of the Century* (San Francisco: Book Club of California, 1952), 8, 53–54; Lawrence Ferlinghetti and Nancy J. Peters, *Literary San Francisco: A Pictorial History from Its Beginnings to the Present Day* (San Francisco: City Lights and Harper & Row, 1980).

9. "Gottardo Piazzoni," California Art Research, WPA Monograph, WPA Project 2874, vol. 7, 1937.

10. Shirley Staschen Triest, *A Life on the First Waves of Radical Bohemianism in San Francisco*, transcript of interview, 1995–96, University of California/Berkeley Regional Oral History Office, Bancroft, 49–50; Samuel Dickson, *Tales of San Francisco* (Stanford: Stanford University Press, 1957), 669–70; "Lee Randolph," California Art Research, WPA Monograph, WPA Project 2874, vol. 7, 1937.

11. Idwal Jones, *Ark of Empire: San Francisco's Montgomery Block* (Garden City, New York: Doubleday, 1951), 23.

12. Dickson, *Tales of San Francisco*, 669–70.

13. Robert O'Brien, *This is San Francisco: A Classic Portrait of the City* (San Francisco: Chronicle Books, 1994), 33.

14. Emily Hahn, *Romantic Rebels: An Informal History of Bohemianism in America* (Boston: Houghton Mifflin, 1967), 46–47, 69.

15. Andrée Marechal Workman, "Modernism and the Desert: Maynard Dixon," *Vanguard*, March 1982, 23.

16. The limited information about Lillian West Tobey Dixon comes from "Recollections of Constance (Consie) Dixon," January 10, 1977, September 8, 1977, and February 5, 1978, typescript, given to author by Consie Dixon's daughter Becky Jenkins; from http://genforum.genealogy.com/tobey/messages/251.html; Dixon papers, mss. 73/81, 1: folder Lummis, Bancroft; and http://www.askart.com/askart/t/lillian_west_tobey/lillian_west_tobey.aspx. Her career after the divorce does not fit with the story of complete collapse: After further study at the California College of Arts and Crafts, she was an adjunct instructor at UC Berkeley in 1918. She had a studio on San Francisco's Russian Hill before moving to Salt Lake City, where she died in 1925 or 1926.

17. MD diary.

18. Workman, "Modernism and the Desert," 25.

19. CD to MM, July 6, 1976.

20. In those days, the only gentlemanly thing to do was to get the wife to be the plaintiff.

21. MD diary.

22. Remembrance by Constance Dixon in Dixon, *Images of the Native American*, 64–65. I wonder if Dixon perceived the irony in Indian children playing at being Indians.

23. CD to MM, October 25, 1976.

24. His mood is evident in his early responses to her in his extremely terse notes. For example: "Dorothea and hope—her encouragement" (MD diary).

25. Notes typed from Lange's handwritten original, JDC; KQED 12.

26. 1920 manuscript census.

27. MM interview with IC, March 17, 1976.

28. Quoted in Wallace, "Maynard Dixon," 76.

29. Notes typed from Lange's handwritten original, JDC.

30. *San Francisco Examiner*, January 22, 1920, 12; *San Francisco Chronicle*, January 22, 1920.

31. California Division of Vital Statistics.

### 5. Working Mother in Bohemia

1. The Herbert Fleishhackers, one of San Francisco's wealthiest families and among Dorothea's clients, invited them to dinner once. Dorothea reciprocated and no doubt put great effort into her preparations for having them at her home; then the Fleishhackers invited the Dixons for a weekend at their country house, where servants waited to fulfill their every desire. TH interview with Roger Sturtevant, n.d., transcript 9, OM.

2. CD to MM, October 20, 1976.

3. TH interview with Sturtevant; CD to MM, June 23, 1976.

4. *San Francisco News*, March 24, 1920; *San Francisco Chronicle*, March 25, 1920.

5. Milton Meltzer, *Dorothea Lange: A Photographer's Life* (New York: Farrar, Straus and Giroux, 1978), 49.

6. Riess, 92.

7. MD diary. All subsequent Dixon quotes from this source unless otherwise noted.

8. CD to MM, November 4, 1976.

9. Erika Doss, "Between Modernity and 'the Real Thing,'" *American Art* 18 no. 3 (2004): 25; Linda Jones Gibbs, with Deborah Brown Rasiel, *Escape to Reality: The Western World of Maynard Dixon* (Provo, Utah: Brigham Young University Museum of Art, 2000), 140.

10. Donald T. Hagerty, *Desert Dreams: The Art and Life of Maynard Dixon* (Salt Lake City: Gibbs Smith, 1998), chapter 6; unpublished biography of Maynard Dixon, California Art Research, WPA Project 2874, AAA. Recently, Dixon's paintings have sold for as much as $1.7 million; see www.maynarddixon.org/auction.php, accessed March 26, 2008.

11. TH interview with Sturtevant.

12. Grant, "Maynard Dixon: Biography and Works," California Art Research, WPA Monograph, WPA Project 2874, vol. 8, 1937, 8–9, 82.

13. Many years later, in 1938 or 1939, Maynard told Consie that he had talked Lillian into having a baby because he believed it would "straighten her out." When Consie asked why he had left her with Lillian, he gave the same reason: "'Everyone said that the child would help straighten L out.'" Consie added the underscoring in the transcript of this interview to emphasize that he referred to her, to her face, in the third person. "Recollections of Constance Dixon," January 10, 1977, September 8, 1977, and February 5, 1978. CD to MM, July 6, 1976.

14. CD to MM, June 21 and October 25, 1976; Consie Dixon, "Recollections."

15. CD to MM, October 25, November 4, and November 10, 1976; CD, "Recollections."

16. Riess, 122.

17. HM interview with Nora Elliott and Jeff Lustig, June 28, 2000; HM interview with Jon Elkus, April 18, 2000.

18. Elizabeth Partridge, ed., *Dorothea Lange: A Visual Life* (Washington: Smithsonian Institution Press, 1994), 93. This photograph was used as a cover photo for Mary Karr's memoir, *The Liars' Club*.

19. Meltzer, *Dorothea Lange*, 109.

20. Partridge, *Dorothea Lange*, 94.

21. Now Presidio Hill School.

22. CD to MM, January 10, 1977.

23. *San Francisco Chronicle*, August 20, 1922; Wallace, "Maynard Dixon," 82.

24. Reiss, 126.

25. DL to Margot Fanger, February 1960.

26. Author's interview with Malcolm and Mary Collier, July 19, 2007.

27. John Collier practiced through photography what he called "visual anthropology," which his wife, Mary, traced to Lange's mastery of showing context in photography. It is as if, Mary Collier said, John represented a second generation, bringing Lange's intuitive ideas into full elaboration. Author's interview with Malcolm and Mary Collier.

28. W. L. Rusho, *Everett Ruess: A Vagabond for Beauty* (Salt Lake City: Gibbs Smith, 1983).

29. Everett Ruess to Stella Knight Ruess, letter dated November 5, 1933, in Rusho, *Everett Ruess*, 182.

30. Maynard wrote Mrs. Ruess a hopeful letter, pointing out from personal experience that wanderers often dropped out of sight for a time and then reappeared. MD to Stella Knight Ruess, March 1935, in Rusho, *Everett Ruess*, 118. In 2008 Ruess's body was finally found, and in 2009 definitively identified through DNA, near Comb Ridge, Utah. The unconfirmed story was that Aneth Nez, a Navajo, had actually seen him killed by Ute Indians (traditional enemies of the Navajo) and buried him afterward; Nez never told anyone except a medicine man he consulted, who in turn told the story to another patient in 2008 who reported it. *National Geographic Adventure*, April/May 2009; *Salt Lake Tribune*, April 26, 2009.

31. Hagerty, *Desert Dreams*, 149.

32. Ibid.

33. These and other stunts are recounted in HM interview with RP, July 7, 1999; Arnold Genthe, *As I Remember* (New York: Reynal & Hitchcock, 1936), 64–65; Meltzer, *Dorothea Lange*, 61–62; TH interview with RP and CG, August 26, 1975.

34. For his "cold as Christian charity" remark, see Winona Tomanoczy, "Remembrances of a Friend," in Maynard Dixon, *Images of the Native American* (San Francisco: California Academy of Sciences, 1981), 80. On anti-Semitism, see HM interviews with RP and with Edith Arnstein Jenkins, September 4, 1998. In 1938, MD wrote in a letter, "What gets me about the Jew bunch is always belly aken about the jewish problem . . . ther aint no jew problem only what they make hollering about it." He then added, "Shure they like the Money but I have saw plenty Pale Faces . . . that's got the same itch." MD to Tom Moriarty, June 6, 1938, quoted in Doss, "Between Modernity and 'The Real Thing,'" 24.

35. Suzanne Riess, interview with Helen Arnstein Salz, 1973–74, University of California/Berkeley, Regional Oral History Office; Oscar Lewis, *To Remember Albert Micky Bender: Notes for a Biography* (Oakland: Grabhorn and Hoyem, 1973), 6–8.

36. TH interview with AA, September 15, 1976.

37. He acknowledged sadly, ". . . growing difference of opinion from other artists . . . less and less contact with them." MD diary.

38. HM interview with RP. Dixon was also annoyed, perhaps more understandably, that other artists fawned over Bender—yet he put up with absurd demands from his patron Anita Baldwin.

39. CD to MM, October 25, 1976.

40. Beatrice Judd Ryan, "The Rise of Modern Art in the Bay Area," *California Historical Quarterly*, March 1959, 1–5.

41. MD diary.

42. Quoted by Robert J. Samuelson, "Great Depression," in *Concise Encyclopedia of Economics*, at http://www.econlib.org/LIBRARY/Enc/GreatDepression.html.

43. Transcript of Mildred Constantine interview with Anita Brenner, Getty Research Institute, Los Angeles. On Mexican art influence in San Francisco, see Belisario R.Contreras, *Tradition and Innovation in New Deal Art* (Lewisburg, Pennsylvania: Bucknell University Press, 1983); Laurance P. Hurlburt, *The Mexican Muralists in the United States* (Albuquerque: University of New Mexico Press, 1989); Anthony W. Lee, *Painting on the Left: Diego Rivera, Radical Politics, and San Francisco's Public Murals* (Berkeley: University of California Press, 1999); Patricia Hills, *Social Concern and Urban Realism: American Painting of the 1930s*

(Boston: Boston University Art Gallery, 1983); Francis V. O'Connor, "The Influence of Diego Rivera on the Art of the United States During the 1930s and After," in *Diego Rivera: A Retrospective* (Detroit: Founders Society, Detroit Institute of Arts, 1986).

44. Quoted in Terence Pitts, *Photography in the American Grain: Discovering a Native American Aesthetic, 1923–1941* (Tucson: Center for Creative Photography, 1988), 13.

45. This was a common nickname for the three; see Helen Langa, *Radical Art: Printmaking and the Left in 1930s New York* (Berkeley: University of California Press, 2004), 61.

46. Diego Rivera to Albert Bender, August 25, 1926, Bender Papers, Archives of American Art.

47. Lee, *Painting on the Left*, 42–43.

48. MD Diary; Hurlburt, *Mexican Muralists*, 99.

49. Quoted in Lee, *Painting on the Left*, 64.

50. CD to MM, November 13, 1976.

51. The State Department had been particularly angered by his participation in the Mexican Hands Off Nicaragua Committee, which displayed a U.S. flag captured by General Sandino in 1928.

52. Hayden Herrera, *Frida: A Biography of Frida Kahlo* (New York: Harper & Row, 1983), 116–118.

53. Hagerty, *Desert Dreams*, 169.

54. Patrick Marnham, *Dreaming with His Eyes Open: A Life of Diego Rivera* (New York: Alfred A. Knopf, 1998), 232.

55. There are contrasting recollections about whose studio Kahlo actually used.

56. Herrera, *Frida*, 120–21, 282; Isabel Alcántara and Sandra Egnolff, *Frida Kahlo and Diego Rivera* (Munich: Prestel, 1999); Eloesser's papers are in the Hoover Institution at Stanford and in the Stanford University Medical Center.

57. Lee, *Painting on the Left*, 47 ff.

58. They might also have crossed paths with Robinson and Una Jeffers, Leopold Stokowski and his Mexican composer friend, Carlos Chávez. Flannery Burke, *From Greenwich Village to Taos: Primitivism and Place at Mabel Dodge Luhan's* (Lawrence: University Press of Kansas, 2008).

59. In recounting this decades later, Lange said that at the time she couldn't have conceived of photographing outside alone, but this was a false memory, since she already knew outdoor work by photographers like Anne Brigman, Arnold Genthe, Clarence White, Alfred Stieglitz, Ansel Adams, and Imogen Cunningham.

60. Maynard's friend Antonio Mirabal offered to share what he had with them, an extraordinary offer of fellowship: "'If it gets too tough come back and I'll share with you.'" MD diary.

61. MD diary.

## Scene 2

1. Nat Herz, "Dorothea Lange in Perspective: A Reappraisal of the FSA and an Interview," *Infinity* 12, no. 4 (1963): 10.

2. Riess, 149.

3. Martin Lange to Paul S. Taylor, undated letter (written well after Dorothea Lange's death), JDC.

4. Herz, "Dorothea Lange in Perspective," 10.

5. Riess, 144.

6. Herz, "Dorothea Lange in Perspective," 10.

7. Doud, DL.

## 6. Leaving the Children, Leaving the Studio

1. Riess, 140.

2. Riess, 141.

3. Lewis Ferbrache, interview with Bernard Zakheim, 1964, AAA.

4. Nancy Dustin Wall Moure, *California Art* (Los Angeles: Dustin Publications, 1998); Belisario R. Contreras, *Tradition and Innovation in New Deal Art* (Lewisburg, Pennsylvania: Bucknell University Press, 1983), 29–30.

5. Lange and Dixon had to consider applying for relief until his painting of the unemployed, *Shapes of Fear*, was purchased by the Ranger Fund for the Brooklyn Institute of Arts and Sciences. Maynard got $1,000 of the $1,500 sale price. Then his *Navajoland* also sold for $1,500, so they could relax for a while. The painting *Shapes of Fear* is now in the collection of the Smithsonian American Art Museum in Washington, D.C.

6. MD diary.

7. TH interview with RP and CG, August 26, 1975.

8. Anna Sommer, *San Francisco News*, February 11, 1932.

9. Dorothea Lange et al., *The Thunderbird Remembered: Maynard Dixon, The Man and the Artist* (Los Angeles: Gene Autry Western Heritage Museum, 1994), 56.

10. Lange's contemporary and friend, photographer Nell Dorr, for example, left her children with relatives in Florida in order to work in New York. Naomi Rosenblum, *History of Women Photographers* (New York: Abbeville Press, 1994), 173. Ben and Bernarda Shahn would leave their children with others so that she could accompany him when he was on the road photographing. HM interview with Louise Rosskam, July 30, 1999. Even the wealthy might do this: Ernest Bloch's daughter Suzanne was sent to live with one of Lange's elite client families, the Sterns. Box 1, Elise Stern Haas Family Papers, Bancroft mss. 92/810c.

11. Elizabeth Rose, *A Mother's Job: The History of Day Care, 1890–1960* (New York: Oxford University Press, 1999), especially 167–68.

12. Riess, 102.

13. Lange et al., *The Thunderbird Remembered*, 56.

14. One Lange scholar wrote that she lacked maternal instinct and that her father's "desertion" had weakened her ability to bond—a judgment based on the assumption that devotion to one's children and to an art or craft are mutually exclusive. Pierre Borhan, *Dorothea Lange: The Heart and Mind of a Photographer* (New York: Little, Brown, 2002), 20.

15. Riess, 147.

16. Lange's previous biographer, Milton Meltzer, wrote that she had retaliated with affairs of her own. Milton Meltzer, *Dorothea Lange: A Photographer's Life*. (New York: Farrar, Straus and Giroux, 1978), 125. (Meltzer told me that he could not remember where he learned this.) Robert Coles repeats the infidelity claim in his essay in *Dorothea Lange, Photographs of a Lifetime* (Millerton, New York: Aperture, 1982), 12. None of the many people I interviewed could confirm the claim.

17. Riess, 123.

18. Author's interviews with John Dixon, February 2003.

19. Lange seems to have conflated two different foster-care locations in her recollection thirty years later.

20. Recollections about the 1932 vacation are from Lange et al., *The Thunderbird Remembered*, 59; TH interview with RP and CG; Dan Dixon's email to the author, March 4, 2008.

21. Riess, 148.

22. Naomi Rosenblum, "Modernist Eye Responsive Heart: The Work of Dorothea Lange," in *Dorothea Lange: The Human Face* (Paris: NBC Editions, 1998), 14.

23. She destroyed these photographs, as she often did with work that did not meet her standards.

24. Riess, 148.

25. Doud, DL.

26. Quotations from FDR's speeches can be found at http://www.americanrhetoric.com/speeches/fdrcommonwealth.html and http://newdeal.feri.org/speeches/1932c.htm.

27. Sally Stein, "The President's Two Bodies: Stagings and Restagings of FDR and the New Deal Body Politics," *American Art*, Spring 2004, 35. The July 1931 interview appeared in *Liberty*, a middlebrow general-interest magazine that featured interviews with celebrities and excerpts from famous authors.

28. Quoted in Karin Becker Ohrn, *Dorothea Lange and the Documentary Tradition* (Baton Rouge: Louisiana State University Press, 1980), 23.

29. Doud, John Collier, Jr.

30. Its founder, Australian immigrant Lois Jordan, had been led by a vision of Jesus Christ to feed unemployed sailors on the San Francisco waterfront. She developed a multiservice center, providing showers, barbers, even some medical care, and was feeding 2,000 a day when Lange passed by the enterprise. Mother Lois Jordan, *The Work of the White Angel Jungle* (San Francisco: self-published pamphlet, 1935), and miscellaneous newspaper clippings.

31. She made it under uncomfortable conditions: "When I took [the picture] I was very timid about it since I was working with a 4 x 5 Autographic. It makes you very conspicuous. I took three shots, then I got out of there." Quoted in Nat Herz, "Dorothea Lange in Perspective: A Reappraisal of the FSA and an Interview," *Infinity* 12, no. 4 (1963): 10. The Autographic was a Kodak sold from 1928 to 1933, called a vanity camera because it came in colors and had a satin-lined case. It used roll film and it allowed the photographer to write notations directly on the film with a stylus.

32. Martin Lange to PST, undated but written well after Dorothea Lange's death, JDC.

33. Nat Herz, "Dorothea Lange in Perspective," 9.

34. TH interview with Sturtevant; Meltzer, *Dorothea Lange*, 71.

35. Herz, "Dorothea Lange in Perspective," 10.

36. Laura Wexler, "Techniques of the Imagery Nation: Engendering Family Photography," in *Race and the Production of Modern American Nationalism*, ed. Reynolds J. Scott-Childress (New York: Garland, 1999), 99.

37. But the group was loose enough that membership was not clear, and the photographers and scholars disagree about who was in and who out. On f/64, see Anne Hammond, "Ansel Adams and Objectivism: Making a Photograph with Group f/64," *History of Photography* 22, no. 2 (Summer 1998): 169–78; Mary Street Alinder, *Ansel Adams. A Biography* (New York: Henry Holt, 1996); Ansel Adams, *Ansel Adams: An Autobiography* (Boston: Little, Brown, 1988); John Raeburn, *A Staggering Revolution: A Cultural History of Thirties Photography* (Urbana: University of Illinois Press, 2006); Jean S. Tucker, *Group f/64* (St. Louis: University of Missouri Press, 1978); George Craven, *The Group f/64 Controversy: An Introduction to the Henry F. Swift Memorial Collection of the San Francisco Museum of Art*, (San Francisco: San Francisco Museum of Art, 1963).

38. Sally Stein, "Starting from Pictorialism: Notable Continuities in the Modernization of California Photography," in *Capturing Light: Masterpieces of California Photography, 1850 to the Present*, ed. Drew Heath Johnson (New York: W. W. Norton, 2001); Hammond, "Ansel Adams and Objectivism," 169–78; Richard Lorenz, *Imogen Cunningham: Ideas Without End* (San Francisco: Chronicle Books, 1993), 33–34.

39. *Camera Craft*, passim; Adams, *An Autobiography*, 112; Imogen Cunningham, interview by Edna Tartaul Daniel, typescript, Bancroft, 143.

40. S. Satterwhite, "Dialogue: Willard Van Dyke," *Photograph* 1, no. 4 (1977); Martha A. Sandweiss, "The Way to Realism: 1930–40," in *Decade by Decade: Twentieth-Century American Photography from the Collection of the Center for Creative Photography*, ed. James Enyeart (Boston: Little, Brown, 1989), 35n.

41. Christian A. Peterson, *Pictorialism in America* (Minneapolis: Minneapolis Institute of Arts, 1983), 55; Michael G. Wilson and Dennis Reed, *Pictorialism in California: Photographs, 1900–1940* (Malibu, California: J. Paul Getty Museum and Henry E. Huntington Library and Art Gallery, 1994); Doug Harvey, "The Other Coast: West Meets East in 'The Modern West,'" exhibit review, *Los Angeles Weekly*, March 28, 2007.

42. Sara Halprin, *Seema's Show: A Life on the Left* (Albuquerque: University of New Mexico Press, 2005), 87.

43. Once, some roosters had been rescued from an Easter display and given to Weston. One of the birds had a Raggedy Ann doll "and he would screw that doll up and down the front lawn." It took a meeting of the town council in Carmel to make Edward get rid of the rooster. James Alinder, "The Preston Holder Story," *Exposure* 13, no. 1 (1975): 45.

44. Alinder, "The Preston Holder Story," 5.

45. TH interview with AA, September 15, 1976, OM.

46. Donald T. Hagerty, *Desert Dreams: The Art and Life of Maynard Dixon* (Salt Lake City: Gibbs Smith, 1998), 191.

## 7. A New Deal for Artists

1. Martin Lange to John Dixon or PST, undated but written after Lange's death, OM.

2. Linda Gordon, "Harry Hopkins Brings Relief," in *Days of Destiny*, ed. James McPherson and Alan Brinkley (New York: DK Publishing, 2001).

3. MD diary.

4. The New Deal's PWA helped build the $78 million Bay Bridge and the $35 million Golden Gate Bridge. Richard Lowitt, *The New Deal and the West* (Bloomington: Indiana University Press, 1984), 174.

5. Donald J. Hagerty, *Desert Dreams: The Art and Life of Maynard Dixon* (Salt Lake City: Gibbs Smith, 1998), 171–73.

6. HM interview with Alan Temko, June 27, 2000; HM interviews with Margot and Donald Fanger, January 24 and April 16, 1999.

7. William H. Mullins, *The Depression and the Urban West Coast, 1929–1933* (Bloomington: Indiana University Press, 1991).

8. Meg Jacobs, *Pocketbook Politics: Economic Citizenship in Twentieth-Century America* (Princeton, New Jersey: Princeton University Press, 2005), 113; quotation, 111.

9. Joel F. Handler and Yeheskel Hasenfeld, *We the Poor People: Work, Poverty, and Welfare* (New Haven: Yale University Press, 1997).

10. U.S. Works Progress Administration, *Final Report on the WPA Program 1935–1943* (Washington, D.C.: Government Printing Office, 1946).

11. Daniel Geary, "Carey McWilliams and Antifascism, 1934–1943," *Journal of American History* 90, no. 3; Carey McWilliams, "Fascism in American Law," *American Mercury* 32 (1934); quotation in John Terry, "The Terror in San Jose," *The Nation*, August 8, 1934, 161–62.

12. Geary, "Carey McWilliams and Antifascism, 1934–1943." Targeting "pink" Hollywood, these attacks resemble today's conservative attacks on liberal and "immoral" Hollywood.

13. Carey McWilliams, "Hollywood Plays with Fascism," *The Nation*, May 29, 1935, 623–24.

14. See, for example, the 1936 American Artists' Congress proceedings, in the David Alfaro Siqueiros Papers, GRI; Matthew Baigell and Julie Williams, eds., *Artists Against War and Facism* (New Brunswick, New Jersey: Rutgers University Press, 1986); Hilton Kramer, "The Big Red Paintpot," *New York Times*, April 27, 1986. Few progressives and intellectuals at this time perceived the Soviet Union as totalitarian.

15. Michael Denning, *The Cultural Front: The Laboring of American Culture in the Twentieth Century* (London: Verso, 1997); Linda Nochlin, "The Realist Criminal," *Art in America*, September/October and November/December 1973; Heinz Ickstadt, introduction to *The Thirties: Politics and Culture in a Time of Broken Dreams*, ed. Rob Kroes and Brian Lee (Amsterdam: Free University Press, 1987); Andrew Hemingway, "Fictional Unities: 'Antifascism' and 'Antifascist Art' in 30s America," *Oxford Art Journal* 14, no. 1 (1991): 107–17.

16. Jane De Hart Matthews, "Arts and the People: The New Deal Quest for a Cultural Democracy," *Journal of American History* 62, no. 2 (1975): 324.

17. Adams feared that the New Deal would begin to regulate photography. Sally Stein, "On Location: The Placement (and Replacement) of California in 1930s Photography," in *Read-

*ing California: Art, Image, and Identity, 1900–2000*, ed. Stephanie Barron et al. (Los Angeles: University of California Press, 2000), 195, n. 19.

18. The Communist party grew rapidly in Depression California, from 438 members in 1926 to 1,800 in 1934. Robert W. Cherny, Richard Griswold del Castillo, and Gretchen Lemke-Santangelo, *Competing Visions: A History of California* (Boston: Houghton Mifflin, 2005), 250.

19. Riess, 151.

20. Shirley Staschen Triest, *A life on the First Waves of Radical Bohemianism in San Francisco*, University of California/Berkeley Regional Oral History Office.

21. Mary McChesney interview with Hansel Hagel, October 8, 1964, AAA; Dolores Flamiano, "Meaning, Memory and Misogyny: LIFE Photographer Hansel Mieth's Monkey Portrait," *Afterimage*, September/October 2005; Sally Stein, "Hansel Mieth and Otto Hagel," in Amy Rule and Nancy Solomon, *Original Sources: Art and Archives at the Center for Creative Photography* (Tucson: Center for Creative Photography, University of Arizona, 2002), 127–31; Mieth interview in John Loengard, *Life Photographers: What They Saw* (New York: Little, Brown, 1998).

22. Marlene Park and Gerald E. Markowitz, *New Deal for Art* (Hamilton, New York: Gallery Association of New York State, 1977), xii, 2; Florence Loeb Kellogg, "Art Becomes Public Works," *Survey Graphic* 23, no. 6 (1934): 279; Jonathan Harris, *Federal Art and National Culture: The Politics of Identity in New Deal America* (Cambridge: Cambridge University Press, 1995), 113; Richard D. McKinzie, *The New Deal for Artists* (Princeton, New Jersey: Princeton University Press, 1973), 176; Forrest A. Walker, *The Civil Works Administration: An Experiment in Federal Work Relief, 1933–1934* (New York: Garland, 1979), 96, 100.

    "Few living American artists over the age of forty did not do something or other" for at least one of the four government art agencies," writes Erica Beckh in "Government Art in the Roosevelt Era: An Appraisal of Federal Art Patronage in the Light of Present Needs," *Art Journal* 20, no. 1 (Autumn 1960): 5. The WPA payroll included Nelson Algren, Thomas Hart Benton, John Cheever, Willem de Kooning, Katherine Dunham, Ralph Ellison, Arshile Gorky, Zora Neale Hurston, Jacob Lawrence, Reginald Marsh, Robert Motherwell, Kenneth Patchen, Jackson Pollock, Kenneth Rexroth, Mark Rothko, Muriel Rukeyser, Isaac, Moses, and Raphael Soyer, Joseph Stella, Studs Terkel, Margaret Walker, and Richard Wright, to name but a few.

23. Terence R. Pitts, introduction to *Sonya Noskowiak Archive* (Tucson: University of Arizona, 1982), 5.

24. Ferbrache interview with Zakheim; Masha Zakheim Jewett, *Coit Tower San Francisco: Its History and Art* (San Francisco: Volcano Press, 1983).

25. Zakheim Jewett, *Coit Tower San Francisco*, 32; Ferbrache interview with Zakheim.

26. MD diary.

27. Christopher DeNoon, "Social Messages: Graphic Artists of the WPA," *Magazine of International Design* 33 (1986): 56–59; undated, Maynard Dixon Papers, AAA, reel 822.

28. Anthony W. Lee, *Painting on the Left: Diego Rivera, Radical Politics, and San Francisco's Public Murals* (Berkeley: University of California Press, 1999), 135.

29. Zakheim Jewett, *Coit Tower San Francisco*, 47–54.

30. Steven M. Gelber, "Working to Prosperity: California's New Deal Murals," *California History* 58 (Summer 1979): 106.

31. Hagerty, *Desert Dreams*, 196–200; Grant Wallace, "Maynard Dixon Biography and Works," California Art Research, WPA Monograph, WPA Project 2874, vol. 8. Dixon received $450 for this work, although he believed its value was more than $3,000.

32. These paintings were exhibited at San Francisco's de Young museum and then sent off to Washington, where they were lost. MD diary; LaVerne Bradley Rollin, typescript memoir of Dixon, 1967, in the author's possession; Grant Wallace, "Maynard Dixon Biography and Works."

33. Winona Tomanoczy, "Remembrances of a Friend," in Maynard Dixon, *Images of the Native American* (San Francisco: California Academy of Sciences, 1981), 81.

34. TH interview with AA, September 15, 1976.

35. Hagerty, *Desert Dreams*, 206.

36. TH interview with AA, who felt strongly that Dixon's Depression paintings were inauthentic.

37. MacLeish, quoted in Belisario R. Contreras, *Tradition and Innovation in New Deal Art* (Lewisburg, Pennsylvania: Bucknell University Press, 1983), 170. One hundred and seven federally funded community arts centers served more than eight million adults and children. The Federal Art Project produced gallery tours and traveling exhibits, and allocated funds for long-term displays of artworks in public buildings.

38. William B. Scott and Peter M. Rutkoff, *New York Modern: The Arts and the City* (Baltimore: Johns Hopkins University Press, 2001), 291–92. The rules imposed by the Treasury Department's Section of Fine Arts led artists to coin the phrase "painting section," meaning sticking to pleasant and agreeable imagery. Open conflicts were uncommon, usually because artists knew enough to avoid provocative subjects. News of the conflicts that did happen spread quickly and created further self-censorship. Roy Rosenzweig and Barbara Melosh, "Government and the Arts: Voices from the New Deal Era," *Journal of American History* 77, no. 2 (1990): 596–608; Catherine Barnett, "The Writing on the Wall," *Art and Antiques* (March 1988), 90–99, 124–28.

39. These photographs, in OM, are numbered LNG3305, LNG34021, LNG34008.1.

40. Lester Balog, from the radical New York Photo League, who was temporarily in the West, may have been the organizing force behind the group. Unfortunately, nothing more seems to be known about this exhibit. Barbara Head Millstein and Sarah M. Lowe, *Consuelo Kanaga: An American Photographer* (Seattle: University of Washington Press, 1992), 35.

41. Doud, DL; Riess, 150.

42. A copy of the poster is in box 21, folder 22, Alexander Meiklejohn Papers, Wisconsin Historical Society, Madison, Wisconsin.

43. Some curators have identified this photograph as May Day 1933, but that is unlikely, because it poured on May Day that year, while in this picture, the day is dry. Another expert dated it 1936. Elsewhere it has been identified as the San Francisco general strike of 1934, but this is also unlikely, because the signs protest Japanese aggression against China (including several signs in Chinese). Lange likely made this picture at a Chinatown demonstra-

tion directed specifically at that issue. The photograph appears, for example, in Dorothea Lange, *Photographs of a Lifetime* (Millerton, New York: Aperture, 1982), dated 1934; Therese Thau Heyman, Sandra S. Phillips, and John Szarkowski, eds., *Dorothea Lange: American Photographs* (San Francisco: San Francisco Museum of Modern Art and Chronicle Books (1994), dated 1934; Keith F. Davis, *The Photographs of Dorothea Lange* (New York: Hallmark Cards, 1995), dated 1933; Mark Durden, *Dorothea Lange* (New York: Phaidon, 2001), dated 1934.

44. Dock workers were so numerous that two-thirds of the city residents were male and a full one-quarter were male blue-collar workers. Kevin Starr, *Endangered Dreams: The Great Depression in California* (New York: Oxford University Press, 1996), 84.

45. Paul S. Taylor and Norman Leon Gold, "San Francisco and the General Strike," *Survey Graphic* 23, no. 6 (1934): 405 ff.; "Helen Hosmer, A Radical Critic of California Agribusiness in the 1930s," interview by Randall Jarrell, Santa Cruz, 1992, transcript, UCLA, 72.

46. Wesley M. Burnside, *Maynard Dixon: Painter of the West* (Provo, Utah: Brigham Young University Press, 1974), 114.

47. Nicholas Natanson, *The Black Image in the New Deal: The Politics of FSA Photography* (Knoxville: University of Tennessee Press, 1992), 26.

48. Dorothea Lange et al., *The Thunderbird Remembered: Maynard Dixon, the Man and the Artist* (Los Angeles: Gene Autry Western Heritage Museum, 1994), 56–57.

49. It was this visit that interested Maynard in painting the dam.

50. Lange et al., *The Thunderbird Remembered*, 61.

51. Riess, 123.

52. This account was taken from Joan Bowly's diary of the trip, JDC.

53. MD diary.

## 8. Paul Schuster Taylor, Maverick Economist

1. All biographical material on Taylor, unless otherwise cited, was taken from Riess/PST.

2. Anne Dewees interview with PST, February 17, 1941, RG 83, BAE, NARA; Abraham Hoffman, "Unusual Monument: Paul S. Taylor's *Mexican Labor in the United States* Monograph Series," *Pacific Historical Review* 45 (1976); 255—70.

3. Paul Schuster Taylor, "Goodby to the Homestead Farm," *Harper's Magazine*, May 1941, 589—97; Richard Stewart Kirkendall, *Social Scientists and Farm Politics in the Age of Roosevelt* (Columbia: University of Missouri, 1966), 113.

4. PST Bancroft, carton 88. In 1959 X-rays showed he still had a long abnormality on the right border of the upper mediastinum; I. Kurita, M.D., to I.C.A., August 3, 1959, in box 29, folder 33, PST Bancroft.

5. Carton 88, folder 19, PST Bancroft.

6. He cherished a rifle and a box of smaller WWI mementos he had brought home with him, and he liked to wear his Purple Heart. All his life, he loved military band music and found John Philip Sousa particularly stirring. Author's interview with Anne Taylor, April 14, 2004; HM interview with Margot and Don Fanger, January 24, 1999.

7. Riess/PST, vol. 1, 97 ff.

8. He had been interested in cameras as a child, and took one into combat, photographing from his foxhole in the Verdun. He got the idea of using photography in scholarship from UC Berkeley anthropologist Arthur Kroeber, who photographed the Indians he studied.

9. Hoffman, "Unusual Monument," 264.

10. Since primary elections were ostensibly private affairs, run by political parties, not governments, it was legal to exclude nonwhites. Since the South was a one-party, Democratic region at the time, the primaries determined who held office and the general elections were insignificant.

11. Riess/PST, vol. 1., 17.

12. The Durán letters are in PST Bancroft.

13. Norris, quoted in Robert Dawson and Gray Brechin, *Farewell, Promised Land: Waking from the California Dream* (Berkeley: University of California Press, 1999), 51–52.

14. Its holding company, Transamerica, owned more than half a million acres by 1936. Alan L. Olmstead and Paul W. Rhode, "An Overview of the History of California Agriculture, Working Paper number 89, Agricultural History Center, University of California, Davis, 1997, 10; Dawson and Brechin, *Farewell, Promised Land,* 69; Riess/PST, vol. 2, 135.

15. State Relief Administration of California, "Migratory Labor in California," mimeographed report, 1936, 8. This uneven demand for labor was much greater in California than, for example, in the Southeast, because California's relative freedom from weeds and pests meant that its farms required less labor before harvest time.

16. Jack Temple Kirby, *Rural Worlds Lost: The American South, 1920–1960* (Baton Rouge: Louisiana State University Press, 1987), 7; Richard Steven Street, "Poverty in the Valley of Plenty: The National Farm Labor Union, DiGiorgio Farms, and Suppression of Documentary Photography in California, 1947–66," *Labor History* 48, no. 1 (2007): 25–48.

17. Moses S. Musoke and Alan L. Olmstead, "A History of Cotton in California: A Comparative Perspective," Working Paper number 6, Agricultural History Center, University of California, Davis, 1980, 20.

18. The burden was heavy. Kern County spent $4.3 million for relief in the 1938–1939 fiscal year, while the value of the cotton crop that year was about $5 million. Richard Lowitt, *The New Deal and the West* (Bloomington: Indiana University Press, 1984), 186–87.

19. The system constituted a seasonal taxpayer-funded unemployment insurance: private employers could lay off workers in slack times and let the state pay them a low subsistence, cutting them off when employers wanted help. When the New Deal brought in federal relief, growers fought to continue these cutoffs, because with continuous relief, farmworkers could demand wages at least above relief levels. Linda Gordon, "Shareholders in Relief: The Political Culture of Relief and Public Jobs in the Depression," Russell Sage Foundation Working Paper number 135, 1998; Martha Gellhorn to Harry Hopkins, November 19, 1934, box 66, Harry L. Hopkins Papers, FDR Library, Hyde Park, New York; Wayne Parrish to Harry Hopkins, December 1, 1934, box 65, Harry L. Hopkins Papers.

20. In cherries in 1936, one contractor got 35 to 45 cents a bucket and paid his workers 20 to 30 cents a bucket; his only expense was running a truck to get workers to the fields.

Louis Adamic, "Cherries Are Red in San Joaquin," *The Nation*, June 27, 1936; comments of Helen Horn, from minutes of Resettlement Administration conference on transients and migratory agricultural labor, San Francisco, December 14, 1936, box 4, folder 21, FSA papers, mss. CR, Bancroft.

21. Riess/PST, vol. 2, 16; "Helen Hosmer, A Radical Critic of California Agribusiness in the 1930s," interview by Randall Jarrell, Santa Cruz, 1992, transcript, UCLA, 40–42.

22. Lamar B. Jones, "Labor and Management in California Agriculture," *Labor History* 11 (1970): 23–40.

23. Quoted in Richard A. Walker, *The Conquest of Bread: 150 Years of Agribusiness in California* (New York: New Press, 2004), 67–69.

24. Leonard Leader, *Los Angeles and the Great Depression* (New York: Garland, 1991); Ramón D. Chacón, "Labor Unrest and Industrialized Agriculture: The Case of the 1933 San Joaquin Valley Cotton Strike," *Social Science Quarterly* 65 (1984): 336–53.

25. The 1930 and 1940 U.S. censuses show a 40 percent decrease in the Mexican-origin population. But censuses and legal immigration controls were even less reliable then than now, so these numbers are unreliable. On deportation/repatriation, see Mae Ngai, *Impossible Subjects* (Princeton, New Jersey: Princeton University Press, 2004); Abraham Hoffman, *Unwanted Mexican Americans During the Depression* (Tucson: University of Arizona Press, 1974); Francisco E. Balderrama and Raymond Rodríguez, *Decade of Betrayal: Mexican Repatriation in the 1930s* (Albuquerque: University of New Mexico Press, 1995); Guerin-Gonzales, *Mexican Workers & American Dreams*; Stein, *California and the Dust Bowl Migration*.

26. Quoted in Jorge L. Chinea, "Ethnic Prejudice and Anti-Immigration Policies in Times of Economic Stress: Mexican Repatriation from the United States, 1929 to 1939," at http://www.people.memphis.edu/~kenichls/2602MexRepatration.html.

27. Paul Taylor, "Uprisings on the Farms," *Survey Graphic*, January 1935; State Relief Administration of California, *Migratory Labor in California*, Special Surveys and Studies, 1936, 61–62; Jerold S. Auerbach, *Labor and Liberty: The La Follette Committee and the New Deal* (Indianapolis: Bobbs-Merrill, 1966), 177; Gilbert G. González, *Labor and Community: Mexican Citrus Worker Villages in a Southern California County, 1900–1950* (Urbana: University of Illinois, 1994), 139; Robert W. Cherny, Richard Griswold del Castillo, and Gretchen Lemke-Santangelo, *Competing Visions: A History of California* (Boston: Houghton Mifflin, 2005), 251.

28. Two thousand large farms dominated cotton. Its profitability was so great that growers quadrupled their acreage between 1932 and 1936. James N. Gregory, *American Exodus: The Dust Bowl Migration and Okie Culture in California* (New York: Oxford University Press, 1989), 25. Strikers were refusing to pick for 60 cents per 100 pounds, especially since they were aware that growers' profits had been raised by New Deal price guarantees.

29. Clark Kerr, Taylor's graduate student, later to be chancellor of the University of California at Berkeley, described it as "a world of hatred, of exploitation, of ideologies right and left, of the raw power of guns and hunger and damaged crops," noting how the situation exposed the falsity of the prevailing (among economists) competition model of wages. Clark Kerr report, box 8, PST Bancroft.

30. John Steinbeck, "Starvation Under the Orange Trees," *Monterey Trader*, April 15, 1938.

31. They advanced the Brentwood Plan, by which law officers would coordinate with AF, giving each worker an identity card, thus enabling the effective blacklisting of union sympathizers. U.S. Senate Committee on Education and Labor, *Employers' Associations and Collective Bargaining in California*, report no. 398, part 4, 1308–9, 78th Cong., 1st–2nd sess., 1943–1944.

32. *New York Times*, October 22, 1933.

33. Carey McWilliams, "The Farmers Get Tough," *American Mercury*, October 1934, 241–45; Carey McWilliams and Clive Belmont, "Farm Fascism," *Pacific Weekly*, April 6, 1936, 181–88; Carey McWilliams, speech in Los Angeles, March 21, 1940, box 14, Carey McWilliams Papers, University of California, Los Angeles; Steinbeck, quoted in Carey McWilliams, "A Man, A Place, and a Time," *American West* 7, no. 3 (1970): 63.

34. Taylor had some trouble getting his work published, as the University of California Press committee thought his scholarship was not really economics. Riess/PST vol. 1, 100, 109. Luckily, he had backing from other progressives in the department, including three senior women—Jessica Peixotto, Barbara Nachtrieb Armstrong, and Emily Huntington—who worked on issues such as welfare, poverty, and social reform, thus introducing social structure into their analyses (there was no sociology department at this time).

35. Ann Foley Scheuring, "A Learned Profession: A History of Agriculture at the University of California," Working Paper number 61, Agricultural History Center, University of California, Davis, 1990, 182–211.

36. Making him still more threatening to the agricultural tycoons, Taylor developed collegially supportive connections with reformers and with Mexican scholars, such as Manuel Gamio, Mexico's most distinguished anthropologist, whose studies of individual Mexican immigrants to the United States formed a companion piece to Taylor's work, and historian and writer Ernesto Galarza, who wrote about and helped to organize farmworkers.

37. John Kenneth Galbraith, "Berkeley in the Thirties," in *Economics, Peace and Laughter* (Boston: Houghton Mifflin, 1971), repr. in *Berkeley: A Literary Tribute*, ed. Danielle La France (Berkeley: Heyday Books, 1997), 46–47.

38. Correspondence with Monroe Deutsch, October 1933, box 5, folder 7, PST Bancroft.

39. Paul Taylor and Clark Kerr, "Documentary History of the Strike of the Cotton Pickers in California 1933," Hearings Before a Subcommittee on Education and Labor, U.S. Senate, 76th Cong., 3rd sess., part 54: *Agricultural Labor in California*; Riess/PST, vol. 2, 1–5; Kevin Starr, *Endangered Dreams: The Great Depression in California* (New York: Oxford University Press, 1996), 80. The report included photographs that Taylor got from Otto Hagel, a friend of Lange, whom Taylor had not yet met. The desperate situation of farmworkers intensified Taylor's conviction that he needed the power of photographs to provide evidence and move people to action. Richard Steven Street, *Photographing Farmworkers in California* (Stanford: Stanford University Press, 2004), 79.

40. "Intimate Journey: the Autobiography of Katharine Whiteside Taylor," typescript, author's possession.

41. Oddly enough, many years later, after the divorce, Katharine reported that E. A. Ross asked her to marry him.

42. HM interviews with Clark Kerr, April 21, 1999, and Greta Mitchell, May 21, 1999.

43. HM interview with Mary Spivey, May 13, 1999. Katharine's "crushes" included John Haynes Holmes, a prominent Unitarian minister; Paul Douglas, an economist and Quaker who was to become a three-term U.S. senator; and Jaime D'Angulo, an anthropologist who became part of the Carmel artist crowd. At D'Angulo's rustic "gypsy-like house" there were parties "wild and free beyond anything I had imagined. . . . Much wine . . . very free dancing, and lovemaking to a degree I never dreamed would go on with others present," Katharine wrote.

44. HM interview with Fangers, January 24, 1999. A friend of Margot's, Mary Spivey, heard a different version of the story: When Margot was seven, Aunt Ethel gave Kathy and Ross "edelweiss" pins. Margot asked where hers was, and Ethel said, "Hasn't anyone told this child?" HM interview with Spivey.

45. HM interviews with Spivey and Margot Fanger.

46. "She had a lifelong yearning for 'real' status . . . The yearning was . . . rooted in a basic lack, i.e., she was female. So she tried, time after time, to get it through a prestigious lover." Margot's handwritten annotation in her mother's memoir.

## 9. The Romance of Love, The Romance of the Cause

1. Van Dyke typescript, "683 Brockhurst," in Beaumont and Nancy Newhall Papers, box 122, folder 22, GRI; TH interview with Willard Van Dyke, 1977, OM.

2. Riess/PST, vol. 1, 112.

3. The project was funded by the Social Science Research Council and a Rockefeller Grant.

4. Clark Kerr, "Productive Enterprises of the Unemployed" (Ph.D. diss., University of California/Berkeley, 1949); John Curl, *History of Work Cooperation in America: Cooperatives, Cooperative Movements, Collectivity and Communalism from Early America to the Present* (Berkeley, California: Homeward Press, 1980); John Curl, "Living in the U.X.A.," at http://www.red-coral.net/UXA.html; Richard Lowitt, *The New Deal and the West* (Bloomington: Indiana University Press, 1984).

5. Van Dyke, "683 Brockhurst."

6. Riess, 166.

7. Riess/PST, vol. 1, 125.

8. Ibid., 122.

9. Riess, 165–66.

10. Doud, DL.

11. See PST to Tom Blaisdell, Jr. (of the Social Security Board), June 2, 1937, and June 14, 1937, carton 16, folder 13, PST Bancroft; DL to RS, June 30, 1937, RSS mss. Lange scribbled in her notebook, "The West is Being Re-fenced." Lange's 1936 notebook is in PST Bancroft.

12. The agency's name was changed to the Farm Security Administration in 1937 as part of the Bankhead-Jones Act. For simplicity's sake, and because the photography project continued the same across this administrative change, I refer to the agency as the FSA both before and after 1937.

13. Doud, C. B. Baldwin.

14. The fact that her name was not given in Taylor's records suggests her status. In an interview thirty years later, Dorothea called her "a wonderful creature," a disturbingly nonhuman label. Riess, 161–62.

15. Doud, DL.

16. Lange was on the State Emergency Relief Administration payroll starting in late 1934. DL to PST, undated but probably November 3, 1934, box 89, folder 54, PST Bancroft. Contrary to Lange's recollection, in Riess, 159, that she worked for seven weeks, her expense-reimbursement requests show that she was working fairly continuously from February through April and then again in June and July. She was not happy about her salary, and Taylor tried to get her a raise on the grounds of her previous high earnings, but he failed, despite her powerful references—John Collier, commissioner of Indian Affairs; the director of J. Barth & Co. brokerage; the president of Mills College; the wife of a federal judge; Anita Baldwin; and a few others. PST to Harry Drobish, memo dated February 24, 1935, FSA, Bancroft; Civilian National Personnel Records Center, St. Louis (hereafter CNPRC).

17. Riess, 160–61. This is almost $27 in 2007 dollars.

18. Travel expense voucher, January 24, 1935 through January 27, 1936, CNPRC.

19. Riess/PST, vol. 1, 131–32.

20. Ibid., 133.

21. Jessie de Los Angeles Cruz and Lillie Gasca-Cuéllar, quoted in Devra Weber, *Dark Sweat, White Gold: California Farm Workers, Cotton, and the New Deal* (Berkeley: University of California Press, 1994), 73.

22. Lange supplied the photographs, printed and bound the mimeographed reports, and later found a bindery to apply a spiral binding and cardboard for the covers, which she hand-waxed.

23. Lange field notes, March/April 1935, OM.

24. Report number 3, Sacramento, May 22, 1935, OM.

25. Weber, *Dark Sweat, White Gold*, 127.

26. A Mexican American woman in the Coachella Valley explained the low-wage versus relief problem personally in Spanish, which was translated for Lange: "We have never been so well off as we are now that we are on relief. We are getting $14 and $15 a week, because now we have a very good president. I don't vote but all my children do. First we give thanks to God for what we have and then our President." Lange field note to photograph number 35059.1, OM; reports to Harry Hopkins from his field investigators, November/December 1934, boxes 65 and 66, Harry L. Hopkins Papers, FDR Library, Hyde Park, New York; Lorena Hickok, *One-Third of a Nation: Lorena Hickok Reports on the Great Depression*, ed. Richard Lowitt and Maurine Beasley (Champaign: University of Illinois, 1981), 196 ff.

27. Reporting from Arizona, Eleanor Roosevelt's friend Lorena Hickok defined two classes of relief recipients: "[1] Whites . . . with white standards of living, for whom relief, as it is now, is anything but adequate. . . . [2] Mexicans—or, East of the Mississippi, Negroes—with low standards of living, to whom relief is adequate and attractive. . . ." Hickok, *One-Third of a Nation*, 238, 225–26, 231, 238–41, 244. The same division prevailed in the Southeast between whites and blacks and between whites and "white trash." William R. Brock,

*Welfare, Democracy, and the New Deal* (Cambridge: Cambridge University Press, 1988), 223–24.

28. Francisco E. Balderrama and Raymond Rodríguez, *Decade of Betrayal: Mexican Repatriation in the 1930s* (Albuquerque: University of New Mexico Press, 1995), 78, 87; Albert Croutch, "Housing Migratory Agricultural Laborers in CA" (M.A. thesis, University of California/Berkeley, 1948), written under PST's supervision.

29. My categorization is based on appearance when it provides clear identification, but also on clothing and the types of shacks built by the workers—e.g., Mexicans built huts of cactus, branches, palm fronds, etc.

30. Lange field notes, undated.

31. PST to Paul Kellogg, April 7, 1935, PST Bancroft. The RA/FSA soon began putting out press releases citing Taylor's findings: RA Division of Information, press release, January 9, 1936, IF-FRS No. 34, copy in vol. 2, misc. material, OM.

32. Sidney Baldwin, *Poverty and Politics: The Rise and Decline of the Farm Security Administration* (Chapel Hill: University of North Carolina, 1968), 221. The size of the Okie migration is often exaggerated, with some reports indicating a figure as high as 1.25 million. Bureau of Agricultural Economics news release, March 16, 1940, in vol. 2, misc. material, OM. Taylor's lower and more reliable estimate for the thirty-three months starting July 1, 1935, was 205,477. Taylor, "Refugee Labor Migration to California," *Monthly Labor Review,* April 1939, table 1.

33. Doud, DL.

34. Lange field notes, undated.

35. Camp-construction supervisor Irving Wood wrote a stinging response—"The right to evict would sooner or later be claimed on the same grounds. . . . If we permitted private growers to literally control the camps, their advantage over labor in the conduct of collective bargaining would be greatly enhanced"—and got Drobish to hold firm: The state would appoint a camp director, and the camp would have to be open to all who would abide by camp rules. George D. Nickel, director, SERA Kern County, to Harry Drobish, March 30, 1935; Taylor handwritten draft; Harry Drobish to George D. Nickel, April 5, 1935, and April 12, 1935, RG 96, box 10, file 028, NARA.

36. Riess/PST, vol. 1, 138.

37. Maynard Dixon hand-lettered the captions for the first two reports; later Lange printed or typed them.

38. MD diary.

39. TH interview with Van Dyke.

40. Ibid.

41. These quotations from Paul Taylor's letters to Dorothea are from JDC.

42. This was a Depression-era regulation officially aimed at distributing employment where it was needed most; underlying it was the common view of the time that married women did not have a need for or a right to employment.

43. He first told Larry Hewes, a former colleague in California's emergency relief program, then administrative assistant to Tugwell, Hewes first responded that there was no way this

could happen. Taylor threatened to resign in order to be with Dorothea. This may have begun as a tactical threat, but it was soon a real possibility in his love-intoxicated mind. He wrote Lange that he would resign rather than have her lose the opportunity that, he knew, would mean so much to her. He strategized about how he might get the Rockefeller Foundation to fund his work so that he could travel with her without being a federal employee.

44. They assembled a group of her photographs, printed in a fourteen-by-eighteen-inch format and mounted, and presented them in a portfolio to Tugwell. Tugwell wanted to show them to the president, but this did not happen.

45. Doud, Ben Shahn, April 14, 1964.

46. Taylor wrote to Lange that Stryker thought "you and Ward [sic] Evans . . . are in a class by yourselves. . . ." PST to DL, undated letter (1935), box 89, folder 54, PST Bancroft. Taylor's plan was to announce their marriage only after she was on the payroll. She was uneasy with this tactic, but he responded that they should face problems as they arose rather than anticipate them.

47. Riess/PST, vol. 2, 27.

48. The FERA would not pay for this. Taylor enlisted Walter Packard of the FSA to ask for funds from the Rockefeller Foundation, but Will Alexander, head of the FSA, prohibited this. Packard to Alexander, September 21, 1935, and Alexander to Packard, September 25, 1935, in box 13, folder 17, PST Bancroft.

49. Riess/PST, vol. 2, 28.

50. Walter J. Stein, *California and the Dust Bowl Migration* (Westport, Connecticut: Greenwood Press, 1973), 151–58. Historians disagree about how many RA/FSA camps were ever built. Richard Lowitt says there were ten permanent camps and five mobile camps by 1940; *The New Deal and the West*, 187. Don Mitchell says twelve permanent and three mobile; *The Lie of the Land: Migrant Workers and the California Landscape* (Minneapolis: University of Minnesota Press, 1996), 182. Anne Loftis says sixteen in California and Arizona; *Witness to the Struggle: Imaging the 1930s California Labor Movement* (Reno: University of Nevada Press, 1998), 143. The discrepancy probably results from different decisions about which camps should be included.

51. PST to DL, undated letter (from the Capitol Limited train, summer 1935), JDC.

52. PST to DL, undated letter, box 89, folder 54, PST Bancroft.

53. Dorothea told Imogen Cunningham that Maynard had helped her come to the decision. MM interview with IC, quoted in Milton Meltzer, *Dorothea Lange: A Photographer's Life* (New York: Farrar, Straus and Giroux, 1978), 126. Taylor said that there was total cooperation. Riess/PST, vol. 1, 149. Maynard, on the other hand, wrote, "Beginning of break-up of family. Leave for Nevada; residence in Carson; trip to Las Vegas, visit Martin Lange; go to . . . Death Valley, Rhyolite, Beatty; cloudburst, great beauty of color; landscape sketches. . . . Sell paintings in Reno. Tragic interlude: divorce. Return to S.F.: begin bachelor life in studio." MD diary.

54. Dorothea Lange et al., *The Thunderbird Remembered: Maynard Dixon, The Man and the Artist* (Los Angeles: Gene Autry Western Heritage Museum, 1994), 63.

55. TH interview with Van Dyke.

56. Ansel Adams recalled that Imogen Cunningham was in his San Francisco studio when Dorothea came in and announced grimly, "'I'm leaving Maynard.' Imogen burst into tears. Harrowing half hour!" TH interview with AA, September 15, 1976, OM.

57. Ironically, Cunningham had also objected fifteen years earlier when Dorothea announced that she was marrying Maynard, saying he was too old for Dorothea.

58. TH interview with Sturtevant.

59. "At first I wept bitterly . . . but then realized the rightness of it, for me as well as for him. I had been told when I awoke at the hospital that during my long sleep I had taken off both my wedding and engagement rings and put them down saying, 'for Dorothea.' My inner self wanted to give over the marriage to her. For me it had not been fulfilling." She later felt cheated by their financial settlement, getting what she described as a "meagre sum for my own 'rehabilitation' . . . and a minimal monthly allowance for each child." This allegation is mysterious, because Paul kept the children most of the time after the divorce. Katharine also said Paul had threatened that no judge would give her more because of her sins. "Yet I learned later that . . . I would have had half the estate since there was 'immorality' on both sides." "Intimate Journey: the Autobiography of Katharine Whiteside Taylor," typescript, in the author's possession.

60. Riess/PST, vol. 1, 149.

61. HM interview with Fangers, April 16, 1999.

62. The eldest, thirteen-year-old Kathy, was sent to her grandmother Rose and great-aunt Ethel, but they soon felt they could not manage, so she was moved first to the home of her Aunt Edna, Paul's sister-in-law, and then, when that did not work out, either, to that of a stranger, Mrs. Robinson. Ross went to the Gay family, who ran a summer camp and had participated in the day-care center the Taylor children attended. Margot was also moved twice, staying with two different families.

## 10. Blending a Family

1. PST to DL, undated (1935), JDC.

2. Author's interviews with John Dixon, February 2003.

3. PST to Paul Kellogg, March 23, 1936, PST Bancroft.

4. Handwritten note by DL, November 14, 1951, OM.

5. The house is important enough to be the feature of an article by John Ribovich, "Artist's Retreat: Maybeck and Magic in the Berkeley Hills," *American Bungalow* 56 (Winter 2007): 32–43.

6. "Intimate Journey: the Autobiography of Katharine Whiteside Taylor," typescript, author's possession.

7. Honored as the founder of progressive nursery school principles, Katharine was the author of three books on raising adolescents, including one for the Commission on Human Relations. In 1996, seven years after her death, she was inducted into the Cooperative Hall of Fame. The citation accompanying this honor credits her for, among other things, organizing California's first cooperative preschool, developing family-life and parent-education

programs in Baltimore, Denver, Seattle, and California, and publishing in 1954 a guide for parents in co-op preschools, a book is still in use. St. Lawrence College established an award in her name for a student of early-childhood education. She died in 1989.

8. Margot recalled that she went to 21 schools in 21 years. HM interview with Margot Fanger, April 16, 1999.

9. "Intimate Journey"; Riess/PST, vol. 1, 148–52.

10. Riess, 147.

11. Information about Taylor/Lange family relationships and feelings, unless otherwise cited, comes from the author's interviews with Andrew Dixon, Daniel Dixon, Gregor Dixon, Helen Dixon, John Dixon, Donald Fanger, Becky Jenkins, Rondal Partridge, Lisa Dixon Perrin, Dyanna Taylor, and Onnie Taylor. Margot and Ross Taylor died before I began this research, but I have the transcripts of interviews by others and I was able to speak with their spouses. Katharine Taylor Loesch lives in Chicago, and I interviewed her by phone.

12. Dorothea Lange et al. *The Thunderbird Remembered: Maynard Dixon, The Man and the Artist* (Los Angeles: Gene Autry Western Heritage Museum, 1994), 75.

13. Several of John's 1935 letters to his parents survive. Reading them with the knowledge of his situation makes them poignant, though if one did not know the context, they might seem like sweet and ordinary letters from a child away from his parents, perhaps at camp.

Dear Father (or Dad)

I am feeling good. I have a chart. I have 4 stars on my chart. I jumped 62 inches. I jumped and also I jumped 63 inches and I draw trees and leaves. I will see you next week, now I am having fun. . . . I sleep on the couch. Jimmy is a bad boy. Robert is a good boy. . . . Will you come over for me to get me on the train to go. JDC.

14. John Dixon, "Recapturing the Spirit," in Maynard Dixon, *Images of the Native American* (San Francisco: California Academy of Sciences, 1981), 73.

15. HM interview with Mary Spivey, May 13, 1999.

16. Dan Dixon, introduction to *Dorothea Lange: Eloquent Witness* (Chicago: Edwynn Houk Gallery, n.d.).

17. HM interview with Spivey.

18. KQED, 19.

19. Riess/PST, vol. 2, 69–70. He had longed for these rituals, even if he had been unaware. Before their marriage, he had written Dorothea, "Wish I might have spent Saturday afternoon and evening with you and the boys. As never before I am coming to want that kind of experience. . . . It will be a real reorientation of my life, and I want it, now, I think, in something like the same way I want my work to increase its effectiveness." Undated, JDC.

20. They married legally in 1941, when they already considered their relationship "doomed," to protect Becky from the stigma of illegitimacy. Lisa Rubens interviews with David Jenkins, 1987–1988, University of California/Berkeley Regional Oral History Office, Bancroft, 36, 123.

21. After Consie and Dave separated, Becky remained with her depressed, economically unstable mother until she was eight. When Dave remarried she was taken permanently into the close, vibrant family Dave and his new wife, Edith Arnstein Jenkins, formed. Becky

believes this saved her life. Edith Jenkins became her true mother and adopted her when she was an adult, Consie having resisted this for years. Later, Consie spent some time in a mental hospital and finally got some security from a Social Security disability stipend. Becky Jenkins to author, November 11, 2007, and November 19, 2007, and John Collier, Jr., to Becky Jenkins, undated letter on Consie's death, author's possession.

22. Becky Jenkins to author.

23. Dimitri Shipounoff, introduction to Charles Keeler, *The Simple Home* (orig. San Francisco: P. Elder, 1904; repr. Santa Barbara: Peregrine Smith, 1979), xxiv.

24. Charles Wollenberg, *Berkeley: A City in History* (Berkeley: University of California Press, 2008), chapter 6.

25. Henry F. May, *Coming to Terms: A Study in Memory and History* (Berkeley: University of California Press, 1987), 200–202. John Kenneth Galbraith recalled, "The graduate students with whom I associated in the thirties were uniformly radical and the most distinguished were Communists. I listened to them eagerly and would have liked to have joined both the conversation and the Party but here my agricultural background was a real handicap." John Kenneth Galbraith, quoted in Irving Stone, ed., *There was Light: Autobiography of a University, Berkeley: 1868-1968* (Garden City, New York: Doubleday, 1970), 25.

26. HM interview with Clark Kerr, April 21, 1999.

27. Author's interview with Walter Goldschmidt, February 3, 2003.


### Scene 3

1. Doud, DL.


### 11. Father Stryker and the Beloved Community

1. Roy Emerson Stryker and Nancy Wood, *In This Proud Land: America 1935–1943 As Seen in the FSA Photographs* (Greenwich, Connecticut: New York Graphic Society, 1973), 10.

2. My discussion of FSA politics is based on Sidney Baldwin, *Poverty and Politics: The Rise And Decline of the Farm Security Administration* (Chapel Hill: University of North Carolina Press, 1968).

3. Tugwell's proposed interpretation of the AAA law was drafted by Alger Hiss, who had become an expert on cotton agriculture in particular. John C. Culver and John Hyde, *American Dreamer: The Life and Times of Henry A. Wallace* (New York: W. W. Norton, 2000), 155.

4. Grant McConnell, *The Decline of Agrarian Democracy* (New York: Atheneum, 1977), 89, 93.

5. The RA's budgetary orphanhood set up competition between Tugwell and FERA head Harry Hopkins, who wanted to centralize all relief programs under the WPA as the price of funding.

6. Laurence Hewes, *Boxcar in the Sand* (New York: Alfred A. Knopf, 1957), 57–61; Baldwin, *Poverty and Politics*, 221 ff.; Culver and Hyde, *American Dreamer*, 153.

7. Brenda J. Taylor, "The Farm Security Administration and Rural Families in the South: Economists, Nurses, and Farmers, 1933–1946," in *The New Deal and Beyond: Social Welfare in the South Since 1930,* ed. Elna Green (Athens: The University of Georgia Press, 2003), 30–46.

8. Will Alexander, FSA administrator, to Secretary of Labor, June 7, 1939, RG16, E17, box 3019, NARA.

9. Memo and report from Alex McC. Ashley to W. A. Jump, Director of Finance, November 16, 1939, ibid.

10. Johanna Schoen, *Choice & Coercion: Birth Control, Sterilization, and Abortion in Public Health and Welfare* (Chapel Hill: University of North Carolina Press, 2005), 37–40; Baldwin, *Poverty and Politics,* 299.

11. The FSA was distinctly more racially progressive than the rest of the Department of Agriculture. Jess Gilbert and Alice O'Connor, "Leaving the Land Behind: Struggles for Land Reform in US Federal Policy, 1933–1965," in *Who Owns America? Social Conflict over Property Rights* ed. Harvey M. Jacobs (Madison: University of Wisconsin Press, 1998), 115.

12. Quoted in Nicholas Natanson, *The Black Image in the New Deal: The Politics of FSA Photography* (Knoxville: University of Tennessee Press, 1992), 52–53.

13. Doud, C. B. Baldwin, February 26, 1965.

14. Natanson, *The Black Image in the New Deal,* 215–23.

15. Cara A. Finnegan, *Picturing Poverty: Print Culture and FSA Photographs* (Washington, D. C.: Smithsonian Institution Press, 2003), 74.

16. The single exception was the National Youth Administration, an unusually daring agency due to its leaders, Mary McLeod Bethune and Aubrey Williams. Natanson, *The Black Image in the New Deal,* 37.

17. Barbara Melosh, *Engendering Culture: Manhood and Womanhood in New Deal Public Art and Theater* (Washington, D.C.: Smithsonian Institution Press, 1991), 71.

18. Lange thought that Tugwell's motive was "a combination of something he really wanted to do and taking care of one of his boys." Transcript of a conversation with Roy Stryker and photographers, 1952, box 10, John Vachon Papers, Manuscript Division, Library of Congress, Washington, D.C. (cited hereafter as Conversation with Stryker and photographers).

19. James Curtis, *Mind's Eye, Mind's Truth: FSA Photography Reconsidered* (Philadelphia: Temple University Press, 1989), 9.

20. Conversation with Stryker and photographers.

21. Doud, DL.

22. The pay scale discriminated against women: Office manager Clara Wakeham received just barely more than the lowest-paid men, for example.

23. In 2007 dollars, this would be $981,000. Salaries had gone up since Lange was hired, but not by much: Stryker earned $5,600, the top photographers $2,600, Rosskam $3,200, and the senior secretary/office manager, Clara "Toots" Wakeham, $1,680. The lowest-paid man got $1,620 and clerk/typist Charlotte Aiken $1,500.

24. Other government agencies used not only photographs but information. In the early days of the project, whenever photographers came in from the field, they were "shipped across

the street to the Department of Agriculture. And we would be pumped dry by . . . desk-rooted specialists who couldn't care less about our photographs." Richard Doud, John Collier, January 18, 1965.

25. RS to Peter Pollack, October 15, 1957, in Pollack papers, box 5, folder 39, GRI.

26. "Could the man read? What interested him? What did he see about him? . . . a sincere, passionate love of people, and respect for people." Doud, Stryker, 1963–1965.

27. F. Jack Hurley, *Portrait of a Decade: Roy Stryker and the Development of Documentary Photography in the Thirties* (Baton Rouge: Louisiana University Press, 1972), 40.

28. Doud, Stryker. Rothstein went on to become a photographic intellectual, writing about the development of documentary photography, as well as the head photographer for *Look* magazine.

29. Quotation in Edwin Locke, "FSA," *U.S. Camera*, February 1941, 23. Ernestine Evans, introduction to *The Frescoes of Diego Rivera* (New York: Harcourt, Brace, 1929). See also mention of her in Diego Rivera, *My Art, My Life* (New York: Dover, 1991), viii, and in Bertram D. Wolfe, *Diego Rivera, His Life and Times* (New York: Alfred A. Knopf, 1939), 63. Ernestine Evans knew and loved Mexico and the southwestern United States; interested in rammed-earth houses, she secured for Walker an assignment to photograph these for the FSA; he did a poor job, but Stryker quickly sensed his potential. Stryker recalled, "If somebody were going to Europe and they talked to Ernestine and she gave them a series of letters" of introduction, he would return and report, "even the President's letters weren't as good as a couple of her letters." Doud, Stryker.

30. Richard B. Woodward, "Revising a Classic," *Doubletake*, Spring 2000, 116–119.

31. Doud interview with Ben Shahn, April 14, 1964. The attraction can be explained by Evans's commitment to high culture, his disdain for conventional respectability and for everything pretentious, corny, or vulgar, and the "negative personal magnetism which is his only and suicidal claim on people," as Evans's friend Lincoln Kirstein put it. Kirstein, quoted in James R. Mellow, *Walker Evans* (New York: Basic Books, 1999), 142.

32. HM interview with Louise Rosskam, July 30, 1999.

33. Doud, Mydans, April 29, 1964.

34. Lange's early federal personnel records are inconsistent, contradictory, confused, and confusing—a situation typical in New Deal agencies being run at an emergency pace—about when she started. Throughout 1935, her salary came from several different agencies. She was first hired as a temp and then given a long-term contract, but even that appointment was dependent on the availability of emergency funds. Paul Taylor was at first Lange's supervisor. He signed her letter of introduction, saying that she was a "field investigator-photographer" for the federal government and that "Any courtesies to Miss Lange will be appreciated." As their romance developed, Taylor arranged to withdraw from his supervisory role.

35. PST to RS, November 9, 1935, and RS to PST, November 15, 1935, RG 96, box 26, file 160, NARA.

36. Karen Becker Ohrn, *Dorothea Lange and the Documentary Tradition* (Baton Rouge: Louisiana State University Press, 1980), 109.

37. R. H. Doherty, Jr., "USA FSA," *Camera*, n.d., quoting *Harvester World* 51, nos. 2–3 (1960), says the FSA produced more than 272,000 pictures; see Beaumont Newhall, untitled paper, box 43, folder 12, Newhall Papers, GRI. The number was 100,000 according to Leah Bendavid-Val, *Propaganda & Dreams: Photographing the 1930s in the USSR and the US* (Zurich: Edition Stemmle, 1999), 52.

38. Conversation with Stryker and photographers.

39. "When Roy said he was trying to get organized," Lange said, "so far as I knew he never really did get organized. The ideas always grew faster than you could keep up with them . . . Maybe the fact that we didn't have any organization, maybe the fact that we grew like Topsy for a while had something to do with" our success. Ibid.

40. Stryker, Tugwell, and FDR never publicly denounced lynching.

41. Doud, Charlotte Aiken and Helen Wool, April 17, 1964.

42. Doud, Marion Post Wolcott, January 18, 1965.

43. Doud, Mydans.

44. Doud, Stryker.

45. Stryker and Wood, *In This Proud Land*, 188.

46. Thomas H. Garver, ed., *Just Before the War: Urban America from 1935 to 1941 As Seen by Photographers of the FSA* (New York: October House, 1968), unpaginated; Arthur Rothstein, *Documentary Photography* (Boston: Focal Press, 1986), Appendix A.

47. Doud, Collier. All the photographers interviewed by Doud were in unanimous agreement on this point.

48. Doud, Stryker.

49. KQED, 16 and 17.

50. Doud, Stryker.

51. Evans repeatedly insisted that his work had no politics whatsoever, that he followed only an inner and exclusively aesthetic imperative, and he denied that Stryker or his fellow photographers influenced him in any way; see John Raeburn, *A Staggering Revolution: A Cultural History of Thirties Photography* (Urbana: University of Illinois Press, 2006), chapters 9 and 10.

52. *U.S. Camera* to DL, July 12, 1936, RS mss. All of Stryker's correspondence is in this collection unless otherwise noted.

53. P. Ingemann Sekaer to Mrs. Franklin Roosevelt, July 24, 1936, and RS to DL, October 22, 1936; RS mss.; Raeburn, *A Staggering Revolution*, 183–93.

54. Doud interview with Romana Javitz, February 23, 1965.

55. Quoted in Catherine L. Preston, "In Retrospect: The Construction and Communication of a National Visual Memory," (Ph.D. diss., University of Pennsylvania, 1995), 124.

56. See, for example, RS to Gardner Cowles (of *Look*), April 22, 1937.

57. He would write formal censuring letters to those who used FSA photographs without permission; for example, see RS to Acme Newspictures, June 29, 1936. On Social Security Board using FSA pictures without permission, see RS to DL, December 2, 1936.

58. RS to Arthur Rothstein, May 19, 1936.

59. RS to Russell Lee, May 17, 1938.

60. Tugwell, in turn, claimed that FDR was his protector. "If we got into any particular criticism, all I had to do was go and tell the President, 'You are going to hear something bad.'" Doud interview with Rex and Grace Tugwell, January 21, 1965. I am skeptical of this claim, given what we know about Roosevelt's political instrumentalism.

61. Each victory made Stryker more skilled and more cutthroat toward the photography project's opponents. He remarked, "... when the lion tastes blood for the first time he likes it. And I didn't forget that taste." Doud, Stryker. In Stryker's various conversations, he regaled interviewers with many stories of fending off attacks.

62. Doud, Stryker; Stryker conversation with photographers.

63. All the FSA photographers Doud interviewed made this point.

64. Doud, Collier.

65. Stryker conversation with photographers.

66. KQED 13 and 20.

67. Stryker conversation with photographers.

68. Doud, Shahn.

69. Stryker conversation with photographers; Doud, Shahn.

70. Jack Delano, *Photographic Memories* (Washington, D.C.: Smithsonian Institution Press, 1997), 35.

71. RS to Arthur Rothstein, February 9, 1937.

72. Stryker conversation with photographers.

73. He told Hine that he lacked funds, but to others he claimed that Hine "is not again going to do the type of work he did in his younger days." RS to Lewis Hine, December 14, 1935; Hine to RS, December 27, 1935; RS to Hine, January 1936; RS to Hine, July 24, 1936; RS to Rexford Tugwell, December 13, 1938. In fairness, we should acknowledge that others may have shared Stryker's judgment at this time. In 1939, Hine was fired, or let go, from a job at the United Fund in New York City (and Jack Delano was hired to replace him); Hank O'Neal *A Vision Shared: A Classic Portrait of America and Its People, 1935–1943* (New York: St. Martin's Press, 1976), 234. A few days after Stryker's last refusal, Hine's wife died. Stryker did, at the urging of Elizabeth McCausland, get Tugwell to lend his name as a sponsor to an exhibit of Hine's work, but it was too late to give Hine a boost—he died broke and depressed in November 1940. Walter Rosenblum's foreword to *America & Lewis Hine: Photographs 1904–1940* (Millerton, New York: Aperture, 1977), 10–11. A month before his death, Hine wrote Stryker to ask for a letter of recommendation for his application for a Guggenheim, for which he had already been turned down twice. Hine to RS, October 17, 1940.

74. Kate Sampsell, "'Three Generations of Grass': Photography, Liberalism and the Myth of the American Yeoman," *History of Photography* 27, no. 4 (Winter 2003): 334; Raeburn, *A Staggering Revolution*, 163.

75. Doud interview with Gordon Parks, December 30, 1964.

76. Doud, Lee, June 2, 1964, 17.

77. Conversation with Stryker and photographers.

78. HM interview with Rosskam.

79. Doud interviews, passim. When Doud asked Russell Lee what he would have changed in the FSA project, he said, nothing, but his wife, Jean, said she would have liked to stay in places with washing machines, because she got sick of washing clothes in hotel bathrooms. Doud, Lee.

80. Bubley was first a copy photographer at the National Archives, then was hired as an FSA darkroom assistant in 1942. Stryker let her try out by making documentary photographs in Washington; they were good, he was impressed, and he hired her at the bitter end of the photography shop for one project, documenting a Greyhound bus trip around the country. My thanks to Beverly Brannan for this information.

81. Melissa A. McEuen, *Seeing America: Women Photographers Between the Wars* (Lexington: University Press of Kentucky, 2004), 147.

82. Doud, Stryker; Doud, Edwin Rosskam, August 3, 1965. My interpretation of how gender worked at the FSA has been influenced especially by the work of Sally Stein. See also Andrea Fisher, *Let Us Now Praise Famous Women: Women Photographers for the U.S. Government, 1935 to 1944* (London: Pandora, 1987); Sharon Ann Musher, "A New Deal for Art" (Ph.D. diss., Columbia University, 2006); McEuen, *Seeing America;* Preston, "In Restropect,"

83. Doud, Stryker.

## 12. On the Road: California

1. Taylor's graduate students included Varden Fuller, Stuart Jamieson, Walter Stein, Walter Goldschmidt, Clark Kerr, Albert Croutch, Zelma Parker, Arthur Ross, Frank Speth, and Samuel Wood.

2. To avoid taxing the reader with repetitive material, I discuss only three main regions where Lange photographed: California, the southern plains drought area, and the Southeast. She did significant photography also in Oregon, Idaho, Utah, Washington, New Jersey, and New York. New England was the only region she never photographed.

3. Unless otherwise noted, all quotations from farmworkers come from Lange's field notes.

4. KQED 17, 21, and 23.

5. Vicki Goldberg, "Propaganda Can Also Tell the Truth," *American Photographer,* December 1978, 17.

6. Conversation with Stryker and photographers; Carl Mydans, *Carl Mydans, Photojournalist* (New York: Harry N. Abrams, 1985), 19.

7. Doud, Jack and Irene Delano, June 12, 1965.

8. Lange field notes, February 21, 1936, San Luis Obispo; conversation with Stryker and photographers.

9. DL to RS, March 2, 1936, RS mss. All Lange-Stryker correspondence is in RS mss. unless otherwise noted.

10. Author's interview with Don Fanger.

11. HM interviews with Alice Hamburg, Tanya Goldsmith, Ernie Goldsmith, and Sonia Ruehl, April 22, 1999, and November 23, 1999.

12. Elizabeth Partridge, ed., *Dorothea Lange: A Visual Life* (Washington, D.C.: Smithsonian Institution Press, 1994), 10.

13. She had to discipline him about his youthful pranks, too. Once, Ron swiped a sugar container from a tiny café/gas station. When, miles down the road, she realized what he'd done, she told him to return it. He drove back, and the waitress said, "I thought I'd be seeing you again." Author's interview with RP, March 21, 2002. Subsequent quotations regarding Lange's working method are taken from this interview.

14. RP, reflections on tape made for MM, 1977; TH interview with RP and CG, August 26, 1975, OM.

15. Author's interview with RP.

16. Therese Thau Heyman, ed., *Celebrating a Collection: The Work of Dorothea Lange* (Oakland, California: Oakland Museum, 1978), 63–64.

17. My search could only bring up photographs with the name of the crop in the caption.

18. Lange field notes.

19. C. M. Johnson to Rep. Toland, May 2, 1940, box 9, PST Bancroft.

20. Michele L. Landis, "Fate, Responsibility, and 'Natural' Disaster Relief: Narrating the American Welfare State," *Law and Society Review* 33, no. 2 (1999): 306.

21. DL to RS (probably February 1936), with box of photographs number 12.

22. Quotation from Lange's field notes included in her letter to RS, May 28, 1937. On farmworker disease in general, see notes of Tom Vasey in PST Bancroft, carton 15; on children's work, see Raymond P. Barry, ed., *A Documentary History of Migratory Farm Labor in California* (Oakland, California: Federal Writers Project, 1938), on-line at http://content.cdlib.org/xtf/view?docId=hb88700929&doc.view=frames&chunk.id=div00122&toc.depth=1&toc.id=div00122&brand=calcultures.

23. Quoted in Walter J. Stein, *California and the Dust Bowl Migration* (Westport, Connecticut: Greenwood Press, 1973), 48.

24. Arthur Miller, "Tragedy and the Common Man," *New York Times*, February 27, 1949; later used as a preface to *Death of a Salesman*.

25. Leah Bendavid-Val, *Propaganda & Dreams: Photographing the 1930s in the USSR and the US* (Zurich: Edition Stemmle, 1999); Simon Dell, "On the Metaphor and Practice of Photography: Socialist Realism, the Popular Front in France and the Dynamics of Cultural Unity," *History of Photography* 25, no. 1 (Spring 2001): 52–60; Pamela Auchincloss and Klaus Ottmann, eds., *Social Strategies: Redefining Social Realism* (New York: Pamela Auchincloss/ Arts Management, 2003); Milton Brown, introduction, *Social Art in America 1930–1945* (New York: ACA Galleries, 1981); Marlene Park and Gerald E. Markowitz, *New Deal for Art* (Hamilton, New York: Gallery Association of New York State, 1977); Jeanine P. Castello-Lin, "Identity and Difference: the Construction of *das Volk* in Nazi Photojournalism, 1930–33" (Ph.D. diss., University of California/Berkeley, 1994); Belisario R. Contreras, *Tradition and Innovation in New Deal Art* (Lewisburg, Pennsylvania: Bucknell University Press, 1983); Susan Noyes Platt, *Art and Politics in the 1930s: Modernism, Marxism, Americanism* (New York: Midmarch Arts Press, 1999); Anthony W. Lee, *Painting on the Left: Diego Rivera, Radical Politics, and San Francisco's Public Murals* (Berkeley: University of California Press,

1999); Donald Drew Egbert, *Socialism and American Art* (Princeton, New Jersey: Princeton University Press, 1967). On New Deal social realism, see Barbara Melosh, *Engendering Culture: Manhood and Womanhood in New Deal Public Art and Theater* (Washington, D.C.: Smithsonian Institution Press, 1991).

26. Nicholas Natanson, *The Black Image in the New Deal: The Politics of FSA Photography* (Knoxville: University of Tennessee Press, 1992), 72. He calculated that Parks led in photographs of nonwhites; then came Lange, 31 percent; Post Wolcott, 24 percent; Rosskam, 24 percent; Evans, 18 percent; Collier, 14 percent; Shahn, 10 percent.

27. Critic Sally Stein calls them "padonna" images. Sally Stein, "Passing Likeness: Dorothea Lange's 'Migrant Mother' and the Paradox of Iconicity," in *Only Skin Deep: Changing Visions of the American Self,* ed. Coco Fusco and Brian Wallis (New York: Harry N. Abrams, 2003); Sally Stein, "Peculiar Grace: Dorothea Lange and the Testimony of the Body," in *Dorothea Lange: A Visual Life,* ed. Elizabeth Partridge (Washington, D.C.: Smithsonian Institution Press, 1994).

28. Linda Gordon, *Pitied But Not Entitled: Single Mothers and the History of Welfare, 1890–1935* (New York: Free Press, 1994).

29. Conversation with Stryker and photographers.

30. A point also made by George P. Elliot in his introduction to *Dorothea Lange* (New York: Museum of Modern Art, 1966). This complexity extends to the way she depicted family and gender. See chapter 13.

31. Riess, 205.

32. KQED 23.

33. She disliked "poetic" captions. Riess, 205–206.

34. Lange caption to LoC 018899-E through 018903-E.

35. Lange caption to LoC 019285-D.

36. Big grower Wofford B. Camp belittled the old idea that " 'Nobody picks cotton but Negroes.' " His racism was not at all biological; he scorned the old belief that the Chinese could not pick cotton because their fingers were short and therefore broke the staple. Workers would do what they had to. Willa K. Baum interview with Wofford B. Camp, 1962–1966, 205, Bancroft.

37. Cletus E. Daniel, *Bitter Harvest: A History of California Farmworkers, 1870–1941* (Ithaca, New York: Cornell University Press, 1981), 67; State Relief Administration of California, "Migratory Labor in California," mimeographed report, 1936, 29–33.

38. From Lange's field notes, OM:

    3. White-Amer (carrots)

    2. Cantaloupe (Mex)

    1. Lettuce Filipinos

39. Raymond P. Barry, ed., *A Documentary History of Migratory Farm Labor in California* (Oakland, California: Federal Writers Project, 1938), on-line at http://content.cdlib.org/xtf/view?docId=hb8870092p&doc.view=frames&chunk.id=div00122&toc.depth=1&toc.id=div00122&brand=calcultures.

40. "Helen Hosmer, A Radical Critique of California Agribusiness in the 1930s," interview

by Randall Jarrell, Santa Cruz, 1992, transcript, University of California Regional Oral History Office, Bancroft, 38.

41. Memo for Will Alexander, December 28, 1938, RG 16, E 17, box 2782, NARA.

42. DL to RS, February 16, 1937.

43. Albert Croutch, "Housing Migratory Agricultural Laborers in CA" (M.A. thesis, University of California, 1948), 49. (This thesis was written under Taylor's supervision.)

44. Eric Thomsen, lecture, January 29, 1937, box 4, folder 15, FSA Bancroft; "Helen Hosmer, A Radical Critique of California Agribusiness in the 1930s," 43.

45. Mercer G. Evans, "Housing for Migratory Agricultural Workers," *Public Welfare News* 7 (1939), 2–4; Paul S. Taylor, "From the Ground Up," *Survey Graphic* 25, no. 7 (1936).

46. Marsha L. Weisiger, *Oklahomans in the Cotton Fields of Arizona, 1933–1942* (Norman: University of Oklahoma Press, 1995), 108.

47. Taylor, "From the Ground Up," 526.

48. Mimeographed newspapers from Shafter Farm Workers Community, 1939; 5/8, in FSA Bancroft; James Frederick Hamilton, "(Re)Writing Communities: Dust-Bowl Migrant Identities and the FSA Camp Newspaper at Arvin, California, 1938–1942" (Ph.D. diss., University of Iowa, 1993), 95.

49. For example, Marysville camp residents listened as a group to a radio broadcast of Paul Taylor's lecture to San Francisco's prestigious Commonwealth Club in 1935. Several listeners said that he knew what he was talking about and that they hoped some growers were listening. Anne Loftis to PST, June 23, 1981, box 10, folder 20, PST Bancroft; Anne Loftis, *Witnesses to the Struggle: Imaging the 1930s California Labor Movement* (Reno: University of Nevada Press, 1998), 149. On January 29, 1937, Eric Thomsen of the FSA gave a lecture on the camps to an educators' forum, entitled "Maverick University: or How the Migrant Gets an Education." He used Alexander Meiklejohn's definition of a liberally educated man as someone "who is trying, with some success, to understand what is happening to him in the midst of the civilization in which he lives." Meiklejohn was in the Bay Area during this period, and he influenced those in Lange and Taylor's network through his advocacy of continuing adult education.

50. Collins, quoted in Charles J. Shindo, *Dust Bowl Migrants in the American Imagination* (Lawrence: University Press of Kansas, 1997), 64.

51. Lange caption to LoC 000825-ZC.

52. Lange general caption #2, May 1939; KQED, 12.

53. La Follette Committee Hearings, part 62, 22637.

54. McWilliams, quoted in Linda C. Majka and Theo J. Majka, *Farm Workers, Agribusiness and the State* (Philadelphia: Temple University Press, 1982), 111.

55. Sanora and Dorothy Babb, *On the Dirty Plate Trail: Remembering the Dust Bowl Refugee Camps*, ed. Douglas Wixson (Austin: University of Texas Press, 2007), 79.

56. Frederick R. Soule to PST, July 3, 1937, box 15, folder 5–8, PST Bancroft; KQED 5.

57. PST to Garst, May 22, 1937, box 6, folders 12–13, PST Bancroft; Loftis, *Witnesses to the Struggle*, 151–52. Taylor succeeded only at Arvin where a new director, Fred Ross—the man who recruited César Chávez to farmworker organizing—overruled the segregation

policy; see Walter J. Stein, "A New Deal Experiment with Guided Democracy: The FSA Migrant Camps in California," *Communications Historiques* (1970): 132–46, 138; Verónica Y. Martínez, "Inside the Federal Labor Camp: Exploring Race, Community and Resistance in the U.S. New Deal Era," 2005, at http://www.utexas.edu/cola/depts/history/content/news/spring_2005/tex_mexico_conf/ponencia_v_martinez.pdf. Photographs of thirty-one actual signs at FSA camps making segregation explicit can be found at http://www.loc.gov.rr/prints/list/085 disc.html, accessed 10/20/2006.

58. One editor sarcastically changed Taylor's title, "From the Ground Up," to "From the Ground Up . . . Into the Air" and posed the usual tough question: "To what extent are government toilets etc a subsidy of the large fruit and vegetable interests . . . ?" VW to BA, June 23, 1936, and VW, notes, n.d., PST Bancroft; Cara A. Finnegan discusses this in *Picturing Poverty: Print Culture and FSA Photographs* (Washington, D.C.: Smithsonian Institution Press, 2003), 112ff.

59. For Taylor's overestimation of the camps' contribution, see Riess/PST, vol. 2, 47. For Lange's, see KQED 17.

60. PST to Paul Kellogg, June 3, 1935, PST Bancroft.

61. DL to RS, February 24, 1936.

62. Carol Shloss, *In Visible Light: Photography and the American Writer: 1840–1940* (New York: Oxford University Press, 1987), 224.

63. KQED 26.

64. Carey McWilliams, *Factories in the Field: The Story of Migratory Farm Labor in California* (Boston: Little, Brown, 1939), 249–251. Growers built stockades prior to strikes or unionizing drives in several locations, including Toppenish, Washington; Lange field notes, August 1939.

65. McWilliams, *Factories in the Field*, 254–59; John Steinbeck, "Poison Gas in America's Salad Bowl: Vigilantes Hunt Reds in the Lettuce Fields of California," *Literary Digest*, October 10, 1936, 5–6.

66. McWilliams, "A Man, a Place, a Time," *The American West* 7, no. 3 (1970): 5.

67. McWilliams, *Factories in the Field*, 236–37.

68. As cotton spread, it changed seasonal migration patterns by providing late-fall and winter employment in picking and early-spring employment in chopping. Workers who had once returned south now stayed to await early spring jobs, establishing homes in the San Joaquin Valley and finding it easier to organize. Ramón D. Chacón, "Labor Unrest and Industrialized Agriculture: The Case of the 1933 San Joaquin Valley Cotton Strike," *Social Science Quarterly* 65 (1984): 336–53.

69. Devra Weber, *Dark Sweat, White Gold: California Farm Workers, Cotton, and the New Deal* (Berkeley: University of California Press, 1994), chapter 7.

70. DL to RS (undated, received November 27, 1938).

71. Sally Stein, "Starting from Pictorialism: Notable Continuities in the Modernization of California Photography," in *Capturing Light: Masterpieces of California Photography, 1850 to the Present*, ed. Drew Heath Johnson (New York: W. W. Norton, 2001).

### 13. *Migrant Mother*

1. Biography of Thompson from her grandson Roger Sprague, at   http://www .migrant-grandson.com/the.htm; and from Geoffrey Dunn, "Photographic License," *New Times*, at http://web.archive.org/web/20020602103656/http://www.newtimes-slo.com/archives/cov_stories2002/cov_01172002.html#top. The various accounts of Thompson's life offer somewhat different chronologies.

2. Lange's narrative is from Dorothea Lange, "The Assignment I'll Never Forget: Migrant Mother," *Popular Photography*, February 1960, 42–43.

3. Ibid.

4. The number and sequencing of Lange's shots is uncertain because her film consisted of unnumbered sheets. I follow the reconstructions of Sally Stein, "Passing Likeness: Dorothea Lange's 'Migrant Mother' and the Paradox of Iconicity," in *Only Skin Deep: Changing Visions of the American Self*, ed. Coco Fusco and Brian Wallis (New York: Harry N. Abrams, 2003); Sally Stein, "Whose Family Romance?: Dorothea Lange, Migrant Mother, and the Biographic Public," unpublished paper presented at Art History and Biography Workshop, Getty Research Institute, February 2003; and James C. Curtis, "Dorothea Lange, Migrant Mother, and the Culture of the Great Depression," *Winterthur Portfolio* 21 (Spring 1986): 1–20.

5. Curtis suggested that she did this because evidence of so many children might raise questions about Thompson's morality, as he also suggests that Lange might have consciously excluded the father of the family from the picture, but he offers no evidence for either charge. James Curtis, *Mind's Eye, Mind's Truth: FSA Photography Reconsidered* (Philadelphia: Temple University Press, 1989), 52.

6. See www.capital-flow-analysis.com/Essays/migrant_mother.htm.

7. Raymond Williams, quoted by John Lucaites and Robert Hariman, "Visual Rhetoric, Photojournalism and Democratic Public Culture," *Rhetoric Review* 20 (Spring 2001): 40.

8. The "Madonna" discussion is indebted to Stein, "Whose Family Romance?" and Wendy Kozol, "Madonnas of the Fields: Photography, Gender, and 1930s Farm Relief," *Genders* 2 (Summer 1988): 1–23.

9. In fact, Stryker and his PR man were as much responsible as Rothstein, for they distributed different versions of the photograph, with captions implying that each skull was from a separate steer. RS to Russell Lee, June 21, 1937.

10. LoC 018227-C. In a group of photographs, a mother holds the hands of two young daughters, an adolescent boy pushes a baby carriage, and a father pulls a wagon with a toddler girl in it. Scholar James Curtis reasoned that Lange had first photographed the family from behind and then asked them to turn around; then, because that turn left the toddler in the wagon facing away from the camera, Lange deliberately tossed out an object to catch the girl's attention and get her to turn toward the camera. To Curtis, it was cheating to move people around. But the full set of negatives, as interpreted by Henry Mayer, suggests that Lange made a series of exposures, starting from when she first saw them walking toward

her, far down the road, and that the shot of the family from behind was made after they had passed Lange. The object that caused the little girl to turn was likely a negative sleeve; whether it was dropped deliberately or accidentally is impossible to know. HM to Beverly Brannan, undated letter, and HM to Sam Stourdze, November 25, 1998, author's collection. This procedure—making numerous photographs of the family, catching the little girl as she turned her head to look at something in order to animate her image, then sending only one negative on to Stryker—was consistent with Lange's customary practice.

Other scholars have challenged the "authenticity" of Lange's several photographs of "tenants without farms" in Hardeman County, Texas, made in 1938. She photographed these men in various groupings and positions. In other words, Lange moved her subjects around, framed her photographs differently, and cropped her prints variously in search of the strongest image.

11. RS to Arthur Rothstein, April 29, 1936. Then Stryker criticized the result: ". . . it looks a little bit too posed . . . men have fountain pens in their hands poised for writing which would be unlikely in an actual situation." RS to Arthur Rothstein, May 29, 1936. Writing Rothstein at another time, he said, ". . . you had best have them do a little staging for you . . . [but] if they [the pictures] aren't good, you may look forward to having your ears knocked off. . . ." RS to Rothstein, February 5, 1937. In 1940, Marion Post Wolcott asked him, "Do you want me to try to pose or 'fake' some of the things . . . which are 'out of season' . . . ?" Marion Post Wolcott to RS, September 25, 1940.

12. William Stott, *Documentary Expression and Thirties America* (New York: Oxford University Press, 1973), 67–73.

13. Maren Stange, " 'Symbols of Ideal Life': Technology, Mass Media, and the FSA Photography Project," *Prospects* 11 (1986): 85.

14. Delano, quoted in Hank O'Neal, *A Vision Shared: A Classic Portrait of America and Its People, 1935–1943* (New York: St. Martin's Press, 1976), 234.

15. Christina Page Gardner, "The Contemplation of Dorothea," unpublished manuscript, author's possession.

16. Riess, 158.

17. Historian Nicholas Natanson computed that in the 60,000 FSA photographs he sampled, blacks constituted about 10 percent of the images, a proportion better than that of any other agency publishing materials on America and Americans. This is, however, 10 percent of the images in the file; of those distributed, far fewer showed any people of color. Nicholas Natanson, *The Black Image in the New Deal: The Politics of FSA Photography* (Knoxville: University of Tennessee Press, 1992), 61–67, 72.

18. *U.S. Camera* sent the letter on to Lange. Previously, at least one other had claimed the woman in the photograph: In 1956, Barbara Crawford wrote to MoMA saying that the woman in the photograph "could easily be my identical twin" and that she hoped to find her in order to donate to "this less fortunate 'sister' . . . if such could be accomplished in a discreet manner." After some delay, the letter got forwarded to Dorothea, who replied on March 5, saying that she could not track down the subject but was "very happy that the photograph has had meaning for you. This is the kind of success that I really wish for."

She added, regarding the woman's neediness, "This is not a story of how it used to be; it still is," and urged Mrs. Crawford to make a donation to the American Friends Service Committee for its efforts on behalf of migrant workers. DL to Barbara Crawford, March 5, 1957, box 68, folder 3, Beaumont and Nancy Newhall Papers, GRI.

19. Author's interview with Helen Nestor, March 20, 2002.

20. Peggy McIntosh speaking to CNN reporters, December 3, 2008, at http://www.cnn .com/2008/LIVING/12/02/dustbowl.photo/. Nevertheless, a few critics have used Thompson's reaction to condemn Lange as instrumental and manipulative and her photography, again, as inauthentic: Mary Street Alinder, *Ansel Adams: A Biography* (New York: Henry Holt, 1996), 228; Curtis, "Dorothea Lange, Migrant Mother."

21. Roger Sprague Web site.

22. Lange field notes, February–March 1937, Imperial Valley.

23. Robert Coles, untitled essay, in *Dorothea Lange, Photographs of a Lifetime* (Millerton, New York: Aperture, 1982), 34.

24. Critic Jacqueline Ellis argues that such pictures close off the possibility of working-class self-representation even as they engender "a sense of social responsibility into the consciences of middle-class Americans." Jacqueline Ellis, *Silent Witnesses: Representations of Working-Class Women in the United States* (Bowling Green, Ohio: Bowling Green University Popular Press, 1998), 22, 29.

25. Judith Keller, ed., *Dorothea Lange: Photographs from the J. Paul Getty Museum* (Los Angeles: J. Paul Getty Museum, 2002), 107.

26. Miscellaneous clippings in OM—for example, *New York Times,* September 17, 1983, and *L.A. Times,* September 17, 1983; Bill Ganzel, *Dust Bowl Descent* (Lincoln: University of Nebraska, 1984). By the time she wrote to Lange, the three daughters in the photograph had all married: The girl on the left is Katherine (Peggy) McIntosh; on the right, Ruby Sprague; and the baby is Norma Rydlewski. In October 2007 the southern California wildfires destroyed the seventy-five-year-old McIntosh's home in Modesto and all her belongings, including a print of the *Migrant Mother* photograph. In late 2008 the Red Cross set up a fund to help her. See articles in *Modesto Bee* of October 27 and November 1, 2007, and December 11, 2008.

## 14. On The Road: The Dust Bowl

1. Lange captured this storm near Mills, in northeastern New Mexico, but was terrified and did not try it again: ". . . it was a death storm . . . we were in this thing before I realized what it was . . . I knew that that much grit would sandblast the lens and . . . get into the gears and I couldn't work the rest of the way. . . ." Another time, she tried to photograph by keeping her head directly on top of the ground glass but found the heat on the back of her neck unbearable. KQED 17.

2. She made 61 pictures labeled as belonging to the dust bowl, 104 identified as drought, and 222 whose captions included the word *Oklahoma*, for example, but these are underestimates, because so many photographs were captioned differently and because so many

people fleeing the drought and dust came from other states.

3. Quoted in James Frederick Hamilton, "(Re)Writing Communities: Dust-Bowl Migrant Identities and the FSA Camp Newspaper at Arvin, California, 1938–1942," (Ph.D. diss., University of Iowa, 1993), 92.

4. Kevin Starr, *Endangered Dreams: The Great Depression in California* (New York: Oxford University Press, 1997), 233.

5. Gerald Haslam, "*Grapes of Wrath:* A Book that Stretched My Soul," at www.californiaauthors .com/essay_haslam.shtml.

6. *Future of the Great Plains,* report of the Great Plains Committee, House of Representatives document no. 144, 75th Cong., 1st sess., 1937, 45.

7. John Opie, "Moral Geography in High Plains History," *Geographical Review* 88, no. 2 (1998): 246–247; Brad D. Lookingbill, *Dust Bowl, USA: Depression American and the Ecological Imagination, 1929–1941* (Athens: Ohio University Press, 2001), 12, 17–18; Timothy Egan, *The Worst Hard Time: The Untold Story of Those Who Survived the Great American Dust Bowl* (Boston: Houghton Mifflin, 2006), 24, quotation on 51.

8. Jack Temple Kirby, *Rural Worlds Lost: The American South 1920–1960* (Baton Rouge: Louisiana State University Press, 1987).

9. C. Vann Woodward, *Origins of the New South, 1877–1913* (Baton Rouge: Louisiana University Press, 1951), 407, 415.

10. Egan, *The Worst Hard Time,* 22, 58.

11. Quoted in Louis Owens, *The Grapes of Wrath: Trouble in the Promised Land* (Boston: Twayne, 1989), 52–53.

12. Lange field notes, box 16, folders 30 and 31, PST Bancroft.

13. Taylor's transcript of remarks of an Oklahoman from Washita County, n.d., box 16, folder 24, PST Bancroft.

14. Caption to BAE 521659.

15. Lange field notes, February 16, 1939, Shafter, California. When this sharecropper said "freed the mules," he was referring to replacing them with tractors.

16. Dorothea Lange and Paul Schuster Taylor, *An American Exodus* (New York: Reynal and Hitchcock, 1939).

17. Egan, *The Worst Hard Times,* 174; W. Richard Fossey, " 'Talkin' Dust Bowl Blues,' A Study of Oklahoma's Cultural Identity During the Great Depression," *Chronicles of Oklahoma* 60, no. 1 (spring 1977): 12–33.

18. California State Relief Administration, *Migratory Labor in California* (San Francisco, 1936), 179.

19. Caption to LoC 002464-E.

20. Starr, *Endangered Dreams,* 241.

21. KQED 13.

22. Field notes, June 8, 1937, as typed out and sent by PST to Thomas Blaisdell, Jr. of the Social Security Board, box 16, folder 20, PST Bancroft.

23. Los Angeles *Herald-Express,* December 11, 1935.

24. These laws were declared unconstitutional in 1941.

25. Leonard Leader, *Los Angeles and the Great Depression* (New York: Garland, 1991), 200.

26. Lange caption to LoC 016251-C.

27. Gregory, *American Exodus: The Dust Bowl Migration and Okie Culture in California* (New York: Oxford, 1989), 98.

28. Los Angeles *Herald-Express*, February 6, 1936.

29. Lange field notes, February 19–20, 1936, south of King City, California. In a letter to Stryker, Lange said she was trying to find the photographs, but I have never seen them in any collection. DL to RS, December 12, 1938.

30. Circular no. 556 from Miss F. M. Warner, State Board of Public Welfare, December 16, 1936, box 14, folder 25, PST Bancroft.

31. Quoted in Owens, *The Grapes of Wrath*, 4.

### 15. On the Road: The South

1. Quoted in Howard M. Levin and Katherine Northrup, eds., *Dorothea Lange: Farm Security Administration Photographs, 1935–1939* (Glencoe, Illinois: Text-Fiche Press, 1980), 39.

2. LoC 019773-C.

3. These strictures limited most New Deal public art. Maynard Dixon had also been constrained by them: Secretary of the Interior Harold Ickes rejected a Dixon mural for the Bureau of Indian Affairs because it showed an Indian farming with an automobile nearby; he said he would approve it only if Dixon eliminated the car and showed "a white man teaching agricultural methods to the Indians." Erika Doss, "Between Modernity and 'the Real Thing,'" *American Art* 18, no. 3 (2004): 15. The FSA photography project's successor agency, the Office of War Information, similarly censored interracial images in its wartime propaganda. George H. Roeder, Jr., *The Censored War: American Visual Experience During World War Two* (New Haven: Yale University Press, 1993).

4. Jack Delano to RS, April 19, 1941; Russell Lee to RS, March 19, 1940.

5. Arthur Rothstein to RS, March 7, 1937.

6. One version of the photograph shows a sliver of Paul Taylor along the left border, doing his usual two jobs—interviewing and holding the subject's attention while Lange did her work. Notice that this man stands in the same posture as that of the Mexican farmworker father with his baby in plate 18. It is a posture of power.

7. Letter to *Washington Times*, August 2, 1938, quoted in Charles Alan Watkins, "The Blurred Image: Documentary Photography and the Depression South" (Ph.D. diss., University of Delaware, 1982), 316.

8. The original caption in Lange's hand is in OM; the LoC caption is 017079-C. Publications featuring FSA photographs frequently cropped blacks out of the images. Pete Daniel et al., *Official Images: New Deal Photography* (Washington, D.C.: Smithsonian Institution Press, 1987), 100.

9. Caption to 017138-C.

10. General captions 7 and 18, North Carolina, LoC.

11. This is a great, though necessary, simplification, and I am grateful to Pete Daniel for help-

ing me with it. The Lange-Taylor interview-photography team had found, to the surprise even of Taylor, an enormous variety of owner-tenant agreements. Many tenants worked under combined wage and share agreements, as the Mexican "patch croppers" in Texas, who received wages plus the produce of a small patch of the owner's land. Some worked independently, provided they made the required payments to owners, while others were supervised as closely as wage laborers, although they earned no wages. Some supplied their own mule and plow and some supplied almost nothing. Pete Daniel, *Breaking the Land: The Transformation of Cotton, Tobacco, and Rice Cultures Since 1880* (Urbana: University of Illinois Press, 1985); Neil Foley, *The White Scourge: Mexicans, Blacks, and Poor Whites in Texas Cotton Culture* (Berkeley: University of California Press, 1997), 177–78; C. Vann Woodward, *Origins of the New South, 1877–1913* (Baton Rouge: Louisiana State Press, 1951); Jonathan M. Wiener, "Class Structure and Economic Development in the American South, 1865–1955," *American Historical Review* 84, no. 4 (1979): 970–92.

12. Arthur F. Raper and Ira De A. Reid, *Sharecroppers All* (Chapel Hill: University of North Carolina Press, 1941), 22; Daniel, *Breaking the Land*, 37. Landowners typically borrowed money at 6.5 percent.

13. This restriction was in violation of the federal antipeonage law, but it happened nevertheless.

14. Wiener, "Class Structures and Economic Development in the American South, 1865–1955," 980.

15. Jack Temple Kirby, *Rural Worlds Lost: The American South 1920–1960* (Baton Rouge: Louisiana State University Press, 1987), 77.

16. Woodward, *Origins of the New South, 1877–1913*, 408.

17. Raper and Reid, *Sharecroppers All*, 21.

18. Examples include LoC 017162-C, 018150-C, 017684-C, 009634-E, 017763-E, and 009303-C.

19. Terrell Cline, FSA representative at Belle Glade, Florida, to John Beecher at FSA Birmingham, May 14, 1939, OM.

20. Cindy Hahamovitch, *The Fruits of Their Labor: Atlantic Coast Farmworkers and the Making of Migrant Poverty* (Chapel Hill: University of North Carolina Press, 1997), 151–81.

21. Daniel, *Breaking the Land*, 181. In photographs LoC 017296-C, 017330-C, 017302-C, and 017595-E, Lange tried to make visual the evictions and the shift to wage labor.

22. U.S. National Emergency Council, *Report on Economic Conditions of the South* (Washington, DC: Government Printing Office, 1938), 9–12. Lange's photographs of erosion include LoC 020035-C, 018071-E, 018086-C, 020160-E; UNC P-3167B 188, 189, 191, and 196.

23. LoC 017969-C. There are several photographs of impoverished African Americans left without livelihood as lumber industries closed in at least three southern states. See 017852-E, 017778-E.

24. Daniel, *Breaking the Land*, 173.

25. Lange made several photographs of this woman's house and yard—019952-E, 019953-E, 020033-C—but apparently none of the woman herself.

26. LoC 018173-C.

27. Interviewed July 4, 1939.

28. Lange field notes, July 4, 1939.

29. Ibid.

30. Arthur Raper, *Tenants of the Almighty* (New York: Macmillan, 1943), quoted in Jess Gilbert, "Can Government Bureaucrats Foment Democracy? The Case of New Deal Agricultural Policy," paper given at Agricultural History Society meeting, June 2006, in author's possession.

31. Lange field notes, nd; DL to M. E. Gilfond, FSA Director of Information, July 20, 1936, RS mss.

32. See, for example, LoC 020204-E. For an ironic story about how one of these country-store pictures was used for World War II propaganda, see page 328.

33. KQED 19.

34. Caption to LoC 019972-C; William Stott, "Introduction to a Never-published Book of Dorothea Lange's Best Photographs of Depression America," *Exposure 22*, no. 3 (Fall 1984): 28.

35. See, for example, LoC 020128-E; KQED 26.

36. UNC P-3167B/45 and P-3167B/316.

37. LoC 018027-E.

38. Arthur Raper calculated that in two counties in Georgia more than 50 percent of white sharecroppers and 40 percent of black sharecroppers owned autos, Kirby, *Rural Worlds Lost*, 257.

39. LoC 019953-E.

40. Thirty years later, she could describe how rice and cotton agriculture produced different social and economic relations. KQED 19.

41. The UNC Press published Paul Taylor's study of binational Mexican workers, *An American-Mexican Frontier*, in 1934. In some ways, the research community that Odum had established around Chapel Hill was analogous to that of Taylor and his students at Berkeley.

42. PST to Arthur Raper, August 9, 1937, box 16, folder 20, PST Bancroft. Raper had worked for the Commission on Interracial Cooperation, a rare, even unique, southern initiative that Will Alexander headed before becoming head of the FSA.

43. Anne Firor Scott, introduction to Margaret Jarman Hagood, *Mothers of the South: Portraiture of the White Tenant Farm Woman* (New York: W. W. Norton, 1977; orig. University of North Carolina Press, 1939). A leading expert in statistics and demography, possibly the first to use analysis of variance and covariance, factor analysis, and principal components in demography and agricultural economics, Hagood helped plan censuses and developed the "level of living" index for each U.S. county, thereby creating the basis for comparative studies.

44. She also helped Lange write captions. Linda Grant, "The Relationships Between Gender, a Feminist Perspective and Research Methods," keynote address, Qualitative Interest Group, University of Georgia, 1993, at http://www.coe.uga.edu/quig/proceedings/Quig93_Proceedings/grant.93.html.

45. See, for example, LoC 020088-E.

46. LoC 019780-E and caption; general caption 13, July 5, 1939, UNC.

47. This account of the STFU was taken from: misc. memos in carton 17, folders 5–6, PST Bancroft; Howard Kester, *Revolt Among the Sharecroppers* (New York: Covici Friede, 1936); H. L. Mitchell, *Mean Things Happening in This Land: The Life and Times of H L Mitchell, Co-Founder of the Southern Tenant Farmers' Union* (Montclair, New Jersey: Allanheld, Osmun, 1979); David Eugene Conrad, *The Forgotten Farmers: The Story of Sharecroppers in the New Deal* (Urbana: University of Illinois Press, 1965); Donald H. Grubbs, *Cry from the Cotton: The Southern Tenant Farmers' Union and the New Deal* (Chapel Hill: University of North Carolina Press, 1971); Greta de Jong, " 'With the Aid of God and the FSA': The Louisiana Farmers' Union and the African American Freedom Struggle in the New Deal Era," *Journal of Social History* 34, no. 1: 105–39; Jess Gilbert and Steve Brown, "Alternative Land Return Proposals in the 1930s: The Nashville Agrarian and the Tenant Farmers' Union," *Agricultural History* 55 (1981): 351–59.

48. Kester, *Revolt Among the Sharecroppers*, 57.

49. KQED 2.

50. Donald Holley, *Uncle Sam's Farmers: The New Deal Communities in the Lower Mississippi Valley* (Urbana: University of Illinois Press, 1975); Joseph W. Eaton, *Exploring Tomorrow's Agriculture: Co-operative Group Farming—A Practical Program of Rural Rehabilitation* (New York: Harper & Brothers, 1943), 199.

51. Colleen McDannell takes Lange to task for not mentioning that this cooperative was funded largely by Eddy, a missionary, attributing this omission to Lange's secular bias. A valid criticism. Colleen McDannell, *Picturing Faith: Photography and the Great Depression* (New Haven: Yale University Press, 2004), 122–23.

52. Lange field notes, July 4, 1936; Jane Cassels Record to MM, December 13, 1976, photocopy in carton 89, folder 21, PST Bancroft.

53. H. L. Mitchell, *Mean Things Happening in This Land*, 133; PST field notes, Carton 14, folder 70, PST Bancroft.

54. KQED 2.

55. LoC 009610-C, 017271-C.

56. The photograph of H.L. Mitchell, 018193-E, is a classic Lange portrait, thanks to the grace of his lean body and worried face; see also J. R. Butler, 018285-C; unidentified black leader, 009549-C; unidentified white leader, 009598-C, all LoC.

## 16. *An American Exodus*

1. Dorothea Lange and Paul Schuster Taylor, *An American* Exodus (New York: Reynal & Hitchcock, 1939). It "pointed the way to a new medium, where words and pictures . . . reinforce one another . . . to produce [a] 'third effect.' " Beaumont Newhall, introduction to *Dorothea Lange Looks at the American Country Woman* (Fort Worth: Amon Carter Museum, 1967), 7. A more recent critic considered it "prophesying and anticipating the multimedia presentation forms of the digital era." A. D. Coleman, "Dust in the Wind: The Legacy of Dorothea Lange and Paul Schuster Taylor's *An American Exodus*," in Pierre Borhan, *Dorothea Lange: The Heart and Mind of a Photographer* (Boston: Little, Brown, 2002), 157.

2. HM, unpublished manuscript, 9, author's possession.

3. Older photo-textual books included Jacob Riis's *How the Other Half Lives* (1890), but both its photographs and text seemed dated by the 1930s and its halftones and woodcut illustrations did not do justice to his photographs. Closer to home, Rexford Tugwell, Thomas Munro, and Roy Stryker's *American Economic Life and the Means of Its Improvement* (1925) was saturated with photos, chosen by Stryker, but the photographers were not the authors of the book. Lewis Hine's *Men at Work* (1932) had little text, only captions. Carleton Beals's *The Crime of Cuba* (1933) featured Walker Evans's photographs. The genre was stimulated from the mainstream side by the new photographic magazines, *Life* and *Look.*

4. Quoted in David P. Peeler, *Hope Among Us Yet: Social Criticism and Social Solace in Depression America* (Athens: University of Georgia Press, 1987), 67.

5. Erskine Caldwell and Margaret Bourke-White, *You Have Seen Their Faces* (New York: Modern Age Books, 1937), note facing half title page.

6. Miles Orvell, *The Real Thing: Imitations and Authenticity in American Culture, 1840–1940* (Chapel Hill: University of North Carolina Press, 1989), 97.

7. Jack Delano to RS, April 9, 1941.

8. Maren Stange, *Symbols of Ideal Life: Social Documentary Photography in America, 1890–1950* (Cambridge, Cambridge University Press, 1989), 120.

9. Archibald MacLeish, *Land of the Free* (New York: Harcourt, Brace, 1938); John Raeburn, *A Staggering Revolution: A Cultural History of Thirties Photography* (Urbana: University of Illinois Press, 2008), 173–176.

10. This may have been in part because MacLeish had never himself seen what the pictures showed. MacLeish, then an editor at *Fortune,* was doing a piece on rural folk and asked Stryker for photographs. According to Ben Shahn, when he saw them, he said he was abandoning his text, "just using your photographs and I'll write a sound track for it. . . ." Doud, Ben Shahn, April 14, 1964.

11. MacLeish, *Land of the Free,* 7.

12. Roy Stryker, quite possibly at Lange's suggestion, envisioned an FSA photographic book about democracy, but it never materialized. Russell Lee to RS, September 22, 1940. Other photo-textual books would follow *An American Exodus,* including James Agee's and Walker Evans's *Let Us Now Praise Famous Men* (1941), Richard Wright's and Edwin Rosskam's *12 Million Black Voices* (1941), and Wright Morris's *The Inhabitants* (1946). But these authors did not notice, did not grasp, or chose not to emulate what Lange and Taylor were doing.

13. Four of the five pictures of people in chapter 1, and eleven of the thirteen in chapter 2 show blacks. The book's second photograph, *Hoe Culture, Alabama, 1937,* shows, in a typical Lange trope, rough hands holding a hoe—no head, no legs—and for quite some time, viewers and critics assumed these worn, dirty hands to be black, while they actually belonged to a white man. This fact underscores, accidentally, an explicit argument of the book: "Rural poverty in cotton is no longer a problem of race." *American Exodus,* 19.

14. Coleman, "Dust in the Wind," in Borhan, *Dorothea Lange,* 162.

15. Sally Stein, " 'Good Fences Make Good Neighbors': American Resistance to Photomontage Between the Wars," in *Montage and Modern Life 1919–1942,* ed. Matthew Teitelbaum (Cambridge: MIT Press, 1992), 129–89.

16. Conversation with Stryker and photographers. Stryker sneered at "the extreme angle German twist," displaying an attitude both populist and nationalist.

17. PST's handwritten note on letter from J. A. McKaughan of Reynal & Hitchcock, September 23, 1939, OM.

18. Ed Locke of the FSA wrote to Stryker about *The Grapes of Wrath*, "When you read it, notice how like the pictures of D. Lange it is." Ed Locke to RS, April 28, 1939. When *Life* and *Look* did stories on the novel, both requested FSA photographs. RS to Arthur Rothstein, May 12, 1939; RS to Russell Lee, June 13, 1939, and June 22, 1939.

19. D. G. Kehl, "Steinbeck's String of Pictures," *Image* 17, no. 1 (1974): 1–10.

20. The title was suggested by Taylor's old friend Paul Kellogg, of *Survey Graphic*. Riess/PST, vol. 1, 113.

21. The pioneer metaphor occurred to other writers, including federal employees, such as David Cushman Coyle, *Depression Pioneers* (Washington, D.C.: Government Printing Office, 1939), 4.

22. It was this strategy in *An American Exodus* that Gary Okihiro and I tried to emulate in *Impounded: Dorothea Lange and the Censored Images of Japanese American Internment* (New York: W. W. Norton, 2006).

23. Riess/PST, vol. 1, 217.

24. Taylor recalled her self-discipline: ". . . if the subject dictated that a certain photograph should be there, one that wouldn't meet the same artistic standard . . . that didn't bother her at all. The criterion for selection of photographs was: What were we trying to say . . . ?" Riess/PST, vol. 1, 295.

25. Roosevelt's column read, "It seems to me that in the pictures and in the spirit [that is, she had not actually read the book], this book marks a high point in artistry and shows us what life means to some of our citizens." "My Day," April 10, 1940, at http://www.gwu.edu/~erpapers/myday/displaydoc.cfm?_y=1940&_f=md055550.

26. AA to "Dorothea and Paul, Paul and Dorothea," January 25, 1940, OM.

27. Edward Weston to "Paul & Dorothea," April 1, 1940, and June 1, 1940, JDC.

28. Paul Strand, *Photo Notes* 4 (1940). Keep in mind that Strand was a Marxist at this point and would have found Taylor's text insufficiently focused on capital/labor relations. Furthermore, he had worked as director of photography and filmmaking for the Mexican Department of Fine Arts; in Mexico, he had been saturated not only with an extraordinary flowering of visual arts but with the intoxicating spirit of seeing the "masses" connect to the arts. James Krippner-Martínez, "Traces, Images, and Fictions: Paul Strand in Mexico, 1932–34," *The Americas* 63, no. 3 (2007): 359–83.

29. DL to RS, January 19, 1940.

### 17. Dorothea and Roy

1. In the summer of 1936, in late December 1936, twice in the summer of 1938, and in June 1939. The trip took four days by train, or nineteen hours by air plus four stops for refueling.

2. RS to DL, October 10, 1935.

3. TH interview with AA, September 15, 1976.

4. These problems continued long after she left the FSA. In 1940, *U.S. Camera* wanted to feature her photography, but she had no prints from which to make a selection. DL to RS, undated (1940).

5. DL to RS, June 18, 1937; for example, see DL to RS, January 12, 1938.

6. Milton Meltzer, *Dorothea Lange: A Photographer's Life* (New York: Farrar, Straus and Giroux, 1978), 169.

7. Charles Alan Watkins, "The Blurred Image: Documentary Photography and the Depression South" (Ph.D. diss., University of Delaware, 1982).

8. DL to RS, October 20, 1937.

9. DL to RS, October 10, 1937.

10. Meltzer, *Dorothea Lange*, 168.

11. Jack Delano, *Photographic Memories* (Washington, D.C.: Smithsonian Institution Press, 1997), 52.

12. DL to Miss Slackman, October 5, 1936, for example; see also DL to RS, February 12, 1936. At some level, Lange knew this. At a 1952 reunion, when the former FSA people were trading memories, John Vachon started to say to her, "I remember you . . ." and Lange responded quickly, "I am always afraid of something terrible when they start remembering me." Conversation with Stryker and photographers.

13. DL to Edwin Locke, September 10, 1936; DL to RS, March 19, 1937.

14. DL to M. E. Gilfond, October 19, 1936; DL to RS, November 11, 1936.

15. DL to RS, December 13, 1936; KQED 20.

16. DL to RS, June 9, 1937.

17. Service Rating Form, May 1939, OM.

18. DL to M. E. Gilfond, March 12, 1937.

19. F. Jack Hurley, *Portrait of a Decade: Roy Stryker and the Development of Documentary Photography in the Thirties* (Baton Rouge: Louisiana University Press, 1972), 60.

20. Evans made half as many photographs as Shahn in an equal period of time, and Shahn was himself not one of the top producers. James R. Mellow, *Walker Evans* (New York: Basic Books, 1999), 271. Evans's low productivity was an irritant because it cost seven hundred dollars a month, over and above wages, to keep a photographer on the road. James Curtis, *Mind's Eye, Mind's Truth: FSA Photography Reconsidered* (Philadelphia: Temple University Press, 1989), 11.

21. Slipping into an odd third-person voice, Stryker continued, "And I imagine some of Stryker's personal feelings were involved. . . ." Doud, Stryker. Historian F. Jack Hurley concluded that Evans never felt that Stryker could teach him anything. Hurley, *Portrait of a Decade*, 60–66.

22. Doud, Shahn, April 14, 1964.

23. DL to RS January 18, 1936; Colleen McDannell, *Picturing Faith: Photography and the Great Depression* (New Haven: Yale University Press, 2004), 153.

24. For example, see DL to RS, January 1, 1936, January 14, 1936, September 30, 1936, February 13, 1937, March 19, 1937, December 12, 1938, January 18, 1939, and March 2, 1939.

25. RS to DL, January 3, 1936, and May 12, 1939.

26. The darkroom workers made the same charge about Marion Post Wolcott's film; was it just coincidence that they complained of the two female photographers? RS to DL, October 7, 1936; email to the author from Professor Sally Stein, January 16, 2007.

27. TH interview with AA. At that time, film was not sealed as well as it is today, Adams recalled. According to Sara Halprin, the film Lange sent to Ansel Adams in Yosemite was actually developed by his assistant Seema Weatherwax. Sara Halprin, *Seema's Show: A Life on the Left* (Albuquerque: University of New Mexico Press, 2005), 111.

28. Halprin, *Seema's Show*, 111.

29. In the 1930s, professional photographers often "bracketed" their shots because film was slower, taking one picture at an exposure that seemed right and others just above and below. Margaret Bourke-White, for example, told Ansel Adams that she set her shutter at 1/200th of a second and then photographed once with every stop she had. Light meters were just coming out in the 1930s. Vicki Goldberg, *Margaret Bourke-White: A Biography* (New York: Harper & Row, 1987), 206; Ansel Adams, *An Autobiography* (Boston: Little, Brown, 1988), 265; Doud, Russell Lee, June 2, 1964.

30. RS to Russell Lee, June 13, 1939.

31. Jonathan Garst to RS, May 13, 1939.

32. Doud, Edwin Rosskam, August 3, 1965.

33. Doud, Marion Post Wolcott, January 18, 1965. Melissa A. McEuen, *Seeing America: Women Photographers Between the Wars* (Lexington: University Press of Kentucky, 2000), 137.

34. Carol J. Payne, "Interactions of Photography and the Mass Media, 1920–1941: The Early Career of Ralph Steiner" (Ph.D. diss., Boston University, 1999), 239.

35. RS to Marion Post, September 21, 1938; Doud, Post Wolcott; McEuen, *Seeing America*, 158.

36. McDannell, *Picturing Faith*, 10.

37. She photographed a pregnant woman without asking permission, and the irate woman stood up so quickly that her chair tipped over backward and dumped her. Marion Post to "Chief Stryker," July 28–29, 1940.

38. Marion Post to RS, February 24, 1940, and March 2, 1940.

39. RS to DL, October 22, 1936.

40. RS to DL, April 16, 1937, May 10, 1937, September 28, 1938, and September 7, 1939.

41. DL to RS, June 9, 1937, and September 30, 1936.

42. Did Stryker harbor some racist attitudes, like virtually all white Americans at the time? Possibly. He referred to one of his staff as a "Negro boy," in a 1960s interview. Doud, Stryker. But Stryker was right that racism in the District was appalling. Parks could not sit with the other photographers in the building cafeteria, could not get his son a soda at a drugstore, could be turned away at a movie theater. It was a "hate-drenched city," Parks wrote. Gordon Parks, *Voices in the Mirror* (New York: Doubleday, 1990), 81.

43. Quoted in Nicholas Natanson, *The Black Image in the New Deal: The Politics of FSA Photography* (Knoxville: University of Tennessee Press, 1992), 4.

44. Doud, Gordon Parks, December 30, 1964.

45. RS to DL, September 19, 1935, and October 30, 1935; PST to RS, October 24, 1935.

46. Therese Heyman thought that Lange expected to get permission to keep a reservoir of photographs in California because of Taylor's connections and influence. Judith Keller, ed., *Dorothea Lange, Photographs from the J. Paul Getty Museum* (Los Angeles: J. Paul Getty Museum, 2002), 113.

47. For example, see DL to RS, December 31, 1935.

48. PST to Thomas C. Blaisdell, Jr., April 25, 1937, and May 2, 1938, carton 16, folder 19, PST Bancroft.

49. DL to RS, December 13, 1936.

50. DL to RS, January 12, 1938.

51. DL to RS, November 16, 1937.

52. Jonathan Garst to RS, November 21, 1939.

53. RS to Jonathan Garst, November 30, 1939.

54. I am inclined to agree with John Raeburn's judgment that firing Lange was "the worst decision [Stryker] ever made. . . . Lange's loyalty . . . was unmistakable, and her contributions . . . extraordinary. If dealing with her was sometimes nettlesome that was a price an administrator ought to have been willing to pay for such superior work." John Raeburn, *A Staggering Revolution: A Cultural History of Thirties Photography* (Urbana: University of Illinois Press, 2006), 160.

55. RS to DL, October 31, 1939, and November 27, 1939.

56. Her response to the first layoff was typical: "I feel very grateful to the Resettlement Administration for the opportunities I have had and a great working experience. For this reason, whether I am on the payroll or off the payroll you may count on me to cooperate in any way I can." DL to RS, October 19, 1936. Her tone continued to be needy and flirtatious, but never resentful. She just wanted to continue as part of the family: "Because I am no longer on the active list—does not mean that you will never write to me and tell me what is happening, does it? You know that I am always one of your people." DL to RS, November 16, 1937.

## Scene 4

1. Riess/PST, vol. 1, 230.

2. Author's interview with Christina Gardner; HM interview with Caleb Foote, September 3, 1998.

3. Caleb Foote to Al Hassler of Fellowship of Reconciliation, August 8, 1942, JDC; hearings before the Select Committee Investigating National Defense Migration, U.S. House of Representatives, 77th Cong., 2nd sess., pursuant to H.Res. 113, part 29, p. 11804K; HM interview with Foote.

## 18. Family Stress

1. She was to photograph in seven western states (Washington, Oregon, Idaho, Utah, California, Nevada, and Arizona), paid at the rate of $3,200 per year, plus travel expenses at $4

per day, to begin February 1, 1940. Impressed with the prestige of the FSA photography and considering it a coup to get the FSA's most popular photographer, the BAE planned a photographic book about rural migration problems, but it had to give up the book project, lower Lange's salary by 20 percent, and limit expense reimbursements because nondefense budgets were being cut. Correspondence of December 1939–October 1940 between DL and Russell Smith, Division of Economic Information, BAE papers, RG 83, NARA (copies in JDC). Approximately 500 Lange BAE images can be traced in the National Archives today, and one has to assume that many were weeded out and a few kept back by Lange. All photographs referred to in this chapter are from this source. The BAE photographs are not well known, partly because they were placed not in the Library of Congress with the FSA's but in the National Archives.

2. As with the famous *Migrant Mother* photograph, she made multiple images of this family, starting from a distance far enough back to get a view of the whole shelter with family members in front and in the doorway, then ending with close-ups of mother and children separately. See, for example, 522203, 522204, 522205, 522526, 522527, 522528, and 522529.

3. DL to PST, June 23, 1939, box 16, folder 34, PST Bancroft.

4. Caption to 521624.

5. 521630; general caption nos. 1 and 2.

6. They shared an interest in Mexican Americans. Moe would later become director of the NEH and president of the American Philosophical Society, and his brother headed the University of California Press.

7. DL to Henry Allen Moe, letter with application materials, October 13, 1940, OM.

8. She had developed the idea after an FSA stop at the Amana Society; and Taylor was interested in cooperatives as a substitute for failing family farms.

9. Lange field notes.

10. DL to Henry Allen Moe, September 5, 1941, OM.

11. This description of Dan's delinquence comes from author's interviews with Dan Dixon, June 18, 2002, and with RP, March 21, 2002.

12. DL to Russell Smith, October 2, 1940, OM.

13. Daniel Dixon to the author, email dated February 5, 2008.

14. Daniel Dixon to DL, April 9, 1954, JDC.

15. Author's interviews with John Dixon, February 2003.

16. Material on Martin Lange is based on author's interviews with Dan Dixon, John Dixon, Donald Fanger, and Rondal Partridge.

17. *Wobbly* is a nickname for a member of the radical union Industrial Workers of the World.

18. The scheme rested on the lack of communication between the department collecting from employers and that paying out benefits. The ring had stolen at least $13,000 in unemployment insurance funds (worth about $181,000 in 2007).

19. Riess, 8.

20. Sledge and Jilk received only probation.

21. Riess, 8. Lange also suspected, as I do, that his immature Wobbly politics made it easier

for him to join the scam: He did not respect white-collar labor as he did blue-collar, and he did not consider stealing from the state an immoral act.

22. It was unnoticed as a widespread problem because previously so many had not survived polio, and because the symptoms of those who did were identified as aspects of normal aging. Daniel J. Wilson, *Living with Polio: The Epidemic and Its Survivors* (Chicago: University of Chicago Press, 2005), 229–30. Today, up to 60 percent of polio survivors experience post-polio syndrome (PPS), the National Institutes of Health estimate. See http://www .ninds.nih.gov/disorders/post_polio/detail_post_polio.htm.

23. In a typical case, not only damaged muscles but muscles previously unaffected become painful and weakened and there is systemic fatigue. But Dorothea could not have known of this syndrome. Polio was poorly understood when it attacked Dorothea in 1902, and the first big epidemic came only fifteen years later, so few survivors were old enough in the 1940s to experience PPS. Although reported in French medical literature in 1875, PPS went unnoticed until the 1970s. Even today, PPS is difficult to diagnose, a process typically accomplished only by excluding other explanations for the symptoms. Lauro S. Halstead, "Post-Polio Syndrome," *Scientific American* 278, no. 4 (1998): 42–47; Marinos C. Dalakas, Harry Bartfeld, and Leonard T. Kurland, "Polio Redux," *The Sciences*, July-August 1995, 30–35.

24. See, for example, DL to Jess Gorkin of OWI, April 13, 1943, OM.

25. They paid $7,500 (worth $110,000 in 2007). They had to borrow money from Mother Rose to do it, partly because they sold the Virginia Street house to Dorothea's brother, Martin, for a low price.

26. HM interview with Donald Fanger, January 24, 1999.

27. It was designed by John White, a partner and brother-in-law of Maybeck.

28. Christina Page Gardner, "The Contemplation of Dorothea," unpublished manuscript, author's possession.

29. Courtesy of the current owners, I visited the house in 2005.

30. After some years, however, trees grew and blocked the view. Author's interview with John Dixon.

### 19. Defiant War Photography: The Japanese Internment

1. The American Legion, the Native Sons and Daughters of the Gold West, and the California Joint Immigration Committee hoped that war with Japan would provide support for their long-term aim of expelling Asians from the United States. Greg Robinson, *By Order of the President: FDR and the Internment of Japanese Americans* (Cambridge: Harvard University Press, 2001), 127. My brief discussion of the development of internment policy comes also from *Personal Justice Denied: Report of the Commission on Wartime Relocation and Internment of Civilians* (Seattle, Washington: University of Washington Press, 1997); Roger Daniels, *Prisoners Without Trial: Japanese Americans in World War II* (New York: Hill & Wang, 1993); Roger Daniels, Sandra Taylor, and Harry H. L. Kitano, eds., *Japanese Americans: From Relocation to Redress* (Salt Lake City: University of Utah Press, 1986); John Armor and Peter Wright, *Manzanar* (New York: Times Books, 1988), 38ff.

2. The FCC denied that there was any shore-to-ship signaling. Armor and Wright, *Manzanar,* 21. The press ratcheted up the fear with headlines such as JAPANESE HERE SEND VITAL DATA TO TOKYO; CAPS ON JAPANESE TOMATO PLANTS POINT TO AIR BASE; AND, MY PARTICULAR FAVORITE, VEGETABLES FOUND FREE OF POISON. Roger Daniels, *The Decision to Relocate the Japanese Americans* (Philadelphia: J. B. Lippincott, 1975), 14.

3. Christina Gardner to the author, July 2004. They announced the goal publicly: A representative of the Grower-Shipper Association of Salinas said, "We're charged with wanting to get rid of the Japs for selfish reasons. We might as well be honest. We do." Quoted in Audrie Girdner and Anne Loftis, *The Great Betrayal: The Evacuation of the Japanese-Americans During World War II* (New York: Macmillan, 1969), 26. I have wondered about the fact that the director of the Manzanar Camp, Ralph Palmer Merritt, was the owner of Sun-Maid raisins.

4. Author's interview with Christina Gardner, Santa Rosa, California, June 16, 2002.

5. They can be seen now in Linda Gordon and Gary Okihiro, eds., *Impounded: Dorothea Lange and the Censored Image of Japanese American Internment* (New York: W. W. Norton, 2006). I have included relatively few photographs in this chapter because they are now available in that book.

6. A member of Los Angeles's prominent community of Japanese American artists and bohemians, in the early 1920s Miyatake was a prominent member of Shaku-do-Sha in Los Angeles, a group dedicated to furthering modern art. He studied with Edward Weston, became Weston's assistant, and opened an extremely successful portrait studio in Little Tokyo in 1923. In 1926, he won a prize in the London International Photography Exhibition. His defiance of Manzanar rules was so risky that he did not even tell his wife what he was doing, and after nine months he was caught. Arguing his case, he got permission to photograph provided a Caucasian snapped the shutter of the camera. After a trouble-free experience of a few months, camp director Merritt agreed to let him do his own work, and soon he was functioning as an official portrait photographer in Manzanar, making, for example, all the photographs for a yearbook put together by Manzanar's high school students.

7. Joel Gardner, interview with Carey McWilliams, July 1978, UCLA Oral History Program, at http://content.cdlib.org/ark:/13030/ft2m3nb08v/.

8. See http://www.who-sucks.com/people/dr-seuss-sucks-7-racist-cartoons-from-the-doctor.

9. Gordon H. Chang, " 'Superman Is About to Visit the Relocation Centers' and the Limits of Wartime Liberalism," *Amerasia Journal* 19, no. 1 (1993): 46.

10. C. L. Dellums (uncle of Ron Dellums, mayor of Oakland, and former congressman) was a leader in the Brotherhood of Sleeping Car Porters. Bayard Rustin, then with the Fellowship of Reconciliation, opposed the camps and spent months in the fall of 1942 traveling, speaking against the policy, and working to protect internees' property. John D'Emilio, *Lost Prophet: The Life and Times of Bayard Rustin* (New York: Free Press, 2003), 44–45; Jervis Anderson, *Bayard Rustin: Troubles I've Seen* (New York: Harper Collins, 1997), 81–82, 340. My thanks to Melissa Milewski for research on Rustin. On the NAACP, see Harry Paxton Howard, "Americans in Concentration Camps," *Crisis* 49, no. 9 (1942): 281–302; Robert

Shaffer, "Cracks in the Consensus: Defending the Rights of Japanese Americans During World War II," *Radical History Review* 72 (1998): 84–120; Greg Robinson's email to the author, November 28, 2006, and his *By Order of the President*.

11. Once someone decided to get photographic documentation, several paths led to Lange. Milton Eisenhower, brother of Dwight, appointed to head the War Relocation Agency, had previously been director of information for the Department of Agriculture; he was certainly in touch with the San Francisco FSA office and probably knew of Paul Taylor, so Lange's reputation at the FSA had likely reached him. Or he might have asked Stryker for a photographer. Therein lies an irony. No doubt Lange had received an enthusiastic recommendation because her work had so perfectly advanced the earlier agency's agenda; the WRA probably expected the same now but did not get it.

12. *Personal Justice Denied*, 6.

13. Jeanie Cooper Carson, "Interpreting National Identity in Time of War: Competing Views in United States Office of War Information (OWI) Photography, 1940–1945" (Ph.D. diss., Boston University, 1995), 76–77.

14. Jason Scott Smith, "New Deal Public Works at War: The WPA and the Japanese American Internment," *Pacific Historical Review* 72, no. 1 (2003): 63–92.

15. FSA staff assisted Japanese Americans in disposing of their belongings; the FSA, along with the San Francisco Federal Reserve, was assigned to hold Japanese American land and property, until the WRA took over the job in 1943. The two Arkansas WRA camps, Rohwer and Jerome, were built on FSA land originally purchased to help settle poor southern families. Some internees who left the camps to take temporary jobs as agricultural laborers in western states lived in settlements run by the FSA. Attorney General Biddle planned to use FSA camps as assembly centers if necessary, but this did not happen, quite possibly due to opposition from West Coast FSA staff. Greg Robinson email and his *By Order of the President*.

16. The Wartime Civil Control Administration originally conducted the evacuation and was succeeded by the War Relocation Authority. I could never quite distinguish the roles of the WCCA, the WRA, and the military police in the internment, not to mention the War Manpower Commission, the Department of Justice, and the FSA, and I suspect my confusion reflects the reality of the situation.

17. Her workhorse was a Rolleiflex, which used 2-1/4" × 3-1/4" roll film. She also carried an older Rolleiflex, which had been Paul's during World War I and during his field work on Mexican labor, in case hers malfunctioned. She also packed her heavier cameras: a Zeiss Juwel, a ground-glass camera, urged upon her by Ansel Adams, and a Graflex, her old favorite for studio work but too heavy to carry around for any length of time. TH interview with RP and CG, August 26, 1975.

18. On several occasions when Christina was not available, Dorothea summoned one of her sons into service, and Paul accompanied her on at least four trips. Box 1, folder 13, PST Bancroft.

19. Dorothea came to see that Christina had no gift for photography—as Christina Gardner herself told me without resentment—but for those months, she was an ideal assistant.

Homer Page, by contrast, became a superb photographer, his work sometimes considered a bridge between Lange and Robert Franks.

20. Broad & Co. of Los Angeles was engaged by the Wartime Civil Control Administration, Public Relations Division.

21. Transcript of conference call, n.d. The participants are identified by letters, but the conversation allowed identification of some participants: Colonel Boekel, Braeden, Colonel Evans, and Colonel Hass, with an an unnamed "B" giving out instructions. RG 499, boxes 1–17, .

22. Author's interview with CG.

23. Riess, 189–194, 182–183, 189; Milton Meltzer, *Dorothea Lange: A Photographer's Life* (New York: Farrar, Straus and Giroux, 1978), 241–242; Dorothea Lange to Dan Jones, letter dated July 13, 1964; Judith Fryer Davidov, " 'The Color of My Skin, the Shape of My Eyes': Photographs of the Japanese American Internment by Dorothea Lange, Ansel Adams, and Toyo Miyatake," *Yale Journal of Criticism* 9, no. 2 (1996): 226.

24. Riess, 189. She got permission to give out one photograph: She had made a set of photographs of the Shibuya family before evacuation; when the elder Mrs. Shibuya died in camp, her daughter asked for one of the pictures. Karen Becker Ohrn, "What You See Is What You Get: Dorothea Lange and Ansel Adams at Manzanar," *Journalism History* 4, no. 1 (Spring 1977): 22.

25. To make this case, she interviewed white employers—far outside her assignment. In the Sacramento delta she made four single-spaced typed pages of notes on interviews with owners of commercial farms regarding the cost of losing Japanese American workers. She heard an argument in which a "Caucasian farmer representing a company was trying to get his workers to continue working in the asparagus fields until Saturday when they were scheduled to leave. The workers wanted to quit tonight in order to have time to get cleaned up, wash their clothes, etc." Lange field notes.

26. War Relocation Authority photographs 537475, 536430, 537530, NARA. All photographs referred to in this chapter are from this source.

27. Elena Tajima Creef, *Imaging Japanese America: The Visual Construction of Citizenship, Nation, and the Body* (New York: NYU Press, 2004), 40. Ironically, while photographing such a sale, she and Paul bought a beautiful *tansu* (chest) for only $25—surprisingly, they did not feel that they were taking unfair advantage. Riess/PST, vol. 1, 234.

28. Riess, 185.

29. Miné Okubo, *Citizen 13660* (New York: Columbia University Press, 1946), 59.

30. Riess, 187–188.

31. Armor and Wright, *Manzanar*, 7. In *Citizen 13660*, Miné Okubo draws scenes like this from memory.

32. Jean Kariya to author, October 24, 2006; Smith, "New Deal Public Works at War," 73.

33. Description from Valerie J. Matsumoto, *Farming the Home Place: A Japanese American Community in California, 1919–1982* (Ithaca: Cornell University Press, 1993), 104–5. When some women complained that men were peering at them over the partition between men's and women's showers, a camp official responded, " 'Are you sure you women are not climbing the walls to look at the men?' " Armor and Wright, *Manzanar*, 9.

34. She wanted to go to Tule Lake, where the WRA was sending the "obstreperous ones," as Lange called those branded "disloyals" by the army, but could not get permission. Riess, 193–94.

35. Riess/PST, vol. 1, 231–33.

36. John C. Welchman, "Turning Japanese (In)," *Artforum* 27 (1989): 152–56; Emily Medvec, introduction to *Born Free and Equal: An Exhibition of Ansel Adams Photographs* (Washington, D.C.: Echolight, 1984).

37. The U.S. Patriot Act after September 11, 2001, stimulated efforts to use U.S. census data for racial- and ethnic-based targeting. William Seltzer and Margo Anderson, "The Dark Side of Numbers: The Role of Population Data Systems in Human Rights Abuses," *Social Research* 68, no. 2 (2001); William Seltzer and Margo Anderson, "Census Confidentiality Under the Second War Powers Act, 1942–1947," at http://www.uwm.edu/~margo/govstat/ Seltzer-AndersonPAA2007paper3-12-2007.documentary.

38. KQED, 15.

## 20. Unruly War Photography:
## The Office of War Information and Defense Workers

1. As a result of the administration's push for propaganda as part of the war effort, by the spring of 1941 there were 153 such offices in the executive branch. The OWI was created in June 1942 in an attempt to coordinate their work. Allan M. Winkler, *The Politics of Propaganda: The Office of War Information 1942–1945* (New Haven: Yale University Press, 1978); Jeanie Cooper Carson, "Interpreting National Identity in Time of War: Competing Views in United States Office of War Information (OWI) Photography, 1940–1945" (Ph.D. diss., Boston University, 1995), 6.

2. It was published in Afrikaans, Arabic, French, Spanish, Italian, and Portuguese. Winkler, *The Politics of Propaganda*, 57.

3. An indication of the OWI's reluctance to challenge racism was that it referred to Negro pilots as "combat flyers [sic];" the label *pilot* was limited to whites in *Victory. Victory* 1, no. 5.

4. All the FSA photographers disdained OWI work: Edwin Locke, "FSA," *U.S. Camera*, February 1941, 25. Ben Shahn raged against its limits: it was run by admen who wanted glitzy, positive propaganda, he charged, never education about Nazism; it even banned the word *Nazi*, and it rejected virtually all of his suggestions. Howard Greenfeld, *Ben Shahn: An Artist's Life* (New York: Random House, 1998), 189 ff. John Vachon disliked " 'your pretty little well planned neatly hedged red and white barned farmsteads, orderly minded Christian Pennsylvania and NY Dutch farmers. . . . They smell bad from where I sit.' " OWI people, in turn, considered the FSA photography project biased and detrimental to the national interest, and accused them of "employing props to create a sense of desolation and despair." Carson, "Interpreting National Identity in Time of War," 129, 165.

5. Carson, "Interpreting National Identity in Time of War," 92, 171–172.

6. David A. Gray, "New Uses for Old Photos: Renovating FSA Photographs in World War II Posters," *American Studies* 47, nos. 3–4 (Fall/Winter 2006): 5–34. Lange's original images are LoC 020006, 020008, 020009, 020010, and 020011-E.

7. DL to Jess Gorkin, July 10, 1943, OM.

8. DL to Gorkin, May 22, 1943, May 31, 1943, and June 10, 1943; Gorkin to DL, May 5, 1943, OM; Riess, 179–81.

9. When you add in the undocumented, about 350,000 Mexicans came to work in the United States during the war. These figures resembled those for the Mexicans expelled from the United States during the Depression. The only Bracero photographs available are among those Lange held back from OWI for her personal collection: LNG42043*, for example.

10. She agreed to a flat fee for the job ($300), but she spent so much time sitting in offices waiting for credentials that she was being paid too little and could not finish by the deadline agreed upon. DL to Gorkin, May 22, 1943, May 31, 1943, and June 10, 1943, OM; Riess, 179–181. After the first assignment, she was paid a per diem fee, $16.53, at the end of her OWI employment. Memo to "Mrs. Taylor, Dorothea Lange," regarding "Separation (Invol.)," March 23, 1946, OM.

11. OWI captions, OM.

12. *Victory* 2, no. 2; OWI captions, OM.

13. Gorkin to DL, March 21, 1944, OM. It was published as "Exchange Students Master Vital Skills in American Universities," *Victory* 2, no. 1, 60–62.

14. Joseph C. Whitnah, *A History of Richmond, California* (Richmond, California: Richmond Chamber of Commerce, 1944), 123–127; Roger W. Lotchin, *The Bad City in the Good War: San Francisco, Los Angeles, Oakland and San Diego* (Bloomington: Indiana University Press, 2003), 194, 214; T. H. Watkins and R. R. Olmsted, *Mirror of the Dream: An Illustrated History of San Francisco* (San Francisco: Scrimshaw Press, 1976), 247–48; Charles Wollenberg, *Photographing the Second Gold Rush: Dorothea Lange and the Bay Area at War, 1941–1945* (Berkeley: Heyday Books, 1995), 12.

15. Lange notes, OM; Robert O. Self, *American Babylon: Race and the Struggle for Postwar Oakland* (Princeton: Princeton University Press, 2003); Wollenberg, *Photographing the Second Gold Rush.*

16. Karen Tsujimoto, *Dorothea Lange: Archive of an Artist* (Oakland: Oakland Museum, 1995), 30–31; Wollenberg, *Photographing the Second Gold Rush,* 17.

17. KQED 22.

18. LNG 42043.8.

19. As always, Lange's best work was critique. By "critique," I do not mean negativity, for she obviously relished some of the changes, but, rather, questions, pointing out contradictions. Adams, by contrast, was more exclusively negative: "At Richmond I was exposed to a cross-section of sheer brutal life that exceeded anything in my experience." AA to Alfred Stieglitz, December 25, 1944, in *Ansel Adams: Letters and Images 1916–1984,* ed. Mary Street Alinder and Andrea Gray Stillman (Boston: Little, Brown, 1988), 154.

20. Wollenberg, *Photographing the Second Gold Rush,* 13.

21. "Richmond Took a Beating," *Fortune,* February 1945, included nineteen of the Adams/ Lange photographs.

22. About her famous "Argument in a Trailer Court," Homer Page recalled that the subjects were a husband and wife "uprooted from Oklahoma . . . to enter a radically different kind of life, and driven apart by the pressures of long and conflicting hours. Their inner rela-

tionship is revealed . . . in that shot. It's the space between that counts." Quoted in Mark Durden, ed., *Dorothea Lange* (London: Phaidon, 2006), introduction, unpaginated.

23. DL to Nancy Newhall, May 13, 1958, Beaumont and Newhall Papers, GRI.

24. OWI captions, OM.

25. LNG 42010.8.

26. Wollenberg, *Photographing the Second Gold Rush*, 69.

27. LNG 42070.2.

28. These recollections are Christina Gardner's. Homer Page and Dorothea's brother, Martin, were already working in the Richmond shipyards. Martin had arranged a job for Dan there, and he tried to discipline his nephew to focus on work, but Dan was fired in six weeks—at a time, Rondal Partridge pointed out, "when even a one-legged carpenter could get work." Author's interview with RP; TH interview with RP and CG, August 26, 1975.

29. Lange quotation from TH interview with Van Dyke. Christina Gardner made a list of the equipment in Adams's car: 2 Juwel cameras, a Contax, a Super Ikonta, two cartons of flash-bulbs, two reflectors, two tripods—"one a massive arrangement guaranteed to withstand a hurricane," a droplight with cord, several boxes of 35-mm. film loose on the seat, plus a carton of various sheet and roll films, two suitcases containing she didn't know what, a few bottles of chemicals, miscellaneous cords and light holders, his ten-gallon hat, a raincoat, a blanket, chains for the car, and a pair of large white tennis shoes. Christina Page Gardner, "The Contemplation of Dorothea," unpublished manuscript, author's possession.

30. Gardner, ibid.

31. TH interview with AA, September 15, 1976.

32. Although "open-minded," Partridge recalled, Lange was firm "about her working methods . . . allowed nothing to interfere with the way she worked, which is why she had so much trouble on the Richmond job with Ansel." TH interview with RP and CG.

33. Lange quoted in Sandra S. Phillips, "Ansel Adams and Dorothea Lange: A Friendship of Differences," in *Ansel Adams/New Light: Essays on His Legacy and Legend* (San Francisco: Friends of Photography, 1993), 51.

34. TH interview with AA.

35. TH interview with AA. Lange was not the only West Coast photographer to question Adams's relatively lavish lifestyle. Most others, including Edward Weston, had to live frugally in order to do the photography they wanted. Brett Weston, Edward's son and a superb photographer himself, commented, "Ansel Adams is touring Scotland right now in a Rolls Royce with a chauffeur. When I go over next month, I'll be in a VW bus." James Danziger and Barnaby Conrad III, *Interviews with Master Photographers* (New York: Paddington Press, 1977), 156.

36. TH interview with AA; Ansel Adams, *An Autobiography* (Boston: Little, Brown, 1988), 225.

37. AA to Edward Weston, November 1938, quoted in James R. Mellow, *Walker Evans* (New York: Basic Books, 1999), 381.

38. Elizabeth Partridge and Sally Stein, *Quizzical Eye: The Photography of Rondal Partridge* (San Francisco: California Historical Society Press, 2003), 25.

39. Alinder and Stillman, eds., *Ansel Adams*, 129, 154.

40. PST to DL, undated letters (1943 and 1944), JDC.

41. PST to DL, "Saturday," from train (1943 or 1944), JDC.

### Scene 5

1. William Kent was a congressman from California. His sons were Roger, a lawyer, and Sherman, a Yale history professor and early CIA analyst, often described as "the father of intelligence analysis."

2. Quotation from Clifton Fadiman, "Who Are They?" in *Milwaukee Journal*, Sunday magazine, February 16, 1952, My thanks to Arthur MacEwan for finding this for me.

3. KQED 23.

### 21. Surviving in the Cold

1. Her weight dropped from 120 to 87 in 1943. US Civil Service Commission, Certificate of Medical Examination, July 28, 1943. She was 5'2".

2. DL to Edward Steichen, July 7, 1954, OM. All Steichen correspondence in this chapter is from OM.

3. The photograph can be found on the Web at http://www.afterimagegallery.com/lifeclarkCPO.htm.

4. Riess/PST, vol. 1, 235.

5. The following medical history comes from notes by one of her physicians (undated), carton 88, folder 19, PST Bancroft. Where possible, I consulted with medical and history of medicine experts to try to explain these treatments, but for several there is too little information available. I am particularly grateful to Jed Appelman, Judith Leavitt, Lewis Leavitt, Jill Lewis, Milton Meltzer, and Helen Nestor for help in understanding Lange's ailments.

6. Called the "Sippy" treatment, it called for three ounces of a mixture of half milk and half cream every hour, along with powders of magnesium and soda and bismuth and soda; eggs, cereal, and creamy foods were to be added gradually after ten days. Oliver T. Osborne and Morris Fishbein, *Handbook of Therapy* (Chicago: American Medical Association, 1920), 295.

7. MM interviews with physicians and PST.

8. Taylor FOIA file, FBI San Francisco memo, February 11, 1949, quoting Professor Edward W. Strong, 9,

9. DL to Nancy Newhall, March 18, 1958, box 68, folder 3, Beaumont and Nancy Newhall Papers, GRI. Lange's typed lists of categories, n.d., JDC.

10. John Morris of Magnum to DL, letters dated April 9, 1955, and June 18, 1955, JDC; MM interview with John Morris; HM interview with Burt Glinn, July 19, 2000.

11. Beaumont Newhall, "The Aspen Photo Conference," *Aperture* 3, no. 3 (1955): 3–4.

12. Lange continued to be connected to the magazine over the long haul. Editor Minor White corresponded with her frequently, as did the first funder, photographer Shirley Burden, great-great-grandson of Cornelius Vanderbilt and an admirer of Lange's work.

13. Shots she mentioned included an aerial view of the town, followed by autumn foliage, battered jeeps next to an old building, and the beautiful brass clock in the lobby of the

hotel where they stayed—not very convincing as a narrative. Newhall, "The Aspen Photo Conference," 5, 7.

14. There must be room "for rearrangement, for probing, for balance, for discard, for embrace." "Aspen Conference," undated typescript, JDC.

15. She may have given the course more often, but there are only two years' worth of documentation in her papers in OM. The fee was $300, which seems high, but it probably included darkroom access and use of cameras. She did not think of this as a continuing commitment, however. DL to Minor White, March 15, 1957, JDC.

16. Copied out by Lange, OM; the poem can be found in Wallace Stevens, *Collected Poetry and Prose* (New York: Library of America, 1997), 70.

17. "Person-to-Person," *New York Times*, March 20, 1955; copy at OM.

18. She urged them to photograph when they first woke, and/or at set intervals, such as 10:00 A.M., noon, and 2:00 P.M. Photographs could be realistic or symbolic, and students could begin by bringing in rough proofs, but by the end of the course they would be expected to bring in folios of good prints. From these, one from each student would be selected and all of these integrated into "a meaningful visual essay which will be submitted to a national picture magazine." I don't think the submissions were ever made, and it seems a typical Lange hubris to think that this could be accomplished with twenty photographs by twenty people.

19. KQED 3.

20. These letters are at OM and in JDC.

21. Mary Ellen Leary, "The Power of a Tenacious Man," *The Nation*, October 12, 1974, 333–38.

22. Greg Mitchell, *Tricky Dick and the Pink Lady: Richard Nixon vs. Helen Gahagan Douglas—Sexual Politics and the Red Scare, 1950* (New York: Random House, 1998), 21.

23. When Lange was hospitalized in 1945, Taylor and Gahagan Douglas corresponded about her condition; PST to Helen Gahagan Douglas, undated letter, box 5, folder 12, PST Bancroft. When Paul sent her a copy of the catalog from Lange's MoMA show, she wrote back, "I walked again in the valleys . . . hand in hand . . . with you and Dorothea." OM.

24. Mitchell, *Tricky Dick and the Pink Lady*, 29. Lawrence Hewes of the FSA believed it was Taylor who convinced her to run. HM interview with Lawrence Hewes, June 6, 1999.

25. Dies's operation became the infamous House Committee on Un-American Activities (HUAC).

26. Goldschmidt "held the fort alone on this 160 A. Limit . . ." PST to DL, April 24, 1944, JDC. At dinner on a trip to Washington, Taylor heard Goldschmidt's story of being called before the Dies Committee, and he wrote to Dorothea, "Fantastic proceedings star chamber. Do you believe in the capitalistic system? Do you believe in God? Do you believe in immortality of the soul? Why did you fight in Spain? . . . Why did you join the Washington coop bookstore?" PST to DL, May 6, 1943, JDC.

27. His FBI file (in the author's possession) is several inches thick. However, like most dossiers released under the Freedom of Information Act, it is only fragmentary—in the several hundred pages I have, more than half the text is blacked out and another 30–40 percent is filler—repeated cross-referencing sheets with no information. Taylor's dossier is entirely unreliable as an account of what he did and thought, but as evidence about McCarthyism,

it is informative. These surveillance and interview reports are notoriously inaccurate. He is frequently referred to as Paul *F.* Taylor and once he was confused with another Paul Taylor, who apparently showed up on a wire tap as an acquaintance of Alger Hiss.

28. Asked by the FBI to list his memberships, Taylor named thirteen, mostly learned societies such as the American Economics Association, but also Veterans of Foreign Wars, the Berkeley Faculty Club, the Washington Cosmos Club, and four political affiliations—the Medical Bureau to Aid Spanish Democracy (UCB faculty and students raised fifteen hundred dollars in 1938 to send an ambulance to the Spanish Loyalists), the Committee on American Principles and Fair Play (opposing the internment of Japanese Americans), the National Consumers League (a Progressive-era organization campaigning for better working conditions through consumer power), of which he was an honorary vice president, and the National Citizens Council for Migrant Labor, of which he was honorary chairman.

29. The only named sources in the FBI reports are representatives of the Associated Farmers, the California Farm Bureau Federation, the Prune and Apricot Growers, and the San Francisco American Legion's "Radical Research Committee." They were explicit, if often misinformed, about the bases on which they judged Taylor a Communist: he favored "too many advantages to the workers at the expense of the employers, and also he advocates dividing up all the lands and giving them to the workers;" or he wanted to restrict their water. A few had probably neither met Taylor nor read his work, such as the author of these statements: "a caustic, acid and fanatically minded person. . . ." "A person of mediocre ability permeated with radicalism." (Someone who had met Taylor would have to hoot at such a mischaracterization.) Others who denounced his anti–big business ideas nevertheless conceded that there was no reason to doubt his loyalty to the United States. One or two (it is impossible to tell when the same source is being quoted in additional reports) witnesses were FBI plants within the Communist party. These people, I have to conclude, were just lying. Supporting that conclusion is the fact that FBI agents added the caveat, following nearly every charge, that the "reliable confidential informant . . . will neither furnish a signed statement nor testify before a Loyalty Hearing Board." Other FBI agents tried and failed to find evidence that he had misused his university or federal position to promote the 160-acre limit.

30. PST/Riess, vol. 1, 303–313.

31. Her FBI file is in the author's possession. The FBI referred to Blitzstein as Blitzenstein. Among other allegations against Lange were telephone calls to Euclid Street from someone under surveillance; her contacts with photographers Hansel Mieth and Otto Hagel, labeled as Reds; membership in the American Artists' Congress, established in 1936 to unite artists against "war, fascism, and reaction"; and her support of the New York Photo League.

32. Supporters of agribusiness dominated the board of regents, two-thirds of whom were corporate lawyers, executives, or bankers, while there was no representative of labor, small farmers, or intellectuals. The board included, for example, A. P. Giannini, the head of Bank of America and the largest agribusiness owner in the state; Charles Collins Teague, a large citrus grower and a major fund-raiser for AF; John Francis Neylan, an attorney for

the Hearst interests and Safeway (tightly integrated with California agribusiness) and also fund-raiser for AF; and Mortimer Fleishhacker.

33. The loyalty oath conflict is related in detail in George R. Stewart et al., *The Year of the Oath: The Fight for Academic Freedom at the University of California* (Garden City, New York: Doubleday, 1950).

34. PST/Riess, vol. 1, 301. Years later, he told his daughter Margot that he would have continued to refuse if he had been younger and Dorothea's health had been better. HM interview with the Fangers, April 16, 1999.

35. PST/Riess, vol. 1, 302–303, 319.

36. Nineteen-twenties Germany led in photo-illustrated newspapers and magazines. Leah Ollman, "The Photo League's Forgotten Past," Anne Tucker, "A History of the Photo League: The Members Speak," and Fiona M. Dejardin, "The Photo League: Left-wing Politics and the Popular Press," all in *History of Photography* 18, no. 2 (Summer 1994); special issue of *Creative Camera* (London), July–August 1983; Terry Dennett and Jo Spence, eds., *Photography/Politics: One* (London: Workshop, 1979). The American group emerged in New York as the Workers' Film and Photo League in 1930, soon dropped Workers' from its name, acknowledging the very different political conditions in the United States, and the film and photographic units separated in 1936.

37. Joseph Entin, "Modernist Documentary: Aaron Siskind's *Harlem Document*," *Yale Journal of Criticism* 12, no. 2 (1999): 360. Its membership reached 80 just before the war, then dropped off, and then rebounded to 200 in 1947.

38. Adams called the League's publication, *Photo Notes*, "'the only real photography journal in the US.'" Quoted in Milton Meltzer, *Dorothea Lange: A Photographer's Life* (New York, Farrar, Straus and Giroux, 1978), 283.

39. Nancy Newhall to Anne Tucker and AA to the Newhalls, undated but late 1940s, box 108, folder 9, Beaumont and Nancy Newhall Papers. Lists of names are also in Lange's FBI dossier.

40. Adams wrote a statement in support, December 10, 1947, when the League was first black-listed, but in 1949 he wrote that "lots of us good-meaning people have been too credulous. . . . No CP member can be trusted to tell the truth. . . . It is perhaps this lack of New England ethics which gripes me. . . ." AA to Nancy Newhall, June 12, 1949; she responded in agreement. Box 108, folder 9, Beaumont and Nancy Newhall Papers.

41. Some West Coast observers thought Lange should have been named as a cocurator. Author's interview with Pirkle Jones, February 2003.

42. Beaumont, educated at Harvard, the University of Paris, and the Courtauld Institute in London, began a Museum of Modern Art career in 1935. Nancy, educated at Smith, replaced her husband as MoMA's curator of photography while he was in the army during World War II.

43. Much of the discussion that follows is taken from John Szarkowski, "The Family of Man," in *The Museum of Modern Art at Mid-Century: At Home and Abroad* (Studies in Modern Art, no. 4, ed. John Elderfield) (New York: Museum of Modern Art, 1994); quotation from Steichen, 21.

44. Exposed first in 1967 in an article by Christopher Lasch, "The Cultural Cold War," *The Nation*, September 11, 1967.

45. Two scholars recently put the argument this way: Photographs can "operate as a political aesthetic that provides crucial social, emotional, and mnemonic resources . . . necessary to a liberal-democratic politics. . . ." John Lucaites and Robert Hariman, "Visual Rhetoric, Photojournalism and Democratic Public Culture," *Rhetoric Review* 20 (Spring 2001): 38.

46. Wayne Miller to Edward Steichen, December 29, 1952, Steichen to DL, July 25, 1952, and January 9, 1953, JDC. All Steichen correspondence is from JDC.

47. DL to Steichen, January 14, 1953, and February 4, 1953.

48. DL to Steichen, May 13, 1953.

49. Wayne Miller to Steichen, May 28, 1953.

50. Wayne Miller to Captain [Steichen], May 12, 1953.

51. Forty photographers came to the first meeting, in March 1953 at the Millers' place in Orinda. (Lange roped two photographers' wives—Joan Miller and Christina Page—into preparing a supper for them all.) She invited more than fifty people by personal telephone call. Steichen flew out for this one. A second meeting, in June, took place at her house and she got Shirley Burden to call a meeting in Los Angeles in September. DL to Steichen, February 2, 1953; DL to Steichen, undated (March 1953).

52. Szarkowski, "The Family of Man," in *The Museum of Modern Art at Mid-Century*, ed. Ziderfield, 33.

53. Eric J. Sandeen, *Picturing an Exhibition: The Family of Man and 1950s America* (Albuquerque: University of New Mexico Press, 1995), 41; Wayne Miller to "Captain" [Steichen], May 12, 1953.

54. Szarkowski, "The Family of Man," in *The Museum of Modern Art at Mid-Century*, ed. Elderfield, 25 and 29; quotation, 26.

55. Monique Berlier, "The *Family of Man*: Readings of an Exhibition," in *Picturing the Past: Media, History and Photography*, ed. Bonnie Brennen and Hanno Hardt (Urbana: University of Illinois, 1999).

56. Szarkowski, "The Family of Man," in *The Museum of Modern Art at Mid-Century*, ed. Elderfield, 33.

57. Allan Sekula, "The Traffic in Photographs," *Art Journal*, Spring 1981, 21.

58. Abigail Solomon-Godeau, " 'The Family of Man': Refurbishing Humanism for a Postmodern Age," in Jean Back and Viktoria Schmidt-Linsenhoff, *The Family of Man 1955–2001: Humanism and Postmodernism: A Reappraisal of the Photo Exhibition by Edward Steichen* (Marburg: Jonas Verlag, 2004), 37.

59. Ibid., 29–55.

60. Olivier Lugon, "Edward Steichen as Exhibition Designer," in Todd Brandow and William A. Ewing, *Edward Steichen: Lives in Photography* (New York: W. W. Norton, 2008), 271; Sandeen, *Picturing an Exhibition*, 49–50; Berlier, "*The Family of Man*, in *Picturing the Past*, ed. Brennen and Hardt, 217.

61. She proposed a three-part organization of photographs—the people, their actions, and a third, untitled group that would include "A Comment on Freedoms" and "Indoctrination (as opposed to Learning)." She also wanted a series on emotions, negative as well

as positive: "Curiosity, Fear, Jealousy, Prejudice, Anger, Hatred, Joy, Love, Rage, Vanity, Loneliness, Anxiety, Gossip, Dismay, Envy." "Dorothea Lange's Group Titles for 'Family of Man,'" OM.

62. DL to Steichen, January 21, 1953.

63. Steichen to DL, January 9, 1953; DL to Steichen, January 7, 1953, and January 21, 1953.

64. Berlier, "The *Family of Man*," in *Picturing the Past*, ed. Brennen and Hardt, 233–34.

65. HM interview with Wayne and Joan Miller, September 28, 1998.

66. She and Paul were happy for Dan, but they nevertheless felt a responsibility to warn Mia of Dan's checkered record. Before they married. Paul called her into his study for a "grave talk" about what she was getting into, i.e., Dan's history of instability; he was not trying to stop the marriage, but he wanted her to be aware, he said. Mia thought she could help stabilize Dan, even bring him back into his family's bosom. HM interview with Mia Dixon, October 5, 1999.

67. She may have avoided talking about her mother in order to keep her father out of sight.

68. HM interview with Margot Fanger, January 24, 1999.

69. Dorothea and Martin received, as well, a small inheritance from their mother, AT&T stock, which Joan had inherited from Bowly. Riess, 6.

70. DL to Margot Fanger, December 15, 1957, author's possession.

71. This number includes her stepgrandchildren.

## 22. Working for *Life*

1. KQED 22.

2. At the Aspen conference, photographers denounced this practice of editors and called for a collective stance against it, part of what Magnum was trying to do. Beaumont Newhall, "The Aspen Photo Conference," *Aperture* 3, no. 3 (1955): 8.

3. Ray Mackland of Time-Life offered them jointly $2,500, including expenses. Ray Mackland to AA, June 27, 1952; AA to Ray Mackland, November 12, 1952; AA to DL, December 3, 1952, OM.

4. Dan, now twenty-seven, thought it the "thrill of a lifetime" to be able to work with his mother and Ansel. Author's interview with Dan Dixon, June 18, 2002.

5. One of Adams's biographers reports that he undertook the job only as a favor to a very ill woman, sensing "that she did not feel strong enough to complete it herself." Mary Street Alinder, *Ansel Adams: A Biography* (New York: Henry Holt, 1996), 244. This is not convincing: With Paul and Dan, she could have managed without Adams, and the job fit his own aspirations: "I feel that now I have come to a point where I must expand my subject material. The work I did with Dorothea Lange is just up my alley; we complement each other in an amazing way. . . . I have a dismal reputation to live down—that of not being interested in people." Adams, quoted in David. L. Jacobs, "Three Mormon Towns," *Exposure* 25, no. 2 (1987): 6.

6. Sociologist Edward Banfield, Taylor's friend, had written about Mormon villages, and he helped them choose. HM interview with Laura Banfield, April 16, 1999.

7. Lange field notes.

8. Quoted in Jacobs, "Three Mormon Towns," 10, 15–16.

9. A good discussion of the permission problem can be found in Jacobs. See also Jonathan Spaulding, *Ansel Adams and the American Landscape: A Biography* (Berkeley: University of California Press, 1995), 277. Coverage of the photography project in St. George's *Washington County News* indicates what local residents thought: "The completed piece of art will possibly be placed on exhibition in museums of modern art throughout the US and abroad as a device to promote understanding." *Washington County News*, September 3, 1953. I could not determine if Taylor's withholding the *Life* publication plan was deliberate. Later, one woman whose picture had appeared in *Life* demanded $1000, complaining that the photographs were unflattering. Taylor convinced her that her financial claim had no merit. AA to DL, October 25, 1954, and December 4, 1954, JDC.

10. Toward the end of her life, speaking more bluntly than usual, she remarked that Nancy gave her "the cold chills . . . I'm scared of her." KQED 15.

11. I was not able to determine how many of the 135 she sent to *Life* were hers and how many Adams's, but I am sure that most of the 1,100 they made were hers, since he worked more slowly. A few of the published photographs cannot be definitely attributed to one or the other of the photographers. Jacobs, "Three Mormon Towns." The editor claimed that Adams's pictures were too fine to reproduce well. Alinder, *Ansel Adams*, 244–45.

12. The sentimentality here foreshadowed "The Family of Man" exhibit, as in a photograph of a blond toddler with a man's rough hand on her silky head, captioned "The hand of love."

13. It appeared as "Three Mormon Towns," *Life*, September 6, 1954, 91–100.

14. Spaulding, *Ansel Adams and the American Landscape*, 277.

15. Author's interview with Dan Dixon.

16. Alinder, *Ansel Adams*, 229, 246.

17. Lange asked *Life* for $5,035, and accepted $3,500, with *Life* providing film, developing, and printing. DL to Ray Mackland, July 9, 1954, and July 31, 1954, OM. Ultimately, nine pages and twenty-two photographs were printed.

18. They stayed in virtually unheated rooms at the Old Ground Hotel. Dan wrote that they were "chilled by the Irish temperatures but warmed by the Irish temperament." Gerry Mullins and Daniel Dixon, eds., *Dorothea Lange's Ireland* (Boulder: Roberts Rinehart, 1998), 14.

19. Ibid., 9, 12.

20. After official closing time, it seems, pubs could legally serve those who came from farther away than three miles—who in turn could share with others—so Dan pulled several all-nighters. Unfortunately, what *Life* wanted from the inexperienced Dan were names, dates, places, and written permissions from subjects, which they had not collected. Still, *Life* thought the photographs good enough to send researchers from London to County Clare with a set of prints in order to identify people and get their permissions. Milton Meltzer, *Dorothea Lange: A Photographer's Life* (New York: Farrar, Straus and Giroux, 1978), 292; Mullins and Dixon, eds., *Dorothea Lange's Ireland*, 15–16.

21. She had read an anthropological study of the county, Conrad Arensberg's *The Irish Countryman* (London: Macmillan, 1937). Her handwritten plans are in OM.

22. Lange was well aware of the emigration. She noted that "1 of 3 boys and girls will be living outside Ireland if they live to the age of 50." Many of her subjects told her of relatives in the

United States, and she went to see one of them in New York. The woman lived on the sixth floor of an old-law cold-water tenement, Lange noted, and "she gave me a drink of whiskey in a tumbler, you know, like cottage cheese used to come in. . . ." Lange asked if she would like to go back to Ireland, and the woman smiled and said, "Too backward. . . ." KQED 5.

23. Lange field notes, quoted in Karen Tsujimoto, *Dorothea Lange: Archive of an Artist* (Oakland, California: Oakland Museum, 1995) 41.

24. "That face. The winds of the Atlantic ocean have blown over it all his life. . . . A very lively intelligence of that soil and wind. . . ." KQED, 19.

25. KQED 9. This is Lange at her most mistakenly self-critical. The OM holds approximately 2,600 of these photographs, and they include scores of her most beautiful. Filmmaker Deirdre Lynch made a lovely video of Lange's Ireland trip, "Pictures to Send," but it has unfortunately had very little distribution.

26. "Irish Country People," *Life*, March 21, 1955. Ansel Adams wrote to *Life*, at Lange's request, asking for credit for Dan Dixon as writer. AA to DL, October 25, 1954, OM.

27. Jones recalled this project as one of "the highlights of my life." As always, Lange's relations with younger photographers were smoother than those with her peers; she became Jones's much-appreciated mentor. Author's interview with Pirkle Jones, February 2003. He would become a renowned photographer, noted particularly for photographic documentation of the Black Panthers.

28. Oral history of Robert McKenzie at http://content.cdlib.org/xtf/view?docId=kt3h4nb1j3&doc. view=frames&chunk.id=doe839&toc.depth=1&toc.id=&brand=calisphere.

29. DL to Ray Mackland, March 5, 1957; Ray Mackland to DL, April 10, 1957, OM. The photographs appeared at the San Francisco Museum of Modern Art and *Aperture* published the photo-essay in 1960. A lovely catalog, edited by Pirkle Jones, appeared with an exhibition in Vacaville in 1994: *Berryessa Valley: The Last Year* (Vacaville, California: Vacaville Museum, 1994).

30. She proposed it to *Life* and got a $1000 commission. In the end, *Life* demanded changes that she would not accept, so she withdrew it. Weirdly (possibly due to Paul's connections), it appeared in the *Manila Chronicle*, August 7, 1960, 24–27. A selection of the photographs appeared in 1964 in a manual for lawyers on civil rights in pleadings and practice. This small pamphlet grew into a 1969 National Lawyers Guild book of 250 pages, *Minimizing Racism in Jury Trials*, making it clear that her photographs, six of them as full-page images and on the cover, were seen by others to underscore the presence of racism. Charles R. Garry, Huey P. Newton, and Ann Fagan Ginger, *Minimizing Racism in Jury Trials: The Voir Dire Conducted by Charles R. Garry in People of California V. Huey P. Newton* (Berkeley, California: National Lawyers Guild, 1969).

31. Her original plan was to follow a single case so that "by the time we have finished the story, we should know not simply about the man but . . . why his office is important to us all." If she could not show through this method the origin of a case—the crime and the arrest— then she would use "flashbacks" to reveal it. Typescript at OM.

32. Euphemisms in her notes intimate the delicacy with which liberal whites spoke about race in those days. She reported that 83 percent of the public defenders' clients came from out of state, largely from Georgia, Texas, and Mississippi—that means, blacks or Okies—but

in all her captions, she never used the word *Negro*, although African American defendants dominated in her pictures.

33. One of seven attorneys in the office, he had handled 2,739 cases in his eight years on the job. Working under Public Defender George Nye, Martin Pulich was, from all accounts, an unusually effective attorney, becoming a judge in the Oakland municipal court in 1963 and in the superior court in 1975.

34. KQED 4.

35. Lange did two more *Life* assignments, the Republican National Convention of 1956 and a UNESCO conference in 1957. Little memorable emerged. The lack of close-up access—at the UNESCO event as in the 1945 UN assignment, she could photograph only from a balcony—produced photographs without faces; the subjects could have been groups of important men in any kind of meeting. At the convention, she sat with the crowd and produced images animated by cheering delegates waving signs, a raucous and not at all contemplative gathering, for which she had little sympathy.

36. KQED 20.

## 23. Diplomat's Wife

1. He served as a consultant on agrarian reform and "community development" for the U.S. State Department, the UN, the U.S. Export-Import Bank, and the Ford Foundation, traveling in Asia, Latin America, and the Middle East.

2. DL to Margot Fanger, June 1, 1958, Fanger family collection. All Fanger correspondence is from this source.

3. KQED, 22.

4. Riess/PST, vol. 1, 266; KQED, 17.

5. DL to Margot Fanger, May 14, 1958.

6. This and all further Lange quotations in this chapter are from her Asia journal, OM, unless otherwise cited.

7. Riess, 101.

8. On Gilmartin, see Riess/PST, vol. 3, 416; on Japan's land reform, see Rehman Sobhan, *Agrarian Reform and Social Transformation* (London: Zed Books, 1993), 29–32.

9. Denounced as a security risk and a Communist sympathizer, Ladejinsky had been fired by the Department of Agriculture in 1954. Rescued by Eisenhower adviser Harold Stassen, he was then appointed to direct land reform in Vietnam for the State Department. At the same time, Arthur Raper, influential in the FSA and particularly on Lange's North Carolina photography, was consulting in Japan, Taiwan, Pakistan, and the Philippines. Al McCoy, "Land Reform as Counter-Revolution: U.S. Foreign Policy and the Tenant Farmers of Asia," *Bulletin of Concerned Asian Scholars* 3, no. 1 (Winter/Spring 1971): 14–49; Mary McAuliffe, "Dwight D. Eisenhower and Wolf Ladejinsky: The Politics of the Declining Red Scare," *Prologue* 14, no. 3 (Fall 1982): 109–27.

10. Taylor considered Jane Addams's work at Hull House his model for community development. Riess/PST, vol. 1, 272.

11. Ngo Dinh Diem's land reform in Vietnam actually took land *away* from peasants who had

acquired it from the Vietminh; Diem not only returned land to the landowning elite but demanded that peasants pay back rents "owed" from the period of the Vietminh government. As a result, many peasants became worse off than they had been before the Vietminh took over. Taylor labeled these programs phony, and criticized U.S. policy—tactfully—for supporting corrupt and authoritarian regimes and refusing to confront egregious repression of free speech. See, for example, PST to Bernard Bell of Ex-Im Bank, July 19, 1952, carton 28, folder 29, PST Bancroft; Paul S. Taylor, "Venezuela: A Case Study of Relationships Between Community Development and Agrarian Reform," mimeographed report, 1960, Bureau of Social Affairs, UN, and memo, September 20, 1958, recapping what he told Ambassador Bohlen, carton 29, folder 7, PST Bancroft.

12. Taylor got it published, however, by the House Committee on Government Operations. Riess/PST, vol. 3, 410.

13. Ibid., 386 ff; quotation, 387.

14. ". . . The lower the level of living of the man on the land, the less he dares experiment with a new technique. He knows what he can do the old way, but . . . he doesn't have an extra acre of rice land on which he dares experiment. . . ." Riess/PST, vol. 3, 389. He had experienced this calculation among the dust-bowl farmers who would not stop plowing.

15. Author's interview with Ray Marshall, April 28, 2004.

16. Riess/PST, vol. 3, 388.

17. He traveled to Sacramento and Washington to lobby not only politicians and officials but also the AFL, the Grange, the Veterans of Foreign Wars, the American Legion, the Farmers Union, and the National Catholic Rural Life Conference; he spoke at meetings and debated growers' representatives on the radio. Riess/PST, vol. 2, 172–75, 195–96; miscellaneous correspondence in carton 31, folders 23 and 28, PST Bancroft.

18. LNG 58213.25.

19. On weekends, Paul helped by trying to distract the crowds, but most of the time she had no help. Riess/PST, vol. 1, 252.

20. "Many things Koreans are not allowed to do in their own country, situation I do not enjoy." DL to Margot Fanger, undated letter.

21. DL to John Dixon, undated letter, JDC.

22. Riess/PST, vol. 1, quotation 254, and vol. 3, 405–6.

23. This interest was not new—they had bought crafts in the United States, as well. CG, "The Contemplation of Dorothea," unpublished manuscript, author's possession. HM interview with Margot and Donald Fanger, January 24 and April 16, 1999. Paul made lists of good stores and other sources of artifacts to purchase: carton 30 passim, PST Bancroft. Interviewed fifteen years later, he still crowed about the excellent bargains they had gotten and praised Dorothea's bargaining skill. They got free shipping to San Francisco through diplomatic channels and had to pay postage only from San Francisco to Berkeley. Riess/PST, vol. 1, 249, 258, 267.

24. Riess/PST, vol. 1, 254; DL to John Dixon, undated letter, JDC. Dorothea was a generous and sensitive gift giver. Author's interview with Onnie Taylor, April 14, 2004.

25. DL to John and Helen Dixon, May 29, 1963, JDC.

26. Riess/PST, vol. 1, 248.

27. DL to Margaret Bourke-White, June 25, 1959, box 26, Margaret Bourke-White Papers, Syracuse Collections Research Center, Syracuse University Library, Syracuse, New York.

28. Hearing about her longing for Paris, Paul's daughter Margot scoffed at Dorothea's hope that she could divert him from visiting that battlefield: he wore his Purple Heart all his life, she said—an exaggeration, but one that captures his feelings.

29. This could be because Taylor was working for the UN in these countries and was therefore associating with people who felt freer to criticize the United States. PST to David Luscombe, Mission Chief in Riobomba, Ecuador, October 10, 1960, carton 31, folder 4, PST Bancroft.

30. KQED 16.

31. DL to Margot Fanger, June 18, 1961, and undated letter.

32. Lange, "Sayings of Aly Agua," in travel diary.

33. DL to the whole family, postcard, March 28, 1963, JDC.

34. PST report to William E. Warne, UNC Ec Coordinator, August 4, 1958, 13, carton 29, folder 20, PST Bancroft.

35. The failure to diagnose this earlier is puzzling, since medical workers in Egypt and Iran should certainly have been familiar with malaria; evidently, hers was an atypical form, because physicians had previously considered and rejected that diagnosis.

36. While there, he read Thomas Mann's *Buddenbrooks*, but it should have been *The Magic Mountain*, because its imagery fit the Interlaken hospital precisely.

37. KQED, 22.

38. Riess, 195–96.

39. Richard Conrat to MM, June 7, 1977, author's possession.

40. Rondal Partridge thought, to the contrary, that it was important to her at that time to be with Paul and to try something new. TH interview with RP and CG, August 26, 1975.

41. She knew that in Asia she would have no regular darkroom access and planned to send exposed film to New York, but the tropical heat made that impossible. So she found labs in several cities to develop her film, mailed the negatives to California, and half of all her work in Japan and Korea went down in a plane crash. DL to John Dixon, October 6, 1958, from Saigon, JDC.

42. KQED, 16.

43. Attitudes toward those photographs divide in the main between left and right, between those whose highest value is social content and those for which it is aesthetics.

44. Conrat to MM, June 7, 1977.

## 24. To a Cabin

1. *Dorothea Lange Looks at the American Country Woman* (Fort Worth: Amon Carter Museum, 1967); Dorothea Lange and Margaretta K. Mitchell, *To a Cabin* (New York: Grossman, 1973). The origin of the former was a 15-photograph collection that Lange had offered to museums for $750 per set. Among those portrayed were Reb Chambers, Maynard's sister, then eighty-one; and beloved Euclid Street neighbor Lyde Wall. After her death, they were published with a preface by Beaumont Newhall.

2. PST diary, OM. Everyone who was with her in those last years understood her will to live long enough to finish the MoMA show. Richard Conrat: "If ever a mind controlled a body, Dorothea's was it." Richard Conrat to MM December 10, 1976, author's collection.

3. KQED, 1 and 2.

4. Helen Nestor to PST, December 7, 1965, OM.

5. She and Paul briefly considered returning to Switzerland to see if the Interlaken physician they loved could help, but he responded that she was better off where she was.

6. KQED 22.

7. He went on, as had others of her assistants, to become a fine photographer, known for environmentalist photography, won a Guggenheim in 1968, and taught at the San Francisco Art Institute. He and his wife, Maisie Conrat, published *Executive Order 9066* in 1972, a collection of photography about the Japanese internment. He worked with Lange four full days a week, and she tried to keep herself working then from nine to five, taking rests when she needed them. Richard Conrat correspondence with MM, author's possession.

8. KQED 15, 18, 19.

9. KQED, 16, 17.

10. Doud, Ben Shahn, April 14, 1964.

11. George Elliott, introductory essay in *Dorothea Lange* (Garden City, New York: Doubleday, 1966), 7; see also George P. Elliott, *A Piece of Lettuce* (New York: Random House, 1964), where he compares Lange to Walker Evans.

12. Weston Naef, interviewed by TH, in Judith Keller, *Dorothea Lange: Photographs from the J. Paul Getty Museum* (Los Angeles: J. Paul Getty Museum, 2002), 101. Another example: "Dorothea Lange lived instinctively . . . photographed spontaneously," Christopher Cox, introductory essay in *Dorothea Lange* (Millerton, New York: Aperture, 1981), 5.

13. KQED 8, 13, 17. Lange was trying to pierce what C. Wright Mills called "sociological ignorance." She sought a socially embedded portraiture. Photographer Susan Meiselas's image of a young Nicaraguan revolutionary throwing a Molotov cocktail became iconized in a similar way, and Meiselas had the same objection to its decontextualization. Joy Garnett and Susan Meiselas, "On the Rights of Molotov Man," *Harper's Magazine*, February 2007, 53–58.

14. KQED 23; Clive Scott, *The Spoken Image: Photography and Language* (London: Reaktion Books, 1999), 81.

15. Raymond Williams, quoted in John Lucaites and Robert Hariman, "Visual Rhetoric, Photojournalism and Democratic Public Culture," *Rhetoric Review* 20 (Spring 2001): 40.

16. Lawrence W. Levine, "The Historian and the Icon: Photography and the History of the American People in the 1930s and 1940s," in *Documenting America, 1935–1943*, ed. Carl Fleischhauer and Beverly W. Brannan (Berkeley: University of California Press, 1988), 25–26.

17. DL to Minor White, May 2, 1961, OM.

18. KQED 3.

19. JZ to DL, July 6, 1965, OM.

20. Therese Heyman, former photography curator at the Oakland Museum, reported that he had to accept it when a trustee of MoMA put up the money, while another source reported that Steichen had insisted on it.

21. KQED 15, 19, 22.

22. HM interview with JZ, March 18, 1999.

23. KQED 10, 11; Szarkowski responded, "All right, you stand in front of that picture during the twelve weeks of the exhibition and make that speech. . . . Then it will be a good picture; without the speech, it's not a good picture." John Szarkowski, untitled lecture, in *Photography Within the Humanities*, ed. Eugenia Parry Janis and Wendy MacNeil (Danbury, New Hampshire: Addison House, 1977), 86.

24. Typed undated statement, OM.

25. By the end of their negotiations, however, neither Lange nor Szarkowski was consistently arguing for an either/or, purely visual or purely historical/topical, organization. In their final correspondence through the spring and summer of 1965, it was he who wanted to scratch the abstract categories such as "Last Ditch," arguing, "The trouble with abstract categories is that they dilute themselves . . ." and "swallow up the experience. Try putting the pictures from this group which are relevant into the California group, and see how the California wall comes alive." KQED, 12; JZ to DL, July 6, 1965, OM.

26. Jacob Deschin, "Dorothea Lange and Her Printer," *Popular Photography*, July 1966.

27. DL to JZ, September 21, 1965, OM.

28. DL to AA, March 15, 1964, OM; Riess, 250; DL to JZ, July 18, 1965, OM.

29. DL to Irving Bernstein, UCLA Institute of Industrial Relations, August 15, 1964, OM.

30. Meltzer, *Dorothea Lange*, 343, citing a letter from Szarkowski.

31. DL to JZ, July 13, 1965, OM. Paul Vanderbilt of the Wisconsin State Historical Society to DL, undated, JDC; DL to Beaumont Newhall, July 29, 1965, box 68, folder 1, Beaumont and Nancy Newhall Papers, GRI.

32. Carton 89, folders 58–59, PST Bancroft. Others made related attempts, such as Cornell Capa's Fund for Concerned Photography, established in 1967; miscellaneous papers in box 6, folder 5, Peter Pollack Papers, GRI.

33. JZ to DL, July 21, 1965, OM.

34. KQED 1 and 2.

35. Maurice Berger, "Photography Changes the Struggle for Racial Justice," in *Click*, on-line journal of the Smithsonian Institution, at http://click.si.edu/Story.aspx?story=29. The project also took on some of the activities of the old Photo League, not only making a photographic record but also teaching photography and making cameras accessible to those who could not afford them. Matt Herron to DL, January 26, 1964, April 28, 1964, and May 2, 1964, and undated letter, OM.

36. "How can we help perpetuate the love and intensity you have brought to our medium?" Homer Page wrote. Homer Page to "Dorrie," September 21, 1964, JDC.

37. KQED 12, 22; IC to Minor White, September 27, 1964, AA to IC, September 18, 1964, IC Papers, AAA.

38. "My children have been just grand, just grand. . . . Dan says I'll give up my job for a year. I'll get a leave of absence, I'll just work with you, I'll help you see it through. And then he had the wonderful idea, that all my photographer friends who will be saying what can I do to help, I should answer yes, come in and help and it could be all part of the film." KQED, 18.

39. KQED, 15. Several of the most moving letters were from Paul Strand. He and Lange had met in New York, probably through the Photo League, but had rarely been together, yet they felt as comrades in spirit. Paul Strand to DL, three letters 1964 and 1965, JDC; IC to Minor White, September 27, 1964, IC Papers.

40. My information about Ross Taylor comes from a musical biography emailed to me by his son, Paul Wegman Taylor, and interviews with Ross's wife, Onnie, and his daughter Dyanna.

41. There was a family argument about this: Ross's mother, Katharine, now a Quaker, wanted him to be a CO, but Paul would not hear of that option.

42. DL to Margot Fanger, March 15, 1964, Fanger family papers. Rondal Partridge recalls that he could hear Ross's mania in the sound of his horn. In January 1964, he was hospitalized, treated, and then released after a few weeks; he returned to his home and to the orchestra, saying that he now knew he had to be a workhorse not a racehorse.

43. The orchestra played a concert in his memory in February 1965, featuring Ross's own arrangements for the French horn repertoire. The concert proceeds were used to start a scholarship fund in Ross's name at San Francisco State, where he taught. His arrangements are still published and played, his students proudly list him as one of their prestigious instructors, and a mouthpiece that he favored on his horn is now called by his name. *San Francisco Chronicle*, February 21, 1965, and *Palo Alto Times*, February 9, 1965.

44. Dorothea, despite her own illness, reached out to Onnie with great sensitivity; author's interview with Onnie Taylor, April 14, 2004.

45. "Doctors are trying to find a way by putting the biggest type of whoozie down. . . ." KQED, 22.

46. KQED 17.

47. KQED 4.

48. KQED 18.

49. KQED 4.

50. "I can have all the dope I want, promised me, I don't have to worry about that. But the food that I want to eat . . ." KQED 10.

51. Richard Conrat to MM, December 10, 1976.

52. DL to Margot Fanger, October 19, 1957.

53. "If Clark had only stepped in there, quick, and told the police to leave, they should never have been allowed there. . . ." When Phil Greene compared it to Little Rock, she responded, "It's cumulative memory . . . becoming a symbol." KQED 20.

54. PST to various family members, December 13, 1964, OM.

55. DL to Margot Fanger, January 10, 1965.

56. KQED 22.

57. She wrote to her cousin Minette: "Suddenly I remembered what you told me years ago, 'let God do it, why don't you let God do it?' Well, that IS what I forgot. . . ." DL to Minette (Minelda Jiras), undated letter, from Jiras.

58. KQED 13.

59. DL to Margot Fanger, September 29, 1959.

60. DL to Margot Fanger, February 10, 1960, and March 15, 1964.

61. Author's interview with John Dixon, February 2003.

62. Handwritten note, undated, JDC.

63. HM interview with Margot Fanger, January 24, 1999; DL correspondence with Margot Fanger, 1959, 1962; KQED 18.

64. KQED 8.

65. DL to Mary ?, undated letter, JDC; she made a similar request to Arthur (Tex) Goldschmidt, undated letter, JDC.

66. Paul had kept a record of events in his typical tiny notebook. Underneath his notation about her time of death, he wrote, "That's the measure of your greatness. I'm not going to try to say it again—you gave me my life." PST diary, JDC; PST notes, OM; PST to Martin Lange, October 13, 1965, OM.

## 25. Photographer of Democracy

1. John Dewey, *Art as Experience* (New York: Minton, Balch & Co., 1934), 325.

2. KQED 20.

3. Sally Stein, "'Good Fences Make Good Neighbors': American Resistance to Photomontage Between the Wars," in *Montage and Modern Life 1919–1942*, ed. Matthew Teitelbaum (Cambridge: MIT Press, 1992), 129–89.

4. KQED 6.

5. KQED 15.

6. KQED 26.

7. KQED 15.

8. Becky was already eighteen by the time of Dorothea's death and remembers her mother's intensity about this decision. Private communication to author.

9. Clippings in the author's possession.

10. Tributes in box 68, folders 2 and 5, Beaumont and Nancy Newhall Papers, GRI.

11. See http://www.eurekareporter.com/article/080531-local-man-does-more-than-take-pictures.

12. Lindsay Warner, "Art for America," *Philadelphia Evening Bulletin*, June 4, 2008.

13. This is true even in Canada; see Zosia Bielski, "Capturing Pride," *National Post*, June 3, 2008.

14. At the time of this writing, Google identifies 130,000 images of it on the Web; there are probably as many or more not identified by this title.

15. See http://www.pbase.com/vhansen/image/67828474.

16. Volume 161, no. 211 (2007).

17. See http://www.neatorama.com/2007/01/02/13-photographs-that-changed-the-world/.

18. This center arose in North Carolina in part as a continuation of the work done there by Howard Odum, Arthur Raper, Margaret Hagood, and Lange.

# PHOTOGRAPH SOURCES

Frontispiece: LC-USF34-009058-C

page xii: LoC 009058-C

Scene 1: LNG57016

1.1: Childhood: Helen Dixon

1.2: Helen Dixon

3.1: LNG

3.2: LNG

3.3: LNG

3.4: LNG

4.1: Cal Hist Society

4.2: Becky Jenkins

4.3: CCP Tucson

5.1: Medicine Man Gallery

5.2: LNG

5.3: LNG

5.4: LNG

5.5: LNG

5.6: LNG

5.7: Malcolm Collier

Scene 2: LNG 33001.1

6.1: LNG7548

8.1: LNG

9.1: Helen Dixon

9.2: Bancroft

9.3: Bancroft

9.4: LoC 016292-E

9.5: LoC 016287-E

9.6: LoC 016613-C

9.7: LoC 017223-E

Scene 3: Rondal Partridge

12.1: LoC 019156-C

12.2: LoC 000826-D

12.3: LoC 016206-E

12.4: LoC 009796-E

12.5: LoC 001735-ZE

12.6: LoC 016070-C

12.7: LoC 009972-C

14.1: LoC 002812-E

14.2: LoC 016272-C

14.3: LoC 009666-E

14.4: LoC 009665-E

14.5: LoC 018281-C

14.6: LoC 018170-C

15.1: LoC 018199-E

15.2: LoC 020258-E

15.3: LoC 019849-E

15.4: UNC P3167B/39

15.5: UNC P-3966/2459

15.6: LoC 019786-E

16.1: *An American Exodus* cover

16.2: *An American Exodus*

Scene 4: NARA, 210-G-2A95

18.1: BAE 522528

18.2: BAE 522026

19.1: NARA, 210-G-1A72

19.2: NARA, 210-G-2C579

20.1: LNG 42043.8

20.2: LNG 42072.6

20.3: LNG 42084.1

20.4: LNG 42059.4

20.5: LNG 42084.4

Scene 5: Helen Dixon

22.1: LNG 54272.4

22.2: LNG 54279.6

22.3: LNG 54282.5

22.4: Pirkle Jones

22.5: Pirkle Jones

22.6: LNG

22.7: LNG 57154.3

22.8: LNG 57063.16

22.9: Helen Dixon

22.10: LNG 55024.6

22.11: LNG 57013.22

22.12: LNG 59242.10

23.1: LNG

23.2: LNG63114.8

23.3: LNG58257.1

23.4: LNG 58210.2

23.5: LNG 60102.4a

23.6: LNG 58218.17

24.1: LNG 59242.10

24.2: Rondal Partridge

24.3: Rondal Partridge

24.4: Shirley Burden, LNG

24.5: Helen Dixon

24.6: Helen Dixon

24.7: Helen Dixon

**Inserts**

1: Studio: LNG 5814

2: LNG2068

3: LNG 6053

4: LNG

5: LoC 016153-E

6: Portraits: BAE 522199

7: LoC 009866-C

8: LNG 35035.1

9: LoC 019300-E

10: Loc 017363-C

11: LoC 018675-D

12: LNG 35057.1

13: LoC 019499-E

14: LNG

15: LoC 019799-E

16: LoC 020397-C

17: LoC 019221-C

18: LoC 016425-C

19: LoC 009915-E

20: LoC 019479-C

21: LoC 020211-E

22: LoC 009959-C

23: LoC

24: LoC 019996-E

25: LoC 099599-C

26: *An American Exodus*

27: LoC 002533

28: LNG 38229.1

29: LNG 38166.5

30: LoC 020250-E

31: LoC 009841-C

32: LoC 018216-E

33 : NARA

34: NARA

35: LNG 45042.6

36: LNG 42102.6

37: LNG

38: LNG 57150.1

39: LNG 56001.7

40: LNG 56002.19

41: LNG 58186.10

42: LNG 93146

43: LNG

44: LNG 63131.3

45: LoC 009270-E

46: LNG 58194.7

47: Helen Dixon

48: LoC 017111-C

# INDEX

Page numbers in *italics* refer to illustrations.